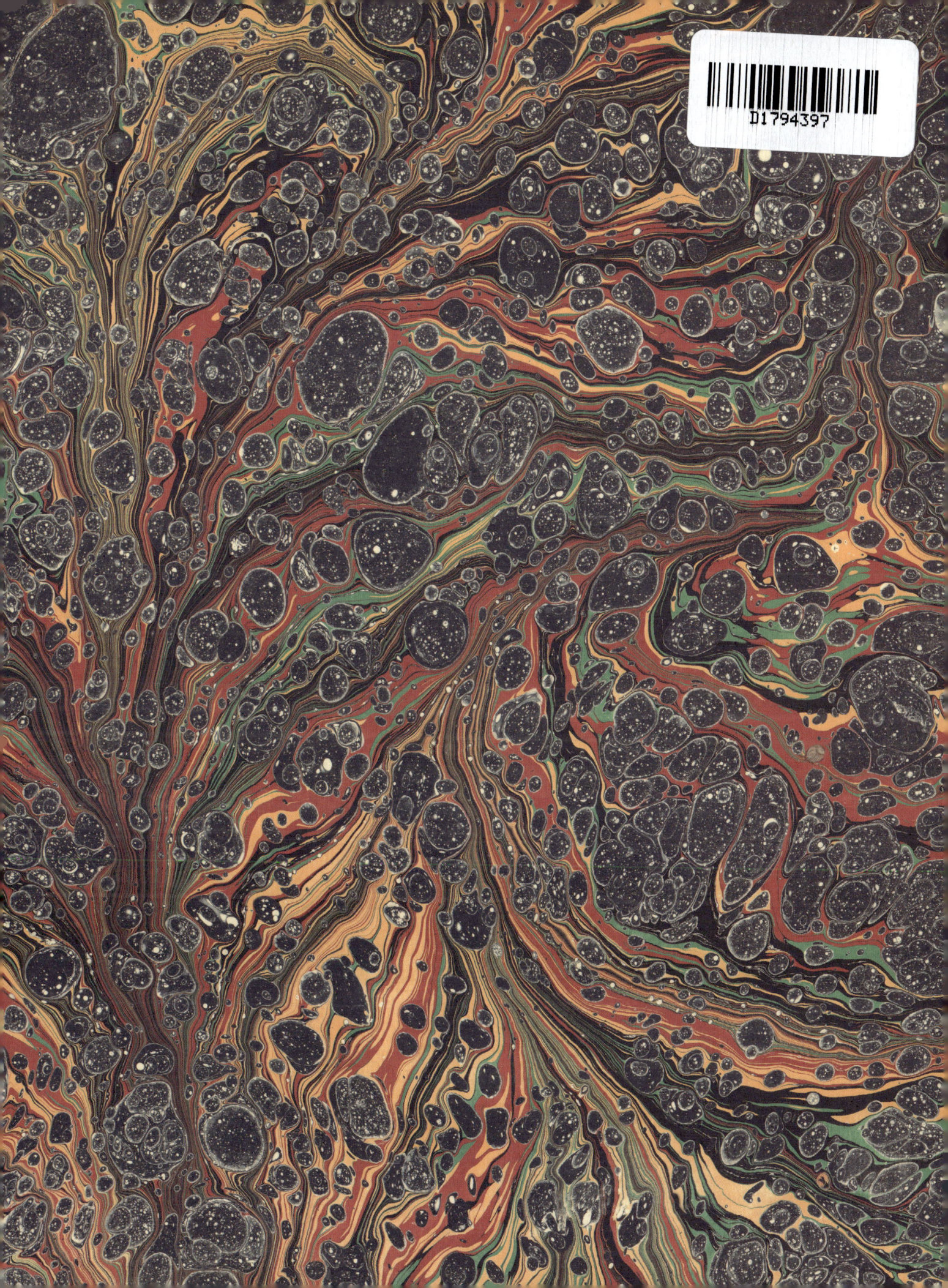

Corsair

Corsair

The Saga
of the
Legendary Bent-Wing Fighter-Bomber

Walter A. Musciano

Schiffer Military History
Atglen, PA

Dedication

To My U.S. Marine Friend and Son-in-law
Rudy Lehner
With Love, Respect, and Admiration

Illustrations by the author except where noted otherwise.

Book Design by Ian Robertson.

Copyright © 2009 by Walter A. Musciano.
Library of Congress Control Number: 2009930667

All rights reserved. No part of this work may be reproduced or used in any forms or by any means – graphic, electronic or mechanical, including photocopying or information storage and retrieval systems – without written permission from the copyright holder.

Printed in China.
ISBN: 978-0-7643-3232-6

We are interested in hearing from authors with book ideas on related topics.

Published by Schiffer Publishing Ltd.
4880 Lower Valley Road
Atglen, PA 19310
Phone: (610) 593-1777
FAX: (610) 593-2002
E-mail: Info@schifferbooks.com.
Visit our web site at: www.schifferbooks.com
Please write for a free catalog.
This book may be purchased from the publisher.
Please include $5.00 postage.
Try your bookstore first.

In Europe, Schiffer books are distributed by:
Bushwood Books
6 Marksbury Avenue
Kew Gardens
Surrey TW9 4JF
England
Phone: 44 (0) 20 8392-8585
FAX: 44 (0) 20 8392-9876
E-mail: Info@bushwoodbooks.co.uk.

Contents

	Acknowledgments	6
	Preface	8
	Foreword	9
	Prologue	10
Chapter I	The Corsair is Born	21
Chapter II	Corsair Development and Production	40
Chapter III	Corsairs into the Solomons	72
Chapter IV	Corsairs Break the Bismarck Barrier	112
Chapter V	Corsairs through the Central Pacific	139
Chapter VI	Corsair Carriers Strike Japan	152
Chapter VII	Corsair Power in Korea	182
Chapter VIII	Aircraft Accidents on Carriers	212
Chapter IX	Corsair Aviators and Decorations	222
Chapter X	Surviving Corsair Aviators	254
Chapter XI	Experimental Corsairs	272
Chapter XII	Surviving Corsairs and Racers	282
	Epilogue	298

Appendices

Appendix A:	Corsair Fighter Organization	303
Appendix B:	Squadron Histories	305
Appendix C:	Corsair Targets and Destruction	309
Appendix D:	Corsair Crash Sites	316
Appendix E:	Foreign Flag Corsairs	319
Appendix F:	Corsair Colors and Insignia	324
	Abbreviations	340
	Bibliography	342

Acknowledgments

The author extends his sincere thanks to the following, who have contributed their time, knowledge, and resources to provide photographs and historic, biographical, and technical information that made this volume possible: Rex Beisel, Jr; Col O K Willams USMC (Ret); Col George F Britt USMC (Ret); David J Ekstrand, VMF-214 Historian; N H "Nick" Hauprich, Aeronautical Engineeer-Goodyear Aircraft Company; H J "Jerry" Dalton, Jr., Paul Bower and Vought Aircraft Company; Sal Marrone; Albert L Lewis; Maj Gen John P Condon USMC (Ret); Arthur L Schoeni and Ling-Temco-Vought; Dottie Sappington and United States Naval Institute; US Army Air Corps; A E Ferko; US Marine Corps; U.S. Information Agency; John Regan for his rare photographs and historic information; E.C. Finney Jr and U.S. Naval Historical Center; Barbara L Burger, Elizabeth Hill, Fred Pernell and U.S. National Archives; U.S. Air Force; David A Mocabee for historic photographs and documents; Capt Donald Edge, USN (Ret); Capt E Earle Rogers II USN (Ret), and the Naval Aviation Museum Foundation; United Aircraft Corporation; French Marine Nationale; Royal New Zealand Air Force; Peter J Doyle, Jr for his superb photographs and historic information; Capt R.L. Rasmussen USN (Ret) Director, National Museum of Naval Aviation; Hap Lanstaff; Dr Louis Antonacci; Jim Larsen for his superb aerial photography and historic information; Alecia Dunn for her photoprint enhancement; and Cecil Weatherly III for interesting photographs.

U.S. Department of Defense; Brewster Aeronautical Corporation; British Information Service; D.C. Bateman and British Ministry of Defense (Navy); Don Berliner for his superb photographs and historic information; Anna Mc Erlean for her expert photographic enhancement; Ed Maloney and The Air Museum Planes Of Fame; Byron Calomiris; American Aviation Historical Society; Michael O' Leary and Air Classics; Henry Tremont; Lt. Col Kenneth Walsh, USMC (Ret); Col T.P. O'Callaghan and the U.S. Marine Corps; Commander D.K. Dagle and the U.S. Navy; Presidential Assistant Benjamin W Fridge; John W Fair and the American Fighter Aces Association; Col James Swett USMC (Ret); CDR Ira C. "Ike" Kepford, USN (Ret); Aero Navale Argentina; Canadian War Museum; Jessica Korniloff for her expert photographic enhancement; Joel Cannon and Greg Henao for their expert drawing reproduction; Anthony Taormina, Chief Researcher of the Lodi Public Library, for expert assistance in conducting research on historic details for this volume; Fuerza Aerea Hondurena; Henry Tremont; Al Lewis and Air Trails; Col. John F. Bolt; USMC (Ret) Col. Aladar Heppes; Jean Jacques Petit; Maj Gen. Robert G. Owens, USMC (Ret); Col. Walter Boyne, USAF (Ret); Alain J. Pelletier; Lt. Loren Stricklin, USMC for contributing rare photographs and information; George A. Page, Chief Engineer; Curtiss Aeroplane and Motor Co.; Peter Hsu for helpful translations; and M.H. Mac Donald and Emil Bueler Aviation Library for excellent photographs.

Michael and Joseph Di Giaimo and Quality Repro Centers Inc. of Elmwood Park, N.J., for excellent photo and drawing reproductions and enhancement.

Special Thanks to Barbara Easton for contributing important photographs and biographical information for this book.

Very Special Thanks to Tommy Borawski for his tireless efforts in producing the accurate typescript for this volume.

Last, but not least, the author thanks Thomas G. Dickinson MD who followed the progress of this book throughout its conception by constantly contributing important information and photographs that enabled the author to complete this work as he envisioned it.

Doctor Dickinson is an ophthalmologist who treated Rex Beisel when the designer retired to Florida. Having served as a flight surgeon during World War Two and having treated many Corsair aviators, he formed a friendship when the man who created the Corsair became one of his patients.

The author extends his Thanks to Dr. Dickinson for the important information he collected for the author to use in this volume (Photos Courtesy of Thomas G Dickinson, MD).

Acknowledgments

Flight Surgeon Tom Dickinson is shown running to a crashed Corsair, somewhere in the Pacific during World War Two, in order to tend to the aviator while mechanics and technicians tend to the plane.

Thomas G Dickinson MD, now living in Florida, smiles to have been of great assistance to the author.

Preface

I fell in love with the Bent-Wing Corsair when the prototype averaged over 400 miles per hour during a 48 mile dash in 1940, and now, more than a half-century later, I still love this magnificent machine. The direct and unbroken lines of the fighter extending to the graceful inverted gull-wing literally take my breath away.

The Corsair was not merely a thing of beauty and grace. The designer blended mission requirements and sound engineering expertise into a unique airplane that outlived most of its contemporaries.

This is the author's second book about the Corsair. The first volume was printed by three publishers; however, that was not enough. More had to be written to bare the very body and soul of this unique creation, including design, construction, modifications, and combat history.

Through its performance as a fighter-bomber, the Corsair became the first strike-fighter; setting the pace for the present-day jet strike-fighters that ended the aerial combat classes of dive bombers and torpedo bombers.

Equally important are the gifted designer, dauntless test pilots, and brave U.S. Navy and Marine Aviators. They have not been neglected in this volume, nor has the historical significance of each operation.

The Corsair suffered the misfortune of being created in accordance with pre-World War Two peacetime requirements. Despite the fact that the design exceeded many of the pre-war specifications, it was constantly required to update while on the production line based upon European wartime innovations. Despite these hardships and setbacks, the Corsair emerged a winner.

Writing this story was exciting and emotionally rewarding. I hope you enjoy reading it as much as I enjoyed writing it.

Walter A. Musciano
Lodi, New Jersey

Foreword

My first glimpse of a Corsair took place on 30 Sept. 1942, on the Hawaiian Island of Maui, and it was an eyeful. My old friend and Mentor, Major Luther S. (Sam) Moore, had learned that the newest and hottest of Navy fighter aircraft was being evaluated on that island, a production model with the Bureau of Aeronautics designation XF4U. Sam and I each flew an F4F-3 Wildcat from Ewa to Maui to have a long anticipated look at this machine, reputed to finally give Naval and Marine Corps pilots a fighter with such superior performance as to cope, on equal or superior terms, with the Japanese Zero. A fighter meeting such a requirement was sorely needed. The number of Marine pilots lost in the recent Battle of Midway was devastating to pilot morale and readiness.

Upon landing on Maui, a surprise awaited me. The Navy lieutenant who greeted us, and who had been assigned the task of making a preliminary evaluation of the new aircraft, was an old friend and Pensacola flight school classmate, Lt. Edward H. (Butch) O'Hare. O'Hare was enthusiastic about the new plane's performance and its future potential as a replacement for the F4F.

The ensuing tests, production, and carrier suitability trials led to a most fortuitous result for the Marine Corps. The result was delivery of the first F4Us to Marine squadrons as replacements for the F4F.

So equipped, and in spite of some minor initial problems, the offensive against Japanese forces up the Solomons chain was now supported by an aircraft of exceptional combat performance.

Walter Musciano has made the story of how this unique aircraft came into being, together with its ensuing combat record, not only interesting, but one that is laudible and inspirational.

No one is better qualified to tell the Corsair story than Walter Musciano.

Col. George F. Britt USMC (Ret)

Prologue

NACA (National Advisory Committee for Aeronautics), later known as NASA, published two Technical Reports by Albert Sherman: NACA Technical Report No. 575 of March 1936, "Interference of Wing and Fuselage from Tests of 28 Combinations in the NACA Variable-Density Tunnel"; and NACA Technical Note No. 1272 of June 1937, "Interference of Wing and Fuselage from Tests of 30 Combinations with Triangular and Elliptical Fuselage in the NACA Variable-Density Tunnel."

The tests revealed that a mid-wing configuration, when the wing juncture with the fuselage surface is at a 90 degree angle, was superior at achieving lower drag or air resistance than a low-wing installation. Further, a 90 degree wing juncture design required no complicated fillet.

The first naval fighter to employ the results of NACA Technical Report No. 575 was the Brewster F2A Buffalo, winner of the U.S. Navy 1936 fighter plane competition. This design featured a midwing installation that required an exceptionally long hydraulically operated retractable landing gear which proved troublesome and contributed to the Buffalo's demise. Following the Buffalo, the U.S. Navy encouraged Grumman to develop a mid-wing design to replace its F4F-1 biplane proposal. The new design became the F4F-2 Wildcat prototype with its typically Grumman fuselage-mounted, hand operated, narrow track, retractable landing gear that posed no problems.

By 1938 Chance Vought Aircraft of East Hartford, Connecticut, a member of United Aircraft Corporation, was completing its SB2U-1 scout-bomber and Kingfisher deliveries, and was eager to obtain more contracts. Fortune smiled when Vought and several other aircraft firms were invited by the U.S. Navy on Feb. 1, 1938, to submit designs for a high-performance aircraft carrier-based naval fighter.

Naval aircraft designers have many more problems to solve than shore-based aircraft designers because naval aircraft are more complex and a breed apart from the conventional shore-based combat planes. Catapult fittings and arresting gear are mandatory, as is a reinforced fuselage and durable landing gear capable of absorbing the stresses of launches and recovery. Folding wings are usually necessary for stowage on carriers and this, alone, can be the biggest problem in naval aircraft design. Some designers, such as Dayton Brown, have intentionally kept the wing span short in his Brewster F2A in order to avoid the necessity of wing folding. The marine environment readily provides an electrolyte between dissimilar metals in the plane's structure and attacks most unprotected metals. The salt water problem is as old as carrier aircraft, having caused rotted wood and mildewed doped fabric on early shipboard planes. Liferafts, flotation gear, and reinforced fuselage and landing gear, plus folding wings have made naval aircraft heavier than their shore-based counterparts.

Vought prepared two proposals for the U.S. Navy in April 1938: the V-166A proposal was to be powered by the Pratt & Whitney R-1830 1,050 hp Twin Wasp engine, one of the most powerful production air-cooled radial engines in the U.S. This was intended to be the conservative proposal. The V-166B proposal was to be powered by the still experimental Pratt & Whitney XR-2800-2 Double Wasp air-cooled radial engine. This 2,000 hp-capable engine was the obvious choice to meet the U.S. Navy's requirements; however, it was an untried powerplant.

The Brewster F2A Buffalo was the first airplane to apply the NACA 90 degree study with this midwing design. Observe the long landing gear leg from wing to the wheel and the shorter strut from wheel to the hydraulic retracting mechanism in the fuselage. The inboard folding strut proved to be the weakness in the system. (US Navy Photo, News Photo Division)

Prologue

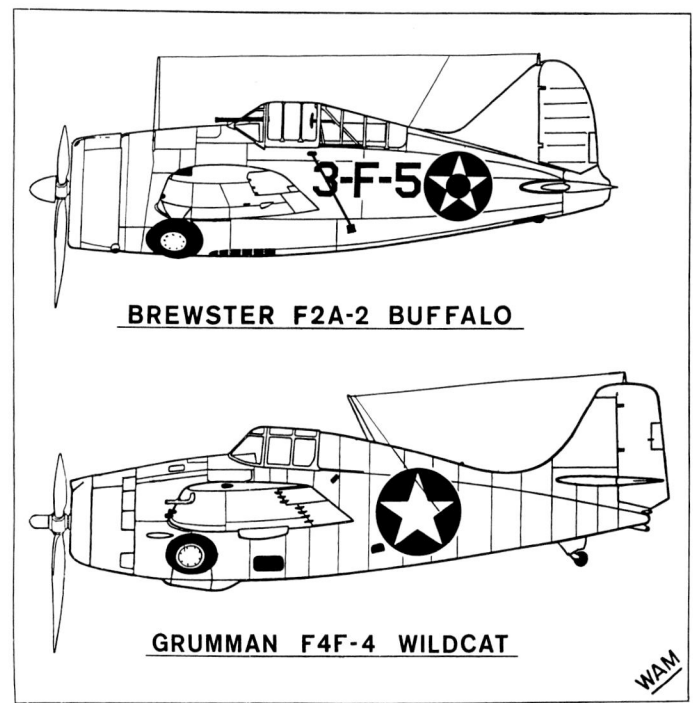

This comparison of the Buffalo and Wildcat shows the wheels retracted into the fuselage, thereby suggesting identical retracting mechanisms. This was not so, because the retracting systems were diametrically opposed; manually operated short struts versus hydraulically operated long struts.

The second U.S. Navy fighter to follow the NACA study was the Grumman XF4F-2 Wildcat, also with a midwing location. This plane used the time-proven, hand operated chain and sprocket, fuselage-mounted, retractable landing gear that had been used on the Grumman biplanes for many years with success. This system had a narrower track than the Brewster. (Grumman Corporation, Courtesy Lois Lovisolo)

Vought engineering manager Rex Buren Beisel decided that "speed is king" and proposed a 400 miles per hour, high-performance, high-speed design built around the newly-developed Pratt & Whitney XR-2800-2 Double Wasp 1,850 horsepower air-cooled radial engine. Pratt & Whitney was also a member of United Aircraft Corporation. This powerful fighter would need a 13-foot, 4-inch, three-bladed propeller that would demand an inordinately long, spindly, and heavy retractable landing gear if the design followed the NACA recommendations requiring a mid-wing design. Further, space in the wing had to be found for the long retractable landing gear. In addition, the mid-wing design would require considerably more headroom for the proposed hydraulically-operated, overhead-folding wing.

In order to resolve the conflicting design requirements Rex Beisel called a meeting in his office with all engineering discipline department heads who led the 90-man engineering staff. The participants included: Alfred J. Sibila (Aerodynamics); James M. Shoemaker (Assistant Chief Engineer); Paul S. Baker (Chief of Aerodynamics and Flight Test); Ernest Mailloux (Chief of Structure); William C. Schoolfield (Head of Aerodynamics); George F. Darracott (Head of Weights); and Fred N. Dickerman (Design).

After an open discussion and assessing all options, Beisel began sketching on his desk pad. As he sketched a front view, he reasoned that if the wing must be at a 90 degree angle to the fuselage surface there is no reason why the wing juncture with the fuselage surface could not be moved downwardly along the fuselage side until the wing root angled

Apparent in this 1940 view of the XF4U-1 prototype is the ingenious wing arrangement that circumvented the midwing pitfall to meet the NACA 90 degree wing-fuselage junction study. (Ling Temco Vought, Courtesy Arthur L. Schoeni)

downward about 30 degrees. The wing outer panels would then be attached to the inclined wing root at 35 degrees to form a five degree dihedral, thus creating an inverted gull-wing. In addition to the right-angled fuselage juncture the inverted gull-wing design reaped supplementary benefits: the landing gear was shorter than for a low-wing design; the inverted gull wing would provide a planing action in the event of an emergency water landing or "ditching" to give the aviator more time to evacuate; it would also provide two hard points for a wheels-up emergency landing; the headroom required for the overhead-folding wing outer panels was less than that for a low-wing design; and greater ground clearance was afforded for the enormous propeller despite the shorter landing gear. The bend in the wing also added rigidity and strength to the structure. The beautiful, graceful curve of the inverted gull-wing was not a mere whim or fancy, but was created by applying good engineering in continuing the important lifting airfoiled surface from fuselage to outer panel without the interruption of a sharp angular break.

The design was conceived in an unfavorable climate. Under pressure from the Army Air Corps, Pratt and Whitney was being urged to concentrate on liquid-cooled engines, thus putting the R-2800 radial air-cooled design on precarious ground. The Army was convinced that the future of high-speed fighters lay with streamlined shapes developed around in-line liquid-cooled types. Current designs (the P-38 and P-40) promised much, and presented far less drag than a big radial engine, such as the proposed R-2800. Pratt and Whitney held that an air-cooled radial was inherently lighter, and that the weight saved was far more important than increased drag. Furthermore, the Navy had always favored radials, and the Corsair was soon to prove that Pratt and Whitney's huge 2,000-horsepower powerplant had what it takes.

Rex Beisel and his design team submitted the Vought Project V-166B fighter design proposal to the U.S. Navy on April 8, 1938, and by June 11, 1938, a contract was awarded for the prototype known as the U.S. Navy XF4U-1.

The detailed design work began at once and continued after an interruption caused by the Chance Vought Aircraft plant move from East Hartford to Stratford, Connecticut, in 1939.

Many factors must be combined to create the conditions in which a fighter plane can arrive at old age and still be considered a first-line weapon. Some of these are operating economics, meeting the tactical situation, and continued armament development; however, most important of all, the aircraft must be of sound basic design, capable of continuous upgrading as combat conditions require. The Bent-Wing Vought, soon to be celebrated as the Corsair, was a design that met all of these requirements.

The man who conceived one of the most recognizable combat aircraft of all time was one of the first certified aeronautical engineers in the U.S., who had supervised the design of many historic and innovative U.S. Navy combat aircraft. Rex Beisel began an aeronautical career that spanned over three decades when he joined the U.S. Navy aircraft design team in 1917.

Born in San Jose, California, on October 24, 1892, young Rex Beisel had several ailments that would discourage anyone. He was deaf in one ear; color blind; had no sense of smell; and suffered from a tremor in his forearms that increased to an obvious shake upon his maturity.

He was also plagued with constant headaches throughout his life, the cause of which was never determined. Having been an aircraft and ship designer for over a half century, the writer can attest to the fact that the arm tremors are a seriously disabling affliction for any designer who must perform drafting as a principal dicipline of his career. Yet, Rex Beisel persevered and became a giant in his chosen profession. Working in coal mines to pay the tuition, Beisel received a B.S. in Mechanical Engineering from the University of Washington of Seattle in 1916. He was then commissioned a lieutenant in the U.S. Army Corps of Engineers.

His application test marks were so high that, by January 1917, he was transferred to Washington, D.C., where the U.S. Navy desperately needed talented engineers in the Aviation Section of the Bureau of Construction and Repair.

Although he knew nothing about airplanes, it really didn't matter because none of the half-dozen engineers in the Aviation Section knew any more than Beisel did about aeronautics. Text books and data about aircraft design were virtually nonexistent, which forced Rex Beisel to "learn by doing" and "profit by experience." In September 1918 he was promoted to Aeronautical Mechanical Engineer, in which capacity he worked on wing design and conducted research in stress analysis. Beisel also designed many seaplane hulls, wing tip floats, and pontoons which require a knowledge of hydrodynamics as well as aeronautics. In November 1919 he was certified as one of the very first Aeronautical Engineers in the United States and transferred to the Scientific Section of the Bureau of Construction and Repair.

By March 1921 Rex Beisel's outstanding and innovative aircraft designing talent prompted the Bureau to award him his most important assignment, which was to be Project Engineer for the design of a single-seat fighter; a type that had never before been designed for the U.S. Navy. By the time the project was completed it had incorporated several "firsts"

As one of the first certified aeronautical engineers, Rex Buren Beisel was selected as Project Engineer to design the U.S. Navy's first fighter plane specially designed for operation from aircraft carriers at age 28. Although afflicted with several physical defects, he worked in coal mines to pay his way through college and persevered to become one of America's finest naval aircraft designers. (Photo Courtesy Rex B. Beisel Jr.)

Prologue

for a U.S. Navy plane: first U.S. Navy production single seat fighter; first U.S. plane designed to use an air-cooled radial engine; first U.S. plane designed to operate from an aircraft carrier; first U.S. Navy fleet fighter; first plane experimentally constructed with a metal framework to compare with the original wooden structure; first U.S. plane fitted with an auxiliary fuel drop-tank; first U.S. airplane to abandon flying and landing rigging wires for rigid struts; and the first U.S. Navy plane to be equipped with double arresting gear systems for both longitudinal and transverse arresting cables.

In April 1921 Beisel spent his unpaid vacation from the Aviation Section to assist the Lewis & Vought Company with the retrofit radial engine installation for the Vought U0-1. He then returned to the Bureau a week later to resume work on the TS-1 design.

Three months later, while Beisel was busy completing the TS-1, President Warren C. Harding converted the Bureau of Construction and Repair into the Bureau of Aeronautics, which is now known as Naval Air Systems Command, or NAVAIRSYSCOM. Rear Admiral William A. Moffett was placed in command of the Bureau of Aeronautics.

The first U.S. shipboard fighter was only the first of many design challenges that were met head-on and conquered by Beisel. The Naval Aircraft Factory TS-1 biplane incorporated several innovative features: the upper wing was set close to the fuselage to give the pilot a good view over and under the upper wing. In order to attain the necessary aerodynamic distance between the wings (gap), the lower wing was suspended below the fuselage on struts that attached to the lower wing center section. Dropping the lower wing in this manner also improved downward visibility. He also used rigid struts between the lower wing center section and the upper wing interplane strut junctions. The rigid struts absorbed the wing's flying load in tension and the wing's landing

Beisel designed and supervised construction of this unusual sesquiplane racer in only a few months in 1922 for the 1922 Pulitzer Race. Observe the barrel type Lamblin radiators and the very advanced streamlined wheel covers. The 650 hp engine seized during the race, plunging the plane into a lake. (U.S. Navy Photos, Author's File)

load in compression, thereby obviating the necessity of fitting the more conventional and complex flying and landing rigging wires.

The NAF TS-1 was the first plane designed expressly for the Lawrence Aero Engine Company J-1 nine-cylinder 200 hp engine that was soon to be known as the Wright J-4 Whirlwind after that corporation's takeover of the Lawrence company.

A ten-gallon auxiliary fuel tank was faired into the underside of the lower wing center-section from where it could be jettisoned by the pilot. Plane was a fabric-covered wooden structure.

Beisel's TS-1 design project was successfully completed in late 1921. His radial engine installation set the pace for U.S. Naval aircraft through the 'thirties and 'forties. Admiral Moffett was so delighted with Beisel's successful radial engine-powered carrier-based airplane that he personally congratulated the young designer.

The U.S. Naval Aircraft Factory built and tested the first TS-1 on the aircraft carrier *USS Langley* (CV-1) with great success. The test craft was also flown with Beisel-designed twin wooden floats. When all went well the NAF constructed five, and the Curtiss Aeroplane and Motor Co. received a contract for 34 more of the design, which were designated FC-1. Thirty-four planes was a very large military order in 1922.

With his TS-1 design project completed Rex Beisel was ordered to help the Curtiss Company convert four of the TS-1 fighters into racing planes for the 1922 Curtiss Marine Flying Race. Airfoils, wings, and engines were changed on the various aircraft, and much was learned about wing/engine combinations. The racing versions were designated TR aircraft. All four were entered in the race, and Beisel's original Lawrence air-cooled radial-powered TR-1 won the contest. Beisel became a "racer expert" overnight.

The designer proved his organizing ability when Admiral Moffett became interested in two new Packard T-2 650 hp Vee, 12 cylinder engines that he wanted to test in the 1922 Pulitzer Race. No existing U.S. Navy airplane could handle such power, so it was decided to design and build a new airframe in a matter of months.

Commander Jerome Hunsaker, Head of the Bureau of Aeronautics Design Section, assigned the task to Rex Beisel, who organized a special team of draftsmen, engineers, and craftsmen requisitioned from Lewis and Vought Corporation and Wright Aeronautical Corporation. Commander Hunsaker had been so impressed by a French Nieuport sesquiplane design that he ordered Beisel to design and build a sesquiplane racer to be

Upper Photo: Rex Beisel employed rigid struts instead of landing and flying rigging wires on his TS-1. This TS-1 was experimentally fitted with a hydrovane to prevent the plane from nosing over in the event of a forced landing on water. Note the wide track landing gear for safer carrier landings. Lower Photo: This USS *Langley*-based Curtiss FC-1 sports the USS *Langley* red tail and a green flight leader's fuselage band. Curtiss had been selected to produce 34 of the Beisel-designed fighters. Two squadrons of this aircraft operated from USS *Langley*. (U.S. Navy Photos, Author's File)

designated Navy Wright-One, or NW-1. A sesquiplane is a biplane with one wing having less than half the area of the other wing.

The new racer was completed in time for the 1922 Pulitzer Race; however, the engine seized during the race, plunging the new plane into a lake with Lt. Sanderson, USMC, at the controls.

As was to be expected with Beisel designs the sesquiplane was novel, having been fitted with the first streamlined wheel covers ever on a racing plane.

Admiral Moffett sent a commendation to Beisel that read in part: "Your selection for this duty was because of the uniform excellence of your work...."

Near the end of 1922 the combined design and production experience of the NW-1 project gave Beisel the urge to expand his scope of design experience to include the perspective from the manufacturer's point of view. Simultaneously, Glenn Curtiss approached Beisel with an offer for the 29 year old designer to prepare Curtiss Pulitzer Trophy racers for the U.S. Army and Navy. Intrigued by the challenge, Beisel agreed to become the design Assistant to the Chief Engineer of the Curtiss Aeroplane and Motor Co. in 1923. He was just in time to begin work on his first project; a biplane racer for the U.S. Navy. The earlier Curtiss CR-1, CR-2, CR-3, and R-6 biplane racers had won the Pulitzer and Schneider Races in the past under U.S. Navy and U.S. Army sponsorship, but now something better was needed for more powerful engines, and to beat the new competing racers. As with the TS-1 and the NW-1, Beisel's approach to the new racing design was innovative and a radical improvement over previous Curtiss designs.

The young engineer developed a remarkably clean biplane racer with pointed propeller spinner, closely cowled 488 hp Curtiss D-12A twelve-cylinder vee liquid-cooled engine and a minimum of wing and landing gear struts. In order to attain the proper wing gap without the use of

Applying his knowledge of hydrodynamics and aeronautics, Beisel converted the three R3C-1 landplane racers into R3C-2 seaplane racers. U.S. Army Air Corps Lt James Doolittle won the 1925 Schneider Race with a record speed of 232.57 mph flying one of Beisel's R3C-2 racers. (U.S. Army Air Corps Photo, Author's File)

Upper Photo: After completing the NW-1 design Beisel accepted a position with Curtiss as Design Assistant to the Chief Engineer and began work on the Navy Curtiss Racer R2C-1 that won the 1923 Pulitzer Trophy Race, and also set a world speed record of 283 mph. Lower Photo: The Curtiss R3C-1 Racer placed second in the 1925 Pulitzer Race, but was faster than the R2C-1 Racer. Note the slot for the streamlined tie-rod in the fixed shock-absorbing wheel hub (arrow). (Curtiss Aeroplane and Motor Co. Photos, Courtesy George A. Page)

cabane struts, or enlarging the fuselage, the wings were attached directly to the fuselage via short wing root stubs that were attached directly to the fuselage structure; the upper stub curving upward and the lower stub curving downward to form miniature gull wings and inverted gull wings. Special care was taken with fillets and other important details to reduce drag to the minimum. Never before had such attention been taken with streamlining.

Engine cooling was accomplished with skin radiators on the upper and lower surfaces of the plywood covered wings.

Streamlined steel tie-rods were used to brace the wings and landing gear in an interdependent trusswork that resulted in an innovative wheel design. A principal flying wire (tie-rod) had to be anchored to the landing gear strut/cross axle juncture; however, the wheels were in the way. Further, the secure bracing permitted very little landing gear flexibility for shock absorbing purposes; therefore, an innovative wheel hub design was developed. The wheel hub was fixed to the landing gear struts and did not rotate, while the rim and tire rotated on the hub, using roller bearings. In addition, a shock-absorbing mechanism was incorporated in the wheel hub in a manner to allow each wheel to move vertically in proportion to the load or impact, while the landing gear components remained in a rigid position. A vertical slot in the stationary hub facilitated this shock absorbing movement without interfering with the steel tie-rod which passed through the hub slot. This Curtiss Navy Racer was designated R2C-1.

Two of Beisel's R2C-1 racers were constructed for the U.S. Navy's participation in the 1923 Pulitzer Race. The planes were assigned to pilots Lt. Al Williams (A-6692) and Lt. Harold Brow (A-6691). The men raced on October 6, 1923, against two U.S. Army Curtiss R-6 Racers, a Verville-Sperry R-3 retractable landing gear monoplane, and two U.S. Navy Wright F2W-1 biplanes. Williams won the Pulitzer Trophy Race with Brow a close second in Beisel's R2C-1. With an average speed of 243.7 miles per hour Al Williams established a world speed record; however, this proved an unofficial record because representatives of the Federation Aeronautique Internationale (FAI) were not present to witness the flight.

Awakened to the speed potential of Beisel's R2C-1 racers, the U.S. Navy made plans to conduct official speed record trials. With National Aeronautic Association (NAA) timers present to represent the FAI, Lt. Al Williams established a new Official Absolute World Speed Record of 266.59 mph on November 3, 1923, with Beisel's R2C-1. The R2C-1 record flight ended the dominance of high speed biplanes, and never again would a two-winged aircraft establish an official Absolute World Speed Record.

Prologue

Rex Buren Beisel sits at his desk in 1925 as Chief Engineer of Curtiss Aeroplane and Motor Co. Inc. He was one of the most talented naval aircraft designers in the United States, having designed many outstanding aircraft from the Curtiss Racers through the famous F4U Bent-Wing Corsair to jet fighters. (Photo Courtesy Rex B. Beisel, Jr.)

Beisel applied his experience with the Curtiss Racer to the development of a fighter design that established a record as soon as it appeared. The XPW-8 fighter resembled an enlarged R2C-1 or R3C-1 with a two-bay wing and fabric covered steel tubing fuselage structure. U.S. Army Lt Russell L. Maugham flew the first Curtiss XPW-8 from New York to San Francisco in 21 hours, 48 minutes, 30 seconds, all during daylight hours. This is remembered as the "Dawn to Dusk Flight." (U.S. Army Air Corps, National Archives)

Beisel's next racer design was ordered by both the U.S. Navy and U.S. Army. Externally, the new design R3C-1 resembled the R2C-1, except for a large fillet at the bottom of the interplane struts. Important improvements included enhanced streamlining and the installation of a more powerful 610 hp Curtiss D-12 engine. An improved airfoil section was also used in a slightly larger wing. This cooperative three-plane venture was divided between the U.S. Army (A-7054) and the U.S. Navy (A-6978) and (A-6979). Beisel's new design enabled Lt. Cyrus Bettis to win the 1925 Pulitzer Race with the Army's R3C-1, while Lt. Al Williams scored second in the Navy's R3C-1.

Delighted with the one-two win with Beisel's R3C-1 in the Pulitzer Race, the Army and Navy brass ordered the three R3C-1 racers converted into seaplanes to compete in the 1925 Schneider Trophy Race, which was to be held that October.

Beisel put his float designing capabilities to advantage by designing twin floats of wooden frames with laminated veneer covering. He directed the construction and installation of the twin floats on the planes, redesignated R3C-2, in time for the Schneider Race.

U.S. Army Lt. James Doolittle won the 1925 Schneider Trophy Race with Rex Beisel's Army R3C-2 seaplane racer with a speed of 232.6 mph, while the two Navy R3C-2 racers dropped out of the race because of engine troubles. An English Gloster III came in second and an Italian Macchi M-33 finished in third place.

Lt. Doolittle also set a world seaplane speed record of 245.72 mph with the R3C-2 in October 1925.

Beisel's successes with the Curtiss Racers earned him a promotion to Chief Designer of the Curtiss Aeroplane and Motor Co. Chief Designer Beisel next applied the Curtiss Racer Experience to a fighter design that vaguely resembled the racers, except that it was larger and had a fabric covered tubing fuselage frame. The fighter retained the wing-skin radiators. The U.S. Army Air Service ordered three test aircraft of the design, designated XPW-8. A production order for twenty-five PW-8 aircraft followed after the second test aircraft was delivered and tested. The XPW-8 became another record-breaking Beisel design when, on June 24, 1924, U.S. Army Lt. Russell L. Maugham flew the first XPW-

Upper Photo: Constant refinement by Rex Beisel of the Curtiss PW-8 included tapered wings, single-bay wing rigging, and replacing the wing-skin radiators with a chin radiator under the engine. This became the first Curtiss Hawk, known in the U.S. Navy as the F6C-1 and F6C-2, and as the U.S. Army P-1. Power was a 400 hp Curtiss D-12 liquid-cooled engine. Lower Photo: This Curtiss F6C-4 Hawk was developed by Beisel from the U.S. Navy F6C-1 by the installation of an air-cooled radial engine. The liquid-cooled engine powered Hawks evolved into the famous Hawk P-6E, while the radial engine Hawks evolved into the equally famous Goshawk series; all timeless classics of the late twenties and early thirties. (Curtiss Aeroplane & Motor Co. Photos, Courtesy George A. Page)

Concurrent with the Hawk, Beisel was studying two swept-back wing fighters: a single-seater and a two-seater. Upper Photo: Rex Beisel designed this jaunty swept-wing single-seat fighter, designated F7C-1 Sea Hawk, in 1927. It was the first Curtiss plane developed expressly for carrier duty with a provision for catapulting. A Sea Hawk won the 1929 Curtiss Marine Trophy. Lower Photo: The two-seater was the F8C-1 Falcon, shown here, flown by the U.S. Navy and U.S. Marine Corps. Designation was changed to 0C observation; however, the armament of machine guns and bombs was retained. The 0C-2 paved the way to serious U.S. Navy dive-bombing. Delivery was in January 1928. (Curtiss Aeroplane and Motor Co. Photos, Author's File)

Inspired by the Falcon, Beisel created the first plane specifically designed for dive-bombing in 1929. Designated XF8C-2 through XF8C-8, the Curtiss Helldiver was an entirely new design from the F8C-1 Falcon. The Helldiver was smaller, carried a heavier bomb load, and had a longer range than the Falcon. Seventy-five Helldivers were constructed for the U.S. Navy and U.S. Marine Corps. Although the designation was changed to 02C-1, its dive-bombing role remained unchanged. (Curtiss Aeroplane & Motor Co., Courtesy George A. Page)

8 from Mitchel Field, New York, to Crissy Field, San Francisco (2,607 miles), in 21 hours, 48 minutes, 30 seconds during daylight hours. This transcontinental performance attracted world-wide attention and is known as the famous "Dawn to Dusk Flight."

Production was stopped after only three PW-8 airframes were completed because the wing-skin radiators were too vulnerable to enemy fire. After a few intermediate modifications, Beisel installed a tunnel radiator under the engine and replaced the constant chord wings with tapered wings, which became a feature of Curtiss fighters for a decade. This design became the first of the famous Curtiss Hawks in 1925, known as the U.S. Army P-1 and the U.S. Navy F6C-1. The design was so enduring that it evolved into the classic U.S. Army Hawk P-6E and U.S. Navy Goshawk BF2C-1 a decade later.

The 1925 Pulitzer Race, previously mentioned, was won by two Beisel-designed Curtiss R3C-1 Navy Racers. Little remembered is the fact that every plane that finished the 1925 Pulitzer race was a Beisel design. Trailing the two Curtiss R3C-1 Racers were: Curtiss Hawk P-1 = third place, and Curtiss PW-8 = fourth, fifth, and sixth places. Never in any air race had the first six places been aircraft created by the same designer.

Tireless Beisel also designed the highly innovative Curtiss Carrier Pigeon purpose-designed mailplane in 1926. The plane was simple to construct and maintain, and featured several interchangeable units, such as rudder, elevator halves, and ailerons. It was also the first production plane to have night landing lights.

Concurrent with the Hawk, Beisel designed the famous Curtiss Falcon flown by the U.S. Navy and U.S. Marine Corps. The innovative swept-back upper wing allowed a greater center of gravity variation, which made the plane stable under a broad range of load conditions. Fuselage structure was riveted dural tubing.

During the same year the prolific designer created the sweptback wing Curtiss F7C-1 Sea Hawk single-seat U.S. Navy fighter. A Beisel-designed Sea Hawk won the 1929 Curtiss Marine Trophy when flown by Lt. W.G. Tomlinson. The F7C-1 resembled a miniature Falcon and was the first Curtiss plane designed expressly for carrier duty.

U.S. Marine Corps' satisfaction with the multi-purpose Curtiss Falcon and the Corps' refinement of dive-bombing techniques led to Beisel's design of the Helldiver in 1929; the first plane specifically designed for dive bombing. Provisions were made to carry one 500 lb. bomb under the fuselage or four 116 lb. bombs under the lower wing. Although the swept-back wing of the Helldiver resembled that of the previous Falcon, the Helldiver was a new design: smaller, heavier bomb load, and longer range. Innovative Rex Beisel tested leading edge slots, wing landing flaps, and Frise (floating) ailerons on the Helldiver, but none were accepted by the U.S. Navy for the production version despite the 50 mph slower landing speed with flaps and slots.

Pioneer aircraft designer and builder Glenn Curtiss died in 1930, and Beisel was not sure in which direction the company would proceed.

That other great aviation pioneer, Chance Vought, also died in 1930. This prompted the president of Chance Vought Division of United Aircraft Corporation, Eugene E. Wilson, to invite Rex Beisel to become Vought's Assistant Chief Engineer "as a substitute for the genius of Chance Vought." Beisel accepted and proceeded to update Chance Vought's classic Corsair biplane designs.

Beisel joined a well established aircraft company that Chance Vought created. It had become one of the leading suppliers of aircraft to the U.S. Navy.

Born in New York City on Feb. 26, 1890, the son of a prominent shipbuilder, Vought attended Pratt Institute, New York University, and University of Pennsylvania.

Prologue

Chauncey Milton Vought, soon to be known as Chance Vought, was an early licensed aviator with Federation Aeronautique Internationale License No.156 dated August 14, 1913. His license is shown here. (Vought Aircraft Company, Courtesy Paul Bower)

Between 1920 and 1924 the U.S. Navy purchased 127 Vought VE-7 "Bluebirds" in several variations, including trainers, single-seat fighters, and attack versions. (U.S. Naval Historical Center, Courtesy Lt Gustav J. Freret, USN (Ret))

Vought left college to work as an engineer for Harold F. Mc Cormick in Chicago and, in a short time, became head of the Experimental Development Department. During this time Vought was "bitten by the flying bug" and completed flying lessons from the Lillie Aviation School. He received his flying license No.156 from the Federation Aeronautique Internationale on Aug. 14, 1912. One year later he filled the position of aeronautical engineer and pilot at the Lillie Aviation School, and then accepted the job as editor of the aviation magazine "Aero and Hydro."

Shortly thereafter he became associated with the Mayo Radiator Works in New Haven, Connecticut, where Vought designed the Mayo-Vought-Simplex, a successful training plane for the British government during the First World War.

Vought's second design was another trainer; the Wright-Martin Model V, in his new position as chief engineer for the Wright-Martin Co., which had absorbed the Simplex Co. At this time he also served as consulting engineer to the Bureau of Aircraft Production in Washington, D.C., and to the Engineering Division of the U.S. Army Signal Corps during World War One.

Chauncy Milton Vought, soon to be known as Chance Vought, started his first airplane company on June 18, 1917, when he joined with Birdseye B. Lewis to form the Lewis and Vought Corporation. Both men had been early aviators and established the plant in the Long Island City district of Queens, New York City.

With two successful designs to his credit, Chance Vought created a new design within a few months which became the successful VE-7 "Bluebird" advanced trainer. Between 1920 and 1924 the U.S. Navy purchased 129 VE-7 trainers, VE-7SF single-seat fighters, and VE-7GF two-seat attack planes.

Constant refinement of the VE-7 resulted in the U.S. Navy OU-1, O2U-1, and O3U-1 whose sobriquet was Corsair. The O2U-1, alone, established four world speed and altitude records.

In April 1921 Rex Beisel assisted Vought in replacing the OU-1 Aeromarine liquid-cooled engines with Lawrence Aero air-cooled radial engines.

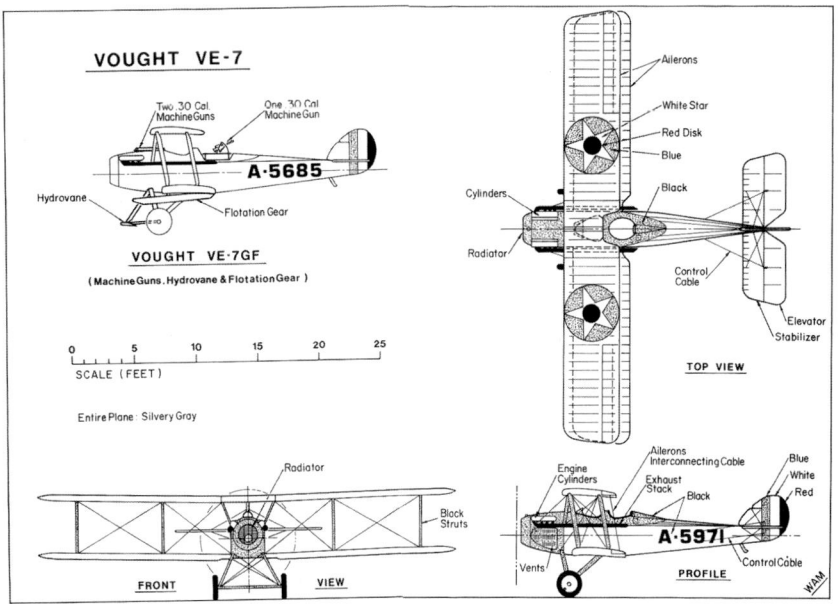

The Vought VE-7 was constructed in single-seat and two-seat versions. The single-seat VE-7SF fighter version made the first carrier takeoff from the American aircraft carrier USS Langley (CV-1) on October 17, 1922, with Lt Comdr Virgil C. "Squash" Griffin at the controls.

This photo of Chance M. Vought was taken about the time that he created three very successful observation biplanes; the first Vought Corsairs. (Vought Aircraft Company, Courtesy H.J. "Jerry" Dalton, Jr.)

The Vought VE-9 was a fighter development of the VE-7, the U.S. Navy UF-1. It was then redesignated to UO-1 (observation). Earlier, the Aeromarine liquid-cooled engine had been replaced with a Lawrence J-1 air-cooled radial engine (arrow). Rex Beisel, having had experience with radial air-cooled engine installations, assisted in the OU-1 installation in April 1921. This was the first Corsair. (Vought Aircraft Company Courtesy Paul Bower)

During the following year the company name changed to the Chance Vought Corporation and, by 1928, the new company had become the largest producer of military aircraft in the United States.

In 1929 Chance Vought Corporation joined with Pratt & Whitney (engines), Hamilton-Standard (propellers), Boeing Airplane Company, and Boeing Air Line to form the United Aircraft and Transport Corporation. In response to Congressional anti-monopoly legislation Boeing Airplane Company and Air Line left the group, whose name was changed to United Aircraft Corporation.

Chance Vought became executive vice-president of the new company; however, shortly after the company moved to East Hartford, Connecticut, he died unexpectedly of blood poisoning on July 25, 1930, after a dental operation. Chance Vought's designing expertise fell on Rex Beisel's shoulders, who met the challenge.

Rex Beisel's first new project with Vought was his response to Bureau of Aeronautics Design Specification 113 for a fighter plane. Beisel developed a two-placed biplane, designated XF3U-1, in 1932. Although the U.S. Navy was pleased with the prototype, Beisel was requested to convert the fighter into the prototype for a new combat classification; scout-bomber. Instead of modifying his older design Beisel proceeded to start anew to develop the very first scout-bomber for the U.S. Navy, the XSBU-1.

The fabric-covered metal frame featured tapered wings for the first time on a Vought product. The new scout-bomber had stronger and larger wings, and greater fuel capacity than the fighter. Provision for a 500 lb. bomb was also made under the fuselage. A twin-row, 14 cylinder, 700 hp Pratt and Whitney Twin Wasp Jr. radial, air-cooled engine was housed in

A squadron of Vought O2U-1 Corsairs are gathered on the USS *Saratoga* (CV-3) in 1926. This design established four speed and altitude records. (Ling Temco Vought, Courtesy Arthur L. Schoeni)

Vought O3U-1 Corsairs were redesignated SU as scouts serving aboard USS *Lexington* (CV-2) and USS *Saratoga* (CV-3). Observe the gunner in the rear cockpit facing aft with his machine gun (arrows). (Vought Aircraft Company, Courtesy Paul Bower)

Prologue

This is one of the last photographs of Chance M. Vought before he died in 1930 at the height of his career. Rex Beisel joined the Chance Vought Corporation in time to continue Chance Vought's design work. (Vought Aircraft Company, Courtesy Paul Bower)

Rex Beisel led his team to design the U.S. Navy's first monoplane scout-bomber in 1934, known as the SB2U-1 Vindicator. This was the first U.S. plane equipped with a fuselage dive-bombing ejection trapeze. The landing gear retracted rearwards, rotating 90 degrees for the wheels to lay flat in the wing. (Vought-Sikorsky Photo, Courtesy H.J. "Jerry" Dalton)

a deep cowl. The XSBU-1 was equipped with a remarkable device, never before fitted on any production aircraft.

Concurrent with the scout-bomber development Beisel had been working on methods of improving the cooling of twin-row air-cooled radial engines. He concluded that by flaring the outlets of a full chord or deep cowl, airflow through the cowl would be increased to improve engine cooling. He then studied methods of controlling the cooling airflow through the cowl and devised the cooling air exit cowl gill opening trailing edge flaps. Cowl flaps became commonplace, without which the multi-row air-cooled radial engine would not be practical.

Beisel experimented with his cowl flaps on a deep cowled XO3U-6 Corsair, which proved his theory was correct. He was granted a U.S. patent for "Engine Cooling Means" that covered improved deep cowl cylinder cooling cowl flaps and cylinder cooling air baffles. On January 23, 1934, Beisel presented a paper on this subject before the Society of Automotive Engineers (SAE) titled "Cowling and Cooling of Radial Air-Cooled Aircraft Engines," for which he was awarded the Manley Memorial Medal and the Wright Brothers Medal for the excellence and timeliness of his invention.

The inventor installed his engine cooling cowl flaps on the XSBU-1 knowing that controlled engine cooling would enable the engine to develop peak power. The XSBU-1 was an immediate success, and a total of 124 of the design was ordered. The maximum speed of 205 mph made the SBU-1 the first U.S. Navy two-seater to exceed 200 mph; a speed that was credited to the installation of Beisel's adjustable engine cooling cowl trailing edge flaps.

In June 1935 Rex Beisel became chief engineer of the Chance Vought Division of United Aircraft Corporation while he was working on another "first" for the U.S. Navy.

Moving to the Chance Vought Division of the United Aircraft Corporation as Assistant Chief Engineer, Beisel worked on improving the Vought Corsair biplanes by adding a full cockpit canopy, full chord cowling, and adjustable engine cowl flaps (arrow). Rex Beisel invented and patented the engine cooling control cowl flaps for which the Society of Automotive Engineers awarded the inventor the Manley Memorial Medal. Beisel also received the Wright Brothers Medal for his cowl flap invention. The Vought XO3U-6 is shown. (Vought Aircraft Company Photo, Courtesy H.J. "Jerry" Dalton)

Beisel's 1933 Vought SBU-1 scout-bomber was the first production aircraft to be fitted with Beisel's adjustable engine cooling cowl flaps, which were considered responsible for the plane's excellent 205 mph speed. This design was the first Vought airplane with tapered wings and the last Vought biplane. A 550 pound bomb could be carried under the fuselage. The U.S. Navy ordered 124 SBU-1 and SBU-2 scout bombers. Photo is an SBU-1. (U.S. Navy Photo, Author's File)

In 1937 Rex Beisel applied his seaplane float design knowledge in the development of the U.S. Navy OS2U Kingfisher, which was the first monoplane to catapult from ships. It was also the very first plane to employ spot-welding in its construction. Observe the unusual double-chine float. Heavily loaded Kingfishers traveled as far as 40 miles in extremely heavy seas. (U.S. Navy Photo (upper) Fleet Air Arm Photo (lower), Author's File)

Vought received another contract from the U.S. Navy on October 11, 1934. Rex Beisel briefed his design team to create one of the U.S. Navy's newest tactical aircraft and the very first U.S. Navy monoplane scout-bomber, the Vought SB2U Vindicator; thereby, again setting the pace for future U.S. Navy tactical aircraft. The Vindicator was also the first U.S. production plane equipped with a fuselage bomb ejection trapeze.

Construction was a basic dural frame covered half with alclad and half with fabric. Outer wing panels folded upward and over the fuselage for storage on aircraft carriers. Fabric covering was used for lightness and ease of repair in the event of battle damage.

Production was ordered on October 26, 1936, and 169 Vindicators were built by late 1940.

U.S. Navy Vindicators served on the pre-war aircraft carriers *Wasp*, *Lexington*, *Saratoga*, and *Ranger*, and saw considerable action in the early years of World War Two dive-bombing Japanese ships.

In 1937 Beisel applied his knowledge of seaplane float design to win a U.S. Navy contract and orders over his nearest competitor. This resulted in the creation of the first U.S. monoplane to catapult from ships. The Vought OS2U Kingfisher could be flown as a landplane or a single float seaplane, although it was predominantly flown as the latter from battleships and large cruisers.

Beisel's innovative application of spot-welding the Kingfisher fuselage and float primary structures was the first time it was used in aircraft construction. This enabled him to create a non-buckling fuselage and float design which gave the all-metal Kingfisher the capability to taxi many miles in rough seas with extremely heavy loads. This construction technique played an important role in the development of future aircraft structures.

Although the Kingfisher was intended for liaison, antisubmarine patrol, shipping attack, spotting naval gunfire, observation, and reconnaissance, it is best known and appreciated for its many World War Two sea rescue operations. These craft are recorded to have traveled as far as 40 miles through rough seas with as many as a half-dozen downed pilots and airmen clinging to or lashed to the wing.

On February 16, 1945, Lt. D.W. Gandy shot down a Zero with his Kingfisher's forward firing guns!

As with most of Beisel's designs, the Kingfisher proved it could properly execute duties for which it was not intended.

In 1938, one year after the Kingfisher design, Rex Beisel began the design for which he is most renowned, the Bent-Wing Corsair. The following chapter describes the basic design of this unique fighter and the efforts required to make it acceptable to the U.S. Navy.

This view of the Corsair fighter-bomber is the most recognizable of all World War Two aircraft. Beisel's selection of the inverted gull wing configuration for the Corsair reduced drag with the correct angle wing/fuselage juncture without the need for large fillets, provided ample ground clearance for the enormous propeller, shortened the landing gear, improved downward visibility, and reduced the height required for the wing folding aboard carriers. (Vought Aircraft Company Photo, Courtesy H.J. "Jerry" Dalton)

I

The Corsair is Born

After the momentous conference in Beisel's office had concluded, and once the Bent-Wing Corsair began to take shape on the drafting boards and artists' conceptions were released to the media, rumors abounded regarding the parentage of the F4U Corsair.

The most prevalent and erroneous conclusion is that the new Corsair design was based upon a 1933 fighter, the Northrop 3A (AKA Northrop XFT). This miniature single-seater Gamma failed to impress the U.S. Army Air Corps and the U.S. Navy. While on a test flight on July 30, 1935, it disappeared over the Pacific Ocean without a trace. Vought's president, Eugene E Wilson, decided to buy the failing Northrop 3A blueprints over the objections of his engineers.

When this Northrop XFT-1 fighter disappeared over the Pacific Ocean on a test flight in 1935, Vought's president, Eugene E Wilson, bought Northrop's blueprints, thereby starting a rumor that the forthcoming Corsair was a copy of the XFT-1. (Author's File)

The Vought designers modified the Northrop, and in just 43 days the new plane, the Vought V-141, was ready for flight. Test flights were not encouraging, but after enlarging the rudder and other modifications the plane was entered in a USAAC fighter competition; however, the V-141 was rejected. A redesign of the plane included a new engine, replacing the tail surfaces with Vought SB2U-1 dive bomber tail surfaces, and lengthening the fuselage by 3 feet-2 inches, thereby converting the V-141 to the V-143. The V-143 even failed to win a contract from Argentina. Finally, the plane and construction drawings were sold to Japan in 1937. The basic design had been a "born loser" and bore no relationship to the yet to emerge Bent-Wing Corsair.

Another candidate for speculation regarding the Corsair's parentage was the Vought-Sikorsky VS-326. This had been another Rex Beisel creation; the XTBU-1 Sea Wolf torpedo-bomber prototype that was contracted by the U.S. Navy on April 22, 1940. The plane first flew on December 22, 1941, and proved so successful that a contract for 1,100 production Sea Wolves was assigned to Consolidated Aircraft Corporation as the TBY-2, because Vought was fully committed to the production of the F4U Corsair and could not produce both aircraft simultaneously.

The idle Vought XTBU-1 prototype was then used for experimental purposes and redesignated VS-326. The underslung torpedo bay and the long cockpit greenhouse were removed and the fuselage was modified to include two individual cockpits.

Vought engineers developed the V-141 design from the XFT drawings (upper photo) and revised the plane into the V-143 (lower photo). The V-143 and the blueprints were sold to Japan in 1937. (Author's File)

The Vought-Sikorsky VS-326 (upper photo) was the prototype test plane for the successful Vought TBU-1 Sea Wolf torpedo bomber of 1941 (lower photo), modified for pressurized-cockpit high altitude tests when it was no longer needed as the bomber prototype. (Ling-Temco-Vought Photos, Courtesy Arthur L. Schoeni)

Rex Buren Beisel declared that "Speed is King" when he conceived the Bent-Wing Corsair, and no effort was spared to achieve this aim. The reduction of air resistance was a primary concern in the design. (Photo Courtesy Rex Beisel Jr.)

One of the primary experiments was a pressurized cabin compartment with two hinged metal hatches. An air scoop just forward of the fin was installed to supply air to the cockpit compressor.

In addition to the high altitude experiments, the VS-326 was used as an experimental test-bed for the 3,000 hp triple-row Pratt & Whitney R-4360 Wasp Major engine that was to power the later to be designed Goodyear F2G fighters.

The foregoing should dispel any thought that the Vought F4U Corsair was not an original design; blending mission requirements and sound engineering expertise into a unique airplane that outlived most of its contemporaries.

On June 11, 1938, the U.S. Navy awarded Chance Vought Aircraft a contract to build the experimental XF4U-1. The Navy specifications described a single-seat fighter with a service ceiling of at least 27,000 ft. With a contract in hand work began at once. For some unknown reason, the Navy Bureau of Aeronautics did not inspect the mockup until February 8, 1940, and when it did, it overlooked problems that would surface later!

Limited production was the rule in 1938, and this meant that Vought could concentrate on the main objective; design the fastest fighter, rather than be concerned about mass production. The inverted gull wing structure presented many design and production problems, and thousands of hours were spent on its design alone.

With the demand for speed and more speed aerodynamic cleanliness received unbridled attention, and the radial engine stigma prompted close attention to reducing drag in every way to offset the very large radial engine frontal area. The fuselage forward of the cockpit was restricted to straight lines with no curves in the tubular shape. Rex Beisel applied his

In addition to interdepartmental meetings, Beisel invited knowledgeable persons to discuss the merits of design details. In upper photograph (L to R) F4U-1 Test Pilot Boone Guyton; Vought Chief Test Pilot Lyman A Bullard; Lt Cdr John T "Tommy" Blackburn, USN; and Vought Engineering Manager Rex B Beisel appear to be viewing the Bent-Wing Corsair XF4U-1 prototype. Lt Cdr Blackburn commanded the very successful Corsair squadron VF-17 "Jolly Rogers" in the Pacific during WWII. In lower photograph Vought engineering personnel conduct a meeting with Lt Cdr Blackburn in 1942. (L to R) Vought Corsair Project Engineer Russell Clark; Asst Chief Engineer James Shoemaker; Chief Engineer Paul S Baker; Lt Cdr JT Blackburn, USN; Vought Chief Test Pilot Lyman A Bullard; and F4U-1 Test Pilot Boone T Guyton. (Ling-Temco-Vought Photos, Courtesy Arthur L. Schoeni)

Chapter I: The Corsair is Born

The Bent-Wing Corsair XF4U-1 prototype strikes a beautiful pose in its silver and yellow mantle. This prototype flew the 48 miles from Stratford to Hartford, Connecticut, at an average speed of 405 miles per-hour; a mythical speed for single engine military aircraft. The plane attained 550 mph in a dive. (Vought Aircraft Photos, Courtesy Paul Bower)

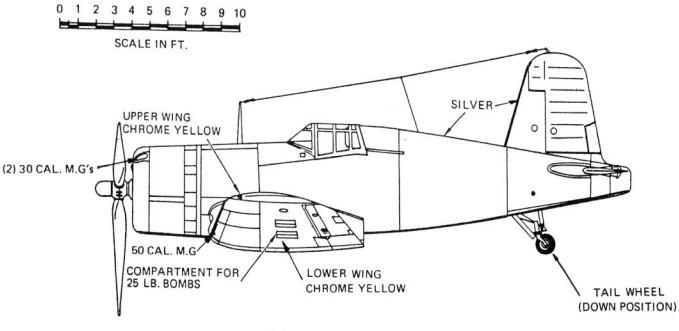

This profile illustrates the simple lines of the Bent-Wing Corsair prototype. Note the pre-war requirement for antiaircraft bombs and four gun armament. (Vought Aircraft Artwork, enhanced by Author)

engine cooling baffles and cowl cooling expertise to design the closest fitting engine cowl possible to reduce air resistance.

The engineering department chiefs held frequent meetings to exchange ideas and resolve problems. Naval and Marine aviators, test pilots, and other informed personnel were invited to discuss design problems and forward opinions on the basis of their experience.

The XF4U-1 was powered by an XR-2800-4 air-cooled, radial, 18 cylinder, 1,850 hp engine for takeoff and 1,460 hp at 21,500 ft. Empty weight was 7,505 lbs and 9,357 lbs in normal loaded condition. Initial rate of climb was 2,660 ft per min and service ceiling was 35,200 ft. Wingspan was 41 ft-3 in, length 32 ft-1 in, and maximum speed was 407.5 mph. The full size plane underwent wind tunnel tests in late 1941.

The Chance Vought Company merged with Sikorsky to become the Vought-Sikorsky Division of United Aircraft Corporation in 1939, which prompted Vought to move to Stratford, Connecticut, to improve production. Sikorsky separated from Vought in late 1943, and Rex Beisel became General manager of Chance Vought Division of United Aircraft Corporation.

The XF4U-1 Bent-Wing Corsair is shown at the NACA facility at Langley Field, Virginia, for drag reduction tests in the full scale wind tunnel during late 1941. Note the long instrument rod extending from the wing leading edge. (U.S. Navy Photo via U.S. National Archives)

The closely cowled radial engine is very evident in this photo of an F4U-1 production Corsair. Careful engine cooling baffles and cowl flap design increased the top speed of the Corsair. (Vought Aircraft Photo, Courtesy H.J. "Jerry" Dalton, Jr.)

Corsair: The Saga of the Legendary Bent-Wing Fighter-Bomber

Vought Chief Test Pilot Lyman Bullard, Jr took the XF4U-1 on its initial flight on May 29, 1940. He is shown here recycling the landing gear and testing the enormous wing flaps. (U.S. Navy Photo via U.S. National Archives)

Boone Guyton was conducting cabin pressure tests in this XF4U-1 prototype when he was confronted by life-threatening weather that caused a serious accident. (U.S. Navy Photo via U.S. National Archives)

After several days of preliminary taxi runs and engine tests, Vought Chief Test Pilot Lyman Bullard, Jr. was ready to fly the Vought XF4U-1 (BuNo 1443) from Stratford's Bridgeport Municipal Airport for its initial test flight on May 29, 1940.

This would be the "moment of truth" for the two years of engineering, design, meticulous drafting, trade-offs, redesign, and the tireless dedication of the experimental shop artists and craftsmen.

Attendees at the airport to observe this momentous flight included Pratt & Whitney powerplant engineers, aerodynamicists, and service department representatives, plus United Aircraft and Vought-Sikorsky executives.

During the 38 minute flight Bullard climbed the prototype to 12,000 ft, where he put the silver and yellow beauty through a variety of standard maneuvers, including sensing the controls at various flap settings and cycling the retractable landing gear. During this simple routine the plane began shaking violently, combined with heavy elevator forces on the control column. Bullard returned to the airport at once, making a no-flaps straight-in approach to a perfect landing.

Upon inspection, it was found that the vibration problem was caused by elevator flutter because the elevator spring tabs had shimmied off the elevator during the flight. Otherwise, the test plane had performed well and this minor problem was easily corrected.

Boone T Guyton was a former U.S. Navy carrier aviator who had flown a Grumman Wildcat from Florida to California in a single day. He had test-flown the SB2U Vindicator and became the Vought technical representative in France. Now, Guyton was named the Primary Test Pilot for the XF4U-1.

The Test Pilot was performing canopy structure and cabin pressure tests during an overcast July 11, 1940, afternoon to prepare the XF4U-1 for later high-speed dive tests when it began to rain. After three of the four required speed runs were complete, a squall confronted the plane, forcing Guyton to turn back. The blinking fuel warning light forced the pilot to switch to reserve tanks as darkness began to envelop the area. Fortunately, during a brief respite of the bad weather, Guyton spotted a golf course and decided to make an emergency landing there instead of trying to reach his airport.

Hanging the Corsair prototype on its huge propeller, the pilot slowed as much as possible and three-pointed on the fairway. Braking as soon as he dared, Boone discovered that the wet, closely mown grass was as slick as ice! He even kicked the rudder hard to ground loop, but to no avail, as the powerless plane skidded toward a bank of saplings. As the heavy Corsair hit the trees they bent and then straightened, flipping the plane on its back and allowing it to slither down a ravine inverted, tail first, and smash into a huge tree stump that tore off the plane's right wing as it came to rest!

Hanging inverted in the eerie darkness, Boone heard a voice! It was a policeman who witnessed the crash and had summoned a doctor. They rushed Guyton to a local inn where the doctor stitched a torn lip and cheek and treated assorted contusions. Nothing was broken. Despite the crash landing, the data on Boone's knee pad proved very valuable to the Vought Aerodynamics Department.

The plane was retrieved and completely rebuilt by the last week of September, 1940.

Primary Test Pilot for the XF4U-1, Boone Guyton was a former U.S. Navy carrier aviator who had test-flown the Vought SB2U Vindicator scout-bomber and was the Vought technical representative in France. He experienced several dangerous incidents while testing the Bent-Wing Corsair. (Ling-Temco-Vought Photo, Courtesy Arthur L. Schoeni)

Chapter I: The Corsair is Born

Lyman Bullard resumed the XF4U-1 flight testing, and on October 1, 1940, he sped the 48 miles from Stratford to Hartford, Connecticut, at an average speed of 405 mph!

Rear Admiral John Towers, U.S. Navy aviation pioneer and Chief of the Navy's Bureau of Aeronautics, witnessed the flight and told the media that they had seen the most powerful and fastest naval fighter in America. At a time when 400 miles per hour was almost a mythical figure, the Corsair's performance was ample proof that Pratt & Whitney's faith in the air-cooled radial engine had been successful.

When Major General Henry (Hap) Arnold, Chief of the U.S. Army Air Corps, learned of the Corsair's capability with the radial engine he instructed Jack Horner, the president of Pratt & Whitney, to cancel its liquid-cooled engine research contract. At the same time he encouraged the company to concentrate its energies in the air-cooled radial engine field.

Gen. Arnold also influenced Republic Aviation Corp to use the Pratt & Whitney R-2800 Double Wasp engine in their P-47 Thunderbolt fighter design, while the U.S. Navy instructed Grumman to use the Pratt & Whitney R-2800 Double Wasp engine in their F6F Hellcat fighter design then underway.

In addition, after learning about the Corsair's remarkable performance, the future U.S. Navy Grumman F7F Tigercat and F8F Bearcat fighters and U.S. Army Air Corp's Northrop P-61 night fighter, Curtiss C-46 transport, and Martin B-26 bomber were all fitted with the Pratt & Whitney R-2800 series Double Wasp engines. The Corsair no longer had a monopoly of the engine.

The Corsair wing airfoil sections were NACA 2300; 18% root thickness; 15% fold thickness; and 9% tip thickness.

While attempting a forced landing on a wet golf course Boone Guyton's XF4U-1 skidded on the wet grass into a bank of saplings and then skidded into a ravine tail first, inverted. Upper photo shows the skid marks, while lower photo shows the inverted plane in the ravine. (Ling-Temco-Vought Photo, Courtesy Arthur L. Schoeni)

On October 24, 1940, the XF4U-1 was flown to Anocostia, Washington, DC, for preliminary flight testing by U.S. Navy pilots. Although the tests revealed inadequate lateral stability and poor spin recovery properties, the U.S. Navy requested proposals from Vought for a production design on November 28, 1940, to be designated the F4U-1. In many ways instability adds to maneuverability in the hands of an expert aviator.

Despite that, at the onset, the U.S. Navy had specified the fairly standard armament of the time, consisting of one .30 caliber and one .50 caliber machine gun in the nose, synchronized to fire through the propeller arc; one .50 caliber machine gun in each wing; plus ten 25 lb bombs in each wing intended to be dropped on enemy bomber formations. Combat experience in the European air fighting dictated that from four to six wing guns were necessary. This changed the Navy's mind, and the F4U-1 armament was finalized at six Colt-Browning M-2 .50 caliber wing machine guns. This armament became the standard firepower for most U.S. fighter aircraft during the Second World War.

Each of the two inboard guns on each side was supplied with a 400 round magazine, while the remaining outboard guns were supplied with a 375 round magazine. The guns were installed so the 1.6 oz bullets converged at 300 yards, creating a devastating impact at that point. Initially, the magazines were loaded with the following bullet sequence: armor piercing, incendiary, armor piercing, incendiary, and tracer, and then the sequence was repeated.

The success with self-sealing, multi-layered, bladder fuel tanks in European fighters convinced the U.S. Navy that this was also necessary on the F4U-1. The armament and fuel tank changes became synergistic, but with dire consequences.

The integral fuel tanks in the wing leading edges were transformed into a single 237 gallon laminated bladder tank in the fuselage, thereby, clearing a space for the new wing guns. This was the good news.

The bad news was that the logical location for this single large bladder tank was at the center of gravity or balance point of the plane in order to retain the plane's maneuverability and to prevent any imbalance to the aircraft as the fuel was consumed. Unfortunately, the cockpit was located at this location and was forced to relocate 32" back to the rear to provide space for the tank. In addition, the fuselage of the F4U-1 was lengthened 17 in forward of the cockpit to make room for the fuel tank, thereby adding almost four feet ahead of the cockpit. The distance from the cowl front to the windshield was now eleven feet! The tank and cockpit relocation excacerbated the originally inferior forward view for the aviator because of the enormous width and length of the forward fuselage that now obstructed his vision. Aviators were forced to land all future Corsairs tail-high; no more three-point landings. The seat was raised eight inches, but this did not cure the problem.

In late February 1941 Boone Guyton conducted spin tests with the XF4U-1. A drogue parachute had been fabricated with a 50 ft. tether attached to the aft end of the XF4U-1 fuselage. A container for the 'chute was fitted in the fuselage tail cone. The 'chute was to be deployed in the event that the spins became uncontrollable. When released the drogue would then raise the tail and, with a nose-down atitude, the plane could recover from the spin. A special red handle was installed in the cockpit for the aviator to pull and release the parachute when necessary.

The first spins were smooth and controllable with left and right spirals. About 1,500 feet of altitude was lost with each single rotation and recovery was normal. When Guyton went into a double spin, recovery became impossible because the controls were frozen in place. With an altitude loss of 1,500 feet per rotation Boone had to calculate how many rotations he could afford before bailing out! But, to bailout he would be in danger of striking the tail surfaces or the enormous propeller. He

Corsair: The Saga of the Legendary Bent-Wing Fighter-Bomber

This full-size F4U-1 was tested in the NACA wind tunnel in Langley, Virginia, to reduce the effects of drag on the plane. Every separation in the plane's skin was taped to not interfere with the tests conducted during October 1942. (Vought Aircraft Photo, Courtesy H.J. "Jerry" Dalton, Jr.)

This early F4U-1 clearly reveals the concave turtledeck side to improve rearward visibility for the aviator (open arrow). Also of interest is the landing gear position indicator on the wing (black arrow). Both features were discarded on later Corsairs. (Ling-Temco-Voght Photo, Cortesy Arthur L. Schoeni)

could not see the ground clearly because the plane's nose was in line with the horizon; he was in a flat spin! After about a dozen rotations Lyman Bullard spoke into the radio to tell Boone it was time to release the spin 'chute. Guyton pulled on the red handle at once. The tail came up and the XF4U-1 stopped its macabre rotating. A safe landing was made from a one thousand foot altitude.

Bullard counted 13 rotations from the ground while Guyton counted only ten in the air.

Boone Guyton repeated the spin test on April 2, 1941, with the same results; pull on the red handle and release the drogue parachute to raise the tail and dive to safety.

No known spin problems were reported during the Corsair's long term of service; perhaps because the aviators were warned not to spin the Corsair.

After considering the harrowing spin tests the U.S. Navy Bureau of Aeronautics eliminated the two-rotation spin requirement from the final acceptance tests and required that the F4U-1 be restricted to only one rotation. Later, the Corsair pilot's handbook stated "WARNING-No intentional spinning is permitted."

During October 1942 a full-size F4U-1 was tested in the NACA wind tunnel at Langley, Virginia, to detect and eliminate parasitic drag. Corrections included an arresting hook fuselage opening fairing, smooth surface wing walks, and tighter fitting wing access doors.

As one of the pioneers in high speed single-engine fighters, the Vought XF4U-1 was one of the first aircraft to encounter compressibility in a dive; a phenomenon that was also to plague the Republic P-47 Thunderbolt.

The Corsair was capable of attaining diving speeds in excess of 500 mph in the thin air of high altitudes. The combinations of high speed and altitude made the airflow over the wing, fuselage, and propeller tips actually break up, literally splashing over the aircraft in a very disturbed pattern instead of flowing smoothly. This forced the plane to dive steeper and faster.

When a plane's high speed, high altitude dive approached the vertical, if the control stick was pulled back too soon without allowing the plane to reach denser air, it could suffer serious damage.

In 1941, test pilot Ralph Verdon encountered the little-understood compressibility during a test dive with the Lockheed YP-38 Lightning. Verdon tried to level off from the high speed dive at a high altitude, causing the entire tail to tear off his plane, killing the brave aviator.

High speed record-breaking aircraft never encountered the compressibility phenomenon because they flew at low altitude at all times and never reached critical speeds at high altitudes.

On April 18, 1941, the U.S. Navy placed an order for 625 F4U-1 production Corsairs in Bureau of Aeronautics contract No 82811.

The Bent-Wing Corsair was no "draft horse"; it was a "thoroughbred stallion" that had to be tamed before it could prove its worth. About two-score modifications were necessary to tame the F4U-1.

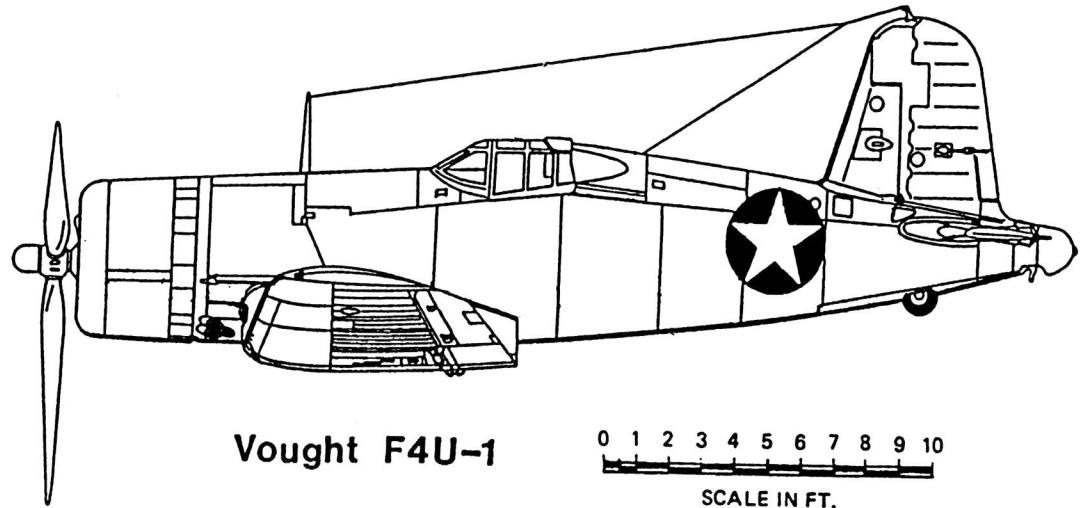

With 17 inches added to the nose length, the already marginal forward visibility of the F4U-1 worsened and became unbearable when the U.S. Navy forced the cockpit back from its original location. (Vought Aircraft Photo, enhanced by Author)

Chapter I: The Corsair is Born

Brewster Aeronautical Corporation was contracted to construct Corsairs on November 1, 1941. The planes were designated F3A-1. Brewster constructed one of the first Corsair bomb racks. This is the first F3A-1 flown by Brewster test pilot Ralph Romaine. (Brewster Aeronautical Corp, Courtesy Ray Hill)

In December 1941, Goodyear Aircraft Corp was contracted to build Corsairs, designated FG-1. This is the first FG-1 taking off at the Akron, Ohio, factory with Art Chapman at the controls. (Goodyear Aircraft Photo, Courtesy Nick Houprich)

The Corsair suffered the misfortune to be designed at a time of transition from the peacetime 1930s to the wartime 1940s. It fulfilled and surpassed the naval fighter requirements of its time, but then endured the agony of being unduly criticized for not meeting the later wartime requirements. Later American fighter aircraft benefited from the Corsair's growing pains without the necessity of constant time-consuming refinements.

Aileron span of the XF4U-1 was increased on the F4U-1 to overcome the inertia created by the U.S. Navy addition of two heavy machine guns and 775 rounds of .50 calibre ammunition in each wing. This change preserved the XF4U-1's excellent rate of roll that was to become the Corsair's maneuvering trademark. The hydraulic system was also modified to fold the much heavier wing panels.

Armor weighing 170 lbs was specified by the U.S. Navy to protect the oil tank, cockpit seat, and back. A bulletproof windshield was also added to protect the aviator. An automatically released life raft was specified for a few Corsairs but was soon discontinued; however, a jettisonable canopy was added and retained. Wing flotation bags were discarded to save weight.

The F4U-1 engine was an uprated P&W R-2800-8 (B) that produced 2,000 hp for takeoff. Length was 33 ft.-4 in, wingspan was 41 ft-3 in, and height was 15 ft-3 in. Loaded weight was 12,050 lbs. Rate of climb at sea level was 3,000 ft per min. Maximum speed was 419.37 miles per hour at 19,900 ft. Service ceiling was 36,900 feet. Despite the added weight the F4U-1 range was a repectable 1,070 miles.

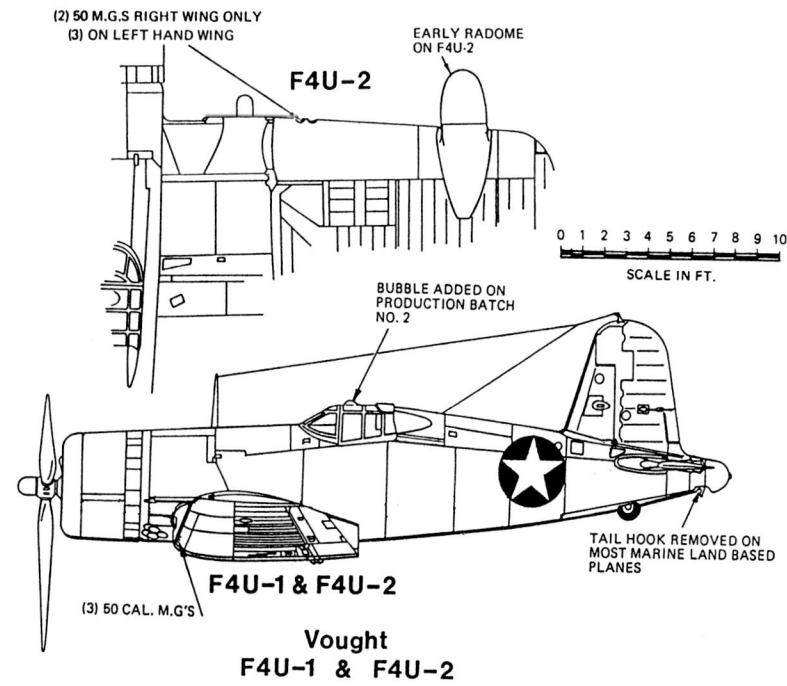

Before the first F4U-1 left the assembly line the Bureau of Aeronautics proposed that a number of the F4U-1 Corsairs be converted to night fighters, designated F4U-2. The conversion work was accomplished by Naval Aircraft Factory Philadelphia, Pennsylvania, and Naval Air Station Quonset Point, Rhode Island, in order not to disrupt the Vought F4U-1 production. (Vought Aircraft Artwork, enhanced by Author)

U.S. Navy demanded more Corsairs than Vought could produce. Further, the Vought engineers, test pilots, and experimental shop craftsmen were fully occupied with the constant U.S. Navy refinement of the Bent-Wing Corsair. Vought-Sikorsky needed production partners.

On November 1, 1941, the Brewster Aeronautical Corporation of New York City and Johnsville, Pennsylvania, a builder of naval aircraft, was contracted to build the F4U-1, designated the F3A-1.

During December 1941 Goodyear Aircraft Corp, a division of Goodyear Tire & Rubber Co, was also contracted to build Corsairs in Akron, Ohio, designated the FG-1. Goodyear had experience building planes and dirigibles. Vought, Brewster, and Goodyear were to build identical Corsairs with all parts interchangeable.

Although the production F4U-1 Corsair was on its way, additional tests were requested by the U.S. Navy with the experimental XF4U-1 (the very first Corsair) in an apparent attempt to find a flaw in the design.

On April 19, 1941, Boone Guyton flew to Naval Air Station (NAS) Anacostia, where the XF4U-1 was weight-checked and inspected. Boone began testing/demonstrating the XF4U-1 with Lt. Frederick Traprell, USN, as the check/chase pilot in a Wildcat. After completing the required maneuvers, including spin tests, the XF4U-1 was approved.

With its intended purpose over, the XF4U-1 was flown to NACA in Langley, Virginia, on June 14, 1941, then to Anacostia, Washington, D.C., and then to Naval Aircraft Factory, Philadelphia, by August 1, 1941. After stays at Vought, NAF, and Anacostia, U.S. Navy aviators had the chance to fly the original Bent Wing Corsair; then back to Vought and off to NAS Anacostia in May 1942. One year later, June 30, 1943, the XF4U-1 appeared at NAS Patuxant River, Maryland. Its final days were spent at the Technical Training Center at Norman, Oklahoma.

Instead of preserving this magnificent and historic airplane, the Vought XF4U-1 was apparently scrapped by the U.S. Navy in December 1943.

Even before the first F4U-1 Corsair left the assembly line, the Bureau of Aeronautics proposed another change. In response to the U.S. Navy's request, Vought-Sikorsky submitted its proposal VS-325 to the Bureau of Aeronautics on January 6, 1942, for an AI radar-equipped night-fighter version of the Corsair, designated the XF4U-2. The night-fighter mock-up was inspected and approved by the Navy 22 days later at the Stratford plant. The U.S. Navy's plan was for Vought to deliver completed F4U-1 Corsairs to the Naval Aircraft Factory, Philadelphia, Pennsylvania, where the electronic equipment was to be installed in order not to interrupt F4U-1 production.

Airborne radar had its start when U.S. Navy Commander Dr A Hoyt Taylor began research of "pulse radar" in 1934 and, two years later, RM Page and RC Guthrie of the Naval research Lab, NAS Anacostia, Washington, DC, extended the range to 25 miles.

The U.S. Army Air Corps also began experimenting with airborne radar because it was discovered that when enemy intruders, such as bombers, are repeatedly interrupted in daylight they resorted to nocturnal intrusions. In early 1941 the Massachusetts Institute of Technology Radiation Laboratory built several experimental models of British AI radar for the Northrop P-61 Black Widow night-fighter program.

U.S. Marine Corps aviation also started a night-fighter program shortly after the Pearl Harbor attack. On January 21, 1942, Marine Lt. Col Harold C Major sent a memo to Col Ralph J Mitchell, Director of Marine Corps Aviation, telling him that U.S. Navy Capt Ralph E Davison of the Bureau of Aeronautics stated on January 20, 1942, that the job of the Marines is to seize a beachhead and hold it until replaced by the Army and, to do this successfully, night fighters would be necessary.

With all three U.S. air forces in agreement there would be no impediment to the development of radar-equipped night-fighter aircraft.

F4U-2 Corsair night-fighters were among the first Corsairs to serve on U.S. aircraft carriers. A trio of F4U-2 Corsairs is about to takeoff from a carrier for a nocturnal mission. (U.S. Navy Photo, via National Archives)

In addition to the foregoing, an exchange of information with British experts, who had considerable radar experience, convinced the BuAer to order a number of radar-equipped fighters, including the Corsair.

In the fall of 1942, under Project Roger, 34 F4U-1 Corsairs were converted into F4U-2 night-fighters; 32 F4U-1 models that had the old "birdcage" canopy were converted by Naval Aircraft Factory, and two F4U-1A models with blown glass canopies were converted in the field by VMF (N) 532 Marine Corps mechanics.

The radar system consisted of an 18 inch AIA (Airborne Intercept type A) parabolic antenna mounted in an aerodynamically shaped pod in the outboard leading edge panel of the starboard or right wing. To counter the 308 lb antennae assembly and make room for the electronics the outboard .50 Cal machine gun was removed from the starboard wing and the overall ammunition was reduced to 250 rounds per gun.

The F4U-2 radar had a search range of two miles at altitudes above 2,000 ft and a minimum range of 500 feet. This radar installation reduced the F4U-2 speed by 11.5 mph. A three-inch radar scope was mounted on the F4U-2 instrument panel and instrument lighting was modified.

The NAF elongated the engine exhaust stacks to dampen the flame in order to preserve the aviator's night vision. A small air scoop was installed

In addition to the antenna pod, electronic equipment, and armament change, the Corsair night-fighters were fitted with engine exhaust stack extensions, dampening the flame to preserve the aviators' night vision (black arrow). The air-driven radar electrical power generator scoop is on the side of the fuselage (white arrow). (U.S. Marine Corps Photo, Author's File)

Chapter I: The Corsair is Born

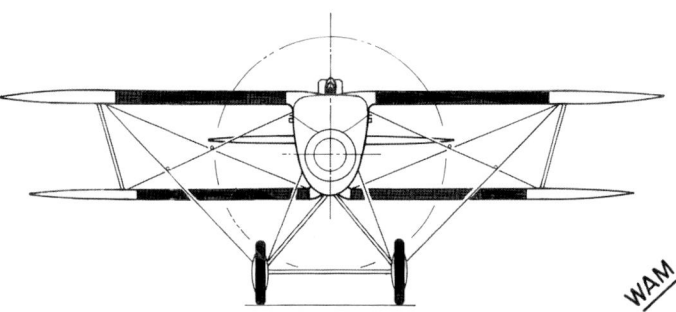

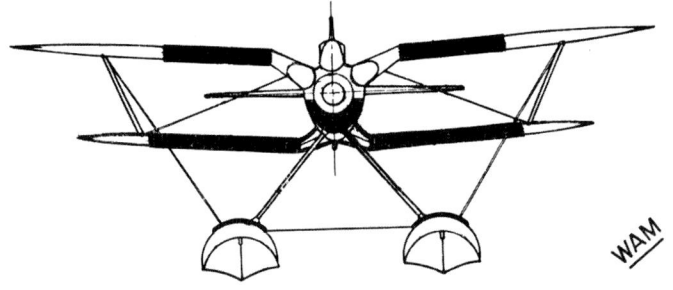

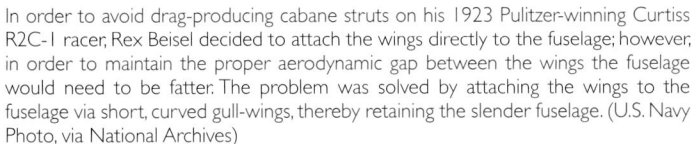

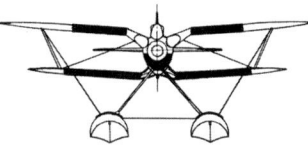

In order to avoid drag-producing cabane struts on his 1923 Pulitzer-winning Curtiss R2C-1 racer, Rex Beisel decided to attach the wings directly to the fuselage; however, in order to maintain the proper aerodynamic gap between the wings the fuselage would need to be fatter. The problem was solved by attaching the wings to the fuselage via short, curved gull-wings, thereby retaining the slender fuselage. (U.S. Navy Photo, via National Archives)

on the right side of the fuselage, midway between the cockpit and engine, to power the air-driven radar power electrical generator. Armor plating was added to the radio compartment.

The NAF F4U-2 (N) radar conversion process required six weeks and doubled the cost of the original F4U-1. Naval Air Station, Quonset Point, Rhode Island, had the task of making the final adjustments to the radar and associated equipment.

The first production F4U-1 BuAer No 02153 was flown by Boone Guyton on June 25, 1942. This plane was to become the first F4U-2 night fighter.

The name, Corsair, became official; having been selected to honor Chance Vought's successful Corsair biplanes of the 1920s. The U.S. Navy received its first F4U-1 Corsair on July 31, 1942.

The Bent-Wing Corsair is often described as having the "most powerful engine (2,000 hp) on a single engine fighter," and as "having the largest propeller (13 ft 4in) of any fighter yet built." As much as the author loves and admires this magnificent machine we must face the facts: the RAF Hawker Typhoon fighter first flew on June 6, 1940, powered by a 2,020 hp Napier-Sabre engine swinging a 3-bladed 14 ft dia propeller. This is mentioned here only to correct those misapprehensions and not to detract from the wonderful Bent-Wing Corsair!

Another misconception is the invention of the inverted gull-wing that is, at times, attributed to Rex Beisel with his Bent-Wing Corsair. In fact, the first known gull-wing/inverted gull-wing design was indeed by Rex Beisel in his 1923 Curtiss Pulitzer Trophy Winning Racer. It was repeated in the 1926 Gloster IV B Schneider Trophy Racer; 1927 Blackburn Ripon I torpedo bomber; 1932 Heinkel He-70 mail/ passenger transport; 1933 Bellanca Air Cruiser light passenger/personal transport; 1934 Supermarine

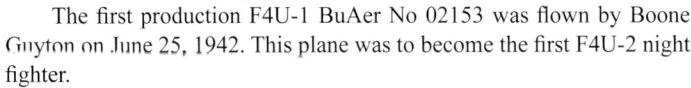

The 1926 British Gloster IV B Schneider Trophy racer featured very pronounced gull and inverted gull wings. Powered by a 12 cylinder, "W" type engine, the plane dropped out of the 1927 race during the fourth lap. (Author's File)

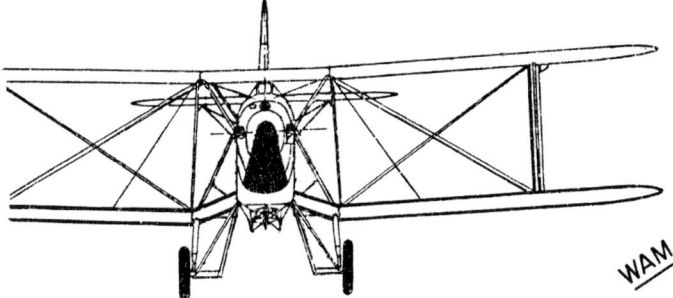

Conceived in 1927, the Royal Navy Blackburn Ripon torpedo bomber resorted to an inverted gull lower wing in order to have adequate clearance for the torpedo with a shorter landing gear. (Air Ministry (Navy), Author's File)

Corsair: The Saga of the Legendary Bent-Wing Fighter-Bomber

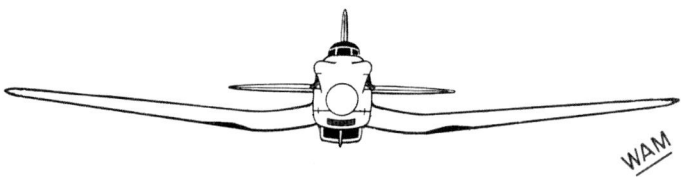

The German Heinkel He 70 of 1932 was designed as a four-passenger high-speed mailplane with a crew of two. The shallow inverted gull-wing could have been for aesthetic effect; however, the right angle juncture with the rounded lower corner of the fuselage antedated the NACA study. (Author's File)

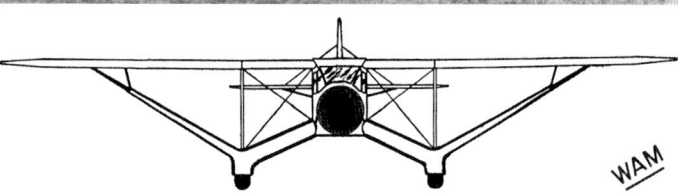

This 1933 Bellanca 15-passenger Air Cruiser featured a combination inverted gull-wing, wing strut, and landing gear. Giuseppe Bellanca patented this inverted gull-wing in 1931 and sued Vought, whom he claimed infringed upon his patent with the Corsair design. (The Aircraft Year Book-1933, Courtesy Oliver L. Parks)

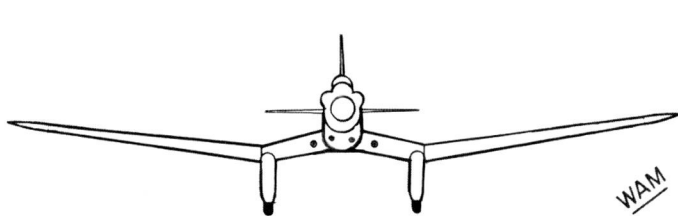

An intermediate design between the 1931 Supermarine S6B Schneider Trophy winner and the Spitfire of WWII, the Supermarine Type 224 four-gun fighter followed Air Ministry Spec F.7/30 with an inverted gull-wing in 1934. As with the Heinkel He 70, the wing is at right angles to the fuselage surface. (Author's File)

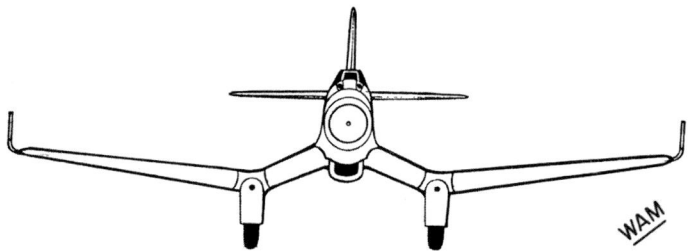

In 1935 the German conglomerate Blohm and Voss introduced the Hamburg 137 single seat fighter-dive bomber. The inverted gull-wing was adopted to accommodate the bombs. The plane never entered production. (Author's File)

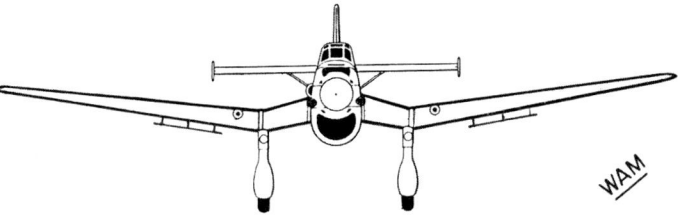

The well publicized Junkers Ju-87 "Stuka" of WWII also employed the inverted gull-wing to accommodate a large under-fuselage bomb. Design stems from 1934. (Photo Courtesy Col. Aladar de Heppes)

Chapter 1: The Corsair is Born

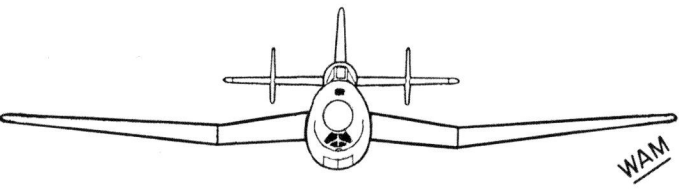

Making its appearance in 1950, the Royal Navy's Fairey Gannet was designed with an inverted gull-wing to clear the enormous radar dome and the weapons bay without an inordinately long landing gear. (Fairey Aircraft Photo, Author's File)

The most recognized inverted gull-wing design is the graceful Bent-Wing Corsair, conceived in 1938. (Vought Aircraft Photo, Courtesy Paul Bower)

224 fighter (called "Spitfire"); 1934 Junkers Ju 87 Stuka Dive Bomber; 1938 Vought Corsair Fighter F4U-1; and 1949 Fairey Gannet Early Warning, anti-Submarine strike aircraft, to name a few.

Despite the many precedents, the Corsair Bent-Wing remains the most graceful and recognizable of all.

On October 26, 1931, Giuseppe M Bellanca, world-famous aircraft designer and CEO of the Bellanca Aircraft Corporation, New Castle, Delaware, applied for a U.S. Patent covering an inverted gull-wing. Bellanca was awarded U.S. Patent No 2,014,366 for an inverted gull wing on Sept. 17, 1935 (*see* pp 32-33).

When Giuseppe Bellanca learned of the large U.S. Navy orders for the Vought F4U-1 he wrote to Igor Sikorsky, president of Vought-Sikorsky Aircraft, regarding the possible infringement of his patent by the F4U-1 in his letter dated Jan. 9, 1941. This requested compensation on a per-unit-construction basis.

On April 24, 1942, Charles A. Hatfield, secretary of the United Aircraft Corporation, wrote to Bellanca that many aircraft had been designed and built with inverted gull-wings that pre-dated and post-dated Bellanca's patent.

Bellanca replied that neither he nor the U.S. Patent Office could verify the existence of other inverted gull-wing designs!

Cooper, Kerr & Dunham, United Aircraft's attorneys, responded with a list of pre-Patent proposed and constructed inverted gull-wing designs that included some of the previously mentioned aircraft.

Upon consultation with the Bureau of Aeronautics, Vought was relieved of any obligation in this matter.

An interesting aspect of the Corsair's enormous wing flap design, hardly ever mentioned, is that the flap angle automatically decreased from

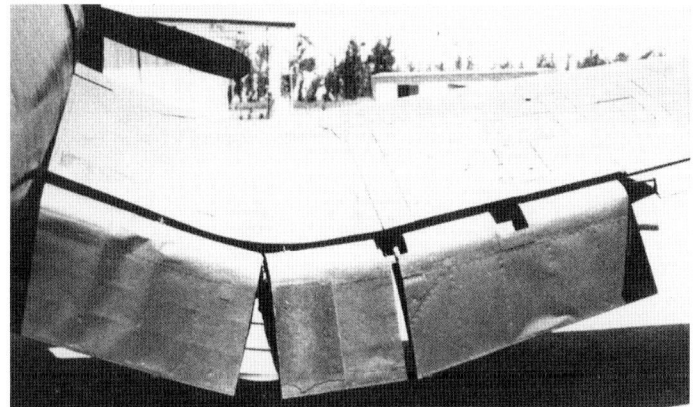

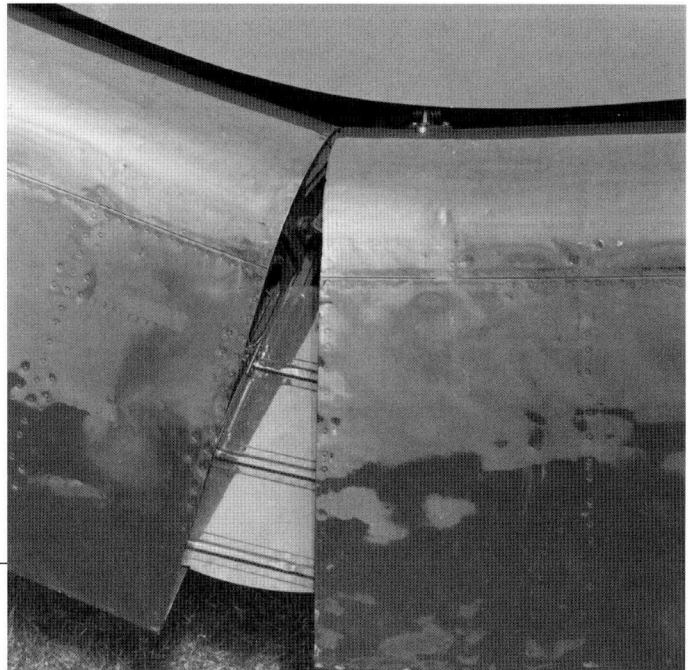

The Corsair's large three-section wing flaps assisted the aviator during maneuvers and automatically decreased its set angle when confronted by excessive airflow pressure. (Alain Pelletier Photo, Author's File)

First page of Bellanca Patent (Author's File)

UNITED STATES PATENT OFFICE

2,014,366
AIRPLANE

Giuseppe M. Bellanca, New Castle, Del.

Application October 26, 1931, Serial No. 571,165

12 Claims. (Cl. 244—12)

This invention relates to an improved airplane.

An object of the invention is to design an airplane which combines the advantages of high speed, inherent stability and easy maneuverability.

Another object of the invention is to provide an airplane with a novel type of landing gear.

Yet another object is to provide a well braced monoplane capable of high speed performance.

A further object is to provide a low wing monoplane having a relatively high center of pressure.

A still further object is to provide an airplane structure with a novel type of cabane strut.

With these and other equally important objects in view the invention resides in the concept of providing a low wing monoplane which is so designed as to present improved lateral stability and in which the landing gear is positioned relatively closely to the wing, while at the same time providing a relatively high center of pressure.

In order to enable a more ready comprehension of the invention typical physical embodiments are shown in the accompanying drawing, in which:

Fig. 1 is a front elevation of the improved airplane.

Fig. 2 is a side view thereof; and

Fig. 3 is a front view of a modification.

As shown in the drawing, the airplane comprises a fuselage 1 in the front end of which is provided a power plant 2 and a tractor propeller 3. In the rear of the fuselage is mounted the empennage structure shown generally at 4. Preferably the airplane is of the close coupled type so as to provide easy maneuverability with minimum area of control surface. The airplane shown in the drawing is of the closed cabin type but it will be readily comprehended that the fuselage may be of any other design, such for example as the open cockpit type.

As noted hereinbefore, an object of the invention is to provide a low wing monoplane having a relatively high center of lift and in the preferred embodiment the wings are so designed as to bring the center of pressure of the wings up closely adjacent to the center of gravity of the plane. As will be seen particularly in Figs. 1 and 3, this is accomplished by providing a single piece wing having a downwardly extending inner section 5 and an upwardly projecting extension 6. This wing preferably is of the thin section high speed type and is of rugged construction. Such thin section cantilever wing, for example, may have a ratio of camber to chord of approximately 12% and may comprise a section such as Bellanca 4414. Such an airfoil, for example, may have a middle camber line maximum ordinate of 4% of the chord located at 40% of the chord, and a fineness ratio of 14%. It will be observed that the monoplane wing comprises largely the dihedral section 6. The dihedral angle of the wing may of course be varied depending upon the desired compromise between maximum stability and lift and minimum resistance.

The inner wing section 5, near its connection to the fuselage, is preferably filleted, as shown at 7, so as to diminish or minimize interference effects. It will be observed that by extending the inner short section of the wing 5 downwardly and the outer main section of the wing upwardly, as shown, a low wing monoplane structure is obtained while providing a center of pressure which is spaced considerably above the lowermost portion of the wing.

The lowermost section of the wing, that is to say the point 9, can thus be positioned very close to the ground, and considerably closer than any other monoplane structure having a center of pressure which approaches the horizontal position of the center of gravity.

In the preferred embodiment of the invention this depression of a portion of the wing is utilized as the mounting point for the landing gear. It will be observed that this at once presents an opportunity to mount the landing gear very ruggedly on the wing and to considerably shorten the landing wheel struts. In order to secure maximum speed during flight the landing gear is made retractable by utilizing any effective mechanism. As shown in Fig. 2, the landing gear comprises the two landing wheels 10 mounted upon the axles 11 from which an extension or extensions 12 extend upwardly to and are pivoted upon structural elements of the wing, such as the front and/or rear spars. The landing gear mechanism is provided with operating devices, indicated generally by the numerals 12 and 13, for extending the gear into landing position or retracting them within the contour of the wing, as shown by the dotted line position 14. It will be observed, as noted before, that for this type of wing structure the landing gear can be relatively rugged and positioned very closely adjacent the main lift surface.

Another improvement of the invention comprises the rigidification of the wing so as to en-

---

Second page of Bellanca Patent (Author's File)

2,014,366

able it to withstand the relatively high stresses resulting from high speed flight. As shown in Figs. 1 and 2, a stream lined member 15 extends downwardly from the underside of the fuselage and is effectively stream lined so as to eliminate parasitic resistance. This member, in the airplane shown in Figs. 1 and 2, serves the function of the cabane strut; while in Fig. 3 it serves a double function, as a cabane strut and a mount for the auxiliary or supplemental wheel 10'. To the cabane strut are attached the flying wires 16 extending and connected to the wing surfaces and preferably at or near the lowermost portion, as shown clearly in Fig. 1. As shown in Fig. 2, the lower flying wires may be duplicated so as to provide two wires, 16 and 16', extending from the cabane strut respectively to the front and rear spars of the wing. Preferably the flying wires and the other wiring of the plane are stream lined to diminish parasitic resistance.

The rigidity of the airplane is further enhanced by providing the landing wires 17 connected each at one end to its corresponding wing and at the other end to an upper section of the fuselage. If desired, to further insure the rigidity and immovability of the wing incidence wires 18 and 19 may be provided which are attached to the front and rear wing spars and extend diagonally therefrom to the fuselage in the usual manner. Similar incidence wires 20 and 21 may be provided on the underside of the wing which extend therefrom diagonally to a point of attachment on the cabane strut.

It will be appreciated that this type of structure insures an airplane which is particularly useful in high speed flying, such as for military purposes. The close coupling provides for easy maneuverability with minimum area of control surfaces and hence diminishes resistance. The provision of a low wing monoplane structure having, in fact, a center of pressure corresponding to or approximating a high wing monoplane, brings the center of pressure up coincident with or closely adjacent the center of gravity of the plane and thus insures inherent stability. The utilization of the double dihedral section wing not only provides for effective lateral stability but also permits the utilization of a low position of the landing gear with the minimum length of landing gear strut. In view of the low permissive position of the point of attachment for the landing gear, this structure may be made very rugged to withstand the high stresses necessarily resulting in landing a high speed plane. This is conceived to be a marked improvement, particularly in view of the fact that a large proportion of airplane accidents are due to defective landing gears. The provision of a landing gear which is retractable into the wing minimizes parasitic resistance during flying. It is particularly to be noted that the present structure is particularly suitable for retractable landing wheels in view of the fact that the wing designed provides for a short landing wheel strut and consequently a corresponding rapid movement of the landing wheel from its extended operative position to its retracted inoperative position within the wing.

As shown in Fig. 3, if desired the cabane strut structure may be utilized to perform a double function. To do this the supplemental landing wheel 10' may be mounted on or within the cabane strut. In the preferred modification of the invention this landing wheel is mounted well within the stream line cabane strut so that only a small portion is extended. An advantage of this type of structure is that in the event one of the landing wheels fails to operate, which often occurs, it is still possible for the pilot to ground the plane without particular difficulty or danger due to the fact that the two point support is provided. Furthermore, in the event that both of the retractable landing wheels become inoperative for any reason, a rotating surface is still provided upon which the plane may be balanced. Since this auxiliary wheel is in the center of the machine and since it may be ruggedly mounted, there is little danger of it becoming inoperative. It will be appreciated, of course, that the retractable landing wheels 10 and auxiliary landing wheel 10' may be provided with suitable shock absorbing mechanisms, such as oleo gears and the like.

It will now be observed that an improved airplane has been provided. The plane combines the structural advantages of a low wing monoplane and the aerodynamic advantages of a high wing plane. Furthermore, due to the design of the wing, that is to say due to the lateral dihedral, improved lateral stability is obtained. In addition to the improved lateral stability, resulting from the design of the wing, an improved landing gear is permitted. The plane therefore combines the advantages of improved stability with high speed and safe landing conditions.

While improved modifications of the invention have been described, it is to be understood that these are given merely by way of example and the invention is intended not to be restricted to the specific device as shown, except as such restrictions are clearly imposed by the appended claims.

I claim:

1. A monoplane comprising a fuselage, a wing attached to the fuselage at a bottom portion thereof, the wing having a short span section adjacent the fuselage of negative dihedral and the remaining long wing portion of positive dihedral, and tension means attached respectively to the fuselage and wings to brace the wing.

2. A low wing monoplane, the sustenation surface of which has a short span section of negative dihedral and a longer span continuous section of positive dihedral.

3. A low wing monoplane comprising a fuselage, sustenation surface attached to a lower portion of the fuselage such surfaces having an inner short span wing section of negative dihedral and an outer longer span of positive dihedral, and a landing wheel positioned at the lowermost portion of the wing the said lowermost portion being spaced below a plane including the bottom of the fuselage.

4. A low wing monoplane, each wing of which comprises a short span root section of negative dihedral a portion of which extends below the bottom of the fuselage and an outer section of positive dihedral, the said sections being so designed and arranged that the plane of the center of pressure of the wing is positioned above the transverse plane defining the lowermost section of the wing, and a retractable landing wheel attached to the wing substantially in the said transverse plane.

5. A low wing monoplane, each wing of which has a negative root section and an outer positive dihedral portion, a landing wheel mounted at the intersection of said portions and a third wheel directly mounted on the fuselage between the said wheels.

Chapter I: The Corsair is Born

2,014,366

6. A low wing monoplane comprising a fuselage, sustenation surfaces attached at each side and at the lower portion of the fuselage, each sustenation surface comprising a short span root section of decided negative dihedral and an outer continuous section of positive dihedral so designed that the joint between the positive and negative sections extends below a horizontal plane comprehending the lower portion of the fuselage; the outer portion of the wing having a wing tip positioned vertically above the point of attachment of the root section to the fuselage; retractable landing wheels mounted directly on each wing at the lowermost portion thereof, a cabane strut mounted on the longitudinal axis of the fuselage and extending downwardly therefrom and terminating in a horizontal plane below the horizontal plane including the point of attachment of the retractable landing wheels to the said wings, a non-retractable landing wheel mounted within the cabane strut and largely enclosed thereby; and tension wires attached at one end to the cabane strut and at other ends to the wing structure.

7. A low wing monoplane comprising a fuselage, a cantilever wing attached to the fuselage at a lower portion thereof, the wing having a short span section of negative dihedral adjacent the fuselage and the remaining longer portion of positive dihedral, a cabane strut extending below the fuselage and tension means attached respectively to the wing and cabane strut to brace the wing.

8. A low wing monoplane, the sustenation surface of which has a short span root section of negative dihedral and a longer span continuous section of positive dihedral and a landing wheel mounted at the end of the short span section.

9. A low wing monoplane, each wing of which has a short span root section of negative dihedral and a continuous outer section of positive dihedral, a retractable landing wheel mounted at the end of the short span section, and a non-retractable landing wheel mounted on the fuselage between the said wheels.

10. A low wing monoplane, each wing of which has a short span root section of negative dihedral and a continuous outer section of positive dihedral, a landing wheel mounted at the end of each short span section, a cabane strut positioned substantially on the longitudinal center of the fuselage and extending downwardly therefrom, tension means attached respectively to the strut and wings to brace the wings, and a third landing wheel carried by the cabane strut.

11. A low wing monoplane, each wing of which is of cantilever construction and which also has a short span root section of negative dihedral and a continuous outer section, a landing wheel mounted at the end of each short span section, a cabane strut positioned substantially on the longitudinal center of the fuselage and extending downwardly therefrom, the cabane strut extending forwardly and rearwardly of the center of gravity of the plan, tension means attached respectively to the strut and wings to brace the wings.

12. An airplane comprising a fuselage, a thin section cantilever wing attached to a lower portion of the fuselage to form a low wing monoplane; a cabane strut positioned substantially on the longitudinal center of the fuselage and extending downwardly therefrom and terminating in a horizontal plane below the plane of the wing, and adapted to serve as an emergency landing skid; retractable landing wheels mounted directly on the wing sections, tension means attached at one end to the cabane strut and at the other end to the wings substantially at the area of connection of the landing wheels to the wing, other tension means attached at one end to the fuselage and at the other to the wings at said area, whereby the said tension means serve to brace the landing gear, wing and the cabane skid.

GIUSEPPE M. BELLANCA.

Third page of Bellanca Patent (Author's File)

Sept. 17, 1935. G. M. BELLANCA 2,014,366
AIRPLANE
Filed Oct. 26, 1931

Inventor
GIUSEPPE M. BELLANCA
By Semmes & Semmes
Attorneys

Fourth page of Bellanca Patent (Author's File)

the set angle when met with excessive airflow pressure. This amazing system could be used to advantage during combat by popping the flaps to decrease the radius of a turn.

In addition, the Corsair aviator had the advantage to be able to set the flaps in ten degree increments from zero to fifty degrees instead of only zero degrees up or fifty degrees down as in most contemporary fighters.

Although F4U-1 production aircraft were already in action against the Japanese in the Solomon Islands, more test flights were necessary to improve the Corsair's control and handling, as well as correct the powerful engine's problems.

When operating at altitudes above 30,000 feet the engine often lost power and/or stalled. It was discovered that this was caused by inadequate pressurization of the distributors, allowing the sparks to jump the gap and burn out the distributor points. This sparking also interfered with radio reception. P&W service representatives, with kits of parts and instructions, rushed to the affected squadrons in the war zones to cure this problem in the field by increasing the air pressure to the distributor.

Another engine problem was the intake and exhaust valve rocker arm box covers that were made from magnesium. It appears that the powerful engine magnesium box covers warped because of the heat and, with the seal broken, the boxes leaked oil badly. It was discovered that the 1,200 hp Pratt & Whitney R-1830 engine aluminum rocker arm box covers were interchangeable with the R-2800 engine rocker arm box covers; therefore, many Corsairs were modified with exchanged covers from Wildcat fighters and Liberator bombers!

Problems were also created by the engine temperature control cowl flaps. The initial installation consisted of a hydraulic actuator for each individual flap in order to insure that the remaining flaps would continue to function in the event of an actuator failure. Unfortunately, the small actuators leaked hydraulic fluid that sprayed onto the windshield. This was cured by installing a master actuator that operated all the cooling flaps via a cable and roller mechanism. The upper three cowl cooling flaps were sealed closed to guarantee that no leakage would strike the windshield.

The huge Hamilton Standard Hydromatic propeller required a control accumulator that provided the necessary oil pressure to keep the propeller blade at any angle set by the aviator. A negative G force, without the control accumulator, would allow the propeller to enter its low-pitch position, overspeed in the airstream, and ruin the engine main bearing, thereby destroying the powerplant. Early in the production phase of the Corsair, propeller control accumulator delivery often lagged behind the intense Corsair production schedule.

On March 15, 1943, Boone Guyton flew from Bridgeport Airport in F4U-1 BuNo 02157 for a series of engine and aircraft tests. At 230 mph the test pilot put the Corsair into a shallow dive with flaps depressed and recorded a "back-off" angle of 25 degrees where the flaps stabilized; a successful test. Boone then climbed to 25,000 ft for a full power run.

The run was to be at full military power without water injection. The run had to be at 24,500 ft, so the test pilot put the Corsair into a shallow dive to gain speed for the run. As Guyton checked the engine cylinder temperatures the plane began shaking; lightly at first, but then increasingly violently. By the time the Corsair had fallen to 20,000 feet, the aviator's head was slamming against the narrow "birdcage" canopy while black oil was streaming from the engine. The normal engine roar had become a loud metallic rattle of explosions because the propeller had shifted to low pitch and was leading the engine to destruction. At 15,000 ft. altitude Guyton considered taking to his parachute, but decided not to because it would be "the last straw," so he returned the ailing Corsair to the airport while trailing black smoke. The edge of the runway was separated from a marsh by an earthen dike to keep the water of Long Island Sound from flooding the runway at high tides or during storms. With flaps full down and descending rapidly the Corsair fuselage hit the dike, broke in half at the cockpit, and catapulted the seat, with Guyton in it, forty feet through the air. The wings had shorn off, converting the once beautiful Corsair into piles of junk.

The injured aviator was rushed to the Bridgeport Hospital emergency room where it was discovered that he suffered two fractured vertebrae, fractured kneecaps, and assorted lacerations.

Among Guyton's visitors was a close friend, famous aviator Charles A. Lindbergh, who had a working arrangement with Vought as a consulting aeronautical engineer. Lindbergh not only attended conferences, but had been test flying Corsairs at the plant, at Naval Air Stations and Test Centers, as well as in the Pacific Theatre of Operations since January 1943.

Boone Guyton's injuries kept him in hospital for three months, after which his recovery was rapid.

While Guyton was recuperating in hospital the U.S. Navy authorized a new design cockpit canopy on March 27, 1943, that facilitated raising the seat of the F4U-1, improving visibility from the cockpit. This was only one of the major improvements that created the F4U-1A beginning with the 689th F4U-1 production aircraft.

A blown glass bubble replaced the heavily framed "birdcage" canopy that was still standard on some contemporary U.S. fighter designs,

Boone Guyton's crash with F4U-1 BuNo 02157 (upper photo) resulted in a destroyed airplane (lower photo) when it struck a dike during an emergency landing. The pilot, still in his seat, was catapulted forty feet into the air and seriously injured. (Vought Aircraft Photo, Courtesy Paul Bower)

Chapter I: The Corsair is Born

This photo of the Vought test pilots was taken while Boone Guyton was in hospital recovering from his near-fatal crash. Chief Test Pilot Lyman Bullard, Jr stands at the center. (Ling-Temco-Vought, Courtesy Arthur L. Schoeni)

This F4U-1, BuNo 02158, was the sixth production Corsair. It became the test F4U-1A when it was fitted with the blown glass bubble canopy; adjustable aviator's seat; strengthened overturn structure; new instrument panel; and other improvements. The entire Corsair production was later converted to building the F4U-1A. (Ling-Temco-Vought Photo, Courtesy Arthur L. Schoeni)

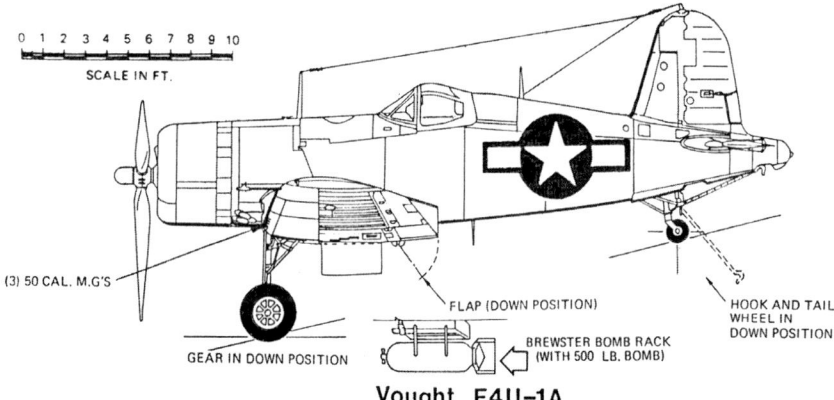

The Brewster bomb rack replaced the jury-rigged bomb racks made by squadron mechanics in the field. Both bomb racks introduced bombing by the Corsairs. (Vought Aircraft Drawing, enhanced by Author)

The clean, uncluttered, straight and direct lines of the Corsair are evident in this profile photo of a production F4U-1A. Famous World War II author and cartoonist Bill Mauldin described the Corsair's appearance as "old fashioned classiness." (Ling-Temco-Vought Photo, Courtesy Arthur L. Schoeni)

Corsair: The Saga of the Legendary Bent-Wing Fighter-Bomber

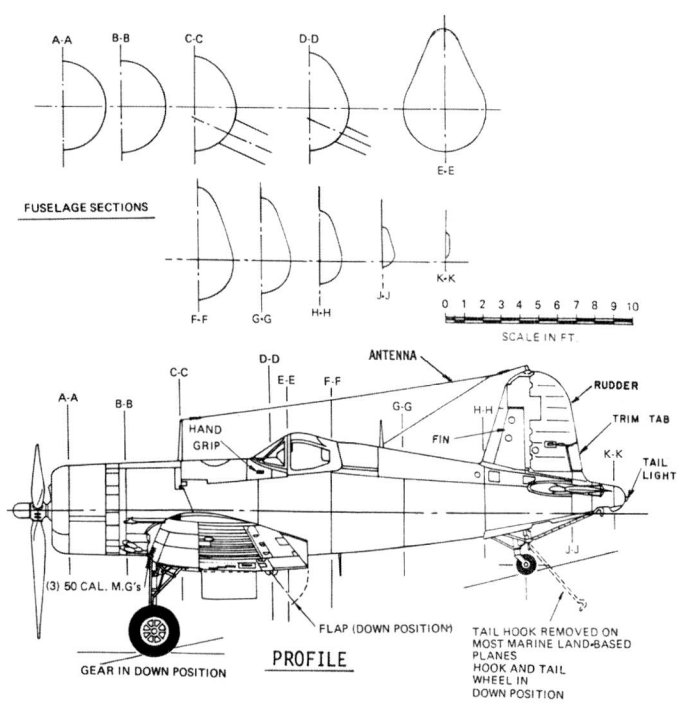

Vought F4U-1A

This detailed profile reveals the fuselage sections. Note that the tail hook was removed on many U.S. Marine land-based Corsairs as was the wing folding mechanism at times, thereby saving weight and improving performance. (Vought Aircraft Artwork, enhanced by Author)

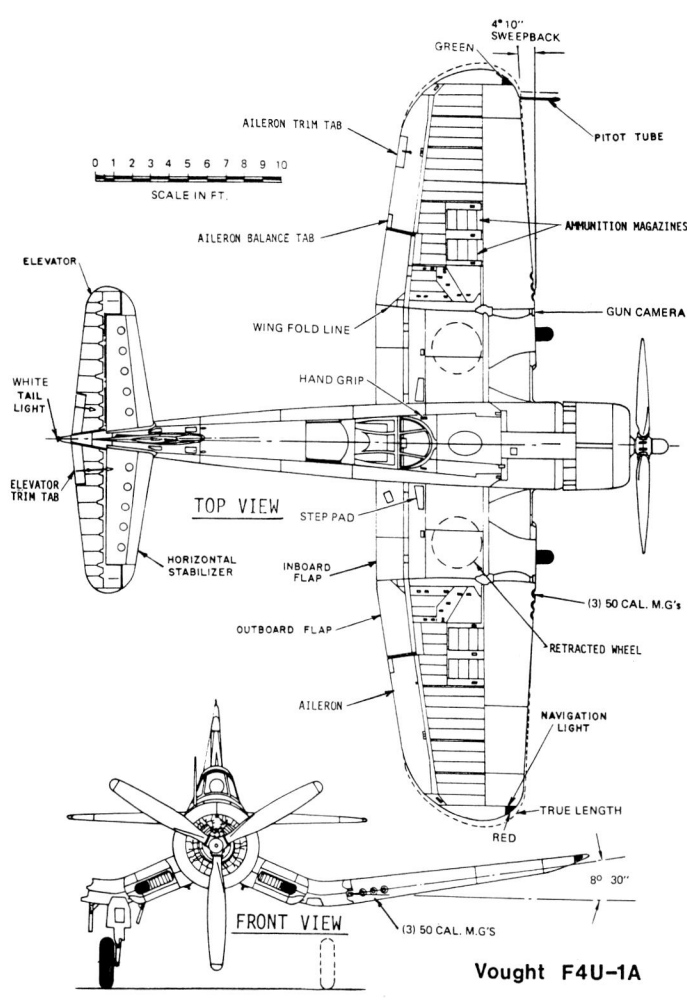

Vought F4U-1A

The basic Corsair was constructed of aluminum alloys, wood, and fabric. The framework was aluminum alloy with Alclad covering, except the rudder, elevator, and that portion of the wing outboard of the ammunition magazines, which was fabric covered. The ailerons were of wood. (Ling-Temco-Vought Artwork, enhanced by Author)

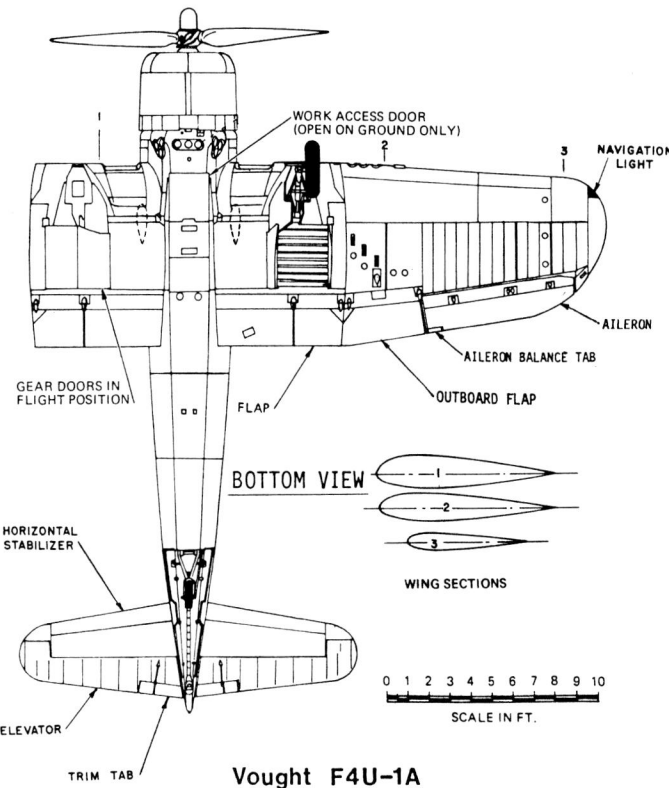

Vought F4U-1A

This underside drawing of the F4U-1A reveals the engine exhaust stack clusters, machine gun shell ejection ports, and landing gear in extended and retracted conditions. The landing gear turned 90 degrees as it retracted with the wheel flat inside the wing root. (Vought Aircraft Artwork, enhanced by Author)

A trio of F4U-1A Corsairs fly by in formation showing their three color camouflage. Although an improvement, it was not the finest of Corsairs, but it set the pace for Corsairs to come. (Official U.S. Navy Photo, via U.S. National Archives)

Chapter 1: The Corsair is Born

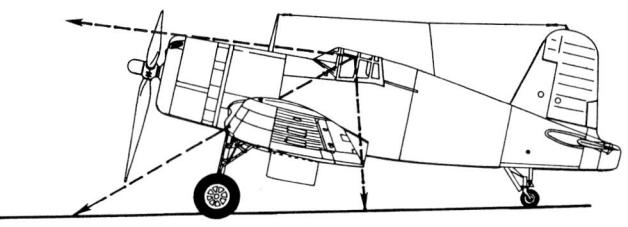

Vought XF4U-1

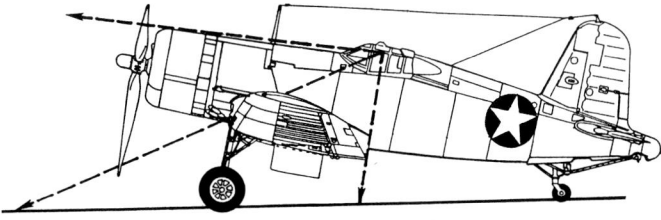

Vought F4U-1

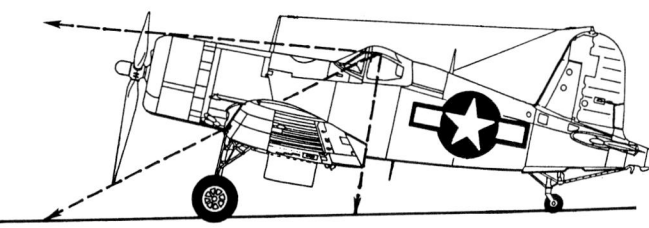

Vought F4U-1A

The aviatior's lines of sight were marginal in the XF4U-1 and deteriorated because of U.S. Navy changes for the production F4U-1. Raising the seat and replacing the birdcage canopy with a blown glass bubble in the F4U-1A improved the lines of sight except the forward ground distance, which never returned to that of the XF4U-1.

The Corsair's basic instrument panel is fairly conventional for the military instrument arrangement of the early WWII era. (Vought Photo, Courtesy Paul Bower)

The left hand console contains the landing gear retracting lever (arrow); throttle (open arrow); wing folding control (curved arrow); CO_2 bottle for emergency landing gear extending (open curved arrow); trim tab control (tailed arrow); and hydraulic system hand pump (box-tail arrow). (Vought Photo, Courtesy Paul Bower)

including the Wildcat, Hellcat, razor-back Thunderbolt, and razor-back Mustang. The only reinforcing structure on the new Corsair canopy was two longitudinal bars at the upper corners of the bubble. This modified Corsair was soon to be known as the F4U-1A.

Simultaneous with the canopy change, the following design changes were accomplished: Gun sight modified; seat made adjustable to be raised or lowered nine inches; control stick lengthened; rudder/brake pedals modified; new instrument panel installed; wheel brake cylinders modified; fuel tank attachment to fuselage structure strengthened; machine gun belt feed improved; horizontal stabilizer reinforced; overturn structure strengthened; and turtledeck modified to fair into the canopy bubble.

In order to extend the Corsair's range, two 56 gal. wing fuel tanks were reinstalled, located in the leading edge, outboard of the guns. When twin pylon-mounted 154 gallon droppable fuel tanks were developed on future Corsair designs, the wing tanks were no longer incorporated.

A water injection system had been developed by Thompson Products Inc. and Pratt & Whitney to temporarily increase the power of the engine without overheating the cylinders. This was named "War Emergency Power" and consisted of one 5.9 gallon center tank and two 2.3 gallon left and right tanks, plus a pump regulator that metered the water to the

The defense workers of Walter Kidde & Co, Inc, designers and manufacturers of fire extinguishing equipment and systems, contributed the $75,000 needed to buy this Vought F4U-1A Corsair for the U.S. Navy. Left to right, the attendees at the ceremony were: Rex Beisel (manufacturer); Navy Commander (recipient); and representatives of Walter Kidde & Co and Walter Kidde & Co employees (donors). Ceremony was in June 1943. (Walter Kidde & Co. Photo, Courtesy Thomas G. Dickinson, M.D.)

carburetor. The system was energized by moving the throttle full-forward, breaking a safety-wire and tripping a switch that turned the water injection system "on." Pulling the throttle back to a normal operating position turned the water injection system "off." The "water" was actually a water-alcohol mixture of 40 percent alcohol that was needed to keep the water from freezing. Further, the alcohol burned cooler than gasoline.

The theory behind WEP (War Emergency Power) is to restrain detonation. This, combined with the capability to operate the engine at the ideal power while the superior cooling of the water permits a higher intake manifold pressure to be used, creating more power in the event of an emergency without overheating the cylinders.

The WEP Water Injection increased the engine horsepower to 2,450 and pushed the engine manifold pressure into the danger zone as engine temperature grew. Fuel burned at an enormous rate when WEP was actuated, boosting speeds to 365 miles per hour at sea level.

War Emergency Power was not to be in operation longer than five minutes; throttle to remain on Full Open; and propeller control maintained at 2700 RPM. Engines fitted with water injection were designated R-2800-8W.

The WEP was responsible for saving the lives of many U.S. Navy and U.S. Marine aviators having been introduced after 1,550 F4U-1s had been built.

During WWII many defense industry workers contributed a part of their salary to buy important weapons so they could give a tank, plane, or ship that they built to the U.S. Army, Navy, or Marine Corps.

The first F4U-1 Corsair aircraft carrier trials were flown from the escort carrier *USS Sangamon* CVE-26 in Chesapeake Bay, Virginia, on Sept. 25, 1943. Flying the seventh production F4U-1, BuNo 02159, Lt. Cdr Sam Porter, USN, made four takeoffs and landings, and reported that the Corsair did not yet qualify for aircraft carrier duty for the following reasons:

The plane had very poor visibility in the three-point landing altitude which encouraged tail-high landings.

The landing gear revealed stiff oleo shock absorbers causing a high bounce upon touch-down.

What had, at the onset, appeared to be a bountiful advantage proved to be an unexpected disadvantage. The short landing gear created by the inverted gull-wing had caused the bounce because many aircraft with longer landing gear oleos are able to absorb the impact of a landing aircraft

MAIN GEAR DETAIL

The Corsair's short landing gear resulted in a short oleo cylinder that could not absorb the sudden shock of a carrier landing and, therefore, rebounded suddenly. Increasing the air of the air-oil ratio in the cylinder softened the absorption of the landing shock. (Vought Drawing, enhanced by Author)

This Hawker Sea Fury demonstrates how a long-stroke oleo strut absorbs a hard landing on an aircraft carrier. The long cylinder allows the piston to travel further and rebound softer. See white arrow. (Author's File)

Chapter I: The Corsair is Born

on a rolling and pitching deck. The weight-saving and simplification of stowage when retracted resulted in a short-stroke oleo strut that could not absorb the sudden shock of landing and rebounded suddenly.

The Corsair also exhibited a twitch or sudden directional bank in landing caused by the stalling of the left or port wing due to propeller upwash, often rolling the plane to the left.

The small hard rubber tailwheel and short yoke increased the plane's ground angle, placing the big trailing edge flaps very close to the deck, diminishing control and creating directional instability.

Some Corsairs exhibited lateral instability that required aileron trim tab adjustment of from 8 to 10 degrees of the allowable 15 degree tab adjustment.

This fighter, that had been designed for aircraft carrier-based missions, was now relegated to land-based operations and was not to operate from American aircraft carriers in the Pacific until two years later.

This disappointment provided the Corsair with the opportunity to prove its superiority in the capable hands of the U.S. Marine Corps during the South-West Pacific fighting in the Solomon Islands to break the Bismarck Barrier.

"Program Dog" was instituted. This consisted of the diligent, troubleshooting Vought field service representatives Ray De Leva, Malcolm Raffo, Frank R Goetz, and Russ Clark led by Vought field service manager Jack Hospers, who worked long hours with Corsair squadron personnel and Col Stanley Ridderhoff, USMC, to remedy the abovementioned problems and others. Very often the Vought field service representatives brought Vought-prepared kits to simplify and hasten the remedy of problems on-site.

The stiff landing gear oleo strut was improved by replacing the air pressure loading Schradar check value with another model and then changing the air-to-oil ratio, increasing the proportion of air to the oil.

The three-point attitude problems were corrected by replacing the small solid rubber tailwheel with a larger pneumatic tailwheel connected to a longer yoke; however, this tire was prone to suffer blow-outs on hard landings, forcing the return to a solid wheel. The longer tailwheel yoke did alleviate the problem somewhat.

The sudden directional roll to the left was corrected by the addition of a six inch triangular strip of metal or wood to the right, or starboard wing. This "spoiler" made both halves of the wing stall simultaneously, thereby preventing the roll to the left. This remedy was first installed on the 943rd Corsair and future aircraft.

The lateral instability was corrected by the addition of a 1/8 in X 8 in strip of wood glued to the underside of the aileron that was on the wing that was light. When aileron balance tabs were fitted on the F4U-4 and following Corsair models the wooden strips were no longer required.

One item left over from the original Navy requirements was the fact that the Corsair cockpit had no flooring. Two rudder heel-rest troughs were the only structure between the pilot and the dark chasm below. The absence of a floor was specified by the Navy because, in the original U.S. Navy concept, windows in the fuselage bottom were needed in order to aim the anti-bomber 25 lb bombs. When that scheme was abandoned the U.S. Navy failed to specify full flooring for the Corsair.

Vought field service representative Frank Goetz sits on the propeller as he guides Marine mechanics working on a Corsair engine in the Solomons air field at Munda. Goetz spent a year on Pacific air fields getting Corsairs battle-ready. (Vought Aircraft Company, Courtesy H.J. "Jerry" Dalton, Jr.)

To prepare the Corsair for combat operations a modification center was formed at Air Base Group Two, Fleet Marine Force West Coast, in November 1942 under the command of Col Ridderhoff. After 25 days of round-the-clock work, 22 Corsairs were issued to VMF-124 on December 22, 1942, and an additional 22 were ready for VF-12 by January 22, 1943.

A total of 2,814 F4U-1, F4U-1A, and F4U-2 Corsairs were constructed and delivered. It is most interesting to learn how this naval fighter was transformed to perform a myriad of functions for which it was never intended.

II

Corsair Development and Production

The Vought Corsair construction was unique in many ways. As Beisel had successfully employed on the Kingfisher fuselage and float, spot-welding instead of riveting was used in the construction of the Corsair. This avoided the added weight and air resistance of rivets, producing an extremely smooth drag-reducing external finish.

Rex Beisel kept the Bent-Wing Corsair airframe as small as possible and could still safely accommodate the powerful 2,000hp engine. Despite the fact that the F4U-1 had 800 more horsepower than the Wildcat, it had only a three ft larger wingspan and was only 4.5 ft longer, much of which was occupied by the F4U-1 tail cone.

The Vought XF4U-1 tail surface construction and configuration followed that of the Vought SB2U-1 Vindicator and Vought OS2U-1 Kingfisher, while the landing gear rotated 90 degrees and folded back into the wing similar to the Vindicator.

The fuselage was constructed in three sections: the forward section began at the wing root and main bulkhead, and included the bladder fuel cell compartment, as well as the cockpit that contained the seat, hydraulic cylinder, controls, battery, oxygen flask, carbon-dioxide cylinder for emergency landing gear operation, and instruments.

The midsection included all the communications equipment, including Very High Frequency (VHF) and Identification Friend or Foe (IFF).

The aft section included the tail surfaces and the hydraulic systems for retracting the tailwheel and extending the tailwheel.

The power-pod that contained the engine and ancillary equipment, including magneto, carburetor, engine mounts, oil tank, supercharger, injection water tanks, and supercharger intercooler, was located forward of the main bulkhead and suspended by it.

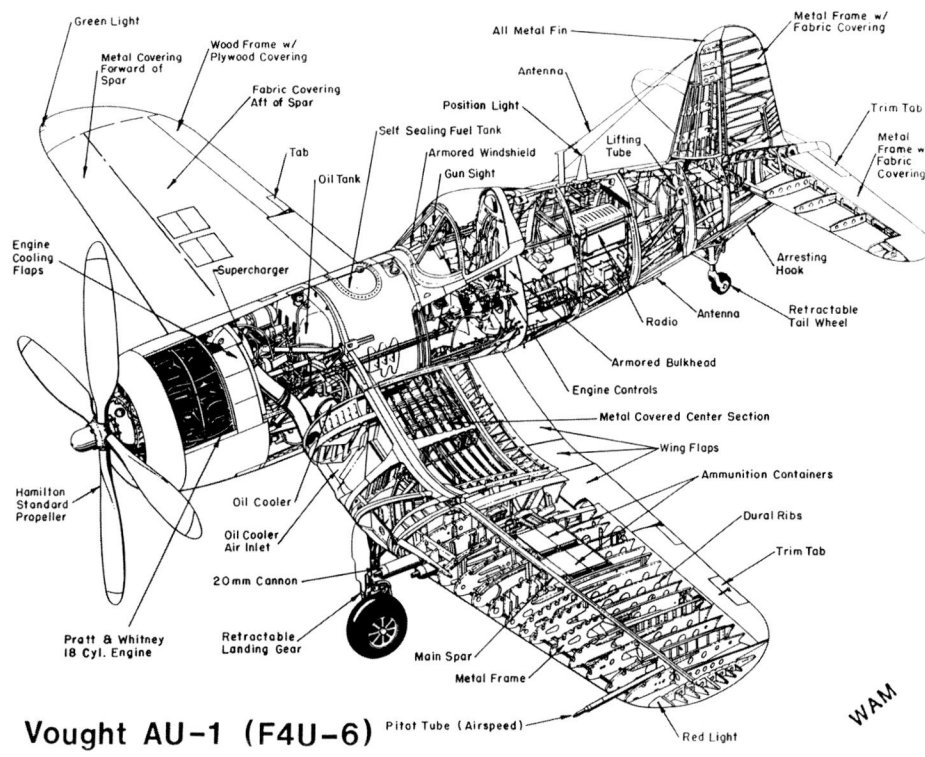

Vought AU-1 (F4U-6)

The three fuselage sections and the power-pod are shown assembled in this composite drawing. The power-pod was not considered to be part of the fuselage structure, but was mounted on the main bulkhead and massive wing root spar. Observe the several transverse structures in the inverted gull-wing root. (Chance Vought Aircraft Photo, Courtesy H.J. "Jerry" Dalton, Jr.)

Chapter II: Corsair Development and Production

This view of the bare and incomplete Corsair cockpit area was taken looking forward to the fuel bladder bulkhead. Observe the myriad of tubing running along the bulkhead. The remainder of the cockpit will be added when work is complete in this area. Note the control quadrant on the upper left side. (Goodyear Aircraft Photo, Courtesy Nick Hauprich)

Looking aft into the fuselage aft section tailwheel and tailhook compartment the longitudinal channels are clearly evident. Interesting items in this photo are the chain and sprocket mechanisms to open and close the tailwheel and tailhook doors. The tailwheel and tailhook are yet to be installed, along with their hydraulic actuators. (Goodyear Aircraft Photo, Courtesy Nick Hauprich)

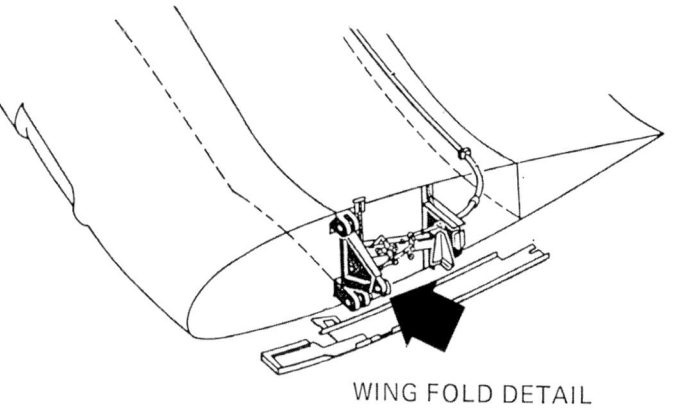

Naval aircraft folding wings are extremely complex, especially those that are hydraulically operated and can be folded and/or extended while taxiing. The Corsair has this ability. Note plate and rod to support the outer panel (Arrow). Observe the profusion of hydraulic tubing, electrical wiring, hydraulic cylinders, and push rods that must be designed to flex or clear the movement of the outer wing (above in the photo) as it opens and closes the cavity. (Alain Pelletier Photo) (Vought Aircraft Drawing)

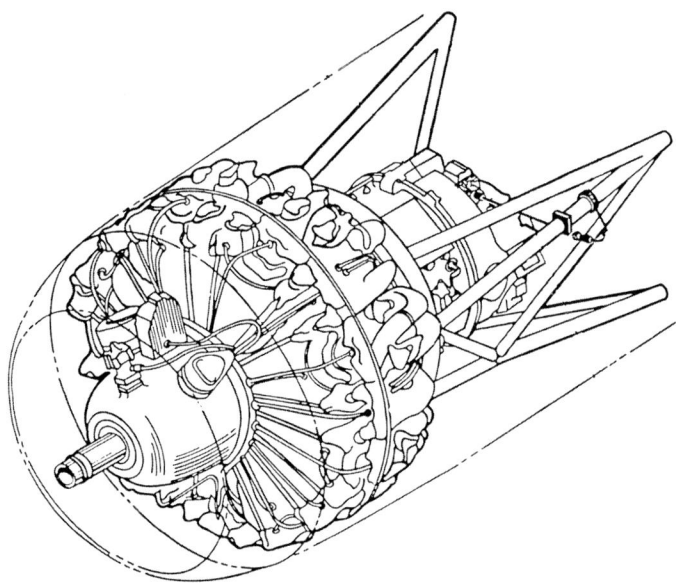
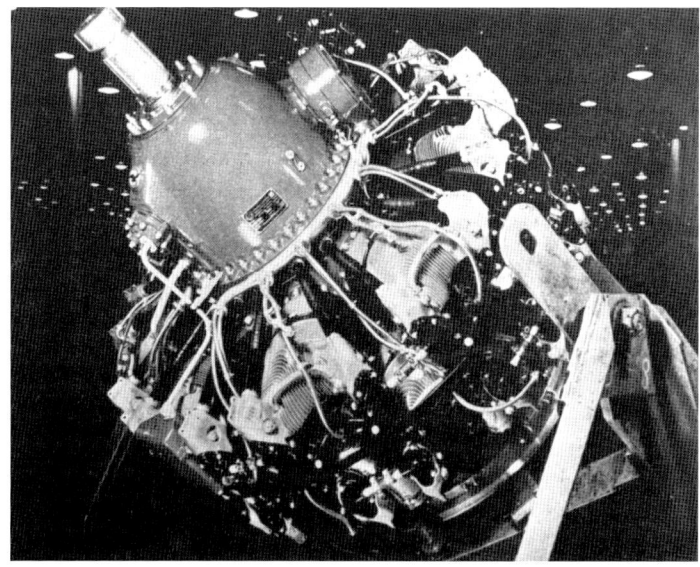

The P&W engine that produced 1,850hp for the XF4U-1 was improved and uprated to 2,300hp for the F4U-5 and AU-1. The entire engine and ancillary equipment were mounted on the main bulkhead. (Vought Photo and Artwork, Courtesy H.J. "Jerry" Dalton)

Longitudinal channel beams joined the sections with assistance from the spot-welding monocoque skin.

The wing was constructed in three sections: two outer panels and a rugged center-section spar that formed the inverted gull-wing. This strength member supported the main bulkhead, landing gear, outer wing panels and, in combination with the main bulkhead, the power-pod.

Constructed over a huge spar, the center section structure consisted mainly of transverse members forming the smooth curvature of the inverted gull-wing. The only longitudinal structures were two high-strength full ribs and two false ribs. Sheeting the compound curves of the center section with Alclad required meticulous pattern-making, but the finished product made all the effort worthwhile.

The principal strength member of the Corsair was the wing center section spar that supported the main bulkhead, landing gear, outer wing panels, and power-pod. This key structural member of the Corsair was constructed by Wyman Gordon Fabricators using a jig supplied by the Vought Tool Department. This photo at the Wyman Gordon factory shows the immense space where the Corsair main spars were fabricated. The spars in the foreground are stowed inverted, while those in the background are stowed upright. Observe the strong "plate" that connects with the folding wing outer panel. (Arrows) (Wyman Gordon Photo, Author's File)

This Hamilton Standard craftsman is giving the blades of the huge Corsair propeller a final polishing. Each blade weighed 95 lbs, while the entire propeller weighed 405 lbs. (Hamilton Standard Photo, Author's File)

Chapter II: Corsair Development and Production

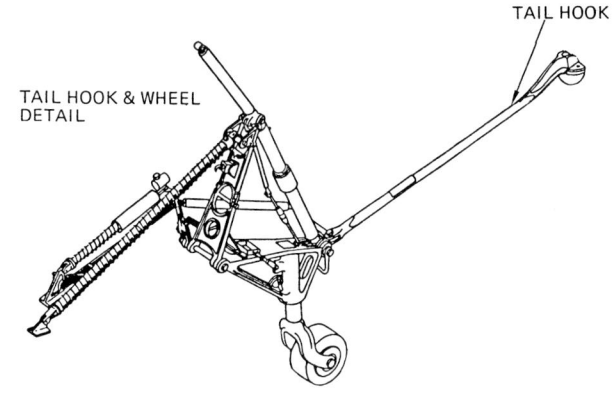

The subcontracted Corsair tailwheel yoke and tailhook were the largest forgings used on any aircraft at that time. (Ling-Temco-Vought Photo, Courtesy Arthur L. Schoeni)

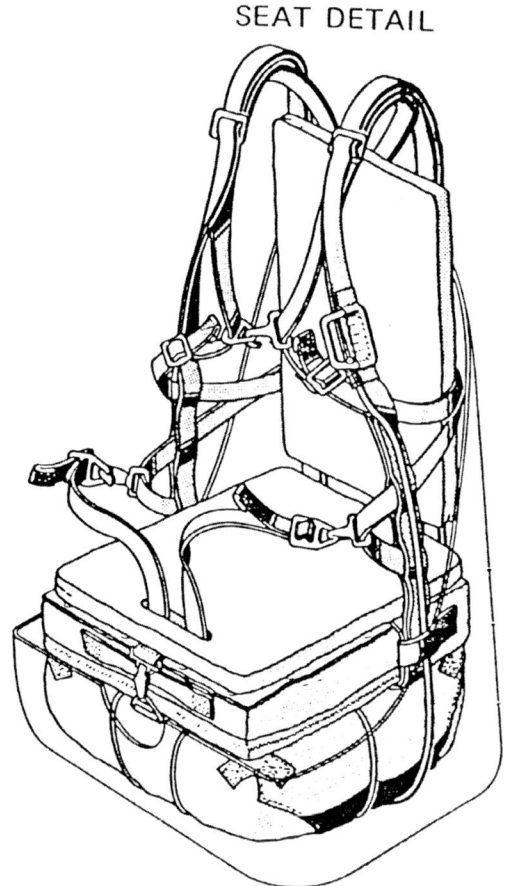

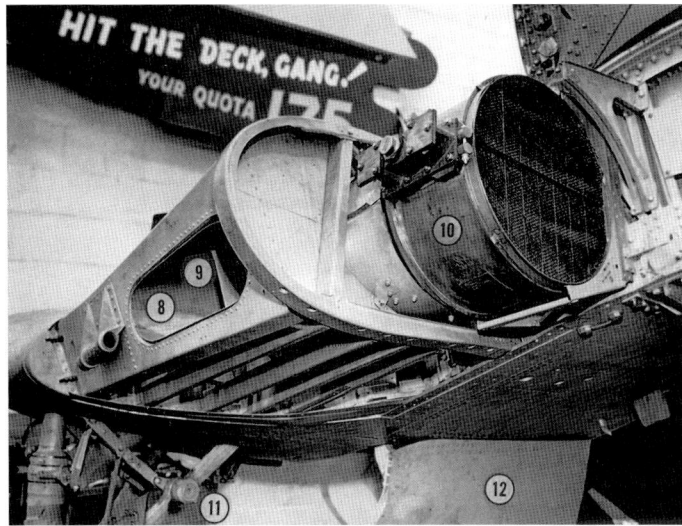

One of the least understood aspects of the inverted gull-wing center-section is the path of the air entering the leading edge inlets. As the air enters the opening, No.8, turning vanes, No.9, guide and separate the incoming air to the oil cooler, No.10, and the air inlet to the engine. After cooling the oil, the air is expelled into the airstream via the underside of the plane. The leading edge inlet provides high-pressure ram air to the carburetor, enhancing engine power. Other items of interest are the landing gear retracting mechanism, No.11, and the landing gear inboard door, No.12. (Goodyear Aircraft Photo, Courtesy Nick Hauprich)

The Corsair, as with most production aircraft, subcontracted the aviator's seat complete with harness, as well as the intricate reflector gunsight. To be forced to fabricate these items would delay production of the airplane. (Chance Vought Aircraft Photo, Courtesy H.J. "Jerry" Dalton, Jr.)

About ten workers are busy assembling each Corsair at this early stage. The gull-wing structure and main bulkhead are the center of the primary assembly. The first fuselage section has been attached to the main bulkhead, as has been the oil tank. Observe the strong points on the bulkhead for the engine mounts (curved arrows) and the engine air inlet (arrow) to be connected to the supercharger. (National Archives, Courtesy Fred Pernell)

Corsair: The Saga of the Legendary Bent-Wing Fighter-Bomber

Vought technicians test the hydraulically folding wing panels. Tests such as this are accomplished away from the Corsair assembly line to insure proper concentration to evaluate the results. F4U-1A shown. (Chance Vought Aircraft Photo, Courtesy H.J. "Jerry" Dalton, Jr.)

A technician carefully tests this F4U-1A hydraulically retractable landing gear. Observe that the plane is propped so the wheels do not touch the rolling platform. Landing gear function is a common failure during the life of most aircraft. (Chance Vought Aircraft Photo, Courtesy H.J. "Jerry" Dalton, Jr.)

The wing outer panels consisted of a full-depth spar and stamped dural ribs. That portion forward of the spar was Alclad covered, as were those areas aft and inboard of the ammunition boxes (magazines). The remainder of the wing outer panels was fabric covered for ease of repair and for lightness.

Virtually all construction enterprises require subcontractors; not only to speed production, but to draw upon the subcontractor's expertise in a specialized field that is essential to the completion of the project. The Corsair production scheme included several subcontractors.

The principal strength member was the wing center-section spar that supported the main bulkhead, landing gear, outer wing panels, and engine mounts. This key structural member was constructed by Wyman Gordon Fabricators of Worcester and Springfield, Massachusetts, using a massive jig fixture assembly built by the artisans in the Vought tool department.

The 13 ft-4in diameter propeller was constructed by Hamilton Standard of Windsor Locks, Connecticut, a member of United Aircraft Corporation.

Nash-Kelvinator Corporation, manufacturers of Nash automobiles and Kelvinator refrigerators, was an important subcontractor that built entire P&W Double Wasp radial engines to power the Corsairs, supplementary to those constructed by Pratt & Whitney.

The largest and most complex subcontracted Corsair component was the wing outer panels constructed by Briggs Manufacturing Co.

Thompson Aircraft Products Co produced the water injection mechanism for the P&W Double Wasp engine previously described.

The ailerons were designed to be fabric covered metal structures; however, it appears that the aileron subcontractor was unable to meet the required delivery dates. Rather than risk endangering the production schedule, innovative Rex Beisel ordered the wood shop to make the ailerons from sheet plywood over a wooden framework with fabric covering doped over the finished aileron. Initially intended only for the early Corsairs, the idea was so successful that the wooden ailerons were used on production models as well.

This Dec. 23, 1942, photo depicts the final assembly line at the Vought-Sikorsky Stratford facility. Shown are early "Birdcage" canopy F4U-1 Corsairs. (Vought-Sikorsky Photo, Courtesy Paul Bower)

Chapter II: Corsair Development and Production

Goodyear Aircraft's first Corsair was the FG-1, which was identical to the Vought F4U-1A. Left photo illustrates virtually completed FG-1 Corsairs at the Akron, Ohio, plant, while the right photo shows FG-1 Corsairs lined up for predelivery flight checks as a successful flight concludes with a flypast. (Goodyear Aircraft Photos, Courtesy Nick Hauprich)

Other subcontracted items were wheels, oleo struts, seats, instruments, wheel brakes, radio, gun sight, and tailwheel yoke and tail hook forging that was the largest forging used on any aircraft at that time.

The distribution of subcontracted items to the three widely separated Corsair manufacturing plants was a task in itself.

The years 1937-1938 witnessed a resurgence in America's aviation industry as the effects of the "Great Depression" began to wane:

Consolidated left its Buffalo, New York, plant and moved into a brand new factory in San Diego, California, with big contracts for PBY Catalina patrol planes. Meanwhile, newcomer Larry Bell moved into the empty consolidated plant in Buffalo for his AFM Airacuda "bomber killer" and the XP-39 Aircobra fighter production.

Curtiss, America's largest airplane company, was struggling for U.S. Army Air Corps fighter plane contracts against relative newcomer Seversky; P-35 versus P-36.

Lockheed, who had moved from its "wooden wonders" factory, was developing the P-38 Lightning in a converted pottery plant in Los Angeles, while Boeing and Douglas were concentrating on large bombers and commercial transport planes.

Northrop became the El Segundo division of Douglas, garnering contracts for the SBD Dauntless.

On Long Island, relative newcomer Grumman bought many tons of steel girders from the dismantled New York City elevated railway to build a state of the art airplane factory.

Another newcomer, North American Aviation, built a one-million sq ft mass production plant in Inglewood, California, based upon German fighter plane assembly plant production. The new firm was producing Texan trainers, B-25 bombers, and the P-51 fighter prototype.

It appears that the relative newcomers were preparing for mass production, while some of the older aircraft manufacturers were content with building quality planes one plane at a time. Vought had fallen into the latter mind-set; therefore, the move to Stratford was an attempt to increase production for the important Corsair contract.

Vought testing of all production aircraft was very carefully made in separate areas from the production line in order to ensure a meaningful evaluation.

In order to increase production, Brewster Aeronautical Corporation and Goodyear Aircraft Corporation joined Corsair production (previously

About 400 Goodyear FG-1B Corsairs were supplied to the Royal Navy Fleet AirArm. Notice the squared-off wingtip that made each wing outer panel eight inches shorter than the U.S. Corsairs in order to clear the overhead when the wings were folded on the smaller British carriers. Observe the conventional British cockade that was used in the European and Mediterranean Theatres of Operation. (Goodyear Aircraft Photos, Courtesy Nick Hauprich)

Corsair: The Saga of the Legendary Bent-Wing Fighter-Bomber

This beautifully restored Corsair is part of the Canadian Warplane Heritage collection. Flown by Dennis Bradley, the craft displays the insignia used by Fleet Air Arm Corsairs in the Pacific Theatre of Operations. (Jim Larsen Photo, Courtesy Jim Larsen)

Although the F4U-1C is known as the "cannon-toting Corsair," it initiated many improvements that enhanced the quality of subsequent models. Improved engine starters and deletion of internal bomb racks and towing apparatus are only some of the improvements. (U.S. Navy Photo, National Archives, Courtesy Arthur L. Schoeni)

described). Brewster had been using Vought's old building in Long Island City, New York, and now opened a new factory in Johnsville, Pennsylvania. The U.S. Navy terminated Brewster's contract in the summer of 1944, claiming it failed to meet production schedules; however, according to Ralph O. Romaine, Brewster production manager and engineering test pilot, from March through June 1944 Brewster completed 111 Corsairs with 4,000 workers, while Goodyear completed 205 Corsairs with 12,000 workers. If the figures are correct it appears that Brewster required only 36 workers to build a Corsair, while Goodyear required 58.5 workers to build a Corsair. Despite these figures Brewster was forced to close its Johnsville Plant in 1944. Goodyear delivered over one-third of all the Corsairs constructed.

The Royal Navy Fleet Air Arm received 70 Vought F4U-1B (Corsair I) Corsairs; 300 Brewster F3A-1 (Corsair II) Corsairs; 440 F4U-1A Corsairs; 100 Brewster F3A-1D (Corsair III) Corsairs; 300 Goodyear FG-1D (Corsair IV) Corsairs; and 400 Goodyear FG-1B Corsairs. The Fleet Air Arm flew the Corsair in the European and Pacific Theatres of Operation. Most of the Royal Navy Fleet Air Arm Corsairs operating along the European littoral wore their usual cockade; however, those that fought the Japanese in the Pacific Theatre added the American rectangular "wing" to each side of the cockade and removed the red center in order to distinguish it from the Japanese "rising sun" insignia. This made the Royal Navy insignia resemble that of the Royal New Zealand Air Force.

We have seen how the BuAer requested and encouraged changes to the F4U-1 as Vought was struggling to increase production; namely the F4U-1A bubble canopy etc. improvements, F4U-2 night fighter, and Fleet Air Arm F4U-1B.

The second F4U-1, BuNo 02154, was selected as a test vehicle for a four-cannon installation to replace the six-machine guns. Apparently reports from European air fighting regarding the use of cannon influenced the BuAer to examine the possibility of cannon-armed Corsairs.

The first test in August 1943 prompted a decision to convert 200 F4U-1 airframes to cannon Corsairs for F4U-1C deliveries scheduled for June 15, 1944.

Installing the four Hispano M2 20mm cannon, with 220 rounds per gun, was not the only F4U-1C modification: the internal wing bomb

When "field mod" bomb racks constructed by U.S. Marine mechanics and ground crew members proved successful, Brewster Aeronautical Corporation designed and produced the centerline "Brewster Bomb Rack" for the F4U-1A that led to the development of the F4U-1D. The 1,000 lb bomb rack is shown. (Ling Temco Vought Photos, Courtesy Arthur L. Schoeni)

Chapter II: Corsair Development and Production

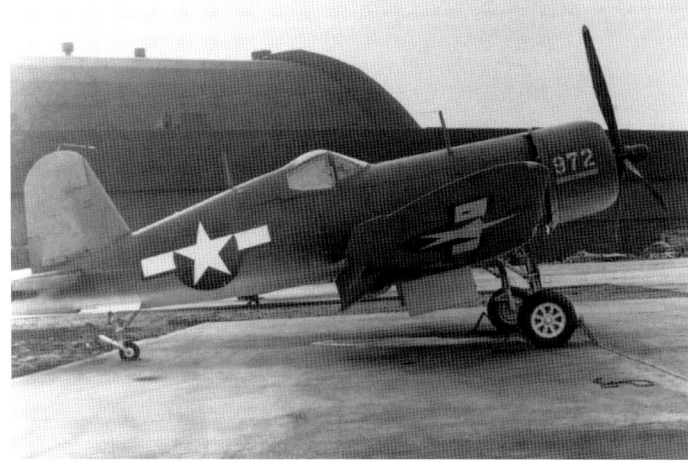

Goodyear FG-1D (Vought F4U-1D) Corsairs await predelivery flight checks in upper photo as an FG-1D taxies with wings folded. The aviator-controlled wing folding was a great advantage over many naval aircraft that required from three to five ground crew to fold one wing half. Lower photo is an early FG-1D (BuNo 13972) on March 28, 1944. The sleek lines make the Corsair appear smaller than its actual size. (Goodyear Aircraft Photos, Courtesy Nick Hauprich)

racks were deleted; target towing equipment was also deleted; the canopy longitudinal brace was deleted; and the longtime gunpowder cartridge engine-starting system was replaced with an electric starter. The non-cannon modifications continued through most subsequent Corsairs.

Although the 20mm (.75in) cannon shell possessed more destructive power than the Browning .50in caliber shell, the rate of fire was less than the machine gun. This made the cannon-armed F4U-1C Corsair more adaptable to surface targets rather than air-to-air combat. The F4U-1C's combat debut was over Okinawa during Spring 1945.

As the war in the Pacific progressed, the Allied air forces evolved to the offensive, while the Japanese air forces found themselves on the defensive as they were forced back toward their homeland. This does not imply that the Japanese fighter had become impotent; therefore, the U.S. felt the need for a multifaceted aircraft that could handle attack as well as interception, escort, and patrol assignments. The Vought Corsair was selected and a redesigned F4U-1A became the F4U-1D.

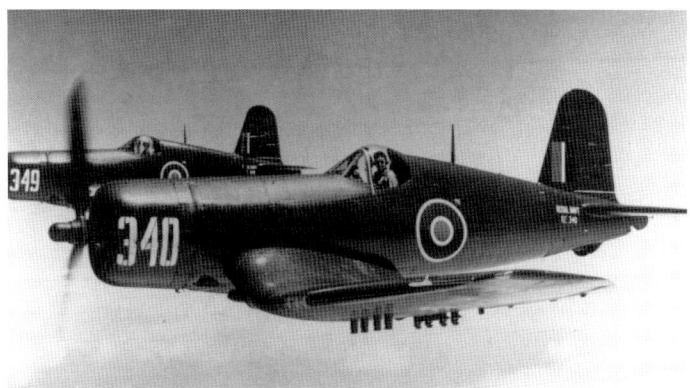

A Royal Navy element of Goodyear FG-1D Corsairs (Corsair IV) displays the underwing HVAR rails and the unbraced blown canopies. Photo taken July 3, 1945. (Goodyear Aircraft Photo, Courtesy Nick Hauprich)

Two interesting items in this Goodyear FG-1D photo are the clear, unbraced blown canopy similar to the F4U-1C and the standard HVAR (High Velocity Air Rocket) rails under the wing. The F4U-1D and FG-1D appear to be the transition Corsairs from braced to unbraced blown canopies. (Howard Levy Photo, Courtesy Albert L. Lewis)

This division of F4U-1D Corsairs from U.S. Navy Fighter squadron VF-89 are flying in formation on a training flight in the U.S. The markings are the prewar scheme, indicating the squadron number (89), the service of the unit (F) fighting, and the aircraft number. (Official U.S. Navy Photo, Author's File)

Corsair: The Saga of the Legendary Bent-Wing Fighter-Bomber

Evident in this Vought F4U-1D photo is the lengthened tailwheel yoke that improved pilot visibility and increased the distance between the large wing flaps and the ground, thereby correcting the instability during landing. (Vought Aircraft Photo, Courtesy H.J. "Jerry" Dalton, Jr.)

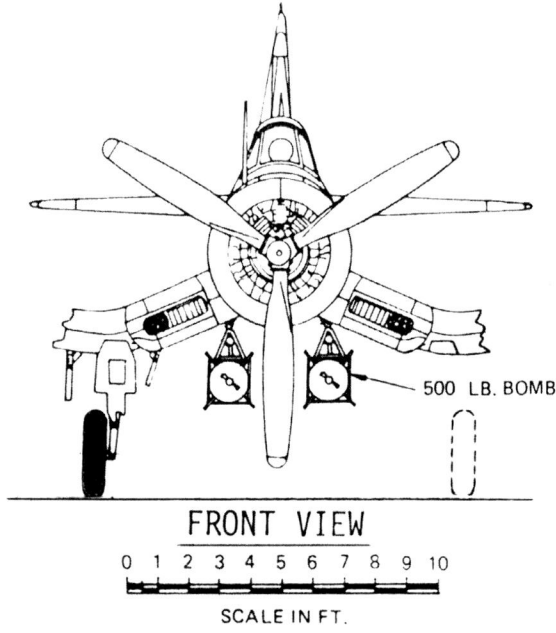

Vought F4U-1D

The two strong points on the F4U-1D could accommodate 500 or 1,000 lb bombs. The strong points are often described in various reports as both wing mounted and fuselage mounted. (Vought Aircraft Artwork)

The centerline rack on the F4U-1D could accommodate a napalm bomb or a droppable fuel tank. Note the fabric covering of the central portion of the wing and the clarity of the engine air inlet and oil cooler air scoop. (U.S. Navy Photo, Author's File)

The Vought F4U-1D was capable of loading bombs, droppable fuel tanks, or napalm bombs on three strong points. Two 1,000 lb bombs are shown on this F4U-1D Corsair. (U.S. Navy Photos, Author's File)

Chapter II: Corsair Development and Production

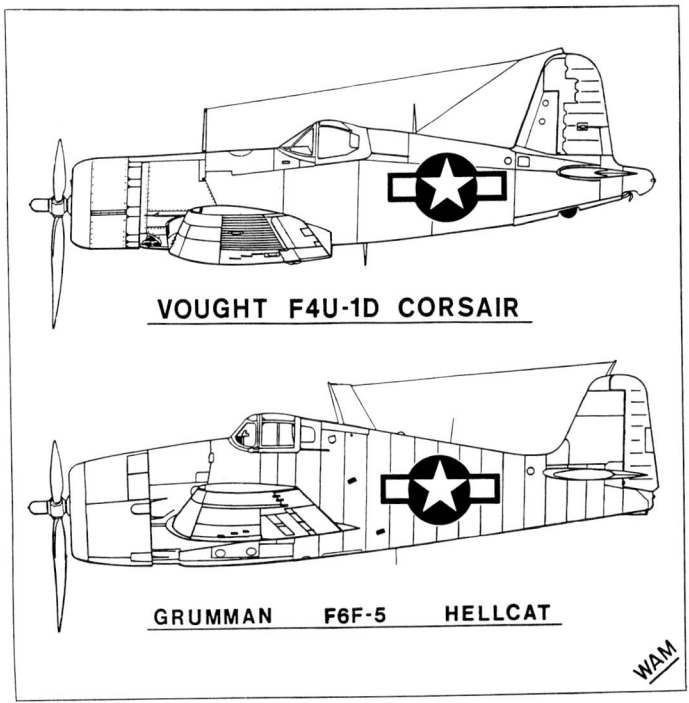

This study of Corsair and Hellcat profiles compares the slender straight-line Corsair lines with the more conventional Hellcat lines.

With the same engine, same armament, and virtually the same weight, the performance, appearance, and construction of the Corsair (upper photo) and the Hellcat varied considerably. When Rex Beisel stated "Speed is King," his team produced a sleek "straight-line design" Corsair toward that end, whereas the Hellcat was conventional and functional. The Hellcat (lower photo) cost $10,000 less to build because of its conventional construction and mass production techniques.

It all began when U.S. Marine aviators, aircraft mechanics, and ordnancemen, realizing that they were now on the offensive, began fabricating ever-increasingly stronger bomb racks for their Corsairs. Their "field-mod" racks would eventually handle a one thousand lb bomb!

Aware of this "Corsair Revolution," the much-maligned Brewster Aeronautical Corporation designed and produced the Brewster centerline bomb rack that proved the Corsair was an extraordinary fighter-bomber.

As a result of the above successful experiments, the BuAer decided to convert two F4U-1A Corsairs into experimental XF4U-1D fighter-bombers. In addition to the standard six machine guns, four five-inch HVAR (High Velocity Air Rockets) rocket rails under each wing and two strong points under the wing roots were fitted. Each strong point could carry a 1,000 lb bomb, a Napalm bomb, or droppable fuel tank. Corsair external fuel tanks were available in three sizes: 154 gal. U.S. Navy Std. (approx. 1,100 lbs full); 174 gal. Lockheed (approx. 1,200 lbs. full); and 178 gal. Firestone Duramold (approx. 1,250 lbs full). The F4U-1A internal fuel tanks were deleted on the F4U-1D.

The first F4U-1D was accepted by the U.S. Navy on April 22, 1944, and this modification paved the way for the outstanding F4U-4.

Basic dimensions, power, and weight of the F4U-1D were the same as the F4U-1; however, the Goodyear FG-1D and the Brewster F3A-1 were powered by the R-2800-8W engine that enabled their new Corsairs to attain a 425 mph maximum speed at 20,000ft. In addition, the FG-1D and F3A-1 were able to carry two 1,000lb bombs compared to one 1,000lb bomb for the F4U-1.

At this time it appears appropriate to compare the Corsair to its U.S. Navy stablemate; the Grumman Hellcat. Having had the foresight to prepare for mass production, Grumman's Hellcat saw action 14 months after its first flight, but the Corsair did not see action until 34 months after its first flight. Of course, much of this gap was caused by the extensive modifications required by the Bureau of Aeronautics based upon the European air war. The Hellcat design benefited from BuAer Corsair modifications while it was still on the drawing board.

When compared to the sleek uncluttered lines of the Corsair the Grumman test pilots preferred to call the Hellcat "functional-looking." The Hellcat located the fuel tank under the cockpit, raising the aviator to a location where he had perfect visibility with an eight degree downward view over the nose.

The Corsair was not as easy to fly as the Hellcat, which made it preferred by experienced pilots; however, the Hellcat was friendly, stable, and steady at low speed approaches that was appreciated by neophytes.

With its ten degree increments wing flap setting from zero to fifty degrees the Corsair responded faster to commands, whether powering up or slowing down, than the Hellcat's flap setting of full up or fifty degrees down with no intermediate positions.

With the same basic powerplant, the Corsair was noisyest on the outside but quietist in the cockpit than the Hellcat, but afforded up to ten percent better fuel economy despite its average cruising speed of about 23 mph faster than the Hellcat's. The Corsair operated better than the Hellcat at altitudes above 20,000ft and was extremely tough at absorbing enemy fire and incidental damage.

All maneuvers were easy in the Hellcat with plenty of stall warning; however, when a mistake was made in the Corsair, the results were more violent. At higher speeds the Hellcat required more control stick input than in the Corsair.

Comparative tests of F6F-3 Hellcats versus F4U-1D Corsairs were conducted by U.S. Navy squadron V0F-2 aboard the Casablanca Class (sometimes erroneously called Kaiser Class) escort carrier *USS Tulagi* (CVE-72) during "Operation Dragoon." Dragoons were heavily armed mounted troops that also conducted scouting operations.

Corsair: The Saga of the Legendary Bent-Wing Fighter-Bomber

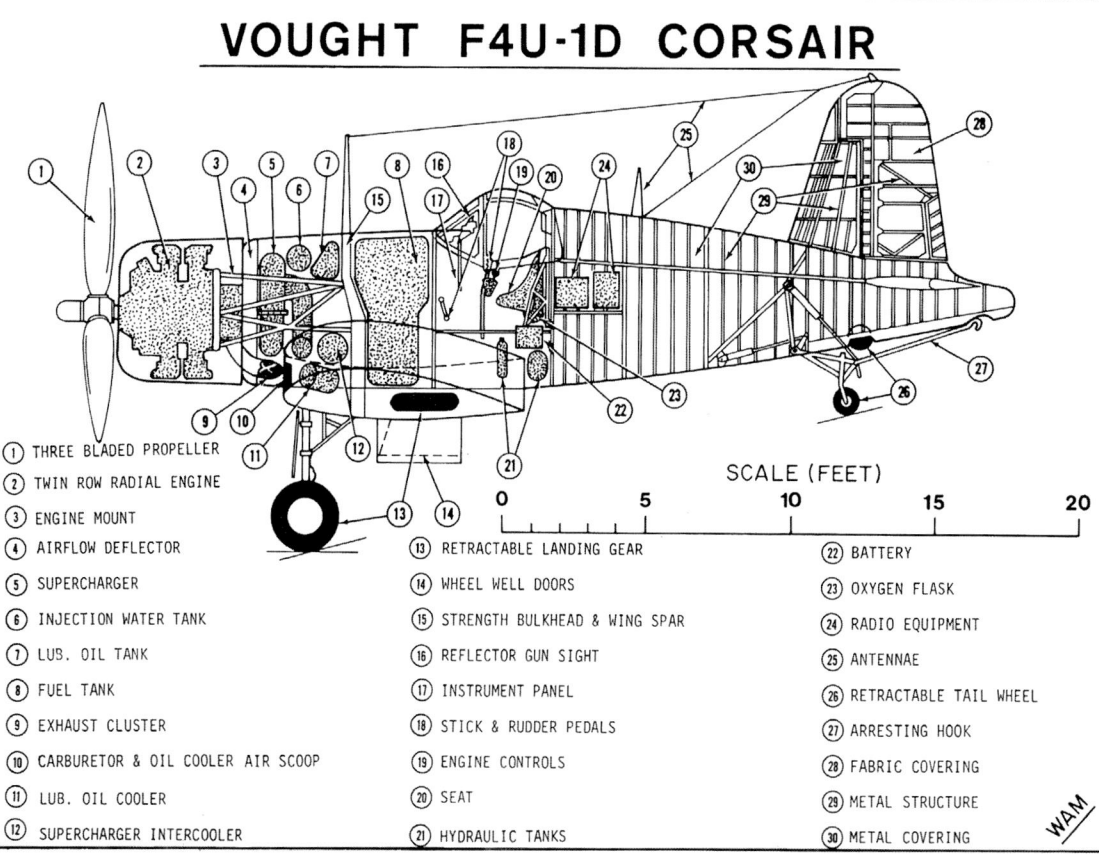

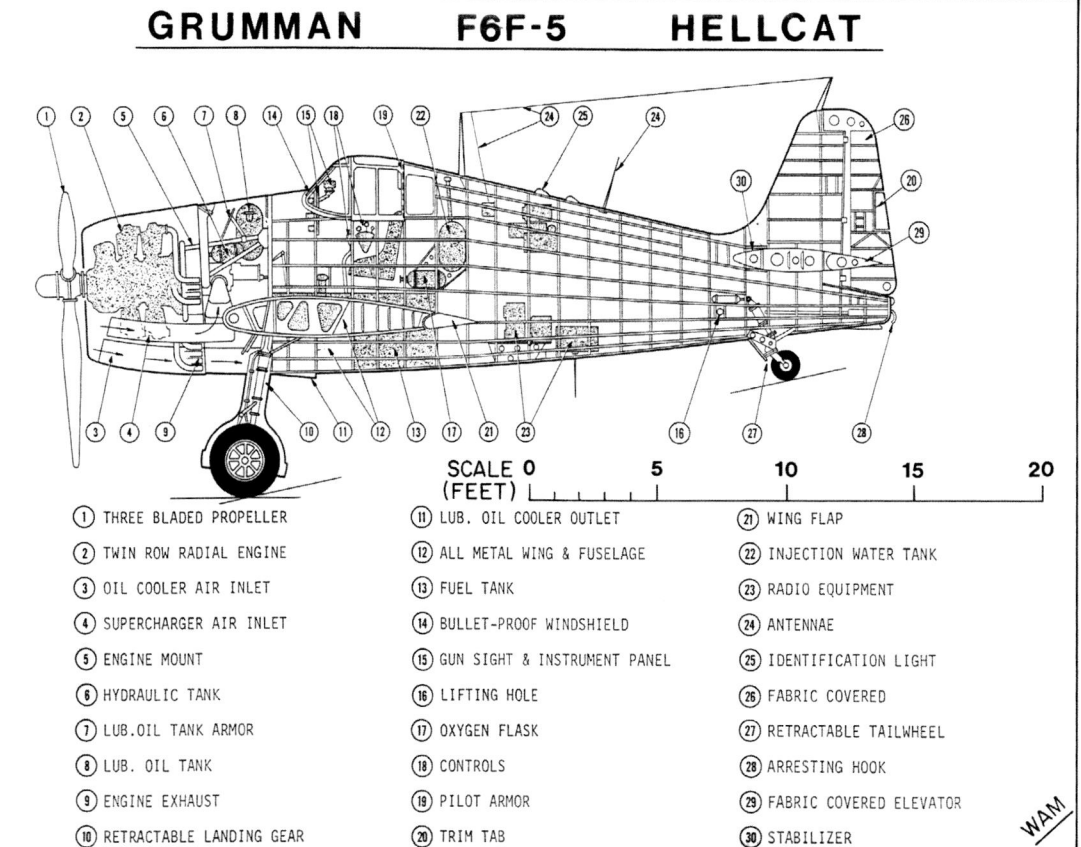

A study of the interior profiles illustrates that, on aircraft intended for similar functions, all principal and ancillary equipment tends to be identically located. The fuel tank and injection water tank appear to be the only equipment differently located on the Corsair and Hellcat. The landing gear of both designs rotated 90 degrees as it folded back into the wing.

Chapter II: Corsair Development and Production

Lt Cdr W.F. BRINGLE

U.S.S. TULAGI, CVE-72

HELLCAT vs CORSAIR

1. The Hellcat was operated from the U.S.S. TULAGI under conditions of no surface wind without difficulty. The landings with light wind conditions on the whole were excellent. The pilots used a slightly longer approach in the groove in order to slow up as much as possible. Under light winds, all planes were launched satisfactorily by catapult with an average interval of approximately 45 to 50 seconds. A CVE of the Kaiser class can best operate about 24 Hellcats; more begins to complicate operations. The availability of aircraft was exceptional during the operation due to a fine organization in the Air Department and outstanding maintenance personnel. Another contributing factor was, that the TULAGI CASD personnel had been servicing the squadron for three months before the squadron came on board. It is my opinion that the Hellcat or Corsair are both suitable for operation aboard the CVE (Kaiser Class).

2. In considering a comparison of other types of planes for the operations involved, this squadron is definitely prejudiced. The Hellcat is a fine plane and there can be no denying that it performed well in all respects during the Operation Dragoon. On the other hand, it is felt that the F4U-1D would be even better suited for a similar operation. The extra speed and faster acceleration of the Corsair would be a big advantage in evading anti-aircraft fire. The Corsair again aids in avoiding intense anti-aircraft fire which was encountered. It was found during the operation that the flak would uncannily open up at the correct altitude, but normally either to one side or slightly astern. Evasive action consisted of speed, course and altitude changes. The Corsair is better suited for spotting naval gunfire; one reason is the good visibility both downward due to position of cockpit aft of wing and forward over leading edge. The second good reason is that speed and maneuverability is essential when forced to stay over intense flak areas or investigate targets at comparatively low altitudes.

The greater range of the Corsair would have increased our effectiveness considerably. It cannot be denied that the Corsair cruises at a faster speed and more economically than the Hellcat. The length of the armed reconnaissances flights necessitated the use of high power settings and consequently a belly tank was needed on the majority of the long-range reconnaissance missions.

-9-   Appendix "D"

U.S.S. TULAGI, CVE-72

The Corsair is a fine plane as it holds its speed and can readily zoom back up to altitude. It would seem to be an ideal plane for rocket firing because of extremely light stick forces and steadiness in a glide. The pilots were greatly handicapped in the F6F in dive bombing, rocket firing and strafing because of the necessity of using rudder trim tabs as speed increased. The Corsair is an excellent fixed gunnery plane. The twin-pylon bomb rack arrangement on the F4U-1D would have been ideal for the fighter bomber missions carried out by this squadron during the past operation.

The question of availability can be discussed pro and con. The Hellcat has a great advantage in accessibility, yet this squadron enjoyed practically as good an availability as the F6F-3 squadrons when operating at NAS, Atlantic City even though we had the first group of Corsairs at that station. After experienced personnel, such as are aboard the TULAGI, are familiar with the Corsair it is felt that availability would compare favorably with the Hellcat (at least not as many flak holes). Ordnance work and servicing is considered considerably easier on the Corsair. The vulnerability of the arresting hook installation on the Hellcat appears to be a greater problem than all reports indicate. A small piece of flak damaging the hook track prevents the hook from extending and thus causes in most cases, a water landing. The hook installation on the Corsair is greatly simplified. It does not have to be extended, but, being connected to the tail wheel installation, would normally drop down with landing gear in case of damage to the hook control system. This hook also has no tendency to bounce over wires.

The question of landing the Corsair aboard a CVE under no wind conditions leaves some doubt in a great number of minds. But upon investigation that doubt is usually based on supposition, not having actually experienced carrier landings in the Corsair or observed them under light wind conditions. Until this operation I do not know of any Hellcats being operated from the CVE's under no wind conditions. This area necessitated operating with no surface wind and there was no difficulty with the Hellcat. From records on board the U.S.S. TULAGI, on which ship, VOF-2 qualified in Corsairs, the average pull-out of arresting wire was at least 10 feet less for the Corsair under similar wind conditions. This was due to the fast deceleration because of large flap area. The Corsair has excellent visibility coming aboard a carrier with not as much tendency to lose the signal officer as in the Hellcat. The approaches are much smoother as the pilot is able to trim plane and does not have to hold hard right rudder. The plane answers the throttle smoothly and more quickly. The majority of the pilots of this squadron consider it an easier plane to land aboard a carrier than the Hellcat.

-10-   Appendix "D"

U.S.S. TULAGI, CVE-72

Tests conducted aboard the U.S.S. CHARGER by Lt. Cdr. Deacon proved that the Corsair could make good landings with winds across the deck as low as 17 knots. It is felt that the Corsair would have no difficulty in landings with no surface wind.

The Hellcat performed well in this operation and the pilots have a great deal of respect for the aircraft. It has a wonderful reputation in combat. Nevertheless, the pilots of this squadron, having approximately equal time in both planes, would much prefer to fly the Corsair under all circumstances and particularily in an operation similiar to the one just completed.

This image contains a reduced copy of the original three-page final official U.S. Navy report for "Operation Dragoon," comparing Corsairs with Hellcats. Inset are two views of a Casablanca Class CVE aircraft carrier; the type that participated in "Operation Dragoon." (Official U.S. Navy Photos Naval Photographic Center; Courtesy Lt. Loren C. Stricklin)

Corsair: The Saga of the Legendary Bent-Wing Fighter-Bomber

The Casablanca Class carriers protected troop landings in the Pacific by moving in close to shore and launching fighters and dive bombers to destroy enemy gun emplacements and other tactical defenses. The objective of the tests was to employ fighters to not only attack the enemy emplacements, but to conduct high-speed, low altitude scouting of enemy forces further inland; hence the name "Operation Dragoon."

All fifty Casablanca carriers had a 500ft long flight deck. When compared to the 800ft USS Enterprise flight deck and 870ft USS Essex flight deck, the USS Tulagi flight deck was only two-thirds the length of the larger carriers, which made landings more difficult. Further, Essex class carriers displaced 33,000 tons while the Casablanca class displaced only 10,300 tons, one third of the larger carrier, and thus adding to landing difficulties.

The following is a transcription of the final U.S. Navy report for the "Operation Dragoon" Hellcat/ Corsair comparison tests conducted in the summer of 1944:

"LCDR W.F. Bringle
Hellcat vs. Corsair
USS TULAGI, CVE-72

1. The Hellcat was operated from the USS TULAGI under conditions of no surface wind without difficulty. The landings with light wind conditions on the whole were excellent. The pilots used a slightly longer approach in the groove in order to slow up as much as possible. Under light winds, all planes were launched satisfactorily by catapult with an average interval of approximately 45 to 50 seconds. A CVE of the Kaiser class can best operate about 24 Hellcats; more begins to complicate operations. The availability of aircraft was exceptional during the operation due to a fine organization in the Air Department and outstanding maintenance personnel. Another contributing factor was, that the TULAGI CASD personnel had been servicing the squadron for three months before the squadron came on board. It is my opinion that the Hellcat or Corsair are both suitable for operation aboard the CVE (Kaiser Class).

2. In considering a comparison of other types of planes for the operations involved, this squadron is definitely prejudiced. The Hellcat is a fine plane and there can be no denying that it performed well in all respects during the Operation Dragoon. On the other hand, it is felt that the F4U-1D would be even better suited for a similar operation. The extra speed and faster acceleration of the Corsair would be a big advantage in evading anti-aircraft fire. The Corsair again aids in avoiding intense anti-aircraft fire which was encountered. It was found during the operation that the flak would uncannily open up at the correct altitude, but normally either to one side or slightly astern. Evasive action consisted of speed, course and altitude changes. The Corsair is better suited for spotting naval gunfire; one reason is the good visibility both downward due to position of cockpit aft of wing and forward over leading edge. The second good reason is that speed and maneuverability is essential when forced to stay over intense flak areas or investigate targets at comparatively low altitudes.

The greater range of the Corsair would have increased our effectiveness considerably. It cannot be denied that the Corsair cruises at a faster speed and more economically than the Hellcat. The length of the armed reconnaissances flights necessitated the use of high power settings and consequently a belly tank was needed on the majority of the long-range reconnaissance missions.

The Corsair is a fine plane as it holds its speed and can readily zoom back up to altitude. It would seem to be an ideal plane for rocket firing because of extremely light stick forces and steadiness in a glide. The pilots were greatly handicapped in the F6F in dive bombing, rocket firing and strafing because of the necessity of using rudder trim tabs as speed increased. The Corsair is an excellent fixed gunnery plane. The twin-pylon bomb rack arrangement on the F4U-1D would have been ideal for the fighter bomber missions carried out by this squadron during the past operation.

The question of availability can be discussed pro and con. The Hellcat has a great advantage in accessability, yet this squadron enjoyed practically as good an availability as the F6F-3 squadrons when operating at NAS, Atlantic City even though we had the first group of Corsairs at that station. After experienced personnel, such as are aboard the TULAGI, are familiar with the Corsair it is felt that availability would compare favorably with the Hellcat (at least not as many flak holes). Ordnance work and servicing is considered considerably easier on the Corsair. The vulnerability of the arresting hook installation on the Hellcat appears to be a greater problem than all reports indicate. A small piece of flak damaging the hook track prevents the hook from extending and thus causes, in most cases, a water landing. The hook installation on the Corsair is greatly simplified. It does not have to be extended, but, being connected to the tailwheel installation, would normally drop down with the landing gear in case of damage to the hook control system. This hook also has no tendency to bounce over wires.

The question of landing the Corsair aboard a CVE under no wind conditions leaves some doubt in a great number of minds. But upon investigation that doubt is usually based on supposition, not having actually experienced carrier landings in the Corsair or observed them under light wind conditions. Until this operation I do not know of any Hellcats being operated from the CVE's under no wind conditions. This area necessitated operating with no surface wind and there was no difficulty with the Hellcat. From records on board the USS TULAGI, on which ship V0F-2 qualified in Corsairs, the average pull-out of arresting wire was at least 10 feet less for the Corsair under similar wind conditions. This was due to the fast deceleration because of large flap area. The Corsair has excellent visibility coming aboard a carrier with not as much tendency to lose the signal officer as in the Hellcat. The approaches are much smoother as the pilot is able to trim plane and does not have to hold hard right rudder. The plane answers the throttle smoothly and more quickly. The majority of the pilots of this squadron consider it an easier plane to land aboard a carrier than the Hellcat.

Tests conducted aboard the USS CHARGER by Lt. Cdr Deacon proved that the Corsair could make good landings with winds across the deck as low as 17 knots. It is felt that the Corsair would have no difficulty in landings with no surface wind.

The Hellcat performed well in this operation and the pilots have a great deal of respect for the aircraft. It has a wonderful reputation in combat. Nevertheless, the pilots of this squadron, having approximately equal time in both planes, would much prefer to fly the Corsair under all circumstances and particularily in an operation similar to the one just completed.

END OF REPORT"

The report reveals several differences between the two naval fighters that are not generally known: 1. The Corsair requires less stopping distance when landing on a carrier, pulling out 10 feet less of the arresting cable; 2. The Hellcat arresting hook is more prone to damage; 3. The Corsair exhibited faster acceleration and speed, course, and altitude changes to avoid flak; and 4. According to the report, in view of the above and its better downward visibility, the Corsair was better suited for spotting naval gunfire.

Chapter II: Corsair Development and Production

The second of five production prototype XF4U-4 Corsairs is shown carrying a 154 gallon Firestone Duramold drop-tank (1,000 lbs) and a half-ton bomb (upper photo). The craft is at the Naval Air Test Center (NATC) Patuxent River, Maryland, in January 1945. The engine cowl is colored yellow, red, and black for test identification (BuNo 80760). (National Archives, Author's File) Lower photo is the F4U-4 assembly line. Observe that the wing outer panels are painted, insignia added, and delivered by the subcontractor for final assembly. (Ling-Temco-Vought, Courtesy Arthur L. Schoeni)

This row of F4U-4 Corsairs is waiting for predelivery flight checks at the Vought Stratford plant. Of interest in this photo is the wing-fuselage brace to protect the upright wing from undue stresses, such as wind gusts. Note the outer panels are vertical and are not folded over the fuselage as on aircraft carriers. (Ling-Temco-Vought, Courtesy Arthur L. Schoeni)

When the 5,156 planes shot down Hellcat victory score is compared to the 2,140 planes shot down Corsair victory score, it suggests that the Hellcat was a far superior fighter than the Corsair. Both planes were great; however, the Hellcat happened to be in the right places at the right times. While the Corsair was banned from carriers and relegated to the U.S. Marines in the Solomons, mainly in troop support missions, Navy Hellcat squadrons were flying from carriers as early as Adm. Charles A Pownall's 1943 Task Force 50 raids into the Central Pacific as far as Makin and Tarawa; and in Adm. Frederick Sherman's Task Force 38 carrier raid on Rabaul in Autumn 1943.

Grumman's production capability enabled the company to deliver over 11,500 Hellcats by the end of World War Two while it was not until 1952 that 12,571 Corsairs had been built by three factories.

In 1943 Beisel became General Manager of Chance Vought Division and was appointed to the Committee on Aeronautics of the NACA. During the following year he was on the Board of Directors of the Aircraft Production Council.

Aviators, mechanics, and historians have used many sobriquets for the Corsair, such as "Bent Wing Bird," "Ensign Eliminator," "Hog Nose," and "Hose Nose"; however, only the F4U-4 has received the superlatives "Iron Bird," "Ultimate Corsair," and "Le Grande Oiseau." Whichever the sobriquet, the F4U-4 was the "top of the line" of Corsairs, not even to be equaled by future modifications.

The idea for the F4U-4 came simultaneously from U.S. Navy planners and Vought engineers. The basic concept was to mate the new P&W water-injected 2,100hp R-2800-18W engine to the basic F4U-1 airframe. U.S. Navy Contract No.198, Amendment No.58, ordered the conversion of two F4U-1 Corsairs into F4U-4X prototypes (BuNo 49763 and 50301). Vought engineering began the project in May 1943.

In addition to increasing the power of the F4U-1A, the following improvements and modifications were incorporated to create the F4U-4: the fuselage fuel tank capacity was reduced to 230 gal with necessary range made up with the drop tanks; a full cockpit floor was installed to replace the two foot channels; flat bullet-proof windshield replaced the curved glass windshield; water-alcohol injection system converted to a single tank; engine air intake scoop relocated to the bottom of the engine cowl because more air was required for the high-altitude stage of the supercharger; oil coolers were enlarged; added battery capacity enabled the F4U-4 to power the Jack and Heinz electric starter for the engine without depending upon an outside power source; redesigned engine

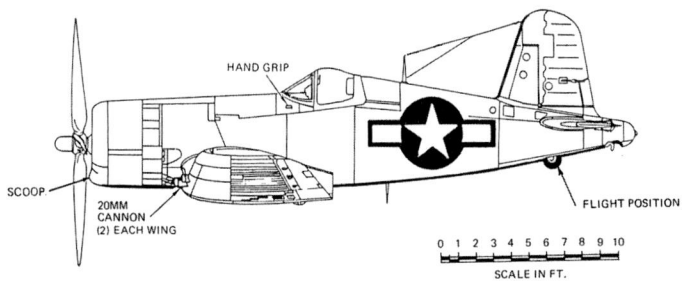

Vought F4U-4

The principal external modifications for the F4U-4 are the chin air scoop, relocated engine exhaust cluster, the flat bullet-proof windshield, and the unbraced bubble canopy. Only the F4U-4B was cannon-armed. (Vought Aircraft Artwork, Enhanced by Author)

53

This interesting photo has been variously described as an F4U-4 and an F4U-4B. The two "Tiny Tim" rockets suggest the F4U-4B; however, the six machine ports say it is an F4U-4. We believe it is the latter. (Vought Aircraft Photo, Courtesy Paul Bower)

A rolling climb was a favorite maneuver for Corsair aviators because of the remarkable effectiveness of the ailerons. This unusual view of an F4U-4 illustrates the aileron size and range of movement. (Author's File)

exhaust discharge tailpipes were relocated from below the wing to above and below the wing; and a new 21.5 gal lub oil tank that could operate during continuous inverted flight and negative G forces was installed, as were enlarged fuel lines. In order to absorb the new engine's power a Hamilton Standard four-bladed 13ft-1in dia propeller was fitted to the F4U-4. New cockpit controls and instrumentation were also installed.

On April 19, 1944, Boone Guyton made the first test flight in F4U-4X BuNo 49763. Top speed was 450 mph at 26,200ft and rate of climb approached 4,000 fpm. The test proved that the F4U-4 service ceiling was 41,500ft and that it was the best flying version of the Corsair.

On the basis of the 450 mph speed attained with the F4U-4X at higher altitudes, the U.S. Navy awarded Contract No. 2720 for production of the F4U-4 on January 25, 1944. In advance of production, five production prototypes were necessary for U.S. Navy testing (BuNo 80759-80763).

The wingspan, length, and weight of the F4U-4 exceeded that of the F4U-1: span 41ft-11.7in; length 34ft-6in; weight 12,500 lbs. Top speed was 446 mph at 26,200ft, and rate of climb was 3,894 feet per minute. Service ceiling was 41,500ft. The engine produced 2,100hp at takeoff and 2,450hp with water injection. Armament was a lethal six .50in caliber machine guns with 2,400 rounds of ammunition; eight five inch HVAR missiles; two 1,000 lb bombs or two 11.75in, 1,200 lb Tiny Tim rockets that had a range of one mile.

This was the only F4U-4N Corsair constructed. The plane provided considerable data for the design and construction of the F4U-5N and F4U-5NL Corsairs. (United Aircraft Corporation Photo, Courtesy Arthur L. Schoeni)

The F4U-4B Corsair was able to carry a variety of equipment on the strong points. Left photo has armorers D.O. Bray and L.A. Wigley installing a 500 lb "Daisy Cutter" anti-personnel bomb. Observe the extension on the bomb's nose to detonate the bomb before it penetrates a solid object. A napalm bomb is mounted on the other strong point. The right photo illustrates a Firestone bullet-proof droppable fuel tank and a 500 lb bomb on the strong points. Note the underwing rockets. Upper photo is on USS Philippine Sea while lower photo is on USS Sicily. Both photos taken in September, 1950 preparing for a Korean strike. (U.S. Navy Photos, Author's File)

Chapter II: Corsair Development and Production

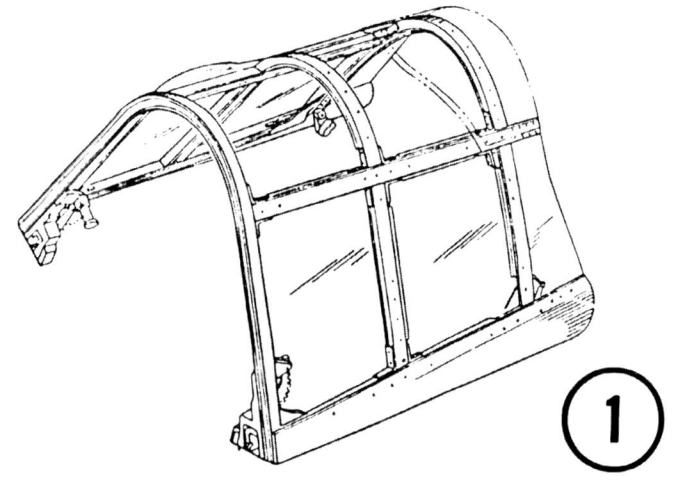

This F4U-4 Corsair (BuNo 97364) was re-engined with the new Pratt & Whitney R-2800-32W rated at 2,300hp at 26,000ft. The plane was a prototype for the F4U-5 and redesignated XF4U-5. (Howard Levy Collection, Courtesy Albert L. Lewis)

The BuAer, again, turned to cannon for surface attack power when it ordered 297 F4U-4 Corsairs equipped with four Masden M3 20mm cannon with 984 rounds to replace the six .50cal machine guns with their 2,400 rounds. The cannon-fitted F4U-4 Corsairs were redesignated F4U-4B. The remainder of the armament remained the same as the F4U-4.

Goodyear Aircraft Corporation also received a BuAer contract to construct 2,370 F4U-4 Corsairs, re-designated FG-4. With 17 FG-4 Corsairs under construction, the Japanese surrendered in August 1945 and the contract was cancelled. The Goodyear Corsairs under construction were scrapped.

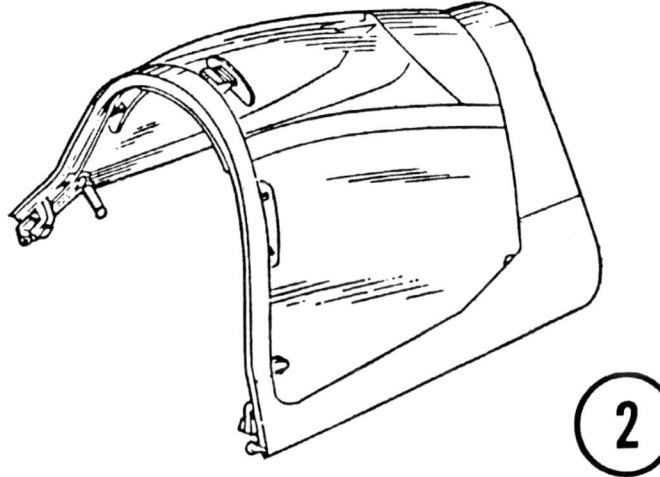

Corsair development continued during the postwar years when a single F4U-4N (BuNo 97361) was equipped with an improved APS-6 radar installation in March 1946. It remained at the Vought plant for testing until May 1947 when the F4U-4N was transferred to Naval Air Station, Patuxent River, Maryland, for electronics testing. In January 1948 the experimental Corsair was sent to the aircraft pool at Cherry Point, South Carolina, where it remained until March. The F4U-4N provided considerable data that was applied to the development of the Vought F4U-5N and F4U-5NL Corsairs of the Korean War.

The normal pattern in aircraft design is that the airplane searches for an appropriate engine; however, in our next subject, it is the engine that waits for an appropriate airplane. When the engine finally mated with the airframe, the result became a unique airplane; intended to be a killing machine, but entertaining thousands of spectators instead.

It all started in early 1943, during one of Gen Henry (Hap) Arnold's visits to United Aircraft Corporation, when UAC president F.B. Rentschler convinced the General that work on the new Pratt & Whitney 3,000hp, 28-cylinder, quadruple-row, air-cooled radial engine was most promising and a contract would accelerate progress. General Arnold agreed and U.S. Navy BuAer contract Noa(s) 596 ordered work to proceed on the new powerplant. The Navy became involved because Vought and Pratt & Whitney held existing U.S. Navy contracts. The 4,360 cu in displacement XR-4360 Pratt & Whitney Wasp Major (commercial version TSB1-G) was ready for flight-testing by Spring.

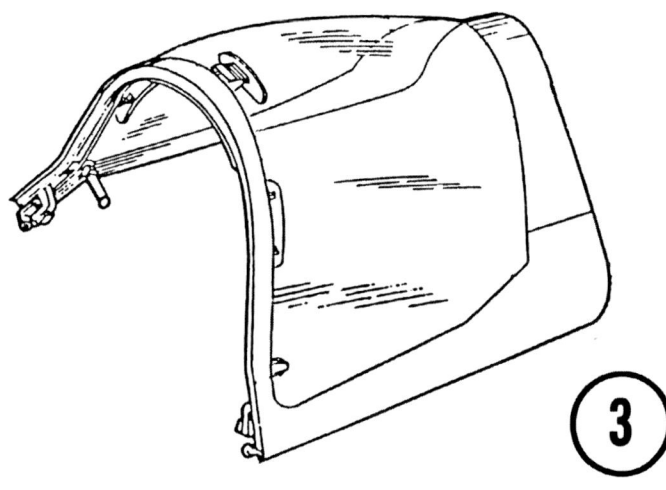

Three steps in Corsair cockpit canopy development: No.1 is the framed "Birdcage" style of the F4U-1; No.2 is the first blown glass bubble installed on the F4U-1A through the F4U-1D; and No.3 is the final unbraced design canopy of the F4U-4 and subsequent models. (Vought Aircraft Artwork, enhanced by Author)

Corsair: The Saga of the Legendary Bent-Wing Fighter-Bomber

The Wasp Major R-4360 quadruple-row, 28 cylinder, air-cooled radial engine could produce one horsepower for every 0.93 lbs of engine weight. Notice that the four seven-cylinder radial rows are staggered for adequate air cooling and proper firing order. (United Technologies Photo, Courtesy Paul Bower)

An early F4U-1 Corsair BuNo 02460 was selected for the test, redesignated F4U-1M. The test Corsair's engine was removed, and Pratt & Whitney accomplished the TSB1-G powerplant installation at East Hartford, Connecticut. The initial flight on September 12, 1943, and subsequent test flights found the engine and airframe to be compatible, thereby proving the feasibility of the Super Corsair project.

The Wasp Major engine weighed 3,400 lbs and developed 3,650hp at emergency power, which gave the powerplant a 0.93 lbs per horsepower ratio that was superior to most engines in the world.

The Pacific fleet had been harassed by Japanese reconnaissance aircraft for some time and, to compound the problem, organized Kamikaze attacks began on October 25, 1944, during the Battle of Leyte Gulf. This double threat resulted in a Pacific Fleet High Command conference at Pearl Harbor during November 24-26, 1944. A decision was made to increase the number of fighters aboard aircraft carriers for intruder interception, which led to plans for extensive re-equipment with production Corsairs. This decision quickly changed to preference for the Wasp Major powered Super Corsair then under development, because it could better fulfill the need for a fast-climbing interceptor.

Inspectors at the Pratt & Whitney R-4360 engine assembly line are making final adjustments. Observe that the engines extend to below the wooden scaffolding where other inspectors are working (See arrow). (United Technologies Photo, Courtesy Paul Bower)

The accessory-end of the Wasp Major engine reveals the many yards of tubing and wiring, as well as the welded steel tubing engine mount. The mount must not only support the weight of this 3,400 lbs engine, but must also transfer the enormous thrust of the engine to the 13,290 lb Super Corsair. (Goodyear Aircraft Photo, Courtesy Nick Hauprich)

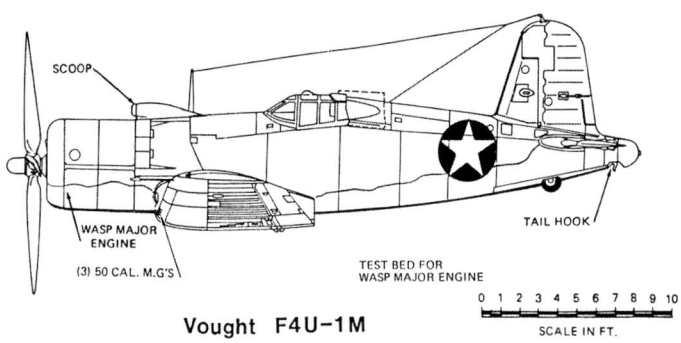

In Autumn 1943 a P&W 3,650hp Wasp Major, 28 cylinder engine was installed in a Vought F4U-1 (BuNo 02460) redesignated XF4U-1M. Flight tests in September proved the success of the experiment. Note the four-bladed propeller to utilize the immeuse power of this engine. (Chance Vought Photo, Author's File)

Chapter II: Corsair Development and Production

This interesting photo illustrates the comparison between the standard Vought F4U-1 Corsair (right) and the Vought XF4U-1M fitted with the Wasp Major engine. The XF4U-1M was only 12in longer with the new engine than the standard F4U-1 Corsair. (Vought Aircraft Photo, Courtesy H.J. "Jerry" Dalton)

The extent of the dorsal fin addition is clearly defined in this photo. This experiment, although a dire necessity, was deemed a failure, and the designers resorted to a taller fin and rudder. (Goodyear Aircraft Photo, Courtesy Nick Hauprich)

The XF2G-1 prototype (left photo) had the Wasp Major engine installed in a standard Goodyear FG-1A. The right photo shows the XF2G-1 with bubble canopy. The loss of turtledeck area and increased engine cowl side area prompted an increase in vertical fin and rudder area. Note the large experimental dorsal attached to the standard FG-1 fin. (Goodyear Aircraft Photos, Courtesy Nick Hauprich)

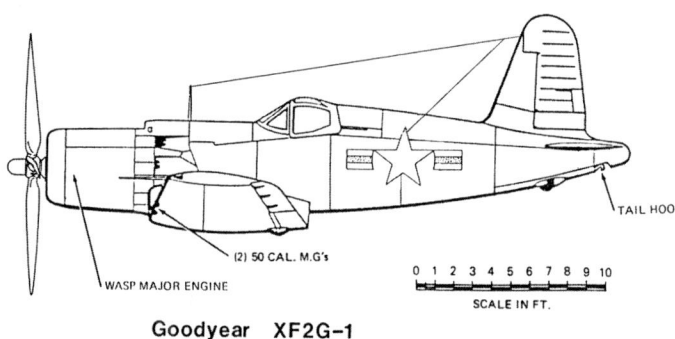
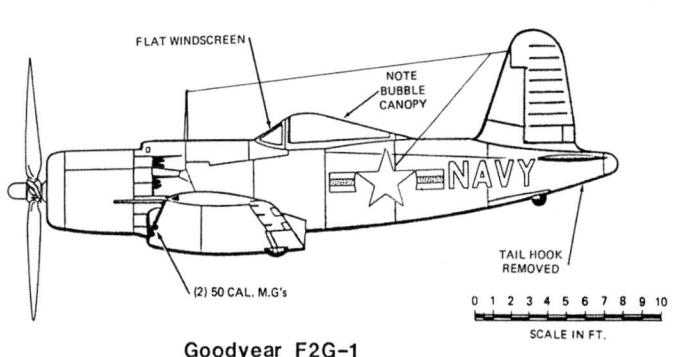

The two F2G profiles illustrate the differences between the XF2G-1 and the F2G-1: the bubble canopy has been added, creating a loss of aft lateral area; and tailhook has been removed because the F2G-1 was to be shore-based (not a Kamikaze killer). Fin and rudder area has yet to be increased. (Goodyear Aircraft Artwork, enhanced by Author)

The left photo is a Goodyear FG-1 with an experimental bubble canopy installed and turtledeck reduced. Fin and rudder are standard FG-1. This plane is often mistaken for an F2G. The right photo shows Don Armstrong, Goodyear Chief engineering Test Pilot, about to embark on an XF2G-1 test flight. This could be when he flew the plane to a joint Army-Navy fighter conference at NAS Patuxent River, Maryland, and stunned the spectators with aerobatics and phomenal acceleration and climbing ability. (Goodyear Aircraft Photos, Courtesy Nick Hauprich)

The F2G bubble canopy's 360 degree visibility is reminiscent of the 1936 Brewster Buffalo. This advanced canopy still did not improve the Corsair's forward visibility over the long nose. Observe the roll-over braces. (Goodyear Aircraft Photo, Courtesy Nick Hauprich)

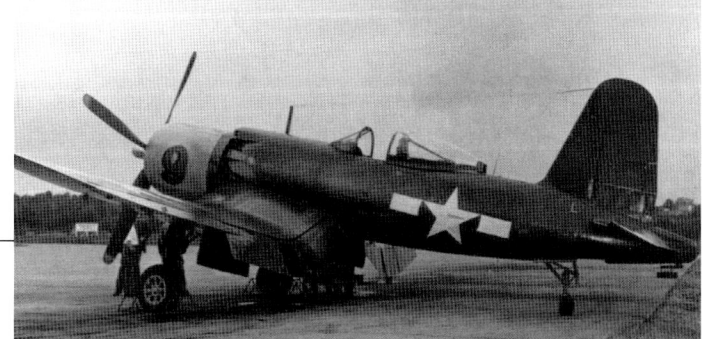

Right photos: XF2G-1 "yellow nose nine" (BuNo 14691) is shown, with Don Armstrong at the controls, during test flights and after-flight checks. Note the enlarged fin and rudder. (Goodyear Aircraft Photos, Courtesy Nick Hauprich)

Chapter II: Corsair Development and Production

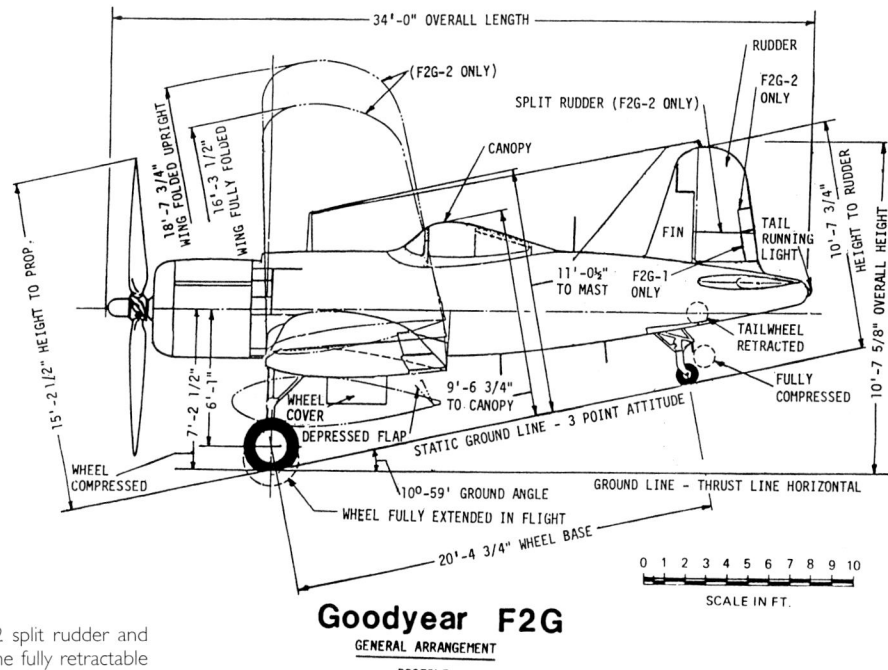

This dimensioned F2G-1/F2G-2 profile illustrates the F2G-2 split rudder and the absence of an arresting hook on the F2G-1. Observe the fully retractable tailwheel. (Goodyear Aircraft Artwork, enhanced by Author)

Meanwhile, work had been progressing on the Super Corsair engine and production of the Super Corsair was implemented. Unwilling to disturb Vought's production line and the design of new Corsair models, the BuAer Engineering Division, Fighter Design Desk had the foresight to issue Directive 4705, assigning contract number 2971 to Goodyear Aircraft Corporation on March 22, 1944, to design and construct 418 Wasp Major powered F2G-1 shore-based Super Corsairs and ten service-test F2G-2 carrier-based models. It had become obvious that the F2G-1 was intended for the U.S. Marines to support invasion landings, while the F2G-2 was intended to intercept reconnaissance and Kamikaze intrusions.

Basic specifications for the Super-Corsair required a top speed of not less than 428 mph for the F2G-1 (shore based) and not less than 426 mph for the F2G-2 (carrier based) at 16,500ft, with sea level climb rate to exceed 4,000 fpm. The specifications required a bubble canopy, and two FG-1 Corsairs (BuNos 14091 and 14092) were test-fitted with bubble canopies and cut-down turtle decks. It was learned that an enlarged fin and rudder were required to replace the lost lateral area of the turtle decks. These craft are often assumed to be F2G Corsairs, which they were not.

The first two XF2G-1 Corsairs were modified FG-1s and stricken from the records; however, the third XF2G-1 (BuNo 14691) was the first Super Corsair built as an XF2G-1 and passed its first flight on October 15, 1944. Donald Armstrong was the Chief Engineering Test Pilot for Goodyear and the supervisor of all test pilots and flight test programs. He flew the new XF2G-1 to the joint Army-Navy fighter conference at NAS Patuxent River, Maryland, and demonstrated the 13,290 lb Super Corsair with a very impressive aerobatic routine on October 22, 1944, only a week

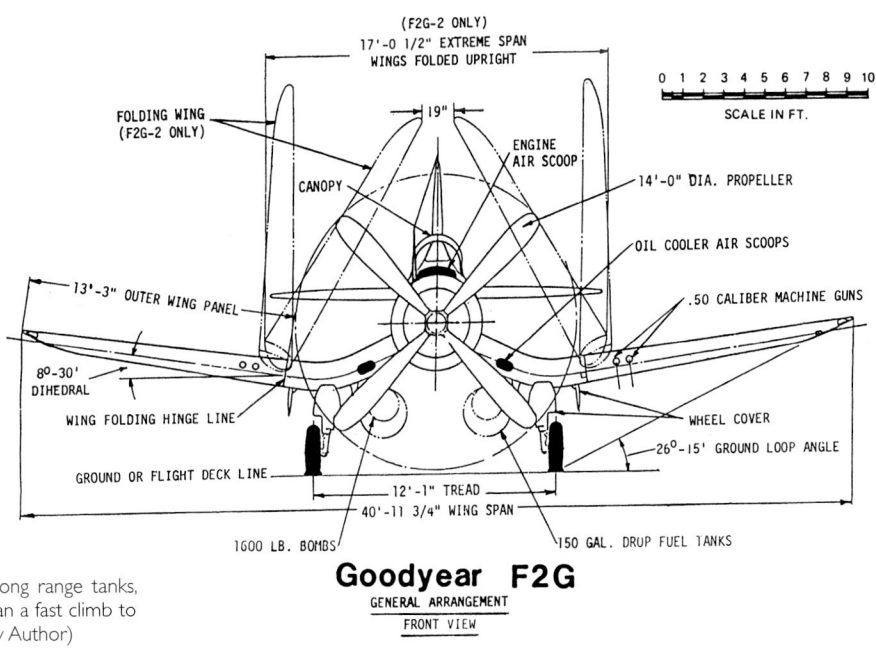

The dimensioned front view drawing illustrates bombs and long range tanks, indicative of long range to a battle or invasion beach rather than a fast climb to intercept an intruder. (Goodyear Aircraft Artwork, enhanced by Author)

Corsair: The Saga of the Legendary Bent-Wing Fighter-Bomber

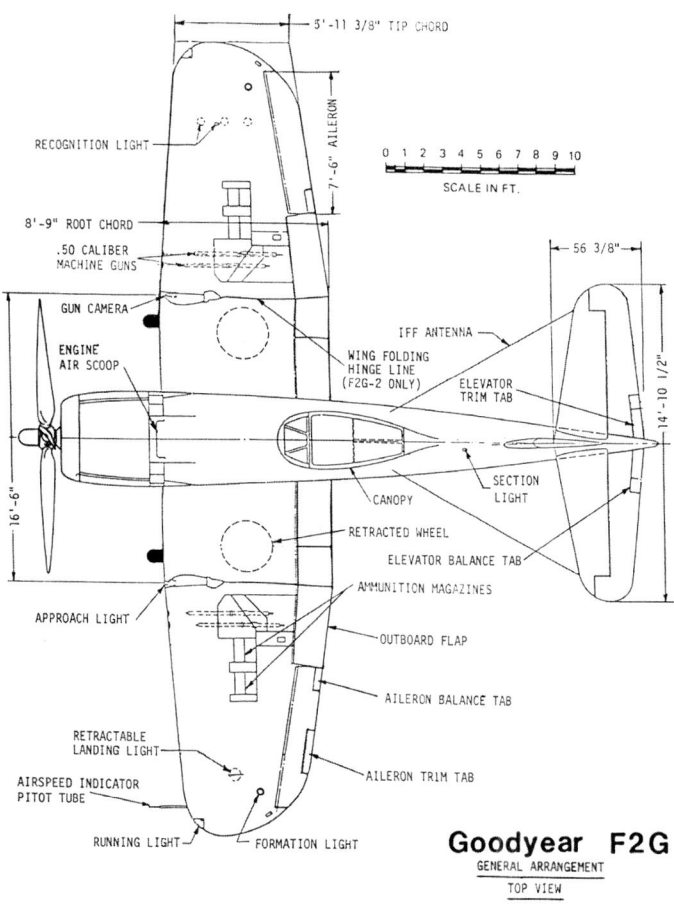

Basic dimensions of the F2G are the same as the F4U, except for the overall length. Observe that only F2G-2 is equipped with wing folding. (Goodyear Aircraft Artwork, enhanced by Author)

after its first flight. The demonstration revealed a short 450 mph takeoff run and a fantastic 60 degree climb to 8,000ft. The Super Corsair could reach 30,000ft in four minutes.

After producing seven experimental Super Corsairs, the first production Super Corsair was scheduled for completion in July 1945; however, on May 8, 1945, BuAer altered the F2G contract to reduce production by 418 planes, requesting that the remaining ten Super Corsairs be divided into two groups: five aircraft (BuNos 88454-88458) to be constructed as F2G-1 shore-based aircraft, and the remaining five aircraft (BuNos 88459-88463) to be constructed as F2G-2 carrier-based Super Corsairs.

A very innovative rudder design was installed in the F2G to counteract the dangerous pull to port (to the left) during a high-power carrier wave-off. The lower 12 inches of the rudder was separated from the rudder and connected to the tailwheel position. Whenever the tailwheel was lowered the lower rudder automatically offset to the right regardless of the main

This Goodyear F2G-1D (BuNo 88454) was filmed at NATC Patuxent River, Maryland. Observe the "Split Rudder." The lower 12" of the rudder operates automatically, separately from the main rudder, by offsetting for a right turn whenever the tailwheel was lowered. (Howard Levy Collection, Courtesy Albert L. Lewis)

Upper Photo: F4U-1 cockpit array below the main instrument panel showing the heel-troughs instead of cockpit floor. This was necessary to aim the 25lb anti-bomber bombs through glass panels in the fuselage bottom. (Vought Aircraft Photo, Author's File) Lower Photo: Later Corsairs cancelled the bombing idea, thereby eliminating the glass windows and installing a more conventional cockpit floor. F2G cockpit shown. (Goodyear Aircraft Photo, Courtesy Nick Hauprich)

Chapter II: Corsair Development and Production

Another F2G convenience inherited from the F4U-4 was the starboard side communication console. The drum-shaped item above the console is the oxygen diluting regulator. (Goodyear Aircraft Photo, Courtesy Nick Hauprich)

rudder's position. This acted as a large trim tab, producing the effect of a neutral rudder position.

The first flight of the new fast-climbing Grumman XF8F-1 single seat fighter occurred on August 21, 1944. The Bearcat was a diminutive fighter, weighing 12,947 lbs and powered with a P&W 2,100hp, R-2800-34W, 18 cylinder engine. The craft attained 421 mph at 19,700ft. Is it possible that the appearance of the Bearcat hastened the demise of the Super Corsair?

It will be remembered that the soon to be Grumman Wildcat was "waiting in the wings" after the Brewster monoplane received a U.S. Navy fighter contract, and the Grumman Hellcat appeared when the Vought Corsair entered production. Nevertheless, the Super Corsair program was terminated, but the Bearcat went on to receive production contracts.

The remaining ten Super Corsairs were distributed to Naval Air Stations and naval technical centers for analysis and testing. Pilots at the Tactical Test Branch of NAS Patuxent River were assigned to compare the F2G's performance with other contemporary U.S. Navy fighters, including the F4U-4 Corsair, F6F-5 Hellcat, F7F-3 Tigercat, and F8F-1 Bearcat. None could compare with the Super Corsair. On January 9, 1947, the Tactical Test Branch claimed that the F2G met the tactical demands for which it was designed.

One F2G can be seen at the Champlin Fighter Museum, Mesa, Arizona, while the other Super Corsairs were sold to private owners, many of whom created a sensation at the air races by beating the other U.S. fighter plane entries.

The part played by the Goodyear F2G program in the continuation of the R-4360 Wasp Major engine development was not wasted. Eventually, Pratt & Whitney and Ford Motor Company produced thousands of R-4360 Wasp Major engines that were used to power hundreds of six-engine Convair B-36 intercontinental bombers and other aircraft, such as the Martin Mauler, during the "Cold War" with the Soviet Union.

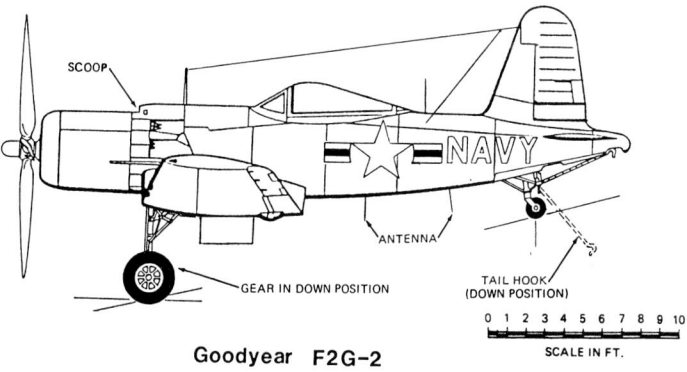

The F2G-2 carrier-version Super Corsair was to be a reconnaissance and Kamikaze interceptor; however, only ten examples were ordered, compared to an order for 418 F2G-1 shore-based invasion-support versions. (Goodyear Aircraft Photo, Courtesy Nick Hauprich)

The Corsair assembly is centered on the principal strength member; the inverted gull-wing structure. Top: the fuselage forward section is attached to the gull-wing structure. Center: Oil tank, water injection tank, and other accessories are mounted on the bulkhead. Bottom: Fuselage midsection and aft section are fixed to the forward section while the engine is attached to the bulkhead and wing outer panels are hinged to the gull center section on the F2G-2. (Goodyear Aircraft Photos, Courtesy Nick Hauprich)

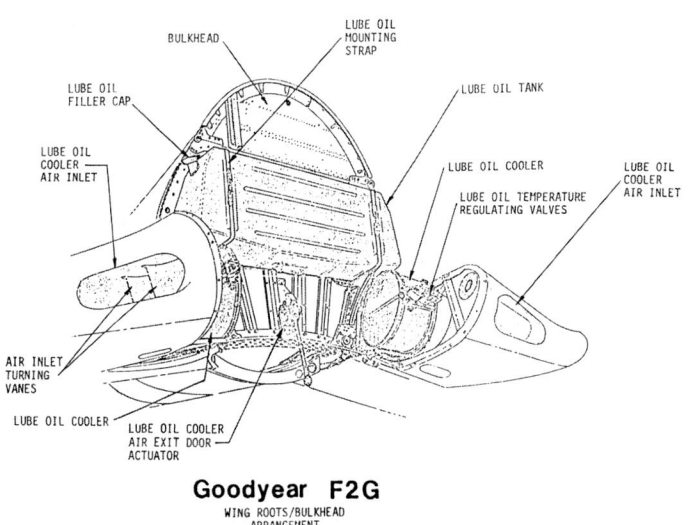

Goodyear F2G
WING ROOTS/BULKHEAD ARRANGEMENT

The gull-wing air inlets on the F2G only serve the oil coolers because the enormous engine demands a separate air supply. The lube oil cooler air exit door is fitted with a weighted counterbalance arm to make the door open at the slightest internal air pressure. The engine air inlet is above the cowl via a separate scoop. (Goodyear Aircraft Artwork, enhanced by Author)

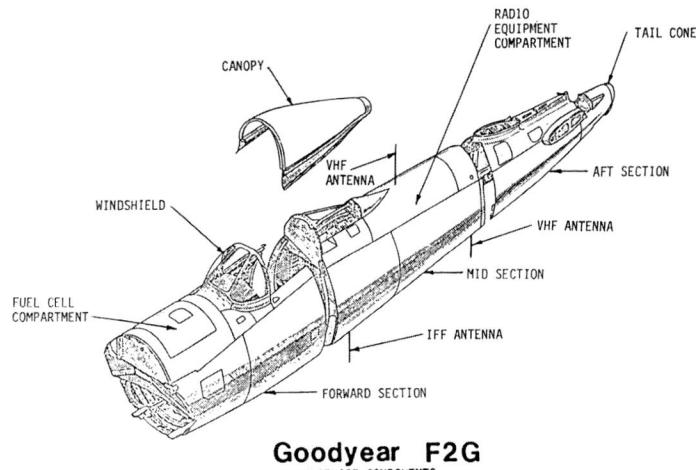

Goodyear F2G
FUSELAGE COMPONENTS

The three basic fuselage sections are defined in this illustration. Prefabricating each section shortens construction time. (Goodyear Aircraft Artwork, Courtesy Nick Hauprich)

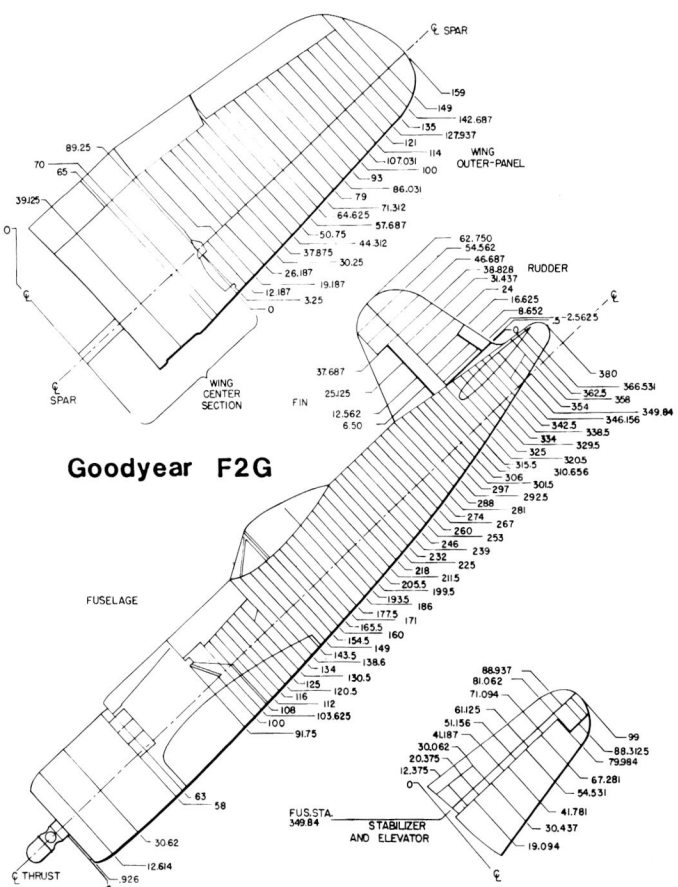

Goodyear F2G

Of interest in this installed P&W Wasp major engine are the individual exhaust pipes, rather than collect them in a header. (Goodyear Aircraft Photo, Courtesy Nick Hauprich)

Wing, fuselage, and tail surface station contour drafting is a painstaking exercise. Every station must be accurately drafted to insure that structures such as wing ribs and fuselage frames and bulkheads can be accurately fabricated. Station locations are shown. (Goodyear Aircraft Artwork, Courtesy Nick Hauprich)

Chapter II: Corsair Development and Production

Looking forward into the engine cooling air outlet, the engine exhaust pipes are evident. By exhausting toward the rear, they not only add propulsive power to the plane but also induce the flow of engine cooling air. (Goodyear Aircraft Photo, Courtesy Nick Hauprich)

A non-structural but important component as the engine air inlet scoop requires an aluminum casting, spot-welding, and sheet metal forming to perform its important function. (Goodyear Aircraft Photo, Courtesy Nick Hauprich)

On March 15, 1944, one month before the optimum F4U-4 Corsair's first flight, the BuAer requested a proposal from Vought for a high altitude Corsair with increased performance, automation, and armament. In response, Vought proposed design V-351 on July 27, 1944, three months after the F4U-4's first flight. A contract for five test F4U-5 prototypes was awarded on December 21, 1944.

At the onset, three F4U-4 Corsairs were used as prototype test XF4U-5 Corsairs: F4U-4 (BuNo 97296) and F4U-4 (BuNo 97415) were the first to arrive for conversion to XF4U-5 test Corsairs. Vought test pilot Bill Moran made the first flight in XF4U-5 BuNo 97296 on July 3, 1946, but did not like the plane because many of the automated features malfunctioned to the point of being dangerous.

Five days later another Vought test pilot, Dick Borroughs, experienced engine failure in the same plane that Bill Horan had flown. Dick attempted an emergency dead-stick landing at Stratford, Connecticut; however, XF4U-5 BuNo 97296 crashed on the airfield, killing the test pilot. Vought XF4U-5 (formerly F4U-4 BuNo 97364) replaced the destroyed BuNo 97296.

The XF4U-5's performance presented a remarkable improvement for the Corsair; therefore, a production contract was awarded to Vought on February 6, 1946. The first F4U-5 production flight was when Bill Horan flew BuNo 121796 from Stratford on October 1, 1947.

The new Corsair was powered by the P&W R-2800-32W air cooled radial engine that produced 2,300hp at sea level. This powerplant propelled the F4U-5 to a maximum speed of 480 mph at 26,800ft. Rate of climb was 5,240 fpm. Service ceiling was 44,100ft. In order to improve forward vision the engine was lowered to afford the aviator a two degrees downward view along the nose of the aircraft. The single engine air

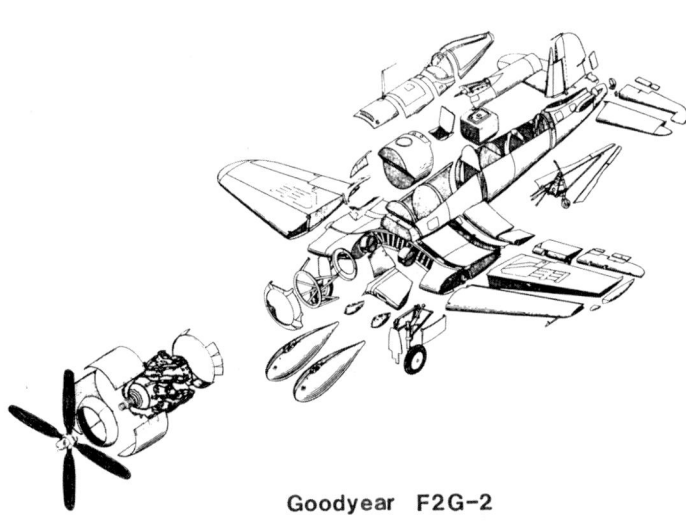

Goodyear F2G-2
BASIC COMPONENTS

The basic components belie the fact that each component is composed of hundreds or thousands of fabricated mini-assemblies. This illustration helps the non-technical reader understand the complexity of fighting aircraft. (Goodyear Aircraft Artwork, Courtesy Nick Hauprich)

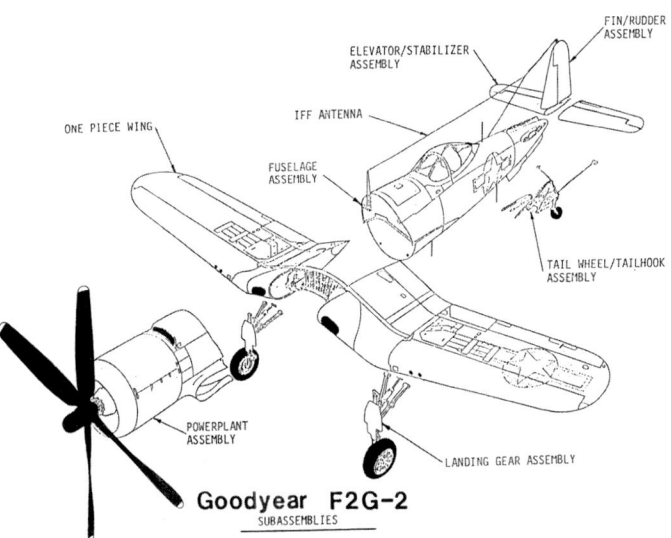

Goodyear F2G-2
SUBASSEMBLIES

Subassemblies include all the Basic Components assembled into recognizable shapes that fall into place to create a magnificent flying machine. (Goodyear Aircraft Artwork, Courtesy Nick Hauprich)

Corsair: The Saga of the Legendary Bent-Wing Fighter-Bomber

This XF4U-5 was the reworked F4U-4 (BuNo 97364) that replaced XF4U-4 (BuNo 97296) after the latter crashed during a deadstick landing attempt at Stratford, killing the test pilot. (Howard Levy Collection, Courtesy Albert L. Lewis)

An early production F4U-5 is undergoing an engine check, as the powerplant is revved up while the wheels are safely chocked. Note the two cheek engine air inlet ducts. (United Aircraft Corp. Photo, Courtesy Albert L. Lewis)

This division of U.S. Navy Vought F4U-5 Corsairs from USS Tarawa (CV-40) makes an over-water flight in December 1951. The F4U-5 canopy was made higher and wider. (National Archives, Courtesy Fred Pernell)

A U.S. Marine F4U-5 Corsair is ready to lift off USS Coral Sea (CVB-43) with tail high and flaps down in November 1950. Long-range drop tanks suggest a long flight. (National Archives, Courtesy Barbara L. Burger)

Chapter II: Corsair Development and Production

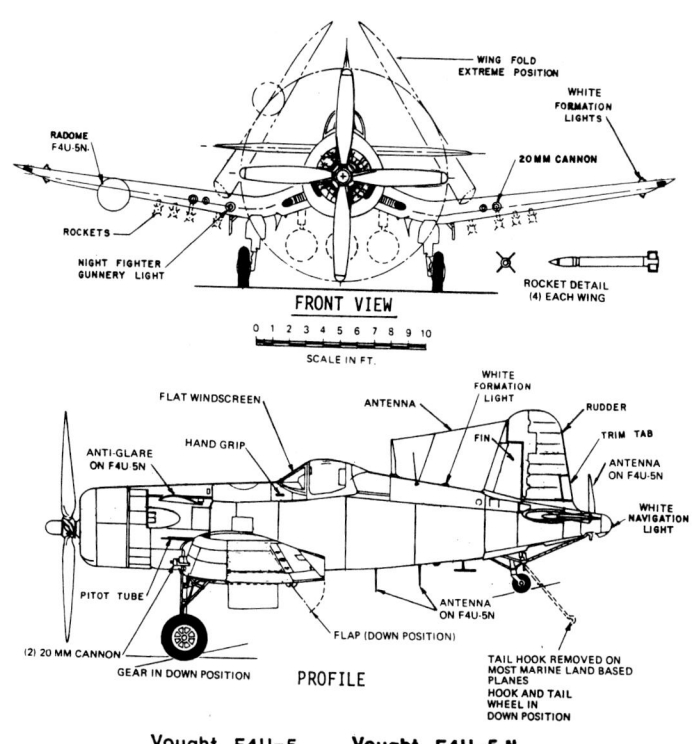

The F4U-5 appeared to be designed for troop-supporting ground-attack work, while the F4U-5N and F4U-5NL night fighters were anti-intruder interceptors. Observe the multiple rockets, 20mm cannon, and strong points for bombs, fuel tanks, or napalm. (Vought Aircraft Artwork, enhanced by Author)

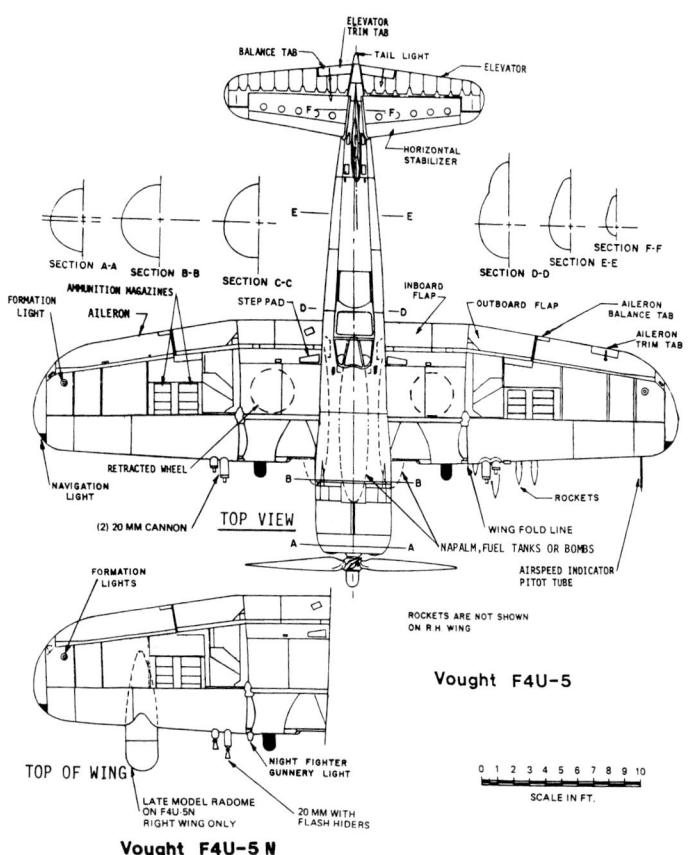

The F4U-5 series was the only Corsair to have the entire wing metal-covered. The night fighter 80 candle-power gunnery light played an important part in properly aiming at an adversary in the inky darkness. (Vought Aircraft Artwork, enhanced by Author)

inlet duct of the F4U-4 was changed to two cowl cheek inlets to feed the increased engine horsepower.

Outer wing panels were revised by replacing the six .50 caliber machine guns with four M-3 20mm rapid-fire cannon. In addition, for the first time, the non-loading, normally fabric covered outer wing panels were alclad dural covered because of the new design's high speed.

In addition to the wing cannon, the F4U-5 had three strong point pylons under the wing center section, two of which could each carry a 1,000 lb bomb. For long-range missions, two 150 gal (1,000 lbs) drop tanks and one 150 gal (1,000 lbs) belly tank could be installed.

The blown bubble canopy was increased in height and width to improve vision and greater head movement.

New automated and luxury appointments included: cigarette lighter; new adjustable seat with folding arm rests; electric elevator and aileron trim control; swing-down rudder pedals that served as leg rests; automatic engine cooling cowl flaps; automatic intercooler doors and oil cooler air-flow exit doors; and spring tabs were fitted to elevator and rudder to reduce the pilots effort by as much as 40 percent.

The automatic double side-wheel, two-stage supercharger increased the engine horsepower to 2,450. The cannon bays and airspeed pitot were electrically heated and the tailwheel was fully retractable.

The modifications increased the F4U-4's 12,500 lbs to the 13,800 lbs of the F4U-5N and -NL—a 1,300 lb increase!

Unfortunately, the F4U-5 was not received with open arms by the aviators, as their approval had been expected, because many of the BuAer-required automated aviator assists were hindering the aviators instead of helping them. The Mark 8 gyroscopic target-lead computer gunsight, intended to simplify deflection shots, required so much attention that it would become useless during combat; the electric elevator, aileron, and rudder trim controls gave the aviator no feedback and required too much of his attention; the automatic cowl flaps were prone to misinterpreting the specific aircraft operating condition requiring the proper flaps setting, especially during formation flying; and for some unexplained reason the formerly hydraulically-retracted tail hook on Corsairs was now required to be manually retracted after a carrier landing.

Probably the most dangerous automated "improvement" was the Automatic Power Unit that decided when the F4U-5 needed extra power. After reading the ambient air temperature, atmospheric temperature, propeller pitch, engine manifold pressure, engine speed (RPM), and the plane's air speed the APU blower cut in with no advance warning to the pilot.

The F4U-5 entered production as the last F4U-4 left the assembly line in June 1947. When the last F4U-5 left the production line 233 of the new model Corsair had been completed.

While the F4U-5 was still under construction Chance Vought Aircraft relocated from Stratford, Connecticut, to Dallas, Texas, in early 1948. This was the largest industrial move at that time, and Rex Beisel was the administrator in charge of this monumental achievement. Specialized equipment and more than 1,500 key workers moved to Texas and occupied the former North American Aviation plant on Jefferson Street, next to the

This interesting comparison between the F4U-5N (upper photo) and the F4U-5 reveals the basic differences between the two models. The F4U-5N is fitted with a radome and 80 candlepower light beam projector (arrows) while the F4U-5 is not. Both models do have cameras (open arrows). (Vought Aircraft Photo, Author's File)

As vice president of Chance Vought, Rex Beisel administered the company's move from Stratford, Connecticut, to Dallas, Texas, in early 1948. The F4U-5 variants were in production at that time; however, the transfer of machinery and personnel was made with no delays. This was the biggest industrial move at that time and was covered extensively in the prestigious periodical "Business Week," which featured a photo of Beisel on its August 14, 1948, cover. (Business Week Photo, Courtesy Thomas G. Dickinson MD)

Temco plant. There was no interruption in F4U-5 production because of the careful planning. By 1965 Chance Vought Aircraft had merged with Temco to be part of Ling-Temco-Vought.

The Korean War started in 1950, and the Chinese nocturnal infiltration of men and supplies into Korea spurred the need for heavy-hitting U.S. day and night fighters, and the F4U-5 and F4U-5N were selected for this role. Airborne intercept radar had made amazing progress since the early F4U-2 night fighters that made the F4U-5N most effective.

The F4U-5N was a standard F4U-5 with a radar suite installation. AN/ASP-19 and AN/ASP-19A radar was installed in all F4U-5N and F4U-5NL Corsairs; the difference in the radar being that the AN/ASP-

The complicated night aiming system included three prisms located on each wingtip and in the tail of the F4U-5N and F4U-5NL Corsairs (See arrows). The prisms detect whether the aviator's aim is "on target." (U.S. Navy Photo, Courtesy Albert L. Lewis)

An element of F4U-5NL Corsairs from VC-4 are shown on a training mission. Designed for the cold Korean nights, the plane was fitted with inflatable deicer boots on the wing, stabilizer, and rudder leading edges. (U.S. Navy Photo, Author's File)

Chapter II: Corsair Development and Production

The F4U-5P Photo-Reconnaissance Corsair was equipped with three cameras to film enemy damage during or after surface strikes. This F4U-5P was an early model with a single transparent bubble under the fuselage for the three cameras (See arrow). Note the streamline blister on the fin for the relocated remote indicating compass. (Howard Levy Collection, Courtesy Albert L. Lewis)

19A featured a control to dim the radar screen; and the difference in the Corsairs was that the F4U-5NL was specially designed for operations in the cold Korean weather.

The radar equipment was fitted with four available modes: SEARCH was able to detect land or sea surface targets as far as 100 miles distant; INTERCEPT could detect an airborne target within 20 miles; BEACON was an assist to navigation; and AIM could locate and fire at an airborne target within 1,500 yards distance.

The radar screen in the center of the instrument panel displayed a dot in the center that represented the Corsair. The hunted aircraft appeared as a blip on the radar screen, indicating its location and movement relative to the Corsair.

The gun-aiming system included three prisms on the wing tips and the tail; an 80 candlepower light beam projector in the right (starboard) wing panels inboard of the guns; and the standard gun camera. When the Corsair aviator sighted his target and pressed his gun trigger a light beam shined on the enemy. When the light beam was on target, it would be reflected from all three prisms at the enemy. Should less than all three prisms return the light the aim was declared inadequate; either too high or too low, etc., and the exercise must be repeated. Not easy! F4U-5N construction reached 240 aircraft.

The F4U-5NL night fighter was specially equipped with protection from the Korean cold. Inflatable leading edge deicer boots were added to the outer wing panels, stabilizer, and fin. Glycol was used to deice

Upper photo shows Vought F4U-6 Corsairs (later known as Vought AU-1) near the end of the Dallas production line. Lower photo is AU-1 BuNo. 129380 recycling the landing gear during a trial flight. Note the landing gear is partially rotated between retracted and extended. (Vought Aircraft Photos, Author's File)

This Vought XAU-1 (F4U-6) is loaded with ten 250 lb bombs at NATC Patuxent River. Instead of the bombs ten five inch rockets can be fitted. Strong points under the fuselage can carry Tiny Tim rockets, bombs, long-range fuel tanks, or napalm. Although this XAU-1 sports "Navy" affiliation, the AU-1 was supplied exclusively to the U.S. Marines starting in 1952. (Vought Aircraft Photo, Courtesy H.J. "Jerry" Dalton)

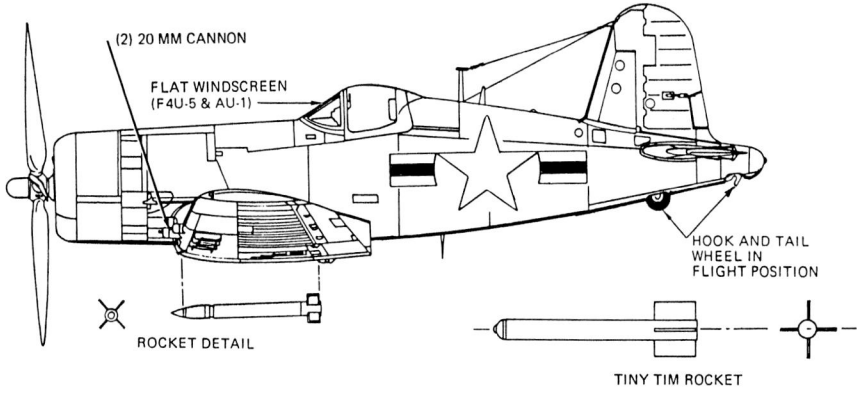

The ground attack Vought AU-1 Corsair used bombs, napalm, rockets, and cannon to pound enemy troops, vehicles, gun emplacements, camps, and ships. (Vought Aircraft Artwork, enhanced by Author)

This factory-fresh Vought AU-1 Corsair shows off its smooth and attractive lines. The high gloss finish reflects the fabric covered outer wing panels that had been abandoned for the F4U-5 models. Observe the above-wing engine exhaust. (Vought Aircraft Photo, Courtesy H.J. "Jerry" Dalton)

Chapter II: Corsair Development and Production

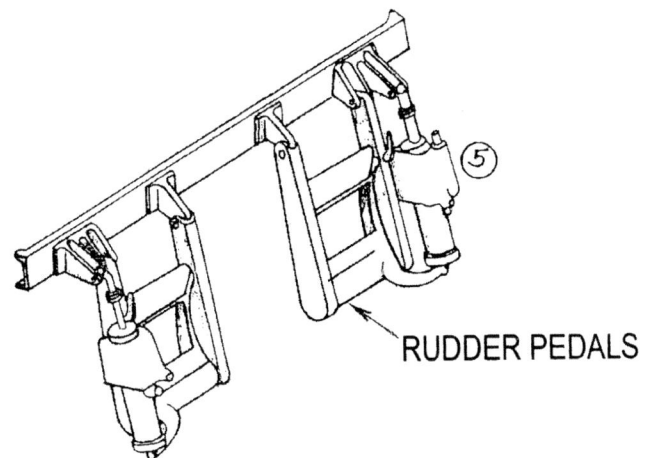

RUDDER PEDALS

The hydraulic cylinders for the steering system are identified (No.5). Observe that the pedals are suspended from an overhead beam.

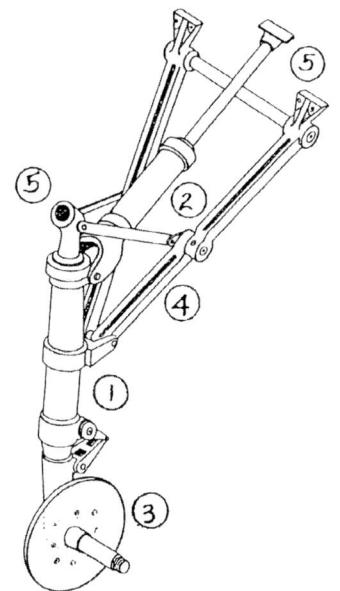

MAIN LANDING GEAR ASSEMBLY

the windshield and propeller; however, the glycol was deteriorating the windshield rubber seals and clouding the plastic canopies and was deleted.

The deicer boots placed some restrictions on the operation of the F4U-5NL aircraft: the F4U-5NL must not dive or land with the deicer boots inflated, nor fly the plane at any speed above 276 mph, nor less than 121 mph. Seventy-five F4U-5NL Corsairs were constructed.

In 1950, a Photo-Reconnaissance version of the F4U-5 (F4U-5P) was introduced on the production line at the Vought Dallas plant where 40 were built.

Three cameras were installed in the radio compartment behind the cockpit: one taking photos vertically downward and the others obliquely downward. The cameras forced the remote indicating compass to relocate into a streamlined blister on the fin.

The F4U-5P tactics were to provide post-strike intelligence as well as photographing the damage wrought while striking targets. The F4U-5P operated in shore-based VC-60 and VC-61 as well as in the USS Leyte-based VC-62.

After creating the high-altitude F4U-5 Corsair and the basic F4U-1M for the fast climbing Goodyear F2G Corsair, Vought was asked to make an about-face and design a low-level ground attack Corsair. This was to become the last Corsair created for the U.S. Armed Forces.

Except for the fabric covered outer wing panels the F4U-6 resembled the F4U-5. The F4U-6 used the same cowl as the F4U-5; however, the two cheek engine air inlets were blanked, and engine air was admitted via the two wing root leading edge air inlets as on the F4U-1.

Soon after the contract was signed the F4U-6 designation was changed to AU-1 because the Corsair had undergone a metamorphosis from fighter to attack mode. "A" was the U.S. Military "attack" designation as "U" was the assigned designation for Vought aircraft.

The AU-1 was powered by a single-speed, single-stage supercharger-equipped Pratt & Whitney R-2800-83W air-cooled radial engine. This engine produced 2,100hp at 3,000ft altitude, dropping to 1,700hp at 16,000ft.

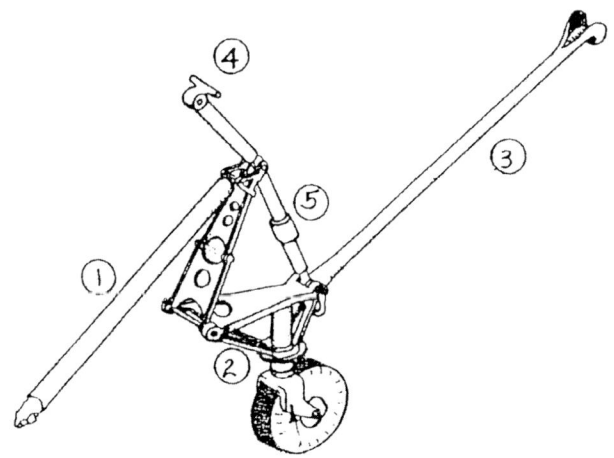

TAILWHEEL ASSEMBLY

Upper Drawing: Main Landing Gear Assembly major components are as follows: (No.1) Hydraulic Shock Strut; (No.2) Hydraulic Retracting Strut; (No.3) Wheel Mounting Disc; (No.4) 90 degree Rotating Struts; and (No.5) Fuselage attachments. Lower Drawing: Tailwheel Assembly major components are as follows: (No.1) Hydraulic Retracting Strut; (No.2) Major assembly structure; (No.3) Arresting Hook; (No.4) Fuselage Attachment; and (No.5) Hydraulic Shock Strut.

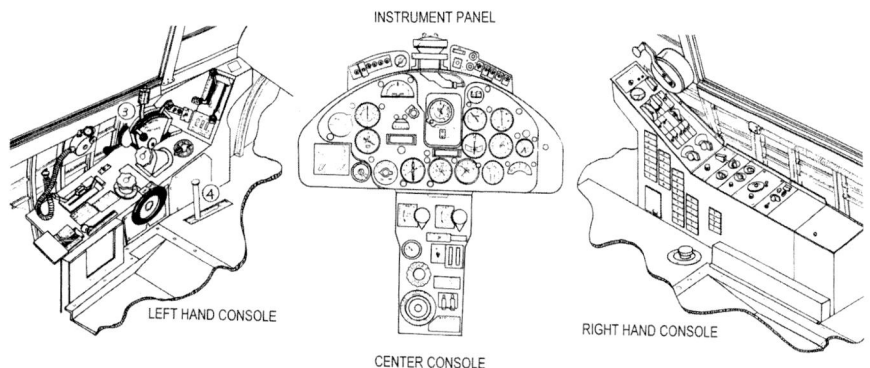

COCKPIT INSTRUMENT PANEL AND CONTROL CONSOLE

The Corsair gauges are assembled on an instrument panel located below the windshield. Three control consoles are placed on the left and right side of the pilot; and below the instrument panel. Control knobs marked (No.3) are the throttle, mixture control, and spark advance, while the control rod marked (No.4) controls the retractable landing gear.

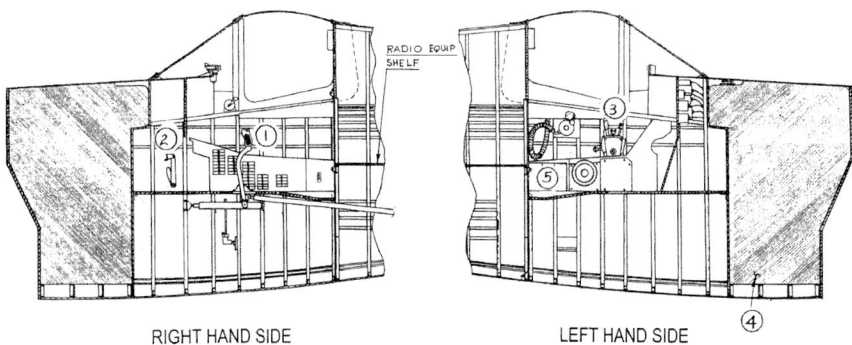

COCKPIT INSTALLATION

The cockpit profiles reveal the Joyce-stick, generally called the Joy-stick, that operates the elevators and the ailerons (No.1); rudder pedals (No.2); engine controls (No.3); bladder fuel tank (No.4); and map case (No.5).

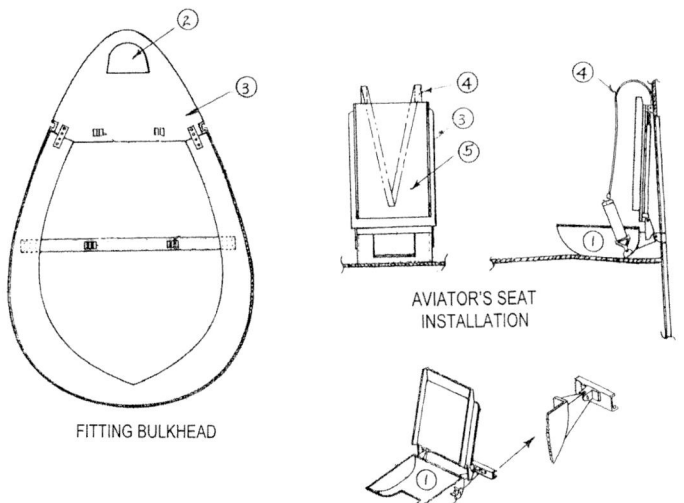

AVIATOR'S SEAT INSTALLATION

Armament consisted of up to ten five inch HVAR rockets or ten 250 lb bombs on underwing mounts, plus two 500 lb bombs, droppable fuel tanks, or napalm bombs on the under-fuselage strong points. Four 20mm rapid-fire wing-mounted cannon round off the armament.

In view of the low altitude missions flown, the AU-1 Corsair was usually met by a barrage of small arms fire and rapid-fire antiaircraft guns. The attacking AU-1 Corsair often returned to base with battle-damage or wounded aviators despite the fact that vital components, such as the oil coolers, and the aviators were protected by armor. Some planes never returned at all because of withering enemy ground fire.

The following chapters will follow the Corsair variants into battle from Guadalcanal to the Indian Ocean, Central Pacific Ocean, Korea, Africa, and Central America.

Aviator's seat (No.1) resembles a bucket until the aviator's parachute pack fits into it. When the aviator sits on the parachute pack it becomes a cushion that will not slide off; (No.2) is the aviator's head rest; (No.3) is armor plate; (No.4) is the aviator's shoulder harness; is buckled to the lap safety belt; and (No.5) is the seat back cushion.

Chapter II: Corsair Development and Production

WING SECTIONS

Airfoils and rib sections reveal the structure and aerodynamic shape of the inner and outer wing panels. The outer panels show only the aerodynamic contours of various sections, while the inner panel reveals the structure as well as the aerodynamic contour. Observe manner in which the wing skin is led over the leading edge of the flap to reduce turbulence.

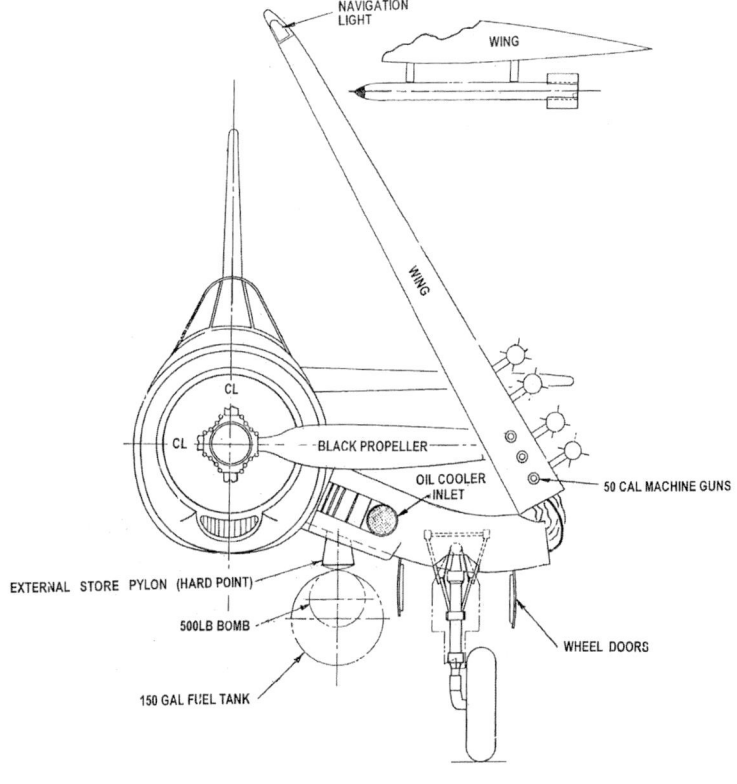

The Vought Bent-Wing Corsair was one of the first airplanes to feature wings that can be mechanically folded from controls in the cockpit while the plane is taxiing. This has the immense advantage over the average naval aircraft that requires six to eight strong men to rotate the wing and fold it back along the fuselage side while the plane remains stationary. The advantage of the remote wing folding is readily apparent, however, the complexity of the design to accomplish this advantage is often overlooked by the casual observer. Countless electrical cables, hydraulic lines, and mechanical connections that run from the fuselage to the outer wing panels to operate the ailerons and flaps; fire rockets and machine guns; illuminate navigation and formation lights; and relay instrument readings to the cockpit all require careful design and installation. Upper photo illustrates the abundance of connections between the inner wing panel and outer wing panel. Photo by Jean-Jacques Petit (Courtesy Alain J. Pelletier) The lower sketch illustrates the sharp angle of the folded wing that increases the outward, open angle, forcing the wiring, tubing, etc. to follow a greater arc.

III

Corsairs into the Solomons

Concurrent with the Japanese attack on Pearl Harbor, Japanese armed forces invaded the Philippine Islands; Dutch East Indies (Indonesia); Burma; French Indo-China (Vietnam, Laos, and Cambodia); Manchuria (Manchukuo); Thailand (Siam); China; USSR; Malaya; Sarawak; Marshall Islands; Gilbert Islands; Solomon Islands; Aleutian Islands; New Guinea (Papua); New Britain; and Formosa (Taiwan).

The majority of the conquests were for raw materials necessary for industrialization of the Japanese economy. This included oil, rubber, coal, tin, zinc, lead, molybdenum, iron, copper, and other industrial necessities. However, not all the conquests were for economics, because many had no intrinsic value, but were strategically necessary to protect and defend the valued conquests.

The South Pacific and Southwest Pacific areas were geographically important to Japan because control of the area would secure its hold on the raw materials of French Indo-China and the Dutch East Indies. Conversely, if the U.S. controlled the area it would threaten Japan's Southeast Asia strategic resources and prevent further expansion or lose what was attained.

Japan lost no time to build airfields and navy bases on New Guinea, Solomon Islands, and Bismarck Archipelago. Rabaul, on the island of New Britain, possessed the finest harbor in the Southwest Pacific, and Japan rushed to make it a bastion with a naval base surrounded by airfields. Rabaul created the "Bismarck Barrier" to protect Japan's SE Asia possessions.

The first wartime Washington Conference (called Arcadia) had begun on December 23, 1941, and came to a conclusion on January 14, 1942. President Roosevelt and Prime Minister Churchill of Britain decided that, although the war was to concentrate on the defeat of Germany and Italy,

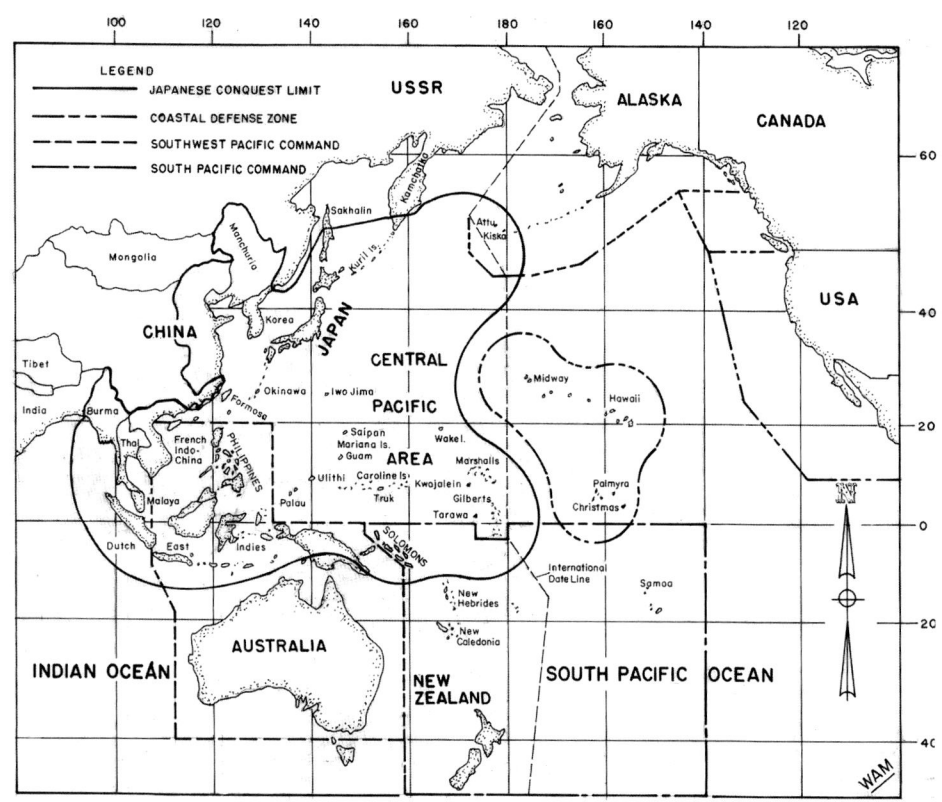

The amazing extent of Japanese conquest ending in August 1942 and the Allied Southwest Pacific and South Pacific Command demarcations illustrated on this map should be of interest to the reader. Also worthy of attention are the North American Coastal Defense Zones.

Chapter III: Corsairs into the Solomons

Australia and the Sea Lines Of Communications (SLOC) with the U.S., ie New Caledonia, the Fiji Islands, and American Samoa, must be held against Japan. It was agreed that America was to take on the responsibility of fighting the Pacific War.

Initially, the Americans had planned to use aircraft carriers to pound the Japanese bastion of Rabaul; however, the U.S. aircraft carriers *Yorktown, Hornet, Wasp, Enterprise, Lexington, Saratoga,* and *Langley* were either sunk or severely damaged in early Pacific battles and engagements. This forced the U.S. to resort to an island-hopping strategy through the Solomons to Rabaul. Neither the Japanese nor the Americans dared risk their remaining carriers alone to attack Rabaul or the American Solomon's invasion because of the restricted waters and enemy aircraft carriers.

The sole purpose of the island-hopping strategy was to possess airfields from which short-range fighter planes could operate. The Solomon Islands now took the place of a fleet of aircraft carriers and became stepping stones to the island of Bougainville, the closest Solomon Island to Rabaul. In effect, it was the "springboard to Rabaul."

The Solomon Island chain is about 550 miles long, with Guadalcanal the largest of the southeastern islands and Bougainville the largest at

Vila, the capitol of New Hebrides, was located beyond the area of Japanese conquest. It featured a hospital and a small airfield. Marines landed in March 1942 using the hospital for wounded and malaria-ridden Marines. Note the roofed movie screen for hospital patients (arrow). (U.S. Navy Photo, Courtesy John Regan)

Upper Photo: Japanese dive bombers pound *USS Yorktown* CV-5 during the Battle of Midway on June 4, 1942, while a torpedo-bomber fires two torpedoes into the carrier's port side, sinking the ship. Lower Photo: *USS Wasp* is afire and sinking after being torpedoed east of Guadalcanal on September 15, 1942. The loss of U.S. carriers prompted an island-hopping Solomons strategy. (U.S. Navy Photos, Author's File)

Upper Photo: *USS Lexington* CV-2 is afire as the crew abandons ship during the Coral Sea battle on May 8, 1942. The ship sank. Center Photo: *USS Enterprise* CV-6 was disabled by Japanese aircraft during the Battle of Santa Cruz on Oct. 26, 1942. Note the explosion at the port (left) side of the bow. Lower Photo: *USS Hornet* CV-8 was severely damaged and listing at the end of October 1942 in the Santa Cruz Battle. Observe the Val dive bomber diving on the ship. *USS Hornet* was abandoned before it sank. (U.S. Navy Photos, Author's File)

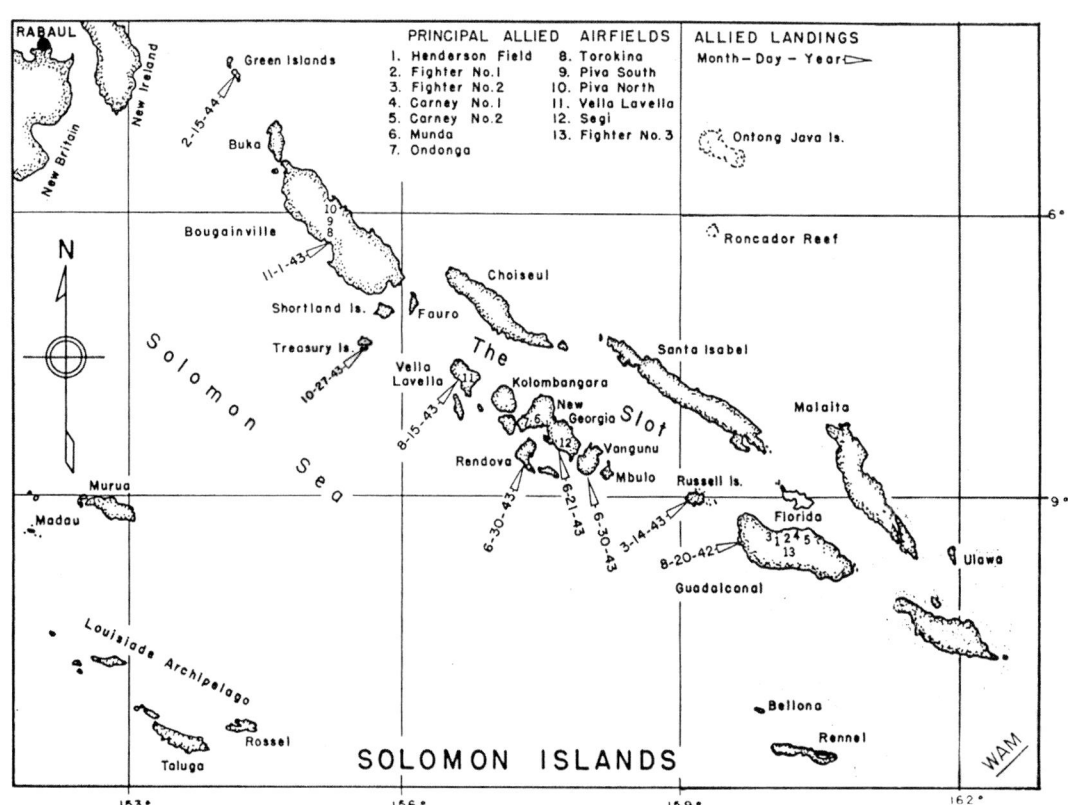

This Solomons map illustrates how the islands are arranged as stepping stones toward Rabaul, with Bougainville being the "Springboard to Rabaul." Observe the many U.S. airfields established throughout the Solomons by the end of 1943.

Bauer Field in Efate, New Hebrides, was used for Corsair training and absorbing replacements. The main runway and secondary area for maintenance and repair were cut out of dense rainforest. The field was named to honor Lt Harold W Bauer, an early Marine ace who gave his life for his country. (USMC Photo, Author's Collection)

This ingenious Pallikulo airfield control tower on Espiritu Santo was built on one of the few leaf-bearing trees on the island. Apparently the control crew remained on station for long periods of time; witness the hoist dangling from the platform. (USMC Photo, Author's Files)

Chapter III: Corsairs into the Solomons

the northwestern end. The islands roughly form two rows with a water passage between them. This is called the "Slot," and became the scene of considerable naval and aerial activity as the Japanese reinforced their manpower and supplies to Guadalcanal via the "Slot."

U.S. Forces were quick to occupy New Caledonia, a French possession, on May 11, 1942, and New Hebrides, a British-French protectorate, on May 27, 1942. New Caledonia is about 350 miles south of Guadalcanal, while the New Hebrides are about 250 miles south of Guadalcanal. The islands became important locations for the Solomons fighting.

The New Caledonia and New Hebrides islands served as supply stations, training areas, staging centers, and wounded care hospitals. Their location beyond the Japanese occupation perimeter gave them a measure of safety and importance.

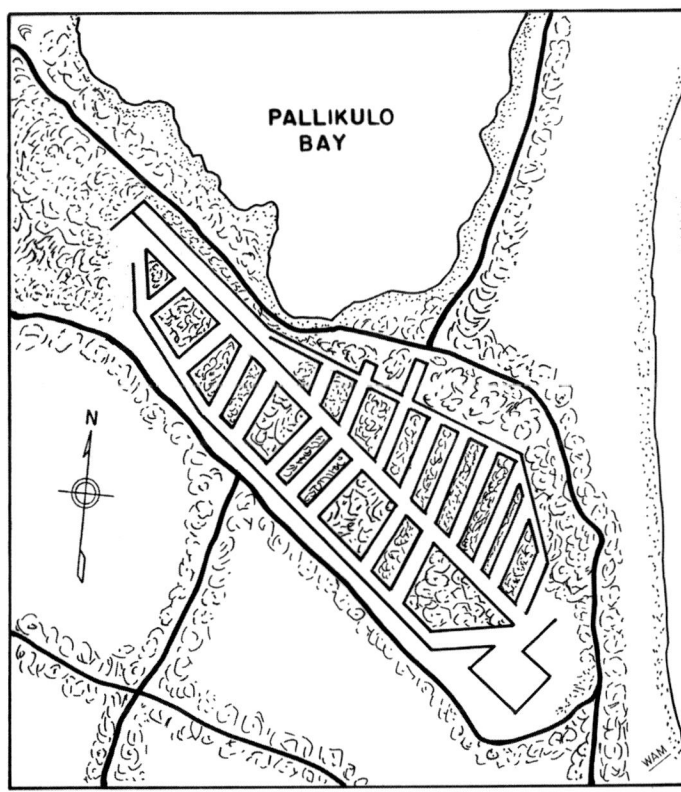

The incomplete Henderson Field is shown in the upper photograph while the finished field is shown in the lower photo. Japanese troops still occupy the hill in the distant right. (USMC Photos, Author's File)

Pallikulo airstrip on Espiritu Santo, in the New Hebrides, was a good staging airfield early in the Solomons campaign. Upper Photo: Avenger TBF torpedo bombers are shown in a revetment. The main operating runway is where the coral dust is rising in the distance (arrow). The field was cut out of an enormous coconut plantation. Lower Photo: Drawing reveals the main runway and revetments near Pallikulo Bay and proximity to roads. (USMC Photo, Courtesy John Regan)

Major Lofton Henderson, USMC, is the Battle of Midway Hero in whose honor Henderson Field is named. (U.S. National Archives, Author's File)

Commander-in-Chief of the Japanese Combined Fleet and Supreme Commander of the entire Japanese-controlled Pacific, IJN ADM Isoruku Yamamoto, opposed war with the United States, but was ordered to plan the Pearl Harbor Attack and other assaults throughout the Pacific. (U.S. National Archives, Author's Collection)

When the U.S. Military learned the Japanese were constructing an airfield on the northern coast of Guadalcanal it planned an invasion of the island, code-named "Operation Watchtower."

The American attack was not a mere raid, but rather a full-fledged amphibious invasion that set the pace for all future Pacific Island assaults. The Force included 14 destroyers; five cargo ships; eight cruisers; 19 troop transports; and five mine-sweepers, plus the aircraft carrier battle groups of *USS Wasp*, *USS Enterprise*, and *USS Saratoga* that provided air support from a distance offshore south of Guadalcanal. The principal objective was the incomplete Japanese airfield.

Simultaneous American attacks were conducted against Tulagi and Florida Islands, 30 miles north of Guadalcanal, while the American Force assaulted the primary target. The attack started on August 7, 1942, and by August 20, 1942, the Marines had aircraft based in Guadalcanal. On 22 and 27 August U.S. Army Air Corps fighters joined the Marine aircraft on Guadalcanal; however, the bloody battle for Guadalcanal did not end in victory for the Allied armies until early in 1943.

Admiral Aubrey Fitch named the partially complete captured Japanese airfield on Guadalcanal "Henderson Field"; a name that has

Marston Mat was a 6ft x 6in earth-gripping, perforated, interlocking strip of steel that, when assembled, became an excellent Henderson Field airfield runway. It is usually assembled into a three-strip unit prior to installation. Upper photo shows stacks of three-strip assemblies ready to install. Center photo has a Marine and a construction worker installing an assembled mat. Lower photo illustrates a completed Marston Mat runway. (USMC Photos, Author's File)

Chapter III: Corsairs into the Solomons

The U.S. Joint Chiefs of Staff met during Autumn 1942 to plan the Solomons campaign. L to R: Lt Gen Henry H Arnold; ADM William D Leahy; ADM Ernest J King; and Gen George C Marshall. (National Archives, Author's File)

FADM Ernest J King CNO was the U.S. Navy Chief of Naval Operations and oversaw high-ranking appointments and strategies. (U.S. Naval Historical Center Photo, Author's File)

been recognized until this day by the average American citizen. The field was named to honor U.S. Marine hero aviator Major Lofton Henderson who led the dive bombers of VMS-241 in strikes against the Japanese ships during the Battle of Midway. With his plane afire Maj Henderson intentionally dived his Douglas Dauntless into a Japanese aircraft carrier and was posthumously awarded the Navy Cross. The code name for Guadalcanal was "Cactus." It was also called "The Canal." All aircraft that flew from Guadalcanal were known as the "Cactus Air Force."

Once the captured airfield was complete, secure, and in operation, five more airfields were built on Guadalcanal to accommodate U.S. Army Air Corps, U.S. Navy, and Royal New Zealand Air Force planes. The Japanese airfield was really worth fighting for.

Marston Mat is credited with transforming the incomplete Japanese airfield into an operating military airfield. The interlocking, perforated strips of steel form a durable airfield runway and is considered the reason for the success of Allied airfields in the Solomons and elsewhere in the Pacific.

During Autumn 1942, the U.S. Joint Chiefs of Staff met to confirm the division of commands for the war in the Pacific. Admiral William D Leahy (Aide to the President), Lt. Gen Henry H Arnold (commander U.S. Army Air Corps); Admiral Ernest J King, Chief of Naval Operations (CNO); and General George C Marshall (Chairman of the JCS) agreed on

FADM Chester W Nimitz was the Commander In Chief Pacific Fleet and Commander In Chief Pacific Ocean Area. (National Archives, Author's File)

FADM Chester W Nimitz, CINCPAC (seated), studies a map of the Solomon Islands with VADM Robert L Ghormley in Nimitz's Pearl Harbor office. (U.S. Naval Historical Center Photo, Author's File)

VADM Robert L Ghormley (Com So Pac) was assigned the capture of the Guadalcanal airfield soon to be known as Henderson Field. (National Archives, Author's File)

VADM Aubrey W Fitch (Com Air So Pac) commanded all aerial activities in the South Pacific Area. He designated Henderson Field as a Marine Corps Air Base on November 15, 1942. Fitch moved nine more squadrons into Guadalcanal in time for the October-November 1942 battles. (National Archives, Author's File)

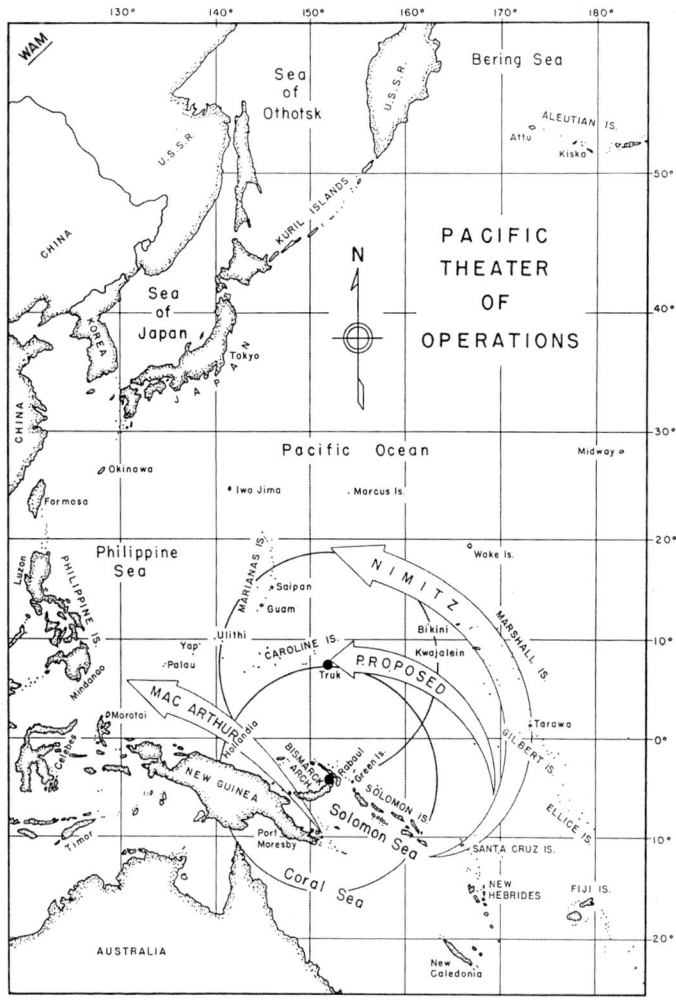

In this map of the Pacific Theatre of operations, observe that Adm Nimitz's original plan of attack was to strike at the Japanese bastion of Truk; however, the plan was altered to strike through the Gilbert and Marshall Islands, bypassing Truk. Also note how Rabaul's and Truk's striking radius overlap to provide mutual defensive and offensive power. Rabaul and Truk are 640 miles apart.

the following responsibilities: General Douglas Mac Arthur, Commander In Chief of the Southwest Pacific Area (Cinc SWPA); FADM Chester W Nimitz, Commander In Chief Pacific Fleet (Cinc Pac); and Commander In Chief Pacific Ocean Area (Cinc Poa) was in overall command of the Central Pacific; VADM Robert L Gormley was Commander South Pacific Area and South Pacific Force (Com So Pac), who reported to Admiral Nimitz; and VADM Aubrey W Fitch was in command of air activities in the South Pacific (ComAirSoPac).

The Director of Marine Corps Aviation was Brig Gen Ralph J Mitchell who served until March 20, 1943, when he was succeeded by Maj Gen Roy S Geiger.

The first year of the war in the Pacific consisted of holding on, but the Casablanca conference between Roosevelt and Churchill in January 1943 confirmed certain long-range Pacific missions: continuation up from New Guinea and Guadalcanal until Rabaul was captured and the Bismarck Barrier broken, plus an advance westward toward Truk and Guam.

The master plan was to have MacArthur's land forces advance westward along the coast of New Guinea to the Philippine Islands, protecting communications between the U.S. and Australia, while the naval effort under Nimitz would be directed toward the powerful Japanese stronghold of Truk Atoll, in the Caroline Island chain. The principal enemy bastion standing in the way of this strategy was the Japanese base of Rabaul, on the northeastern tip of Island of New Britain in the Bismarck Archipelago.

Rabaul controlled the path from New Guinea and the Solomons to the Philippines. It also served as a barrier for attacks on Truk from the south. Located as it was 700 miles south of Truk, 560 miles northwest of Guadalcanal, and only 445 miles northeast of Port Moresby, on the southern coast of New Guinea, Rabaul was in the perfect defensive position to prevent the proposed Allied advance. This was known as the Bismark Barrier. Offensively, it was from Rabaul that the Japanese planned to dominate the Solomons, New Guinea, and the coast of Australia. As a result, with both belligerents keenly aware of the strategic importance of Rabaul, the stage was set for a long battle in which airpower was to play the decisive role.

Lost to Australia by Germany during the First World War, Rabaul was taken from the Australians during the Japanese advance in January 1942. Rabaul was blessed with one of the finest harbors in the South

Chapter III: Corsairs into the Solomons

Maj Gen Roy Geiger was the Director of Marine Corps Aviation from March 20, 1943, to October 15, 1943, and became Director again on July 17, 1944. With the General is Lt Harold W "Joe" Bauer, an 11 victory Ace and commanding officer of VMF-212, who was forced to ditch his plane and was last seen floating in his "Mae West." Bauer airfield in Efate, New Hebrides, was named in his honor. (USMC Photo, Author's File)

Directors of Marine Corps Aviation Brig Gen Ralph J Mitchell, March 11, 1939, to March 20, 1943 (left), and Brig Gen Louis E woods, October 15, 1943, to July 17, 1944, are seen together after a high-level planning session. (USMC Photo, Author's File)

The various military disciplines engaged in the Solomons exhibited the epitome of cooperation with each other. This was truly a Joint Command. From left to right: Brig Gen Francis P Mulcahy, USMC (Cactus Air Force Commander), RADM Charles P Mason, USN (Commander Air Solomons), and Maj Gen AM Patch, USA (Commander Ground Troops on Guadalcanal) remain at Henderson Field, while VADM Aubrey W Fitch (Commander Air South Pacific) boards a PBY for a return to his base after a conference in May 1943. (U.S. Naval Historical Center Photo, Courtesy U.S. Naval Institute)

Pacific, protected by six volcanic mountains, and the Japanese lost no time in making it an impregnable fortress. After the fall of Guadalcanal the importance of Rabaul increased tremendously, and the strength of the bastion was built up even more until, by November 1943, there were 98,000 Japanese on New Britain. Almost 400 aircraft were based on Rabaul's four principal airfields at Lakunai, Vunakanau, Rapopo, and Tobero to bomb Allied ships and bases, as well as to defend the base against the impending Allied attack. It was quite evident that the Japanese were prepared to hold Rabaul at any cost.

The rank of ComAirSols (Commander Air Solomons) evolved, quite by accident, when General Geiger, commanding general of the First Marine Air Wing, landed in Henderson Field on September 3, 1943. He had decided to remain in combat area Guadalcanal despite the fact that Wing Headquarters was based on non-combat area Espiritu Santo. As the senior aviator on Guadalcanal he assumed the unofficial title of ComAirCactus that was responsible to ComAirSoPac.

ComAirCactus eventually evolved into ComAirSols as American airfields emerged on other Solomon Islands. In view of the fact that Marine aircraft were joined by U.S. Army Air Corps, U.S. Navy, and New Zealand planes, ComAirSols became very democratic and a true joint command with alternating leaders, including Adm Charles P Mason, Adm

Corsair: The Saga of the Legendary Bent-Wing Fighter-Bomber

Marc J Mitscher, Maj Gen Ralph J Mitchell USMC, Brig Gen Francis P Mulcahy USA, and others.

FADM Chester W Nimitz, CincPac, selected VADM William Halsey to succeed VADM Ghormley as ComSoPac on October 20, 1942.

In 1942-1943 Japanese aircraft manufacturers' names such as Aichi, Kawasaki, Mitsubishi, Kawanishi, and Yokosuka were not as familiar in the West as they became in the post-war years.

In December 1942, to avoid confusion and mispronounciation leading to error, U.S. Army Capt Frank T Mc Coy Jr devised a system whereby Japanese fighters would be identified with masculine code names, and Japanese bombers, flying boats, and reconnaissance aircraft would be identified with feminine code names.

The Mitsubishi Zero Sen code name was to be Zeke or Hamp, depending upon the model. Following is a list of the more commonly used code names, including the Japanese manufacturer and the plane's basic performance:

BETTY: Mitsubishi G4M2a; (2) 1850hp; 272mph; 2,262 mi range. (Medium bomber)
CLAUDE: Mitsubishi A5M4; 710hp; 273mph; 746 mi range. (Single-Seat Fighter)
DINAH: Mitsubishi Ki 46-111; (2) 1500hp; 396mph; 2,485 mi range. (Two-Seat Long Range Reconnaissance)
GEORGE: Kawanishi N1K2-J Shiden-Kai; 1990hp; 369mph; 1066 mi range. (Single-Seat Fighter) Four 20mm cannon
HAMP: Mitsubishi A6M8C Zero-Sen; 1,560hp; 356mph; 900 mi range. (Single-seat fighter-clipped-wing Zero)
JACK: Mitsubishi J2M3 Raiden; 1820hp; 371mph; 655 mi range. (Single-Seat Fighter)
JAKE: Watanabe (Aichi) E13A1; 1,000hp; 234mph; 954 mi range. (Three-Seat Reconnaissance-Float Seaplane)
JUDY: Aichi D4Y3 Suisei; 1560hp; 350mph; 944 mi range. (Shipboard dive-bomber)
KATE: Nakajima B5N2: 1,000hp; 235mph; 609 mi range. (Shipboard torpedo-bomber)
MAVIS: Kawanishi H6K4; (4) 1070hp; 211mph; 3107 mi range. (Reconnaissance-bomber flying boat)
MYRT: Nakajima C6N1: 1990hp; 379mph; 3306 mi range. (long range reconnaissance)
NATE: Nakajima Ki.27b: 710hp; 286mph; 389 mi range. (land based fighter)
OSCAR: Nakajima Ki.43.11B Hayabusa; 1,130hp; 320mph; 1006 mi range. (land-based fighter)
REX: Kawanishi N1K1 Kyofu; 1460hp; 302mph; 1060 mi range. (Float Fighter)
RUFE: Nakajima A6M2-N; 925hp; 270mph (Float Fighter-Zero Modification)
SALLY: Mitsubishi Ki.21 Type 97; (2) 1490hp; 397mph; 1595 mi range. (Heavy Bomber)
TOJO: Nakajima Ki-44-11b Shoki; 1520hp; 376mph; 497 mi range. (Land-based fighter)
TONY: Kawasaki Ki.61-2b Hien: 1500hp; 373mph; 746 mi range. (land-based Army fighter)
VAL: Aichi D3A2: 1300hp; 399mph; 970 mi range. (Shipboard Dive Bomber)
ZEKE: Mitsubishi A6M5c; 1130hp; 346mph; 975 mi range. (single-seat fighter-Zero modification)

Tropical Paradise?

Somewhere in the Pacific
where the heat is like a curse,
and each day is followed
by another slightly worse.
Where the coral dust blows thicker
than the shifting desert sands,
and the white man dreams & wishes
for the greener, fairer lands.

Somewhere in the South Pacific
where a girl is never seen.
Where the skies are always cloudy
and the grass is ugly green.
Where the bats are nightly howling
robs a man of blessed sleep
Where there isn't any whiskey
and the beer is never cheap.

Somewhere in the Pacific
where the nights were made for love.
Where the moon is like a searchlight
and the Southern Cross above
sparkles like a diamond
in the balmy tropic night.
It's a shameful waste of beauty
when there's not a girl in sight.

Somewhere in the Pacific
where the mail is always late,
and a Christmas card in April
is considered up-to-date.
Where we never have a payday
and we never get a cent,
but we never miss the money
'cause we never get it spent.

Somewhere in the Pacific
where the ants and buzzards play,
and a hundred fresh mosquitoes
replace each one you slay.
So take me back to 'Frisco,
let me hear the Mission Bell.
For this God-forsaken outpost
is a substitute for Hell!

To the left of the photo is a poem written on a piece of tissue by a member of VMF-214 "Swashbucklers." To the right of the photo is a typed transcription of the original poem. (Unknown Author, Courtesy Lt Col OK Williams, USMC, Ret)

Chapter III: Corsairs into the Solomons

FADM Nimitz (left) briefs VADM Halsey for his new assignment as Commander South Pacific (Com So Pac) when Halsey succeeded Admiral Ghormley on October 20, 1942. (U.S. Navy Photo, Author's File)

In the following battle descriptions the Zero Sen will be described as either Zero or Zeke; however, other Japanese aircraft will be called by their American code names.

The Vought F4U Corsair, ideally suited to both defensive as well as offensive roles, was the perfect weapon for the island-hopping strategy employed in the Solomons. After repelling the early Japanese raids down the "Slot," the Corsair became the escort for United States Army and Navy heavy bombers. It fit in smoothly with the Army escort fighters due to its superior performance at intermediate altitudes. With the bombers normally flying at 20,000 feet, the low-flying Curtiss P-40 afforded little protection from the higher-flying Zero. The twin-engined Lockheed P-38 Lightning, on the other hand, was more at home at altitudes above 30,000 feet.

With the advent of the Corsair, a standard escort pattern was developed for the increasingly larger bombing raids directed against Rabaul. The big bombers lumbered along at 20,000 feet with the P-40 providing low protection and the P-38 supplying top cover. The Marine Corsairs flew between 20,000 and 30,000 feet in loose staggered formation with four to eight airplanes per layer. Weaving over an area two to four miles wide, the F4U could give immediate protection to the bombers. Because the intercepting Japanese fighters invariably went directly to the egg-laying giants, the Corsair pilots were usually the first to engage the Zeroes, often with the odds very much in favor of the enemy. That the Corsair in the hands of a skillful pilot was more than a match for the best Japan could offer was quickly demonstrated.

The men flew against great odds. In addition to being pitted against the finest fliers in Japan, they were forced to live under unbelievable conditions. Soaring temperatures, fantastic humidity, and torrential rains were bad enough, but on many occasions powdered eggs, dried beef, and weevil-ridden bread were the finer delicacies adding to living during these difficult days. Engines were balky in the heat, and it was not uncommon for a pilot to be forced to return to his base due to low oil pressure or an overheated engine.

As soon as he left his formation an Allied pilot would invariably be jumped by a Zero, for the Japanese fighters were on the constant prowl for stragglers. A lone American could expect to find a Zero waiting for him as far south as New Georgia, and as a result none of the sky over the islands was considered safe territory. This required a constant vigil by the Solomons pilots during every flying moment. Furthermore, Japanese snipers often crept close to the jungle airstrip and fired at the aircraft and pilots as they prepared to take off. With this combination of adverse conditions, it is indeed surprising that the men had any will left with which to carry on the fight.

The Marine fighter squadrons that experienced the major portion of the action in the Solomon Islands and Rabaul were VMF-122, 124, 211, 212, 213, 214, 215, and 221. These eight outstanding units are officially credited with the destruction of 903 Japanese aircraft. Of the token force of U.S. Navy fighter aircraft that participated in the campaign, VF-17 is unquestionably the most famous with 156 Solomons victories to its credit.

Sixty-four percent of all United States Marine aerial victories during the Second World War were gained in the Solomon Islands-Rabaul area of operations. The twelve Marine fighter squadrons in the area all flew Corsairs, but due to the prescribed rotation policy only four to six

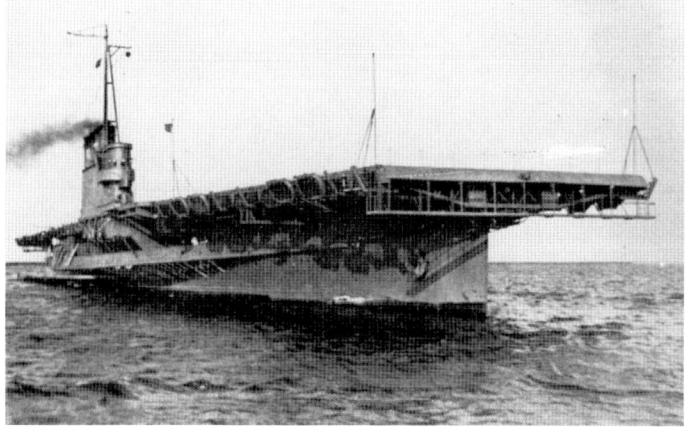

Upper Photo: The training carrier USS Sable was converted from a Great Lakes paddle-wheel passenger steamer that remained in the Great Lakes after conversion. Lower Photo: An F4U-1 Corsair, F4F-4 Wildcat, and two TBF-1 Avengers are poised on the after deck of USS Sable awaiting carrier trials. Observe the rescue boat following the carrier and the letter "S" on the aft end of the Flight Deck. (U.S. Navy Photos, Author's File)

The first U.S. Navy squadron to receive Corsairs was VF(N) 75, which began flying its F4U-2 Nightfighters from Munda on Sept. 11, 1942. Experiments were also conducted on the escort carrier USS Windham Bay (CVE-92) in late 1943 (shown here). (National Archives, Author's File)

squadrons were in action at any given time. It was customary for a unit to remain in a forward combat zone of from four to six weeks, after which it was given one week leave and transported to Sydney, Australia, or Aukland, New Zealand, for a holiday. This was followed by two to four weeks in a back area on a relatively quiet island such as Espiritu Santo or Efate, in the New Hebrides, for regrouping and additional training, if required. The unit then returned to action on Guadalcanal, New Georgia, Vella Lavella, or Bougainville.

On many occasions, only a select few left the squadrons and were replaced by fresh aviators. On other occasions, entire units were dissolved for leave and their places were taken by new men.

The Southwest Pacific and South Pacific had no Western amenities. All food, building materials, fuel, armament, vehicles, communications, spare parts, and medical supplies, etc, were usually flown in because there were so few harbors worthy of the name. The area was truly hostile to civilized man; one of the most primitive places on the planet, fraught with dense rain forests, mountains, deep rivers, heat, humidity, and insects; however, the Japanese defended the Solomon Islands tenaciously because of their tactical and strategic value.

Training of aviators and testing of carrier aircraft not only took aircraft carriers out of combat service but placed them in jeopardy of sinking by marauding enemy submarines. The first thought was to construct escort-type carriers on the Great Lakes for training on the landlocked Great Lakes, between the United States and Canada. Then, upon further cogitation, it was agreed to convert two aging paddle-wheel steamers "Greater Buffalo" and "Seeandbee" into training auxiliary aircraft carriers USS Sable and USS Wolverine, respectively.

The large superstructure was replaced with a flight deck and standard starboard island. The two conversions became the world's only side paddle-wheel aircraft carriers, serving thousands of airmen and a variety of dive bomber, torpedo bomber, and fighter aircraft.

The first U.S. Navy unit to receive Corsairs was VF(N)-75, which began flying its F4U-2 Nightfighters from Munda on Sept 11, 1942. The six pilots of LCDR WJ "Gus" Widhelm's unit could boast about 2000 hours of flying time, some of which was on an Escort Carrier. Manufacturing delays with the hand-built radar sets hampered proper operation of the converted F4U-1 Corsairs.

This photo is reported to be the only group photograph taken of the original VMF-124 aviators. Photo was taken on February 28, 1943. The men are, from left to right: Top Row: Capt Joseph F Quilty, Jr; Lt James English; Lt William J Badford; Lt Carl R Newman, USNR (medical Officer); Lt Willam E Cannon; and Lt Thomas R Mutz. Center Row: Lt Walter A Franklin, Jr; Lt Lee Langer; Lt David C McDowell; Lt William P Spencer; Lt Kenneth A Walsh; Lt David C McDowell; Lt John D Kuhn; Lt William M Johnston, Jr; SSgt Troy M Shelton; Lt Lloyd B Pearson; and Lt Mervin L Taylor. Bottom Row: Capt Cecil B Brewer; Lt George W Kaseman; Lt Gilman B Rood; Lt Howard J Finn; Maj William E Gise (C0); Lt William E Crowe; Capt Lawrence A Hart (Ground Intell Off); and Lt Edmund P Hartsock. Absent from photo: Lt John Hurst, Lt Benjamin E Dale Jr, and Lt Richard J Webster were in hospital; Lt Gordon L Lyon and Lt Harold R Stewart were killed in action Feb 14, 1943; and Lt Robert L Gately was killed in a crash Feb 27, 1943. (Photo Courtesy Col Kenneth Walsh, USMC [Ret.])

Chapter III: Corsairs into the Solomons

Taken on February 12, 1942, this photo captured the first Corsair to land on Guadalcanal. Belonging to VMF-124, the aviator's name is assumed to be Maj William Gise, the squadron's commanding officer. (USMC Photo, Author's File)

Lt Walsh warms the engine of his "white thirteen" in preparation for a sortie to Bougainville. Observe the extra "gun port" placed there by his ground crew. (USMC Photo, Courtesy Col Kenneth Walsh USMC (Ret))

The very first Marine Corsair squadron in the Solomons was Maj William E Gise's Marine VMF-124, organized in Camp Kearney, California, on September 7, 1942. The unit received its first Corsairs on October 26, 1942. Maj Gise and 27 officers, 232 enlisted men, 8 corpsmen, and one civilian sailed on the passenger liner SS *Lurline* to Numea, New Caledonia, and then transferred to Espiritu Santo, arriving on January 27, 1943. Their Corsairs were transported to Espiritu Santo on an Escort Aircraft Carrier.

Col Edward Pugh, USMC, had almost cancelled the VMF-124 fighters because of his conviction that the planes couldn't be ready by the deadline. Jack Hospers of Chance Vought and Maj Gen Roy S Geiger persuaded Pugh that the job of making combat modifications could be done. Combat ready changes made on the airplanes totaled 159.

While on a practice flight from Espiritu Santo on February 1, 1943, Lt. Kenneth A Walsh was flying at about 30,000 feet when he suffered engine failure. Apparently the engine's distributor points had arced because of

Lt Kenneth A Walsh returns from a successful mission with his F4U-1 Corsair. The Ace fought some of Japan's finest combat aviators early in World War II as well as Japan's finest fighter planes late in the war. (Photo Courtesy Col Ken Walsh USMC (Ret))

Jubilant Ken Walsh smiles for the photographer after scoring his first victories on April 1, 1943. This was only the beginning of a long string of victories culminating in number 21! (USMC Photo, National Archives)

The members of Lt Walsh's VMF-124 "C" Flight division scored a total of 27 victories during the Solomons Campaign. From left to right: Lt William Johnston (2V); Lt Kenneth Walsh (20V); Lt Dean Raymond (2V); and MSG Troy Shelton (3V). (USMC Photo, Courtesy Col Kenneth Walsh, USMC (Ret))

Capt Crowe's VMF-124 "D" Flight division scored 17.5 victories. Standing L to R: Lt Howard J "Mickey" Finn (6V) and Lt Marvin L Taylor (3V). Kneeling L to R: Capt William Crowe (7V) and Lt Tom R Mutz (3V). (USMC Photo, Courtesy Col Kenneth Walsh, USMC (Ret))

insufficient air pressure, as had happened during Boone Guyton's test flight. Walsh prepared for the water ditching unaware of the Corsair's planing action because this was the first known Corsair ditching.

The Corsair began sinking at once, taking the aviator down with it. After a strenuous struggle, Walsh broke free of the cockpit at a depth of about 150 feet. He quickly inflated his Mae West flotation vest and bobbed to the surface. He was soon rescued.

After readying the Corsairs and, because the inexperienced aviators had several mishaps while conducting practice flights, the 24-plane squadron was reduced to 20 planes available for duty. The aviators then flew to Guadalcanal's No 2 Fighter Airstrip. The bloody struggle for Guadalcanal had just begun to wane when VMF-124 landed on the island on the morning of February 12, 1943.

Only one hour after VMF-124 landed twelve Corsairs were assigned to a rescue mission, escorting a PBY Catalina to Sandfly Bay, Vella Lavella, to pick up two shot-down Wildcat pilots. The twelve VMF-124 aviators had logged nine hours on that first day; a good indication of how much the Marines would be flying their new Corsairs. The only mishap of VMF-124's first day was when Lt. Richard J Webster crashed on takeoff and was hospitalized for his injuries.

A Corsair is caught during takeoff from the Espiritu Santo "Turtle Bay" strip heading toward Turtle bay. Corsairs entered the strip from lower right-hand corner behind coconut trees. Mavea Island is seen in the background. Espiritu Santo continued to be an important base throughout the Solomons Campaign. (U.S. Navy Photo, Courtesy John Regan)

Three Aces of VMF-124 compare combat techniques because each had his own methods. Lt Howard J "Mick" (for Mickey) Finn demonstrates a climbing roll that was a favorite Corsair maneuver. L to R the Aces are Capt William E Crowe (7V), Lt Ken Walsh (21V), and Lt Finn (6V). (Photo Courtesy Col Ken Walsh USMC (Ret))

Chapter III: Corsairs into the Solomons

On the following day, 13 February, twelve VMF-124 Corsairs escorted Navy Consolidated PB4Y bombers (U.S. Navy version of four-engined Liberators) for a raid on Japanese shipping in Buin Harbor, on the southern end of Bougainville. The target was more than 300 miles from Guadalcanal; a distance that had previously been difficult with a Wildcat escort. This was the farthest that any Allied fighter had flown up the Solomons. The raid met with no interception, probably because the Japanese had never experienced a bombing attack this close to Rabaul or the Bougainville airfields.

A lone Zeke approached the homeward-bound raiders and flew alongside at a distance, long enough to study the new and unusual Bent-Wing Corsairs. Little did the Japanese aviator realize that the planes he was studying were the first fighters that could outperform his own.

On the following day, February 14, 1943, VMF-124 aviators were part of a mixed fighter escort for a half dozen Navy PB4Y Liberator bombers in a strike on Kahili airfield, on Bougainville. The bombers flew at 20,000 feet, with a half-dozen U.S. Army Air Corps Curtiss P-40s flying low in front, four Lockheed P-38 Lightnings flying top cover, and a dozen Corsairs weaving over the bombers.

After experiencing the Bougainville raid of the previous day the Japanese were wary of another raid on this St Valentine's Day. As the raiders approached Kahili, they were surprised by about four-dozen Mitsubishi Zeros (Zekes) whose aviators fought with skill and aggressiveness.

The Japanese aviators shot down two bombers, all four Lightnings, two P-40s, and two Corsairs, killing VMF-124 aviators Lt. Gordon L Lyon and Lt. Harold R Stewart. Lt. Lyon was killed when a Zeke that he scored crashed into his Corsair. Lt. Stewart's Corsair was raked with 20 mm cannon fire across his bladder fuel tank, causing the fuel to pour out through dozens of holes. When his Corsair ran out of fuel and headed down to ditch in the sea a few Zekes followed, firing all the way down. Lt. Stewart was never seen again.

This first encounter with Japanese fighters was a painful blow, not only for the squadron's aviators, but also to the Guadalcanal-based flyers of all services. The encounter is remembered as the "Saint Valentine's Day Massacre," paraphrasing a mobster "rub out" during the American Prohibition two decades before. VMF-124 scored three Zekes on that catastrophic day.

Capt Kenneth Walsh posed in a Japanese plane graveyard on New Georgia after his thirteenth victory over the Vella Lavella beachead. A fellow aviator snapped this photograph. The Ace never missed the opportunity to visit Japanese aircraft wreckage to study the location of fuel tanks and other sensitive equipment, as well as the plane's structure. (Col Kenneth Walsh USMC (Ret) Photo, Courtesy AE Ferko)

Another identical mission had been planned for the following day but was cancelled before takeoff.

The second of the eagerly waiting U.S. Navy squadrons to receive Corsairs was LCDR Joseph C "Jumpin Joe" Clifton's VF-12, receiving their Corsairs at NAS North Island, San Diego, California, in October 1942. By April 1943 the squadron had become carrier qualified aboard the *USS Saratoga* (CV-3), but when the unit was ordered deployed to the Pacific, it was forced to give up its Corsairs on Espirito Santo. It received Hellcats in exchange for the Corsairs when the unit was assigned to carriers.

The U.S. Navy's lame explanation for the exchange of planes was that Hellcats were already operating from carriers, and the Navy was initiating a system of employing logistic support for only one dive bomber, one torpedo bomber, and one fighter design on all aircraft carriers. Therefore,

LCDR Joseph C "Jumpin Joe" Clifton's VF-12 was the second U.S. Navy squadron to receive the Corsair. Photo shows Clifton leading a division of VF-12 F4U-1 Corsairs. Inset photo caught VADM Lord Louis Mountbatten, Supreme Allied Commander SE Asia, congratulating "Jumpin Joe" on the performance of his Air Group 12 in the Dutch East Indies (Indonesia). (U.S. Navy Photos via National Archives)

only Hellcat spares and maintenance tools were available for fighters on all carriers. All Navy Corsairs were relegated to shoreside bases to fight alongside Marine Corsairs. Eventually, the new U.S. Navy scheme was to disintegrate when Corsairs and Hellcats flew from the same carrier flight deck not too long after this episode.

Meanwhile, Admiral Halsey made his first move up the Solomons toward Bougainville on February 23, 1943, with an unopposed landing on Banika, in the Russell Islands, about 50 miles from Guadalcanal. Banika was secured on March 14, 1943.

In the following month Japanese Imperial Headquarters became alarmed that Japan had lost Guadalcanal and Banika, knowing that New Georgia would be next on the American drive to Bougainville.

The American gains moved toward Bougainville with such constancy that Admiral Isoruku Yamamoto, commander of the Imperial Japanese Combined Fleet (equal in rank to U.S. Admiral Nimitz), was so concerned that he traveled to Rabaul, taking personal charge of his forces to thwart the Allied advance. This scheme was called "I-go Sakusen," which translated to "I-Operation," and consisted of ordering his carrier aviators and aircraft off the Japanese aircraft carriers *Zuiho, Junyo, Zuikaku,* and *Hiyo* into Rabaul airfields. This included 96 fighters, 65 dive bombers, and a few torpedo planes to join the Rabaul-based 86 fighters, 27 dive bombers, 72 twin-engine bombers, and a few torpedo planes; an impressive array of aerial might.

The initial onslaught consisted of 58 Zekes and Val dive bombers attacking Banika and Guadalcanal on April 1, 1943, in an attempt to destroy the American fighter planes. In the ensuing air battles the attackers lost 18 Zekes, but shot down six of the defenders. Two Zekes and a Val fell before the guns of Lt. Kenneth Walsh's VMF-124 Corsair. Walsh was then ordered to R&R, during which time he partly spent examining crashed enemy aircraft.

Further Japanese "I-Operation" air raids were minimally successful by sinking some small ships near Tulagi and Guadalcanal for a prohibitive loss of aircraft, which influenced ADM Yamamoto to discontinue "I-Operation" on April 16, 1943, and send the remaining carrier-based aircraft back to their ships.

Two days later Yamamoto and his staff planned to leave Rabaul in two Betty bombers converted to VIP transports for a stopover in Kahili,

Upon becoming an Ace and the first Corsair Ace after his sixth victory on May 13, 1943, the U.S. Marine Corps placed five instead of six Japanese victory flags on Walsh's Corsair. Photo was taken for the "Folks back home" to show "how well our boys were doing," and they were doing very well. (USMC Photo by Cpl Wm G Wilson, Author's File)

Imperial Japanese Navy Admiral Mineichi Koga succeeded ADM Yamamoto in April 1943 as Commander of the Combined Fleet (*Rengo Kantai*). He tried to follow the combat plans of his predecessor. Koga was killed in a plane crash during a tropical storm in March 1944. (U.S. Information Agency Photo, Author's File)

the important air base on Bougainville. When this became known in Pearl Harbor, orders were sent to ComAirSols to be certain that Yamamoto must not return to Tokyo alive. A plan was hatched to shoot down the Bettys. U.S. Army Air Corps P-38 Lightnings were selected for the task: four in the "trigger section" (the shooters) and twelve for top cover. Two of the shooters failed to takeoff, but the remaining planes continued in order to meet Yamamoto over Kahili at 11:35 AM of April 18, 1943, because that was the Admiral's schedule and he had a penchant for promptness.

Captain Thomas G. Lanphier, USAAC, shot down one of the Bettys, sending ADM Yamamoto crashing into the rain forest to his death. The second Betty was shot down into the sea by Lt. Rex T Barber, injuring Yamamoto's Chief of Staff, VADM Ugaki. The greatest Japanese admiral was dead, and it is a matter of speculation how this event affected the remaining air and sea battles of the Pacific fighting.

ADM Yamamoto was succeeded by ADM Mineichi Koga, who tried to continue Yamamoto's plans. On May 10, 1943, ADM Koga ordered 58 Zekes and 49 Betty bombers from Truk to Rabaul.

In one of the last major Japanese air raids against Guadalcanal on May 13, 1943, USAAC Lightnings and Marine Corsair fighters intercepted 25 Zekes escorting a reconnaissance Betty checking on the number of Guadalcanal airfields. Sixteen Zekes were shot down: three by Lt. Ken Walsh; four by Capt Archie Donahue of VMF-112; and one by a P-38 Lightning. The remaining eight victories were scored by Marine Corsairs.

Major William Gise and two other Marine aviators were shot down and killed. Capt Cecil B Brewer succeeded Major Gise as commanding officer of VMF-124.

The three Japanese fighters shot down by Ken Walsh brought his score to six victories; the first VMF-124 aviator to achieve Ace status and the very first Corsair Ace.

Upon scoring his third victory of the day, Walsh was surprised to find a Zeke flying alongside his left wing. As soon as the Japanese aviator realized that he was seen he barrel rolled and suddenly set up about 500 feet behind the Corsair, peppering Walsh's wingtips. This was a challenge for mortal combat. The American knew it was foolish to engage a Zeke

Chapter III: Corsairs into the Solomons

in a dogfight so he rolled into a split-ess dive and firewalled his throttle, simultaneously adjusting his mixture and propeller pitch and headed for home. Upon landing he examined the damage and discovered that the bullet holes were from the 7.7 mm machine guns and not the 20 mm cannon. Had they been from the latter, it could have been the end of the new Ace's career.

On June 5, 1943, Ken Walsh's division of Marine Corsairs was assigned to escort Navy Dauntless dive bombers and Avenger torpedo bombers on a mission to Buin Harbor, at the southern end of Bougainville. Naval officer CDR Weldon Hamilton, the Commander of Air Group 11, was to personally lead the strike in the lead Avenger, and Walsh was responsible to protect Hamilton from intercepting Japanese fighters.

As Walsh listened on his radio to Hamilton directing the strike force he was impressed with his leadership and professionalism. He planned to look up the naval officer some day to congratulate him on his performance.

While still over the target Walsh's wingman, who was having engine problems, was attacked by a Zero. Ken's quick reaction put his Corsair into a dive and then zoomed into a high speed climb, drawing the enemy to follow. The Zero's slow speed caused it to stall, at which time the Corsair rolled out of the climb, dived on the enemy, and scored another victory.

Suddenly, the Ace realized that his involuntary reaction to save his wingman caused him to neglect his assignment to protect CDR Hamilton. As he sped to close with the lead Avenger, Ken spotted a Japanese "Pete" seaplane moving in on Hamilton's tail. A quick maneuver and a long range burst of fire scored another victory for Walsh. When another "Pete" appeared Ken maneuvered into firing position, but none of the six guns would fire. Intimidated by the Corsair, the "Pete" turned away and sped to safety. Hamilton waved a "Well done" sign to the Ace.

When finally Ken Walsh had a day off, he made his way to the island where Hamilton was based. Upon his arrival, Walsh was told the terrible news that CDR Weldon Hamilton had died in an airplane accident the day before!

In 1996 Lt. Col Kenneth A Walsh and prominent aviation artist Stan Stokes planned a painting about one of Walsh's combat experiences, and the Ace selected the previously related experience titled "Mission to Buin Harbor."

Exactly what ADM Yamamoto had expected was about to happen; the American invasion of the New Georgia Group of islands between Guadalcanal and Bougainville began on June 30, 1943.

Vice Admiral Fitch's deputy, RADM Marc A Mitscher ComAirSols, had tactical command of all land-based planes that were to fly from

The American occupation of the New Georgia Islands was a strategic move of great importance because they became a springboard to Bougainville. (Upper Photo) The obscure New Georgia Island of Arundel boasted a two-strip airfield. The island of New Georgia, where Munda Airfield is located, can be seen in the distance. (Lower Photo) This view of the reconstructed captured Munda airstrip reveals the destruction wrought on the surrounding trees that resulted from the fierce fighting to win the airfield. (U.S. Navy Photos, Author's File)

Eighteen and one-half victory Marine Ace Capt Marine E Carl scored his first kill at the Battle of Midway on June 4, 1942, flying a Wildcat. While flying F4U-1 Corsairs, he scored two final victories on December 23 and December 27, 1943. Carl flew 78 Combat missions for a total of 150 hours. When asked how he liked the Corsair, he replied "The Corsair was a great mount. It was head and shoulders above its contemporaries. An airplane like the Corsair only comes along occasionally." Major Carl is shown here with one of his Corsairs when he was CO of VMF-223. (Defense Dept Photo (Marine Corps), Author's File)

Corsair: The Saga of the Legendary Bent-Wing Fighter-Bomber

Marine Major Joe Foss scored all of his 26 victories as a member of VMF-121. He then became CO of VMF-115 in February 1944 flying Corsairs from Emirau. Although he extolled the Corsair, Maj Foss scored no more victories after training because most of his duties consisted of bombing and strafing ground targets. He was ordered to CONUS (CONtinental United States) in September 1944. (Official U.S. Navy Photo, Author's File)

Lt Wilbur J Thomas of VMF-213 shot down four Japanese fighters during the New Georgia Group invasion. His F4U-1 was named "GUS'S GOPHER."

Guadalcanal and Banika. The New Georgia Group included the main islands of Vangunu, Rendova, Arundel, New Georgia, Kolombangara, and Vella Lavella. As was usually the prime objective, Japanese airfields were coveted during the battle.

The battle for the New Georgia Islands introduced the Corsair as an infantry support weapon by fighting side-by-side with Dauntless and Avenger bombers; an added load for Corsair aviators.

Among the U.S. Marine Corsair Aviators that scored victories during the New Georgia Island Campaign were the following: VMF-213 "Hellhawk's" CO Major Gregory J Weisenberger shot down three Zekes in one minute before a fourth Zeke shot him down. The Major parachuted from one thousand feet; however, his chest struck the plane's tail. Fortunately, he landed close to a destroyer that hauled him aboard. Maj Weisenberger was succeeded by Major James R Anderson.

Lt. Wilbur J Thomas of VMF-213 "Hellhawks" scored four Japanese fighters in one flight over New Georgia.

VMF-213 commanding officer Maj Gregory J Weisenberger shot down three Zekes in one minute in July 1943 over the New Georgia Islands before a fourth Zeke shot him down. Weisenberger parachuted from about one thousand feet; his plane's tail struck him in the chest, but he landed close to a destroyer that hauled him aboard. Major Weisenberger was succeeded by Maj James R Anderson on August 22, 1943. Upper photo: With engine cranking to start, a ground crewman stands at the ready with a fire extinguisher. Lower photo: The crewman adjusts the Major's harness prior to takeoff. (USMC Photos, Author's File)

Chapter III: Corsairs into the Solomons

Lt Harold E "Murderous Manny" Segal of VMF-221 "Fighting Falcons" shot down three Japanese Betty bombers during the New Georgia Campaign on July 14, 1943, to become an Ace. He is shown here in his F4U-1 with two victory flags before his Ace status. His total was 12 victories. (USMC Photo, Author's File)

Capt James N Cupp of VMF-213 scored his first victories on July 15, 1943, by destroying three Bettys. He became an Ace two days later when he shot down two more Japanese planes over New Georgia. (USMC Photo, Author's File)

Lt. Harold Segal of VMF-221 "Fighting Falcons" shot down three Bettys on July 14, 1943, to become an Ace during the New Georgia Islands campaign.

Capt James N Cupp of VMF-213 scored his first two victories, a Zeke and a Betty, on July 15, 1943, and two more Japanese planes fell before his guns two days later.

On July 18, 1943, four Corsairs of VMF-214 "Swashbucklers" from Espiritu Santo, led by Maj William H Pace, shot down three Nell bombers.

Munda airfield, on New Georgia Island, fell to American Forces on August 5, 1943, and the diligent Seebees were working on the airstrip even before the entire strip was in American hands! By 14 August, VMF-123 and VMF-214 were operating from Munda airfield.

Lt. Edward O Shaw of VMF-213 "Hellhawks" shot down two Japanese float planes; two and one-half twin-engine bombers; plus three Zeros from June 18 to July 18, 1943. Lt. Shaw was awarded the Distinguished Flying Cross for the above actions.

The fourth U.S. squadron to receive Corsairs and the first U.S. Navy squadron to fly Corsairs in action was VF-17; known as "Blackburn's Irregulars" or "Jolly Rogers" because of their "skull and cross bones" squadron insignia.

The squadron was formed in Norfolk, Virginia, on January 1, 1943, consisting of ten ensigns and two aviators with combat experience. LCDR John T "Tommy" Blackburn, who had been a consultant during the final

Lt Edward O Shaw of VMF-213 shot down five fighters and two and one-half Bettys in the New Georgia Campaign from June 18 to July 18, 1943. (U.S. Navy Photo via National Archives)

Lt Ira Cassius Kepford, USN, was the leading VF-17 Ace with sixteen official and one probable victory, making him the fifth leading Ace in the U.S. Navy. (U.S. Navy Photo, Courtesy Albert L. Lewis)

VF-17 Lt John M Smith (10V) smiles for the camera in the glaring heat of the South Pacific sun. (U.S. Navy Photo, Author's File)

factory modifications to the Corsair, was the unit's Commanding Officer, with LCDR Roger Hedrick as the Executive Officer.

This U.S. Navy squadron would boast 15 aces: Ira "Ike" Kepford (16); Roger Hedrick (12); John Blackburn (11); John M Smith (10); DC Freeman (9); E May (8.5); 0I Chenoweth (8.5); CD Gile (8); HM Burris (7.5); P Cordray (7); DG Davenport (7); DG Cunningham (7); and R Mims (6).

After basic trials on the escort carrier *USS Charger* (CVE-30) the squadron sailed from Norfolk on the aircraft carrier *USS Bunker Hill* (CV-17) in September 1943 for the squadron's carrier qualification cruise.

All went well with only one landing mishap. The Air Group Commander was very pleased with the "Jolly Rogers" performance, and

This informal photo of VF-17 aviators includes LCDR Roger Hedrick (12V), tall in center, and Lt 0I Chenoweth (8.5V) to the right of Hedrick. (U.S. Navy Photo, Author's File)

A VF-17 Corsair is caught about to touch-down on the escort carrier *USS Charger* in Chesapeake Bay. Although one wheel is a bit high, it was considered a perfect landing. (U.S. Navy Photo, Author's File)

Chapter III: Corsairs into the Solomons

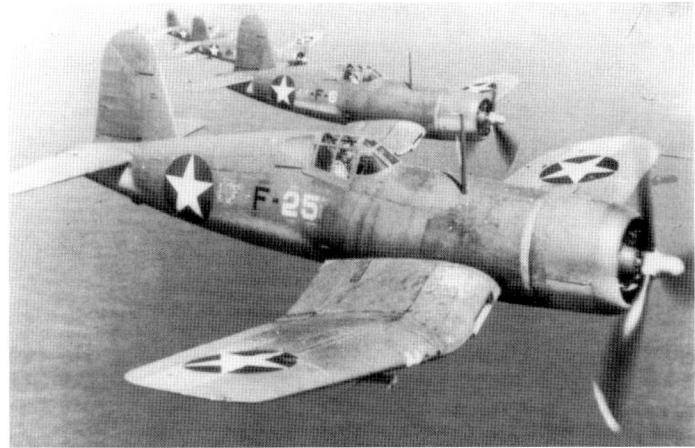

Squadron VF-17 is shown in route to rendezvous with USS Bunker Hill for a carrier qualification cruise. (U.S. Navy Photo, Author's File)

During the "Jolly Rogers" carrier qualification cruise aboard USS Bunker Hill in September 1943, all aspects of carrier operations with their Corsairs were successful. Upper Photo: A Corsair is just airborne as the bridle drops away in this catapult test. Lower Photo: This VF-17 Corsair awaits its turn for catapulting. Note the "skull and crossbones" insignia on the engine cowl. ID lettering indicates 17 (squadron); F (fighter); 8 (plane number). (U.S. Navy Photos, Author's File)

their F4U-1 Corsairs were exchanged for the improved F4U-1A with blown canopy.

Despite the unit's fine performance on the carrier, VF-17 was ordered to report to ComAirSols because it was to become a land-based squadron in the Solomons. The reason given was that carriers had no spare parts, etc, for Corsairs!

By August 15, 1943, Kolombangara was bypassed and Vella Lavella was captured; only 90 miles from Kahili airfield. On that day Capt Ken Walsh shot down his eleventh, twelfth, and thirteenth victories while fighting off the defenders of the Vella Lavella beachhead. Then Walsh was attacked by five Zekes at 10,000 ft. He chased one for five miles north of Vella Lavella before he shot it down for his fourteenth victory.

Having flown so far north of Vella Lavella, the Ace found himself surrounded by Japanese planes flying to Vella Lavella from Kahili; Val Dive bombers below and Zekes flying top cover! He quickly dived past the Vals and came up under them, firing into their blind spots, and scored two Vals. Then all hell broke loose! Vals and Zekes attacked the lone Corsair, cutting the hydraulic line, shreddin the elevator, and putting 20 mm holes in his right wing and a punctured tire, plus numerous machine gun holes throughout the plane. Walsh managed to escape, and was cheered when he

This "Jolly Roger" demonstrates a perfect arrested landing aboard USS Bunker Hill (CV-17) with his F4U-1 "Birdcage" Corsair. After the qualification cruise the F4U-1A "blown canopy" Corsairs were issued to VF-17. (U.S. Navy Photo, Author's File)

This was the only "Jolly Roger" mishap during the VF-17 carrier qualification cruise aboard USS Bunker Hill. (National Archives, Author's File)

President Franklin D Roosevelt congratulates Capt Walsh after he awarded the Ace America's highest military decoration, the Medal of Honor. The Ace's wife, the former Beulah Barinott, smiles proudly on this happy occasion on February 8, 1944. (U.S. Naval Historic Center, Author's File)

This popular USMC photo was taken after Capt Walsh scored his twentieth victory. Photos showing Aces between two propeller blades decorated with Japanese flags indicating the number of victories were a popular device to illustrate the successes of America's fighting aviators. (USMC Photo, Author's File)

made a safe landing at Munda, on New Georgia Island. His Corsair, being beyond repair, was junked.

On 30 August, two weeks later, Ken Walsh had engine trouble and landed his Corsair at Munda. The intrepid Ace commandeered another Corsair and sped to rejoin his squadron near Kahili, where he tangled with a fleet of about 50 Japanese fighters heading for the New Georgia group. After scoring four more victories, his Corsair was so shot up that Walsh was forced to dead-stick on the coast of Vella Lavella.

For these amazing exploits, Capt Kenneth A Walsh was awarded the Medal of Honor by President Franklin D Roosevelt in the White House on February 8, 1944.

VMF-124 was credited with 69 Japanese destroyed in aerial combat. This tally includes a Zeke shot down by Major Bechtol, a USAAC aviator, who flew on a bomber escort mission with VMF-124 on September 2, 1943. This record also includes 20 probables whose destruction could not be confirmed. The squadron lost seven aviators. Eleven Corsairs were lost in combat and 21 in operational accidents. VMF-124 could boast three fighter aces: Capt Ken Walsh (20); Capt William E Crowe (7); and Lt. Howard J Finn (5).

Capt Walsh celebrated his twentieth victory by posing between propeller blades for an official USMC photograph.

Before every mission all aviators were issued the Mission Briefing, which they must memorize regarding altitudes, target location, rendezvous locations, time, participating aircraft, mission description, and mission route.

While the aviators were concentrating to remember the important details of the mission they were forced to repel Japanese interceptors. This required an exceptional combination of memory and combat reflexes to accomplish the mission successfully. (Courtesy Lt. Col OK Williams, USMC (Ret)

The Mitsubishi Zero-Sen A6M was the most numerous Japanese fighter engaged by Allied aviators in the Pacific War. The latest version of this premiere Japanese fighter was the A6M 8-C that weighed 6,944 lbs loaded; only about half the weight of a Corsair. The light weight of the

The Mitsubishi Zero-Sen was the Japanese fighter most often fought by Allied aviators throughout World War II. Early in the war, the Zero or Zeke enjoyed a measure of aerial supremacy until the arrival of the Corsair. Observe the Inflatable Flotation Bag in an attempt to save aviator and/or plane in the event of ditching. (National Archives, Author's File)

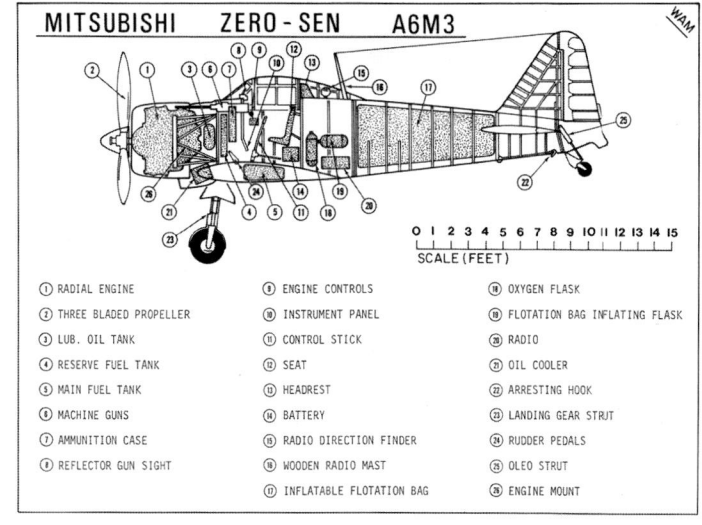

Chapter III: Corsairs into the Solomons

FIGHTER COMMAND
NEW GEORGIA AIR FORCE

18 October 1943.

ESCORT MISSION

STRIKE PLANES

- Number: 42
- Type: 30 SBD's - 12 TBF's
- Bombing Altitude: Dive Bombing
- Route out: Direct to Munia Island (Southern Fauro) then to target.
- Target: SBD's - AA positions on Ballale.
  TBF's - The runway on Ballale.
- Time of attack: 1022
- Route back: Direct to Rally Point then home.
- Rally Point: 8 miles down slot from target about halfway between Shortland and Fauro.
- Calls: SBD's - Silver 1-30
  TBF's - Silver 50-61

STRIKE COVER

- Number: 56 VF (24 Segi P39's)(12 Munda F4U's)
  (12 Vella LaVella F4U's)(8 P40's Gold)
- Type: P39's - P40's - F4U's
- Time of Rendezvous: 0925 (on course 0932)
- Rendezvous Pt.: Baniata Point, Rendova
- Rendezvous Altitude: 12,000'
- Calls: SBD Cover - 24 P39's G 30-35 (close cover)
  12 F4U's D 1-3 (medium cover)
  TBF Cover - 8 P40's (NZ) G 40-41 (close cover)
  12 F4U's D 4-6 (medium cover)

REMARKS:

Close cover will go down in column spaced at intervals of about 5 or 6 bombers.

3 squadrons of heavies will hit Ballale Air Field at 1030, covered by 16 P38's.

Maintain Radio Silence for all units.

A. R. STACY
Major, USMC

Distribution:

ComAirNG	(1)
Air Intelligence	(1)
Squadron Intelligence	(1)
Fighter Intelligence	(1)
Fighter Line	(2)
F D O	(1)
File	(1)

A Mission Briefing, similar to that shown here, is issued to every member of every mission to be memorized for recall throughout the operation. (USMC, Courtesy Lt Col OK Williams)

This seaplane version of the Zero A6M2-N (code-named "Rufe") was built by Nakajima as an interim type pending completion of the Kawanishi Kiofu seaplane fighter design. Despite the large float, Rufe proved to be extremely agile. Observe the large number of seaplanes at this beachfront seaplane base. (National Archives, Author's File)

Corsair: The Saga of the Legendary Bent-Wing Fighter-Bomber

Upper Photo: The Kawanishi Kiofu (code name "Rex") seaplane fighter's performance approached that of many contemporary fighters. In a rare transition, the seaplane Kiofu was developed into a state of the art land-based fighter Shiden (Lightning Flash). Lower Photo: This Kawanishi Shiden ("George" in the allied Code) was a heavily armed, high speed fighter developed from the Kiofu seaplane. (National Archives, Author's File)

Zero was partly to attain a very maneuverable design and partly because Japan always experienced a shortage of strategic materials.

Armament consisted of two 20 mm cannon (.75 inches) in the wing and two 7.7 mm (.31 inches) machine guns buried in the forward fuselage, with the gun breeches projecting into the cockpit. Later models mounted two 13.2 mm (.528 inches) machine guns in the fuselage.

The designer, Jiro Horikoshi, was considered one of the world's great aeronautical engineers, who brought Japan out of the copycat plane design age into original pre-world war two designs such as the Zero. The word Zero marked the 2,600 anniversary of the ascension of the legendary Emperor Jimmo to the Japanese Throne.

Upper Photo: Japanese fighter aviators watch as a fellow aviator describes how he scored his most recent victory. Lower Photo: Japanese bomber aviators discuss their next mission while their bomber is serviced. This Mitsubishi G4M2-a medium bomber ("Betty" in the Allied Code) was well-manned with a crew of seven. The 33,070 lb loaded bomber was armed with four 20mm cannon and one 7.7mm machine gun plus a 2,200 lb load of bombs (The normal Corsair bomb load). A total of 2,479 "Betty's" were constructed. (National Archives, Author's File)

LTJG Saburo Sakai scored virtually all of his 64 victories with Zeros. He is Japan's fourth leading Ace and the highest scoring Japanese Ace to survive the war. (Saburo Sakai Photo, Author's File)

Jiro Horikoshi developed a 360 degree visibility cockpit canopy on the Zero such as was done on the Brewster Buffalo, instead of the standard pre-World War Two metal turtledeck. This was a very advanced design feature that did not become universal until late in the war years. Top speed was 356mph at 19,600 ft. Service ceiling was 36,745 ft. About 10,000 Zero (Zeke) fighters were constructed; more than any other Japanese fighter.

When the American aviators first encountered the Zero they had to forget everything they were taught during their advanced training; aerobatics and dogfighting. The Zero had phenomenal maneuverability at slow speeds (230-250mph) and could easily turn inside any American fighter. Wildcats that were surprised by a Zero had to remain and fight their way clear; however, the Corsair had the speed to leave the fight and return at a more propitious moment. The Zero could not stay with the Corsair in a hard diving turn at speeds of about 275mph or more. The best tactic for the Corsair was to attack at high speed, hit and run, and then repeat the attack. Using this high speed tactic multiple victories were fairly common; often destroying up to a half-dozen Zeros in one mission.

Fire power was clearly in the Corsair's favor, with six .50 caliber (12.7 mm) machine guns in the wing, each firing a 1.6 ounce bullet at a muzzle velocity of 2,240 feet per second, with a rate of 1,200 rounds per

Chapter III: Corsairs into the Solomons

minute! This was a total devastating 7,200 rounds per minute when all six guns were firing. The guns were bore sighted to converge at 300 yards; further than the length of two football fields, at which range they could seriously damage or sink ships up to destroyer size.

It was important that the armorers and/or aviators had to remember to wipe the Corsair's gun mechanism free of oil before flight because the oil froze at 20,000-30,000 feet, causing the guns to misfire or jam.

Despite the fact that the Japanese cannon fired a heavier round of 2.4 ounces, the rate was only 550 rounds per minute with a muzzle velocity less than 2,000 ft per second. This made it less effective than the Corsair's Colt-Browning M-2 machine guns.

Another major disadvantage of the Zero's armament was the fact that the machine gun breeches extended into the cockpit, giving off acrid fumes and smoke when fired. In addition, the machine guns had to be charged by hand, using a lever mounted on the inner sides of the breeches. The cannon were fired by a lever, mounted just forward of the throttle. The more conventional control stick button was not used, which prevented the Japanese aviator from working the throttle and stick simultaneously when he fired his guns.

The Mitsubishi Zero fuel tanks were located in the wing roots near the center of gravity for better maneuverability, and that is where most Allied aviators aimed their guns. The Zero appeared to burn ferociously; perhaps because flammable magnesium was used in part of its construction to promote a light weight. Later models were fitted with a two-inch bullet-resistant windshield and an automatic carbon dioxide fire extinguishing system was installed in the fuel tanks. Many Zero drop-tanks were made of bamboo because of a shortage of materials.

Despite its shortcomings the Zero produced many high-scoring Japanese aces and demonstrated dependable service throughout the Second World War.

Hiroyoshi Nishizawa, Japan's highest scoring ace, downed the vast majority of his 87 victories while flying the Zero, and Japan's highest scoring surviving Ace, Saburo Sakai (64 Vict), also scored many of his victories while flying the Zero.

The Japanese military construction organization was not as well equipped with heavy machinery as the American Construction Battalions (See Bees) and, therefore, required more time and effort to construct airfields. This forced the Japanese Naval Air Force to depend on fighters that were independent of land airfields. It was for this reason that the Japanese resorted to seaplanes and seaplane bases. The latter were often mere strips of sandy beaches with a few shacks for supplies and maintenance. Single-float designs seemed to predominate the fighter and reconnaissance types, while many twin-float designs were submarine-based.

Early in WWII a single-float version of the Zero fighter appeared and was given the Allied code name "Rufe." Constructed by Nakajima, the fighter was designated A6M2-N. Powered by a 925hp radial engine, Rufe attained a top speed of 270mph at 14,111 ft. The craft had a three foot larger wingspan than the landplane Zero. Service ceiling was 32,020 feet. Despite the enormous single float, Rufe possessed exceptionally good maneuverability. About 327 Rufes were completed and placed in service as an inerim type pending delivery of the Kawanishi Kiofu seaplane fighter.

The Kawanishi N1K1 Kiofu (Mighty Wind), named "Rex" in the Allied code, was a single-float midwing fighter powered by a 1,460hp, 14 cylinder, twin-row radial engine. Maximum speed was 302mph at 18,700 ft. Service ceiling was 34,645 ft and loaded weight was 8,184 lbs. After only 97 Kiofus were built the design was converted to a potent landplane; the Kawanishi N1K1-J and N1K2-J Shiden (Lightning Flash), named "George" in the Allied code.

Powered by a 1,990hp radial engine, the N1K1-J attained a top speed of 369mph at 17,715 ft. Service ceiling was 39,700, and loaded weight rose to 9,526 lbs. Armament was four 20 mm cannon and two 7.7 mm machine guns. Over 1,000 N1K1-J Shidens were constructed. George was encounted over the Philippines, Formosa, Okinawa, and over Japan. This was the first time that a float plane design evolved into a landplane.

The Japanese work on seaplane fighters stimulated U.S. Navy interest, resulting in a test version of a Wildcat fighter seaplane; however, the idea was abandoned as American airfields were developed.

The fifth squadron to receive Corsairs after VF(N)-101, VF-12, VMF-124, and VF-17 was VMF-213 "Hellhawks," organized on July 1, 1942, at Ewa, Hawaii, under the command of Capt Herbert T Merrill. The "Hellhawks" three leading Aces were Capt Wilbur J Thomas (18.5 vict); Lt. Edward O Shaw (14.5 vict); and Capt James N Cupp (12.5 vict).

Lt. John D Kuhn and Lt. Edmund P Hartsock of VMF-124 flew to Espiritu Santo from Guadalcanal to brief the VMF-213 aviators all about their new Corsairs. Such was the comradery between Corsair squadrons in the South Pacific.

Major Wade H Britt Jr commanded VMF-213 from October 1, 1942, to April 13, 1943, when, during an early morning takeoff, he ran off the runway. His Corsair struck two other planes and the Major died in the ensuing explosion. Maj Gregory J Weissenberger, previously mentioned, succeeded Major Britt.

Of the 117 victories attained by the "Hellhawks" Lt. Thomas scored 18.5 kills, which makes this Corsair aviator the highest ranking ace of

The highest ranking Ace of VMF-213 "Hellhawks," Capt Wilbur J "Gus" Thomas, earned the Navy Cross for his multiple victories, scoring 18 ½ kills to become the eighth ranking Ace in the U.S. Marine Corps. (National Archives, Author's File)

Lt Edward Oliver Shaw scored 14.5 victories to become the second ranking Ace of the Hellhawks. He was once arrested for flying his Corsair and engaging in unauthorized combat with the enemy. He was awarded the Distinguished Flying Cross and the Gold Star in lieu of a second Distinguished Flying Cross. (USMC Photo, Author's File)

Capt James Norman Cupp logged more than 200 combat hours in the Solomons scoring 12.5 victories to make him the third ranking Ace of VMF-213 "Hellhawks." "Daphne" on the Corsair's cowl is to honor the captain's wife. (National Archives, Author's File)

VMF-213 and the eighth on the list of United States Marine Aces. "Gus" Thomas joined the "Hellhawks" on June 18, 1943.

Twelve days later, on 30 June, his division of Corsairs was protecting amphibious landings in Wickham Anchorage, on Vanguna Island, when 15 Zekes were upon the leathernecks firing cannon and machine guns. "Gus" became separated from his flight and found himself over Rendova Island. Before he could rejoin his comrades, seven of the Zeros had boxed-in the Corsair for an easy kill. As with most outstanding "aerial swordsmen," Thomas turned on his attackers, placing them on the defensive. The Marine maneuvered with such fierce determination that first one, then another, still another, and then the fourth Japanese fighter fell in rapid succession before his six blazing guns. The remaining Mitsubishi fighters broke off the engagement and sped for home. Upon landing, Lt. Thomas had nothing to say except "my plane performed wonderfully," thereby modestly giving the credit to his Corsair.

On July 15, 1943, Thomas engaged in a strafing raid on a Japanese cargo ship in which he played an important part, leaving the vessel burning and sinking. When this assignment was complete "Gus'" two-division formation intercepted a huge formation of Japanese bombers and Zeros.

Thomas was in the center of the melee and, at the onset, sent a bomber and a fighter down in flames. As the Corsair leveled off, the Marine felt the sickening thuds of cannon shells. A Zero was on the Corsair's tail, firing furiously. Thomas avoided the Japanese fighter with a series of sharp turns and rolls, soon placing himself in a striking position. A short burst and it was all over; his third victory of the day plunged into the sea.

Two days later "Red" Thomas and his wingman attacked seven enemy twin-engine bombers and an undetermined number of Zeros. The Japanese fighters fought valiantly to keep the Corsairs away from the bombers, but Thomas found an opening in the Zero cordon and blasted away at the bombers over Kolombangara Island and, as he scored one, the Japanese formation quickly turned and left the scene.

Wilbur J Thomas was promoted to the rank of captain in February 1944, and was awarded the Distinguished Flying Cross and the Navy Cross.

Lt. Edward Oliver Shaw joined VMF-213 in January 1943 as Squadron Materiel Officer and became the squadron's second ranking ace.

On June 18, 1943, Shaw and his Corsair division encountered nine Japanese float-planes over Rendova. Shaw attacked at once, scoring two of the enemy. Shortly thereafter he attacked eight Betty bombers, destroying two and sharing a third with another Corsair pilot. The intrepid Marine scored three Zeros on July 18, 1943.

The Ace was involved in an unusual incident that resulted in his arrest on November 10, 1943, and he was confined to quarters for a period

Chapter III: Corsairs into the Solomons

of five days. Apparently Edward Shaw violated flight regulations by flying his Corsair and engaging in combat without authorization; such was this Ace's enthusiasm and devotion to destroy his country's enemies.

On December 20, 1943, Lt. Edward Shaw was promoted to the rank of captain. He was sent to CONUS (San Diego), arriving on December 31, 1943.

On July 31, 1944, Engineering Officer Shaw of VMF-213 was testing a Corsair when the plane suddenly crashed to earth 2.5 miles northeast of Mojave, California. Capt Shaw was killed at once. His remains were cremated and given to his father, Harold A Shaw. The reason for the crash is unknown.

Capt Edward O Shaw was awarded the Distinguished Flying Cross and the Gold Star in lieu of a second Distinguished Flying Cross.

With 12.5 official victories, Capt James Norman Cupp was the third ranking ace of VMF-213.

Based on Guadalcanal, Capt Cupp scored his first two victories during his second tour on July 15, 1943, when Cupp shot down a Betty bomber and a Zero over Kolombangara Island. The bombers were attacking Munda airfield, and the novice made five passes before he flamed a Betty that crashed into the sea. Cupp then observed the Zero circling the bomber wreckage and fired four short bursts, sending the fighter into the water.

Two days later the "Hellhawks" were escorting bombers on a raid over Kahili Harbor. The bombers had completed their runs and were on their way home when intercepting Zeros appeared. Capt Cupp attacked at once and scored two Zeros. He also assisted his wingman in scoring another Zero. Now he was credited with 4.5 victories; one-half victory from becoming an ace.

On the following day, July 18, 1943, Cupp was part of a patrol that engaged a Zero formation over Rendova Island. In the ensuing melee he shot down one of the Japanese fighters in flames to breech the portals of Acedom, but the Ace did not stop there.

September 11, 1943, saw Major Cupp score a Japanese Army "Tony" (Kawasaki Ki-61) and a Zero for his sixth and seventh victories.

Major James N Cupp logged more than 200 combat hours in the Solomons.

Major Donald H Stapp scored eleven of the 50 victories shot down by VMF-222 "Flying Deuces" in the Solomons. He participated in the first fighter sweep over Rabaul on December 17, 1943, as the Squadron Executive Officer.

Major Donald H Stapp escorted bombers and conducted fighter sweeps and strafing missions, scoring bombers, Zeros, and landing barges. He became a double-Ace with four probables while flying with VMF-222 "Flying Deuces." He was awarded the Distinguished Flying Cross and the Navy Cross. Major Stapp was born Donald Sapp but legally changed his name to Stapp in Feb 1956. (National Archives, Author's File)

Left Photo: An RNZAF Curtiss P-40 is about to pass a parked U.S. Marine Corsair. The aviator is probably wondering when will he be issued one of those beautiful bent wing fighters. (U.S. Navy Photo, Author's File) Right Photo: RNZAF No 14 Fighter Squadron Corsairs lined up in Bougainville in 1945. Nearest Corsair was flown by Flt Sgt Teschner, who was killed when he crashed 2000 yards east of Vanaukani Air Strip-Jacquinot Bay on New Britain, Sept 20, 1945. (John Regan Photo)

Capt Archie Donahue was the leading Ace of his squadron with 14 of the VMF-112 "Wolfpack's" 83 victories. He became an Ace during a single engagement. Donahue also helped in sinking three enemy ships. (USMC Photo, Author's File)

Major Stapp was awarded the Distinguished Flying Cross on January 30, 1944, for the following heroic feats: from September 5 to October 11, 1943, he led his division on strafing attacks on Kahili, inflicting serious damage; on September 14, 1943, Maj Stapp led a bomber escort over Kahili and engaged intercepting Zeros, scoring two. He also shot down a twin-engine bomber. During an attack on Japanese landing barges on October 4, 1943, his division destroyed eight barges and seriously damaged four others; and seven days later, while escorting bombers, Maj Stapp led his division around heavy antiaircraft fire, simultaneously protecting the bombers and destroyed an intercepting Zero at 23,000ft.

After participating in 92 strike escorts, strafing missions, and fighter sweeps, plus having scored ten victories, the Ace was awarded the Navy Cross in September 1944.

The Royal Navy Fleet Air Arm began receiving Corsairs in May 1943, while the Royal New Zealand Air Force had to continue flying their Curtiss P-40 Kittyhawks and Curtiss P-40K Tomahawks for another year before they received their eagerly-awaited Corsairs. Upon delivery to the RNZAF, several weeks were spent on Guadalcanal learning all about the Bent Wings with bombing and gunnery practice to ready the Kiwis for action.

The sixth U.S. squadron that was issued Corsairs was VMF-121; organized on June 24, 1941 in Quantico, Virginia, under the leadership of Maj Sam S Jack. VMF-121 aces were Capt KM Ford (5V); Maj HH Long (10V); Lt. HA Mc Cartney (5V); Capt FE Pierce, Jr (6V); Maj RB Porter (5V); and Capt PL Shuman, (6V).

Number seven of the squadrons to receive the Corsair was VMF-112 "Wolfpack" squadron; organized on March 1, 1942, in Camp Kearney, California, with Maj Wilfred H Huffman in command. Capt Archie Donahue was the squadron's top Ace with 14 of the unit's 83 victories. Other Aces were Maj H Hansen, Jr (5.5V); Maj JB Maas, Jr (5.5V); Capt DC Owen (5V); Lt. JG Percy (6V); and Lt. ST Synar (5V).

Capt Archie Glenn Donahue scored 14 official victories in the Solomons and while attacking Japan. He is one of only seven Marine Aviators to become an ace during a single engagement.

While flying with VMF-112 "Wolfpack" (MAG-11) on May 13, 1943, Donahue intercepted a Japanese reconnaissance plane escorted by 25 Zeros and destroyed four of the fighters, forcing the enemy to abort their mission. Later, the aviator took part in an attack on enemy shipping, sinking three vessels and damaging a fourth. On the way back to Guadalcanal his division was attacked by fifteen Zeros and ten float fighters. Twelve of the enemy were destroyed, with Captain Donahue scoring two of the total and becoming an ace in one day.

Two days later, 15 May, Donahue and 29 comrades engaged 40 Zeros over the Russell Islands and Archie scored again, bringing his total to seven victories.

Captain Donahue was awarded the Distinguished Flying Cross in November 1943.

The eighth squadron to be equipped with Corsairs was VMF-221 "Fighting Falcons"; organized on July 11, 1941, in San Diego, California, with Capt Kirk Armistad as CO.

Of the 185 victories credited to VMF-221 "Fighting Falcons," Capt James E Swett shot down 15.5; Capt Harold "Murderous Manny" Segal scored twelve; Capt William N Snider 11.5 victories; and Capt Donald L Balch is credited with five victories. Seventy-one of the squadron's victories were attained in one month over New Britain.

Capt Segal earned three Distinguished Flying Crosses, four Air Medals, and the Purple Heart. His first victories were scored on June 25, 1943, over the coast of New Georgia when "Murderous Manny" shot down one bomber and one fighter.

Segal became an Ace on July 14, 1943 (previously mentioned), when he and another Corsair aviator attacked fifteen Japanese Mitsubishi G4M Betty twin-engine bombers escorted by Zekes. Wounded by cannon shell fragments, the diminutive 5ft-6 inch tall aviator continued to attack the

Photo taken on January 10, 1944, shows Capt Harold E "Murderous Manny" Segal with his Corsair. The victor over twelve Japanese planes, Segal is renown for his multiple victories. (Defense Dept Photo, Marine Corps, Author's File)

Chapter III: Corsairs into the Solomons

bombers while his feet were slipping off the rudder pedals, eventually shooting down three of the Bettys. When he broke away, pursued by the Zekes, he finally ditched off New Georgia and was rescued. Capt Segal was in the air again on July 18, 1943, scoring three more Japanese planes!

Capt Donald L Balch experienced his most harrowing aerial encounter on July 6, 1943, when two divisions of VMF-221 were diverted from the Russell Islands to New Georgia and were attacked by several Zeros. The divisions quickly split, each heading in a different direction. Balch tied on to a Zero and scored his second victory.

While he searched for the remainder of his division (aerial combat is a team effort) all hell broke loose, as his F4U-1 cockpit canopy fragmented, as did his instrument panel. He had been surprised by the enemy! Balch rolled to port (left) and pulled out at about 6,000ft. His wingman joined him, but they could not communicate because Balch's instruments and radio had been shattered in the Zero attack. His wingman kept pointing at Don Balch's Corsair tail on the way back to the airfield, and as Balch flared out in landing he lost all control, with the Corsair slamming to

Capt William N Snider of VMF-221 "Fighting Falcons" shot down 11.5 enemy aircraft over the Solomon Islands to become the third leading ace of his squadron while flying Corsairs. (National Archives, Author's File)

Capt Donald L Balch, five victory Ace of VMF-221, sits by his shot-up Corsair enjoying his safe return on July 6, 1943. The effects of his shot-away controls and the hard landing are evident in the collapsed tailwheel assembly and shredded elevator. The Ace had been jumped by Zeros over New Georgia. (USMC Photo, Courtesy FJ Delear, Chance Vought)

Upper Photo: Lt Alvin J Jensen and two other former "Swashbuckler" Technical Sergeants were promoted upon Captain Britt's recommendation. Lt Jensen scored seven victories in aerial combat. Lower Photo: F4U-1 Corsairs of VMF-214 taking off "Knucklehead" strip in the Russell Islands for a mission against the enemy. (USMC Photos, Courtesy Lt Col OK Williams USMC (Ret))

The original members of VMF-214 were photographed in Hawaii before they shipped out to the Solomons Islands. Standing, the aviators are L to R: Luthi; Lincoln Deetz; Jackson Petit; Henry W Hallmeyer; Richard Sigel; David W Rankin; Bennie P O'Dell; Robert T Hoover; Hartwell V Scarborough; and Otto K Williams. Sitting, the aviators are: Schaefer; Vincent W Carpenter; Charles C Lanphier, Henry S Miller; John R Burnett; Henry Ellis; George F Britt; William H Pace; George Kraft; Carol DC Bernard; Howard L Cavanaugh; John L Fidler; and Ledyard B Hazelwood. (USMC Photo, Courtesy Lt Col OK Williams USMC (Ret))

earth. The aviator emerged unhurt, but his Corsair required a considerable amount of repair before it flew again.

VMF-122 was the ninth squadron to receive Corsairs; organized on March 1, 1942, in Camp Kearney, California, under the command of Capt Elmer E Bracket, Jr. Among the Aces were maj JH Reinburg (7 vict) and Capt EA Powell (5 vict).

The tenth squadron to receive Corsairs was VMF-214 "Swashbucklers"; organized on July 1, 1942, in Ewa, Hawaii. The squadron leadership comprised officers from VMF-211, which squadron had been redesignated from VMF-2 and fighting at Wake Island.

Capt Charles W Somers, a Midway veteran, took command of a "paper squadron" with no aircraft and no aviators or enlisted personnel. By July 21, 1942, Capt George F Britt, former Executive Officer for half of VMF-211, assumed command of VMF-214 "Swashbucklers" while Capt Henry A Ellis, also a VMF-211 veteran, became the "Swashbuckler's" Executive Officer.

The "Swashbucklers" formed part of MAG-21 that also included VMF-213 "Hellhawks" and VMF-221 "Fighting Falcons." As soon as each squadron had 27 aviators, one doctor, one intelligence officer, and a squadron adjutant they headed for the Solomons, arriving in early March 1943. The aviators were told each squadron was scheduled for three tours of from six to nine weeks depending upon the demands for combat.

VMF-214 reached operational strength in mid-September 1942 with fresh and eager Lieutenants, plus four Technical Sergeants. Upon Captain Britt's recommendation three of the sergeants were promoted to lieutenants. This included Alvin J Jensen, who was to accomplish one of the most amazing ground attack strikes of all time.

Combat operations stopped on May 13, 1943, after completing the longest tour of any squadron to date (two months). Two days later the flight echelon flew to Sydney, Australia, for R&R.

During June 5-6, 1943, the VMF-214 flight echelon regrouped at Efate, New Hebrides, to train with its new Corsairs.

Capt George Britt was promoted to the rank of major and assigned as Operations Officer for MAG-21 (Marine Aircraft Group-21) on June 8, 1943. MAG-21 included Squadrons VMF-213, VMF-214, and VMF-221.

Operations Officers planned and coordinated air strikes, escort missions, and other aircraft combat activities. Major Henry Ellis succeeded

Two VMF-214 "Swashbuckler" heroes of the Kahili airfield strafing raid of August 28, 1943, destroyed a total of 24 Japanese aircraft in one day. Upper Photo: Lt Alvin Jensen flamed 13 enemy aircraft in a lone strike on Kahili. Lower Photo: In a separate lone raid after Lt Jensen's, Lt Charles Lanphier destroyed 11 enemy aircraft on the Kahili runway, but was shot down and captured. Later reconnaissance flights confirmed 24 destroyed aircraft on the Kahili runway. (USMC Photos, Courtesy Lt Col OK Williams USMC (Ret))

Chapter III: Corsairs into the Solomons

Lt O Keith Williams, VMF-214 "Swashbucklers" Propeller Officer and Asst Engineering Officer, was a close air support and strafing expert. He is shown here with his F4U-1A Corsair. Lt Williams conducted countless surface attacks, always surprising the enemy. He was truly a "down to earth" Marine aviator. (USMC Photo, Courtesy Lt Col OK Williams USMC (Ret))

Major Britt as Squadron Commander; however, on 11 July, he was ordered to CONUS.

The new Squadron CO was Major William H Pace. On 18 July, Maj Pace led the squadron to provide close air support for the crippled seaplane tender *USS Chincoteague* that was under attack by three Japanese bombers. All three bombers were shot down.

The "Swashbucklers" were based on Banika Island, in the Russells, supporting the Munda-Rendova invasions, when Lt. Lanphier scored a Zero on August 4, 1943. Three days later Major Pace's engine was hit during a strafing raid, but the intrepid aviator decided to return to Banika rather than ditch the Corsair. As he attempted to land the engine seized due to oil starvation. Bailing out at a very low altitude, his parachute had just started to open when he hit the shallow water at the end of the landing strip, sustaining fatal injuries.

Lt. OK Williams and Lt. Dave Rankin made a cross from a broken propeller and placed it on Major Pace's grave.

Captain John RB Burnett succeeded Major Pace.

The most satisfactory aspect of the Solomons Campaign regarding U.S. Marine Aviation was the progress made in close air support for the troops and strafing enemy ground targets, such as gun emplacements, landing craft, and parked aircraft. Corsair squadrons were ideal for this task by virtue of the high approach speed, bomb load, and lethal firepower of six .50 caliber machine guns.

Contrary to what numerous aviation historians have written and many "armchair aviators" believe, the combat aviators were not "bored" when ordered to a close air support mission or a strafing assignment. Every Pacific air war veteran fighter aviator that the Author has contacted agreed that close air support or strafing was far more dangerous than air-to-air combat. In air-to-air combat, the aviator has the option to maneuver in three-dimensional space to elude or press the attack against his opponent. Conversely, the ground attack aviator is restricted in his maneuvers once he makes his run on the surface target. During his run, the attacker is being pounded by enemy ground fire ranging from rifle fire, machine gun fire, and 20 mm and 40 mm antiaircraft fire, and at times, heavier artillery fire!

It must be remembered that the basic reason for Marines having airplanes is for the close support of Marine ground troops.

The word "strafe" evolved from the German word to punish, "Strafen."

There are two types of strafing attacks: "Penetrating" or "Assigned Target" and "Raking" or "Targets of Opportunity."

In a "Penetrating" or "Assigned Target" attack the Corsair approaches the target at altitude and aims at the specifically assigned target, such as a ship, landing barge, or building. The attacker dives at great speed for surprise and levels off at two or three thousand feet. In this event the enemy has seen the attacker coming and the Corsair is met with devastating antiaircraft fire.

In a "Raking" or "Targets of Opportunity" attack, the Corsair remains at an extremely low altitude all the way to the unassigned targets, selecting those subjects to cause the most damage and that are the least protected to surprise the enemy. The attacker can change from target to target, confusing the enemy and receiving very little return fire.

Either attack is fraught with danger for the attacker.

It is of utmost importance that the attack be a complete surprise, preferably with the sun behind the attacker. The attack must be restricted to a simultaneous single run or pass for all targets because the enemy will be at the ready with AA fire if a second run is attempted.

The only complaints regarding a strafing attack assignment apparently came from the few so-called "Glory Seekers" who felt that they were being denied the opportunity to shoot down more enemy planes and become an ace.

On August 15, 1943, the ground echelon of VMF-214 went to Espiritu Santo, while the flight echelon arrived at the newly completed airstrip at Munda, on New Georgia, where VFM-214 joined its Corsairs.

Twelve days later five Corsairs from VMF 214 and three from VMF-215 (Fighting Corsairs), led by Maj Robert G Owens (CO VMF-215), were assigned a strafing mission to "beat up" enemy aircraft on the Kahili bomber field on Bougainville. As the Marines approached the target the formation was scattered by a sudden violent tropical storm. Lt. Alvin Jensen's Corsair was tossed about like a leaf when, suddenly, he emerged from the storm upside down directly over the Kahili Airfield!

Rolling his Corsair into a dive, he lined up with the Japanese planes parked on the runway and, starting at the north end, he flamed thirteen Japanese aircraft in one pass. Maj Britt's confidence in Lt. Jensen's ability was rewarded.

When Major Owens and his wingman emerged from the storm and found 24 flaming planes on the runway he aborted the mission because of the intense antiaircraft fire. Twenty-four flaming planes when Jensen claimed only thirteen! None of the surviving aviators claimed any destroyed aircraft. Strange?

Reconnaissance photographs confirmed that no less than 24 grounded Japanese aircraft had been destroyed on Kahili airfield.

The only casualty of the raid was Lt. Charles C Lanphier, brother of Capt Thomas G Lanphier USAAC, the aviator who killed Adm Yamamoto. Lt. Lanphier had been shot down by antiaircraft fire and was taken prisoner by the Japanese.

Capt James Mc Murria USAAC, a captured B-24 pilot, was in the same POW camp as Lt. Charles Lanphier. After the war Capt Mc Murria quoted Lt. Lanphier recalling his last mission, saying: "We really shot the Hell out of Kahili." Lt. Charles Lanphier died of malnutrition in a POW camp.

Unfounded rumors abounded that the Japanese purposely starved the aviator to death in order to punish his brother for killing Admiral Yamamoto.

Apparently, Lt. Charles Lanphier flamed the remaining eleven planes in Kahili and died a hero. Seeing Lt. Jensen's burning planes, Lt. Lanphier probably finished off the remaining eleven; however, the alerted Japanese shot him down.

Lt. Jensen was awarded the Navy Cross for his outstanding achievement in strafing the airfield.

Lt. OK Williams of VMF-214 "Swashbucklers" became an expert at the "down-to-earth" art of strafing, giving up many flying opportunities to score victories. Very often, high-ranking officers with little or no combat experience issued orders that were virtually impossible to execute. During the Summer of 1943, Henderson Field Fighter Command issued an order to search and destroy any landing barge activity in the Central Solomons.

After his Corsair division searched for about an hour, "OK" discovered a barge covered with palm boughs in a cove. After the pass, two barrels of oil on the barge caught fire but the barge did not sink, because it was made from huge logs tied together.

When Lt. Williams reported to the Fighter Command Colonel that the barge did not sink, the officer became "unglued and very upset." The aviator wanted to tell the Colonel that he was very familiar with logs, having worked in a lumber camp during his high school and college days, and knew that the log barge could not be sunk with machine gun fire, but Lt. Williams was ordered to "get out."

Four months later the aviator discovered that the Colonel had recommended him for the Air Medal!

Colonel Raymond E Hopper USMC was the MAG-21 Commanding Officer who believed that happy warriors are better warriors. Major Britt joined with Col Hopper, and together they created "Boomtown" on Banika, in the Russell Islands.

Still within bombing range for the Japanese, "Boomtown" featured a hamburger stand; screened portable living quarters; one-day laundry service; running water; a solid mahogany mess hall; a "Good Humor Man"; and free beer for enlisted personnel. Most important is the fact that Hopper selected high, level ground on which to establish camp.

The idea for "Boomtown" grew out of Col Hopper's military experience in Cuba, Puerto Rico, Guam, and other remote outposts. The Marines brought along special equipment and construction material

Col Raymond E Hopper, CO of Marine Aircraft Group 21 (MAG-21), and Maj George F Britt, Operations Officer (MAG-21), were responsible for "Boomtown" on Banika in the New Georgia Islands. "Boomtown" was known as the "Shangri-la" of the Solomons and entertained many Marines who made the trip to the "Shrine." Col Hopper is shown here. (USMC Photo, SSG E Hart, Jr, Author's File)

Upper Photo: "Boomtown's" screened-in latrine was a comfort but lacked privacy. Note the luxury of toilet tissue. Lower Photo: "Boomtown's" scramble, standby, and ready room featured a large table for reading maps and charts and preparing reports. (Swashbucklers Photo, Courtesy Lt Col OK Williams USMC (Ret))

Chapter III: Corsairs into the Solomons

Upper Photo: Artie Shaw's band was a sensation in the 'Forties, and the group visited "Boomtown" to entertain the "Swashbuckler" aviators. Howard J Cavanaugh is in pajamas and Dave Rankin is standing at extreme right. Remaining five are members of Artie Shaw's band. Rankin had been an All-American football player at Purdue 1939-1940. Lower Photo: Sign at "Boomtown" announces the "Pilot Club" where the aviators could relax. Observe the sturdy buildings in the background. (Swashbuckler Photos, Courtesy Lt Col OK Williams USMC (Ret))

Upper Photo: "Boomtown" sleeping, resting, and/ or relaxing area was high and dry with large tents for officers and enlisted personnel. Lower Photo: Dave Rankin, VMF-214 CO Henry Ellis, and OK Williams with a damaged Japanese tank. (Swashbucklers Photos, Courtesy Lt Col OK Williams USMC (Ret))

as well as a well-digger, portable laundry, sawmill, and refrigerators. "Boomtown" became known as the Solomons' "Shangri-la" and was visited by any Marine who could travel to this oasis! All visitors were welcome.

Major George Britt, as Operations Officer for MAG-21, found it necessary to travel to the three squadrons of MAG-21 as well as other Marine squadrons in the sector in order to plan and coordinate contemplated aerial offensives.

Conversations via radio were too vulnerable. They would be overheard by the Japanese and, further, conversation is not sufficient nor precise enough because visual discussion with maps was necessary. In view of the above, it was imperative for Major Britt to fly his Corsair to the various units involved. This meant that he could not fly alone because, if he was shot down by the Japanese, his plans would be revealed to the enemy. Conversely, if he was to fly with an escort, it would arouse attention and a confrontation would result. The only viable solution was to build the fastest plane in the Pacific!

The Headquarters Squadron Engineering Section of MAG-21 had access to many wrecked Corsairs and spare parts for the Corsair. Major Britt consulted with Tech Sgt Jack Downs, engineering chief of MAG-21, and decided to build a special Corsair from the wreckage and spare parts! This had to be a very fast Corsair to beat any plane the Japanese had, to enable Major Britt to make his trips safely.

"Boomtown" featured a laundry washing machine; a rarity in the Solomons. Clothes driers were not popular at that time, so clothes had to be dried the old fashioned way. (Swashbucklers Photo, Courtesy David J Ekstrand)

Corsair: The Saga of the Legendary Bent-Wing Fighter-Bomber

"Boomtown" was apparently a distance away from the airstrip, so this improvised bus transported the aviators to their Corsairs. Standing L to R: James Taylor, Alvin Jensen, Richard Sigel, and Victor Scarborough. Kneeling L to R: David Rankin, Harry Hollmeyer, and Jackson Petit. (Swashbucklers Photo, Courtesy David J Ekstrand)

Whenever the "Swashbucklers" were in Espiritu Santo they never failed to visit this "swimming hole." Compare this facility with the Royal New Zealand Air Force "swimming hole" in Chapter Four, and how this "swimming hole" appears today in Chapter Ten. (Swashbucklers Photo, Courtesy Lt Col OK Williams USMC (Ret))

The "Swashbucklers" were so pleased with their Corsairs that they insisted on having their photograph taken with one of their "Bent-Wing Birds." Top Row, L to R: Pettit, McCall, Hollmeyer, Sigel, Scarborough, Knipping, Fiddler, and Rankin. Second Row, L to R: Cavanaugh, Synar, Hatch, Miller, Burnett, Brookman, Eisele, and Carpenter. Third Row, L to R: Hernan, Hazelwood, Moak, Bernard, Williams, Jensen, and Dunbar. Bottom Row, L to R: Taylor, Tomlinson, Deetz, Hunter, Curran, and O'Dell. (Swashbucklers Photo, Courtesy Lt Col OK Williams USMC (Ret))

Marine Aircraft Group 21's CO, Col Raymond Hopper (L), and MAG-21's Operations Officer, Maj George Britt (R), welcome the first Corsair Ace, Lt Ken Walsh, to "Boomtown" for a short stay on Banika. (USMC Photo Courtesy David J. Ekstrand)

Chapter III: Corsairs into the Solomons

Marine Aircraft Group 21 officers (VMF-213, VMF-214, and VMF-221) assembled in the Russell Islands during September 1943 for this photo with the MAG-21 Commanding Officer, Col Raymond Hopper. Front row only L to R (Kneeling): Capt Wynn Mendous, Ordnance Officer; Capt Morris Flater, Radar Officer; LCDR George Kraft (MD), USN, Flight Surgeon; and Capt Douglas J Peaches, Supply Offier. Seated: Lt Col Tom Noon, Executive Officer; Col Raymond E. Hopper, Commanding Officer; and Maj George F Britt, Operations Officer. Kneeling: Maj Charles Endweiss, Asst Operations Officer; and Capt Cain, Adjutant. (USMC Photo, Courtesy Col George F Britt USMC (Ret))

Lt Robert M Hanson stands with his cannon-damaged Corsair on August 4, 1943. As a member of VMF-214 "Swashbucklers," Hanson was "mixing it up" with Tonys and Zekes when a Zeke peppered the Corsair's starboard wing. Hanson then scored a Tony with his damaged plane for his first of 25 victories, the highest scoring Corsair Ace. (USMC Photo, Author's File)

Jim Swett was a member of VMF-221, which squadron was part of MAG-21, and therefore he enjoyed the advantages of "Boomtown." He is shown here before his quarters in April 1943. (MAG-21 Photo, Courtesy Lt Col OK Williams USMC (Ret))

L to R: Robert Hanson, DE McCall, Ed Hernan, and Keith Williams of VMF-214 "Swashbucklers" appear to be agog about some nurses in the darkness of night on Espirito Santo. Hanson and Williams soon transferred to VMF-215 when "Swashbucklers" was disbanded. (Swashbucklers Photo, Courtesy Lt Col O Keith Williams USMC (Ret))

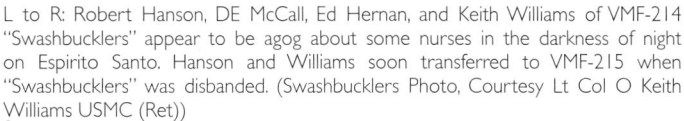

Left: Capt James E Swett is shown with his Corsair. Having scored 8.5 Corsair victories of his total 15.5 victories, he can truly be named a Corsair Ace. Right: Capt Swett was awarded the Medal of Honor in the field on October 9, 1943, for shooting down seven Japanese bombers single handedly in one day during a two-hour battle on April 7, 1943. Swett was also shot down in the fight, but was rescued after he ditched his plane. This was the first time in the history of the Marine Corps that this medal has been awarded in the field. (USMC Marine Corps Photos, Courtesy National Archives)

Maj Gen Roy Stanley Geiger, Director of Marine Corps Aviation, and Maj Joseph Foss discuss Corsair combat tactics. Gen Geiger was Naval Aviator No 49. He was given command of Marine Troop Landings on October 15, 1943. (USMC Photo, Author's File)

Right: "No BuNo" belies its parentage of wreckage and spare parts as Major Britt poses proudly with his new mount. Weighing one-ton less than the production F4U-1, "No BuNo" was faster than any fighter plane in the Solomons. (USMC Photo, Courtesy Col George F Britt USMC (Ret))

Brave Corsair aviators received medals in a revetment on November 20, 1943. The awards committee, L to R: Lt Robert E Clark; Maj Robert G Owens, Jr; Maj James L Neefus; and Lt Col Herbert H Williamson. The recipients, L to R: Lt Lincoln F Deetz (Gold Star); Lt Bennie P O'Dell (Air Medal); Lt David R Moak (Air Medal); Capt Don Aldrich (Purple Heart); Lt Drury E Mc Call (Air Medal); Lt Robert M Hanson (Air Medal); Lt Thomas M Tomlinson (Air Medal); Lt Otto K Williams (Air Medal); and Lt Grafton S Stidger (Purple Heart). Lt Williams was recommended for the Air Medal by the same Colonel who became very upset when log barges were not sunk by Williams' machine gun fire! Bob Hanson's bandaged hand was injured in a freak accident according to Col Williams, who was there: "I was standing on a revetment one day at Munda air strip watching 215 and 221 scramble to intercept some Japs. Hansen began his takeoff from one end of the strip and another pilot was taking off from the opposite end. There was no 'tower control,' they hit head-on doing around 70 miles per hour. Both left wings hit, and 100 gallons of high-octane exploded. Hansen had his left hand exposed, and I think he lost a finger or two in the crash, thus the bandage…." (Defense Dept Photo-USMC, Author's File)

The talent of the MAG-21 Headquarters Squadron Engineering Section created "No BuNo" from Corsair wreckage and spare parts. The dedication of these craftsmen kept the Corsairs of three squadrons "on the ready" for action. They pose here in October 1943 with a Corsair under their care in the Russell Islands. (USMC Photo, Courtesy Col George F Britt USMC (Ret))

Chapter III: Corsairs into the Solomons

Major Britt sits proudly in "No-Bu-No," which he flew to participating combat units to plan and coordinate missions against the Japanese. The MAG-21 Operations Officer traveled alone without an escort, depending upon his one-of-a-kind Corsair's speed for safety. Photo taken in Russell Islands in October 1943. (USMC Photo, Courtesy Col George F Britt USMC (Ret))

This Corsair, flown by Major Robert G Owens, was the first U.S. airplane to land on Munda Airfield after the airfield's capture and reconstruction by U.S. forces. We will meet Major Owens in the following chapter as Commanding Officer of the very successful VMF-215 "Fighting Corsairs." (National Archives, Author's File)

The talented craftsmen of MAG-21 Headquarters Squadron Engineering Section began to work at once to create this one-of-a-kind Corsair. It was a conventional F4U-1, except that it had no armor; no tailhook; no wing folding mechanism; no guns or ammunition boxes (magazines); and no wing fuel tanks. The savings in weight alone was over one ton! The only new items installed were the engine and propeller. This was the "hot-rod" of all military Corsairs.

Major Britt's Corsair was "Illegitimate" because it had no Bureau of Aeronautics Number; therefore, the plane was call "NoBuNo" (**NO BU**reau of Aeronautics **N**umber "N**O**"). With speeds approaching 450mph "NoBuNo" was the fastest plane in the South Pacific at that time. The "NoBuNo" performance was demonstrated one day as Major Britt was about to takeoff from the Munda airstrip on his way to Vella Lavella or Guadalcanal, or both. A USAAC Lockheed P-38 Lightning taxied into a wing position on Britt's Corsair, obviously challenging the Major to the takeoff and climbout. Major Britt recalls the event as follows:

"I'm sure that smart-aleck P-38 pilot was shocked a minute or so later when he found himself far behind and below me. I've always wondered if he told his squadron mates about it."

Major Boyington never failed to brief the VMF-122 aviators before a mission so that the squadron would operate like a "well oiled machine." The aviators are as follows: Left Photo, Standing (L to R): WN Case; RN Rinabarger; DH Fisher; HM Bourgeois; JF Begert; RT Ewing; D Groover, Jr; and BL Tucker. Kneeling (L to R): G Boyington; SR Bailey; VG Ray; and RA Alexander. Right Photo (L to R): RN Rinabarger; G Boyington; HM Bourgeois; and JF Begert. (USMC Photos, Courtesy David A Mocabee)

Major Gregory "Pappy" Boyington taxies into a revetment under the direction of a ground controller after landing at Torokina Airfield on Bougainville as the Black Sheep leader. (USMC Photo, Author's File)

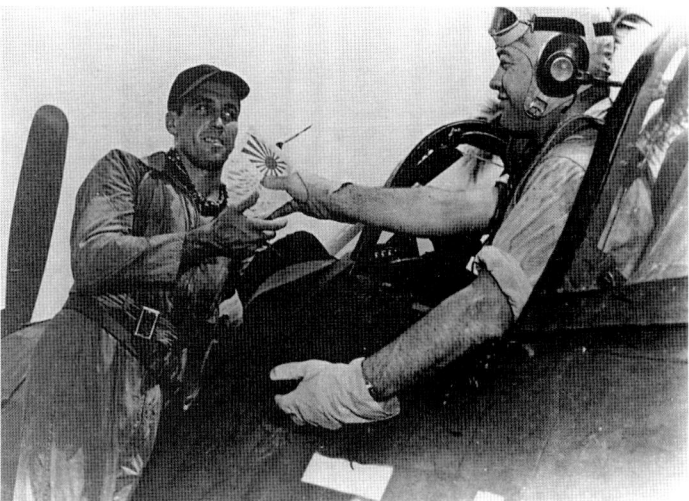

Shown here are two "Black Sheep" publicity photos regarding baseball caps and victory flags. Upper Photo: Second ranking "Black Sheep" ace Lt Chris Magee (9 Vict) trades St Louis Cardinal baseball caps for victory flags with Major Boyington. Black Sheep pilots received a baseball cap from World Series players for every Japanese plane shot down. Lower Photo: Maj Boyington discussing his Corsair with Chance Vought field representative and troubleshooter Ray De Leva in Espiritu Santo. "Lulubelle" and flags were later removed. Boyington never flew with victory flags because the Japanese would "gang up" on him if he did. (Ling-Temco-Vought Photo, Courtesy Arthur L Schoeni)

This November 20, 1943, publicity photo of the Black Sheep Squadron was taken on Vella Lavella after the St Louis Baseball Team gave the celebrated aviators baseball caps and bats. Aviators on the Corsair wing, who had not yet become aces, are (L to R): Sims; Ashmun; Matheson; Hill; Olander; Bragdon; Walton; Harper, Enrich; Heier; Tucker; and Moore. Aviators who were aces when the photo was taken are standing before the Corsair wearing baseball caps and holding baseball bats. Thay are (L to R): Christopher L Magee; Robert W Mc Clurg; Paul A Mullen; Gregory Boyington; John F Bolt; and Don H Fisher. (USMC Photo, Courtesy Lt Col John Bolt USMC (Ret))

Chapter III: Corsairs into the Solomons

This amusing incident must have given the Operations Officer tremendous confidence in his "scrapyard Corsair" during future flights.

VMF-214 Swashbucklers went to Sydney, Australia, on August 31, 1943, for R&R (Rest and Recreation or Rest and Recuperation) after completing their second combat tour.

Upon its return to Espiritu Santo the squadron was surprised to learn it had been disbanded. Some aviators were ordered to CONUS, while six were transferred to other squadrons as replacements. Lt. OK Williams and Lt. Robert M Hanson joined VMF-215 Fighting Corsairs.

The number VMF-214 was to be transferred to another squadron; however, "Swashbucklers" would remain a cherished memory.

Major Gregory R "Pappy" Boyington had flown with the Flying Tigers in China and had been the CO of VMF-112 and VMF-122. He was then actively agitating for the command of a new squadron for multi-squadron aggressive fighter sweeps, which resulted in giving Boyington command of VMF-214 on September 7, 1943, for fighter sweeps.

The VMF-214 number continued, but the "Swashbucklers," who had fought and died to make the early Allied advances in the South Pacific, did not fade from memory. Major Boyington's squadron was called "Black Sheep," perhaps because it was "illegitimate," having taken another squadron's number. At times he was referred to as "Pappy" because, at 30 years old, he was older than the other "Black Sheep" aviators, some of whom were 19-22 years old.

Maj Boyington led the Black Sheep on their first mission on September 14, 1943, escorting B-24 bombers in a raid over Kahili, Bougainville.

Two days later 20 Black Sheep Corsairs were escorting 150 Dauntless dive bombers and Avenger torpedo planes when they were intercepted by 40 Zekes over Ballale, Bougainville. When the battle was over, sixteen Zekes were confirmed shot down, while nine others were probables. Capt Robert Ewing was shot down and killed.

Black Sheep aviators run to their Corsairs for a fighter sweep over Rabaul. Fighter sweeps were a means to "flush out" enemy fighters to engage in aerial combat, similar to "throwing down the gauntlet" in medieval times! (USMC Photo, Author's File)

The Black Sheep relocated to Munda, in the New Georgia Islands, and became part of MAG-11 on September 17, 1943. On September 30, 1943, the Squadron suffered its third loss when Lt. Robert Alexander's Corsair was mistaken for a Japanese plane by a U.S. Navy PT boat and was shot down, crashing on Kolombangara Island.

Black Sheep aviator Lt. John F Bolt had been experimenting to discover the optimum machine gun belt-loading combination for setting Japanese aircraft afire. Instead of the U.S. Navy-specified standard of one tracer, one armor-piercing, and one incendiary bullet, Lt. Bolt discovered through his own experiments, firing various combinations into oil-filled floating drums, that the optimum combination was one armor-piercing, two incendiary, and one tracer bullet. After the Squadron's second tour, the U.S. Navy adopted Lt. Bolt's belt loading discovery for all Navy and Marine aircraft.

Major Boyington was leading about a dozen Corsairs to escort USAAC B-24 Liberator bombers when the target area clouded over, solid. The lower-flying bombers disappeared into the overcast and the Black Sheep turned back and headed in the direction of Munda. When the flight passed over Kahili and Ballale Island it sighted a tremendous amount of enemy barge activity. With the clouds down to about a thousand feet the barges were ideal targets, but Boyington ordered "Nobody Shoot." Those Corsairs that were low on fuel landed at Vella Lavella for refueling.

After his gunsight was serviced at Vella Lavella Lt. Bolt tried to convince the half-dozen aviators who had landed to fly back and strafe the barges. None dared to disobey "Pappy" Boyington's orders, but Bolt decided to go alone because it was his duty.

When Lt. Bolt arrived over Kahili he shot up three or four barges and, after making a run inland on one of the barges, he spotted a barge staging area about ten miles east of Kahili, in Tonolei Harbor. The intrepid Aviator shot up the barges and a tugboat, then returned to Munda.

Major Boyington was livid when he learned about Bolt's escapade and "chewed out" the errant aviator for disobeying orders.

A few days later VADM Halsey expressed his pleasure about Lt. Bolt's strafing attack in a message to ComAirSols.

On October 22, 1943, the Squadron went to Sydney, Australia, for R&R. Upon their return to the Russells, a search party was organized

Corsair designer Rex Beisel discusses the merits of the Bent-Wing Bird with aeronautical engineer and famous Corsair Ace Gregory "Pappy" Boyington. Boyington scored 22 victories with the Corsair, second only to Robert M "Butcher Bob" Hanson, who scored 25 victories with Corsairs. (Photo Courtesy Rex Beisel Jr)

to locate Lt. Alexander's crash site. This included "Pappy" Boyington; Robert W Mc Clurg; Paul A Mullen; Frank E Walton; Donald J Moore; Barney Tucker; and Flight Surgeon James M Reames. All traveled to Kolombangara in a PT boat.

After cutting their way through the rain forest the group came upon Lt. Alexander's Corsair. His body had been thrown from the wreckage and was located a short distance from his plane. The search party buried the fallen comrade facing toward Japan "so he can follow our advance all the way to Tokyo," as Intelligence Officer Frank E Walton wrote in his book *Once They Were Eagles*. A broken propeller blade served for Lt. Alexander's tombstone.

Maj Boyington detested paperwork. All he wanted to do was fight the Japanese. At the conclusion of a pilots' briefing prior to a fighter sweep, the CO of another squadron asked tactical commander Boyington what tactics he would use when sighting Zeros. "Tactics," replied Pappy, "Hell, you don't need any tactics, when you see 'em just shoot 'em down, that's all!" It was fortunate for Boyington that he had a very efficient executive officer, Major Henry S Miller, who handled maintenance, supply, and personnel problems for the Commanding Officer.

Boyington's first fighter sweep of Rabaul was flown on Decmeber 17, 1943, when 32 Marine Corsairs, 24 Navy Hellcats, and 24 New Zealand Kittyhawks headed for Rabaul. Japanese aerial reaction to the sweep was low, probably because the Japanese could not afford fighter-versus-fighter combat without a strategic mission. The "Black Sheep" scored three victories during the fighter sweep to bring their score to 60.

Lt. Bolt scored two victories on December 23, 1943, to make him the fifth Black Sheep Ace of the eight Black Sheep Aces.

By Christmas Day 1943 the "Black Sheep" were credited with 76 victories and 27 probables, and by January 2, 1944, the squadron could boast 88 victories.

On the following day Maj Boyington led a sixty-plane fighter sweep that comprised VMF-214 Corsairs and VF-33 Hellcats. At about five o'clock in the morning the armada was spotted by a Japanese combat patrol, which alerted the 204 Kokutai Air Group from Lakunai Airfield commanded by Lt. Sadao Yamaguchi and 253 Kokutai Air Group from Tobera Airfield led by Lt. Kenji Nakagawa. Both Japanese units consisted of over a dozen aces with victory records of from ten to 202 victories! Seventy Zeros sortied to intercept the Americans.

Boyington's division included his wingman, Capt George Ashmun, plus Second Element Leader Lt. Bruce Matheson and his wingman, Lt. Rufus Chatham.

After making a circular sweep over Rapopo Airfield Boyington spotted a flight of six Zeros below him at about 15,000ft. The heavy cloud overcast prevented the Japanese aviators from seeing the two Corsairs diving to the attack. Firing at "tail-end Charlie" at 1,200ft range, Boyington scored his twenty-sixth victory as the Zero exploded. This victory was official because it was witnessed by several "Black Sheep" aviators.

Separated from the Second Element, Boyington and Ashmun found themselves surrounded by Zeros. Ashmun scored one Zero as his Corsair was mortally hit and smoking. Boyington saw his wingman crash into St George Channel as his own Corsair was riddled with cannon shells, wounding the Major and setting his fuel tank afire. What happened next is steeped in controversy. Initially Major Boyington claimed he bailed out of his plane at 100ft altitude and drifted in his inflatable raft; however, when the Japanese submarine I-181 picked up the Ace he was near Cape St George, located at the southern tip of the island of New Ireland, a distance of about 50 miles from Rabaul. It is quite possible that he eluded the Zeroes and managed to nurse his damaged Corsair to Cape St George and ditched the plane there. His only additional injury was a broken ankle.

```
SECRET                          PRIORITY
              170500

FROM:  SEGI AERO
  TO:  COMAIRSOLS
INFO:  COMAIR NEW GEORGIA

THAT ONE MAN WAR X YOUR SIXTEEN ZERO FOUR FIFTEEN X CONDUCTED

BY LIEUT BOLT AGAINST JAP STUFF IN TONOLEI WARM HEART X HALSEY X


REF: 160415 : LIEUT BOLT CMA ONE OF THE TWO CORSAIRS THAT

LANDED VELLA FROM KARA STRIKE CMA REFUELED AND RETURNED TO

TONOLEI HARBOR WHERE HE HAD PREVIOUSLY SEEN SEVERAL BARGES X....
```

Disobeying Maj Boyington's orders, Lt John F Bolt successfully strafed several Japanese landing barges and a tugboat. Despite Boyington's anger, VADM Halsey was very pleased with Lt Bolt when he learned about the strafing attack. The actual message is shown below the photograph of Lt Bolt. (USMC Photo & Document, Courtesy Lt Col John F Bolt USMC (Ret))

Major Gregory Boyington spent the remainder of World War Two in a Japanese POW camp.

Adding credence to the ditching theory is the fact that the only American Corsair losses in the fighter sweep were those flown by Ashmun and Boyington. Capt Ashmun was killed but Boyington survived. When the Black Sheep returned to Munda some of the aviators reported a distress call from an unidentified Corsair aviator who stated that he was about to ditch his damaged plane. This call had to be from Major Boyington. In a 1983 letter Boyington stated that he ended up in the water almost abreast of Cape St George.

Aerial combat is an unnerving experience, even for those aviators blessed with Sang-Froid. Many individuals have little or no recollection of the danger and excitement endured less than an hour ago. Therefore, it would be quite normal for Boyington to have dissimilar recollections of what happened 39 years before.

Chapter III: Corsairs into the Solomons

Maj Gregory Boyington claimed 22 victories with the Corsair in addition to six claimed victories with the AVG (Flying Tigers) for a total of 28 victories.

Major Henry S Miller was appointed VMF-214 Commanding Officer on January 4, 1944.

During January 4 and 5, 1944, the Black Sheep searched for Capt Ashmun and Maj Boyington. At this time Lt. John Bolt scored his sixth victory, Lt. Denmark Groover his first, and Lt. Paul Mullin his seventh victory.

The Corsair aviators continued to contribute immensely to the successful Allied invasion and construction of airfields on the island of Bougainville, the "Springboard to Rabaul." Breaching the "Bismarck Barrier" became within the realm of possibility, but there was much more fighting ahead for the Corsair aviators as they flew from Bougainville airfields.

The question of whether Corsair aviators were issued their personal fighter or flew any plane that was available and fully serviced has always been a subject of argument among military and aero historians. It appears that the decision rested with the squadron commander. Two diverse opinions are revealed in this example: Commander John T Blackburn, CO of VF-17, did not assign specific aircraft to his aviators, and they rarely flew the same Corsair more than once. Conversely, major William E Gise, CO of VF-124, assigned a specific Corsair to each aviator. Further, VMF-124 aviators were required to work on their Corsair with the crewchiefs to become familiar with their mount, understanding the construction and equipment in the plane much as a cavalryman must know the health of his horse.

Another subject worthy of explanation is the surprisingly short term that commanding officers served as squadron leaders. The exceptionally high mortality rate of squadron Commanding officers during Spring-Summer 1943 pressured ComAirSoPac to institute a policy that all squadron Commanding Officers (COs) be removed from their command after one combat tour.

The fourth squadron to receive Corsairs, after VMF-124, VF-12, and VF-17, was VMF-213 "Hellhawks"; organized on July 1, 1942, at Ewa, Hawaii, under the command of Capt Herbert T Merrill. The "Hellhawks" three leading Aces were Capt Wilbur J Thomas (18.5 vict); Lt. Edward O Shaw (14.5 vict); and Capt James N Cupp (12.5 vict). Lt. John D Kuhn and 2nd Lt. Edmund P Hartsock of VMF-124 flew to Espiritu Santo from Guadalcanal to brief the VMF-213 aviators all about their new Corsairs. Such was the comradery between Corsair squadrons in the South Pacific.

IV

Corsairs Break the Bismarck Barrier

Aware that U.S. Strategy was aimed at destroying Rabaul, Japanese Imperial Headquarters issued a special directive on September 30, 1943, as follows:

"Make every effort to hold the important southeastern area extending eastward from the eastern part of New Guinea to the Solomon Islands and repulsing all enemy attacks in the area. To accomplish this purpose: (a) Consider Rabaul as the center and make every effort for a protracted defense of important positions in the Bismarck Archipelago and Bougainville Areas. (b) Endeavor to hold out in the northern New Guinea area by reinforcing important positions in this area. (c) Endeavor to destroy the attacking enemy before landings are made by using air and surface forces. (d) In case the enemy succeeds in landing operations endeavor to destroy him before he consolidates his position, thereby disrupting his plan for counterattack. (e) Endeavor to concentrate military supplies for high speed transport to the above-mentioned important positions, particularly to those in New Guinea."

This order strengthened the already impregnable fortress Rabaul with 170 more planes and 10 more ships, plus military supplies. More than 370 planes were based on Rabaul by November 1, 1943.

On October 1, 1943, Admiral Halsey informed General MacArthur that he decided to invade Bougainville on November 1, 1943—"Dog Day" (later changed to "Love Day")—at Cape Torokina, in Empress Augusta Bay, midway up the western side of Bougainville. The General agreed and promised all possible air support for the landings that included B-24 and

Prior to the scheduled Bougainville invasion, Stirling Island and Mono Island, in the Treasury Group, were invaded by New Zealand's 8 Brigade Group on October 27, 1943. An airstrip and taxiway were constructed at once on Stirling. These are shown to the right on this photograph. (U.S. Navy Photo, Author's File)

Lt Robert M. Hanson of VMF-215 shot down three Kate Torpedo bombers within a few minutes on "Love Day," but was shot down by a Kate gunner. He ditched his Corsair and was in action a few days later. Hanson became the leading Corsair Ace and is shown with one of his Corsairs. (Defense Dept. USMC, Author's File)

Chapter IV: Corsairs Break the Bismarck Barrier

Rear Admiral Frederick Carl Sherman dared to approach and attack northern Bougainville and Rabaul Airfields with his carriers to assist the Empress Augusta Bay invasion. He is shown here receiving good news from CDR Joseph "Jumpin Joe" Clifton, fighter group commander of the raids on Japanese airfields. During the twelve-day assault more than 130 Japanese aircraft were destroyed. The officers are aboard USS Saratoga (CV-3). (U.S. Naval Historical Center Photo, National Archives)

B-25 bombers and P-38 fighters. The invasion was Code-Named "Cherry Blossom." Rabaul was the target marked for strangulation by the aviators, and Bougainville airfields were needed to accomplish the task.

In order to defend the Empress Augusta Bay invasion forces against attacking Japanese aircraft, Acting ComAirSols Maj Gen Ralph J. Mitchell ordered a constant 32-fighter plane patrol over the beaches.

Five Marine fighter squadrons and one Navy fighter squadron were in action against the Japanese from the beginning of the Bougainville operation: VMF-211 "Wake Avengers," Maj Robert A. Harvey; VMF-212 "Musketeers," Maj Hugh M. Elwood; VMF-215 "Fighting Corsairs"; Maj Robert G. Owens; VMF-221 "Fighting Falcons" Maj Nathan T. Post Jr.; VMF (N)-531 "Gray Ghosts" Lt. Col Frank H. Schwable; and VF-17 "Jolly Rogers" LCDR John T. "Tommy" Blackburn. All were flying Corsairs.

Two landings were made on Stirling and Mono Islands in the Treasury Group on October 27, 1943.

One of the first patrols included VMF-215 "Fighting Corsairs" led by Lt. Col Herbert H. Williamson (who was succeeded by Maj Robert G. Owens on December 6, 1943). A VMF-215 division intercepted approximately 25 Zeros and Kate torpedo bombers about noon and shot down five, of which Lt. Robert M. Hanson destroyed three in a few minutes before he was shot down by a Kate's rear gunner.

Hanson made a safe landing with his Corsair, skimming on the water of the Bay. He drifted in his rubber dinghy until late afternoon when he was rescued by a destroyer and was back at the VMF-215 airstrip on Vella Lavella within a few days. Hanson had been listed as missing in action.

The "Jolly Rogers" arrived at Ondonga airfield, on the island of New Georgia, on October 27, 1943, in time to join Marine fighter squadrons for the November 1, 1943, assault on Bougainville.

RADM Frederick C. Sherman's carrier group, including USS Saratoga (CV-3) and light carrier USS Princeton (CVL-23), approached Rabaul from the east on Love Day, November 1, 1943, to attack Bougainville airfields at Bonis and Buka. The use of carriers in the Solomons would have been considered suicidal one year before.

VF-17 first tasted combat on November 1, 1943, during the invasion of Cape Torokina, in Bougainville, when Vals and Zekes with some Tony fighters appeared over Empress Augusta Bay at 0900. The "Jolly Rogers" intercepted the aerial armada and shot down six Zekes, helping to break

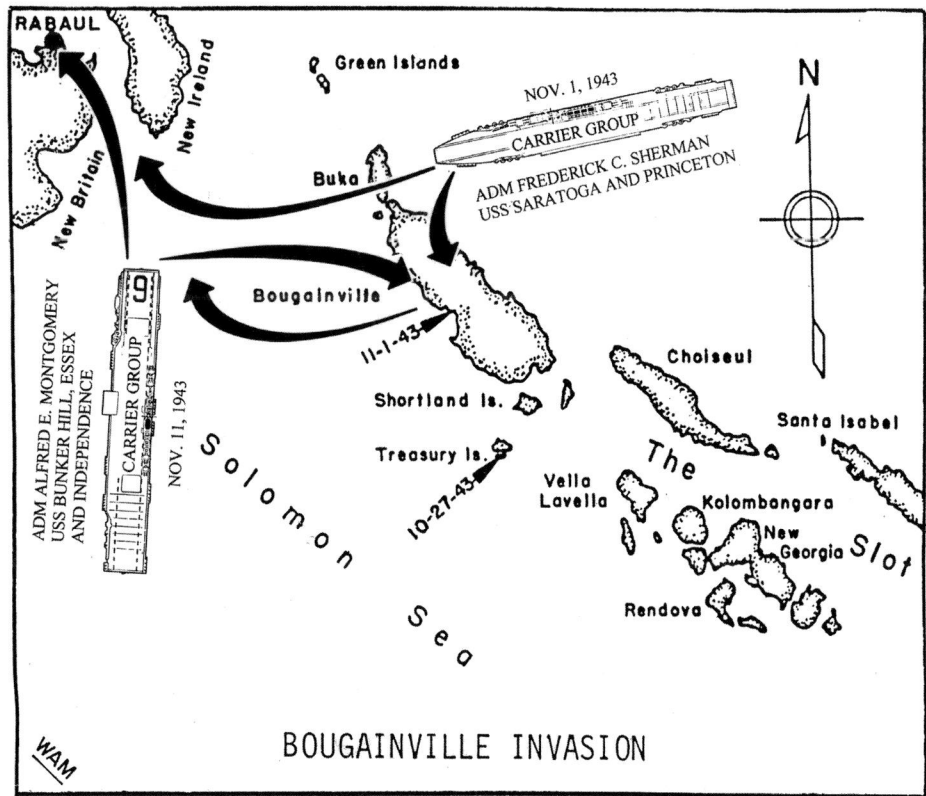

The air attack on Rabaul and Bougainville was conducted by U.S. land-based and carrier-based aircraft in a well-coordinated operation.

ENS Ira C. "Ike" Kepford flew Combat Air Patrol for U.S. carriers raiding Rabaul on November 11, 1943. Alone, and never before in combat, he shot down four attacking Japanese aircraft; saved a U.S. aircraft carrier from destruction; landed on a U.S. carrier to refuel and rearm; and then made the one and one-half hour flight back to his airfield. He earned the Navy Cross for his heroism. (Courtesy of LCDR Ira C. Kepford)

up the attack. LCDR Roger Hedrick scored his first victory during this interception, destroying a Japanese Army Tony fighter.

Capt James E. Swett of VMF-221, who had lost contact with the remainder of his Corsair division, joined USAAF Lightnings and shot down two Val dive bombers. He then dived down to rescue a New Zealand Kittyhawk pilot who had several Tonys on his tail, setting one afire.

Ten days later, November 11, 1943, Adm. Alfred E. Montgomery joined RADM Sherman with his aircraft carriers USS Bunker Hill (CV-17), USS Essex (CV-9), and the light aircraft carrier USS Independence (CVL-22) approaching Rabaul from south of the bastion and launched air attacks. One of the objectives was also to lure the hundreds of Rabaul airplanes away from the Empress Augusta Bay invasion.

By the end of 1943 the U.S. Navy had received sufficient numbers of new Essex Class aircraft carriers and Independence Class light aircraft carriers, constructed by a half-dozen shipyards, to risk employing aircraft carriers to break the Bismarck Barrier.

"Jolly Rogers" arrived at the carriers shortly after a carrier strike had launched, so they joined a Hellcat squadron from the carriers to assist in Combat Air Patrol. The VMF-17 Corsairs landed and took off from the carriers to refuel and rearm, despite the fact that this was forbidden by "regulations" because the Corsair was not "qualified" for carrier operation!

ENS Ira C. "Ike" Kepford, a 24 year old former star quarterback at Northwestern University who had never experienced combat, became part of the carriers' CAP. After the "Jolly Rogers" had been on station for three hours without sighting any Japanese aircraft, LCDR Blackburn decided to return to Ondonga, New Georgia. Shortly after he made this decision all hell broke loose; more than 100 Val dive bombers, Kate torpedo bombers, and Zero and Tony fighters bore down on Adm Montgomery's carriers.

As ENS Kepford turned back to the carriers he ran into a group of Vals that had already dropped their load of bombs and were returning to Rabaul. Alone, "Ike" attacked at once and, in his first taste of combat, shot down three and damaged a fourth dive bomber. Nearing USS Bunker Hill, the lone aviator spotted a single Kate torpedo bomber trailing the carrier ready to launch its torpedo into the carrier's wake. As the Kate ran into a hail of antiaircraft fire, Kepford was right behind the Japanese, closing fast and braving the ship's guns. The tyro moved in close and blasted the Kate with all six guns, sending the torpedo bomber into the Bunker Hill's turbulent wake. ENS Ira C. "Ike" Kepford had saved the aircraft carrier single-handedly!

The Corsairs had been operating beyond the limit of their range, forcing two to ditch into the sea. ENS Robert H. Hill destroyed a dive bomber before he ran out of fuel and was rescued by a PT Boat. ENS Bradford W. Baker flamed a Zero before his engine stopped and he also ditched. He was picked up by a Catalina.

Kepford's fuel was so low that he knew he couldn't make the return flight to Ondonga. He was also out of ammunition. When a third Japanese strike appeared, Kepford was helpless and was forced to circle slowly overhead, watching the battle. At the first opportunity the intrepid aviator landed on Bunker Hill to replenish his fuel and ammunition.

When ENS Kepford finally made the one and one-half hour flight back to Ondonga, he had flown eleven of the previous fourteen hours and shot down four Japanese aircraft of the 18.5 claimed by VF-17 on that day. He also made two carrier landings and earned the Navy Cross for his heroism.

LCDR John T. Blackburn scored his fourth victory on that day, November 11, 1943. ENS Frederick J. Streig also scored a victory.

Three "Jolly Rogers" that scored victories during the Bougainville invasion stand before one of their beloved Corsairs. L to R: VF-17 XO LCDR Roger R. Hedrick shot down the first of his twelve victory score on November 1, 1943; VF-17 CO LCDR John T. "Tommy" Blackburn destroyed four of his eleven victory score on November 11, 1943; and LTJG Ira C. "Ike" Kepford shot down four of his 16 victory score on November 11, 1943. (National Archives, Author's File)

Chapter IV: Corsairs Break the Bismarck Barrier

"Jolly Roger" Lt Merl W. "Butch" Davenport scored 6.25 of VF-17's 127 Solomons victory total. At the time this photo was taken Davenport was credited with 5.25 victories and officially an Ace. (U.S. Navy (USMC) Photo, Courtesy A.E. Ferko)

The twin runways of the Japanese-built Torokina airfield on Bougainville's Empress Augusta Bay were renovated by U.S. Construction Battalions. This water's-edge field is much larger than it appears. The specks at the near end of the field are Corsairs. (U.S. Navy Photo, USMC, Author's File)

Late in the morning of November 17, 1943, 55 Zekes escorted ten dive bombers to attack eight troop transports and ten destroyers in Empress Augusta Bay; however, a large patrol of U.S. Army, Navy, and Marine planes was waiting for them and shot down 16 of the raiders. Three were shot down by VMF-221 CO Major Nathan T. Post Jr., and another three were destroyed by Lt. Harold E. Segal of the same squadron.

Three days later Major Donald H. Stapp of VMF-222 shot down a prowling Betty reconnaissance-bomber at 7,000 ft for his fourth victory.

The final episode of the "Jolly Rogers" participation in the Empress Augusta Bay confrontation occurred on 21 November when Lt. Merl W. "Butch" Davenport's division intercepted a half-dozen Zekes while the Japanese were involved in early morning strafing of U.S. troops and equipment. All six Zekes were destroyed, two by Lt. Davenport.

The "Jolly Rogers" had earned R&R and were not to return to action until January 1944.

The Solomon Islands had been taken by Britain in 1900, then by the Japanese in 1942. Captured by U.S. forces in 1943, they became an independent country in 1978.

Lost to Australia by Germany during the First World War, Rabaul and the Bismarck Archipelago fell to the Japanese advance in January 1942. The Bismarck Archipelago is named after Prince Otto von Bismarck, Chancellor of Imperial Germany before the First World War.

The island of Bougainville is named for Louis-Antoine de Bougainville (1729-1891), a French navigator and explorer.

The success of "Operation Cherryblossom," the Empress Augusta Bay invasion, opened a beachhead of six by eight miles through which Allied troops poured ashore on Bougainville. The objective was not to occupy all of this largest of the Solomon Islands that was fraught with volcanic peaks and impenetrable rain forests. The plan was to operate from airfields near the beachhead, isolating several thousand Japanese to the South while battering them and the 40,000 Japanese in the North with air power.

An airstrip was quickly constructed on Stirling Island on October 27, 1943. In rapid succession three airfields were completed on Bougainville: one on Torokina Point and the two airstrips of Piva South (Yoke) and Piva North (Uncle), which were less than half the distance to Rabaul than those on Guadalcanal, facilitating fighter strikes against Rabaul from the "springboard."

The stage was set for the strangulation of Rabaul and destroying the "Bismarck Barrier" with air power. The three Bougainville Allied airfields

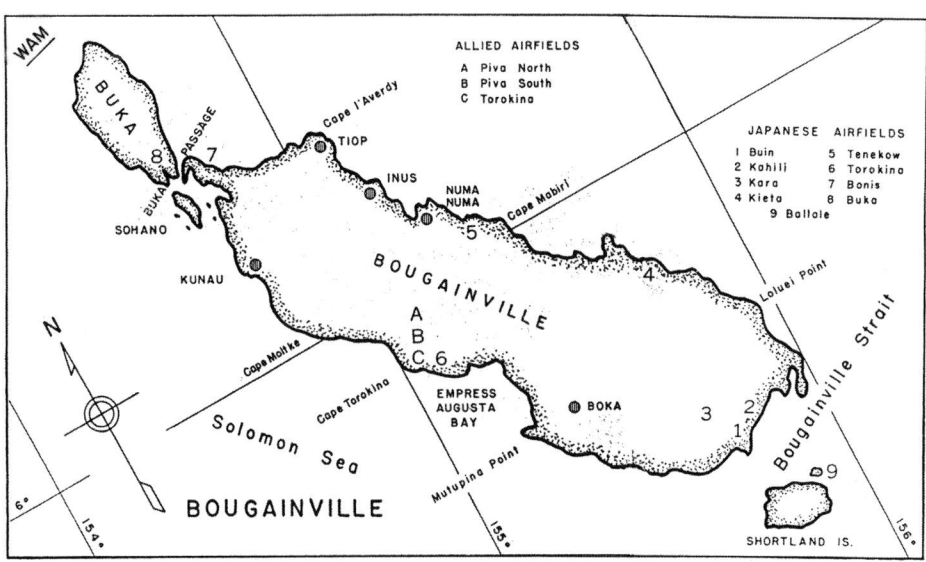

With nine Japanese airfields surrounding three Allied airfields, it required a superhuman effort to simultaneously suppress the Bougainville airfields and pound the Rabaul airfields.

115

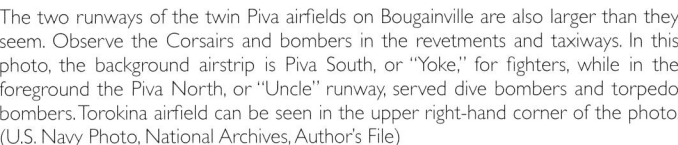

The two runways of the twin Piva airfields on Bougainville are also larger than they seem. Observe the Corsairs and bombers in the revetments and taxiways. In this photo, the background airstrip is Piva South, or "Yoke," for fighters, while in the foreground the Piva North, or "Uncle" runway, served dive bombers and torpedo bombers. Torokina airfield can be seen in the upper right-hand corner of the photo. (U.S. Navy Photo, National Archives, Author's File)

This unusual photo shows the overrun area at the left end of Piva Yoke airstrip. In an emergency landing aircraft that could not stop at the end of the runway were able to continue into the overrun area rather than crash into the tropical forest or coconut plantation. (Photo by and Courtesy of Lt. Loren C Stricklin, VMF-211)

were mainly for the "short-legged" fighters, dive bombers, and torpedo bombers, while the heavy B-24, PB4Y, and medium B-25 bombers were usually based at more remote airfields.

At the onset, the three American airfields were surrounded by nine well-established Japanese airfields that menaced the new airfields. The Bougainville Corsair aviators had to neutralize the existing Japanese airfields while attacking Rabaul's airfields.

Upon his arrival in Bougainville with VF-17, Lt. Merl W. "Butch" Davenport scored two more Zekes on January 3, 1944, and became an Ace when he shot down another for his 5.25 victory on 5 February. His final total was 6.25 Japanese aircraft destroyed.

After establishing three airfields in Bougainville in November 1943, Allied commanders turned their attention to the neutralization of Rabaul.

Air Sols, USAAF, USMC, and USN aerial armadas bombed and strafed the area while U.S. Navy surface ships and submarines cut its supply lines.

VF-17 and VMF-215 were two of the many fighter squadrons that contributed to the more than 3,000 sorties during the first three weeks of February 1944. Second in importance after Rabaul, on the island of New Britain, was Kavieng, on the Northwestern tip of New Ireland. Both are in the Bismarck Archipelago.

Rabaul is located at the Northeastern tip of the island of New Britain and was protected by five airfields. It is also located in a harbor, within a bay, and volcanic peaks that afford more protection. A total of twelve airfields defended the island of New Britain. The naval commander of Rabaul was the very competent Rear Admiral Jinichi Kusaka, who was

Corsairs as far as the eye can see! Either just returning from a mission or preparing for a new mission, this gathering of Corsairs on Piva South (Yoke) airfield is awe inspiring. (Vought Aircraft Photo, Courtesy H.J. "Jerry" Dalton, Jr.)

Rear Admiral Jinichi Kusaka was the naval commander at Rabaul. A competent leader, Kusaka was overwhelmed by the incessant aerial bombardment and strafing, and the wavering support of Admiral Koga. (National Archives, Author's File)

Chapter IV: Corsairs Break the Bismarck Barrier

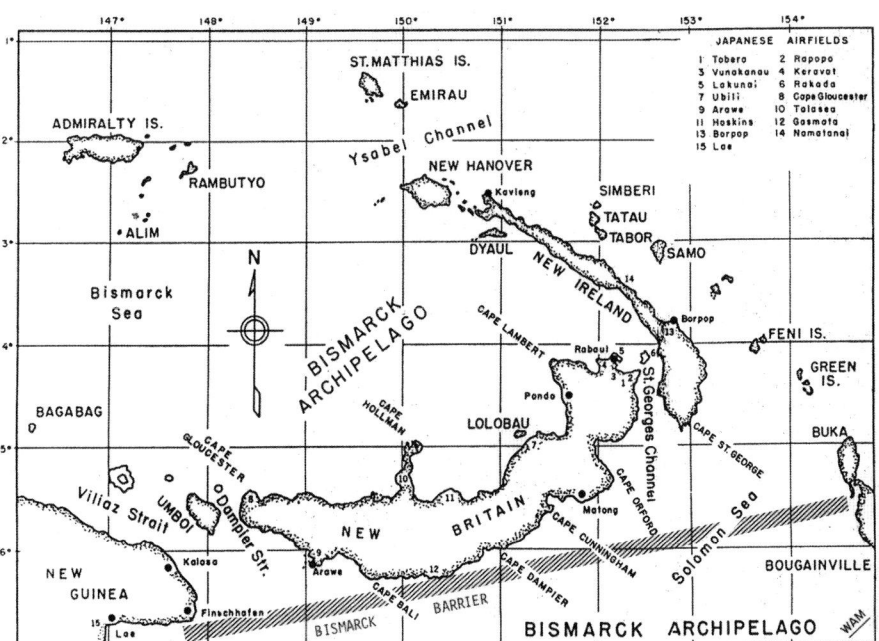

Protected by New Ireland and several airfields, Rabaul was in the ideal location to control the "Bismarck Barrier" and fend off air and sea attacks. After losing some outer islands the bastion was vanquished by the Allies.

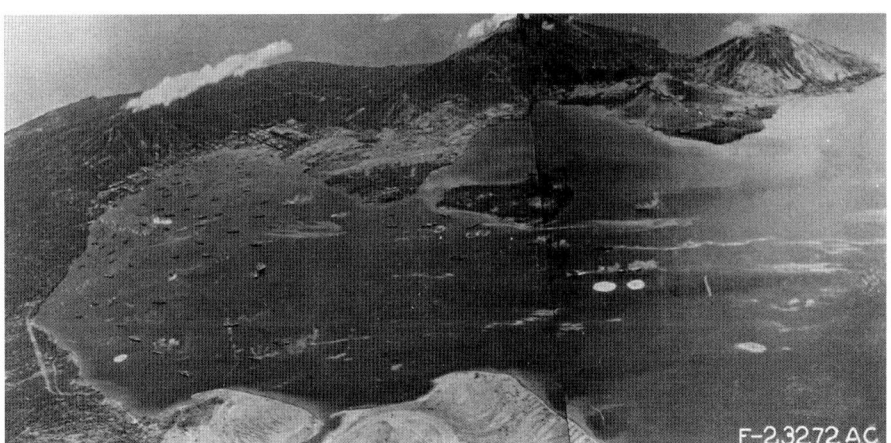

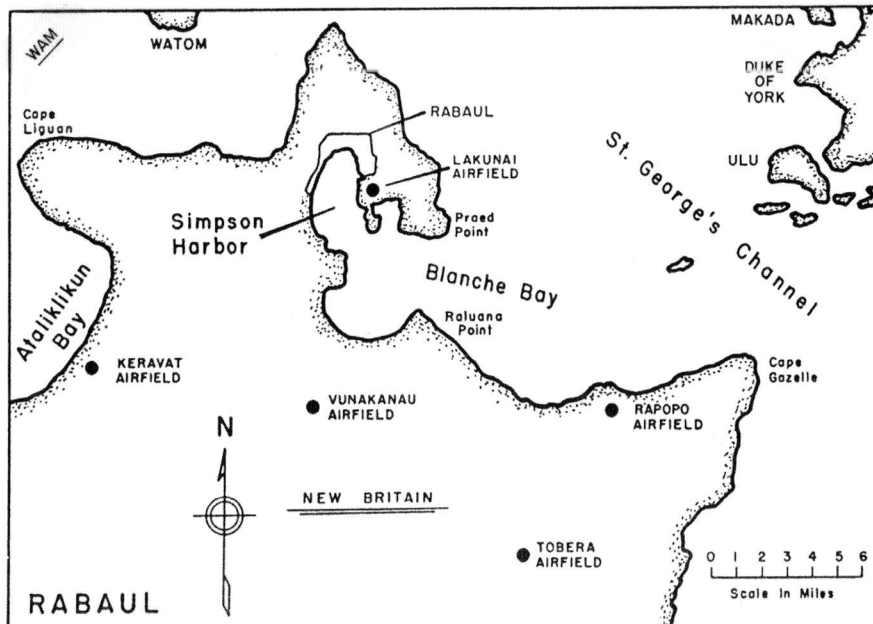

Ideally located within Simpson Harbor and protected by Blanche Bay and volcanic peaks, Rabaul was well suited to defend itself. Photo was taken during an anti-shipping raid by USAAC bombers. Note the bomb explosion rings in the water and the abundance of ships in the harbor. (U.S. Army Air Corps Photo, Author's File)

This close-up of Rabaul reveals a sizeable city and not a mere settlement. It also appears to have a railway linking two ends of the city. (U.S. Navy Photo, Author's File)

not able to hold the Bismarck Barrier because of incessant U.S. air attacks and the indecisive support of Admiral Koga.

By January 14, 1944, Blanche Bay and Simpson Harbor was still busy with shipping, delivering guns, ammunition, food, and other necessities of life. The U.S. Marines' first shipping strike on that date consisted of 16 Avenger Torpedo bombers and 36 Dauntless dive bombers with an umbrella of Corsairs.

Nine hits were made on seven ships; all were seriously damaged but none sank. Of the armada of intercepting fighters, 29 were shot down, 19 of them by VMF-115 led by Maj Robert Owens.

A veteran of the Pearl Harbor attack, Major Robert G. Owens, Jr succeeded Lt. Col Herbert H. Williamson as CO of VMF-215 "Fighting Corsairs" on December 6, 1943, after serving as the unit's Executive Officer.

Major Owens was a dedicated leader who not only conducted squadron business, but led his unit into battle without seeking victories at his aviators' expense. The author received a letter from one of Major Owens' former aviators, who stated "He was an excellent CO and a damned fine leader. We all liked him." Major Owens scored seven official victories and was awarded the Navy Cross, Distinguished Flying Cross with four Gold Stars in lieu of second through eleventh awards for the Solomons/Bismarck fighting.

Major Robert G. Owens Jr, CO of VMF-215, scored seven victories and four probables. He scored official victories as follows: Zero (August 21, 1943); Zero (August 22, 1943; Zero (August 30, 1943); two Zeros (January 14, 1944); Zero (January 22, 1943); and a Tojo (January 24, 1944). Major Owens had 160 combat hours to his credit during 55 missions. Bob Owens' Corsair F4U-1 "My Fran" is named in honor of his wife, the former Frances Hart. (Defense Dept. Photo, USMC)

From left to right, the three leading Aces of VMF-215 "Fighting Corsairs" are: Lt Robert M. Hanson, 25 victories; Capt Donald N. Aldrich, 20 victories; and Capt Harold L. Spears, 15 victories. Observe the abbreviated attire necessary in the tropics. (Defense Dept. Photo, National Archives)

Chapter IV: Corsairs Break the Bismarck Barrier

Robert M. "Butcher Bob" Hanson scored 20 victories in only 13 days. The victor over 25 Japanese planes was the No.2 U.S. Marine Ace and the highest scoring Corsair Ace, having shot down all of his victories while flying a Corsair. (Defense Dept. Photo, USMC, Author's File)

Operations from Torokina began in December with bomber escorts and fighter sweeps over Rabaul. Major Owens' quiet leadership instilled confidence and accomplishment in the VMF-215 aviators that three rose above the average as the "Fighting Corsairs" star performers.

Top scorers of VMF-215 were Lt. Robert M. Hanson (25 Vict); Capt Donald N. Aldrich (20 Vict); and Capt Harold L. Spears (15 Vict). Their combined scores of 60 victories almost equaled half of the squadron's total of 135.5 official victories!

Lt. Robert M. Hanson became the second highest scoring Ace of the USMC in WW-2. He had completed two tours of duty while hammering Bougainville during Autumn 1943. Despite the fact that he was eligible to receive R&R after his first tour, he elected to remain on duty. "Butcher Bob" scored five victories during his first and second combat tours. He reasoned that with this combat experience he would be more valuable during his third combat tour and he was right.

Flying from Torokina during Hanson's first flight into the Rabaul area, the "Fighting Corsairs" were escorting USAAC Mitchell B-25 bombers on a ship bombing run in Simpson Harbor on January 18, 1944. Intercepted by a force of 70 Japanese fighters, the "Fighting Corsairs" promptly attacked and an enormous battle ensued. "Butcher Bob" sped into the center of the melee in his customary fashion, disregarding danger and death and, when he emerged, he had become a double ace with five more victories!

On his second and third sorties, Hanson shot down one and three Japanese aircraft respectively. The Ace's fourth flight was another bombing raid over Simpson harbor on 24 January. The lone Corsair struck at the Zeros with such devastating fury that he not only eluded certain death, but shot down four Zeros and forced the Japanese to break off their attack on the bombers. "Butcher Bob" was on his way to becoming the U.S. Marine Ace of Aces. His next sortie added three more to the growing score. Hanson's following sortie added three more victories to his score, and he now had 21 victories.

In the late afternoon of 30 January, VMF-215 escorted Grumman TBF Avenger torpedo bombers to the Rabaul area and protected the bombers as they sank a 3,000 ton Japanese ship. Of the 21 Japanese planes shot down during this action, Hanson destroyed four to bring his total to 25. His last 20 victories were scored in only 13 days!

First Lieutenant Robert M. Hanson was in great spirits as he prepared to take off in his Corsair on the morning of February 3, 1944. It was the day before his 24th birthday, and his third tour of duty would be over in a few days. The Ace had planned to go to the United States for a well-earned rest and then return to the South Pacific to continue his phenomenal military career. The task that morning was to escort bombers to Rabaul and then strafe gun emplacements near Cape St. George, on the island of New Ireland. Cape St. George is only about 50 miles from Rabaul and in the path of any planes flying from Bougainville to Rabaul. Surely, the Japanese at the gun emplacements either saw or heard the Americans heading toward Rabaul and were "on the ready" for the returning bombers and Corsairs. The element of surprise that was so important for any strafing attack was non-existent.

Capt Donald N. Aldrich scored 20 victories in an action-packed career in VMF-215 and became the fifth highest scoring ace of the USMC in WWII. Even when wounded he pressed the fight against the enemy. (Defense Dept. Photo, USMC, Author's File)

Don Aldrich is shown in one of the Corsairs he flew to victory. At least two of the Ace's Corsairs were so badly damaged in dogfights that they had to be scrapped when he returned to his airfield. Capt Aldrich was twice wounded by shrapnel from Zero cannon but he continued the fight. (Defense Dept., USMC, Courtesy A.E. Ferko)

shrapnel from the exploding cannon shells. Instead of leaving the dogfight, however, the intrepid aviator remained with the bombers and, through his superior flying, he not only assisted in driving off the Japanese fighters, but even succeeded in scoring one of his attackers.

During another bomber escort mission in the Solomons on September 2, 1943, the three guns in one wing sustained cannon hits and failed to fire. Undaunted, Don Aldrich pressed the fight on the enemy interceptors, drove them off, and destroyed one Zero.

Aldrich ended his first combat tour with five victories, which classified him as an ace. During his second combat tour he ran his victories up to 20 by scoring fifteen victories in less than a month while protecting bombers on raids over Rabaul! During this time, on January 28, 1944, Don was occupied with his job of protecting the bombers over Rabaul when Japanese interceptors appeared in force. While absorbed with sending one of the enemy to his doom Aldrich was jumped by six Zeros. He failed to see the attackers until it was too late, and 20mm shells were already tearing into the rugged Corsair. Suddenly, a shell exploded in the cockpit, sending razor-sharp pieces of jagged shrapnel deep into his shoulder and leg. Aldrich, instead of breaking away and speeding for his airfield, turned and attacked his adversaries.

The Japanese aviators were caught by surprise and Don Aldrich shot down three more Zeros in rapid succession. The last Mitsubishi erupted in flames after it was hit by a short burst at long range. Captain Aldrich then

During the strafing runs, anti-aircraft fire increased with each successive attack. When Hanson put his Corsair into a shallow dive, aiming at the ground targets, he was met by withering anti-aircraft fire from large and small caliber weapons. Suddenly Hanson's six machine guns ceased firing, but the Corsair remained on course. The nose then rose slightly and the Bent-Wing Corsair raced across the target and out over the waters of St. George's Channel. Still, it maintained its earth-bound attitude: lower, lower, then a tremendous splash. When the churned waters were still again, the aviator and his aircraft had disappeared. The Solomon Sea had swallowed the brave, young American, and a careful search of the area revealed no trace of man nor machine. Apparently the intense anti-aircraft fire had killed or seriously wounded Hanson, causing him to lose control of his Corsair over the target. A terrible example of strafing without surprise, following inept planning by those who direct but don't fly.

The Medal of Honor was posthumously awarded to the heroic Lieutenant for gallantry during the actions of November 1, 1943, and January 24, 1944. The highest United States medal was presented to the Ace's mother, Mrs. Harry A. Hanson, by Maj Gen Lewis G. Murrit on August 19, 1944.

There is no doubt, in some quarters, that had the fatal accident not occurred, Lt. Robert M. Hanson, with his tremendous potential, would have continued to increase his score and possibly become the leading Allied ace of the war. He was, however, the leading Corsair Ace of all time.

Capt Donald N. Aldrich became the fifth highest scoring Ace of the USMC in WW-2, shooting down every one of his 20 victories more than 200 miles from the nearest friendly airfield.

On August 26, 1943, while escorting bombers Capt Aldrich was attacked by several intercepting Zeros. The Japanese shooting was most accurate, and the American found his Corsair full of gaping holes that caused serious damage. Furthermore, his body was pierced with flying

Known for his relentlessly furious and aggressive attacks on intercepting fighters, Capt Harold L. Spears scored 15 victories in six months. He returned to CONUS, where he was integrated into the regular Marine Corps from the Reserves on November 1, 1944. (Defense Dept. Photo, USMC, Author's File)

Chapter IV: Corsairs Break the Bismarck Barrier

nursed the Corsair for 200 miles back to Torokina airstrip, on Bougainville, where he landed with no flaps, one flat tire, and 105 bullet holes in the aircraft. His great flying ability and the ruggedness of his Corsair enabled the wounded Ace to walk away (with assistance) from the landing.

One week later saw Aldrich back in action when he shot down two more Zeros on February 7, 1944.

Two days later, February 9, 1944, the rugged, 180lb six foot Ace was in the air again, scoring his 20th victory to conclude his combat carrier.

The Ace was awarded the Distinguished Flying Cross, Air Medal, Purple Heart, and Gold Star in lieu of a second Purple Heart.

Tenth on the list of USMC Aces was Capt Harold L. Spears, who fought through the Solomons campaign up to Rabaul, scoring 15 official victories. He scored his first four victories on August 18 and 19 and on September 2, 1943, for which he received the Air Medal. Spears was awarded a second Air Medal for his strafing attacks against ground targets on Bougainville and was promoted to Captain in December.

By January 18, 1944, the action had moved to Rabaul. On this day, Spears became an ace when he shot down his fifth, sixth, and seventh Zeros while escorting USAAC B-25 Mitchell bombers on a raid over this Japanese stronghold. Two more Zeros went down before his blazing guns two days later, and on the 22nd of that month he scored his tenth victory, becoming a double-ace. Four days later he destroyed his 11th and 12th Zeros over New Britain.

Captain Spears was awarded the Distinguished Flying Cross for heroism in early February when he became a division leader.

The Ace was escorting bombers on February 3, 1944, when several flights of Japanese fighters slipped between the bombers and the fighters. Spears' division was closest to the interceptors, but the Corsairs were heavily outnumbered. Despite this disadvantage the Marine Ace sped after the Japanese and, with relentless fury, he broke up the attack on the bombers. During the melee Spears shot down two more Japanese fighters. Under virtually the same conditions the Captain destroyed his 15th fighter over Rabaul on February 7, 1944.

Spears was ordered to return to the United States and was stationed at the Marine Corps Air Station, El Toro, California. On November 1, 1944, Spears was integrated into the regular Marine Corps from the Reserves, and he planned to make a career in that service. He was assigned to VMF-462 at El Toro pending another tour of duty in the Pacific.

On December 6, 1944, Capt Spears had just completed a routine flight and was in the process of landing when the plane crashed into the ground, killing the Ace.

A half-dozen VMF-215 Corsairs are being maintained in a Torokina revetment on January 18, 1944. Corsair No. 735 was flown by Capt A. Roger Conent after he scored a Zero—one of his six victories. Observe the incomplete insignia bar. (USMC-National Archives, Author's File)

At the time of his death, Capt Harold L. Spears was survived by his wife, the former Mary Anderson, and his mother Mrs. Stanton Davis.

On January 24, 1944, the unbelievable happened; Major Robert Owens, VMF-215 CO, was shot down by his own wingman! Capt Arthur Roger Conant (known as Roger Conant) had been Maj Owens' wingman for a long time, and then was assigned to command his own flight. Recruits in the squadron averaged age 18 or 19 years old and were shepardrd by the experienced aviators, assigned as wingmen. One of the inexperienced youngsters became Major Owens' wingman, replacing Capt Conant.

The new wingman's first sortie with the squadron was escorting Dauntless dive bombers and Avenger torpedo bombers. As the "Fighting Corsairs" approach their target they intercepted Japanese Val dive bombers attacking shipping while escorted by Zeros. As Owens went into a shallow dive to cover the American bombers his novice wingman passed him about three times! Apparently confused and/or frightened the young wingman was everywhere except where he belonged; alongside the leader, slightly behind and above.

With the mission accomplished, the Americans regrouped and headed south, with the Corsairs covering the bombers from above and behind. Maj Owens flew in a wide circle to cover any stragglers when he spotted a lone Tony stalking the stragglers. The Major closed in with a short burst

Recuperating Major Robert Owens and VMF-215 "Fighting Corsairs" aviators, ground crew, and mechanic well-wishers were filmed at Vella Lavella shortly after the Major was shot down by his tyro wingman. Owens' official wingman, Capt Conant, is shown kneeling at extreme left (with cap). (USMC Photo, Courtesy Maj Gen Robert G. Owens Jr, USMC)

The "Boneyard" at Torokina includes USAAF, Navy, and Marine aircraft: Upper Photo: Corsairs with bent propellers. Center Photo: A badly damaged P-39 Aircobra. Lower Photo: This Corsair has a bubble canopy stowed on the fuselage, possibly intended to replace the "birdcage" canopy as a "field-mod?" (USMC Photos, Author's File)

Four "Jolly Rogers" fly in echelon formation: No.29, LTJG Ira Cassius "Ike" Kepford (16 Vict.); No.8, LTJG Robert "Hal" Jackson (4.5 Vict.); No.3, LTJG Frederick J Streig (5.5 Vict.); and No.28, ENS Wilbert P. Popp (3 Vict.). (U.S. Navy Photo, Courtesy Ling-Temco-Vought, Arthur L Schoeni)

as both planes were turning, knocking off a Tony wing at the root. The sudden loss of lift on one side flipped the Tony into the Corsair's curving path, forcing Owens to reverse his flight path.

Suddenly, the Major's Corsair shuddered with a loud noise and burst into flame. Owens quickly ditched his burning plane while his aviators threw their dye markers in the water to mark Maj. Owens' location. Within a half-hour a PBY Catalina rescued the downed Major from Blanche Bay.

Apparently Owens' inexperienced wingman had also been firing at the Tony and, when the Major was forced to change course, he flew into his wingman's barrage of .50 caliber bullets. Of course, the youngster should not have been shooting at all!

When the story got to ComAirSols it was assumed that Maj Owens was shot down by his well-known wingman, Capt Conant.

On February 26, 1944, Major Robert G. Owens Jr was assigned to Marine Fleet Air, West Coast, as Commander of Marine Air Group Six aboard aircraft carriers.

VMF-215 reformed with new personnel in March 1944 under command of Maj James K. Dill and served on Emerau in the summer of 1944. In September the "Fighting Corsairs" left Emerau for CONUS as a replacement-training squadron under command of Lt. Col William A. Millington.

A VMF-222 "Flying Deuces" crewman is "running through" the propeller of a Corsair F4U-1 in spring 1944. Propeller need be only partially rotated to prime the engine while the ignition switch is off. VMF-222 aces were 2nd Lieut CD Jones (6 Vict) and Maj DH Stapp (10 Vict). (U.S. Navy Photo, USMC, Author's File)

Chapter IV: Corsairs Break the Bismarck Barrier

LCDR John T. "Tommy" Blackburn (in Pith Helmet) poses with members of VF-17 before his F4U-1A Corsair "Big Hog" that refers to the Corsair's long cylindrical nose resembling a swine's snout. Radiating to the left of Blackburn are March, Guttenhurst, and Wharton. Radiating to the right of Blackburn are Dr. Hermann (Flight Surgeon) and LTJG Taylor. (U.S. Navy Photo, Author's File)

Upper Photo: Double Ace LTJG John M. Smith scored ten victories while flying with VF-17 "Jolly Rogers" and VF-84. During several raids on Vunakanau and Lakunai airfields on New Britain, Smith shot down Japanese interceptors without abandoning the bombers he was escorting. He was awarded the Air Medal and Gold Star for this achievement. (U.S. Navy Photo, U.S. National Archives) Lower Photo: The six "Jolly Rogers" in flight gear are L to R Standing: Lt Harry A. "Dirty Harry" March Jr. (5 Vict.); Lt Carl W. Gilbert (1 Vict.); and Lt Walter J. Schub (4.25 Vict.). Kneeling: LTJG Whitney C. Wharton (2 Vict.); ENS Frank A. Jagger (2 Vict.); and LTJG Harold J. Bitzegaio (2 Vict.). (U.S. Navy Photo, Author's File)

"Jolly Rogers" pose with propeller blades emblazoned with 47 victory flags of their final 156 victories. Observe the living quarters constructed of wood and canvas and the towering coconut trees. (U.S. Navy Photo, Author's File)

Corsair: The Saga of the Legendary Bent-Wing Fighter-Bomber

LTJG Kepford's battered Corsair rests where it stopped, adjoining the Piva Yoke runway, as mechanics inspect the damage. Observe the crumpled fuselage rear, flat tire, and perforated wing and wing flap. The fuselage sports only ten victory flags in lieu of the thirteen victories the Ace had scored before this fateful flight on February 19, 1944. (Photo by and Courtesy of Lt. Loren C Stricklin, VMF-211)

One of the several preliminaries required before an aircraft engine is started is called "running through" the propeller in order to draw a spray of fuel into the engine cylinders called "priming" to insure prompt ignition when the starter is actuated. The operation can be done manually because the propeller need be only partially rotated.

VF-17 "Jolly Rogers" had 13 aces; more than any other Navy squadron in WW-2. In 76 days of combat the unit shot down 156 enemy aircraft and sank five transport ships and invasion barges. After flying 8,577 combat man-hours, VF-17 lost only 20 planes and 12 aviators, four to antiaircraft fire. No ship covered by the "Jolly Rogers" was ever hit by bomb or torpedo, nor any bomber escorted by VF-17 ever shot down!

Returning from R&R the "Jolly Rogers" of VF-17 were flying from Piva Yoke (South) airfield by early January 1944. By this time Ira C. Kepford had been promoted to Lieutenant Junior Grade (LTJG).

On January 29, 1944, LTJG Kepford was part of a bomber escort on a strike against Tobero airfield, on New Britain, which defended the Japanese base of Rabaul. The defending Japanese fighters outnumbered the Corsairs, but the former football hero led his wingman, ENS Don Mc Queen, in an attack on twelve enemy fighters, resulting in four victories for Kepford, which brought his score to thirteen victories.

Before the ground crew had time to finish adding all the new victory flags to Kepford's Corsair, the Ace was flying one of 26 Corsairs led by VF-17 XO Roger Hedrick. The "Jolly Rogers" joined with 72 Dauntless Dive Bombers and Grumman Avenger Torpedo Bombers to "beat-up" airfields in the Rabaul area. This foray was to be the most harrowing combat experience that LTJG "Ike" Kepford ever experienced.

It might be of interest that many of the American aviators wore only a pair of shorts, tennis shoes, and a summer coverall flying suit on combat missions because of the oppressive heat and humidity.

On Saturday, February 19, 1944, Hedrick's force assembled at 8:00 in the morning and headed for Rabaul. As Kepford's division approached New Ireland, his wingman was forced to fly back to Bougainville because of engine trouble. Under normal conditions Kepford would also be compelled to leave the flight because the skies near Rabaul were full of Japanese fighters, and no Allied plane was permitted in the area without his wingman. Mission leader Hedrick made an exception in Kepford's case, but when the Americans arrived at the target area the Ace was ordered to return to Piva Yoke because of the strong Japanese interception.

LCDR Roger R. Hedrick, XO of VF-17, led the February 19, 1944, raid on New Britain. He is credited with nine official victories in "Jolly Rogers" and another three victories as CO of VF-84 in 1945 flying Corsairs. (U.S. Navy Photo, National Archives, Author's File)

Lt Oscar I. "Oc" Chenoweth, former XO of VF-38 with two planes to his credit, scored seven victories in the February 19, 1944, raid on Tobera airfield. His final official tally is 10.5 victories. He is quoted as saying this about the Corsair: "It would run circles around any other aircraft in the Pacific." (U.S. Navy Photo, National Archives, Author's File)

Chapter IV: Corsairs Break the Bismarck Barrier

ENS Andrew Jagger exhibits unrestrained enthusiasm as he describes his 19 February victory over New Britain to Lt H.A. "Dirty Harry" March. (U.S. Navy Photo, National Archives, Author's File)

As Kepford lost sight of the "Jolly Rogers" he spotted a lone Rufe floatplane fighter far below. A quick dive and a short six-gun burst sent the smoking Rufe into St. Georges Channel. "Ike" Kepford had little time to enjoy his fourteenth victory because when he looked up he saw an armada of Zero and Tojo fighters high above at 16,000ft and between him and Bougainville. The Ace dropped to wavetop level hoping that the forty-odd enemy fighters would not detect his Corsair because it was dark blue, as was the water. Too late; two Tojos and two Zeros peeled off the formation and dived at the lone Corsair for what they expected would be an easy kill.

The Ace opened his throttle and banked away from the impending doom swooping down upon him. The diving Japanese fighters had gained tremendous speed during their dive and, therefore, as the leading Zero opened fire, Kepford "popped" his flaps only about 50 feet above the water, forcing the Japanese aviator to overrun his target. As the Zero flashed by "Ike" opened fire for a split second and shattered the Mitsubishi stabilizer, sending the plane crashing into the waves for victory No.14.

The remaining Japanese fighters now had the Corsair neatly boxed, with two Tojos on the right and the Zero on the left. Furthermore, the American found himself speeding in the wrong direction, and every second of this chase brought him closer toward Japanese-held islands. In fact, he was virtually over the tip of Japanese-held New Ireland.

In desperation Kepford remembered the water/alcohol injection system and forced the throttle beyond its normal full power position, breaking the stop wire, and cutting in the injection system, which produced unbelievable power for a few minutes. The big fighter shuddered and then surged forward with a burst of speed. Kepford observed that his pursuers were dropping farther and farther behind, but he could no longer continue in the wrong direction. In a sudden maneuver he turned violently to the left in an effort to escape the trap, but the Zero began to turn inside of the Corsair's flight path. As he skimmed over the water, Kepford fought to keep his Corsair from stalling while the Zero pilot began firing.

Suddenly, the Zero wingtip dug into the water and the plane cartwheeled across the surface, disintegrated, and sank. The two Tojo fighters, meanwhile, had been sucked wide during the turn and now fell so far behind the Corsair that they gave up the chase.

Throttled back and leaning the mixture to conserve fuel, Kepford headed for Piva Yoke airstrip on Bougainville, under the unbearably hot sun two hundred miles away. Slowly, almost by rote, the Ace made his approach over Empress Augusta Bay. In the air over four hours, he was exhausted and his fuel was almost gone. Dropping his speed to 115 mph, he made a rough landing that caused his propeller to chop at the runway and stall the engine. Kepford's trusty Corsair then rolled off the runway to a grinding stop.

LTJG Kepford sat limp in the cockpit. There were tears in his eyes, and he was trembling in shock. He had looked death in the eye and won! Unable to speak, he was put to bed for a few days until he could be debriefed and tell his story. He had perspired so heavily that it rolled down his legs and turned his tennis shoes green!

The Corsair's flaps were in tatters, wings punctured, the fuselage rear was mangled, the stabilizer was seriously damaged, and both tires had been punctured.

The plane could never fly again.

Kepford's use of "popping flaps" (extending the wing flaps during maneuvers) and using the water/alcohol injection was one of the first deployments of these life-saving tactics in combat.

With sleeves rolled up, .45 automatic at his hip, and a smile on his face, Lt Ira C. "Ike" Kepford exudes an air of confidence after his combat experience of 19 February. (U.S. Navy Photo, National Archives)

125

This photo of Lt Kepford's F4U-1A Corsair is interesting because it illustrates the victory flags on the right (starboard) side of his plane. Many aircraft have victory flags only on one side of the fuselage, usually the left (port) side. (U.S. Navy Photo, National Archives)

By mid-March 1944 Lt. Kepford was back to normal and became the "Jolly Rogers" highest scoring Ace with 16 official victories. He had a replacement F4U-1A Corsair emblazoned with his white "29" and 16 flags neatly arranged in a four-by-four box. This is the plane that is the most associated with the famous Ace.

From March to June 1944 Kepford was attached to the Fleet Air, Alameda Command and then served with VF-84 until December 1944, when he joined the Staff of Commander Fleet Air, West Coast, where he remained until after the Japanese surrender. Lieutenant Commander Kepford was released from active duty on November 7, 1945.

Ira Cassius Kepford was awarded the Distinguished Flying Cross; Navy Cross with Gold Star; Silver Star Medal; Ribbon for the Navy Unit commendation; American Defense Medal; American Campaign Medal; Asiatic-Pacific Campaign Medal; and the World War II Victory Medal.

Lt. Oscar I "Oc" Chenoweth, former XO of VF-38, transferred to the "Jolly Rogers" when his squadron returned to CONUS. LCDR Blackburn had been his flight instructor.

During the 19 February raid on New Britain, Chenowith and his wingman tore into a flight of 16 Japanese fighters and scored seven victories. While LTJG Kepford was fighting for his life the remaining 25 VF-17 aviators were scoring 16 victories with no losses. "Oc" had scored two victories with VF-38 and added 8.5 kills in VF-17 to become a double Ace.

"Ike" Kepford flies his last Corsair on one of his last combat missions. Of interest is how vibration and the slipstream have chipped off the paint on the wing root, and the wing, fin, and stabilizer leading edges. (U.S. Navy Photo, Courtesy Air Progress, Albert L. Lewis)

LCDR "Tommy" Blackburn on the left and Vought Service manager Jack Hospers take "time out" to pose for the photographer before returning to investigate and solve reported problems with operational Corsairs. "Big Hog" No.1 is Blackburn's personal F4U-1A. (Vought Aircraft Photo, Courtesy Paul Bower)

Chapter IV: Corsairs Break the Bismarck Barrier

LCDR John T. "Tommy" Blackburn stands before the VF-17 "Jolly Rogers" scoreboard at Piva Yoke (South) airstrip in February 1944. His squadron scored 156 victories; flying 8,577 combat man-hours, and lost only 12 aviators. (U.S. Navy Photo, National Archives)

RADM J.J. Ballantine, Chief of Staff, Air Force, Pacific Fleet, met with leading aviators of VF-17 regarding their rotation out of the Central Solomon's Combat Zone on March 22, 1944. L to R: Lt Harry A. March (5 Vict.); LCDR Roger R. Hedrick (11 Vict.); RADM Ballantine; LCDR John T. Blackburn VF-17 CO (11 Vict.); and Lt Ira C. Kepford (16 Vict.). Blackburn joined the Bureau of Aeronautics and then became CO of Carrier Air Group (CAG) 74. Kepford joined the Fleet Air, Alemeda, Command. Hedrick went on to become CO of VF-84 aboard USS Bunker Hill (CV-17). (U.S. Navy Photo, National Archives)

Maj Gen Ralph J. Mitchell, USMC (ComAirSols), congratulates LCDR John T. Blackburn after awarding the "Jolly Rogers" CO the Distinguished Flying Cross for "Commander Blackburn's keen foresight in planning for the assaults and his expert training of personnel directly contributed to the splendid record of the squadron…." (U.S. Navy Photo, National Archives)

CDR Marshall U. Beebe, USN, became the new CO of VF-17 on April 18, 1944. He led the squadron into the Central Pacific to the shores of Japan aboard USS Hornet. (U.S. Navy Photo, Author's File)

Precariously perched on the wing, two ground crewmen guide VF-17 Corsairs onto the runway prior to takeoff during heavy "traffic." A fall from the wing at that height could cause a serious injury. Some aviators "fishtail" to the runway viewing the ground ahead through the bend in the wing. (U.S. Navy Photo, National Archives)

In a great spirit of cooperation U.S. Marine mechanics service a U.S. Navy VF-17 Corsair in the darkness of night. Of special interest are the temporary folding scaffold walkways on each side of the nose that are supported by special fittings built into the Corsair's structure. The Corsair designers apparently realized that work on the engine would be impossible without a structure from the ground, so they designed this clever arrangement. (U.S. Navy Photo, USMC, Author's File)

LCDR John T. "Tommy" Blackburn, USN, was the model of Annapolis discipline to mold a squadron of high-spirited aviators into one of the most effective squadrons in the Pacific. His knowledge of aircraft and tactics also proved invaluable in the development of the Corsair during the design phase, and in the field working closely with Vought Service Manager Jack Hospers to update Corsairs when necessary.

LCDR Blackburn is credited with eleven official victories. He was awarded the Distinguished Flying Cross and a Gold Star in lieu of a second Distinguished Flying Cross. LCDR John T. Blackburn competed the Naval War College course in Strategy and Tactics, which contributed considerably to his outstanding leadership.

CDR "Tommy" Blackburn joined the Bureau of Aeronautics on June 15, 1944, followed by command of Combat Air Group (CAG) 74, and

Green Island is a coral atoll composed of two principal islands (Pinepil and Nissan) plus lesser islands. Siezed by New Zealand troops, it became a base for Royal New Zealand Air Force fighters and bombers. Observe the runways, taxiways, and revetments. (RNZAF Photo, Author's File)

Capt Phillip C. DeLong of VMF-212 "Hell Hounds" was a master at multiple victories, often scoring two and three kills at a time. He scored 11.5 victories in 145 combat hours on 45 combat missions. (U.S. Navy Photo, USMC, National Archives)

Chapter IV: Corsairs Break the Bismarck Barrier

Capt Phillip C. DeLong has his picture taken as he flies one of his Corsairs, an F4U-1D. This must have been one of his last Corsairs, because the 11.5 victory flags equal his final score in World War II. (Vought Aircraft Photo, Courtesy Paul Bower)

Captain of the Battle Aircraft Carrier USS *Midway* (CBV-41) on May 11, 1945.

VF-17 was officially reorganized on April 18, 1944, at NAS Alameda under the command of ten-victory ace CDR Marshall U. Beebe, USN. He led VF-17 aboard the aircraft carrier USS *Hornet* on February 1, 1945, into the Central Pacific as part of Task Force 58.

After mid-February 1944, Rabaul's interception to U.S. air raids ranged from meager to non-existent. It was now time to move into the surrounding islands and to isolate and bypass Rabaul; on to Kavieng, New Ireland; and second only to Rabaul in importance.

Under cover of eight Marine squadrons, Green Island, 115 miles east of Rabaul, was invaded by New Zealand troops on 15 February and secured by March 6, 1944.

VMF-212 "Hell Hounds" was on duty during Green Islands invasion day when 15 Val dive bombers attacked U.S. ships unloading vital war cargoes on the beachhead. Capt Phillip Cunliffe DeLong dived through intense U.S. antiaircraft fire and shot down three Vals. The remaining Japanese planes left the scene without dropping a bomb. Capt DeLong was awarded the Distinguished Flying Cross for his skill and bravery during this action.

During Lt. DeLong's first tour of duty he specialized in strafing the Treasury Islands and the Shortland Islands.

He made his first contact with Japanese aircraft during his second tour when he shot down two Zeros in flames over Rabaul on January 9, 1944.

While escorting Marine dive bombers on January 17, 1944, he destroyed his third and fourth Zeros, also over Rabaul.

Lt. DeLong divided a kill with five victory Ace and VMF-212 CO Maj Hugh M Elwood on January 23, 1944, over Tobera Airfield, New Britain, and one week later he shot down his fifth Zero over the same airfield.

Two days later DeLong destroyed his sixth Zero over Rabaul and scored his seventh victory over the same city on January 31, 1944.

One week before his third tour he scored his eighth victory, and during the last day of his second tour he shot down three dive bombers on

The VMF-211 "Wake Avengers" scoreboard proudly announces that the squadron scored 74 victories in 33 days. Observe the Corsair in the background. (Photo by and Courtesy of Lt. Loren C Stricklin, VMF-211)

Upper Photo: A gathering of Eagles! Corsairs as far as the eye can see on Torokina Airfield, Bougainville, are preparing for a fighter sweep over New Britain. VMF-211 "Wake Avengers" and VMF-215 "Fighting Corsairs" are among the squadrons awaiting action. Lower Photo: A VMF-211 Corsair F4U-1 sits in the hot sun in a revetment off Piva Yoke, Bougainville, airstrip undergoing repairs. Note the mechanics in the shade of the wing preparing spare parts. Observe the missing stabilizer tip on the Corsair. (Photo by and Courtesy of Lt. Loren C Stricklin, VMF-211)

Only sixty days after U.S. Marines landed on Emerau, the Construction Battalions had completed this airfield ready for operation. Corsairs pounded Kavieng on New Ireland from this airstrip. (U.S. Defense Dept, USMC, Author's File)

February 15, 1944, for which he was awarded the Distinguished Flying Cross.

At the end of his third tour he logged more than 145 combat hours and participated in 45 combat missions. He is officially credited with 11.5 victories, scored in less than 18 weeks of combat flying.

VMF-211 "Wake Avengers" (descendant of VMF-2 of Wake Is) was one of the first squadrons to arrive at Green Island on March 20, 1944, led by Maj Thomas V. Murto Jr. In December 1944 the unit was transferred to Leyte, Philippine Islands, to cover the Ormoc and Mindoro landings.

VMF-211 aces included Lt. J C Hundley (8 Vict); Maj J W Ireland (5 Vict); Lt. J L Morgan (8.5 Vict); and Lt. F C Thomas Jr (9 Vict).

Emirau Island, 76 miles northwest of Kavieng, was occupied by the 4th Marines on March 20, 1944. Landings by U.S. forces were also made on the Admiralty Islands, Cape Hollman and Cape Gloucester on New Britain, and Lae on New Guinea, forging a virtual ring around Rabaul.

VMF-211 "Wake Avengers" Corsair F4U-1Ds are being repaired or maintained in a repair depot on one of the Green Islands in March 1944. The squadron was transferred to Emerau and then to Leyte, Philippines, by the end of the year. (U.S. Navy Photo, USMC, Courtesy Lt. Loren C Stricklin (VMF-211)

Chapter IV: Corsairs Break the Bismarck Barrier

Upper Photo: United Aircraft "tech rep" Charles A "Lindy" Lindbergh met with famous aces Joe Foss (at left) and Marion Carl (center) in Emirau on May 24, 1944, to discuss Corsair combat performance. "Lindy" flew Corsairs on combat missions in the South and Central Pacific. U.S. Defense Dept (USMC) Lower Photo: In an attack on Wotje Atoll, in the Marshall Islands, Lindbergh dive-bombed a target with a 12,000lb Corsair carrying 4,000lbs of bombs. 4,000lbs is the normal bomb load carried by a 53,000lb, four-engine, ten-man crew B-17 Flying Fortress bomber, shown here. U.S. Defense Dept (USAAC)

Now, the remaining Corsair squadrons in the South/Southwest Pacific had to continue pounding Rabaul and Kavieng to keep the bastions impotent.

World-famous long-distance aviator, Transcontinental Speed Record Holder, and Airline Routes Trailblazer Charles A. Lindbergh arrived at Green Island in May 1944 to improve range and dive bombing tactics for Corsairs during combat missions.

Before the Pearl Harbor attack, Lindbergh was strongly opposed to any U.S. involvement in the European war and openly criticized President Roosevelt, as did other leading aviators, such as Al Williams. Denied military service because of his opposition to the Roosevelt Administration, the famous aviator and engineer, and former U.S. Army and airmail pilot, was working as a consultant to several aviation companies. This position as "civilian technician" enabled him to obtain U.S. Government permission to enter combat zones and fly on combat missions in combat aircraft.

The Corsair missions were invariably low-level "down to earth" strafing or bombing runs. On his first mission, May 22, 1944, "Lindy" actually fired his six guns at the target, in violation of the Geneva Convention agreements. The MAG-14 CO Lt. Col Roger T. Carlson was quite disturbed, because if Lindberg fell into Japanese hands he could be legally executed! This, apparently, made no impression on the aviator, because it was part of the risk that he was willing to accept!

Charles Lindbergh flew his last mission in the Bismarck Archipelago on 9 May, and left for Espiritu Santo on the following day to investigate a Corsair hydraulic wing-folding mechanism failure. His next project was in New Guinea to analyze combat flying Lockheed P-38 Lightning fighters. He also flew Thunderbolts and Liberators in combat.

As a United Aircraft "tech rep," Lindbergh did not desert the Corsair when he took off in an F4U-1D with a 4,000 pound bomb load and 65 degree dive-bombed a target on Wotje Atoll, in the Marshall Islands. This is the same weight of bombs normally carried by the four-engined B-17 Flying Fortress bomber!

It is rumored that the "Lone Eagle" also shot down a Japanese fighter in combat!

About twenty-one thousand tons of bombs rained on Rabaul during the siege. After the middle of February only token Japanese air resistance was met by Marine fliers. On February 20, 1944, the Japanese evacuated as many aircraft as they could to Truk; a definite sign that the 90,000 troops in the Bismarck Archipeligo were being abandoned to defend themselves as best they could. Rabaul's last contact with the homeland was during April 1944, when a Japanese cargo submarine entered Simpson Harbor undetected by the Allied blockade.

It was, indeed, fortunate that an invasion of Rabaul was not necessary, because the loss of Allied soldiers during such a frontal assault would have been enormous.

Despite the fact that her air power had been decimated and her supply route severed, Rabaul was well prepared to combat an invasion of any magnitude. All beaches were fortified with underwater mines, concrete anti-boat blocks, land mines, pill boxes, barbed wire, and plenty of ammunition!

Three hundred and fifty miles of underground caves and tunnels afforded the Japanese excellent shelter from the shower of Allied bombs. In fact, it took about four tons of bombs to kill one Japanese soldier during the entire campaign! Rabaul's radar afforded them from one half hour to a full hour advance warning of an air attack, which made surprise raids by the Allies an impossibility.

In addition to an abundance of ammunition, Rabaul had plenty of food supplemented with extensive vegetable gardens. Even items such as toothpaste and soap were in plentiful supply. Morale on Rabaul was always high. Yes, it can definitely be said that the victory of the Corsair fighter aviators in the skies over the Solomons and Bismarcks was the principal factor in canceling the Rabaul invasion, thereby saving the lives of countless thousands of Allied infantrymen.

Even more important than the cancellation of the Rabaul invasion itself was the fact that the Solomons air battles sapped the strength of the Imperial Japanese Naval Air Service. Realizing the importance of Rabaul, the Japanese fought tenaciously to hold the fortress against the Allied fighters. However, Admiral Koga underestimated the ability of the U.S. Marine and Navy aviators and their Corsairs; committing his fighter strength piecemeal, hoping that each succeeding air battle would end the threat to Rabaul. The Admiral can be compared to a gambler at the gaming tables who enters a losing streak. In order to recoup his losses he borrows on his life's savings and bets it a little at a time, hoping to strike a winning number, only to find himself broke with no hope of ever regaining solvency.

When the Solomons air battles were but an echo, Japan's finest combat pilots were dead. Like the gambler, Koga overextended his air power and committed more aircraft to the defense of Rabaul than Japan could afford. In fact, Koga never planned to risk as many aircraft as he actually placed in combat. Their best pilots gone, the Japanese could not

During July 1944 President Franklin D. Roosevelt met with Gen Douglas MacArthur and Adm Chester W. Nimitz in Pearl Harbor, Hawaii. At this momentous meeting it was decided to recapture the Philippines. (U.S. Information Agency, Author's File)

produce airmen with the degree of training that was sufficient to meet the demand of actual air-to-air combat. This lack of skilled pilots became evident during the invasion of Saipan, in the Marianas Islands, when on June 19, 1944, the U.S. Navy fliers destroyed no less than 383 Japanese aircraft on that single day! This is known as the "Marianas Turkey Shoot" thanks to the earlier fighter victories at Rabaul.

The Japanese aviators defending Rabaul and the Solomons fought with great skill and determination; they were the finest aviators in the Imperial Navy. Yet, they were no match for the Corsair aviators, who were so thorough in their job that from that time to the end of the war the Japanese air arm would be an ineffective weapon, and the Japanese Combined Fleet would be without air support during crucial battles in the Central Pacific.

During July 1944 President Franklin D Roosevelt met with Gen Douglas Mac Arthur and Adm Chester W Nimitz in Pearl Harbor, Hawaii.

The conferees decided to recapture the Philippine Islands and attack Japan. This required the movement of Marines from the Solomons, in Melanesia, to the Central Pacific through Micronesia, the Gilberts, Marshalls, Carolines, and Marianas to Okinawa and Iwo Jima.

As soon as it was apparent that the advance up the Solomons was effective and that Rabaul could no longer seriously interfere with the Allied advance, MacArthur and Nimitz went into action. The General's American, Australian, and New Zealand troops began their march northwestward along the coast of New Guinea and captured the important Japanese base of Lae on September 16, 1944. Finchhafen fell two weeks later, and the troops were well on their way to the Philippines. Nimitz began his drive against the Japanese on Truk. However, here again, it was decided to bypass this Japanese base which could no longer depend upon Rabaul for assistance. Truk was isolated from Japan by the Allied drives into the Gilbert, Marshall, Caroline, and Marianas Islands. Japanese aerial resistance during these campaigns was quite meager thanks to the effectiveness of the Solomons airmen. Thus, the superb performance of the Marine pilots in their Corsairs had far-reaching results, and contributed in great measure to the ultimate victory.

It was agreed that the Royal New Zealand Air Force (RNZAF) would continue to batter the bypassed Japanese installations.

During World War II, the diminutive twin-island nation of New Zealand had a population of only one and one half million; however, on a per-capita basis it provided the largest number of airmen (57,000) and the largest number of fighter aces (94) of any Allied nation. Also, on a per-capita basis the country suffered the largest number of airmen killed.

Starting in May 1944 the U.S. provided the Royal New Zealand Air Force (RNZAF) with 424 Corsairs under the terms of Lend Lease consisting of: 237 F4U-1A Corsairs; 127 F4U-1D Corsairs; and 60 Goodyear FG-1D Corsairs.

The Corsairs phased out the aging Curtiss P-40 Kittyhawk fighters that the RNZAF had flown so well, scoring about 100 victories.

The disassembled Corsairs were shipped to the RNZAF Base Depot Workshops in Espiritu Santo, where the planes were assembled and made ready for flight. All completed Corsairs were flight tested before assignment to squadrons.

This large formation of sixteen RNZAF No.18 Squadron Corsairs are flying along the Guadalcanal coast to attack Japanese pockets of resistance. This formation includes eight two-plane elements or four four-plane divisions. F4U-1A and F4U-1D Corsairs were supplied to the RNZAF under the Lend Lease agreement. (RNZAF Photo, Courtesy Al Lewis, Air Progress)

Chapter IV: Corsairs Break the Bismarck Barrier

This interesting photo is of the first RNZAF Corsair landing on Espiritu Santo; returning from a test flight after having been assembled on that island. (RNZAF Photo, Courtesy John Regan)

RNZAF mechanics are completing the assembly of a Corsair that was shipped, entirely disassembled from the U.S. to Espiritu Santo, New Hebrides (now Republic of Vanuatu). Each mechanic is working on his speciality. Observe the armorers installing the huge .50 caliber machine guns. (RNZAF Photo, Author's File)

Left Photo: RNZAF Corsair F4U-1D is filmed at No.4 FOTU (Flying Operational Training Unit) at Ohakea, New Zealand, for flight training methods. Right Photo: Another F4U-1D is undergoing a landing gear retracting test at Ardmore airfield, New Zealand. (RNZAF Photos, Courtesy John Regan)

The RNZAF No.18 Squadron Corsair shown here displays the identification number 303 on the engine cowl and rudder which number is part of the serial number NZ 5303. (RNZAF Photo, Courtesy John Regan)

This New Zealand Corsair aviator's tropical flight gear is standard U.S. Navy issue except that it includes about 65 pounds of survival gear. His clothing consists of a lightweight flash burn-resistant coverall over a pair of underwear shorts plus standard boots. By the time this aviator climbs up into his cockpit he will be perspiring profusely. (RNZAF Photo, Author's File)

Upper Photo: RNZAF Corsairs under the trees on Guadalcanal are being repaired or maintained. The mechanics can work efficiently despite the primitive setting. Lower Photo: Pilot officer Pat Crump exits his Corsair with care because of his 65lb load. (RNZAF Photo, Author's File)

Left Photo: Three Corsairs returning from a mission (Photo taken by the fourth Corsair of the division). Note the water and the coastline. Right Photo: At least two islands in the Solomons and New Britain have active volcanoes. This unusual photograph shows a Corsair near the erupting volcano Mount Bagana on Bougainville. (RNZAF Photos, Courtesy John Regan)

Chapter IV: Corsairs Break the Bismarck Barrier

Five RNZAF No.14 Squadron aviators pose before a Corsair. They are L to R: Neale Sutherland; Chuck Offen; John Claydon; Warren Eades; and Bernie Nelson. Observe the dimensions marked on the Corsair insignia to guide the conversion of the U.S. insignia into the RNZAF insignia. (RNZAF Photo, Author's File)

Upper Photo: Members of No.14 Squadron, RNZAF, in this photograph are (L to R) Bottom Row: Neale C. Sutherland; R. Barnett; W. Blundell; B.S. Hay; S/L D.W. Cocks; P.S. Tennent; H. "Pat" Crump; L. Strawbridge; and Don Walther. Center Row: Stan Sparrow; D.A. "Sam" Corbett; Chuck Offen; I. Munro; Richard Soar; J. McArthur; Ronald R. Mitchell; J. M. Wilson; and F.C. Keefe. Top Row: A.R. Horn; A. Cook; I. Thornburn; A.N. Sayward; L. Jeffs; John Claydon; P.G. Moore; Eric Green; A. Ewart; and C. Brown. Lower Photo: Aviators of No.14 Squadron are shown with one of their Corsairs before raiding Japanese positions (L to R): Stan Sparrow; Don Walther; Ronald R. Mitchell; Richard Soar; Information Officer Fred Smith; D.A. "Sam" Corbett; and Eric Green. (RNZAF Photos, Author's File)

This RNZAF "swimming hole" on Bougainville is fully equipped with diving platforms and diving boards, as well as marked lanes for racing to an enormous float. Compare with the "Swashbucklers" swimming hole on Espiritu Santo in Chapter Three. (RNZAF Photo, Author's File)

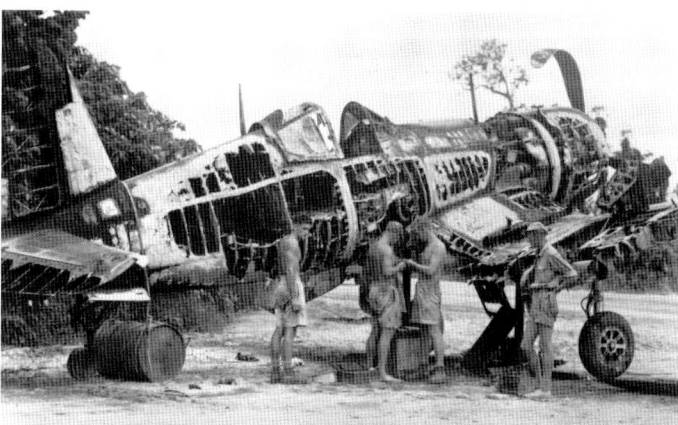

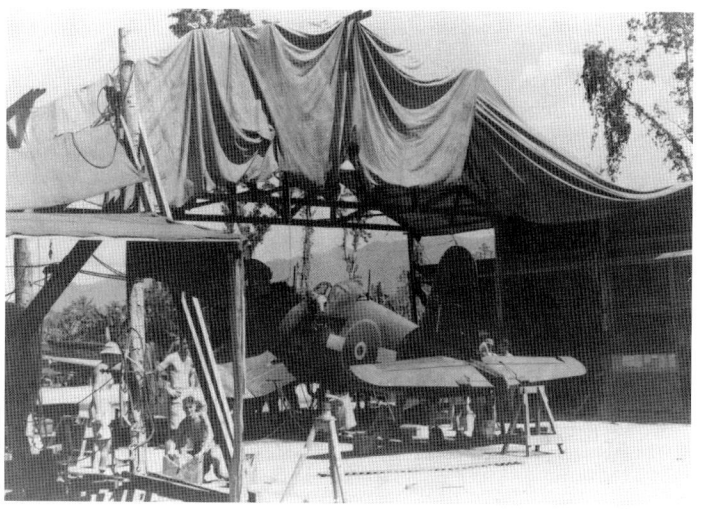

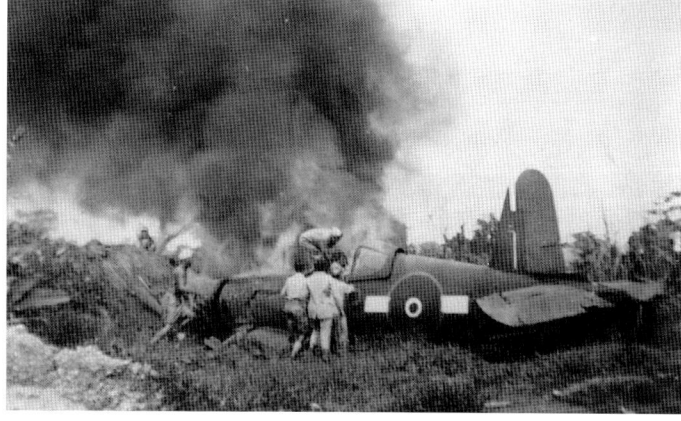

Every sortie is fraught with danger. Upper Photo: Pilot Officer N.W. McCready was on a test flight from Green Island on February 12, 1945, when his F4U-1A caught fire. McCready returned to base and escaped from the cockpit to safety. Center Photo: Flight Lieutenant F.E. Bradley from No.26 Squadron belly landed on Piva North (Uncle), Bougainville, on April 13, 1945, when the wheels failed to lower. The left (port) side of the fuselage remained undamaged. Lower Photo: Flight Sergeant H. Wigg was badly burned when he was trapped in the cockpit after a crash landing at Piva North, Bougainville, on September 15, 1945. (RNZAF Photos, Courtesy John Regan)

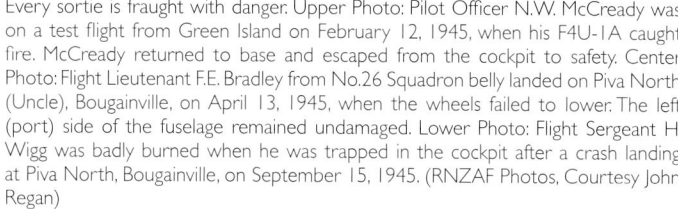

Maintenance and repair of aircraft are never-ending operations. Observe the canvas-covered wooden structures that serve as shelter for RNZAF aircraft and engine mechanics at the Piva Strip, Bougainville. Palm and coconut tree trunks are not suitable for cutting into lumber, therefore, deciduous trees were cut down and cut into lumber with the RNZAF sawmill on Piva. Suitable wood in the area is mostly mahogany. (RNZAF Photos, Courtesy John Regan)

Chapter IV: Corsairs Break the Bismarck Barrier

RNZAF ground crew removes wheel blocks from a Corsair before a sortie from Piva North (Uncle) airstrip in Bougainville. Observe the one-thousand pound bomb fitted with a "Daisy Cutter" fuse to make the bomb detonate before it strikes the ground. The blast was devastating to enemy personnel and equipment. (RNZAF Photo, Author's File)

Aviators of RNZAF No.23 "Ghost" Squadron discuss the raid from which they just returned on Aug. 6, 1945. Observe the "Ghost" insignia and "Marie." Plane is an F4U-1D Corsair. (RNZAF Photo, Author's File)

Thirteen RNZAF fighter squadrons were equipped with Corsairs (No.14 through No.26) flying from the Admiralty Islands, Green Island, Emirau, Espiritu Santo, Bougainville, and Guadalcanal, attacking bypassed targets on New Britain, New Ireland, and the Solomons. The Corsair shown is from No.18 squadron.

The RNZAF fighter aviator wore standard U.S. Navy/USMC tropical flight gear, which was much different from his European counterpart. Instead of a heavy fur-lined leather jacket with fur collar, the Solomons/Bismarck aviator flight gear consisted of a lightweight tropical coverall, chemically treated to resist flash burns. The coverall was worn over a pair of underwear shorts. That is all.

This was similar to what U.S. Navy VF-17 aviator "Ike" Kepford wore, as described earlier in this chapter.

The principal difference was that the RNZAF aviator was required to wear field boots in the event he was forced down in the rain forest.

In addition to a cloth helmet with earphones, throat microphone, goggles, light leather gloves, and oxygen mask, the South Pacific fighter aviator carried the all-important survival gear that weighed about 65lbs: .38 cal revolver (RNZAF); .45 cal automatic (U.S.); extra ammunition; hunting knife; canteen of water; and the "Mae West" inflatable life vest that contained a flashing light, whistle, sea marker dye, and shark repellant. The aviator's rain forest survival pack included maps, signaling mirror, compass, fishing gear and bait, first aid supplies, booklet illustrating edible plants and fish, water purifying tablets, large folding machete for cutting vines and underbrush, and a morphine syringe for extreme emergencies. Also included were the large parachute pack and an inflatable dinghy.

Perspiration was not only a nuisance but a health hazard as well, making salt tablets essential. By the time the aviator had climbed up to and entered the big Corsair with his survival pack he was perspiring heavily. Once in the cockpit with engine started many aviators placed their arms outside the cockpit, hands facing forward, so the propeller slipstream could rush into their sleeves and "air condition" the interior of their coveralls.

In addition to flying over large areas of water and hostile rain forests, the RNZAF Corsairs were forced to fly dangerously close to active volcano peaks on at least two islands.

Twenty-victory U.S. Marine Ace Capt Don Aldrich, USMC, took time off to join Combat Radio Correspondent Sgt George Theeringer in a War Bond Drive radio broadcast in 1945. Broadcast was made in the USMC Air Station in Santa Barbara, California. (USMC Photo, Author's File)

The aviators of No.14 Fighter Squadron RNZAF were very active in the drive against the bypassed Japanese strongholds.

The brave men were normally calm and cheerful, despite knowing that they face serious injury or death in their next sortie.

In order to relieve the tension of constant "down to earth" missions, efforts were made to develop diversionary activities. One such diversion for the aviators was a rather enormous swimming pool in Bougainville.

Although bypassed by Allied forces, the Japanese targets still possessed defensive power in their antiaircraft batteries to ward off any aerial attacks, as well as aircraft to intercept the attackers.

The official New Zealand orders regarding RNZAF activities are as follows:

"(1) To reduce the enemy forces, to disrupt their organization and weaken their morale. (2) To destroy or damage their means of living, camps, bivouacs, supply dumps, vegetable gardens and livestock. (3) To eliminate or disrupt their transport system by destroying or damaging barges, motor vehicles, jetties, bridges and roads. (4) To eliminate or reduce their capacity for defensive action by destroying or damaging coastal or antiaircraft artillery positions, airfields and ammunition dumps."

The orders required strafing and other low-level activities that are more dangerous than high level aerial combat. More has been written about the U.S., British, and Japanese air effort than the Royal New Zealand Air Force; therefore, little known is the fact that in the Pacific War, the relatively small RNZAF was operating over an area that is one-third larger than the entire continent of Europe with only twenty-three Allied airfields available.

The Royal New Zealand Air Force (RNZAF) performed Yeomanly Duty by keeping pressure on the remaining pockets of Japanese resistance in the Solomons and Bismarcks by destroying the Japanese ability to not only wage war, but to exist at all.

The attacking Corsairs strafed with their six .50 caliber machine guns and destroyed buildings, tents, ammunition, gardens, planes, vehicles, and personnel with 500lb and 1,000lb bombs fitted with "daisy cutters." This attachment detonated the bomb a few feet above the ground, creating a forceful blast effect that could overturn vehicles and aircraft and sweep away wooden buildings, tents, and foliage, such as gardens, without scoring a direct hit on the target. The explosion also scattered shrapnel that was grossly lethal to personnel. In addition, 250lb naval depth charge bombs were used on ground targets. The charges detonated upon impact with the ground and were so forceful that the blast could obliterate overgrown rain forest foliage that hid military installations. It was a program of total destruction of man, animals, machines, dwellings, farms, and the forest.

This operation continued while U.S. Marine, U.S. Navy, and Royal Navy Corsairs were assigned to press the Japanese toward the North and West in the Central Pacific Area and Dutch East Indies as land-based and carrier-based forces.

V

Corsairs through the Central Pacific

Near the end of March 1944 Admiral Mineichi Koga, Commander-in-Chief of the Imperial Combined Fleet, was killed in an airplane crash. He was succeeded by Admiral Soemu Toyoda.

While the Bismarck Barrier was being breached and the RNZAF rained destruction on the Japanese in the Solomons, Bismarcks, and elsewhere in the Southwest Pacific, the U.S. Navy, U.S. Marines, and the Royal Navy Fleet Air Arm (RNFAA) were taking Corsairs into the Central Pacific, Philippines, East Indies, and the shores of Europe.

Of the seven countries that flew the Corsair as part of their armed forces, the British Royal Navy Fleet Air Arm's 2,012 Corsairs were second in number only to the combined U.S. Navy and U.S. Marine Corps Corsairs; sufficient to equip more than 47 RNFAA Squadrons.

The only problem was that, when folded, the vertical dimension of the Corsair wingtip was 16'-3.5" above the aircraft carrier deck; however, the Royal Navy aircraft carriers, being smaller than the American carriers, had a hangar headroom of only 16 feet. After long discussions and numerous suggestions, LCDR R.M. Smeeton, RN (British Corsair Liaison Officer), suggested that all RNFAA Corsair wing tips be shortened by eight inches. The approved procedure to achieve this was to remove eighteen inches from each wingtip and replace this with a ten-inch wooden wingtip shaped similar to the blunt wingtip of the Messerschmitt 109E and the P-51 Mustang.

Briggs Manufacturing Company, subcontractor of the Corsair wing outer panels, incorporated the wooden tips on newly constructed wings for the FAA, while the Blackburn Aeroplane and Motor Co. Ltd. modified the wingtips on Corsairs that had already been delivered to the Fleet Air Arm. Brewster was the first to deliver clipped wing Corsairs to the FAA.

The first Royal Navy Corsairs were delivered starting on May 20, 1943. The four Corsair models delivered to the Fleet Air Arm were: F4U-1 (Corsair Mark I); F4U-1A and F4U-1D (Corsair Mark II); and FG-1D (Corsair IV); some F3A-1; and all F3A-1D (Corsair III).

It was discovered that the shorter, blunt wingtip increased the sink rate; reduced the floating tendency in landing; less roll during a stall; and increased the takeoff run by about 15 feet in a 25K (28.8 mph) headwind.

The "clipped wing" is very evident in this photo of a Royal Navy FAA Corsair Mark II. Note the flat finish camouflage. The majority of Fleet Air Arm Corsairs were based on aircraft carriers. (Royal Navy Photo, Courtesy Henry Tremont)

Corsair: The Saga of the Legendary Bent-Wing Fighter-Bomber

Royal Navy aircraft carriers operating in the Indian Ocean and Bay of Bengal striking at the Dutch East Indies (now Indonesia) relied on British India for logistics, and Corsair repair and replacement. Very often sections of India were lacking in sophisticated machinery, such as tractors. Here we find a Corsair being towed by an Indian elephant when a tractor could not be found near the airfield. (Royal Navy Photo, Courtesy LTV, Arthur L. Schoeni)

Carrier-based Royal Navy Corsairs flew cover for FAA bombers during a raid on the German battleship *Tirpitz* on April 3, 1944, in Altenfjord, Norway. Observe the heavy clothing worn by the plane handlers to brave the cold North Sea winds. Upper Photo: A Fleet Air Arm Corsair II taxis to its takeoff point as it extends its wings. Lower Photo: After escorting the bombers a Corsair II taxis on the carrier after landing. (Royal Navy Photos, Author's File)

Less than one year after receiving its first Corsair the FAA assigned 28 Corsairs from Nos. 1834 and 1836 Squadrons, based on *HMS Victorious*, to provide top cover for "Operation Tungsten." This was a bombing attack on the German battleship *Tripitz* that was being repaired in Altenfjord, Norway. Escorting the bombers and torpedo planes in two waves from *HMS Victorious* and *HMS Furious* on April 3, 1944, the Corsairs met no intercepting German aircraft. Fourteen hits were made on the battleship during this raid. Corsairs flew top cover in four more attacks on *Tirpitz*.

Concurrent with "Operation Tungsten," Royal Navy carrier-based Corsairs were in action in the Indian Ocean when Nos. 1830 and 1833 Squadrons flew from *HMS Illustrious* east of Ceylon (now Sri Lanka) to sweep the sea of Japanese commerce raiders. *HMS Illustrious* worked very closely with *USS Saratoga* in this operation; however, the American carrier had no Corsairs aboard!

During July 1944, *HMS Victorious* joined *HMS Illustrious* with 42 Corsairs, including No 1836 Squadron, increasing the number of Corsair II fighters in the task group to 84. This enlarged force flew top cover for

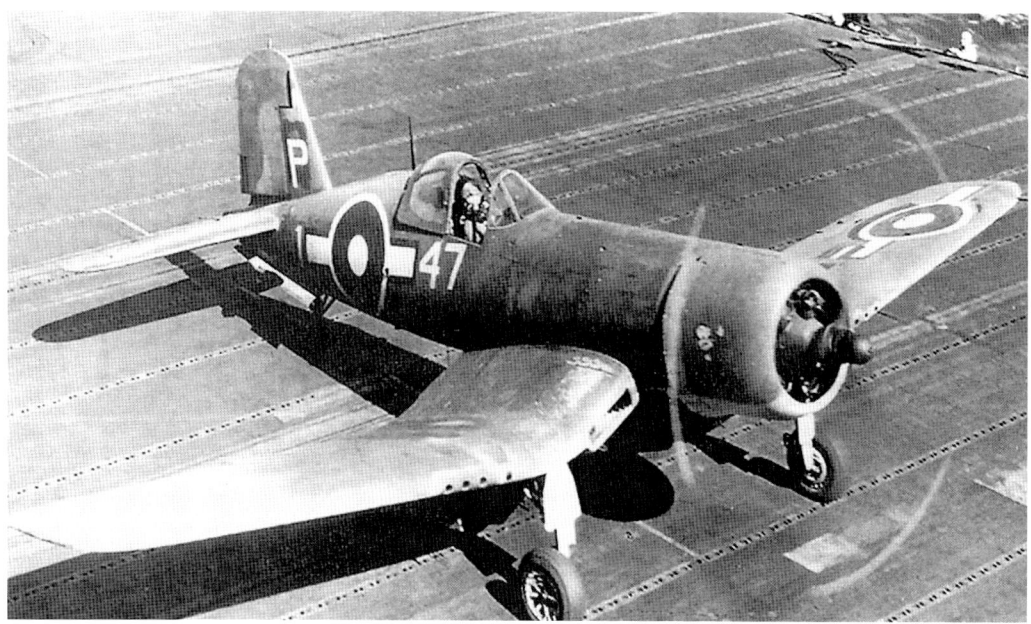

Forty-two Corsairs from NOS 1830, 1833, and 1836 FAA Squadrons from *HMS Victorious* and *Illustrious* flew cover for surface ships bombarding oil refinery and storage installations on Sabang Island, Sumatra. Note the modified cockade with the addition of wings or bars, similar to the U.S. and RNZAF insignia. This was necessary to distinguish it from the Japanese red disk that has been omitted. This Corsair II is from No 1836 Squadron aboard *HMS Victorious*. (Royal Navy FAA Photo, Author's File)

Chapter V: Corsairs through the Central Pacific

An FAA "batsman" guides a Corsair to a landing on an Indian airfield: Arms spread= maintain power; arms raised= increase power; arms lowered= reduce power; and arms crossed= cut power. (Royal Navy Photos, Courtesy United Aircraft Corporation)

Two potent, long-range "Tiny Tim" rocket-powered, 1,200lb air to surface missiles are shown nestled under the wing-fuselage joint of two Corsairs. Left Photo: This well-armed Corsair F4U-1A has the firepower of some naval destroyers and destroyer escorts with two "Tiny Tims", eight five inch HVAR missiles, and six .50 cal machine guns. (Released Naval History Photo, Author's File) Right Photo: This Corsair F4U-4B, with two "Tiny Tims," has the power to sink some cargo ships and warships, and could have raised havoc with the V-1 "Buzz Bomb" missile launchers. (U.S. Navy Photo, USMC, Author's File)

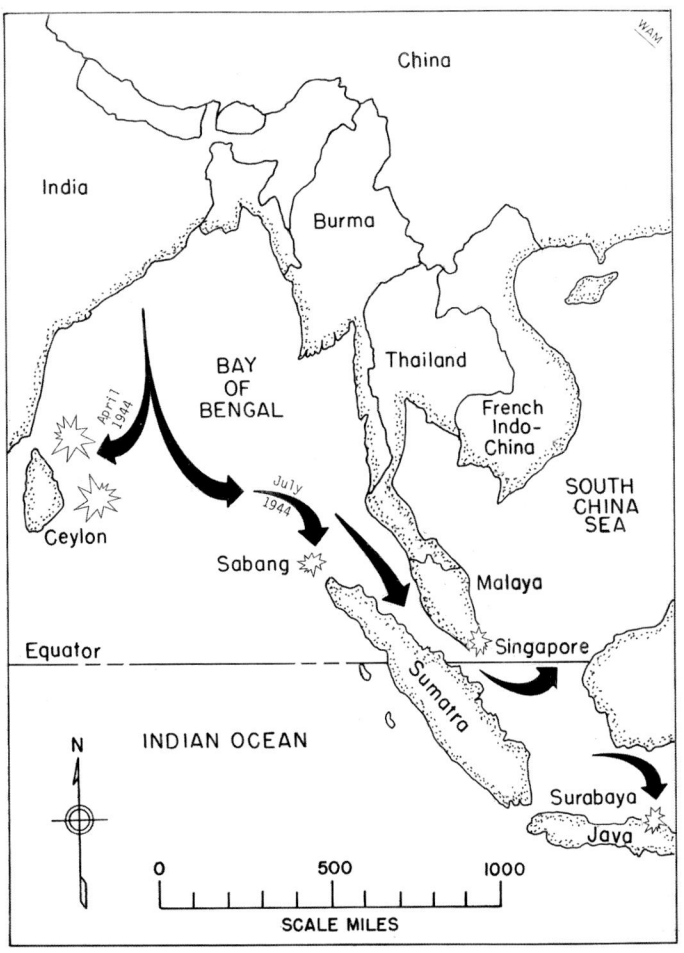

From bases in India, Royal Navy aircraft carriers traveled to Sabang and Surabaya to launch Fleet Air Arm Corsairs on raids over oil refinery and storage installations. Japanese shipping near Ceylon was also attacked as shown on this schematic. The Corsairs performed well from the Royal Navy Carriers.

battleships, cruisers, and destroyers that were bombarding the port and oil storage sites of Sabang Island, at the northern tip of Sumatra, East Indies. As the bombarding ships withdrew they were attacked by Sally bombers escorted by Zekes. No 1833 Squadron Corsairs scored two Zekes and a Sally, while No 1830 Squadron Corsairs destroyed three Zekes. Another Corsair from temporarily assigned No 1838 Squadron on *HMS Victorious* scored another Zeke.

These successes were the first aerial victories scored by carrier-based Corsairs and the first of many victories scored by FAA Corsairs. U.S. Military Corsairs had yet to be approved for operation from U.S. Navy aircraft carriers.

On July 1, 1944, MAG-51, consisting of VMF-511, VMF-512, VMF-513, and VMF-514, was assigned highest priority for training with large air-to-ground rockets. Twenty-seven aviators from each squadron were sent to Boca Chica, Florida, and Manteo, North Carolina, while 42 other aviators were sent to NAS Quonset Point, Rhode Island, for training.

VMF-351, already in shape for combat, was assigned to MAG-51 to be part of the project.

The reason for this preparation was that Germany began launching V-1 "Buzz-Bomb" missiles over England after D-Day, and the Marine squadrons were selected to destroy the V-1 launching installations with their Corsairs. The plan was officially designated "Project Crossbow," but was known as "Danny" to the Marines.

The Joint Chiefs of Staff selected the "Tiny Tim" rocket-powered surface attack missile as the weapon to destroy the V-1 launchers. This 11.75in diameter missile was 8ft-9in long and weighed 1,200lbs. The warhead consisted of 150lbs of explosive. Range was one mile. Each Corsair was to carry two "Tiny Tims."

The missile was developed by the scientists at California Institute of Technology; however, the weapon was still in the design stage. Problems also arose regarding safe launching techniques because the "Tiny Tim" was mounted close under the fuselage/wing joint of the Corsair within the propeller arc; nor was it ready for mass production.

The assigned squadrons had completed carrier training and were scheduled to embark on carriers with 60 Corsairs by July 16, 1944, despite the fact that missile-firing training was moving at a very slow pace. Only two missiles per squadron were available for practice, and any additional training was conducted with dummies or standard five-inch rockets. By 30 July Project Crossbow was cancelled.

Tafuna airstrip on Tutuilla, in American Samoa, was one of the first airfields built for the Central Pacific Offensive. Observe that much of the airstrip was constructed on a landfill in the shallow lagoon. (U.S. Navy Photo, Author's File)

Chapter V: Corsairs through the Central Pacific

This wisp of an island is typical of many in the Central Pacific that are very difficult to find after a long flight. Funafuti, in the Ellice Islands, was 700 miles southeast from Tarawa. Note the airstrip that runs down one of the two spits of land that form the island. (U.S. Navy Photo, Author's File)

The American airstrip on Nanumea, the most northwestern island of the Ellice Islands, was only about 450 miles from Tarawa Atoll. Note the slender shape of the land, surrounded by broad shoals, and the two airstrips in the center. (U.S. Army Air Force Photo, Author's File)

It is interesting that, despite the prohibition of the Corsair and Marine aviators on U.S. carriers, Project Crossbow planned to fly both from aircraft carriers in July 1944; four months before Corsairs were officially accepted on U.S. aircraft carriers.

Meanwhile, an offensive in the Central Pacific had been proposed that would become the largest of all World War Two Theaters. The actual proposal was made in February 1943; however, it was not until July 1943 that the Joint Chiefs of Staff instructed FADM Nimitz to plan operations in Samoa, the Ellice Islands, and the Gilbert Islands (operation Galvanic) in preparation for a later thrust into the Marshall Islands (Operation Flintlock).

In August, 1943 the Combined Chiefs of Staff at the Quebec Quadrant Conference authorized the advance into the Central Pacific through the Gilbert Islands, then the Marshall Islands, and the Mariana Islands (Operation Forager) and/or the Caroline Islands. The conference also created the South East Asia Command under the leadership of Lord Louis Mountbatten.

The concept of the Central Pacific thrust began shortly after the Pearl Harbor attack, when U.S. concern was directed at the Samoan Islands, which were just outside of the Japanese conquest limit. This was not only for defense, but as a springboard for a Central Pacific counterattack.

By the spring of 1942 an airstrip had been completed at Tafuna, on Tutuilla, the Eastern (American) Samoan Island. After it was constructed, the 2,500ft runway proved too short. Several hundred thousand tons of volcanic rock and coral was unloaded into an adjacent shallow lagoon, and the runway was extended over this landfill.

A 4,000ft long airstrip was then constructed at Faleolo, on the western Samoan Island of Upolu, by July 1942.

Tarawa Atoll was the prime target in the Gilbert Islands to capture and then use the Japanese airfield on Betio Is. The initial move was to occupy Funafuti Atoll, in the Ellice Islands, and construct an airstrip 700 miles from Tarawa in October 1942.

Simultaneously with the Guadalcanal Campaign, VMF-441 had landed on another Ellice Island (Nanumea, only about 463 miles from Funafuti) on September 28, 1943, while VMF-111 landed on a companion island, Nukufetau, on October 20, 1943.

VADM Raymond A Spruance, the victor of the Battle of Midway and FADM Nimitz's chief of staff, became Commander of the U.S. Fifth Fleet and Task Force 51, Central Pacific Force, on August 5, 1943.

Vice Admiral Marc A. Mitscher, formerly ComAirSols, was appointed Commander of Task Force 58, the aircraft carrier force of the

Vice Admiral Raymond A. Spruance, who won the Battle of Midway, was selected Commander of the U.S. Fifth Fleet and Task Force 51, Central Pacific Force, on August 5, 1943. He had been FADM Nimitz's Chief of Staff. (U.S. Navy Photo, Via National Archives)

Corsair: The Saga of the Legendary Bent-Wing Fighter-Bomber

VADM Marc A. Mitscher became commander of Task Force 58, the aircraft carriers of the Fifth Fleet. This was the most powerful aircraft carrier force in the U.S. Navy. VADM Mitscher had been ComAirSols from March to July 1943. (U.S. Naval History Photo, Via National Archives)

Fourteen hundred miles apart, two Corsairs were fighting on two Pacific fronts at the same time: the South Pacific and Central Pacific. Upper Photo: An FG-1 Corsair of MAG-31 prepares for a sortie in a revetment on Roi, Marshall Islands. (Defense Dept-USMC, Courtesy N.H. Hauprich) Lower Photo: Capt Edwin L. Olander of VMF-214 emerges from his F4U-1 Corsair in a Torokina revetment, Solomon Islands, after a sortie. (Defense Dept-USMC, National Archives)

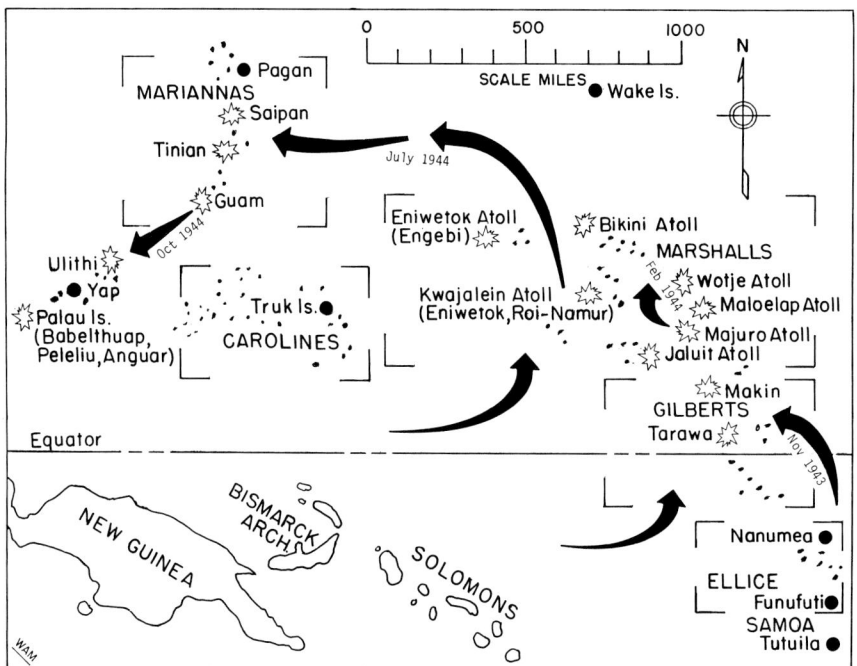

This schematic illustrates the general paths of the American thrusts through the Central Pacific. Observe how the Carolines, with the bastion of Truk, is isolated from the Japanese forces to the north. Also note the large individual Solomon Islands (550 miles total length) that required two years to conquer compared to the multitude of small Central Pacific Islands (2,000 miles total length) that were traversed in one year.

144

Chapter V: Corsairs through the Central Pacific

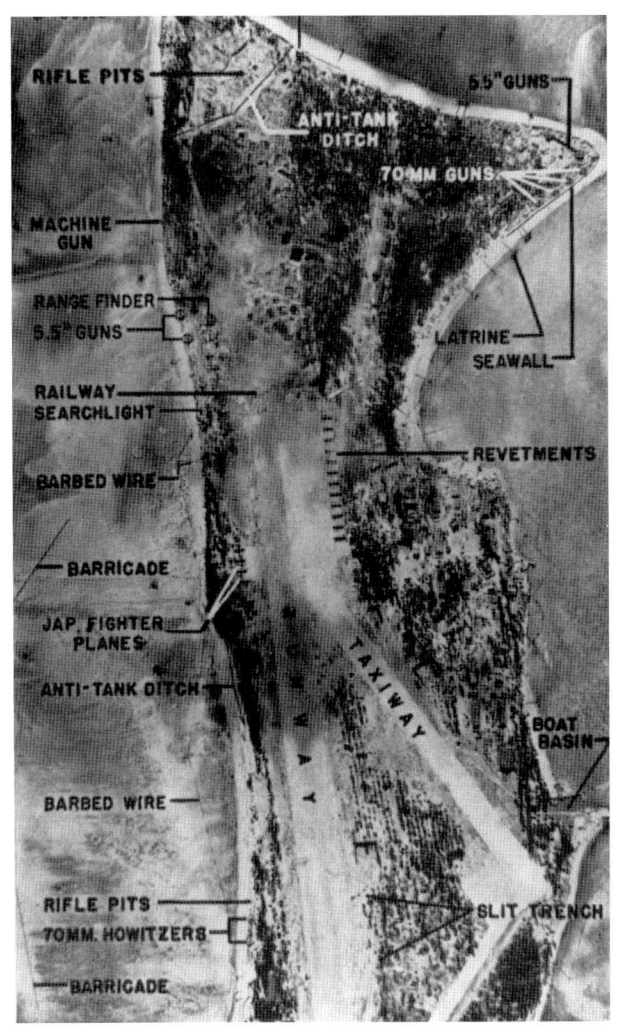

Hawkins Airfield, on Betio Island on Tarawa Atoll in the Gilbert Island chain, was hotly contested because of the airfield. Right photo shows the entire island, while the left photo is a close-up of the airstrips and all defensive installations that are identified by intelligence officers. Observe the curve in the island in the right hand photo, perhaps to conform with the atoll's curvature. Note the immense shoals larger than the island. (USAAC Photos, Author's File)

Flying over the Central Pacific Ocean is traversing a featureless seascape. Even the largest atoll is virtually invisible at altitude. Upper Photo: F4U-1A Corsairs on their way to dive bomb Marshall Island targets with 1,000lb bombs. The Corsair proved itself at dive-bombing in the Central Pacific. Lower Photo: Returning Corsairs appear diminutive in the spacious Pacific sky. (U.S. Navy Photos, Author's File)

U.S. Fifth Fleet. This was the most powerful aircraft carrier force in the U.S. Navy, ideal for assaulting the profusion of atolls and islands in the Central Pacific.

The task was similar to that of the Marine troops with top cover Marine aviators and Corsairs in the Solomons, except that there were no Corsairs or Marine aviators to provide close support for the Marine troops. Marine aviators and Corsairs were forbidden to operate from aircraft carriers; therefore, the Navy provided close support for the Marine troops.

Unlike the Solomon Chain, which was 550 miles long and contained six islands ranging from 75 to 120 miles long, including the New Georgian Group, with six smaller islands overaging 25 miles in diameter, the Central Pacific covered an area of millions of square miles, with hundreds of miniscule islands and atolls through which the U.S. planned a 5,000 mile path from the Ellice Islands to Iwo Jima and Okinawa.

An atoll is a ring of coral reef, not necessarily round, enclosing a lagoon. The atoll is usually separated into segments, and each one is called an island. For example, a few segments of Tarawa Atoll are called the islands of Betio, Bairiki, Eita, and Naanika. Atolls range in size from ten to twenty-five miles wide, usually surrounded by sandy shoals and, because they are composed of about 80 to 95 percent water, it requires exceptional navigation and a sharp eye to locate an atoll from the air.

A tragic example of the dangers in locating atolls and islands in this vast expanse of ocean happened on January 25, 1944, when 23 new VMF-422 F4U-1A Corsairs were ordered to fly from Hawkins Airfield on Tarawa to Nanomea, Ellice Islands (700 miles), and then to Funafuti (237 miles) to prepare for the impending Flintlock (Marshall) operation. Squadron commander Maj John S. McLaughlin Jr. did not request an escort plane.

Confusion in radio communication and changing weather conditions made maps useless in the overcast. Six Marines were lost because of forced landings, ditchings, bail outs, and disappearance in flight, while four others made forced landings and were rescued en route.

The survivors, consisting of thirteen aviators in twelve one-man rubber dinghys, drifted for two days until they were sighted by a Catalina flying boat. The plane was damaged in landing; however, a destroyer rescued the aviators about 100 miles from Funafuti.

A trio of Corsairs is ready to take off to dive-bomb bypassed Japanese islands. The bypassed islands were well prepared for offensive and defensive operations. Bombing in the Marshalls introduced the Corsair to dive-bombing, for which it was celebrated during the next decade. (U.S. Navy Photo, Courtesy Vought Aircraft)

Loss to the squadron was six aviators and 22 Corsairs.

RADM Alfred E. Montgomery's Southern Carrier Group headed northeast, returning from the November 11, 1943, raid on Rabaul, and dropped 115 tons of bombs on Tarawa Atoll on November 18, 1943. On the following day, the Southern Carrier Group dropped an additional 69 tons on the beleaguered atolls. Close air support for the attacking 2nd Marine Division was handled by U.S. Navy planes, flying from eight escort carriers.

Once the Central Pacific Offensive began, the advance forward was so rapid that the bomb-laden, land-based, short-legged Marine Corsairs (compared to large USAAC bombers) could not make the leaps forward from selected atoll to selected atoll. Only USAAF bombers or U.S. Navy carrier-based aircraft could fly to the targeted atolls. The U.S. Marines had been ruled off carriers and could not conduct rear guard action until the fighting was over and new airfields were ready for the bomb-laden Corsairs from which to attack the bypassed atolls that were still manned and armed by Japanese troops.

The U.S. Marine aviators and their Corsairs were relegated to base defense, escorting damaged ships as was done for the torpedoed aircraft carrier USS Independence, and engage in search and patrol of rear areas! The embattled U.S. Marine troops on Tarawa Atoll were bitterly disappointed that no U.S. Marine Corsairs flew close support for them.

The close support of Marine ground troops at Tarawa had been entrusted to carrier-based U.S. Navy pilots; however, in the opinion of Navy and Marine officers, the air support at Tarawa was ineffective because the Navy pilots had never trained with ground troops as a team.

As was discovered in the Solomons and Bismarcks fighting, bypassed enemy strongholds and islands in the Gilbert and Marshall islands did not wither and die just because they were no longer in a tactical front line location. Therefore, it was found prudent to continue to pound the principal pockets of well-armed enemy forces: Wotje; Jaluit; Maleolap; and Mille atolls. The Marine Corsairs were called upon to fulfill this task.

The MAG-22 Corsairs were based on Roi, Kwajalein Atoll, and flew 165 miles to Wotje Atoll; 225 miles to Maloelap Atoll; 320 miles to Mille Atoll; and 240 miles to Jaluit Atoll.

Parked on the Dalap Island airfield on Majuro Atoll in the Marshall Island Chain, a Corsair is ready to strike at the enemy with a single bomb in place. Wing is folded to make the plane fit in a smaller revetment and present a smaller target to the enemy when it is parked. (U.S. Navy Photo, National Archives)

Chapter V: Corsairs through the Central Pacific

Three intense fires are burning on Wotje Atoll, Marshall Islands, as a U.S. Navy observation plane flies past. This is the atoll that Charles Lindbergh 65 degree dive-bombed a Corsair with 4,000lbs of bombs. (U.S. Navy Photo, Office of Public Relations)

Jaluit- 26 of the 66 defending guns were destroyed and half of the Japanese vehicles and boats were damaged.
Wotje- All 14 heavy guns were destroyed; however, about 90 medium and light guns survived.
Maloelap- Fifty of the ninety guns were destroyed and only three command posts survived.
Mille- Two of 122 guns were still working after the raids.

In addition to the gun emplacements, numerous concrete blockhouses and other buildings were destroyed that made life for the bypassed Japanese unbearable.

According to the Casualty Division, Headquarters U.S. Marine Corps, twenty-two Corsairs were shot down during the 21month attack on bypassed targets.

The loss to the Japanese on the four bypassed atolls was that, of the original 13,701 Japanese, 7,440 failed to survive; killed in action, or by starvation or disease caused by food and medical deprivation.

Rear Admiral DeWitt C. Ramsey, Chief of the Bureau of Aeronautics, congratulated the Fourth Marine Air Wing for their work in developing a Corsair fighter-bomber technique for use in large scale operations.

It was during the massive carrier aircraft encounter known as the Battle of the Philippine Sea during Operation Forager in June 1944 that the Japanese first engaged in self-immolation, or Kamikaze. A Nakajima Tenzan "Jill" torpedo bomber was damaged, and perhaps the aviator was wounded, as it made its torpedo run on 19 June, so that Japanese aviator changed course and dived into the U.S. battleship *Indiana*; however, the torpedo failed to explode, but the plane caused considerable damage. This brave action was the pilot's decision and set the stage for future devastating Kamikaze attacks.

Dyess Field, Roi, Kwajalein Atoll, in the Marshalls, was completely rebuilt into a useful Corsair airfield.

A Corsair was the only airplane to ever receive an official citation. Major General Louis E. Woods, USMC, awarded Corsair No.122 from VMF-111 an official citation for completing 100 dive bombing and strafing missions during the Marshalls Campaign: "Without once causing trouble----- without a single time requiring pampering or special favors." Such was the Bent-Wing Corsair.

During a seven-week period in the Marshalls, Corsairs dive-bombed 200,000lbs of bombs on Japanese targets.

The Marine Corsairs attacked the bypassed islands with 500 and 1,000lb bombs. This activity was so successful that the Corsair became an extraordinary fighter-bomber that gave birth to the strike-fighter.

The Fourth Marine Air Wing Corsair fighter-bombers approached their target with a high speed 70-80 degree dive. The usual target was fifty feet diameter or less; however, the average dive-bombing target usually approaches 150 feet diameter. The smaller targets honed the aviators' skill during every following dive. In addition to 12,918 tons of bombs, the Corsairs fired 300 tons of five inch rockets and napalm. The Corsair's six .50 inch caliber machine guns also proved lethal to men and machines.

During the 21 month attack (November 1943 to August 1945) on the bypassed Marshalls, the land-based Corsairs wrought havoc on the very lives and existence of the defending Japanese.

In addition to aircraft and airfield structures, the Marine Corsairs caused the following destruction:

The airfield on Taroa Island, Maloelap Atoll, Marshall Chain is pockmarked with bomb craters; mute testimony of the carnage that U.S. air raids wrought. Bombing such as this saved the lives of countless infantrymen. (U.S. Navy Photo, Author's File)

Jaluit, Jaluit Atoll, Marshall Islands suffers under a cloud of smoke after a severe bombing from Corsairs. (U.S. Navy Photo, Office of Public Relations)

Dyess Airfield on Roi, Kwajalein Atoll, in the Marshall Chain, has well-placed runways and revetments that would be ideal for Corsairs to attack enemy strongholds in the Central Pacific. (U.S. Navy Photo, Author's File)

Once the Marine Corsairs were "let loose" in the Marshall Islands their fantastic record caught the attention of Maj Gen Louis E. Woods, USMC, and he issued the only citation ever given to an airplane. This citation was varnished into the Corsair's cockpit in accordance with the General's order that it "be a part of her permanent record." Corsair 122, an F4U-1D assigned to VMF-111 "Devil-Dogs," was the only aircraft to receive a citation. A plaque affixed to her instrument panel states: "In accomplishing her 100 missions, Corsair 122 logged more than 400 hours flying time; her total hops, included tests and reconnaissance flights, reached an amazing total of 178. Built for air combat, Corsair 122 proved her versatility by accepting 1,000 pound bombs slung from her belly, and without strain or protest developed into the hottest dive bomber with wings. Were there blood in her fuel line instead of 100 octane, she would be wearing the Purple Heart; for the patch on the leading edge of her wing attests to the accuracy of Jap antiaircraft fire. She has covered all the Jap bases in Marshall Islands like the morning dew." (U.S. Marine Corps Photo, Author's File)

In early August 1944 VADM WF "Bull" Halsey relieved VADM RA Spruance as Commander of the U.S. Fifth Fleet and Task Force 58.

During this change of command the Fleet and Task Force number changed from Fifth Fleet to Third Fleet, and Task Force Number 58 changed to 38. When the command returned the number 3 remained with Halsey, while the number 5 remained with Spruance. The objective was to enable the Admiral with no battle command to return to Pearl Harbor and plan the next naval move for when he returned to his command. Same fleet and task force, but different identification numbers depending upon the admiral.

In effect, only the Admiral's Staff changed leadership and took the fleet's number with them. All ships, officers, and crew remained the same except for the designation number. The U.S. Third Fleet and Task Force 38 were the same as U.S. Fifth Fleet and Task Force 58. Not two different fleets or two Task Forces.

The Palau Islands (Peleliu, Angaur, Ngesebus, and Koror) were invaded in September 1944 (Operation Stalemate). The group lay only 500 miles from the Philippines, which made it most important to both Americans and Japanese.

Peleliu was heavily defended; even heavy artillery and offshore naval guns firing for two hours failed to defeat the Japanese defenders; therefore, the Marines of VMF-114 were called to take over with their Corsairs.

Maj Robert F. (Cowboy) Stout's twenty Corsairs of VMF-114 "Death Dealers" bombed and strafed for a half-hour and waited while the artillery tried again for 20 minutes. Then, twenty "Death Dealer" Corsairs strafed the beaches just ahead of the troops for 15 minutes, flying at 50 feet. After that attack the island was taken.

Maj Gen Roy Geiger (Commander Western Force), Maj Gen William H. Rupertus (1st Marine Div), Maj Gen James T. Moore (Group Commander), and Maj Gen Julian C. Smith (Commander Expeditionary Troops and Landing Force) watched the Corsairs perform their amazing attack. Air and ground Marines had only 28 casualties, but they killed 440 enemy and captured 23 prisoners. Maj Stout was heartily congratulated by Gen Rupertus for this outstanding performance.

Major Stout had designed the VMF-114 squadron insignia; a green hand holding the cards "AA488." The two Aces and the Four indicated the squadrons number "114." Being from Wyoming "Cowboy Stout" was steeped in "Western Lore," so he added the two eights to make the cards

This close-up photo of Corsair 122 shows Marine Staff Sgt W. Howard Miller painting 100 bombs on the Corsair's fuselage, while Marine Master Tech Sgt Fred Smith, Squadron Line Chief, supervises. Corp Alex F Gerasimuk, Mechanic, watches from the cockpit. (U.S. Marine Corps Photo, Author's File)

Chapter V: Corsairs through the Central Pacific

Armorers fit a napalm bomb to a VMF-114 F4U-1D Corsair in Peleliu prior to an attack on "Bloody Nose Ridge." In addition to gasoline and the aluminum soaps thickener, used engine oil was sometimes added to the bomb ingredients. (Vought Aircraft Photo, Courtesy Paul Bower)

Vice Admiral William F "Bull" Halsey relieved Vice Admiral Raymond A Spruance as Commander of the U.S. Fifth Fleet and Task Force 58 in August 1944. The Fleet became the U.S. Third Fleet and TF 38 under Halsey's command. (U.S. Navy Photo, Via National Archives)

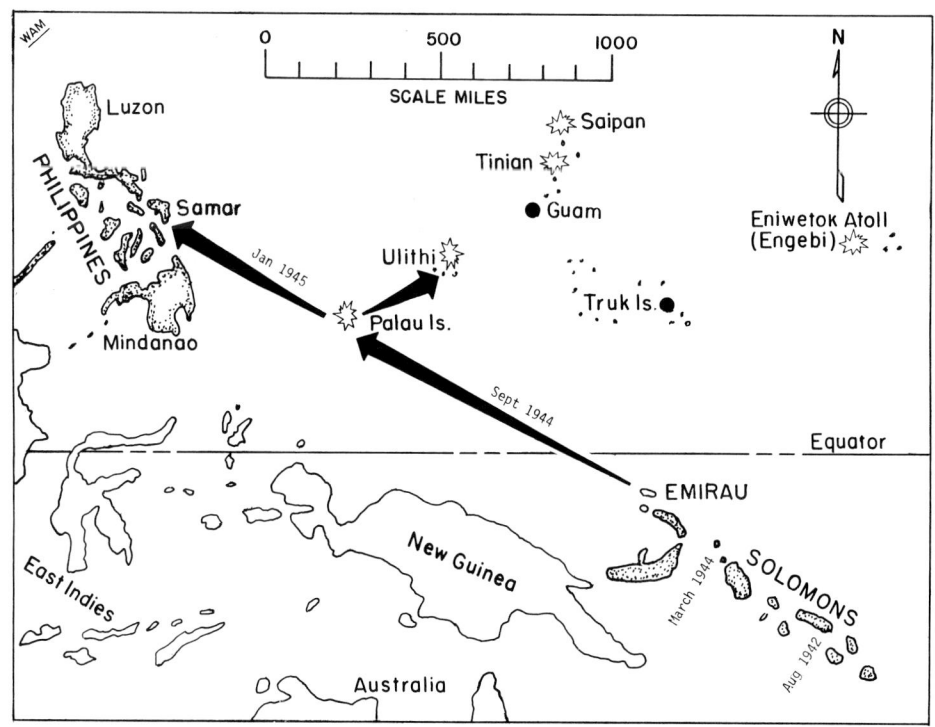

As Guam had been a springboard to Ulithi from the northeast, so were the Palau Islands a springboard to Ulithi from the southwest. Ulithi became the important centrally located American base in the Central Pacific as Truk had been for the Japanese Navy. The Palau Islands were also a springboard to the Philippines.

149

A VMF-114 Corsair has just dropped a napalm bomb on "Bloody Nose Ridge," Peleliu. The target was only a 15 second flight from the airfield, and many pilots did not bother to retract the landing gear. (USMC Photo, Author's File)

This is the precursor of the napalm bomb. It consisted of an auxiliary drop fuel tank filled with gasoline and used engine oil. The detonators were two 22lb bombs tied to the fuel tank. When the assembly hit the ground, the tank ruptured and the bombs exploded, igniting the sticky mixture. The design was conceived by famous German Ace and Inspector Of The Fighters Gen Adolf Galland in 1937. (Gen Adolf Galland, Author's File)

"AA488"; the exact hand that Wild Bill Hickock held when he was shot by Jack McCall. This "hand" of playing cards is known as the "Dead Man's Hand."

The Palau landings were covered by 11 CVE escort carriers; the largest contingent of escort carriers yet assembled. The escort carrier was coming into its own and was to really prove itself in the impending Philippines battle.

The Palaus battle witnessed one of the early Marine applications of airborne napalm. The objective was Bloody Nose Ridge; a promontory of the Umurbrogol Mountains on Peleliu where the Japanese had sought safety in caves and pits.

After the Corsairs of VMF-114 dropped twenty 1,000lb bombs within a 100 yard square area on the caves and pits with no effect they switched to napalm. However, after the aluminum soaps thickener was added to the captured Japanese gasoline the bombs lacked the adhesive effect that was expected. The addition of used engine oil to the mixture restored the adhesive effect desired.

The first known application of used engine oil in an incendiary bomb was conceived by the German Condor Legion during the Spanish Civil War in 1937.

Major Stout's VMF-114 continued the low level bombing and strafing from October 1944 to June 1945, losing only twenty-eight Marine Corsairs, including Major Stout, who was killed by ground fire over Koror on March 4, 1945.

Corsair squadrons operating from Peleliu destroyed 112 barges, 30 small boats, 58 trucks, and a locomotive. The only plane scored by a Marine in the Palaus was a "Jake" shot down by Maj Norman L Mitchell of VMF(N)-541 on October 31, 1944.

Maj William Kellum's F4U-2 Corsairs of VMF(N)-542 landed on the 3,514ft airstrip of Falalop, an island east of Ulithi, on October 29, 1944. The Corsairs were to fly day and night CAP for the 500 U.S. Navy ships anchored at Ulithi, now that Ulithi Atoll, in the Caroline Islands, was the principal American Naval Base in the Central Pacific.

The Corsair was capable of replacing U.S. Navy fast climbing CAP interceptors because the climb was almost 1,000 FPM greater than its closest U.S. Navy competitor.

The Corsair was also capable of diving with a two-thousand pound bomb load that could bring on the demise of dive bombers, thus introducing the fighter-bomber.

The Corsair's advanced performance as a fighter-bomber and an interceptor was one aircraft that could perform air defense and attack phases of aerial combat; one aircraft that can handle both efficiently must be considered worth two specialized airplanes.

Attacking Iwo Jima, Okinawa, and the Philippines, plus the Japanese Home Islands, would be the test for aviator and Corsair flying off and protecting carriers as they were originally intended.

Chapter V: Corsairs through the Central Pacific

Maj William Kellum led his F4U-2 night fighters of VMF(N)-542 to a landing on the 3,514ft airstrip on the island of Falalop, east of Ulithi. The squadron flew day and night CAP for the U.S. Fleet in Ulithi Harbor. (U.S. Navy Photo, Author's File)

U.S. Marine activity in the Palaus consisted of ground attack operations (dive bombing and strafing). Six victory Ace Capt Francis E Pierce Jr of VMF-121 poses by his Corsair named "Mary" in honor of his wife. Plane is a Goodyear FG-1A Corsair. VMF-121 scored 205 victories during its South West and Central Pacific service. (USMC Photo, Author's File)

VI

Corsair Carriers Strike Japan

GDR "Gus" Widhelm's VF(N)-101 Night Fighter Squadron of F4U-2 Corsairs (previously mentioned) detached a four-plane section in August 1943 that was placed under the command of LCDR Richard E. Harmer, while CDR Widhelm took the remainder of his Corsairs and aviators to the Solomons.

LCDR Harmer's detachment was designated VF(N)-75; however, once organized, Harmer's detachment was split again. Night fighters are not deployed en masse as are day fighters; one or two night fighters are sufficient to intercept intruders once they have been directed (vectored to enemy aircraft from land-based or shipboard radar stations).

Lt. Cecil Kullberg led half the Corsairs and aviators to board USS Intrepid (CV-11), while LCDR Harmer was assigned to board USS Enterprise (CV-6) with the remainder on January 9, 1944.

While USS Enterprise was supporting Allied landings in the Dutch East Indies, LCDR Harmer scored two twin-engine bombers on the night of April 24, 1944, off the coast of New Guinea; night victories scored by a carrier-based Corsair.

The uncanny part of Harmer's two victories is that the magnificent Corsair, designed as a day fighter and, for a variety of sporadic reasons, was deemed unsuitable for aircraft carrier duty, scored its first victory as a carrier-borne F4U-2 Corsair night-fighter in early 1944. Unusual?

After the battle of Tarawa in November 1943, Lt. Gen Holland M Smith, USMC, recommended that "consideration be given to assign at least one Marine Aircraft Wing (MAW) specifically for direct air support in landing operations." Unfortunately, the U.S. Navy was against assigning Marines to aircraft carriers or assigning escort carriers to the Marines.

General Roy Geiger (USMC) had stated many times. "The reason for the Marine Corps having airplanes is their use in close support of ground troops." Was anyone listening?

From Guadalcanal to Rabaul, the Marine Air Corps had been land-based. VADM John Towers (ComAirPac) noted that a third of the aviators being qualified for carrier service by the Naval Air Operational Command were Marines. He thought that was wasteful and recommended all Marines carrier training be stopped. Gen Ross E Rowell, USMC, agreed, and FADM Vimitz ordered it so that every new generation of Marine aviators were trained without ever flying from an aircraft carrier deck.

VADM John Towers, the officer who announced the Corsair to the world in 1940 when he was Chief of the Bureau of Ships, insisted Marines didn't want or need carriers. He told Gen Alexander Vandergrift, USMC (Commandant of the Marine Corps) "Your own people don't want carrier."

After making an inspection tour that ended in a Pearl Harbor conference with FADM Nimitz, Gen Vandergrift (RADM), Forrest Sherman, Maj Gen Ross E Rowell, Brig Gen Field Harris (Director of Marine Aviation), Brig Gen Gerald C Thomas, and VADM John Towers were all convinced that Marine aviators belong on aircraft carriers because

Left Photo: LCDR Harmer's VF(N)-75 was divided into two detachments: One was commanded by Lt Cecil L Kullberg and his F4U-2 Corsairs, embarked on USS Intrepid (CV-11). Right Photo: The remaining F4U-2 Corsairs, commanded by LCDR Richard E. Harmer, embarked aboard USS Enterprise (CV-6) on January 9, 1944. (U.S. Navy Photos, Author's File)

Chapter VI: Corsair Carriers Strike Japan

Left Photo: Rear Admiral Arthur C. Davis is shown presenting the Distinguished Flying Cross and Air Medal to Lt Ralph Weymouth while the then Lt Richard Harmer awaits presentation of the Distinguished Flying Cross. Right Photo: Lt Richard E. Harmer during February 1943. (U.S. Navy Photos, Author's File)

Col Clayton C Jerome, USMC (left), Chief of Staff to Maj Gen Ralph J Mitchell, devoted considerable effort to have Marines assigned to aircraft carriers. He became commanding officer of aircraft on the Philippine Islands. The Col is shown here with his driver, Corp L J Blasko. (Defense Dept-Navy, via National Archives, Author's File)

VADM John Towers (ComAirPac)(left) insisted to Gen Alexander A Vandergrift (Commandant of the Marine Corps, right) that the Marine Corps did not want carriers. (Naval Hist Center, Left, USMC; Right Author's File)

153

Corsair: The Saga of the Legendary Bent-Wing Fighter-Bomber

The fast carrier *USS Essex* (CV-9) was the first of its class. Observe two squadrons of Corsairs arranged on the after deck and one Corsair on the starboard catapult. (Official U.S. Navy Photo, Naval Photo Center, Wash DC)

they are the most proficient of all in direct air support operations. The officers recommended that when Marines are engaged in supporting troops during beachhead invasions they must operate from aircraft carriers.

Col Clayton C. Jermoe, USMC (Chief of Staff to Maj Gen Ralph J Mitchell), and Col Albert D Cooley, USMC (asst Director of Marine Aviation), also devoted considerable time and effort to have Marines assigned to aircraft—but what about Marine Corsairs?

F4U-1D BuNo 57157, which had been fitted with modified landing gear shock absorbers, was delivered to Grumman Aircraft Corporation for comparison with the satisfactory shock absorbers of the Hellcat on June 29, 1943. After several shock tests, Grumman chief test pilot Corwin H. Meyer made several landings during which he dropped about 25 feet to the runway and declared that the Corsair shock absorber was comparable to the Hellcat's oleo strut.

CDR T.K. Wright, USN, and Lt. Col John Dobbin, USMC, conducted a series of test landings with a modified shock absorber-fitted Corsair at NAS Jacksonville, Florida. The landings were so encouraging that carrier trials were conducted by VF-301, whose Corsairs completed 113 successful landings on *USS Gambier Bay* (CVE-73) in April 1944. The Corsair was then declared satisfactory for aircraft carrier operation, but that was not the last word.

An increase in Kamikaze activity was noted since a Jill torpedo bomber dived into a U.S. battleship in June 1944 during the Battle of the Philippine Sea in Operation Forager (Chapter Five). This prompted U.S. war planners to request a carrier fighter with better Combat Air Patrol performance than the F6F Hellcat. Time was too short to design and produce a new high-speed, fast-climbing CAP design; therefore, attention was directed to the Corsair's performance. The Corsair bested the Hellcat's cruising speed by about 23 mph, and the rate of climb was better than the Hellcat by about eight hundred feet per minute; therefore, the Corsair was chosen for CAP carrier duty. What happened to all the derogatory comments about Corsairs on carriers?

It was decided in October 1944 that at least two squadrons of Corsairs were to be stationed on each Essex-Class fast carrier for CAP and other duties.

The 33,000 ton deep load displacement Essex-Class carriers were powered by 150-,000 hp geared steam turbines, driving four propellers. Flight deck measured 96 ft x 860 ft.

Normal aircraft complement was two squadrons of fighters (36 aircraft) and two squadrons of dive bombers or torpedo bombers (36 aircraft) for a total of 72 aircraft; however, at times Essex-Class carriers operated with as many as 110 planes.

The Essex-Class carrier range was 15,000 miles at 15 knots (17.27 miles per hour). *USS Essex* (CV-9) was launched on July 31, 1942.

In addition to Fast Carriers and Light Carriers (CVL), the U.S. Navy's carrier inventory was completed with CVE Escort Carriers.

The Escort Carrier, or CVE (Carrier Air Escort), was a smaller, lighter, unarmored, and lightly armed aircraft carrier that depended upon the escorting destroyers for its protection. Initially intended in 1942 to escort convoys across the Atlantic Ocean to Britain, hence the name Escort, the carriers were found more useful sailing close to Pacific

Left Photo: Two squadrons of Corsairs from Air Group 84 arranged on the flight deck of *USS Bunker Hill* (CV-17). Right Photo: Armorers install high velocity air rocket (HVAR) missiles to the underside of the folded wings of Corsairs on flight deck of *USS Bunker Hill*. Planes are part of TF-58 sailing to attack Japan. (Official U.S. Navy Photo, Courtesy U.S. Naval Institute)

Chapter VI: Corsair Carriers Strike Japan

Two views of the Casablanca class Escort carrier USS *Guadalcanal* (CVE-60). Fifteen of these unarmored, lightly armed carriers fought Japanese battleships and cruisers into believing they were Halsey's fast carriers, forcing the Japanese to retreat. Casablanca carriers flew Wildcats and Avengers because Corsairs were still shore-based. (Dept of Defense, U.S. Navy, Author's File)

invasion beachheads and launching aircraft to strike at defending enemy troops and equipment during Allied beachhead invasion operations.

The first Escort Carriers were converted cargo ships and tankers; however, as demand increased for ships to be converted into Aircraft Carriers, so did demand increase for tankers and cargo ships until none were available for conversion.

The idea to make purpose-built Escort Carriers surfaced when west coast shipbuilder Henry J. Kaiser proposed the construction of escort carriers to the U.S. Navy who rejected the idea; however, Admiral Emory S. Land, head of the U.S. Maritime Commission, and President Franklin D. Roosevelt liked the idea and awarded a contract to Kaiser for fifty Escort carriers. Prestigious New York Naval Architect George G. Sharp and his staff was selected to design the mini-carriers in 1942.

This large class of carriers was officially named "Casablanca Class," but is often erroneously called "Kaiser Class." Eventually, the U.S. Navy had to participate in the areas of naval concern, such as arresting gear, aircraft support, catapult, guns, and ammunition. The author was deeply involved in the design of the "Casablanca Class" carriers.

During construction, the Casablanca Class mini-carriers were not permitted to use aluminum or copper to any extent, or to install electric motors, diesel engines, turbines, or gears. These were needed for the first-line combat ships.

The first Casablanca was launched in April 5, 1943, 10 months after the start of the project, and the 50th ship was launched on June 8, 1944.

The main engines were reciprocating steam engines, with each engine directly connected to one of two propellers. Casablancas were very steady and maneuverable. Because electric motors were forbidden, all ventilation and forced draft fans plus all pumps in the engine room were steam driven.

The Casablanca Hulls CVE-55 through CVE-104 displaced 10,200 tons fully loaded. Flight deck dimensions were 85 x 475 feet. Max speed was 19 knots (about 22 miles per hour). Range was 15,000 miles. Twenty-eight planes could be carried.

The Casablanca class has been unduly criticized and ridiculed by misinformed or uninformed writers over the years; however, only six of the 50 Casablancas were sunk by enemy action. A Casablanca was the only carrier to capture a submarine.

The recapture of the Philippine Islands was important not only to the U.S. military strategy, but to General MacArthur as well, because his return to the Islands would signal a victory to the American people. The General's advance to Japan was from Australia to New Guinea and the Philippines, while Admiral Nimitz's path to Japan was through the Mariannas, to Iwo Jima and Okinawa.

Admiral Toyoda and the Japanese Imperial General Staff realized that the American Forces would soon begin another thrust westward, but did not know where the next move would be. Japan envisioned a final decisive battle and made plans for four alternative battle fronts. The plans were called Sho, which is the Japanese word for victory. Sho 1 prepared for an attack on the Philippines; Sho 2 anticipated landings on the Ryukyu

FADM Soemu Toyoda, Supreme Admiral of the Japanese Navy, was willing to fight to keep the Philippine Islands, even if it meant losing the Japanese Navy. (U.S. Naval Historical Center, Author's File)

Islands (Nansei Shoto) and on Formosa (Taiwan); Sho 3 foresaw U.S. landings on all Japanese home islands, especially Kyushu; and Sho 4 assumed a U.S. attack in the north in Hokkaido.

The Japanese Army, Air Force, and Navy were all to take part in the impending battle. The four remaining Japanese aircraft carriers were truly useless because they had no trained aviators and only about 100 planes. The experienced Japanese aviators and carriers had been decimated by Admiral Spruance's Fifth Fleet carrier planes during the Battle of the Philippine Sea; therefore, the Japanese were forced to offer their carriers as sacrificial decoys in all of their Sho plans.

VADM Halsey's aviators had flown a total of 2,400 sorties, or individual flights, during 8 and 9 September against Mindanao and on 12 and 13 September against the Viscayan Sea islands, but the raids were weakly challenged. On the evening of 13 September, VADM Halsey assumed the Philippine Japanese Air Forces were so weak that he should attack as soon as possible. He presented his plan to FADM Nimitz at once and to Gen MacArthur, ADM King, and the Joint Chiefs of Staff. All agreed on 20 October 20; only Halsey was wrong!

The Japanese Air Forces in the Philippines were only holding their planes back and saving them for the U.S. landings they expected to take place very soon.

Another reason for the weak Japanese aerial defense in the southern and central Philippines was that a report had been received in the Japanese Air Operations Center at Clark Field, near Manila, that U.S. Carriers were sailing north. The natural Japanese assumption was that the invasion would be on Luzon; therefore, many Japanese air groups and air divisions had been transferred to Luzon to fight the Americans.

The Third Fleet's Task Force 38 kept pressure on the Japanese with air raids on and around the Philippines as far as Okinawa and Formosa during late September and early October. The objective of the raids was to reduce Japanese air power so it could not protect Japan's oil supply route from Borneo through the South China Sea and into the Philippine Sea.

The American raids also tried to cut Japan's Philippine aircraft supply route from Japan and Okinawa with which Japan supplied Japanese forces in the Philippines with airplanes to oppose the Allies and also used as flying-off bases.

The Japanese fought back by launching shore-based aircraft from the Philippines. These included torpedo-carrying Bettys, Jills, and Kates, but the Task Force 38 Corsair Combat Air Patrols repulsed every Japanese raid, which resulted in very slight damage to the American ships. The untrained and inexperienced Japanese aviators proved impotent against the Corsair CAP defense of the American ships. There was only one solution left to stop the American Juggernaut.

Totally frustrated by their failure to penetrate the Task Force 38 Combat Air Patrols, a group of dedicated Japanese aviators decided to immolate themselves to sink or disable the American carriers as had been done to the American battleship in June 1944. Their decision was apparently a spontaneous and personal action devoid of official sanction. On Sunday, October 14, 1944, this group of Japanese dive-bomber aviators took off for their scheduled sortie, but when confronted by the American carrier Combat Air Patrols, the Japanese aviators plunged their bomb-laden planes into the American carriers.

Obviously, the success of the immolated aviators came to the attention of high-ranking officials in the Imperial Japanese Navy, some of which felt that the suicide tactics should be officially adopted as the only way the American carriers could be destroyed.

By 17 October Gen MacArthur's invasion fleet was moved toward the entrance to Leyte Gulf which made it clear to FADM Toyoda that the Americans planned to attack the Philippines. The Japanese admiral also decided for an all-out defense of the Islands because, he reasoned, the Philippine Islands were more important, defensively, than the weakened Japanese fleet that had lost so many trained pilots.

Sho 1 was placed in operation at once, which included the practice of immolation. VADM Takijiro Onishi arrived in the Philippines to assume command of the First Air Fleet and the "Special Attack" concept of intentional suicide attacks which, it was agreed, was the only way to stop the U.S. Navy "steamroller."

The Japanese named this practice "Kamikaze" or "Divine Wind," which appears to have two conflicting derivations. Both involve an ancient enemy about to invade Japan when a Divine Wind appeared and destroyed the enemy fleet.

One story involves the Mongols of the Thirteenth Century, while the other involves the Koreans of roughly the same period. Admiral Onishi felt that this new Divine Wind, or "Kamikaze," would also destroy Japan's modern-day enemy fleet.

As the practice of Kamikaze progressed, it was refined into a more effective procedure: the bomb-laden attacker released his bombs a few hundred feet above the target and then altered his drive to strike the target a distance away from the bomb explosions, thereby causing more damage; the bomb's explosion in one area and the plane's engine and flaming fuel in another area.

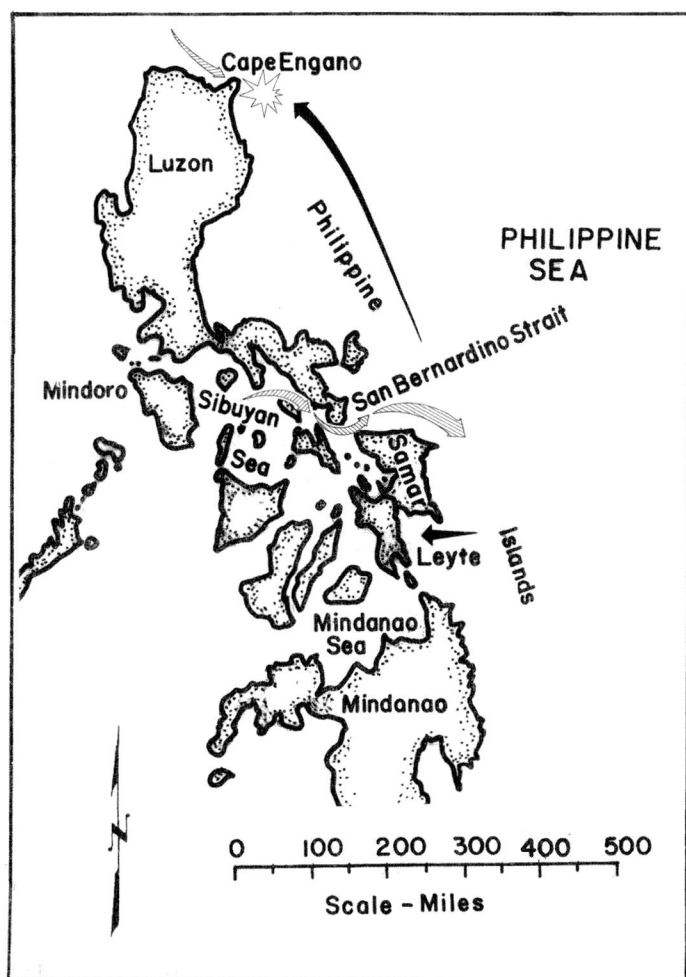

VADM William F. (Bull) Halsey's desire for a victorious carrier vs carrier battle impelled the admiral to take the Third Fleet 500 miles northward, away from its assigned post, to battle a Decoy "Japanese Carrier Fleet." As soon as Halsey sailed north, the Japanese battleship and battle cruisers emerged from the Sibuyan Sea and attacked the Escort Carriers of the Seventh Fleet. Striped arrows are Japanese warships' path.

Chapter VI: Corsair Carriers Strike Japan

By October 20, 1944, Kamikaze attack bases had been established at Mabalacat, on Luzon, and at Davau, on Mindanao. The objective was for the aviator to dive his bomb and plane into American ships, rather than be shot down by the CAP. The preferred Kamikaze targets were U.S. aircraft carriers.

Two U.S. Fleets were heading towards Leyte Gulf:

VADM William F Halsey Jr, commander of the U.S. Navy Third Fleet that included eight fast carriers, with Corsairs aboard, and nine light carriers, plus five battleships and numerous cruisers and destroyers.

VADM Thomas C Kinkaid, commander of the U.S. Seventh Fleet, that consisted of four converted-Sangamon Class tanker CVE escort carriers and 15 Casablanca Class twin-screw escort carriers, plus an assortment of old battleships, cruisers, and destroyers.

Admiral Kinkaid's U.S. Seventh Fleet had worked so often in General MacArthur's campaigns that the Seventh Fleet was often unofficially called "Doug MacArthur's Navy."

The Leyte landings, including sea and air cover, was called "Operation Reno," and was to become the largest battle of World War Two, involving one of the most complicated and bewildering command arrangements of the war.

The American force consisted of three concentric arcs across Leyte Gulf: the innermost arc comprised destroyers, destroyer escorts, cruisers, and battleships enclosing the hundreds of supply ships, troopships, and landing craft; the escort carriers, often called Baby Flattops or Jeep Carriers, formed the center arc, about 70 miles from the beachhead; while the outermost arc comprised Admiral Halsey's Third Fleet that spread over 300 miles of ocean. Task Force 38 carrier aircraft were to engage Japanese shore-based planes to prevent them from reaching the battleships, cruisers, and destroyers, while planes from the Casablanca Class CVE carriers covered the troop landings while bombing and strafing.

Halsey, with his Third Fleet, reported to Nimitz, while Kinkaid, with his Seventh Fleet, reported to MacArthur. Kinkaid was concerned with getting the troops ashore and protecting them while, instead of being concerned with protecting the invasion force, Halsey appeared to be

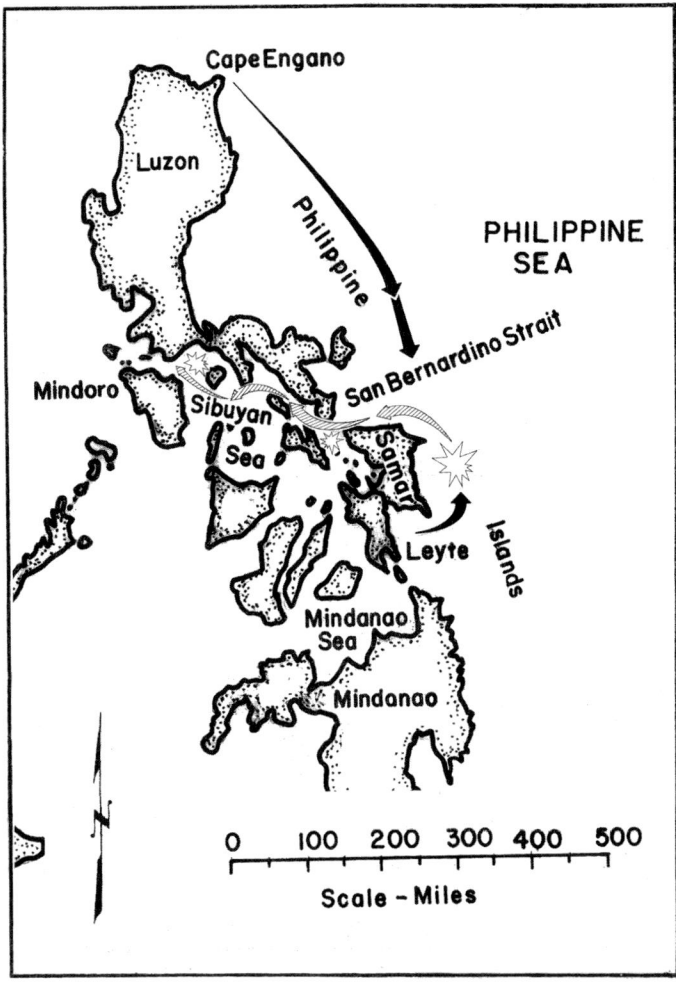

The Escort Carrier's aircraft fought the Japanese battleship and battlecruisers so furiously that the Japanese retreated back through San Bermardino Strait to the Sibuyan Sea. Assuming the Escort Carriers were Halsey's Third Fleet, the Japanese retired from the battle of Samar as the Third Fleet was returning from Cape Engano. Large bomb-burst indicates attacks by Escort Carriers. Small bomb-burst indicates attacks by Third Fleet's aircraft attacking the retiring Japanese ships. Striped arrows are path of Japanese ships.

As soon as VADM Halsey left Leyte Gulf for Cape Engano, Japanese battleships and battle cruisers passed through San Bernardino Strait and bombarded the escort carriers guarding the Allied landing in Leyte Gulf. Observe the Japanese ships firing at the mini-carriers at a seventeen-mile range. (U.S. Navy Photo via U.S. Naval Institute, Author's File)

concerned with a carrier battle. One thousand American ships and 200,000 men were involved in Leyte Gulf and their fate was in the balance.

Knowing Admiral Halsey's interest in a carrier battle, Adm Toyoda conceived SHO-1 to seduce VADM Halsey and his Third Fleet away from Leyte Gulf in order that Admiral Kurit's Japanese battleship force, waiting in Sibuyan Sea, could sail through San Bernardino Strait and attack the Seventh Fleet CVE carriers and escorting destroyers, thereby annihilating the American invading forces in Leyte Gulf while the Third Fleet was away chasing a decoy at Cape Engano.

Without informing Adm Kindaid, Gen MacArthur, or Adm Nimitz, Adm Halsey fell for the ruse and sailed north to battle Admiral Ozawa's "carrier force" that actually consisted of helpless Japanese aircraft carriers with 100 planes plus two battleship/carriers with no aircraft that had been converted by the removal of the aft gun turrets.

When the decoy launched about 20 planes they were shot down by the Task Force 38 CAP Corsairs, followed by the sinking of four carriers and two destroyers by Task Force 38 carrier bombers and torpedo-bombers, including Corsair dive-bombers.

157

Corsair: The Saga of the Legendary Bent-Wing Fighter-Bomber

While the Third Fleet was engaging Admiral Ozawa's decoy force at Cape Engano, Admiral Kurita's battleships and battlecruisers had left Sibuyan Sea and were approaching Leyte Gulf. *USS Fanshaw Bay* (CVE-70) radar detected ships 18 miles to the northwest at 6:42 AM on 25 October. Eleven minutes later ships could be seen on the horizon. Adm Toyoda's Sho 1 was working, and the Japanese battleships began firing 14 and 18 inch shells at a range of 17 miles. The min-carriers launched as many planes as possible loaded with depth charges, bombs, torpedoes, and antipersonnel bombs, or whatever was available.

A Kamikazi was diving at the Casablanca carrier *USS Petrof Bay* (CVE-80); however, thanks to the carrier's excellent maneuverability the carrier was able to dodge the Japanese plane and shoot it down. Another Kamikazi hit *USS Lo* (CVE-63), which sank in 30 minutes.

Other groups of mini-carriers joined the attack, and their Avengers sank the Cruisers *Chickuma*, *Chokai*, and *Suzuya*; however, the CVE *USS Gambier Bay* (CVE-73) was hammered to a wreck by Admiral Kurita's battleship's big guns.

The little carriers and aircraft put up such an admirable fight that Admiral Kurita was not certain whether or not VADM Halsey had "taken the bait" and really left Leyte Gulf. Considering the beatings his battleships and battlecruisers were receiving from the mini-carrier planes, Kurita surmised that Halsey's Third Fleet was still in Leyte Gulf. Knowing his few ships could not battle Halsey's Third Fleet, Adm Kurita retreated his battleships and battlecruisers when they were only about five miles from

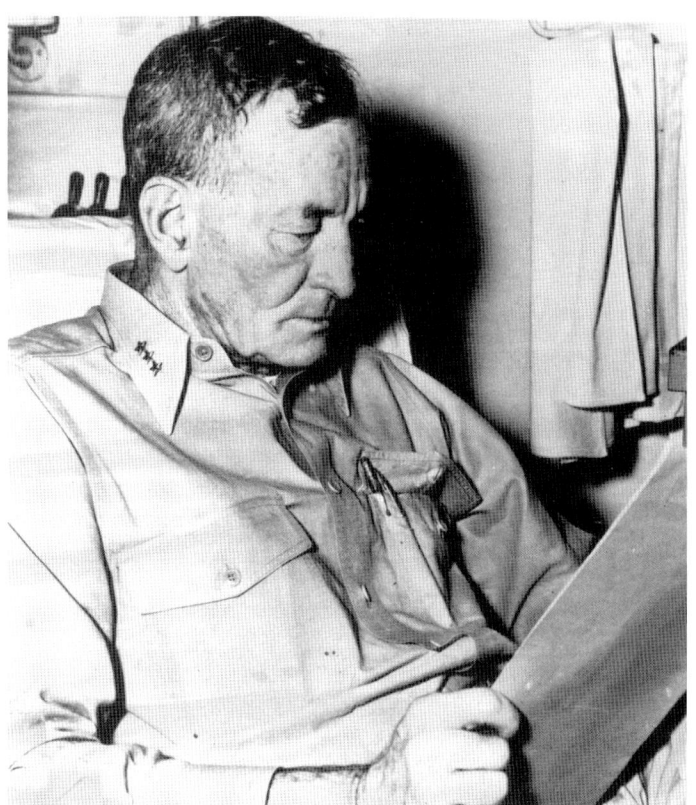

VADM John S McCain, Commander Task Force 38, on board *USS Hancock* (CV-19), ordered continuous fighter sweeps over all known Kamikaze bases with successful results. (U.S. National Archives, Courtesy Fred Pernell)

USS Belleau Wood (CVL-24) was hit by a Kamikaze on October 30, 1944, off the Philippine coast. Flight deck crews are moving TBM Avengers away from the flames while water is sprayed on them. This kept the Avenger loss down to 12 planes. Note another U.S. Carrier aflame in the distance. (U.S. Naval Historical Center, Author's File)

USS Intrepid (CV-11), the most bombed and Kamikazed U.S. aircraft carrier, was hit by Kamikazes on November 25, 1944, during the Philippine campaign. Crewmen attempt to extinguish fires burning below the Flight Deck. (U.S. Navy Photo, Author's File)

Chapter VI: Corsair Carriers Strike Japan

Tacloban airfield, on Leyte, belies the hardships endured during its creation because of deep mud and Kamikaze attacks. (U.S. Army Photo, Author's File)

This "freak accident" may not have been an accident at all: a Japanese plane crashing so close to a row of Corsairs parked at Tacloban Airfield that it burned a Corsair's fabric away and scorched the paint. Thoughts are that a wounded Japanese aviator could have decided to immolate himself and dived into parked Corsairs on the airfield. Incident occurred on December 6, 1944, and the Corsair belonged to VMF-115. (USMC Photo, Author's File)

the invasion beachhead, and passed through San Bernardio Strait into the Sibuyan Sea.

Admiral Kinkaid had asked for battleship support from Admiral Nimitz, who sent this message to Admiral Halsey: "All the world wants to know where is Task Force 34?" (Adm Halsey's Battleship Force).

Upon FADM Nimitz's admonishment Halsey and his Third Fleet returned to Leyte Gulf in time to catch the Japanese battleships passing through Mindoro Straits on October 26-27, 1944, and Halsey's Air strikes sank the Japanese destroyers *Noshiro* and *Hayashime*, plus the cruiser *Abukuma*. The giant battleship Yamato was damaged. It is interesting that the CVE carrier aircraft inflicted more damage to the Japanese ships than had Halsey's Third Fleet aircraft.

After Halsey's rush to Cape Engano (often called "Bull's Run") he replaced VADM Mitcher with VADM John S McCain, possibly because Mitcher disagreed with Halsey's leaving Leyte Gulf for Cape Engano. VADM McCain ordered fighter sweeps over Kamikaze bases as commander of Task Force 38.

When VADM Marc A Mitcher was free, he sped to Washington to testify how well U.S. Marines and Corsairs operated from carriers.

Kamikaze raids increased with Task Force 38 as the prime target, even after the Leyte beachhead became secure.

As with the Solomons campaign, the first task in the Philippines was the construction of airfields. The initial invasion point was Tacloban, Leyte, where a large airstrip was built under the tremendous handicaps of deep

Commencement Bay Class Escort Carrier (Marine Carrier) *USS Cape Gloucester* (CVE-109) appears fresh from the shipyard, revealing construction details clearly. Class is often called "Corsair Carriers." (U.S. Naval Institute, Author's File)

This plaque was mounted on a *USS Cape Gloucester* (CVE-109) bulkhead to relate the carrier's history. Note that the carrier served in the South China Sea and along the Japanese-occupied Chinese coast. Also note the activity of its Corsairs mentioned on the plaque. (USMC Photo, Courtesy Lt Col OK Williams, USMC (Ret))

Members of VMF-351 "Fighting Bulldogs" pose with their newly acquired USS Cape Gloucester (CVE-109). Squadron Commander and Marine Carrier Group Four (MCVG-4) Commanding Officer Lt Col Donald K. Yost, USMC, is seated fifth from left, while Capt O. Kieth Williams, USMC, is seated extreme left. (USMC Photo, Courtesy Lt Col OK Williams, USMC (Ret))

mud and Japanese Kamikaze attacks. Located near Leyte Gulf, the airfield depended on protection from carrier aircraft until it was completed.

During October 1943 U.S. Navy Planners had decided that a U.S. Marine CVE aircraft carrier program must be organized, and work began on the design.

The keels for the first U.S. Marine escort carriers were laid from late 1943 through 1945, during which time critical materials and machinery had become more readily available than when the Casablanca Class was conceived. Seventeen of the new "Commencement Bay" class were constructed (CVE 105 to 121). Flight deck measured 80x495 feet. The 16,000 shaft horsepower steam turbine powerplant developed a maximum speed of 19 knots (about 22 miles per hour). Aircraft complement was 33 planes. Small task groups were to cover amphibious assault operations, while others were to engage in ASW activities. Defensive armament included two 5 inch guns on the Main Deck aft of the Flight Deck in addition to 40mm and 20mm antiaircraft guns.

Now, the U.S. Marines had their own Navy; however, it was necessary for U.S. Navy officers and enlisted men to man the new U.S. Marine aircraft carriers.

The newer and larger "Commencement Bay" escort carrier design was selected for the Marines by December 1943. The Marine CVE training program, under the direction of Col Albert D Cooley, had progressed to the point that it was assigned its first CVE: USS Block Island (CVE-105) with squadrons VMF-511 and VMTB-233, commanded by Lt. Col John F Dobbin; USS Gilbert Islands (CVE-106) with squadrons VMF-512 and VMTB-143, commanded by Col William R Campbell; USS Vella Gulf (CVE-107), commanded by Maj Royce W Coln; USS Kula Gulf (CVE-108); USS Cape Gloucester (CVE-109) with VMF-351 "Fighting Bulldogs," commanded by Lt. Col Donald K Yost.

The Marine CVE (Carrier Aircraft Escort) program consisted of a six-ship Carrier Division, with each CVE to have a Marine Carrier Air Group (MCVG).

Each MCVG consisted of two squadrons: an eighteen-plane fighter squadron VMF (CVS) and a twelve-plane torpedo-bomber squadron VMTB(CVS). The (CVS) indicated that the squadrons were specially trained and were part of the CVE program.

Col. Cooley's pilots were not to be the first Marines to fly from carriers because of the "Kamikaze Terror." Com Third Fleet requested additional fighters, which caused VADM George D Murray (ComAirPac) to state that the "Critical Situation" required Marine VMF squadrons to join the complement of the fast carriers.

The increase in Kamikaze activity demanded more American fighters and fewer dive bombers and fewer torpedo bombers. The current fast carrier complement at that time was 54 VF, 24 VSB, and 18 VTB.

The pressure of Kamikaze attacks increased the demand for aviators to fly Corsair CAP. In view of the fact that dive bombers and torpedo bombers were cut back, many aviators transferred to Corsair fighters. Capt George E. Dooley is one aviator who transferred from VMSB-131 and VMTB-131 to fly Corsairs in VMF-216, which he commanded as Maj George E. Dooley on USS Wasp. (National Archives, Author's File)

Chapter VI: Corsair Carriers Strike Japan

Lt Col William A Millington is given the signal to takeoff in his Corsair on USS Essex flight deck. Observe the moister-laden telltale Corsair propeller helix. (USMC Photo, Author's File)

Capt Howard J. Finn's division was based on USS Essex (CV-9) and raided Okinawa and Japan. Shown here from left to right are: Capt Edmund Hartstock; Lt George B Parker (standing); Capt Finn; and Lt William Mc Gill preparing for a mission. (USMC Photo, Author's File)

The complement change was to add 19 fighters and reduce dive-bombers and torpedo-bombers to 15 planes each. This resulted in a complement of 73 fighters with 15 VSB and VTB each. The U.S. Navy was also short of fighter aviators, and therefore, depended upon U.S. Marine fighter aviators to fly the fast carrier fighters. In addition, dive bomber aviators were encouraged to transfer to Corsair fighter squadrons.

Capt George Dooley gave up his dive and torpedo bombers for the opportunity to fly the Corsair and became Commanding Officer of VMF-216. Many fighter aviators also requested the opportunity to fly Corsair fighters in action.

The first fast carrier to be equipped with U.S. Marines and Corsairs was USS Essex (CV-9).

WMF-124 (Lt. Col William A. Millington) and VMF-213 (Maj David E. Marshall) embarked USS Essex (CV-9) in Ulithi Atoll on December 28, 1944. The two squadrons operated as one, under the command of Millington, except for administrative records, which continued to be kept separately.

Lt. Col William A Millington's VMF-124 began operations at once with his aviators and Corsairs, which confirmed the Corsair to be carrier-qualified.

VMF-124 Corsairs escort an Avenger torpedo bomber returning from the January 3, 1945, Okinawa raid. Observe the long-range fuel tanks on the Corsairs. Planes were based on USS Essex (CV-9). (USMC Photo, Author's File)

Rear Admiral Frederick C Sherman (right) listens intently as Lt Col William A. Millington relates details of his scoring and his wingman's scoring of Japanese fighters on January 3, 1945. Capt C.W. Weber (left), master of USS Essex (CV-9), also listens attentively on the bridge of the Essex. (U.S. Navy Photo, Author's File)

Corsair: The Saga of the Legendary Bent-Wing Fighter-Bomber

Marine Lt. Col William A Millington was promoted to Commander Air Group Four (CAG-4) aboard *USS Essex* when the former Group commander, Navy CDR Otto Kinsman, was hit by antiaircraft fire on 15 January. He ditched safely but disappeared before he could be rescued. Never before had a U.S. Marine officer been placed in command of a U.S. Navy Air Group; however, Col Millington was well qualified for the command. (National Archives, Author's File)

USS Essex sortied from Ulithi on 30 December as part of a Task Force 38 armada that included 30 carriers, 13 of which were fast carriers, and an assortment of almost 800 other ships.

On January 3, 1945, Task Force 38 made a preemptive strike on Okinawa, about 800 miles northeast from Lingayen Gulf, to support MacArthur's proposed landing.

Col Millington was leading a flight of VMF-124 Corsairs on Jan. 3, 1945, escorting VTB-4 Avengers returning from a raid on Okinawa, when two Kawasaki Nick twin-engine fighters attacked the Marines. Millington quickly turned toward the nearest "Nick" and scored the first victory. His wingman destroyed the second Japanese fighter in the same manner.

On that same day other carrier-based Corsairs flew three move strikes, scoring 27 aerial victories, plus 207 aircraft on the ground by strafing and bombing. Capt Howard J. Finn's division scored heavily in this action.

Meanwhile, Gen MacArthur planned to invade Luzon, not only to capture Manila, but to attack the Japanese in the Philippines from the north. He decided upon an amphibious landing in Lingayen Gulf, rather than "island hop" and fight the Japanese in numerous land battles.

As MacArthur's invasion force threaded its more than 600 miles from Leyte Gulf south through Surigao Strait and west into Minidinao Sea, and then north into the Sulu Sea, through the Mindoro Strait, and into the South China Sea to land in Lingayen Gulf.

The General's Casablanca Escort Carrier, destroyers, destroyer escort, cruisers, battleships, troopships, and minesweepers were pounded by more than 50 Kamikaze aircraft from all directions during the entire journey.

One Escort carrier was sunk while four others were damaged. A destroyer, destroyer escort, and cruiser were also damaged, but were able

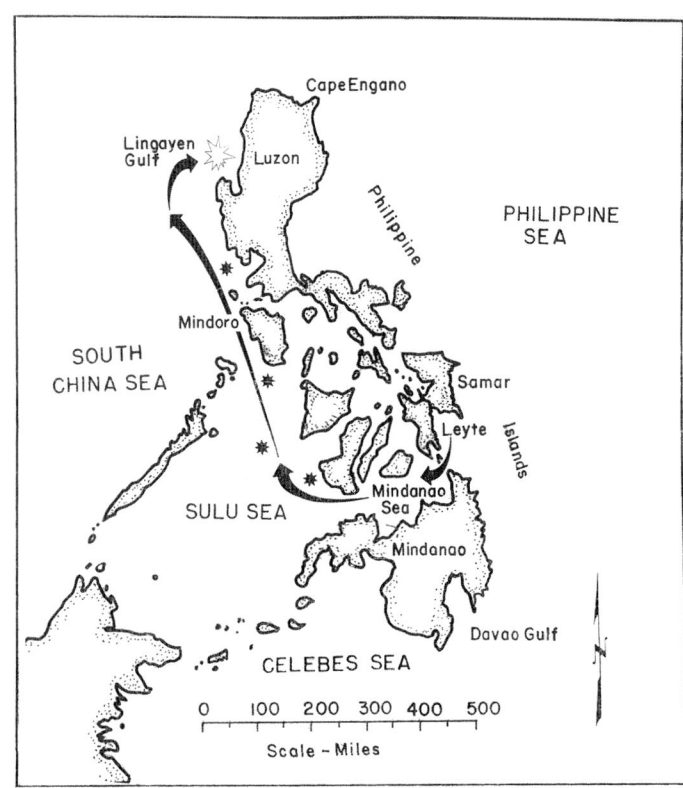

This schematic map illustrates the route taken by Gen Douglas MacArthur from Leyte Gulf to Lingayen Gulf in order to avoid the land battles of an island-hopping route. Although battered by Kamikazes throughout, the water route was considered successful because the troop landings in Lingayen Gulf were made on schedule. Small black stars represent Kamikaze attacks.

Corsair CAP intruder interceptors and fighter-bombers were arranged on the flight decks of TF-38 aircraft carriers, similar to that shown in this photograph, during the invasion of the South China Sea. Note the Avenger Torpedo-Bombers in the after left area of the flight deck. The Corsairs and Avengers often worked as a team. (Sal Marrone Photo, Courtesy Sal Marrone)

Chapter VI: Corsair Carriers Strike Japan

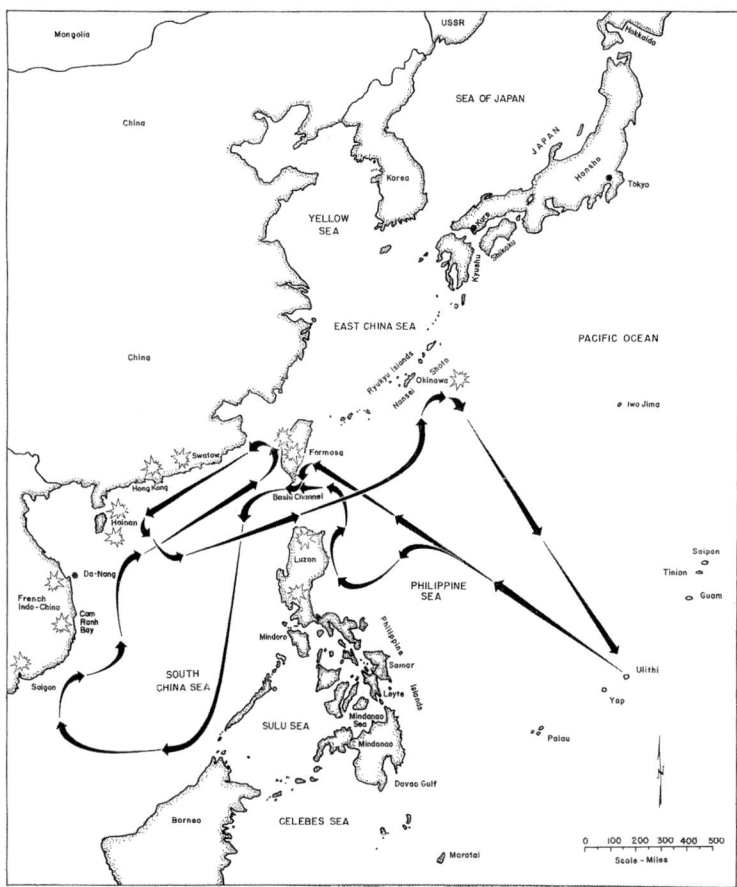

The route of TF-38 in the South China Sea invasion is simplified in this schematic map. TF-38 ships' routes are shown with arrows. Corsair and Avenger flights are not illustrated for simplicity. Planes flew from the carriers to explosion symbols, representing the strikes. The Third Fleet returned to Ulithi on January 26, 1945, where it became the Fifth Fleet once again.

to sail on, and two battleships, two cruisers, and two other destroyers were seriously damaged.

The Escort Carrier Wildcats found it difficult to beat off the swarms of Kamikaze attackers; however, despite the Japanese defense, MacArthur's troops succeeded with their Lingayen Gulf beachhead.

In order to protect MacArthur's Lingayen Gulf landing force, Admiral McCain ordered Corsairs from his Fast Carrier Task Force to Lingayen Gulf on 6 and 7 January to assist MacArthur's invasion force. Task Force 38 Corsairs engaged only eighteen enemy planes in the air, but destroyed more than 200 Japanese aircraft on the ground.

The weather over the Northern Philippines had been so overcast and stormy that seventeen *USS Essex* Corsairs were lost because of navigation errors, killing seven Marine aviators. The surviving Marine aviators rightfully complained that it was impossible to "learn navigation and carrier operations in one week as well as the Navy aviators learned in six months."

This most audacious naval dash, eclipsing that of the celebrated "English Channel Dash," was planned by VADM "Bull" Halsey to send Task Force 38 into the South China Sea during January 1945. Halsey had received intelligence information that Japanese carriers, battleships, marine carriers, cruisers, and destroyers were presumably located at Japanese-occupied Cam Ranh Bay, in French Indo-China. The Admiral wanted revenge by destroying the ships that evaded him in Leyte Gulf, especially if he could also intercept the Japanese ships, as they might sail to stop MacArthur's landing in Lingayen Gulf.

Halsey chose the Bashi Channel, at the southern tip of Formosa, for the Task Force crossing into the South China Sea. This channel was precariously near a Japanese airfield, 80 miles from the southern tip of Formosa; however, the "die was cast" and the Task Force refueled on 8 January.

While MacArthur's troops went ashore at Lingayen Gulf on 9 January, Halsey sent an armada of aircraft against Formosa to thwart any Japanese attack against MacArthur's forces. Very few Japanese aircraft were airborne in the treacherous weather; however, VADM Halsey claimed 15 enemy ships sunk.

In early January 1945, 11 carriers, 6 battleships, 13 cruisers, 48 destroyers, Marine Carriers, two night carriers, and a fuel replenishment force ventured into the South China Sea via the Bashi undetected by the Japanese.

Bomb-carrying Corsairs escorted Avengers, bombing airfields, ships, and petroleum installations with very little opposition except antiaircraft fire. January 12, 1945, was one of the greatest days of the U.S. Navy regarding ships sunk: 33 merchant ships and 14 warships went down in the harbor of Saigon. Also sunk by mistake was the French cruiser *Lamotte-Picquet*, which resulted in French protests. Major Fay V. Domke, USMC, greatly contributed to the sinkings with his Corsair. Two years later the ships were still visible on the harbor bottom; vivid proof to the accuracy of the bombing.

The American armada returned via the China coast, Formosa, Hainan, and Okinawa, arriving at Ulithi by January 26, 1945, in time for Admiral Halsey to transfer the Third Fleet to Admiral Spruance, who led it as the Fifth Fleet. TF-38 became TF-58 under VADM Mitcher.

Now the islands Tinian, Guam, and Sapipan, in the Marianas, were taken by American forces, and they were made ready as Boeing B-29 Superfortress long-range bomber bases for the strategic bombing of Japan. The Marianas are about 1,600 miles to Formosa and to Japan. In 1945, a

3,200 mile non-stop bomber flight was considered extremely hazardous; fraught with danger from mechanical malfunctions and/or from damage inflicted by intercepting Japanese fighters. In either case, the limping bomber would be forced down in the open seas.

Japanese-occupied Iwo Jima, in the Volcano Island group, is about halfway between the Marianas and Japan; in the path of the proposed B-29 route to Japan, Japanese fighters based on Iwo Jima would be a threat to any superfortress enroute to and from Japan.

In American hands, Iwo Jima would be an ideal location for malfunctioning B-29 bombers to land and be repaired. Shot-up and crippled on its return flights to the Marianas, a B-29 could also find safety on Iwo Jima. Therefore, the capture of Iwo Jima was necessary for the success of America's strategic bombing of Japan.

The Boeing B-29 range was 3,250 miles, and barely enough to complete the estimated 3,200 miles; however, the Boeing B-29A's range had increased to 4,100 miles.

The B-29A range increase did not, however, make it immune to Japanese fighters, because Japanese fighters were able to intercept the giant bombers from Okinawa in Ryukyu Island, as well as Iwo Jima.

Four cast carriers of Task Force 58 gathered at Ulithi to support the two Jima invasion: *USS Essex* with squadrons VMF-124 (Deathhead) and VMF-213 (Hellhawks); *USS Bennington* with squadrons VMF-112 (Wolfpack) and VMF-123 (Eight Balls); *USS Wasp* with squadrons VMF-216 (Bulldogs) and VMF-217 (Wild Hares); and *USS Bunker Hill* with squadrons VMF-221 (Fighting Falcons) and VMF-451 (Blue Devils).

The eight Marine fighter squadrons totaled about 145 Marine Corsairs and approximately 220 Marine aviators. Every Marine aviator received navigational training at Ulithi, and was to receive more enroute to the targets if necessary.

The 122 ships of TF-58 departed Ulithi on February 10, 1945, and, as they approached Iwo Jima, 1,000 miles from Ulithi, the Force continued 800 miles further to Tokyo, Japan. The orders were to "soften up" Japanese airfields and other military sites to support the Iwo Jima invasion.

The weather worsened as the Force approached Japan, with low ceilings, driving rain, and heavy seas. A temperature reading, at 25,000 feet, was 55 degrees below zero.

Several well-known aviators and leaders were members of the Task Force, including Capt James Swett, Col William Millington, Maj Archie Donahue, LCDR Roger Hedrick, Maj Henry Ellis, Capt Wilber Thomas, Capt William Snider, Maj David Marshall, and Maj Herman Hansen Jr.

The raids on Japan began early on 16 February with the planes skidding on the wet decks during takeoff, with Tokyo as the target. The planes left the carriers about sixty miles from the largest Japanese island on Honshu, 125 miles from Tokyo.

The majority of the Marine squadron aviators in the Task Force were comprised of inexperienced youngsters; well trained but inexperienced.

Assigned targets were easy to find. Free-hunting VMF-112 (Wolfpack) aviators struck Konoike and Hokoda airfields with strafing and rockets, and Lt. Robert B Hamilton scored a Tojo during the same operation.

Wilbur "Gus" Thomas scored two Zeros, running his score up to eighteen and one half.

When Major Jack Amende's VMF-217 Division was escorting Navy planes to Hamamatsu airfield, where sixty Japanese planes were "sitting ducks," Amende's division flamed six of the enemy planes; however, the CO's Corsair was also set afire by a defending Zero and turned away trailing dense smoke. Lt. Vernon Salisbury shot down the Zero, but Amende fell to his death.

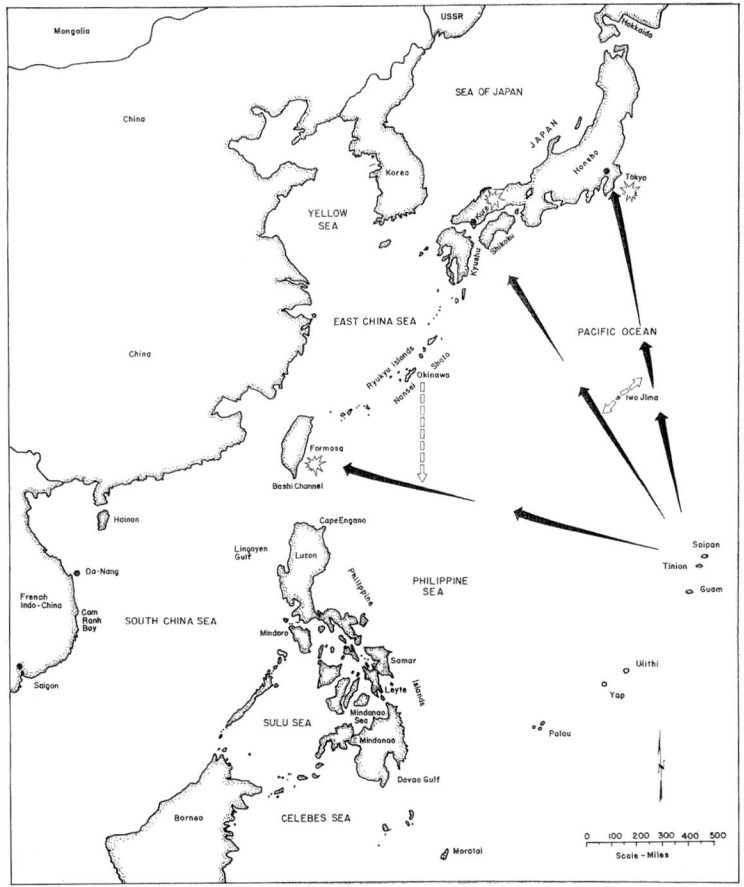

This schematic map illustrates the B-29 bomber routes from Tinian/Saipan to Formosa and Japan, plus the importance of Iwo Jima. Also shown is the key location of Okinawa for Japanese fighters to intercept the B-29 Superfortress bombers on some routes. Open arrows from Iwo Jima and Okinawa illustrate Japanese intercepting fighter routes if the islands remained in Japanese hands.

Chapter VI: Corsair Carriers Strike Japan

USS Bunker Hill Corsairs damaged three cargo ships. One of the corsairs from WMF-451 was hit by antiaircraft and made a water landing, but the pilot was never found.

Leading a VMF-112 CAP division from *USS Bennington*, Maj David Andre intercepted a Betty 35 miles off the Japanese coast. Andre and Lt. Carroll King shared the victory.

During the February 16, 1945, aerial activities the Corsair squadrons lost ten aircraft and eight aviators. Seventeen Japanese planes were shot down by Corsairs on sweeps and CAPs, in addition to enemy aircraft destroyed on the ground.

The weather worsened on 17 February and the raids had to be cut short, allowing only a few missions to be completed.

On 17 February eight VMF-112 *USS Bennington* Corsairs and twenty Corsairs from *USS Wasp* attacked Tokyo airfield with 500lb bombs and five-inch HVAR missiles. Maj Herman "Hap" Hansen scored an Oscar on this mission.

On the same day, Lt. James O Seay shot down an Oscar and Lt. William T Stratton on WMF-217 from *USS Wasp* scored a Zeke during a bombing attack on Haneda airfield, near Tokyo.

Eight VMF-123 *USS Benniton* Corsairs and twenty from *USS Wasp* struck Tateyama and Atsugi airfields, near Tokyo, with five-inch rockets. Maj Everett V Alward scored a Tojo over Tokyo Bay, while Lt. Archie J Clapp shot down a Zero. Maj Alwood flew so low that mud splattered his windshield.

Lt. Edward H Rohrict had his rudder shot off. He baled out but was never seen again.

The Marine aviators were disappointed in the Tokyo strikes because there was far less aerial opposition than was expected; however, the Admirals were happy because factories and airfield installations were heavily bombed.

Official claims stated that 332 Japanese aircraft were shot down, twenty-one of which were credited to the U.S. Marine aviators. Also claimed were 177 Japanese aircraft were destroyed on the ground, sixty of which were credited to U.S. Marine aviators.

February 16 and 17, 1945, saw Japanese airfields beat up; planes shot down; aircraft plants, airfield hangars, and runways bombed around Tokyo. Operations were cancelled on 17 February and TF 58 sped to Iwo Jima.

Task Force 58 planned to arrive at Iwo Jima by February 19, 1945, for the Marine aviators to provide close air support for the Third, Fourth, and Fifth Marine Divisions as they hit the sandy beaches on that day (D day).

Although the Iwo Jima D-day had been delayed because of the "Kamikaze Terror" that created a shortage of fighter aviators, additional aviators were needed to intercept Japanese dive bombers and Kamikaze aircraft that were harassing Task Force 38. Iwo Jima D-day began ahead of the arrival of Task Force 58. It had been planned that the well trained close-support Marine aviators were to fly from eleven Marine CVE carriers (Corsair Carriers); however, Navy aviators were flying from them! The close-support Marine aviators had not completed their Escort carrier training in the U.S. and were forced to launch from the fast carriers 100 miles from the beaches. Iwo Jima had been bombed for 72 straight days by the U.S. Army Air Corps' Seventh Air Force before the assault and, for 20 days after that, Navy fighters and U.S. Army Air Corps Mustang P-51 fighters continued covering the beaches.

Upon the arrival of TF-58 at Iwo Jima CAG-4 Col William Millington, USMC, worked closely with Col Vernon E Megee, USMC, Commander of the Landing Force Air Support Control Unit and Deputy Commander, Aircraft, Landing Force, who controlled all aircraft operating over Iwo Jima.

USS Saratoga (CV-3) was hit by several Kamikaze strikes on February 2, 1945, while she was patrolling the waters around Iwo Jima. Several fires were started, destroying many Corsairs that were deployed on the forward area of the Flight Deck. The ship did not sink and fought on to the end of the war. (U.S. Navy Photo, via National Archives)

In the early morning of Iwo Jima D-Day, February 19, 1945, Col Millington led a flight of twenty-four Marine Corsairs and twenty-four Navy Hellcats dropping napalm, firing 5 inch HVAR rockets, and strafing .50-caliber bullets.

The attack impact areas remained 200 yards ahead of the advancing Marine troopers as they moved closer to the Japanese defenders.

On 20 February 20 *USS Bennington* launched two ground-support strikes of eight Corsairs each, while on the following day *USS Bunker Hill's* VMF-221 and VMF-451 also flew troop-support missions. This action was given a "very well done" by the "Commander Support Aircraft (CSA).

USS Wasp Corsairs flew in a 23-plane ground-support mission followed by a *USS Bunker Hill* squadron in another troop-supporting assignment on February 21, 1945.

The venerable *USS Saratoga* (CV-3) and the escort carrier *USS Bismarck Sea* (CVE-95) were patrolling the waters around Iwo Jima on February 21, 1945, when they were hit by Kamikaze and bombing attacks. *USS Bismarck Sea* sank and many fires were started on *Saratoga*. Quick and efficient response by damage control teams saved the ship from debilitating damage; however, many planes were destroyed on the flight deck.

Later that day *USS Bunker Hill* squadrons VMF-221 and VMF-451 made strikes inland of the beaches, strafing and dropping napalm.

Both *USS Bunker Hill* squadrons flew separate support missions on February 21, 1945.

Also on February 21, 1945, eight of *USS Bennington's* Corsairs flew a special strike with torpedo and dive bombers using both bombs and rockets.

On the same date twelve VMF-216 and VMF-217 Corsairs from *USS Wasp* engaged in a 43-plane strike ordered by CSA (Commander Support Aircraft).

The *Wasp* squadrons attacked an area 400 yards ahead of the Fourth Marine Division's front lines.

Later that day *USS Bunker Hill* squadrons VMF-221 and VMF-451 flew on a support mission. This was followed by eight *USS Bennington*

This is probably the most famous photograph of World War II, showing U.S. Marines erecting the American flag atop Mount Suribachi on Iwo Jima after a hard-won battle. (Iwo Jima 60th Anniversary World War II Veterans Committee, Courtesy The American Studies Center)

Aircraft based on captured Iwo Jima included Corsairs in the foreground, Navy Liberator bombers in center of photograph, and P-51 Mustangs in the distant left. Note the twin, long range fuel tanks on the Corsairs, possibly for escorting the B-29 bombers during part of the flight. (Vought Aircraft Company Photo, Courtesy H.J. "Jerry" Dalton)

Corsairs armed with bombs and HVAR missiles escorting torpedo and dive bombers with twelve *USS Wasp* VMF-216 and VMF-217 Corsairs.

Eight *USS Wasp* Corsairs flew in a twenty-three plane ground-support mission on the next day (Feb. 22). *USS Bunker Hill* VMF-221 and VMF-451 took off for a support mission; however, foul weather set in, forcing the Corsairs to jettison their napalm, bombs, and rockets and return to the carrier. On the following day the Task Force moved north to Chichi Jima, in the Bonin Islands, about 220 miles from Iwo Jima.

The U.S. Marines lost 5,563 men in taking Iwo Jima; however, this sacrifice enabled over 24,700 crewmen and 2,251 B-29 Superfortresses to survive emergency landings on Iwo Jima throughout the remainder of the war.

The victory in Iwo Jima was celebrated by five marines who planted an American flag atop Mount Suribachi. This has since become the symbol of the American victory.

Although not generally known, the February 23, 1944, flag-raising was witnessed by Secretary of the Navy (soon to become Secretary of Defense) James V. Forrestal, who made the voyage from Washington to Iwo Jima in order to congratulate the Marines and stand on the beaches to salute the flag-raising.

As soon as Iwo Jima was taken an airfield was secured for USAAC Mustangs, Thunderbolts, and Black Widow fighters, as well as Marine Corsairs to escort the B-29 bombers and defend the airfield. Navy PB4-Y2 Liberator bombers were also based on Iwo Jima.

CDR Roger Hedrick, former XO of the Jolly Rogers, led 16 VF-84 Corsairs in a strike on Katori airfield firing HVAR missiles. Surprising eight Franks the CO scored two Franks; the second blew up in his path, forcing the leader to fly through the fireball with no perceptible damage to his Corsair.

Following the raids on Japan, Okinawa, in Ryukyu Island, became important because it had become an excellent base for Japanese interceptor aircraft to attack the B-29 Superfortresses. Conversely, it was an ideal base from which the U.S. could invade Japan.

Okinawa had been intermittently attacked by the U.S. Third and Fifth Fleets, but now Okinawa must be eliminated as a threat to the Superfortresses, and for use as a U.S. base for operations against the

Unaware of the impending doom about to engulf their ship, the *USS Franklin* crew go about their tasks. Corsairs on deck are from VMF-5. (Official U.S. Navy Photo, Courtesy U.S. Naval Institute)

Chapter VI: Corsair Carriers Strike Japan

With its after Flight deck filled with folded-wing Corsairs, USS Franklin steams at high speed for an attack on Japan. (Official U.S. Navy Photo, Courtesy U.S. Naval Institute)

Japanese homeland. Okinawa (codenamed Iceberg) has been called the last big battle of the Second World War.

Following the Iwo Jima and Chichi Jima strikes, VADM Raymond Spruance took his fifth fleet back to Japan and coordinated carrier aircraft attacks with 200 Superfortress strikes from Tinian/Saipan. The heavy bombers, dive bombers, and fighters bombed Japan on 25 February in weather worse than the pre-Iwo Jima strikes; however, the CinC Pac reported that at least 158 Japanese planes were destroyed, including 37 in aerial combat.

Avengers, Helldivers, and Corsairs destroyed the Nakajima and Koizimi aviation plants, as well as radar installations and hangars.

Nine U.S. planes and four pilots were lost. Among those who were killed was Maj Everett V Alwood, CO of VMF-123, who was shot down over Tokyo Bay by a Zero. He was succeeded by Maj Thomas E Mobley Jr.

Lt. Col William Millington and Capt Howard J (Mickey) Finn each scored one victory despite the inclement weather.

Task Force 58 returned to Ulithi on 11 March, where VMF-124 and VMF-213 were detached from USS Essex and returned to the United States.

The Essex Class fast carrier USS Franklin (CV-13) joined Task Force-58 with squadrons VMF-214, VMF-452, and VF-5 in preparation for the Okinawa invasion.

On 14 March 14 TF-58 left Ulithi to "soften up" Japan in preparation for the Okinawa invasion that was scheduled for two weeks later.

Previous strikes at Okinawa and Japan were "hit and run" affairs and, therefore, the fleet escaped debilitating damage; however, now TF-58 was to support an invasion and was forced to "remain in the neighborhood."

As it sailed ninety-miles off the coast of Japan in the early morning of March 19, 1945, with Corsairs ready to attack Kure Naval Base with huge "Tiny Tim" missiles, USS Franklin (CV-13) was hit by two 550-pound bombs from a Judy dive bomber that had evaded the U.S. picket ships.

The bombs hit just as the first Corsair made its takeoff. Once airborne, the Corsair shot down the Judy before it could escape. One of the bombs penetrated the Flight Deck, while the second penetrated the hangar deck as well. Both bombs ignited armed planes, ready ammunition, and aviation

Burning gasoline and firemain water pour from the ship's side as smoke billows from the hull of USS Franklin. Many planes were burned on the Flight Deck and on the Hangar Deck. Note the collapsed Corsair almost hidden by the smoke (arrow). Photo taken from attending cruiser USS Santa Fe (CL-60). (Official U.S. Navy Photo, Courtesy U.S. Naval Institute)

USS Franklin (often called "Big Ben") appears to be a doomed ship with towering flames and smoke. It is amazing to see the damage that an eight-thousand pound airplane can create on a twenty-seven thousand ton aircraft carrier! (Official U.S. Navy Photo, Courtesy U.S. Naval Institute)

Escorted by the cruiser USS Santa Fe (CL-60), "Big Ben's" fires are extinguished and the carrier is making six knots (6.9 mph) with its own power. Observe the hot boiler furnace gasses emerging from the Franklin's smoke stack. (Official U.S. Navy Photo, Author's File)

gasoline that turned the ship into a raging inferno. Quick and efficient action by the damage control crews prevented a total disaster. Much of the crew was quickly disembarked to attending cruisers.

Internal explosions wrought considerable damage, such as lifting the thirty-ton forward elevator and dropping it into the elevator opening.

Among the many heroes aboard the *Franklin* was Mr. Donald Russell, a civilian Chance Vought engineering representative with the Marine squadrons who remained on board to help organize the firefighting teams.

The cruiser *USS Pittsburg* towed the blazing carrier beyond the range of Japanese bombers and then towed it to Ulithi. The men struggled for several days to save their ship and, finally, by 28 March all the fires had been extinguished and one boiler was operating. On 3 April Franklin limped into Pearl Harbor for temporary repairs and then sailed 12,000 miles to New York under her own power, listing heavily. Of the 3,450 crew 724 were killed and 265 were wounded. A total of 393 decorations were awarded to the brave *USS Franklin* crew.

Okinawa is the largest of the Ryukyu Islands, which stretched from Kyushu to Formosa. The assault on Okinawa, which is sixty miles long and from two to eighteen miles wide, became the largest and costliest single operation of World War II.

Amphibious forces hit the beach on April 1, 1945—Easter Sunday and April Fools Day—with VADM Richmond K Turner in command of all the forces in and around the Okinawa target area (land, sea, and air) during the amphibious phase of the invasion.

As during the Philippine campaign, Japanese Kamikaze activity increased when it became evident that Okinawa was America's next objective. Kamikaze, or "Special Attack," became a two pronged assault from the Japanese home island of Kyushu and the island of Formosa (Taiwan). Unlike the relatively sporadic Philippine attacks, the Okinawa attacks were a well-organized and regimented operation called "Tengo," or First Special Attack Force, under special orders of ADM Soemu Toyoda. The force consisted of 1,800 planes of the Fifth Air Fleet and Sixth Air Army.

The Japanese attacks abated during the early American Okinawa landings; however, a 355 plane bombing and Kamikaze raid on 6 and 7 April sank six U.S. Navy ships and damaged twenty-one, with over 500 casualties in 19 hours. The Japanese lost almost 400 Kamikaze and escorting fighters during this time.

During the remainder of April 1945 the Kamikaze sank fourteen U.S. ships and damaged 90, while conventional bombing sank one and damaged forty-seven U.S. ships.

Japan's loss during the month of April was over 1,100 aircraft.

The overwhelming Kamikaze attacks prompted a U.S. Navy call for more fighter pilots.

As previously mentioned, many American dive bomber aviators transferred to Corsairs from Dauntless, Helldiver, and Avenger types; for example, Capt George Dooley, who became CO of VMF-216.

Now it was LCDR Fred A Patriarca who gave up his Dauntless for the Corsair and became CO of VBF-831, a fighter/bomber squadron that included thirty-two aviators who also transferred from his previous squadron.

It was at Okinawa that the U.S. Marine aviators were "let loose" to engage in close support of the group troops who called them "Sweethearts," ie "Sweethearts of Okinawa." It was also at Okinawa that the Corsair earned another sobriquet ("Whisting Death") by the Japanese troops who were being attacked by his potent fighter that made a whisting sound when cooling air rushed through the wing hub oil coolers.

Upper Photo: The Yokosuka MXY7 *Ohka* (Cherry Blossom) piloted flying bomb was rocket powered. With a 16 ft wingspan and length of 20 ft, the range was 40 miles at a speed of about 500 mph with the 2,640lb warhead. Photo shows U.S. Army mechanics and engineers dismantling and inspecting a captured *Ohka*. The nose cone has been removed, revealing the bomb. (U.S. Army Photo, Author's File) Lower Photo: This is the powerless version of the *Ohka*. The aviator glides it to the target where it is released. (Photo by Cecil Weatherly III at the Grand Canyon Air Museum, Courtesy of the photographer)

Chapter VI: Corsair Carriers Strike Japan

Royal Navy *HMS Victorious* is photographed with Corsairs filling its foreward Flight Deck. This carrier was part of Task Force 57 when it served with the U.S. Fifth Fleet in the Pacific. (Ministry of Defense (Navy), Author's File)

Unfortunately, the majority of the marine Corsairs that performed so well at Okinawa flew from fast or light carriers, or from land bases. Very few flew from the CVE "Corsair Carriers" that were specially designed and constructed to bring troop-supporting Corsairs over the battlefield. Much of this debacle was caused by inter-service rivalry that was reflected by RADM Calvin T. Durgin, who was in command of the Marine Carriers, when he claimed that:

"Marine Air Groups should be and probably are as flexible as Navy squadrons and groups, and should remain so, and should expect no preferential treatment. --- this command sees, at the present writing, no reason for such assignments and has no intention of allowing it to occur."

The only CVE Marine carrier that covered U.S. Marine Troops in the Okinawa campaign was the *USS Gilbert Islands* for five days. Despite this limited use of CVE Marine carriers the Corsairs were the "Sweethearts of Okinawa."

In order to improve the effectiveness of the conventional bomb-laden single engine Kamikaze plane for use against large warships, the Japanese scientists/engineers developed a two-ton, piloted flying bomb. This was carried by a Mitsubishi G4M Betty twin engine bomber and released near its target.

The MXY7 Ohka (Cherry Blossom) was called Baka (fool in Japanese) by the Americans, and is most recognized by that name.

Only a few Ohkas reached their targets because the heavily laden Battys were easily shot down on the way to the release points; however, those Ohkas that hit their targets either sank the ship or inflicted serious damage.

The first Ohka attack on 21 March sank one U.S. ship and damaged four.

The Royal navy had long been eager to take part in the Pacific war, and now, with the German Navy close to collapse and the Bay of Bengal, Southeast Asia, and Dutch East Indies (Indonesia) under control, it was agreed that Britain would join the U.S. Navy in its drive to Okinawa and the Japanese homeland.

The British Pacific Fleet (BPF) was created in January 1945 and included the aircraft carriers *HMS Victorious*, *HMS Formidable*, *HMS Illustrious*, and *HMS Indefatigable*.

The armored Flight Decks of Royal Navy aircraft carriers often make the difference between the life and death of the ship and crew. This photo was taken shortly after a Kamikaze struck the armored Flight Deck of a Royal Navy carrier. Planes on the deck and the Kamikaze created a pile of rubble, but when this was cleared, the carrier returned to normal operation. (Ministry of Defense (Navy), Author's File)

Upper Photo: It is not easy to move a six-ton airplane, but these Royal Navy plane handlers give it all they've got! Lower Photo: This unusual Royal Navy three-wheel tractor is ready to move this Corsair as soon as the elevator reaches the deck. (Ministry of Defense (Navy), Courtesy United Aircraft Corp.)

Corsair: The Saga of the Legendary Bent-Wing Fighter-Bomber

This Royal Navy flagman signals "cut engine" to the landing Corsair in Dutch East Indies (Indonesia). The plane sports the sea green/ gray matte camouflage for all Royal Navy aircraft before they became part of Task Force 57. The comfortable abbreviated tropical attire exposes the skin and flesh to flash-burns and fire radiation that can cause debilitating injuries. (Ministry of Defense (Navy), Courtesy United Aircraft Corp)

Two views of a Royal Navy Goodyear FG-1D (Corsair IV) division (fourth member took the photos) of Task Force 57 reveal the U.S. Navy glossy sea blue color scheme. Observe the anti-glare treatment forward of the cockpit. (Goodyear Aircraft Photos, Courtesy Nick Hauprich)

This view of Kadena Airfield, on Okinawa, shows it in operation by U.S. Forces with tents, Jeeps, cranes, and Corsairs. The single Japanese runway had been long and wide. (U.S. Army Photo, Courtesy Henry Tremont)

The BPF had attacked oil refineries on Sumatra prior to leaving for the Pacific. Royal Marine Maj Ronald Hay, Co of No47 Wing, was high scorer on this raid, destroying a Tojo and an Oscar.

After R&R in Sydney, Australia, British Admiral Sir Bernard Rawlings placed his entire fleet of carriers, battleships, cruisers, and destroyers under Admiral Spruance's supreme command. This British Force was so equivalent to a U.S. Task Force that it was designated Task Force 57. British TF-57 contributed 110 Corsairs to the Okinawa battle.

The Royal Navy carriers were not as combat-effective as the American carriers in the broad expanse of the Pacific Ocean. Designed for the European and Mediterranean Theatres, the British carriers lacked the range of the U.S. carriers because they did not need it in the confines of the North Sea or Mediterranean Sea; however, they did have an important feature that was lacking in U.S. Carriers—armored Flight Decks? A Kamikaze dived into the Flight Deck of *HMS Indefatigable*, but within a few hours the carrier was operating normally as soon as the rubble of the Kamikaze and parked aircraft had been cleared away! *Indefatigable* was able to continue its support of the Okinawa landings, which had begun on that day, despite the impact and explosion of the Kamikaze.

On April 6, 1945, the Japanese 63,700 ton super-battleship *Yamato* left the Tokuyama Naval Base in Honshu with an escort consisting of the light cruiser *Yahagi* and eight destroyers. The ships carried only enough fuel to reach the American landing beaches and bombarded them with *Yamato's* eighteen inch guns.

This Kamikaze mission was called the Ten-Ichi Operation (Heaven Number One), under the command of VADM Selichi Ito and his Special Surface Attack Force.

U.S. submarines detected the Japanese force late on 6 April, sending Avenger torpedo, Hell Diver dive bomber, and Corsair attack and escort planes to strike the Japanese force at noon of April 7.

The TF-58 carrier planes sank *Yamato* with ten torpedo and five bomb hits; sank *Yahagi* with seven torpedo and twelve bomb hits; and sank four destroyers. Four damaged destroyers escaped to Japan. When the *Yamato* sank it killed 2,487 of its crew. Ten U.S. aircraft were shot down.

By mid-April, Kadena and Yontan airfields on Okinawa were in operation by U.S. Force. The initial assault on the westerley side of the island facilitated capture of the airfield. The captured airfields were under such constant attack by Japanese bombers that combat air patrols (CAP), similar to that used for aircraft carriers, proved successful.

Medal of Honor recipient Capt Ken Walsh served as Operations Officer of VMF-222 in the Okinawa campaign. While flying an F4U-

Chapter VI: Corsair Carriers Strike Japan

The fantastic streaks of light are created by antiaircraft fire across searchlight beams during a Japanese air raid on Yonton Airfield. Searchlights have also silhouetted Corsairs, forming a beautiful but deadly mural in the sky. Raid was on April 16, 1945. (U.S. Army Photo, via National Archives)

Corsair (FG-1D) squadron VMF-312, 2nd Marine Air Group (MAG), scored fifty-nine Kamikaze intruders while the unit flew CAP over Kadena Airfield in April 1945. The spectacular blue and white checkerboard markings on engine cowl and rudder are outstanding. (USMC Photo, Author's File)

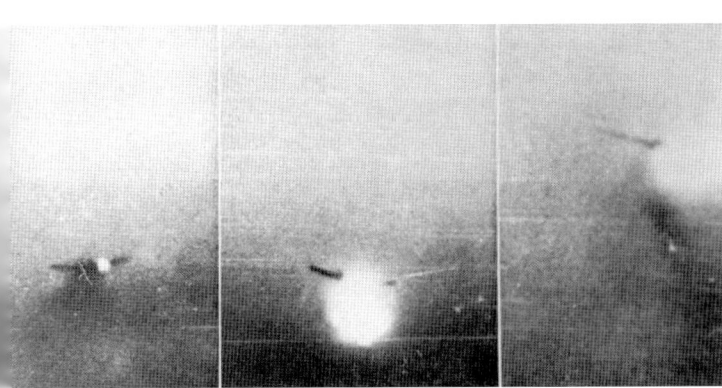

Sequence photos of a Mitsubishi Betty disintegrating before the six guns of a VMF-112 Corsair over Okinawa on March 19, 1945, are spectacular. (USMC Photo, Author's File)

Capt Ken Walsh stands before his new F4U-4 Corsair that he flew in the Okinawa campaign. He considered this variant the finest Corsair of all the Corsairs he had flown. (Ken Walsh Photo, Courtesy Col Kenneth Walsh (USMC) (Ret)

Corsair: The Saga of the Legendary Bent-Wing Fighter-Bomber

With a smile on his face, Capt Walsh appears happy with his F4U-4. The Ace has grown a moustache since his Solomons days. (USMC Photo, Courtesy Col Kenneth Walsh, USMC (Ret))

Capt Kenneth Walsh is congratulated by his crew chief upon his twenty-first and concluding victory. (USMC Photo, Courtesy Col Kenneth Walsh, USMC (Ret))

4 Kenneth Walsh scored his twenty-first and final victory when he shot down a Zero near Okinawa.

The war began with excellent Japanese aviators and good Japanese fighter planes; however, as the war progressed most of the elite Japanese aviators were shot down, leaving poorly-trained beginners to fly the excellent fighters that had been developed during that time. One of the better Japanese fighter planes late in the war was the Kawanishi N1K2-J Shiden-Kai, whose performance was equal to many Allied fighters.

One of the youngest U.S. Marine squadron leaders, Maj George C Axtell Jr, led VMF-323 "Death Rattlers" in action over Okinawa late in the war. Some of the squadron members had never fought a Japanese plane

The very advanced Kawanishi N1K2-J Shiden-Kai (Violet Lightning), or "George" in the Allied Code that appeared late in the war, was powered by a 1990 hp radial engine. Top speed was 369 mph with a range of 1060 miles. Armament was four 20 mm cannon located in the wing outside of the propeller arc. (Photo by Nick Hauprich, Courtesy Nick Hauprich)

172

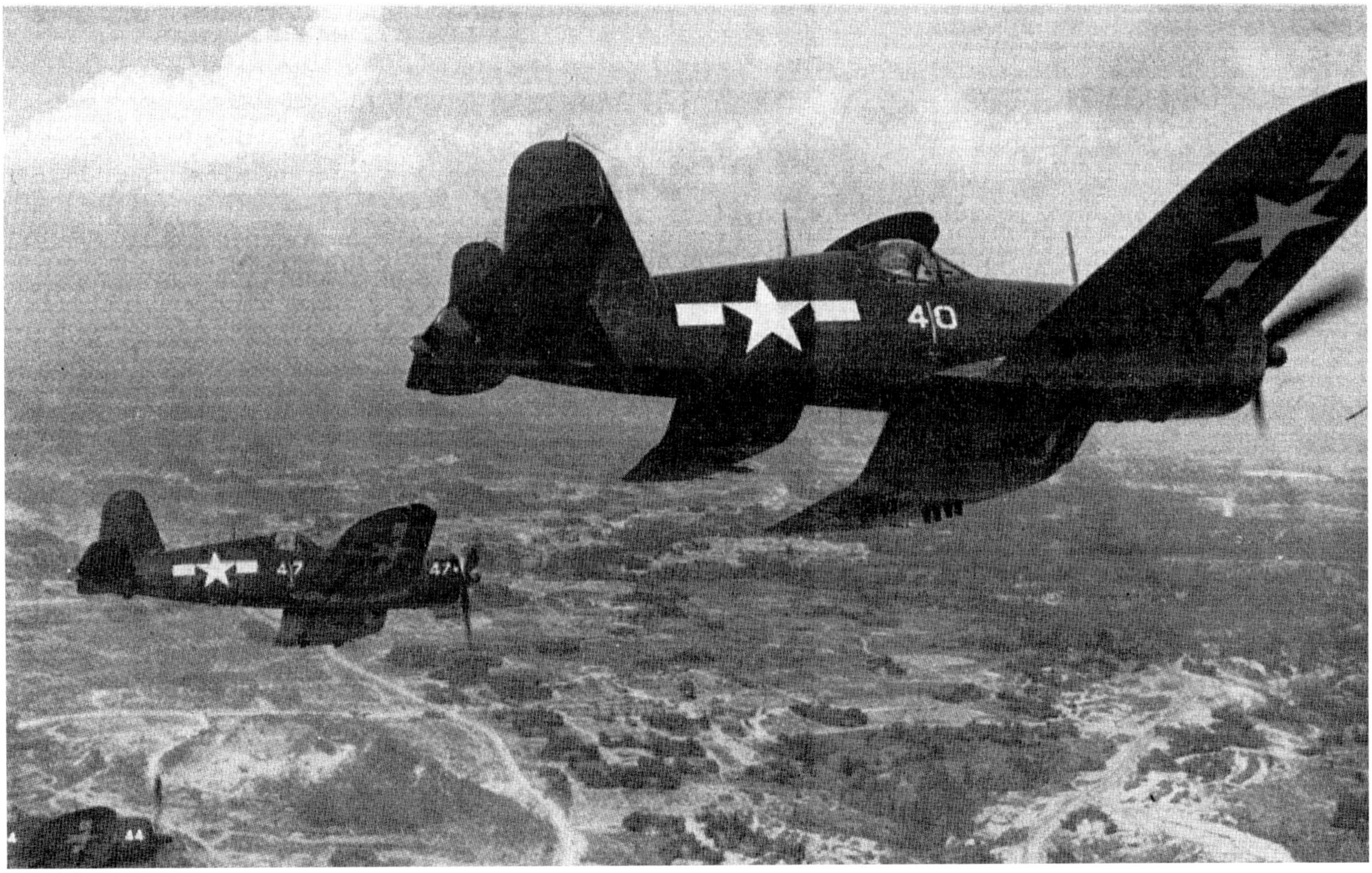

Chapter VI: Corsair Carriers Strike Japan

Three members of VMF-323 "Death Rattlers" who scored well in their first encounter with Japanese aircraft (L to R): CO Maj George C Axtell (6V); Lt Robert Wade (7V); and Lt Joseph V Dillard (6.3V). Bottom photo is a flight of "Death Rattlers" over Okinawa. (Upper Photos USMC; Lower Photo U.S. Army; Author's File)

Lt Jeremiah J O'Keefe of VMF-323 scored five victories during the squadron's initial engagement with Kamikaze attackers. He shot down two more of the enemy in later combats and is shown signaling seven victories while in his Corsair on an Okinawa airfield. (USMC Photo, Author's File)

A Marine ordnance specialist maintains the .50 cal machine guns of a Corsair on one of USS Block Island's (CVE-106) elevators in June 1945 during operations off Okinawa. (USMC Photo, Author's File)

until that day, April 22, 1945, when elements of three Corsair squadrons were ordered to the radar picket line because about eighty kamikazes were endangering destroyers.

Two divisions of VMF-323 led by CO Maj George Axtell Jr and XO Maj Jefferson D Dorrah were the first to arrive. The seven "Death Rattlers" found about forty Vals flying low towards two destroyers and dived to the attack.

Maj Axtell became an Ace when he shot down five of the Vals in fifteen minutes and then damaged three more.

Lt. O'Keefe scored four Vals and flamed a fifth that circled back toward the aviators and, after O'Keefe fired continuously at the oncoming fireball, the Val banked at a fifty-foot range and splashed into the water.

Lt. Robert Wade scored seven; Lt. Joseph V Dillard shot down 6.3; and Lt. Jeff Dorrah scored six.

VMF-323 Death Rattlers scored 124 victories of the 637 victories recorded by the Tactical Air Force of the Okinawa Campaign.

Three divisions of VMF-10 were launched from USS Intrepid early in the morning of 16 June for CAP duty over northern Okinawa. After a half hour on station, the Marines were dived upon Zeros and Tonys; however, the Corsairs scored five Zeros and two Tonys, with the remaining Japanese escaping to safety.

Lt. Philip Kirwood's division split towards two groups of Kamikazes. He and ENS Horace W. Heath remained below while Ensigns Norwald Quiet and Alfred Lerch climbed to attack Vals at 7,000 feet. Quiel scored two Vals and one Nate while Lerch shot down a Val.

Lt. Kirwood paired with ENS Quiet when they picked up a destroyer's distress call; upon their arrival at the destroyer Kirwood shot down four Nates and two Vals and Quiel scored four Nates.

Meanwhile, Ensigns Health and Lerch returned to the original orbit and spotted thirty Nates. The pair chased the pre-war fighters, scoring six for Leach and one for Heath.

Seven victories for ENS Lerch, not only in any day, but in one sortie; a feat of aerial combat equaled by only for other American aviators.

Ensign Alfred Lerch of VF-10 scored seven victories during one sortie on April 16, 1945; a feat matched by only four other American aviators. (U.S. Navy Photo, Author's File)

Chapter VI: Corsair Carriers Strike Japan

Oops! This Corsair aviator accidentally released a 500lb bomb upon takeoff. Fortunately, it missed the aircraft carrier. (U.S. Navy Photo, Courtesy Alain J. Pelletier)

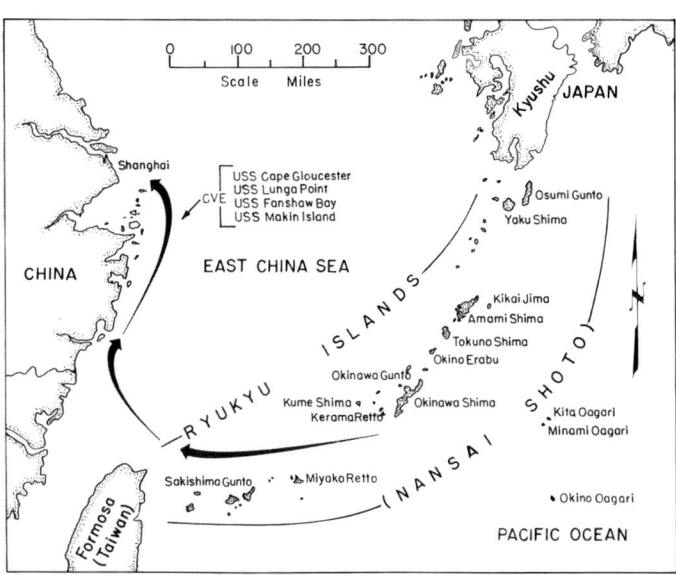

Okinawa is the largest of the Ryukyu Islands, which are often called Nansai Shoto, and is located in the virtual midpoint of the island chain. The ends of the chain are close to Kyushu, Japan, and Formosa (Taiwan), which made it valuable to Japan and U.S. Forces. The islands are literally stepping stones between Formosa and Kyushu. Note the route of the four "Corsair Carriers" from Okinawa to Shanghai.

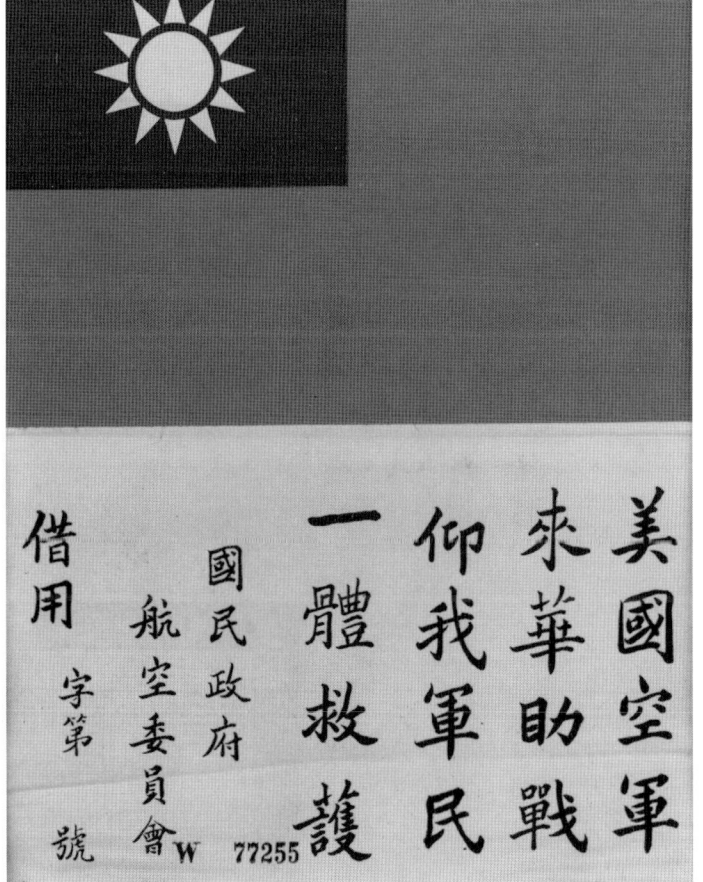

On occasion American aviators and "Corsair Carrier" crewmen found themselves in Japanese controlled China, either by accident or on a mission to free American prisoners of war. In any event, this fabric armband is worn for safety. It contains the Chinese Nationalist flag with a message in Chinese in the event that the American is intercepted by armed native Chinese inhabitants. The message reads as follows: "American airmen came to China to aid the war effort. Let us unite to help as one" Signed by: "China official Air Force Committee W77255" (U.S. Marine Corps Photo, Courtesy Lt Col OK Williams, USMC (Ret), Translated by Peter Hsu)

A "Corsair Carrier," with Corsairs gathered at the bow, cuts through choppy seas. Four Commencement Bay Class escort carriers sailed into the East China Sea from Okinawa to Shanghai along the Japanese-occupied Chinese coast and scored some Japanese interceptor aircraft. (U.S. Navy Photo)

Part of the seventy-two Corsairs of CAG-84 are gathered at the bow of USS Bunker Hill on their way to attack Japan in Spring 1945. They will soon return for the Okinawa engagement. (U.S. Navy Photo, Author's File)

Lt Robert R Klingman scored a Japanese twin-engine Nick with his enormous Corsair propeller when all six of his guns froze at 38,000 feet. Lt Klingman is shown examining his broken propeller on May 10, 1945. (USMC Photo, Author's File)

Four Marine escort carriers (Corsair carriers) were active in the Okinawa campaign: *USS Block Island* (CVE-105) with squadrons VMTB 233 and VMF-511, and *USS Gilbert Islands* (CVE-106) with squadrons VMTB-143 and VMF-512. Later arrivals were *USS Cape Gloucester* (CVE-109) with squadron VMF-351 and *USS Vella Gulf* (CVE-107).

On the first of July, *USS* Cape *Gloucester's* and *USS Vella Gulf's* Corsairs began protecting U.S. Navy minesweepers along the southern coast of Okinawa.

Another four "Corsair Carriers" were busy by early August 1945 when *USS Cape Gloucester* sortied from Okinawa with *USS Lunga Point*, *USS Fanshaw Bay*, and *USS Makin Island* into the East China Sea and along the Chinese coast as far as Shanghai.

The "Corsair Carriers" were not on a carefree cruise. They attacked and were attacked by Chin-based Japanese aircraft as far as Shanghai. On 4 August Lt. Thomas W. Doyle shot down a "snooper" while, on the following day, Col Donald Yost scored his eighth and final victory of the war.

Lt. Robert R. Klingman was flying wingman to Capt Kenneth L Reusser on 10 May in a division on Combat Air Patrol over the island of Ie Shima at 10,000 feet when Klingman performed one of the most unusual and bravest feats in scoring a Japanese plane.

Flying at 10,000 feet, the pair climbed to intercept a photographing twin-engine Nick at 25,000 feet. Capt Reusser and Lt. Klingman fired most of their heavy ammunition to lighten their planes and climb higher to reach the Nick at 38,000 feet.

Capt Reusser used the remainder of his ammunition to damage the nick's wing and left engine. Klingman continued the attack, only to find his guns had frozen. Undaunted, he continued the attack using his huge propeller as a weapon, damaging the ANAick's rudder and sawing into the fuselage near the rear gunner. Klingman's second pass cut off the rudder and damaged the right stabilizer. Klingman decided on a third pass because he believed he didn't have enough fuel to return to an American airfield. This time the huge propeller chewed off the Nick's stabilizer, sending the Japanese plane into a violent spin. Reusser and Klingman witnessed both of the Nick's wings tear off at about 15,000 feet.

The hero made a dead-stick landing at Kadena airfield with part of his propeller missing, and his Corsair's wing, engine cowl, and fuselage full of holes from the ill-fated Nick's rear gunner's gun.

Two days later, Klingman's hydraulic system failed from enemy fire and, rather than risk a crash landing on one landing gear strut, he chose to bail out and made a safe descent on the water. He was picked out of the sea by a destroyer-escort and invited to dinner by Admiral Turner.

At that time (11 May), the Japanese started heavy Kamikaze, bombing, and torpedo attacks against the American and British Fleets. Task Force 58 VADM Marc Mitscher's Flagship was the fast carrier *USS Bunker* (CV-17).

The *Bunker Hill* combat air group (CAG-87) included VMF-221 (18 Corsairs), VMF-451 (18 Corsairs), and VF-84 (36 Corsairs).

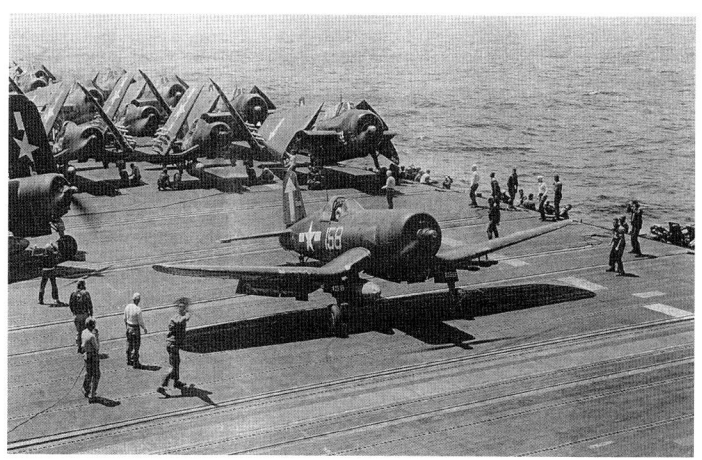

USS Bunker Hill Marine squadron VMF-211 prepares to takeoff just before disaster struck the carrier. Corsairs are armed with 5 inch HVAR missiles for ground attack in support of Marine ground troops. (U.S. Navy Photo, via National Archives)

Chapter VI: Corsair Carriers Strike Japan

Capt James Elms Swett, XO of VMF-211, was in the air when two Kamikaze struck USS Bunker Hill. After saving many men in the water the Ace was instructed to land on USS Enterprise. Then his plane was pushed over the side into the sea! (U.S. Defense Dept Photo, USMC, Author's File)

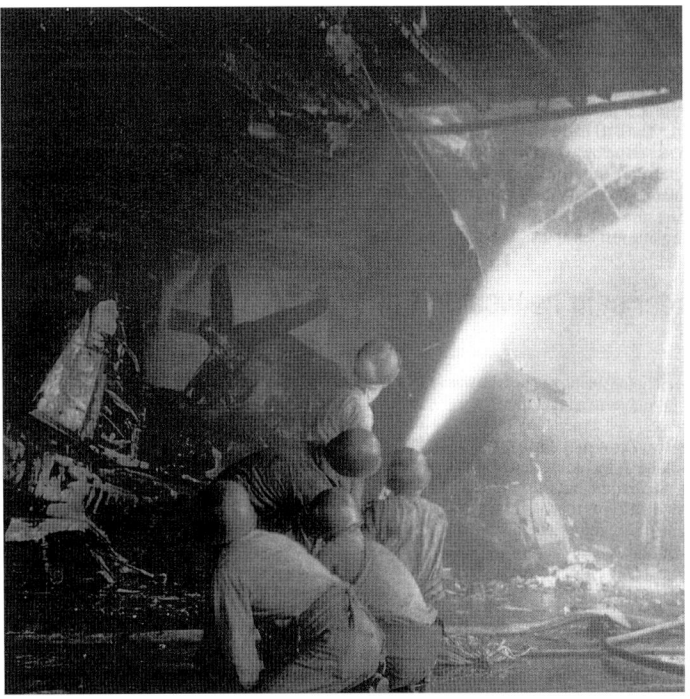

Hangar crewmen and damage control teams fought burning Corsairs in the hangar as well as burning Corsairs that tumbled down from the main deck through the elevator opening. (U.S. Navy Photo, Courtesy National Archives)

CDR Roger Hedrick had been XO of squadron VF-17 "Jolly Rogers" in 1944 and became commander of Group 84 in mid-1945 on *USS Bunker Hill*. He led pre-dawn strikes on an Okinawan airfield before the Japanese could attack the American troops. The Marines on the ground started shooting as soon as Group 84 arrived, creating a coordinated attack.

Capt. James Elms Swett, XO VMF-221, was issued one of the few F4U-1C cannon-armed Corsairs that were produced. Although the 20mm cannon shell possessed more destructive power than the Browning .50mm caliber shell, the rate of fire was less than the machine gun.

During the 11 May Kamikaze attacks Capt Swett's CAP encountered a Jill torpedo bomber that had turned for home. A short burst from the Corsair's cannon tore the Jill to pieces, according to Jim Swett. This victory brought Swett's final score to fifteen and one-half victories.

The powerful cannon shell's slow rate of fire made the weapon more adaptable to surface targets rather than air-to-air combat. Amazing, how this Medal of Honor winner shot down a moving air target with a weapon designed for a surface target.

Actually, the cannon-fitted Corsair F4U-1C was sent to Okinawa for troop support missions, hence the tremendous fire power.

As Capt Swett scored his last victory, he saw a Judy and a Zero drop from the clouds and head for *Bunker Hill*. Before he could intervene the Judy dropped its 500lb bomb, piercing the after deck, with the Judy smashing into the parked aircraft on the deck. The Zero crashed at the base of the island and exploded. Among the many fatalities on board were fifty Navy pilots.

Men were jumping overboard with and without life jackets to escape the roaring flames and choking smoke, so Swett ordered his CAPs to swoop to wave level and drop their dye markings, Mae Wests, shark repellants, inflatable dinghies, and other life saving equipment to help the men in the water.

USS Bunker Hill (CV-17) is still underway as she emits billows of smoke and fumes after being hit by two Kamikazes on the morning of May 11, 1945. The ship did not sink. Photographed from USS Bataan (CVL-29). (U.S. Navy Photo, Courtesy National Archives)

Canadian Lt Robert Hampton Gray, RCN, sacrificed his life to sink a Japanese ship with his Corsair near the coast of Japan on August 9, 1945. He was awarded the Victoria Cross. (Canadian War Museum, Author's File)

VADM Mitscher transferred his flag to the carrier *USS Enterprise* because *USS Bunker Hill's* condition was questionable, and all airborne aircraft were ordered to land on *USS Enterprise*.

As Jim Swett's F4U-1C rolled to a stop on *Enterprise*, a crewman shouted for Swett to "get out" of his plane, and then proceeded to have Swett's cannon-fitted Corsair pushed overboard! Apparently, there was not enough room for Swett's aircraft on the smaller *Enterprise*. This disappointed the Ace, because he had appreciated the short time with his cannon-toting Corsair.

A final attack on the Japanese Naval Base in Kure Harbor, Honshu, was planned for July 24, 1945, in order to thwart any Japanese attack on the U.S. invasion of Japan.

Virtually all the Allied activity in midsummer 1945 concentrated on attacking Japanese shipping along the Kyushu coastline. Much of this activity fell to Task Force 57 Royal Navy aircraft carriers and their Corsairs as Japanese aircraft dwindled.

Among the last victories that fell to 1841 Squadron of *HMS Formidable* was a Kate near the end of July and a Grace on 9 August.

Also on 9 August, a Canadian flight commander, Lt. Robert Hampton Gray of 1841 Squadron, led a flight of Corsairs on an anti-shipping strike off the coast of Honshu, Japan. Lt. Gray was a veteran of the Norwegian Campaign in which he scored many ships performing his matchless style, low and fast.

As he approached his target, the Flight Commander was hit by Flak but continued his run on the target. As he closed to within fifty feet of the ship a violent explosion obscured ship and Corsair, sinking the ship and killing the Canadian aviator.

Heroic Lt. Robert Hampton Gray was awarded the Victoria Cross posthumously, Britain's highest military honor.

Heavily loaded Corsair F4U-4 fighter-bombers escorted Curtiss SB2C Helldivers to the Japanese Naval Base, Kure Harbor, Honshu, in the Inland Sea, Japan. The objective was to destroy the remnants of the Japanese Navy to prevent attacks on American ships. Heavy hits were made on a cruiser and other vessels during the raid.

In reply to the Allied leader's Potsdam Declaration, which called upon Japan to unconditionally surrender or face utter destruction, the Japanese refused to surrender unconditionally.

Heavily loaded Corsair F4U-4 fighter-bombers are ready for catapult launching from fast carrier *USS Princeton* (CV-37) in Summer 1945. (Sal Marrone Photo, Courtesy Sal Marrone)

A Japanese Tone class cruiser under bombardment by U.S. aircraft, including Corsair fighter-bombers. The cruiser suffered serious damage at the Japanese Naval Base in Kure Harbor, Honshu. (U.S. Navy Photo, Courtesy Naval Photo Center Naval Station, Wash, DC)

Chapter VI: Corsair Carriers Strike Japan

Lt T. Hammel Reidi of VF-83, based on US Essex (CV-9), was the last aviator of the squadron to score a victory on Aug. 14, 1945; the day that Japan unconditionally surrendered. The squadron is elated as Lt Reidi describes his victory. (U.S. Navy Photo, Author's File)

Corsairs from Marine Air Group 31 (MAG-31) fly in formation over Mount Fujiyama on Honshu, Japan, to celebrate victory in a hard-fought war. (Official U.S. Marine Corps Photo, Courtesy United Aircraft Corporation)

The Allied reply to Japan's Potsdam Declaration refusal: a B-29 Superfortress dropped an atomic bomb on Hiroshima on August 6, 1946.

Two days later the Soviet Union declared war on a prostrate Japan.

A second atomic bomb was dropped on Japan on Nagasaki on 9 August.

The Japanese Government agreed to an unconditional surrender on August 15, 1945.

The end of the war was celebrated by the American airborne warriors in many ways: special flights over Japanese monuments, and over famous Japanese works of nature. Other popular ways of celebrating the end of the war were the gatherings of American aviators to observe a notable occasion with festivities, such as the aviator who scored the last victory of his squadron during World War II.

INSERT PHOTOS 06-71 TO 06-74 WITH FOLLOWING TEXT

Despite the fact that the Government of Japan accepted the unconditional surrender, there remained hundreds of thousands of individual meetings, surrenders, and agreements throughout the former airfields/battlefields to formalize the cessation of hostilities and return of prisoners.

It was also agreed that all surrendering Japanese aircraft were to be marked with bright green crosses, instead of the red rising sun insignia, for the safety of the conquerors, as well for the safety of the surrendering aviator.

This is only one of the many meetings that were necessary to make the unconditional surrender feasible. Japanese officers are seated at the desk to sign agreements with New Zealand officers regarding the treatment and return of officers and aviators. The New Zealand principal representative is standing at left in the rear row, Air Commodore G.N. Roberts. (RNZAF Photo, Author's File)

This surrendering Japanese Zero fighter has landed on a New Zealand airfield. While Japanese-speaking officers interrogate the pilot, some RNZAF personnel examine the plane, while others are anxious to meet their former enemy. Observe the bright green cross marking under the wing that indicates a surrendering aircraft. (RNZAF Photo, Author's File)

Corsair: The Saga of the Legendary Bent-Wing Fighter-Bomber

Little is ever mentioned about how the natives must have felt, having just gotten accustomed to the Japanese occupiers, and must now accept men from the west with a different language and customs.

The formal Japanese surrender ceremonies were conducted on the American battleship *USS Missouri* (BB-63) in Tokyo Bay on September 2, 1945.

The world rejoiced when this bloodiest of wars was over; however, little did anyone imagine that the U.S. would be to war with another Asian nation five years later.

At a time when the vast majority of U.S. Navy, Marine, and U.S. Army Air Corps fighters were discontinued in favor of jet-powered fighters, Corsair fighters continued with new automated high altitude fighters and low altitude troop support designs as well as World War II designs.

We will follow the Korean War Corsairs and the aviators who flew them in the following chapter.

Native residents at Jacquinot Bay, on New Britain, in the Bismarck Archipelago visit New Zealand aviators and their beautiful Corsairs. The natives were confronted with new occupants speaking a different language and having different customs from the previous Japanese occupants. (RNZAF Photo, Author's File)

Upper Photo is most unusual, because it depicts a New Zealand Air Force Corsair landing on an aircraft carrier. As part of the Occupation Forces, New Zealand Corsairs were landed on HMS Glory in Melanesia and ferried to Japan, where they flew to their occupation airfield (1946-1948). (RNZAF Photo, Courtesy Vought Aircraft) Lower Photo: a RNZAF Corsair being fueled and serviced on a Commonwealth Occupation airfield in Japan (1946-1948). (RNZAF Photo, Courtesy John Regan)

Chapter VI: Corsair Carriers Strike Japan

This view from USS Missouri during the surrender signing shows off the 16 inch/ 50 cal guns of number one turret and the officers and enlisted men in "dress whites" to honor the occasion. Observe the U.S. Navy carrier planes flying in formation to salute the signing. Careful examination will reveal that a good portion of the American planes are Corsairs. (Photo by Lt Barret Gallagher (USA) via National Archives)

VII

Corsair Power in Korea

The years of peace following World war II saw many events:

1. The Marshall Plan was created on June 5, 1947, in which the United States provided economic aid to the war-torn nations of Europe. The Soviet Union and other Communist countries refused to participate in the program.
2. During July 1947, the U.S. adopted a policy of patient but firm containment against Soviet or Communist expansionism, either by peaceful or military means.
3. When the battle carrier *USS Midway* (CVB-41) was launched it was America's largest aircraft carrier, and Capt John T "Tommy" Blackburn, USN, became the Commanding Officer of the huge ship.
4. On April 4, 1949, NATO (The North Atlantic Treaty Organization) was established by the United States, Britain, France, Italy, Canada, Norway, Denmark, Belgium, Netherlands, and Iceland.
5. On March 31, 1948, the Berlin Airlift was organized to fly the necessities of life to west Berlin over the Soviet Blockade. The "Cold War" began here and the "Iron Curtain" became a reality.

The "revolt of the Admirals" was precipitated when the former Secretary of the Navy, James V Forrestal, was named the first U.S. Secretary of Defense as part of the National Security Act of 1947 that unified the U.S. Army Air Corps (now called U.S. Air Force), U.S. Navy, and U.S. Army. The Secretaries of the Army, Navy, and Air Force reported to the Secretary of Defense.

Ignoring the words of Royal Navy Fifth Sea Lord Sir Arthur Lumley St George Lyster, Commander of all British Naval Aviation, who had stated

The Battle Aircraft Carrier *USS Midway* (CVB-41) plows through rough seas in February 1949. Photo taken from *USS Philippine Sea* (CV-47). Observe the Corsairs on *Philippine Sea* and *Midway*. (U.S. Navy Photo, via National Archives)

Captain John T. "Tommy" Blackburn (USN) became the Commanding Officer of the Battle Carrier *USS Midway* (CVB-41). It will be recalled that "Tommy" Blackburn was instrumental in the Corsair development and CO of VF-17 "Jolly Rogers" Corsair squadron. (U.S. Navy Photo, Author's File)

Chapter VII: Corsair Power in Korea

Left Photo: Secretary of Defense James V. Forrestal, a leading Supercarrier advocate, fought for Supercarriers against many enemies until his term of office ended in tragedy. (Defense Dept Photo, via National Archives) Right Photo: Captain John G. Crommelin precipitated the Revolt of The Admirals and was elected into the Carrier Aviation Hall of Fame because he "saved carrier aviation." (U.S. Navy Photo, via National Archives)

This unusual photo of a U.S. Navy North American AJ-2 Savage attack plane refueling a U.S. Navy Vought F7U-3 illustrates the large size of the atom bomb-carrying Savage that demands operation from a Supercarrier. (Vought Aircraft Company, Courtesy Paul Bonner)

that unification virtually destroyed the Fleet Air Arm, President Truman transmitted a special message to Congress in December 1945 outlining a unified Army, Navy, and Air Force! On June 15, 1946, Truman followed this with a specific plan that resulted in the National Security Act of 1947, which also created the U.S. Air Force as an equal to the Army and Navy.

During the summer of 1947 the U.S. House of Representatives Finance Committee held hearings on the Unification Act. Captain John Gevaerdt Crommelin Jr., USN, asked to be called as a witness. John had four brothers who also served in the U.S. Navy during World War II. Crommelin had also been assigned as an aide to Sir Arthur Lumley St George Lyster when Sir Arthur visited the U.S. in 1941. The British naval officer had been commanding officer of *HMS Illustrious* during many actions in the Mediterranean Sea and Atlantic Ocean. He related his experiences to the eager Crommelin, and also volunteered the fact of how Royal Navy Aviation was virtually destroyed by unification of the air services. Crommelin had served as wartime air officer and executive officer of *USS Enterprise* (CV-6), as well as Chief of Staff for a carrier division commander. At this time he was the first commanding officer of *USS Saipan* (CVL-48). Crommelin influenced a Committee member to have Admiral Gerald F. (Gerry) Bogan and Admiral Joseph J (Jocko) Clark testify at the hearings. Captain Crommelin testified after the admirals that carrier aviation, being highly mobile, embodied the Navy's most effective offensive striking power, and to destroy this effective force would endanger U.S. national security. All other testimony concurred with Crommelin's opinions.

Soon the opinionated media got into the act with obviously planted misinformation, which lauded the giant B-36 bomber and condemned

Left Photo: Kim Il Sung, North Korean leader, started the Korean War by sending his army to attack South Korea. (U.S. Army Photo, Courtesy Henry Tremont) Right Photo: General of the Army Douglas MacArthur CINC UN Command since July 10, 1950 (right), and Lt Gen Mathew B Ridgeway, new commander of the U.S. Eighth Army, discuss tactics upon Ridgeways' succeeding Lt Gen Walton H Wheeler, who was KIA in a Jeep accident. (U.S. Army Photo, Courtesy Henry Tremont)

carrier aviation. Publications went as far as to write articles in cooperation with the U.S. Air Force which would, of course, be derogatory towards carrier aviation and in favor of the long-range bomber as the only weapon able to guarantee U.S. national security. Everyone had forgotten the poor record of General George C Kenney's Fifth Air Force B-17 Flying Fortresses when they tried to bomb Japanese ships. Carrier-based dive bombers were far more successful, naturally.

In early 1948 the U.S. Navy carrier force consisted of three 45,000 ton *Midway* class, eight *Essex* class, two *Independence* class, and seven escort carriers. Except for the *Midway* class, the U.S. carriers were inadequate to handle the heavier and faster operational jet aircraft that were being developed.

As previously mentioned, the two developments that influenced carrier aviation during the immediate postwar years were jet-powered aircraft and the atomic bomb.

The specter of U.S. Army, Air Force, and Navy unification became a reality on September 18, 1948, when the National Security Act of 1947 (NSA 47) took effect. NSA 47 combined the three military services under the aegis of a single Department of Defense, with the offices of Secretary of the Army, Navy, and Air Forces as subcabinet posts. On that day John L Sullivan became the 49th Secretary of the Navy, replacing James V Forrestal, who had been appointed America's first Secretary of Defense. Little did Forrestal realize the fuss and fury that was to mar his term of service, ending in tragedy.

Experience with the North American AJ-1 Savage pointed to the fact that the existing U.S. Navy aircraft carriers were not adequate to accommodate a multi-engine, atomic bomb carrying long-range strategic bomber. This led to the inescapable conclusion that a large supercarrier that would be capable of operating long-range nuclear-armed aircraft was desperately needed to give the U.S. Navy the capability of atomic strategic attack against the enemy. Secretary Forrestal had proposed the carrier to Congress, of which four were to be built. Congress approved and funded the project in the autumn 1948.

James V Forrestall was the leading supercarrier advocate. His 65,000 ton ship was conceived to accommodate a 2,000 mile range, 80,000lb strategic bomber carrying nuclear weapons.

Secretary Forrestal had fought hard for the important supercarrier, and the first to criticize the idea of a new carrier was the fledgling U.S. Air Force, which had been recently created by NAS 47. The USAF objected to giving the Navy strategic attack capability. It argued that only the USAF should have the means of strategic attack and claimed the Convair B-36 bomber was the only weapon capable of this mission. The Air Force openly defied the Defense Secretary on appropriations,

and the fair-minded Forrestal even permitted Air Force brass to present their views before Congress. The family fight burst into the open, with the news media accusing Forrestal of not being able to control the Air Force's insubordination.

On February 11, 1949, Assistant Secretary of the Navy for Air, John N Brown, resigned because of the way Naval Aviation was being abused.

Secretary of Defense Forrestal fought for his carrier as long as he was able, but on March 4, 1949, he resigned his post, effective 31 March. He was awarded the Distinguished Service Medal on 29 March and entered Bethesda Naval Hospital on 2 April suffering from nervous exhaustion.

On March 28, 1949, Louis Johnson had been selected to succeed Forrestal.

The keel of *USS United States* (CVA-58) had been laid at Newport News Shipbuilding and Drydock Co. on April 18, 1949, with a minimum of ceremony. With Forrestal out of the picture, five days later Secretary of Defense Johnson announced the cancellation of the supercarrier *United States* (CVA-58) without consulting with or informing Secretary of the Navy Sullivan or Chief of Naval Operations Admiral Louis E. Denfield! Johnson instructed Newport News Shipbuilding to discontinue construction "… at once and at the least possible cost to the Government." News of this abrupt dictatorial cancellation resounded like a thunderclap throughout the U.S. Navy, and those officers who had protested unification now realized that U.S. Navy carrier aviation was doomed to share the fate of the Royal Navy Fleet Air Arm. Secretary of the Navy John L Sullivan resigned at once in protest to this underhanded and unwarranted cancellation.

In the early morning of May 22, 1949, James V Forrestal sat in his room on the 16th floor of Bethesda Naval Hospital reading a passage by Sophocles. Despite the fact that he was hospitalized on the 16th floor, Forrestal, somehow, was transported to the 13th floor, and, at 2:00 o'clock in the morning, he either fell, jumped, or was pushed from the 13th floor window, from which the screen had been carefully removed. Forrestal's tragedy was officially recorded as suicide.

President Truman called him a war casualty and blamed excessive work during and after the war. Military affairs analyst Hanson Baldwin blamed the news media.

It seems that nobody thought about the probability that Forrestal might have been despondent about the supercarrrier cancellation and concerned over the future of U.S. Navy carrier aviation and his country.

Forrestal's death and the supercarrier cancellation infuriated Navy Brass, and a series of events began which led to the Revolt of the Admirals. From June 3 to August 25, 1949, controversy raged over the B-36 bomber, with accusations and reports that this plane had been selected by Secretary of Defense Johnson and Secretary of the Air Force

Chapter VII: Corsair Power in Korea

Stuart Symington for political and personal profit reasons. The U.S. House Armed Services Committee cleared everyone of all charges after a two-month investigation.

On May 25, 1949, Francis P Matthews, a Nebraska businessman and lawyer who had very little experience in naval affairs, was sworn in as Secretary of the Navy.

Frustrated over the steamroller tactics in these dangerous turns of events, Captain John G Crommelin called a press conference on 10 September and assumed the mantle of spokesman for the entire U.S. Navy. He warned that the Joint Chiefs of Staff, acting as a "General Staff," could be controlled by "landlocked concept" members, which is "intolerable." Captain Crommelin stated that the NSA-47 (National Security Act of 1947, which had been amended) was a dangerous piece of legislation, and that the Secretary of Defense was making dangerous decisions which were stripping the Navy of vital offensive power and greatly imperiling the security of the United States.

Crommelin's statements created a sensation in the Sunday papers, and Secretary Matthews quickly sent confidential messages to senior Navy commanders asking for their comments on Crommelin's news releases. This was Matthew's big mistake, because all of the Naval officers he contacted agreed with Crommelin.

Admiral Ernest J King warned that seapower would not receive its proper recognition, and reminded the Secretary that the absorption of Britain's crack Royal Naval Air Service into the RAF destroyed that service and made the Royal Navy a second-rate power by 1940.

Admiral Arthur W Radford, Commander in Chief, U.S. Pacific Fleet, said that the majority of officers in the Pacific Fleet concurred with Captain Crommelin.

The belief that the atom bomb was America's premier weapon became the reason that influenced the approval of the first supercarrier in July 1951, assigned the name *USS Forrestal* (CVA-59) to honor the former Secretary of Defense who had fought and died for the supercarrier. Many of the U.S. Admirals who had protested the cancellation of the suppercarrier *USS United States'* construction were fired, as was the CNO (Chief of Naval Operations) Admiral Louis E Denfield.

Meanwhile, the entire world was shocked when, after a forty-five minute bombardment at four o'clock on the Sunday morning of June 25, 1950, Kim Il Sung, North Korea's leader, ordered six North Korean

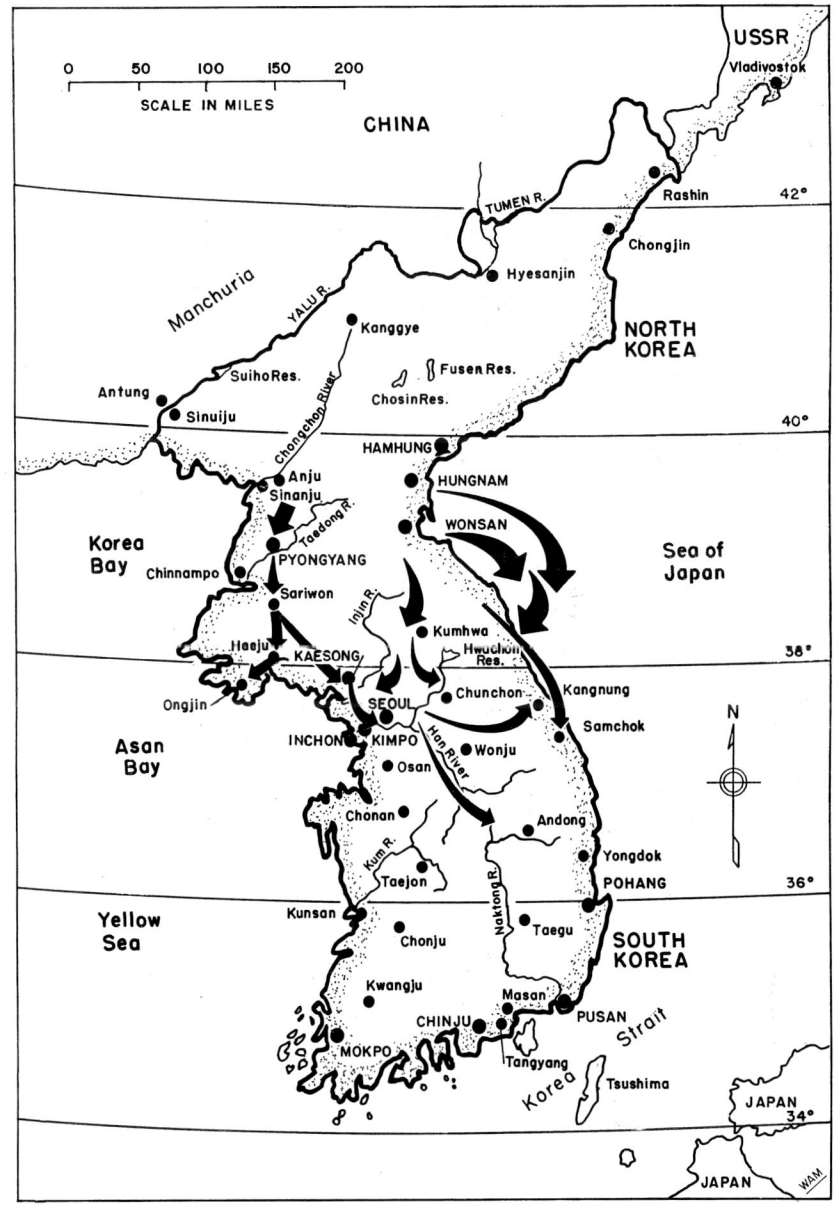

North Korea's lightning military strike against South Korea on June 25, 1950, ignited an international war that included the United States, United Nations, NATO, and China. Map illustrates the North Korean thrusts into South Korea.

VADM Arthur D. Struble commanded Task Force 77, which included all ships, naval aircraft, and U.S. Marines in the Korean conflict. British warships of the Royal Navy also sailed under Task Force 77 representing the United Nations with the U.S. Navy. (U.S. Navy Photograph, Courtesy Naval Photographic Center)

The light carrier USS Wright (CVL-49) was used as a training carrier during the Korean War. A Corsair makes a perfect landing as the ship cruises off the Florida coast. Observe the following rescue boat. (Official U.S. Navy Photo, Author's File)

People's Army (NKPA) infantry divisions and three Communist Border Constabulary Brigades (CBCB), totaling about 100,000 troops, with about 100 Russian-made T-34 and T-70 tanks, to invade the ROK (Republic of Korea, or South Korea).

Simultaneously, another 10,000 North Korean troops landed at Kangnung and Samchok, on the South Korean east coast.

Unprepared, the poorly equipped South Korean Army was unable to stop the superior force and retreated as the NKPA poured across the 38th Parallel. This was obviously the Communist expansion that U.S. policy was determined to contain.

The divided Korea had been formed when, at the end of World War II, Japanese troops north of the 38th Parallel surrendered to Soviet Russian Troops, while Japanese Troops located south of the 38th Parallel surrendered to American troops.

By 1950 the Soviet Russians and North Koreans had made the 38th Parallel an armed border without legal sanction, but with ideas of uniting the entire peninsula under Russian/ North Korean domination.

This North Korean attack precipitated the three-year-long Korean War that involved the United States, United Kingdom, China, NATO, and the United Nations. This war was named a "Police Action" and is now known as the "Forgotten War."

The years of peace after the end of World War II gave the Western Powers a sense of security that was abruptly ended by the North Korean attack; however, as a result of the attack, the United States entered a program of training and weapons construction that often overshadowed that of World War II.

On the same day of the attack, the United Nations Security Council condemned the invasion of South Korea.

The U.S. Navy destroyers De Haven (DD-727) and Mansfield (DD-728) evacuated 700 American and other foreign citizens from Inchon, South Korea, on June 26, 1950.

On the following day President Harry S Truman authorized General Douglas MacArthur, Commander-in-Chief Far East, to use American Air and naval forces in support of South Korea's defenses. The United Nations recommended that UN members also assist South Korea in repelling the attack. By 28 June North Korean forces occupied Seoul, the South Korean capital, and two days later President Truman authorized the use of U.S. ground forces in Korea.

By July 3-4, 1950, two units of VADM Arthur D Struble's Task Force 77—the U.S. Navy carrier USS Valley Forge (CV-45) and the Royal Navy carrier HMS Triumph—delivered the first naval air strikes of the Koran War against military installations in the North Korean capital of Pyongyang.

President Truman proclaimed a blockade of the Korean coast, while General Douglas MacArthur was appointed Supreme Commander of all United Nations forces in Korea.

The President's blockade was only partially effective, because the common border between North Korea and Communist China is about

Chapter VII: Corsair Power in Korea

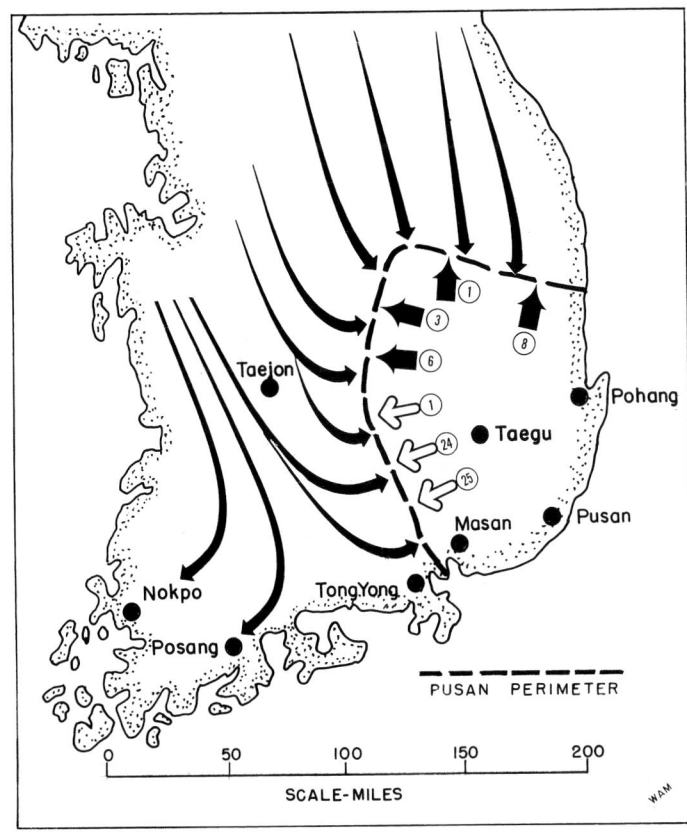

Within a month the North Korean CBCB and NKPA had reached the southern portion of South Korea and trapped four ROK Infantry Divisions and three U.S. Eighth Army Infantry Divisions. Twelve NK Infantry Divisions held the U.S. and ROK divisions in a 100 x 150 mile area. The contained area was called the Pusan Perimeter.

Col William A Willis was the first commander of the First Marine Air Wing in Korea for close air support, bomber escort, and dive bombing. (Defense Dept Photo (USMC), Author's File)

Many World War II Corsairs served in the Korean Conflict. This F4U-4 accomplished 107 bombing missions during World War II and another 43 missions during the Korean Conflict. (Official U.S. Navy Photo, Courtesy United Aircraft Corporation)

The F4U-5 was armed with two "Tiny Tims" and eight HVAR missiles. Observe that two of the rockets are longer than the others for increased range. Also note the 20mm ammunition displayed on the ground. (U.S. Navy Photo, Author's File)

Left Photo: The high altitude cannon-armed F4U-5 Corsair fighter proved to be a very capable low-altitude, troop-supporting, ground-attack performer. (Vought Aircraft Company, Courtesy Paul Bonner) Right Photo: This F4U-4 is armed with two "Tiny Tim" rocket-powered surface attack missiles. Each missile weighs 1,200lbs and has a range of one mile. The Corsair was the only fighter to be equipped with "Tiny Tims." (U.S. Navy Photo, Courtesy Vought Aircraft Company)

four-hundred miles "as the crow flies"; ample contact between the two Communist nations for China to provide military supplies and/ or sustenance to North Korea without much interference.

Col William A Willis became the first Commanding Officer of the First Marine Air Wing in Korea. Col Willis developed many of the successful aerial operations in Korea.

The Corsairs flown in the Korean Conflict consisted of World War II designs, as well as new and updated versions of the "Bent Wing." Some Corsairs also fought in both wars.

At the onset of the Korean War, the available low level, close support Corsairs were the F4U-4; cannon-fitted F4U-4B; and the high-altitude cannon-firing F4U-5.

Early in the conflict the F4U-4 and F4U-5 were accounting for 82 percent of all close air support flown by U.S. Navy and Marine pilots against targets assigned by air support controllers in Korea.

Designed for high altitudes, the F4U-5 proved well-adapted to low-level, close-support operation, for which it was not intended.

Also available at the beginning of the war was the F4U-5N night fighter Corsair.

The F4U-5N night fighter proved susceptible to the cold high altitude of Korea, and therefore was modified to become the F4U-5NL. Modifications included flexible rubber boots on the leading edge of the stabilizer, fin, and wing outer panels that cleared ice that formed on the wing or tail surfaces. An anti-freezing glycol solution system was also

This sequential series of photographs illustrates a Corsair F4U-5 firing five inch HVAR missiles into ground level targets during a low level, close support assignment. (Official U.S. Navy Photograph, Author's File)

Chapter VII: Corsair Power in Korea

This element or section of winterized Vought Corsair F4U-5NL night fighters is test flying over the author's home state of New Jersey. Observe the flexible "boot" on the outer wing panel leading edge. "Winterizing" was necessary to combat the cold Korean weather at altitude. (U.S. Navy Photograph, Courtesy Air Trails Albert L Lewis)

Upper Photo: The sleek lines of the Vought AU-1 are revealed in this photo fresh from the Vought production line. (Vought Aircraft Company, Courtesy Paul Bonner) Lower Photo: This AU-1 is loaded for action with six 250lb bombs under the wings plus one 500lb bomb and one 1,000 bomb at the hard points in addition to the four 20mm cannon. Plane flew in First Air Wing One's VMF-323 "Death Rattler" squadron. (Dept of Defense Photo, USMC, Courtesy H.J "Jerry" Dalton, Jr.)

installed to spray on the propeller and windshield; however, the solution attacked the windshield rubber seals and clouded the cockpit canopy, so the cockpit spray was discontinued.

F4U-5NL aviators were warned not to dive the aircraft or land with the boots inflated because the inflated boots altered the wing's airfoil.

This all-weather fighter was equipped with the AN/APS-19A radar set and flew with VC-3.

Seventy-two of these successful aircraft were constructed and served from land bases as well as aircraft carriers.

The AU-1 was the first specially designed Corsair for Korean low-level close support operations, making its first flight on January 31, 1952. Heavily armed, and provided with well armored pilot's seat, oil coolers, cockpit flooring, fuselage underside, engine, fuel tank, and pressurized fuel areas, the AU-1 performed its tasks without failing.

Originally given the designation F4U-6, this was changed to AU-1, with "A" indicating Attack, and "U" was the U.S. Navy designation for Vought aircraft.

As previously mentioned, low level operations of strafing, rocket firing, and bombing are more dangerous than plane-against-plane fighting at higher altitudes. The low level attacks resulted in sixteen AU-1 losses to anti-aircraft fire between July 1952 and July 1953 despite their armor.

The Corsair and the larger attack plane, the single-seat Douglas AD Skyraider, became a well-matched pair when attacking special targets, such as bridges, factories, oil refineries, airfields, and other tactical targets in Korea.

When the pair operated in daylight, F4U-5 or AU-1 Corsairs flew low in Flak Suppression roles armed with Daisy Cutter-fitted bombs, 20mm cannon, and/or HVAR missiles to disperse or destroy the anti-aircraft battery and personnel. This gave the Skyraiders a free run with 2,000, 1,000, 500, and/or 100 pound bombs to destroy the target.

When flying at night, the Skyraiders depended upon F4U-5N or F4U-5NL Corsairs to guide them to targets over Korea. The Corsair night fighters located the target, dropped flares, and led the Skyraiders to the target, joining in the attack.

The first air strikes of the Korean War began at 5:45 AM on the morning of July 3, 1950, when the Royal Navy aircraft carrier *HMS Triumph*, in the Yellow Sea, launched twelve Firefly fighter-bombers of

The Corsair and Skyraider became the forerunner of the Hunter/Killer team in the brightness of day and the darkness of night. This F4U-5N Corsair night fighter guides the Skyraider to the strategic target, illuminates the target, and joins the Skyraider in the attack. Planes shown here are from VC-3 flying from NAS Moffett Field on a training mission. (U.S. Navy Photograph, Author's File)

Light Aircraft Carrier *USS Bataan* (CVL-29) is underway with F4U-4 Corsairs of VMF-312 (Checkerboard) on the Flight Deck. The Light Aircraft Carriers were constructed on light cruiser hulls. Note the two smokestacks at the far edge of the deck. (U.S. Navy Photo, Courtesy National Archives)

Smoke, flame, and fireballs surge skyward after eleven U.S. Navy Skyraiders and ten U.S. Navy Corsairs attacked the Wonson Oil Refinery on the east coast of Korea on July 18, 1950. Repeated explosions destroyed the entire refinery. (U.S. Navy Photo, Author's File)

827 Squadron and nine rocket-armed Seafires of 800 Squadron to attack hangars at Haeju Airfield. Bridges and railroads were also attacked.

Fifteen minutes later on the same morning, *USS Valley Forge* (CV-45) launched sixteen Corsairs of VF-54, each armed with eight 5 inch HVAR missiles, and twelve Skyraiders of VA-55 armed with two 500lb and six 110lb bombs each. The target was the airfield at the North Korean capital of Pyongyang.

Aircraft from both carriers repeated the raids on Pyongyang in the afternoon of 4 July. Hangars were demolished, runways were pockmarked with craters, and aircraft were destroyed on the ground at the airfield. Elsewhere in the city the Corsairs and Skyraiders strafed, rocketed, and bombed buildings, bridges, roads, locomotives, railroad tracks, and military installations.

Four Skyraiders were slightly damaged by Flak that was generally inaccurate and dispersed.

On July 18, 1950, *USS Valley Forge* (CV-45) launched ten Corsairs and eleven Douglas AD Skyraiders to destroy the Wonson Oil Refinery on the east coast of Korea. After the attack, it was difficult to distinguish portions of the refinery due to the complete destruction. Carrier aircraft power had proven its worth in Korea.

USS Boxer (CV-21) arrived from the United States on July 23, 1950, with a cargo of 145 North American P-51 Mustangs for the Far Eastern Air Force. The carrier steamed across the Pacific Ocean in eight days and was a welcome addition to the carrier force in Korean waters.

By July 25, 1950, Task Force 96.5 was organized to blockade North Korea. The U.S. Navy covered the Korean East Coast, while the British

Left Photo: Armorors are loading bombs on F4U-4 Corsairs on the Flight Deck of *USS Philippine Sea* (CVA-47) in preparation for providing close air support for U.S. Army troops in the Pusan Perimeter. Right Photo: An F4U-4 Corsair has just landed on *USS Leyte* (CV-32) on station off the coast of North Korea. At least two U.S. aircraft carriers were on station at all times off the East coast of North Korea. (U.S. Navy Photos, Author's File)

Chapter VII: Corsair Power in Korea

Essex Class Fast Aircraft Carrier *USS Boxer* (CV-21) steams with F4U-4 Corsairs arranged on the after Flight Deck. Two F4U-5N Corsairs of VC-3 fly-by with Lt John D. Ely leading and LTJG Stranlund in formation. (U.S. Navy Photo, Courtesy National Archives)

U.S. Navy Squadron VF-114 cannon-armed F4U-4B Corsairs are being armed with 200lb bombs aboard *USS Philippine Sea* prior to a low-level close air support mission over Korea. (U.S. Navy Photo, via National Archives)

Commonwealth (Task Group 96.53) covered the Korean West coast. U.S. Naval Forces in Korean waters included three types of aircraft carriers: large fast carriers (CV); light carriers built on light cruiser hulls (CVL); and Marine escort carriers known as Corsair carriers (CVE).

The Royal Navy provided the aircraft carriers *HMS Theseus*, *HMS Triumph*, and *HMS Glory*.

As with the Royal Navy carriers, Royal Navy carrier aircraft were designed for a short range, flying about five 2-1/2 hour missions with a 45 gallon drop tank during a normal day. This cannot compare to the Corsair that was designed for the wide expanses of two oceans.

The North Koreans trapped most of the U.S. Eighth Army and many ROK regiments, forming a perimeter enclosing the seaport of Pusan, at the southeastern corner of South Korea. The U.S. Eighth Army and South Korean regiments were fighting to break out of this 80 x 115 mile Pusan Pocket.

About one month after the war began the United Nations command had lost most of its airfields by destruction or capture by the NKPA. This placed more dependence on the mobile airfields, the aircraft carriers, and carrier aircraft.

Replacement Royal Navy aircraft were brought from Singapore by the replenishment carrier *HMS Unicorn*. Worn or damaged aircraft were returned to Singapore by the same carrier.

The F4U-4B Corsairs on *USS Philippine Sea*, and all other aircraft on this *Essex* class carrier, required careful preparation before the planes

Once armed, the Corsairs start and run engines until they reach operating temperatures; then the planes are taxied along the deck to the flight line. (U.S. Navy Photo, via National Archives)

When the Corsair arrives at the flight line the aviator is signaled to extend the Corsair's wings as he rolls forward to his place in line (left side of photo). (U.S. Navy Photo, via National Archives)

Launch! The Corsair is caught at the moment it leaves the deck; having been catapulted off the *USS Philippine Sea* bow. Note the catapult bridle on the deck. Earlier Corsairs took off sans catapults; however, as later models became heavier with bigger payloads the catapult became necessary. (U.S. Navy Photo, via National Archives)

embarked on a low-level, close air support mission for American and South Korean troops. Upon their return from the mission, every plane was checked for Flak damage and/or any potential mechanical failure.

Aircraft support personnel are the unsung heroes of the Flight Deck. They must be properly clad for Korean weather in clothing light enough to permit them to work, but warm enough to endure the frequent gales and snow squalls, especially during the months from mid-Autumn to mid-Spring.

While the UN and NATO forces were bent on destroying bridges, railroads, and military installations, the North Korean First, Second, Third, Fourth, Fifth, Sixth, Eighth, 12th, 13th, and 15th Infantry Divisions were driving the U.S. Eighth Army, First, 24th, and 25th Infantry Divisions and ROK forces' First, Third, Sixth, and Eighth Infantry Divisions south into a pocket in the southeast corner of South Korea, hereafter called the "Pusan Perimeter." This operation was completed during July and August, 1950.

USS Philippine Sea arrived near Pusan with Carrier Group Eleven on August 1, 1950, which included the Corsairs of VMF-113 and VMF-114 plus one squadron of AD Skyraiders.

On July 25, 1950, Lt. Gen Walton H Walker, commanding the U.S. Eighth Army, requested tactical air support for the Army forces holding the hard-pressed Pusan Perimeter. *USS Philippine Sea* answered the call with Corsairs on 5 August, and continued into September 1950.

About one mouth after the war began, the UN command had lost most of its airfields by destruction or capture by the NKPA. This placed more dependence on the mobile airfields, the aircraft carriers, and carrier aircraft.

The Marines of the First Provisional Marine Brigade at the Pusan perimeter managed to keep six Corsairs over their Brigade throughout daylight-hour fighting.

Further north, at Kaesong, Marine observers detected a column of about one hundred North Korean vehicles heading north. The ground controller called down four Corsairs that made low-level strafing runs, creating chaos in the column. Trucks collided with each other and motorcycles and jeeps were abandoned, while many vehicles ran off the road. Such was the potency of a Corsair low-level attack.

With its mission complete, this Corsair engages the arresting cable for a safe landing on *USS Philippine Sea*. Observe that all bombs have been delivered. (U.S. Navy Photo, via National Archives)

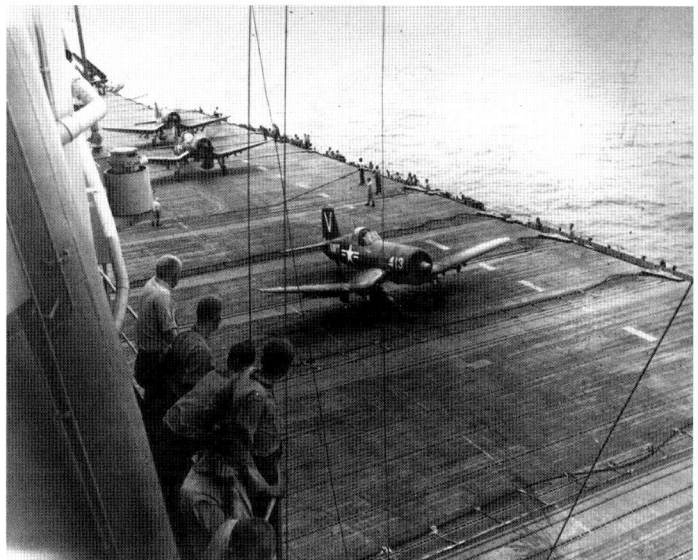

As soon as the Corsairs disengage from the arresting cable they taxi alongside the carrier island where they will be inspected, repaired if necessary, and refueled and rearmed, and made ready for the next sortie. (U.S. Navy Photo, via National Archives)

Chapter VII: Corsair Power in Korea

Maj George Axtell Jr was the youngest squadron commander when his VMF-323 "Death Rattlers" worked closely with VMF-214 "Black Sheep" in Korea. Major Axtell was an Ace with six victories. (Department of Defense, USMC, Author's File)

VMF-214 retained the name "Black Sheep" in Korea just as squadron VMF-214 had used in World War II.

Lt. Col Walter E Lischeid became the first commanding officer on July 8, 1950, and by 12 July the unit had deployed to Kobe, Japan, reporting to MAG 33, First MAW. The squadron arrived at the Pusan Perimeter on August 2, 1950, stationed aboard the Corsair carrier *USS Badoeng Strait* (CVE-116) with their F4U-4B Corsairs.

Flight operations against enemy-held positions began immediately, making VMF-214 the first Marine squadron to fight in Korea.

The Squadron XO, Major Kenneth L Reusser, flew repeated "extreme" close air support runs on August 5, 1950, against enemy troops, tanks, trucks, and a gasoline tanker. His bravery and disregard for danger brought Major Reusser his second Navy Cross. He earned his first Navy Cross in World War II.

The VMF-214 squadron number was originally assigned to the Swashbucklers during the challenging World War II Guadalcanal vs Bougainville battle, and was later known as the Black Sheep under the command of Major Gregory (Pappy) Boyington during the Bougainville vs Rabaul battle.

U.S. Marine troops experienced their baptism of fire in Korea on August 7, 1950. Their assignment was to counterattack against Chinju and Masan, at the southwestern corner of the Pusan Perimeter. The troops had the expert assistance of close air support (50 to 200 yards distance) from two Corsair squadrons: Black Sheep VMF-214 and Death Rattlers VMF-323. Chinju was captured; however, before the troops could take Masan, they were ordered seventy-five miles north to repel a North Korean offensive, crossing the Naktong River.

By 8 August, the UN situation on the ground had deteriorated to the point of collapse. The remnants of the U.S. Eighth Army seemed to be overwhelmed, and carrier aircraft appeared to be the only salvation to redeem the ability to attack the enemy.

USS Valley Forge and *USS Philippine Sea* increased their close air support by flying two consecutive days, with the third day devoted to refuel and rearm.

In view of the dire straits the United Nations found itself, General MacArthur persuaded Admiral Forrest P Sherman, Chief of Naval Operations, and General J Lawton Collins, U.S. Army Chief of Staff, to support his plan for an amphibious assault on Inchon, at the west coast of Korea. The conference was held in Tokyo on August 23, 1950.

Aviators of VMF-214 "Black Sheep" pose for the photographer with the squadron insignia. Flight operations began early in August 1950 with their F4U-4B Corsairs making this the first Marine squadron to fight in Korea. (Dept of Defense, USMC, Courtesy David J Ekstrand)

Upper Photo: Major Kenneth L Ruesser, USMC, XO VMF-214 receives Purple Heart from Capt John S Thach. Ruesser injured his right arm when he was forced to ditch his Corsair. (Dept of Defense, USMC, Courtesy David J Ekstrand) Lower Photo: Major Ruesser models the U.S. Navy's new exposure suit that saved his life when he was forced to ditch his Corsair into frigid Korean waters. (Dept of Defense, USMC, Courtesy David J Ekstrand)

CDR John S Thach, Captain of USS Sicily, developed several aerial combat maneuvers during the early years of World War II. One of his most popular is the "Thach Weave." Photo taken in 1943. (U.S. Navy Photo, Author's File)

Having convinced Admiral Sherman and General Collins of the assault, General MacArthur planned to launch an amphibious attack of incomparable audacity at Inchon, the port of Seoul 150 miles behind enemy lines, on September 15, 1950.

Inchon possessed no "beach" on which to land. The "beach" was a city-type waterfront with sea walls, docks, and barriers. In addition, the tidal range was thirty-feet over a narrow, uncharted, twisting channel (named Flying fish Channel) through acres of mud flats to the harbor.

Despite the hardships, Inchon was only fifteen miles from North Korean-occupied Seoul and less than that from Kimpo airfield. Further, the North Koreans would never expect an assault landing at Inchon with all its handicaps.

Of the several islands in Asan Bay, Wolni-Do and Solni-Do guarded Inchon Harbor. The two islands were connected to each other with a 750 yard long causeway that gave the military personnel the ability to travel from one island to the other without the need for boats. The islands were heavily grown with trees to cover the artillery that was installed.

Preliminaries for the Inchon invasion began on 10 September, when VMF-214 and VMF-323 flew from USS Sicily and USS Badoeng Strait to strafe and napalm Wolni-Do and Solni-Do to burn away the trees and expose the artillery. This was followed by raids on Kimpo airfield and Seoul.

Five days later, Inchon invasion day, Lt. Col Robert D Taplett's G Company, 3rd Battalion, Fifth Marines requested VMF-214 to spread napalm, at dawn, on a North Korean platoon that had dug in at one end

Chapter VII: Corsair Power in Korea

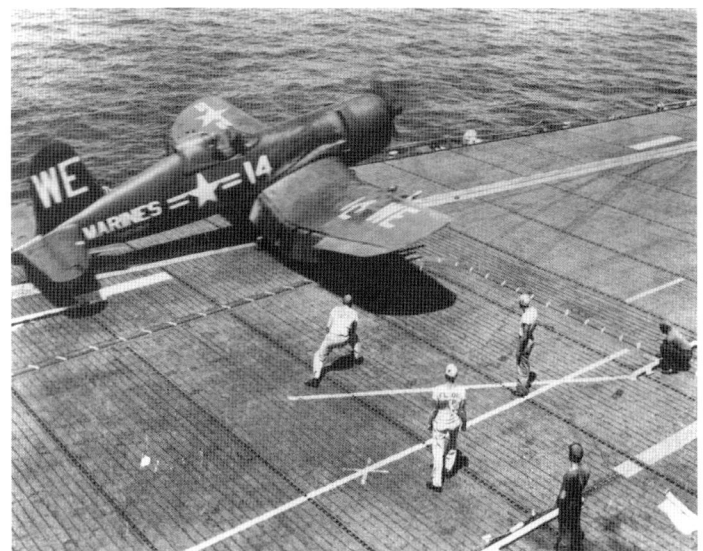

Black Sheep F4U-4B Corsairs takeoff from USS Sicily just prior to the Inchon invasion. The VMF-214 Corsairs attacked Wolmi-Do and Solmi-Do, plus Kimpo Airfield and North Korean-occupied Seoul on Sept. 10, 1950. Observe the HVAR missiles in addition to the four 20mm cannon for close in troop support. (Dept of Defense, USMC, Courtesy David J Ekstrand)

Upper Photo: The "mastermind" of the Inchon invasion, General Douglas MacArthur, observes and controls the Inchon attack on Sept. 15, 1950, from the command ship Mount Mc Kinley. From left to right: Brig Gen Courtney Whitney, General MacArthur, and Maj Gen Edward M Almond. (U.S. Army Photo, via National Archives) Lower Photo: This drawing of Inchon reveals the mud flats and the angular dockside exposed to the waterfront, plus warehouse ashore, instead of the more inviting sloping beach for an amphibious assault.

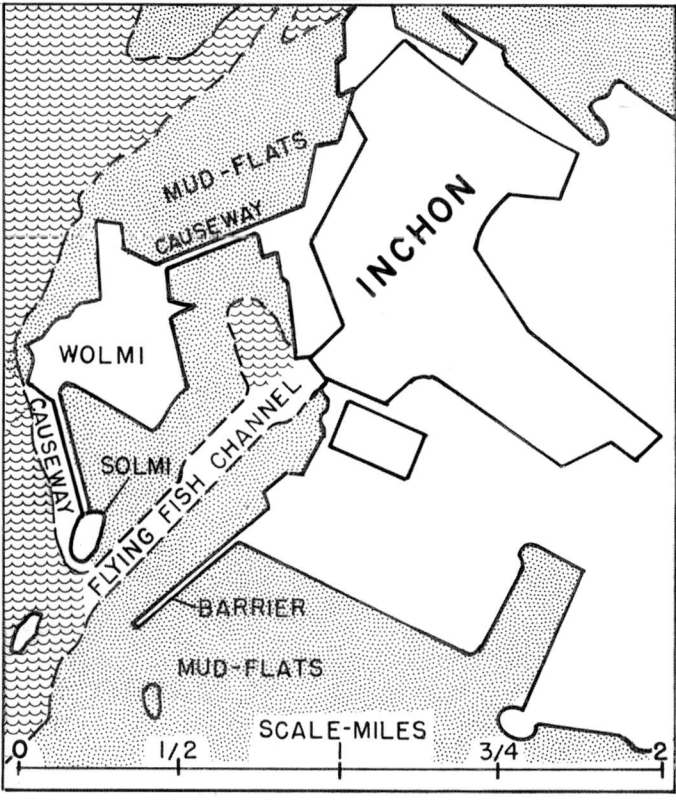

of the inter-island causeway. This enabled the Marine troops to take the islands.

The actual invasion of Inchon on September 15, 1950, required scores of freighters, troopships, and fighting ships with an overhead CAP of Corsairs. As General MacArthur predicted, the Inchon invasion proceeded as planned; the UN armies landed 150 miles behind the North Korean front lines, dividing and heading north to the China/ Korean border, plus south to the Pusan Perimeter.

The immediate post-invasion tasks were to provide close air support for the UN and ROK forces breaking through the Pusan Perimeter and driving north to the Korean/ Chinese border, while General MacArthur went ashore at Inchon to inspect the port facilities to ascertain its ability to accept a flow of military equipment.

The U.S. Air Force system of "Close Air Support" depended on an airborne controller in light liaison-type grasshopper aircraft assigning

This panoramic view of the Inchon invasion reveals one of the several CAP Corsairs from USS Philippine Sea. Observe the islands guarding the harbor. (U.S. Navy Photo, Author's File)

missions to the strike aircraft. It appears that "Close Air Support" under this system meant that anything up to a ten-mile range from the front lines was considered satisfactory.

While the carriers of Task Force 77 were trying to conduct "close air support" according to U.S. Air Force principles learned in World War II, two escort Corsair carriers—*USS Sicily* (CVE-118) and *USS Badoeng Strait* (CVE-116)—arrived with their Marine Corsair squadrons VMF-214 (Black Sheep) and VMF-323 (Death Rattlers). The squadrons began, as part of Task Group 96.8, to demonstrate the fine art of "Close Air Support."

Trooper friends of the author who charged the enemy in Korea under an umbrella of strafing Corsairs testify to the fact that it literally rained ejected .50 cal shell casings as the Corsairs roared overhead! Truly "Close Air Support"!

General MacArthur (center) inspects the Inchon port facilities with VADM A.D. Struble (left) and Maj Gen O.P. Smith, USMC, to ascertain the port's capability for volume and size of future inbound materiel. (U.S. Naval Historical Center Photo, via National Archives)

Lt Col Walter E Lischeid, CO VMF-214 Black Sheep, points to map of Korea where the squadron gave Marine Ground Troop Support "Extra Ordinary." The Colonel is aboard USS Sicily (CVE-118). (Dept of Defense, USMC, Courtesy David J Ekstrand)

Chapter VII: Corsair Power in Korea

Lt Col Lischeid stands proudly with his No. WE-16 F4U-4B Corsair. The squadron leader was killed on September 25, 1950, while leading a low-level Marine Ground Troop Support in number "17." (Dept of Defense, USMC, Courtesy David J Ekstrand)

The Black Sheep's CO, Lt. Col Walter E Lischeid, led his squadron in Corsair No.17 with "extra-ordinary" leadership in low-level close air support to help Marine and Army troopers gain ground and objectives. The CO lost his life from intense antiaircraft fire while leading his men during close air support, low-level operations on September 25, 1950. He was succeeded by Major William Lundin, USMC, on Nov 1, 1950.

Although Lt. Col Lischeid's death was caused by intense AA fire, naval superstition blamed Lt. Col Lischeid's death on the fact that any plane No.17 in the squadron was jinxed: a replacement No.17 killed Tech Sgt George C Underwood when its guns fired while the aircraft was being serviced; and Maj Robert Floeck was killed on 23 Sept while flying another No.17.

After Lt. Col Lischeid's death, the No.17 was banned from all aircraft on board *USS Sicily* by order of Navy Capt John S Thach.

The newly captured Kimpo airfield was placed in service to assist in the UN march to the north, driving the North Korean Armies to the Chinese border.

The Black Sheep were called again, on 18 September, to hit North Korean T-34 tanks that were moving through a village near Inchon. As the Corsairs attacked the tanks with napalm in full view of the Marine ground forces, the Marines cheered; however, when one of the Corsairs was hit by Flak, failed to pull up in time and crashed, the cheering stopped. The aviator, Capt William F Simpson, was killed instantly in Corsair No.17.

On September 20, 1950, Lt. Col Taplett's 3rd Battalion again called upon the Black Sheep. Four VMF-214 Corsairs provided the only close air support for the battalion's crossing of the Han River, South of Seoul, and assault on Hill 125.

The Black Sheep skillfully covered the withdrawal of the 2nd Battalion's E and F Companies at dusk on Sept 21, 1950. The companies had assaulted a ridge overlooking the Inchon-Seoul Highway during

Marine Maj William Lundin, who succeeded Lt Col Walter E. Lischeid as CO of VMF-214 Black Sheep, uses a chart to clearly point out the targets hit in a recent foray to Capt John S Thach. (Dept of Defense, USMC, Courtesy David J Ekstrand)

Black Sheep Lt Robert King holds a flotation life vest as he assists Lt George Dodenhoff don his flight gear. Flight gear must be properly worn for protection in the cold Korean water in the event of a ditching. (Dept of Defense, USMC, Courtesy David J Ekstrand)

Corsair: The Saga of the Legendary Bent-Wing Fighter-Bomber

the day, but at dusk the enemy still held the high ground, forcing a withdrawal.

On 26 September three U.S. Eighth Army Divisions, advancing from the Pusan Perimeter, joined with the Seventh Infantry Division from Inchon.

This severed the NKPA supply line south of Seoul through which the North Korean supply line ran. In effect, the North Korean Army ceased to exist as an organized fighting force.

The U.S. Joint Chiefs of Staff authorized General MacArthur, on September 27, 1950, to pursue the North Korean Army north of the 38th Parallel into North Korea in view of his astounding victory at Inchon.

On October 9, 1950, General MacArthur issued his second surrender ultimatum to the North Korean government as U.S. Forces crossed the 38th Parallel into North Korea.

During the five days ending on November 7, 1950, Col Homer L Litzenberg's Seventh Marine Regiment shattered a series of attacks by the 124th Chinese Communist Division near the Yalu River.

Lt John V Hanes was the first Black Sheep to land his Corsair on the newly captured Kimpo Airfield following a close air support mission flying from USS Sicily. (Dept of Defense, USMC, Courtesy David J Ekstrand)

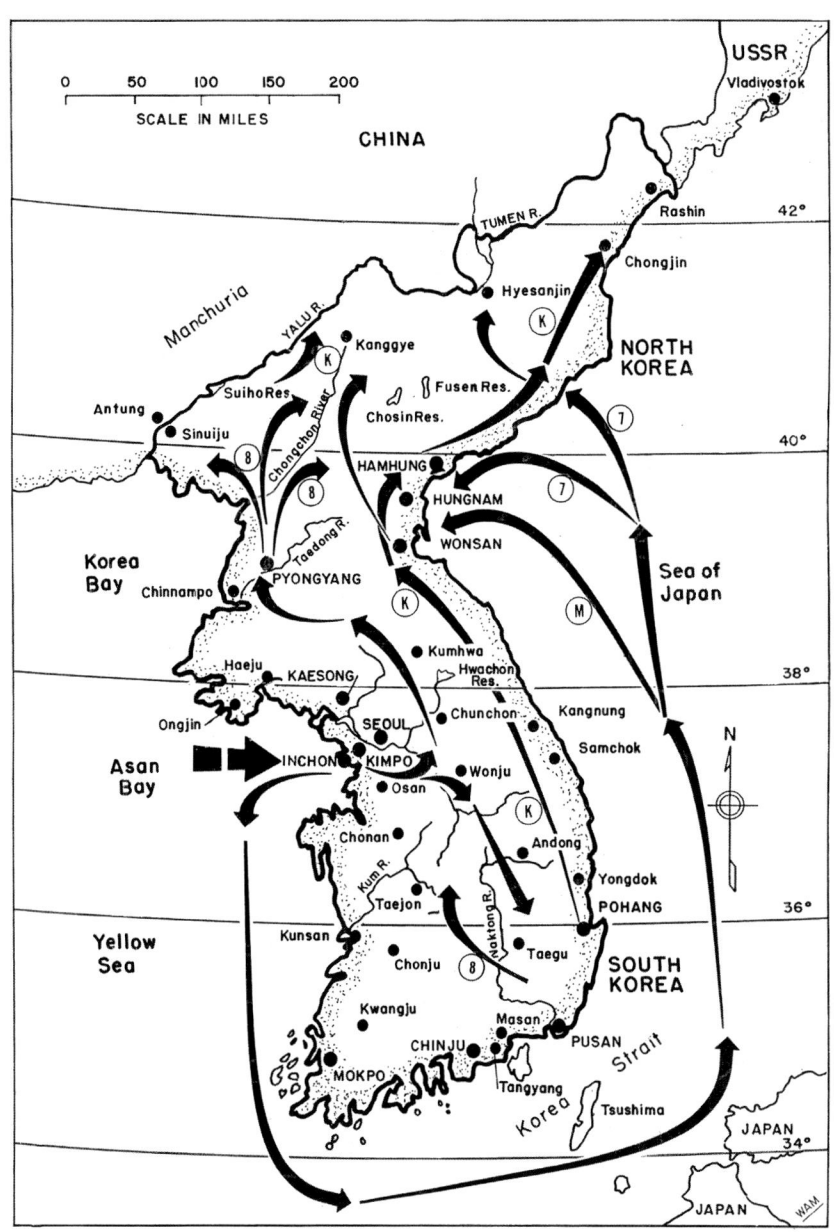

After the successful invasion of Inchon, UN forces headed north and south assisting the Allied Forces in the Pusan Perimeter and forging ahead towards the Yalu river. U.S. Naval forces also landed troops on the Eastern coast of North Korea (K= S. Korean Troops, M= U.S. Marines: 8= U.S. Eighth Army, 7= U.S. Seventh Army).

Chapter VII: Corsair Power in Korea

Left Photo: The cold winter weather of Korea is revealed on the flight deck and planes of this Essex Class aircraft carrier. Note the AD Skyraider on the catapult and the F4U-5N Corsairs in the foreground. Also note the manned snow-clearing cart. Right Photo: Armed with HVAR missiles, F4U-4 Corsairs await take-off to Korea. Note the snow on the deck and catwalk. It is Corsairs such as these that facilitated the Marine's retreat form the Chosin Reservoir. (U.S. Dept of Defense, Navy, Author's File)

During this time General MacArthur officially notified the United Nations of the presence of Chinese Troops in North Korea.

On March 8, 1950, VADM Arthur D Struble ordered his Carrier Task Force 77 to destroy the bridges crossing the Yalu River. The Yalu River forms the border between China and North Korea, and the bridges were the means for the Chinese to cross into North Korea.

The caveat to VADM Struble's order was that the UN aircraft were permitted to attack only the Korean side of the bridges. This was obviously a politically rather than a militarily motivated order.

On November 13, 1950, the U.S. Seventh Marines arrived at the village of Hagaru-Ri, at the southern end of the Chosin Reservoir. Eight days later the Seventh Marines reached the Chinese border at the Yalu River.

In an unforeseen and unforecast counterstroke, about 300,000 white-clad Chinese Communist Force (CCF) troops poured into North Korea blaring loud trumpets, ostensibly to chase evil spirits, on November 27, 1950. The white-clad CCF troops had traveled across the frozen Yalu River, undetected. This massive attack was directed at American and ROK forces near the Chosin Reservoir.

Two days later, eight Chinese divisions attacked the First Marine Division positions to the west and south of the Chosin Reservoir.

The best defense was Corsair close air support with napalm and HVAR missiles that enabled the UN forces to fight their way south to Hamhung, and then to the port of Hungnam, from where General MacArthur ordered the U.S. Navy to evacuate 105,000 military personnel and 91,000 civilian refugees. The carriers *Philippine Sea* (CV-47), *Princeton* (CV-37), *Bataan* (CVL-29), and *Valley Forge* (CV-45), and the "Corsair Carriers" *Badoeng Strait* (CVE-116) and *Sicily* (CVE-118), provided air support for the evacuation.

Before the Chosin Reservoir Battle was over a total of 332 bombing and strafing runs were flown: the First Marine Air Wing flew 136 sorties; U.S. Navy carriers off the coast launched 80 sorties; and U.S. Air Force fighters flew 37 sorties.

Leading elements of the First Marine Division linked up with Marine units heading north making the withdrawal from the Chosin Reservoir, one of the most heroic fighting retreats of all time.

The Marines suffered 4,400 battle casualties that included 730 deaths. Chinese losses are estimated to be 37,500.

At this time of year the Chosin Reservoir was frozen; however, crossing on the ice would be hazardous for men and machines. This retreat is often called the "Battle of the Frozen Chosin," with temperatures of thirty-degrees below zero, plus a wind chill factor that approached 75 miles per hour at times!

Fighter Squadron VF-32 from *USS Leyte* (CV-32) was conducting close air support for the outnumbered Marines at the Chosin Reservoir. Many of the F4U-4B Corsairs often returned with multiple holes in wing and fuselage made by small arms fire from the thousands of white-clad Chinese Communist Forces that were hardly visible from the air.

On December 4, 1950, VF-32 Commanding Officer LCDR Richard Cevoli led a four-plane Corsair division from *USS Leyte* (CV-32) on an armed reconnaissance mission at about 1,500 feet above the mountainous, snow-covered ground. Following was XO LTJG William Koenig, flying

A Marine column, during the Chosin Reservoir Battle breakout, watch a Corsair climb for altitude after it completed a napalm attack (at extreme right) and flies through smoke from a previous Corsair napalm attack on pursuing Chinese troops. (Defense Dept Photo, USMC, Author's File)

Left Photo: Ensign Jesse Brown was a Corsair section leader protecting UN troops at Chosin Reservoir when he had engine trouble and crash landed. Right Photo: LTJG Thomas J Hudner Jr was Ensign Brown's wingman and tried to save his crashed comrade at the risk of his own life. (U.S. Navy Photos, Author's File)

Left Photo: Capt Charles C Ward, USMC, was awarded the Silver Star for extraordinary bravery in his attempt to rescue ENS Jesse L Brown, USNR. The Silver Star is America's third-highest award. (U.S. Navy Photo, Author's File) Right Photo: ENS Jesse Brown was the U.S. Navy's first black commissioned officer and its first black aviator to fire his guns in combat. He was the subject of an intense rescue attempt after he force landed in frigid temperatures and high winds. (U.S. Navy Photo, Courtesy National Archives)

Chapter VII: Corsair Power in Korea

Cevoli's wing, and ENS Jesse L Brown, with LTJG Thomas J Hudner, Jr flying ENS Brown's wing. Hudner was flying the "Tail-End Charlie" position.

ENS Brown was the U.S. Navy's first black commissioned officer and the first black naval aviator to fire his guns in combat.

As the flight circled back towards the Chosin, antiaircraft fire flew up at the Corsairs.

Suddenly, ENS Brown radioed that he was losing power and had to land, apparently hit by antiaircraft fire. A forced landing was most dangerous because the terrain was snow covered and mountainous with many trees. Brown's reply to Cevoli's question was that he could not maintain any power at all.

Brown did spot a small open area and made a rough wheels-up landing on the side of a hill.

The force of the crash landing had bent the Corsair fuselage about 45 degrees at the cockpit, trapping the aviator. The engine had also torn off. The canopy, which had been open for the landing, was now closed; however, ENS Brown opened it after a minute or two and weakly waved. The crash was about ten miles from Chosin Reservoir, and the crippled Corsair had started to smoke, which prompted the XO to radio for a rescue helicopter. It would be at least twenty minutes before the helicopter could arrive, and LT Hudner feared the Corsair would burst into flames with ENS Brown trapped inside.

Without waiting for approval, Tom Hudner decided to save Jesse Brown. He planned to crash-land his Corsair as close as possible to Jesse and pull him from the cockpit, assuming that when the helicopter arrived it could carry both aviators to safety.

Lt. Hudner unloaded all his ordnance, lowered his flaps, and kept his wheels retracted. In this condition, he made practice passes and finally landed about 100 yards from ENS Brown. The only obvious damage to Hudner's Corsair was a shattered windshield, which had become brittle from the extreme cold and the Corsair's impact on the frozen ground.

When the rescuer reached the downed Corsair Jesse Brown was semiconscious. He had taken off his gloves to unbuckle his parachute and seat harness, but dropped them and could not retrieve them in the crushed cockpit.

Hudner could not find the source of the smoke, but scooped up some snow and threw it under the engine cowling, which reduced the smoke somewhat. He noticed that Jesse couldn't get out of his plane because the central control console had jammed his leg, at the calf, against the fuselage side.

Hudner returned to his Corsair and radioed to his XO to have the helicopter bring an ax and fire extinguisher, hoping the ax could free his comrade and the extinguisher to put out the fire.

When Hudner returned to Brown, the Ensign was very calm and spoke coherently. As the helicopter approached Hudner popped the smoke end of his life jacket flare to indicate wind direction for the helicopter. The Helicopter was a U.S. Marine Sikorsky HO3S from squadron VMO-6 flown by Lt. Charles Ward, an acquaintance of Hudner's. Ward and Hudner worked to release ENS Brown manually and with the ax until dusk, to no avail.

As darkness approached the duo had to stop working to release Brown because the helicopter was not equipped for night flying and the terrain was mountainous. It must be remembered that helicopters in 1950 were not as technically advanced as they are today.

The intention to rescue Brown on the following morning was cancelled due to terrible weather, the same as it was for the morning of 5 December.

On December 7, 1950, LTJG Hudner was transferred to *USS Leyte*, and a helicopter was made ready for flight to Jesse Brown with Hudner and a flight surgeon aboard. Thomas Hudner objected on the grounds that it was too dangerous, and that Jesse was already dead. An alternative plan was developed:

Four Corsairs were to fly over the crash site, where everything was the same as Hudner had left it, except that there were hundreds of new footprints around Jesse Brown's Corsair and Jesse had been stripped of his clothing. Apparently local Korean peasants had taken the clothing from the dead body because this had been the coldest Korean winter in 100 years.

The four Corsairs destroyed the two crashed Corsairs and then cremated Ens Jesse Brown's body with napalm. The Corsairs then flew a salute over the brave warrior.

LTJG Thomas Hudner believed he would be court-martialed for crash landing his plane without permission, thereby destroying government property. He also bore a sense of guilt for not being able to save Jesse.

The VF-32 squadron commander LCDR Cevoli broke the news to Tom Hudner that he had been recommended for the Medal of Honor. President Harry S Truman presented the Medal of Honor to LTJG Thomas J Hudner on April 13, 1951; a well deserved award, to risk his life to try to save the life of a comrade.

Left Photo: Although recently applied to military use, helicopters saved lives by speeding the wounded to field hospitals. Shown here is a Sikorski HO3S-1 bringing a wounded Marine to Hagaru. Note the mountain in the background. Right Photo: This HO3S-1 helicopter is being inspected for possible repairs after crashing in mountainous North Korea. It was a helicopter such as this that Capt Charles Ward, USMC, rescued LTJG Hudner with after both tried to rescue ENS Brown. (U.S. Marine Corps Photos, Courtesy National Archives)

President Harry S. Truman presents the Congressional Medal of Honor to LTJG Thomas Jerome Hudner Jr. on April 13, 1951, in a ceremony at the White House, Washington, DC. Among those present were Lt Hudner's proud parents, Mr and Mrs Thomas J Hudner. (U.S. Navy Photo, Courtesy National Archives)

LTJG Thomas J Hudner's Medal of Honor Presentation reads as follows:

"Quickly maneuvering to circle the downed pilot and protect him from enemy troops infesting the area, LTJG Hudner risked his life to save the injured flier who was trapped alive in a burning wreckage. Fully aware of the extreme danger in landing on the rough mountainous terrain, and the scant hope of escape or survival in subzero temperature, he put his plane down skillfully in a deliberate wheels-up landing in the presence of enemy troops. With his bare hands, he packed the fuselage with snow to keep the flames away from the pilot and struggled to pull him free. Unsuccessful in this, he returned to his crashed aircraft and radioed other airborne planes, requesting that a helicopter be dispatched with an ax and fire extinguisher. He then remained on the spot despite the continuing danger from enemy action and, with the assistance of the rescue pilot, renewed a desperate but unavailing battle against time, cold, and flames. LtJG Hudner's exceptionally valiant action and selfless devotion to a shipmate sustain and enhance the highest traditions of the United States Naval Service."

General MacArthur declared that the entry of the Chinese in the Korean War made it an entirely new war. He proclaimed that the war could be won only by invading China against the Chinese "nerve center." It was with this sensible military idea that he clashed with the political judgment of President Truman. When Gen MacArthur persisted, President Truman dismissed the famous general on April 11, 1951, and replaced him with Gen Mathew Ridgeway as C in C United Nations Command. This placed Gen James H van Fleet in command of the U.S. Eighth Army.

The United Nations Command had begun "Operation Killer" in an attempt to inflict the maximum number of enemy casualties upon the Chinese, rather than concentrate on the capture of territory.

Heretofore, the UN planning staffs always hoped to use overwhelming air power to cut the country into manageable sections and destroy, damage, or cut off each section's line of supply. It was hoped to inhibit the sections' ability to fight after interdiction strikes to communications and industry.

When "Operation Killer" failed another plan was hatched.

"Operation Strangle" began in June 1951 when it became obvious that "Operation Killer" had no effect on the Chinese war effort. "Operation Strangle" consisted of an imaginary strip across Korea, one degree in latitude, from 38 degrees 15'N to 39 degrees 15'N that was just behind the Chinese front line, drawn across the country. This latitude strip was divided into eight sections assigned to the Fifth Air Force (Three Secions), First Marine Wing (Three Sections), and Task Force 77 (Two Sections). The objective was to halt Chinese supply and troop traffic across the line.

The air forces were to destroy every vehicle, every bridge, every road, and every target within their section.

For many weeks the assigned aircraft bombed bridges, destroyed railroad tracks, blew craters in roads, fired rockets into tunnels, strafed vehicles, and dropped delayed fused anti-personnel and delayed-action bombs. On June 20, 1951, Task Force 77 aircraft dropped 500 thousand leaflets and used searchlights, flares, and other night-lighting contrivances to prevent the enemy from traveling in the dark.

It appears that the UN underestimated the Chinese resoluteness, because the Communists worked with inexhaustible labor filling bomb craters, repairing railroad tracks, rebuilding bridges, and exploding delayed action bombs with rifle fire or walking around them.

Eleven-victory World War II Ace Capt. Philip C. De Long was leading a division of F4U-4 Corsairs from VMF-312 (Checkerboard) squadron on April 21, 1951, on an interdiction operation southwest of Pyongyang. De Long divided his division into two elements.

Capt Philip C DeLong scored two victories in Korea in addition to his eleven victories during World War II for a total of thirteen victories. Capt DeLong flew F4U-4 Corsairs of VMF-312 (Checkerboard) based at Pohang Airfield and aboard USS Bataan (CVL-29). (U.S. Marine Corps Photo, Author's File)

Chapter VII: Corsair Power in Korea

Capt DeLong is making the 22,000th landing on *USS Bataan* (CVL-29) on April 25, 1951, as he returns from a mission over Korea. Observe the Checkerboard on the engine cowl (VMF-312, Checkerboard squadron). (U.S. Dept of Defense, USMC, Author's File)

Maintenance work on VMF-312 (Checkerboard) squadron F4U-4 Corsairs proceeds with meticulous care. Planes are on the Korean Wonsan airfield; however, the squadron was also based on *USS Bataan* (CVL-29). Careful maintenance can decide the difference between victory or death in aerial activity. (U.S. Defense Dept, USMC, Courtesy David J Ekstrand)

After an hour into the mission, flying over Chinnampo, Capt De Long heard a distress call on his radio that a Corsair in his separated element, flown by Lt. Godbey, had been hit by flak and that the pilot was bailing out. After contacting his carrier *USS Bataan* (CVL-29), Capt De Long ordered his separated element to rendezvous with the rescue helicopter.

De Long and his wingman were climbing and heading north to discharge their ordnance when, at an altitude of about two-thousand feet, four in-line engine powered monoplanes approached two-thousand feet above the Corsairs. Capt Harold Daigh, De Long's wingman, quickly identified the four intruders as U.S. Air Force P-51 Mustang fighters; however, as they came closer they were identified as Soviet-built Yakovlev (YAK) 9 fighters. The planes were Soviet-built, with cannon and machine guns, and had a maximum speed of 332 miles per hour at an altitude of 7,720 feet.

Several enemy machine gun rounds pierced De Long's cockpit and smashed into his radio. The Corsairs were at a disadvantage in the fight because they were still laden with 250 lb bombs and five-inch HVAR missiles.

Lt. Daigh's efforts to dump his ordnance failed, yet despite the weight, he pressed the attack on one of the Yaks and scored, with his victim losing a wing as the YAK fell to earth.

At the time of the initial attack Capt De Long had been studying maps and, as soon as he was fired upon, he executed a quick split-S maneuver to evade his pursuers. The cockpit became full of drifting maps blocking the aviator's visibility until De Long quickly gathered the maps and stowed them while simultaneously evading the attacking Yaks.

As De Long executed a sharp turn, two of the enemy made another pass at the Ace. While he was still in his turn, one of the Yaks crossed in front of the Corsair, which caught the Yak with a burst of .50 caliber fire, sending the enemy straight down trailing thick, black smoke.

Lt. Daigh was chasing another YAK, while the fourth YAK was closing behind Daigh. Capt De Long warned Lt. Daigh of the situation and Daigh cut sharply to the left, causing the chasing YAK to overshoot the Corsair. A few moments later Lt. Daigh scored on the overshooting YAK while Capt De Long shot down the Yak that Lt. Daigh had been stalking.

Two heavily laden corsairs scored against four high performance Soviet-built fighters; good American aviators in good American planes.

On 10 July 10 negotiations for a truce began at Kaesong. While the truce talks were in progress, North Korean troops captured Taejon on 15 July, about 250 miles south of Pyongyang, while on the same day the U.S.

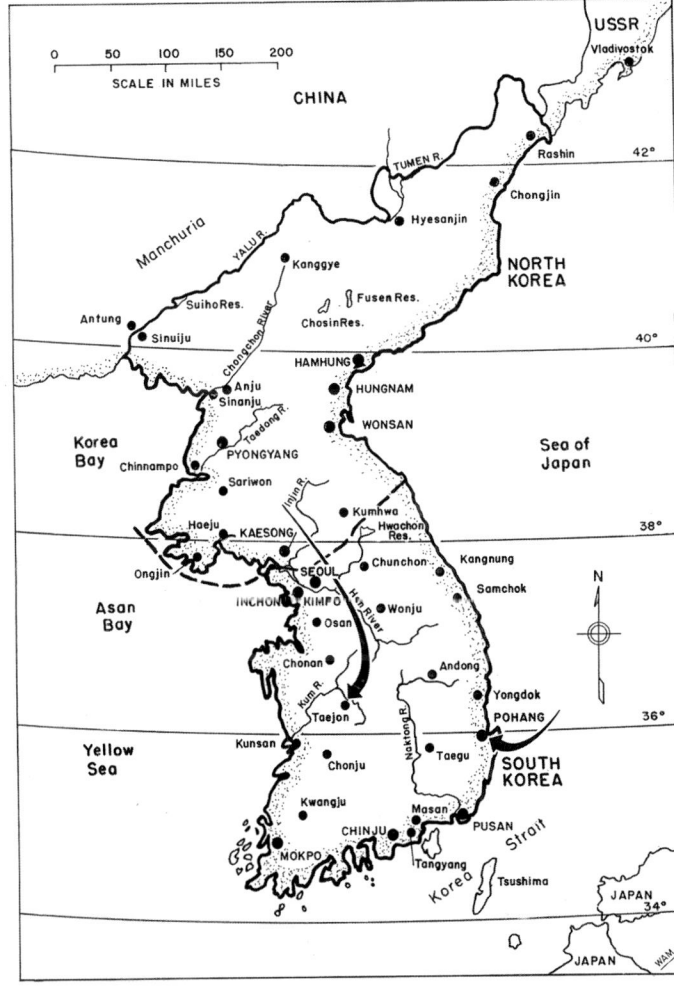

While truce talks were in progress in Kaesong, North Korea, troops captured Taejon on July 15, 1951, about 250 miles south of Pyongyang; while on the same day, the U.S. First Cavalry Division conducted an amphibious invasion at the Port of Pohang. Corsairs from *USS Valley Forge* provided close air support for this daring operation. The dash line across the peninsula is the 1953 demilitarized zone separating North and South Korea.

203

A Black Sheep Corsair lands on USS Sicily in preparation to deploy to Pohang, at the northeastern corner of the Pusan Perimeter. (Dept of Defense, USMC, Courtesy David J Ekstrand)

Cpl William General signals a Black Sheep F4U-4B Corsair into position at Pohang Airfield. Observe the tips of the HVAR missiles and the 20mm cannon projecting from the Corsair wing. The "Checkerboard" Corsair in the background is from VMF-312, which shared Pohang Airfield with VMF-214 and VMF-323. (Dept of Defense, USMC Photo, Courtesy David J Ekstrand)

First Cavalry Division made an amphibious landing at the Port of Pohang, across the peninsula from Taejon. *USS Valley Forge* provided Corsair air cover for this daring operation. Corsairs were quickly flown into the new airfield.

As soon as VMF-214 and VMF-323 arrived at Pohang, the planes were moved to the newly layed Marston Mat and refueled, re-armed, and made ready for flight and fight.

The aerial torpedo was considered an obsolete weapon by 1951 with the advent of rockets and missiles, plus improved high explosive bombs. One of the reasons for its demise was the high torpedo bomber losses for relatively little damage to the targeted ships. Another reason was the torpedo's slow speed and liability to interception.

An example of losses is that, during the Battle of Midway in June 1942, only four of 41 torpedo bombers launched from American carriers managed to return, and 37 were shot down. The Royal Navy suffered similar losses. It appeared that the aerial torpedo was dead as a military weapon until a unique problem arose in the Korean fighting.

Located just north of the 38th parallel was Hwachon Reservoir, created by a dam on the Pukhan River. The dam was a huge concrete structure about 250 ft high with eighteen two ft thick, 40 ft wide, and 20 ft high sluice gates across the dam. The sluice gates could be raised or lowered to control the flow of water downstream in the lower Pukhan River that flows into the important Han River flowing through Chinese recaptured Seoul, for which the water provided water and electricity.

The Hwachan Dam could spell success for the Chinese Communist Forces or for the U.S. Eighth Army, depending on who controlled the dam. At this time the CCF controlled the dam and, if they closed the sluice gates, it would permit the CCF to continue its advance in the knee-deep

Left Photo: Black Sheep Corsairs, newly arrived at Pohang, await final servicing and reloading prior to fighting to free the UN troops in the Pusan Perimeter. (Dept of Defense, USMC Photo, Courtesy David J Ekstrand) Right Photo: From left to right: Black Sheep armorers TSgt Frank C Jewett, Cpl Earl K Branch, and Cpl Clyde Fannor load a five-inch HVAR missile on an F4U-4B Corsair at Pohang. Observe the VMF-214 coat of arms on the engine cowl. (Dept of Defense, USMC Photo, Courtesy David J Ekstrand)

Chapter VII: Corsair Power in Korea

The impressive Boeing B-29 Superfortress was designed for strategic bombing such as cities or huge sprawling industrial sites, and generally failed with tactical pin-point assignments, such as bridges and dams, for which it was not intended. Tactical pin-point bombing can be best accomplished by smaller dive bombing or glide bombing aircraft. One engine nacelle of the huge bomber was larger than a Corsair. (The Boeing Company, Courtesy Marilyn A Phipps)

Skyraiders escorted by Corsairs were a frequent sight during the Korean War. The four Corsairs and four Skyraiders in flight here are from USS Boxer (CV-21). Corsairs are in VF-791 and Skyraiders are in VA-702. (U.S. Navy Photo, via National Archives)

water. However, if the sluice gates were opened, the water would flood and render the Pukhan and Han rivers impassable, blocking the Chinese Communist Forces' advance southward across them. Gen Ridgeway ordered the Hwachan Dam disabled to flood the rivers.

In January 1951, the U.S. Far East Air Force sent two B-29 Superfortresses against the dam, escorted by Corsairs; however, they failed to punch a hole in the target with two six-ton bombs.

On April 9, 1951, the Eighth Army continued its advance northward until the CCF opened the sluice gates of the Hwanchon Dam and flooded the Pukhan River, with the water rising several feet within an hour, washing away UN engineering bridges and other river-crossing contrivances.

In desperation, the Eighth Army captured the dam on 16 April; however, seven days later the CCF counterattacked in force and was, again, in control of the dam.

The Eighth Army Staff decided it was time for another air attack; however, this time it called upon the U.S. Navy. On April 30, 1951, Task Force 77 Commander RADM Ralph A Oftsie, USN, was requested to destroy two or more of the dam's sluice gates.

Three hours later six VA-195 Douglas Skyraiders led by LCDR Harold "Swede" Carlson from USS Princeton (CV-37) were on their way to the dam escorted by five VF-193 Corsairs for flak suppression.

Left Photo: A Douglas Skyraider is on its way to the Hwachon Dam with a torpedo slung under its belly. Torpedoes were successful when powerful bombs were not. (U.S. Navy Photo, Author's File) Right Photo: ENS RE Bennett, USN, of VA-195 poses with his AD-4 Skyraider prior to his participation in the Hwachon Dam torpedoing on May 1, 1951. Observe the enormous torpedo. (U.S. Navy Photo, Author's File)

Of the eight torpedoes launched by Skyraiders against the Hwachon Dam (escorted by twelve Corsairs for Flak suppression and top cover), one torpedo ran erratically while another was a dud. The remaining six ran true on target, destroying one sluice gate and punching a ten-foot hole in another gate. The raid was a success. (U.S. Navy Photo, Author's File)

This bomb-laden VF-791 F4U-4 Corsair is taking off from USS *Boxer* (CV-21), possibly to bomb North Korean bridges in concert with Skyraiders. Note also the long range drop tank, suggesting a long flight to the Yalu River. (U.S. Navy Photo, via National Archives)

Although each Skyraider released two 2,000 pound bombs, only one hole was punched in the dam, with the sluice gates undamaged.

Undaunted, Capt William O Gallery, USN, Skipper of USS *Princeton*, recalled that several MK 13 aerial torpedoes were stowed on his ship and suggested that the torpedoes be used against the dam.

On the morning of May 1, 1951, USS *Princeton* (CV-37) launched eight Skyraiders: three from VA-35 and five from VA-195. The Skyraiders were led by CAG-19 CDR RC Merrick, USN. The important escort consisted of 12 Corsairs from VF-192 and VF-193.

Upon arrival at Hwachon Reservoir the Corsairs quickly braved the flak to silence the CCF defenders, and when their job was done, the Corsairs withdrew to cover the torpedo bombers as they roared into action.

The Skyraiders made their attacks in pairs. All eight torpedoes were dropped; however, one ran erratically and another failed to explode. The remaining six torpedoes exploded against the forty-feet wide sluice gates.

One sluice gate was destroyed while a ten foot hole was punched through another gate, thereby attesting to the success of the raid, as the impounded Hwachon Reservoir water cascaded through the Hwachon Reservoir Dam Gates into the Pukhan River.

Aviators involved in this attack braved the same dangers that had confronted torpedo bombers for decades; however, thanks to the Corsair pre-attack flak suppression and top cover during the attack, no loss of life or aircraft was experienced.

These North Korean rail and road twin-river crossings have been the target of U.S. Navy and U.S. Air Force bombers on many occasions. Observe the missing section of the rail bridge (right) and the pontoon replacement for the road bridges (left). Roadway bridges are more easily repaired than railroad bridges. (U.S. Army Photo, via National Archives)

This F4U-4 Corsair from VF-791 is circling a North Korean highway bridge near Wonson that has been destroyed by Corsairs and Skyraiders. The aviator is Lt R Pitner, USNR, stationed aboard USS *Boxer* (CV-21) in summer of 1951. (U.S. Navy Photo, Naval Photographic Center)

Chapter VII: Corsair Power in Korea

During the summer of 1953 UN "bridge busting" became an art; witness this rail bridge broken in two places. Observe the steam locomotive that has been thrown a distance from the bridge by the U.S. Navy Task Force 77 attack. (U.S. Navy Photo, Naval Photographic Center)

During this brief period on May 1, 1951, the assumed defunct torpedo bomber was reincarnated as a weapon of war. The Skyraider aviators of VA-195, who had twice attacked the dam, first with bombs and then torpedoes, adopted the name "Dambusters."

U.S. Air Force B-29 Superfortresses, flying from bases in Japan, were escorted by Corsairs from *USS Essex* (CV-9) to bomb the major railroad center in Rashin, North Korea, on August 25, 1951. Rashin is only a few miles from the Soviet border.

American aviators returning to Korea for their second tour of duty found that the enemy flak had improved considerably since their first tour. North Korean and Chinese flak had been steadily increasing in accuracy and frequency. It had also grown constantly heavier and more intense. From August 22 through November 30, 1951, the *USS Essex* Air Group Five aircraft were hit 318 times, losing 28 aircraft and 11 aviators. Flak suppression and troop support operations were the most vulnerable to flak damage and injury.

It will be remembered that, on November 8, 1950, VADM Arthur D Struble ordered that the bridges crossing the Yalu River must be destroyed to prevent Chinese troops from entering North Korea. In effect this order applied to all bridges in North Korea. The CMF defended their roads, rail lines, and bridges tenaciously, which increased the number of UN aircraft losses.

Corsair fighter-bombers raised havoc with the straight railroad runs because they were the least defended since they were the easiest to repair. Conversely, bridges that spanned canyons or rivers were heavily defended because they were difficult to repair.

The most efficient combination for "bridge busting" was the Douglas Skyraider and Corsair because their speeds were compatible. Although jet-powered F9F Panthers and F2H Banshees were available, their high speed and short range precluded the ability of the jets and prop jobs arriving at the target simultaneously—a Target Coordinator's nightmare.

The Corsair F4U-4B could carry 500 pound (GP) general purpose bombs for the actual attack, or use the four 20mm cannon with five-inch HVAR missiles and "daisy cutter" bombs for flak suppression. The Corsair was truly a Jack-of-all-trades for bombing bridges, as well as bomber escort and close air support.

The bridge-bombing campaign continued through 1951. During this time the slower attack aircraft (Corsairs and Skyraiders) suffered more losses than the faster jet fighters (Panthers and Banshees). During the last six months of 1951 the U.S. Navy lost 55 Corsairs and 40 Skyraiders, mostly during attacks on bridges, because they flew low for flak suppression.

Analysis of the effect of land and carrier-based airpower on North Korean bridges, railroads, and roads by January 1952 revealed that, regardless of the number of aircraft used, nor how bravely and skillfully they were flown, it was not enough to stop the flow of North Korean and Chinese equipment and soldiers into the combat zones.

Despite this failure, the Task Force 77 carriers on the Korean East Coast opened the new year with plans for night operations using F4U-5N Corsairs and AD4N Skyraiders.

The new system began on 15 January with Operation MOONLIGHT SONATA; a night operation against railways, designed to take advantage of the winter snow and bright moonlight when roads, rails, hills, and valleys would be easy to see at night from the air.

Every MOONLIGHT SONATA operation began at 3 AM, when five Corsairs and five Skyraiders were launched in pairs. Each pair was responsible for fifty-miles of railway and briefed on the most important targets. Unfortunately the bright moonlight, good flying weather, and good targets hardly ever appeared simultaneously. In addition, trains began to appear just as the aircraft were leaving! The Communists had deciphered the MOONLIGHT SONATA timetable!

OPERATION INSOMNIA replaced MOONLIGHT SONATA by launching the attacks one hour earlier; however, this was discontinued during the first half of 1952.

AD Skyraiders and F4U-5 Corsairs from *USS Princeton* wrought havoc on a railroad marshalling yard and bridges during October 1952 near Kowan, North Korea. Corsairs silenced the flak gunners in the marshalling yard with Daisy Cutter bombs (black arrow) and then the Skyraiders destroyed the bridge (white arrow). (U.S. Navy Photo, Author's File)

Corsair: The Saga of the Legendary Bent-Wing Fighter-Bomber

Left Photo: Capt Jesse G Folmar of VMA -312 (Checkerboard Squadron) scored a Soviet-built MiG-15 jet fighter with his Corsair F4U-4B during an encounter in which he was outnumbered. Note the checkerboard scarf and helmet. (U.S. Marine Corps Photo, Author's File) Right Photo: Lt Jesse G Folmar flew a corsair F4U-1 during World War II. Note the name of his Corsair, "Thundering Hog II." Apparently, this was his second Corsair when fighting the Japanese. (USMC Photo, via National Archives)

In May 1952, RADM J.J. "Jocko" Clark, who had commanded TF-77 in 1951, was promoted to Vice Admiral in command of U.S. Seventh Fleet. VADM Clark was an experienced carrier admiral who had commanded a task group in the Pacific under Spruance and Halsey, and ordered continuous bombing and strafing sweeps of North Korean held territory. "Jocko" Clark was a full-blooded Cherokee Indian, which gave rise to calling this series of ground attacks "Cherokee Strikes." This operation kept Corsairs and Skyraiders very busy.

In June 1952 UN carrier aircraft turned to industrial targets with much less emphasis on interdiction and timetables. The U.S. Navy had four aircraft carriers assigned to the Korean coast: two carriers near the coast at a time, with the remaining two at standby. On June 23, 1952, *USS Boxer* and *USS Princeton* were joined by *USS Bon Homme Richard* and *USS Philippine Sea* for a four-day series of strikes by Navy, Marine, and Fifth Air Force aircraft on thirteen power plants in North Korea, destroying about ninety per cent of North Korean power production.

The largest all-Navy air strike of the war was conducted on September 1, 1952. This included twenty-nine aircraft from *USS Essex*: sixty-three from *USS Princeton* and fifty-two from *USS Boxer* that destroyed the Aoji oil refinery.

Also, on the same day Guided Missile Unit No.90, embarked on *USS Boxer*, launched six attacks of "Drones" that were pilotless radio-controlled Second World War F6F Hellcats that were loaded with explosives and fitted with TV guidance systems. The Hellcat Drones were led to their targets by control aircraft, such as Corsairs. This was a very early use of guided missiles from carriers.

Since the advent of the jet-powered fighter it was assumed that this spelled the demise of propeller-driven fighter aircraft. The Korean war was the staging ground where the two fighter types were to meet.

Although a few other Russian-built jet fighters were scored by UN fighters, the best documented was the last victory of a Corsair over a MiG-15 on September 10, 1952.

Capt Jesse G Folmar, a Corsair veteran from WWII, and his wingman, Lt. Walter E. Daniels of VMA-312 (Checkerboard Squadron), took-off from *USS Sicily* (CVE-118) on September 10, 1951, and headed for the Chinnampo area, southwest of Pyongyang. The objective was to strike a heavy enemy troop concentration; however, upon arriving over the target area there was no activity on the ground. The pair continued with interdiction and reconnaissance in the area. As the Corsairs turned toward the coast, Folmar glimpsed two MiG-15 jet fighters preparing to attack the Corsairs.

Folmar knew that, at medium to high altitudes, conventional fighters could not hope to combat the Soviet-made jet fighters; therefore, he and Daniels jettisoned their ordnance and drop tanks and spiraled to a lower altitude.

The MiGs were in loose echelon so Folmar steepened his bank, turning into the jets. Seconds later two more enemy jets appeared, closing fast from Folmar's eight-o'clock position. The Captain tightened his turn into the enemy as the MiGs fired but missed. The American reversed his turn and climbed inside of one of the enemy, firing his 20mm cannon and scoring on the nearest enemy jet.

The MiG belched gray smoke and then streamed a black trail of smoke as it dived to the water. The pilot had taken to his 'chute, and Folmar could see his G-Suit burning before he hit the water.

Just as his victim hit the water, Capt Folmar saw four more MiG-15s approaching in a loose column of two sections. Folmar told his wingman to dive hard and left. As Folmar gained speed he saw fiery tracer balls pass close to the left side of his cockpit. Then he felt a severe jolt and explosion in his left wing.

Controlling the Corsair became impossible. A glance at his left wing revealed that the aileron and four feet of the Corsair's left wing was missing, and the top of the wing was gutted to the inboard gun.

A MiG-15 (Mikoyan-Gurevich) was shot down by a Corsair F4U-4B flown by Capt Jesse G Folmar (USMC) on Sept 10, 1951. This Soviet-built jet fighter had a maximum speed of 668 miles per hour. Armament was one 37mm cannon and one 23mm cannon, both located in the nose. Service ceiling was 51,000 feet. Combat range was 560 miles. (USAF Photo, via National Archives)

Chapter VII: Corsair Power in Korea

After scoring his first two victories on June 29, 1953, Lt Bordelon describes the excellent performance of his F4U-5N Corsair with crew-chief MSG Galland while TSgt Gabear looks on. Note the muzzle flash cone on the cannon. (U.S. Navy Photo, U.S. Naval Photographic Center via Al Lewis and Air Trails)

Lt Guy Bordelon scored his third and fourth victories on July 1, 1953. The photographer insisted on this photo after four red stars were applied to Bordelon's Corsair. (U.S. Navy Photo, via U.S. Naval Photographic Center)

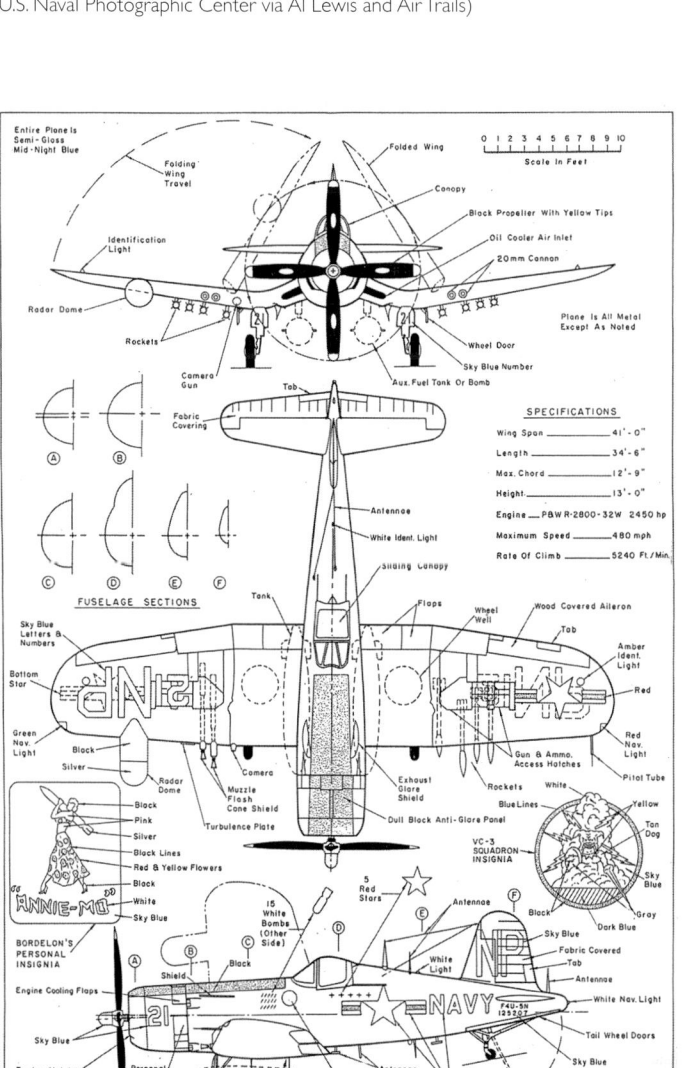

The Corsair began to shudder as if in a high speed stall, and the plane tried to roll left, although the control stick was in the full right position. This made the aviator decide to bail out.

As Folmar transmitted a distress signal, another MiG-15 made a firing pass with all cannon blazing but all missed. At three thousand feet the aviator bailed out, and during his descent he saw the enemy jets firing at his spinning Corsair.

Lt. Daniels circled Capt Folmar's position, and the Captain was rescued within eight minutes of hitting the water.

Capt Jesse G Folmar proved that a good, experienced aviator with an excellent propeller-driven fighter can overcome a superior jet-powered design, even when outnumbered and equipped with guns intended for close air support work.

The hard-pressed CCF and NKPA resorted to a deceptive weapon to weaken the UN and American serviceman with psychological warfare.

Using old Soviet-built YAK-18 aerobatic trainers and ancient LA-11 fighters, the oriental Communists routinely flew the aircraft over U.S. troop concentrations, bases, and airfields in nocturnal nuisance raids. The single-engine, propeller-driven, noisy airplanes usually appeared about 2:00 in the morning, and often dropped small bombs for no strategic or tactical purpose. The objective of the raids was to keep troops and other personnel awake at night, running to shelters or to assigned emergency posts, and thereby destroying their tranquil sleep and replacing it with mind-shattering excitement. By the time the men were at the ready for action with antiaircraft guns, the raiders were but a barely audible drone in the distance.

Constant repetition, night after night, of "Operation Bed Check Charlie" was having its desired effect on the UN personnel, and was close to reducing their combat efficiency.

This scale drawing depicts Lt Bordelon's Corsair night fighter in configuration and markings. For the sake of clarity, guns are shown on the starboard (right) wing only while the rockets are shown on the port (left) wing only. The guns and rockets are actually on both wings as shown in the front view. Observe the exhaust glare shields and the cannon muzzle flash cone shield needed to improve the aviator's visibility in the darkness. Some U.S. Marine Corsair night fighters applied identification lettering in red instead of sky blue.

Upon Lt Bordelon's return to USS Princeton he was met with a tumultuous welcome by officers and crew alike. The banners were so quickly made that all was ready when he returned to his ship. (U.S. Navy Photo, U.S. Naval Photographic Center)

"Bed Check Charlie" had to be stopped, and USAF jet fighters were deployed to erase the nuisance flights. Unfortunately, the raiders were too slow and too agile for the fast jets and easily turned inside and away from their powerful pursuers. It was decided that the only possible way to combat the Communist menace was to employ agile propeller-driven aircraft equipped with search radar and heavy armament. Since there was no U.S. Air Force unit in the area with both suitable aircraft and aviators with adequate night fighting training, the authorities looked for assistance from the U.S. Navy, which was operating late model Corsairs most effectively.

On June 25, 1953, five U.S. Navy Corsair fighters were transferred to Kimpo airfield from the carrier USS Princeton. These craft were part of Composite Squadron Three (VC-3) all weather Night Fighter-Detachment D (Dog), and ordered to operate in close liaison with the Fifth Air Force. Their aircraft were Vought F4U-5N Corsairs, and were numbered 21 to 25.

Detachment D (Dog) was commanded by Lt. Guy P Bordelon Jr, whose personal Corsair was number 21. He christened this aircraft Annie-Mo in honor of the pet name he used for his wife, the former Ann Craig Taylor.

Prior to his assignment to Kimpo, Bordelon successfully completed many combat missions in Korea with bombing and rocket strikes against ground targets in inclement weather.

Four days after arriving at Kimpo the VC-3 Corsairs scrambled into the inky blackness after a flight of "Bedcheck Charlie" that had been reported near Seoul. Using the airborne APS-19A search radar, the instrument-laden Corsairs vectored in on their quarry. Bordelon then spotted the shadowy forms of the "bandits" and closed in for the kill with visual sighting. The moment the Lieutenant pressed the firing button the enemy started to take evasive action, but a slight movement on his rudder pedals directed the 20mm shells into the YAK-18 monoplanes, which erupted into a giant fireball. Although momentarily blinded by the flash, the American peered into the murky darkness and was surprised to see another "Bedcheck Charlie" speeding for the 38th parallel on a zig-zag course. Bordelon slammed the throttle forward and was soon pumping shells into the second Yak-18, which joined its fellow intruder on a hillside north of Seoul.

On July 1, 1953, Bordelon scored again. This time he destroyed two Po.2 biplanes south of the city of Sariwon, and on the sixteenth of that month the Lieutenant became an ace by shooting another Po.2 out of the black Korean sky. Bordelon's success was accomplished during only fifteen nocturnal interception sorties, and his victories came with such rapid succession that they so dampened the enthusiasm of future "Bedcheck Charlie" intruders that not one Red ventured over United Nation's territory during the nights that followed.

Ten days after Bordelon's fifth victory a truce was signed that ended the fighting, and Detachment D returned to USS Princeton. Bordelon received a tumultuous welcome by the officers and crew of the carrier because, not only did he become the only U.S. Navy ace of the Korean Police Action, but the only night fighter ace and the only ace to fly a propeller-driven airplane! His were the last victories scored by an American Corsair.

Lt. Bordelon was presented with the Navy Cross, the U.S. Navy's highest honor, second only to the Medal of Honor, for a job well done.

When truce talks failed at Kaesong the armistice conference transferred to Panmunjom. As the armistice appeared to be reaching a conclusion both belligerents increased their offensive power.

The Communists launched two major offensives in June and July 1953, while Task Force 77 aircraft carriers USS Lake Champlain, Boxer, Philippine Sea, and Princeton aircraft sorties rose from 4,343 in May 1953 to 6,423 in July 1953; close support sorties rose from 256 to 1,690; and tons of bombs, rockets, and cannon shells expended rose from 2,835 in May to 4,606 in July.

The armistice was signed at ten o'clock in the morning of July 27, 1953, and was to come into effect at ten o'clock that evening.

The three TF 77 carriers on station (USS Boxer, USS Lake Champlain, and USS Philippine Sea) flew 250 sorties before ten o'clock in the morning, destroying 23 railroad cars, eleven rail bridges, one tunnel, 69 buildings, nine road bridges, a half mile of trench, and forty road and rail cuts. It was the last punch before the referee's whistle!

It must be remembered that this little limited "Forgotten War" at the other side of the world inflicted almost four million casualties.

Chapter VII: Corsair Power in Korea

The United States suffered casualties of 142,091 killed, wounded, missing, or POW, while other Korean War participant casualties were: United Kingdom 4,286; South Korea 1,313,836, plus one million civilians; Chinese 900,000; and North Korea 520,000, plus one million civilians.

The Korean War, which was, too often, called a "Police Action" during its lifetime and is now, too often, called the "Forgotten War," suffered as many American casualties in only three years of fighting as was suffered in the Vietnam War during eleven years of fighting. Further comparison reveals that Vietnam casualties were at the rate of about 36,000 per year during eleven years, while Korean casualties were about 1.4 million casualties per year during three years.

As a departure from combat inflicted crashes, our next chapter will attempt to concentrate on peacetime mishaps and crashes; some spectacular and others mundane.

Lt Guy Bordelon stands proudly at attention during the ceremony for presentation of the Navy Cross to the Ace. The U.S. Navy award is second only in the U.S. Navy to the Medal of Honor and can be seen beneath his Naval Aviator's Wings. (U.S. Navy Photo, U.S. Naval Photographic Center)

VIII

Aircraft Accidents on Carriers

When flying any airplane, the most difficult and hazardous operation is the landing, and most accidents seem to occur at this time. The faster and more maneuverable fighters and dive bombers appear to be the more difficult to fly and land.

Now, imagine that the airfield is pitching from front to rear and rolling from side to side. This would increase landing dangers and increase the probability of crash landings considerably.

This chapter is devoted to landing and takeoff accidents on those pitching and rolling airfields called aircraft carriers.

The intent of this chapter is to illustrate the results of being inept, careless or, in some cases, following poor decisions from superior officers.

The accompanying photographs illustrate amazing mishaps and crashes in which the aviator has survived in most incidents.

The aviator in this Corsair has just received the "fly" signal. The takeoff is generally uneventful; however, it can be fraught with danger depending on weather and the aviator's experience to takeoff from and alight on the deck safely. (U.S. Navy Photo, Courtesy United Aircraft Corp)

An F4U-5 just recovered from a bad landing on USS *Princeton* (CV-37) and is surrounded by deck crew with all types of fire extinguishers. Note the crumpled starboard side wingtip. (near side). The deck crew is always ready for a fire in the event of a rough landing. (Sal Marrone Photo, Courtesy Sal Marrone)

Chapter VIII: Aircraft Accidents on Carriers

ENS Ardon R. Ives crashed a barrier aboard USS Lexington (CV-16) on February 25, 1945, and his VF-9 Grumman Hellcat burst into flames. The aviator is seen trying to escape from the flames. (Photo from Emil Buehler Naval Aviation Library, Courtesy M.H. MacDonald)

Caught in the middle of an arrested landing, LCDR C.W. Conger Jr tangled his propeller in the arresting cables. The aviator was landing his VF-75 F4U-4 on board USS Franklin D Roosevelt in January 1946. The plane continued the somersault, resting on its back. (U.S. Navy Photo, Author's File)

This F4U-4 Corsair of VF-53 missed the first arrester cables on USS Valley Forge (CV-45) and landed very heavily, smashing the landing gear. Part of the landing gear strut is imbedded in the wooden sheath of the deck behind the plane (solid arrow) while a wheel lays on the deck ahead of the plane (open arrow). (U.S. Navy Photo, U.S. Naval Photo Center)

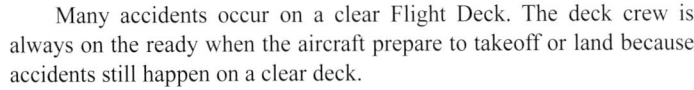

Many accidents occur on a clear Flight Deck. The deck crew is always on the ready when the aircraft prepare to takeoff or land because accidents still happen on a clear deck.

An F4U-1A of VBF-94 approaches USS Prince William (CVE-31) with flaps down and arresting hook extended. (NAVEAR Photo, via National Archives)

Corsair: The Saga of the Legendary Bent-Wing Fighter-Bomber

After engaging the arresting cables at high speed, the hook breaks and the plane bounces into the *Prince William's* island. The starboard wing shears off as the engine tears loose along with the engine mount, forcing the crew on the catwalk to scramble for safety. (NAVEAR Photo, via National Archives)

As the wing crashes to the deck and catwalk, the fuselage settles to the deck with the engine dropping dangerously over the cockpit. Observe the Corsair in the distance, leaving the scene of the accident. Apparently this plane was following the crashed plane in the landing routine and was waved off. (NAVEAR Photo, via National Archives)

With the wing settled on the catwalk, and the fuselage and engine hanging over the cockpit, rescuers scrambled to save the aviator, LTJG Laney. (NAVEAR Photo, via National Archives)

A wheel snags on the island coaming, thereby preventing the engine and fuselage from falling on the cockpit. Meanwhile, the crew has brought water and foam hoses to the deck to fight the gasoline fire surrounding the cockpit. (NAVEAR Photo, via National Archives)

Chapter VIII: Aircraft Accidents on Carriers

All hoses are aimed around the cockpit to save LTJG Laney. Twenty-plus men are working diligently to save the aviator. (NAVEAR Photo, via National Archives)

Full attention is aimed at the cockpit as gasoline flames threaten the aviator. Fortunately, the landing gear snag has prevented the engine and fuselage from dropping on the cockpit. (NAVEAR Photo, via National Archives)

With the fire and water clear of the cockpit the aviator can be seen; injured but alive, with the fuselage, engine, and port wing dangling precariously over the cockpit. (NAVEAR Photo, via National Archives)

Below: This VS-31 Grumman Avenger taking off from USS Saipan (CVL-18) has barely left the deck when it is heading toward the carrier's island. (Photo from the Emil Bueler Aviation Library, Courtesy M.I.I. Mac Donald)

Below: The head-on impact with the small island must have been unbearable for the aviator, ENS Lee Bonner, and his crew, as well as anyone on the island. (Photo from the Emil Bueler Aviation Library, Courtesy M.H. Mac Donald)

Corsair: The Saga of the Legendary Bent-Wing Fighter-Bomber

As the Avenger drops off toward sea fumes hiss from the engine. The aviator and his crew were rescued safely and there were no injuries on the island. (Photo from the Emil Bueler Aviation Library, Courtesy M.H. MacDonald)

Despite the fact that the broad Flight Deck is the ideal landing field (except for the rolling and pitching), taking off and landing aircraft still manage to strike the relatively small Island, located on the extreme starboard side of the Flight Deck.

On occasion, aircraft collide with each other during takeoff and landing operations on the Flight Deck. These are not unusual incidents on crowded flight decks.

Being surrounded by water, it is not unusual that carrier aircraft often plunge into the sea during takeoff and landing operations. These mishaps rarely result in fatalities.

Fire! This is the most feared hazard aboard a ship, whether it be a warship or a commercial vessel. Warships, and aircraft carriers especially, are prone to fire because of the ship's fuel and the aviation fuel, in addition to special aviation armament, such as rockets and bombs. The planes on an aircraft carrier are prone to catch fire and set other fires.

Near the end of World War II a rule emerged that all carrier landings must be made with the drop tank attached, although the old rule required that all drop tanks be released at sea before landing on an aircraft carrier. Aircraft returning with attached drop-tanks increase the fire hazard, not only for the landing aircraft, but for the carrier and parked aircraft, as well.

Collision on the Flight Deck! A Corsair F4U-4 clips another F4U-4 from squadron VF-152. It is not known whether the Corsair leaving the ship was landing or taking off. Note the struck Corsair has lost its fin and rudder. Accident was aboard USS Princeton on February 12, 1953. (U.S. Navy Photo, via National Archives)

ENS Porter has ditched his F4U-4 Corsair alongside USS Franklin on January 10, 1949. The aviator from VF-75 stands on the Corsair's wing waiting for rescue. (U.S. Navy Photo, via National Archives)

Chapter VIII: Aircraft Accidents on Carriers

This F4U-4 from VF-74 missed the arresting cables and "pancaked" into the sea. (Vought Aircraft Photo; Courtesy H.J. "Jerry" Dalton)

LTJG Michael Stachow, USN, scraped the port wing of his F4U-4 Corsair on the *USS Philippine Sea* Flight Deck and, before he could correct the bank, his plane became inverted and plunged into the sea. The landing accident happened on January 10, 1949, and the aviator survived the strange mishap. (U.S. Navy Photo by SN J Wasziewicz, USN; via National Archives)

This Corsair illustrates the late WWII requirement that returning aircraft must land on aircraft carriers without jettisoning the drop tanks. Left Photo: Illustrates a normal takeoff with drop tank in January 1945. (Defense dept Photo (Marine Corps), Courtesy United Aircraft Corporation) Photo aobve: Shows a Corsair about to touch down with drop tank attached. The capacity of some drop tanks is so large that they contain enough fuel to fill ten luxury automobile fuel tanks. (Official U.S. Navy Photograph, Courtesy United Aircraft Corporation)

Lt Charles H Easton, USN, experienced the most fantastic and dangerous fire when he returned to his carrier with inoperable landing flaps and a full drop-tank that burst into flame. The following photographs record the story from his high-speed landing and the enormous ball of flame created by his drop-tank. (U.S. Navy Photograph; Courtesy Mrs Charles Easton)

Lt Ralph Husted, USMC, of VMF-214 returned to the USS Franklin on February 28, 1945, with an ample amount of fuel in his attached drop tank. The landing was soft and slow because of the full flaps and head wind; however, when the arresting hook caught a cable, the sudden stop dislodged the drop tank, which hit the propeller and burst into flame under the stopped plane. The aviator was consumed in the inferno before rescuers arrived. (U.S. Navy Photo, via National Archives)

Right: As 23 year old Lt Easton of VBF-93 neared USS Boxer (CVA-21) in his Corsair, he requested permission to drop his auxiliary fuel tank because his landing flaps had become inoperative and there was no head wind. He insisted that the high speed landing would prove dangerous. His request was denied! He is shown here in his final approach for landing on June 16, 1945. (U.S. Navy Photograph; Courtesy Mrs Charles Easton)

Chapter VIII: Aircraft Accidents on Carriers

Touchdown proved very fast and dangerous, as one wheel hits the deck first. The hook is about to grapple the arresting cable as the second wheel is dropping to the deck. (U.S. Navy Photograph; Courtesy Mrs Charles Easton)

The impact of the remaining wheel striking the deck dislodged the drop tank, thrusting it forward. The tank struck the propeller, spraying gasoline on the hot engine which engulfed the Corsair in flames. Photo taken from the Island a split-second after touchdown. (U.S. Navy Photograph; Courtesy Mrs Charles Easton)

Note that the fire has intensified in the drop tank ahead of the plane and that more of the plane is visible. (U.S. Navy Photograph; Courtesy Mrs Charles Easton)

This photo, taken from the forward Flight Deck, reveals the flaming drop tank rolling well ahead of the stopped Corsair. (U.S. Navy Photograph; Courtesy Mrs Charles Easton)

The flaming drop tank appears to have rolled further ahead of the stopped plane in this photo. Apparently it is rolling well ahead of the plane, taking the fire with it. (U.S. Navy Photograph; Courtesy Mrs Charles Easton)

Corsair: The Saga of the Legendary Bent-Wing Fighter-Bomber

This photo, taken from the carrier's Island, proves that the flaming drop tank is rolling ahead of Lt Easton's plane, spewing flaming gasoline. The Corsair appears to be clear of the flames that are being generated by the drop tank. (U.S. Navy Photograph; Courtesy Mrs Charles Easton)

As the flame-spewing drop tank rolls further ahead of the stationary Corsair, more fire fighters close in on the plane. It is very possible that quick-thinking Lt Easton, realizing his fast landing speed, slowed the plane to a sudden stop, ejecting the drop tank to the deck in order to keep clear of the rolling gasoline-filled drop tank. (U.S. Navy Photograph; Courtesy Mrs Charles Easton)

As soon as the fierce flames moved far enough ahead with the rolling drop tank, rescuers sped to remove Lt Easton from the smoking Corsair. (U.S. Navy Photograph; Courtesy Mrs Charles Easton)

At the moment of rescue, two fireproof-clad firemen struggle to take the Aviator away from the smoke and fumes to awaiting litter bearers. Observe the fire extinguisher equipped crewman on the ready in case of a flare-up. Note the burning tire. (U.S. Navy Photograph; Courtesy Mrs Charles Easton)

Charred but not destroyed, Lt Easton's Corsair remains on the Flight Deck with all fabric covering burned away. The accident left Lt Easton badly burned, and it was several years before his squadron mates learned that he had survived his awful experience. The high speed of the landing combined with Easton's rapid slowing down of the plane thrust the flaming drop tank forward. Lt Charles Easton lived to enjoy the age of seventy-eight. (U.S. Navy Photograph; Courtesy Mrs Charles Easton)

Chapter VIII: Aircraft Accidents on Carriers

A well-trained and dedicated crew can have the damage repaired quickly and the carrier operating normally regardless of the damage.

It is amazing how quickly the damaged Flight Deck could be repaired and placed in operation. This Corsair is speeding to a takeoff, with lowered flaps, down the USS Boxer Flight Deck. (U.S. Navy Photograph; Courtesy Mrs Charles Easton)

IX

Corsair Aviators and Decorations

The author omitted personal statistics, such as date and place of birth and so forth, during aviators' historical and personal coverage in previous chapters in order not to interfere with their heroic activities. Therefore, the personal information and other history are presented in this chapter for those readers who are interested in these statistics.

The data is presented in a somewhat alphabetical order for the convenience of the reader.

CAPT DONALD NATHAN ALDRICH, USMC, was born on October 24, 191, in Moline, Illinois, but when he was one year old the family moved to Chicago. His father, Lyell Aldrich, was a mechanical engineer and a private pilot. He owned a Waco biplane, and father and son went flying at least once a week. By the time Donald was twelve years old he had almost 100 hours in the air. While Donald was in his junior year at Fonger High School in Chicago, his father died and the Waco was sold.

Upon graduation from high school, Don enrolled in the Armour Institute of Technology to study engineering. After two years of college he could not resist the burning desire to fly. He quit school and became employed in the office of the Visking Corporation in order to earn money to fly. The air-minded youth spent every spare moment at Ashburn Field in Chicago and worked out in a Piper Cub owned by Royal Schaefer, his friend and flying instructor.

After logging about 70 hours of solo time in the Cub he longed to fly bigger and faster planes. He had married recently, and found that his job had no promise of rapid advancement for a stable career. Don decided to kill two birds with one stone by joining an air force where he would have a stable job and fly big, powerful planes.

He tried to join the U.S. Army Corps; however, he was refused because the USAAC rejected married applicants. Don joined the Royal Canadian Air Force and received his wings in November 1941. He served as an instructor in the RCAF until October 1942, when the war forced the U.S. to relax the rule against married men. Don, therefore, joined the U.S. Marine Corps as an aviator.

By the summer of 1943 he was sent to Guadalcanal and assigned to fly F4U Corsairs with VMF-215, the "Fighting Corsairs." Aldrich scored well in combat, becoming the fifth leading Ace in the U.S. Marine Corps.

The 180lb, six foot tall Ace remained in the Marine Corps after World War II. On May 3, 1947, he was making a forced landing on unstable ground and crashed to his death while engaged in flying, the activity he loved best, in his native Chicago.

Capt Aldrich left his wife Marjory and a son, Frederick Bruce Aldrich, born in 1945.

The Ace is credited with twenty official and six probable victories.

Capt Aldrich was awarded the following decorations: Navy Cross and Gold Star; Distinguished Flying Cross; Air Medal; and Purple Heart.

Capt Donald N. Aldrich, USMC, learned to fly by the time he was a pre-teenager. He scored twenty official victories with six probables before he died in a forced landing. (U.S. Defense Dept Photo, Marine Corps)

Chapter IX: Corsair Aviators and Decorations

Major George C. Axtell Jr, USMC, was the youngest USMC fighter squadron commander. He scored six victories and led VMF-323 "Death Rattlers." (Official USMC Photo, National Archives)

LCDR John Thomas Blackburn, USN, was the commanding officer of VF-17 "Jolly Rogers," and was generally known as "Tommy." He was the squadron's first "Ace" and made VF-17 the envy of other U.S. Navy and U.S. Marine fighter squadrons during World War II. (Official U.S. Navy Photo)

MAJ GEORGE CLIFTON AXTELL JR, USMC, was the youngest Fighter Squadron Leader in the U.S. Marine Corps when he led VMF-323 "Death Rattlers" from August 1, 1943, to June 14, 1945.

Major Axtell was born in Ambridge, Pennsylvania, on November 29, 1920. After graduating from Ambridge High School in 1938 he attended the University of Alabama before entering the Marine Corps in July 1940 as an Aviation Cadet.

He was commissioned a second lieutenant and designated a Naval Aviator on May 12, 1941.

After flight school he attended the U.S. Navy's postgraduate school to study meteorology and engineering, from which he graduated in March 1943.

Axtell was promoted to the rank of major on May 15, 1943. He was assigned to command the newly formed Marine Fighter Squadron (VMF) 323 at Cherry Point, South Carolina.

The unit was sent to Okinawa, where Major Axtell led the "Death Rattlers" in the destruction of 124 Japanese planes with the VMF-323 Corsairs. "Big Ax" became an ace during his first engagement.

Following the Okinawa campaign he became the CO of MCVG-16 (Marine Carrier Air Group), also known as "Corsair Carriers."

During the Korean War Lt. Col Axtell flew combat with the First Marine Wing.

He is credited with six confirmed victories and three damaged enemy aircraft.

Lt. Col Axtell was awarded the following decorations: Navy Cross; Distinguished Service Medal; Legion of Merit with Combat "V" and two Gold Stars; Distinguished Flying Cross with one Gold Star; and the Air Medal with six Gold Stars.

LCDR JOHN THOMAS BLACKBURN, USN, was born into a Navy family on June 24, 1912, in Annapolis, Maryland.

He entered the Naval Academy in 1929 and graduated on June 1, 1933. "Tommy," as he was often called, served on the battleship USS *Mississippi* until February 1936, at which time he started flight training.

Blackburn won his wings on February 26, 1937, flying with several squadrons over the next four years becoming of VGF-29 on June 18, 1942. Assigned to the escort carrier USS *Santee* during the Allied invasion of North Africa, Blackburn led Wildcats in VF-29 against Vichy French forces during November 1942. Engine trouble forced his Wildcat down at sea, but he was rescued by friendly forces and returned to the United States.

In the U.S. Blackburn organized a new Navy fighter squadron (VF-17), which became the envy of other Navy and Marine squadrons. The squadron was equipped with Corsairs and, because the word "Corsair" is a synonym for "pirate," the VF-17 aviators selected a pirate's skull and crossbones flag as the squadron insignia, and the squadron was called the "Jolly Rogers."

Capt John F Bolt, Jr, USMC, was one of the youngest Marine fighter aviators. He was selected by Maj Boyington for the new squadron that "Pappy" was organizing. Bolt flew Corsairs in the Marine Corps and F-86 Sabre Jets in the Air Force. (via National Archives)

LCDR Blackburn set the example for his men by becoming the squadron's first ace and, led by "Tommy" Blackburn, the "Jolly Rogers" scored 152 victories between October 1943 and March 1944.

LCDR Blackburn is credited with eleven confirmed victories, five probable victories, and three damaged enemy planes.

He was awarded the following decorations: Navy Cross with one Gold Star; Distinguished Flying Cross with one Gold Star; and the Air Medal with two Gold Stars.

LT. COL JOHN F. BOLT, JR, was born on May 19, 1921, in Laurens, South Carolina, during a recession. His family moved to Sanford, Florida, in 1926, where he attended school until college age. He was the president of his class in his Junior and Senior years. Jack's parents were very poor, and he had to provide his own clothes and social expenses from the age of 10.

John Bolt attended the University of Florida for two years, but received very little financial support in college. Although he was supporting himself, he was an honor student and a member of the Freshman Honor Society.

Bolt decided to join the Navy to save money and complete college to earn a low degree. He joined up in July 1941, but he was not called until mid-November, which was only a few weeks before the Pearl Harbor attack.

Flight training began at E-base in Atlanta, and then to Jacksonville, where he trained in the SNJ, followed by Miami, where he practiced gunnery in F3F-1 biplanes.

After a sea voyage to Turtle Bay, Espiritu Santo, Bolt was transferred to the pilot pool. His first flight in the pool was on June 26, 1943, when Major Gregory (Pappy) Boyington selected John Bolt to be part of the squadron Maj Boyington was forming. Bolt remained in the "Black Sheep" as long as Boyington was in the unit.

Following his combat tour in the Solomons Jack Bolt, one of the youngest Marine fighter aviators, took a leave to marry Dottie Wiggins.

When Capt Bolt returned to the Pacific Theatre on a second combat tour in VMF-472, he said of his second tour:

Capt Bolt established a new Corsair endurance record on May 13, 1945. Using standard drop fuel tanks, he logged a flight of 14 hours and seven minutes over Ewa, Hawaii. The only extra items carried on the flight were a rubber seat pad and a spare canteen of water. The left photo shows a weary Capt Bolt as he landed after the record flight, while the right photo shows a jubilant Capt Bolt with a victory cigar. (Nick Hauprich Collection)

Chapter IX: Corsair Aviators and Decorations

"It was kind of a nothing kind of war. We bombed some bypassed islands. We were in a jeep carrier, the *USS Block Island* (CVE-21)."

Capt Bolt established a new Corsair endurance record on May 13, 1945. Using standard drop fuel tanks, he logged a flight of 14 hours and seven minutes over Ewa, Hawaii. The only extra items carried on the flight were a rubber seat pad and a spare canteen of water.

Following World War II he served with Corsair Squadron VMF-452 based on Corsair carrier *USS Badoeng Strait* (CVE-116). Next, he had a staff position in MAG-13.

During the Korean War Major Bolt flew 92 fighter-bomber missions in VMF-211 with Panther jets. By March 1953 he was attached to the USAAF 39th Fighter-Interceptor Squadron flying F-86 Sabrejets.

Retiring from the Marines with the rank of Lt. Col, Jack Bolt moved to Florida.

Col Bolt scored 12 confirmed victories (six in WWII and six in Korea), plus two damaged enemy aircraft.

Col Bolt was awarded the following decorations: Navy Cross; Distinguished Flying Cross with one Gold Star; and Air Medal with one Gold Star (plus one Oak Leaf Cluster from the Air Force).

CAPT DONALD LUTHER BALCH, USMCR, was born in Youngstown, Ohio, on July 6, 1917. He attended Ohio State University, graduating in 1940. Don started Naval Aviation Training in September 1941 and finished July 18, 1942.

Balch went to the Solomon Islands in January 1943 as a 2nd Lieutenant with VMF-221 "Fighting Falcons." He scored in his first engagement on 7 April by shooting down a Zero and damaged another with his Wildcat.

Capt Donald L Balch, USMC, scored a victory on his first engagement with the enemy, but when he flew the Corsair his victories increased to five, thus entering the hallowed halls of Acedom. He flew from the Solomon Islands and the fleet carrier *Bunker Hill*. Balch scored five confirmed and one probable victories. (USMC Photo Courtesy F.J. Delear, Chance Vought)

When the squadron transitioned to the Corsair he scored another victory and continued until he scored four more victories, some of which were made when VMF-221 flew from the fleet carrier *USS Bunker Hill*. He returned to the U.S. in May 1945.

Capt Balch scored five confirmed victories, one probable victory, and two damaged enemy aircraft.

Capt Donald L Balch was awarded the following decorations: Distinguished Flying Cross with one Gold Star and an Air Medal with four Gold Stars.

MAJOR GREGORY "PAPPY" BOYINGTON, USMC, was born in Coeur d'Aene, Idaho, on December 4, 1912, but grew up in Tacoma, Washington. He graduated from the University of Washington in 1934 with a degree in Aeronautical Engineering. Two years later he began Naval Flight Training.

Major Gregory "Pappy" Boyington, USMC, is probably the most celebrated American flying Ace of World War II. He organized and led the most renowned flying fighter group, the "Black Sheep." He also organized sixty-plane fighter sweeps to draw Japanese fighters into massive dog-fights. (USMC Photo)

Boyington received his wings and commission in the Marine Corps; however, he resigned in 1941 to join the American Volunteer Group to fight the Japanese in China. He flew in the AVG "Flying Tigers" for eight months, during which time he scored two victories. He resigned from the AVG in March 1942 and returned to the U.S. and joined the U.S. Marine Corps again in November 1942. Boyington wanted his own squadron.

He was ordered to Espiritu Santo in January 1943 as assistant operations officer and transferred to VMF-112, then transferred to VMF-122 as XO, and in a short time became the squadrons' CO.

Four weeks later he broke his ankle and remained in a Naval hospital for two months. Upon his return to Espiritu Santo he insisted that he be given the "temporary" command of a fighter squadron.

VMF-214 "Swashbucklers" had just completed their second combat tour on August 31, 1943, and went to Sydney, Australia, for R&R (Rest and Recuperation). Upon the "Swashbucklers'" return for their third combat tour, the aviators discovered that their squadron had been disbanded and the number VMF-214 was given to Boyington's new squadron! The "Swashbucklers" were dispersed to other squadrons.

Named the "Black Sheep," the new VMF-214 had been issued Corsairs that pleased Major Boyington. He loved the plane so much that he instructed his men to fight with the engine set at high power all the time.

Apparently Boyington had forgotten or disregarded the axion that the Marines were given airplanes to assist and protect the Marine troops and not to seek dogfights for glory.

In addition to escorting bombers over Rabaul, Boyington conducted fighter sweeps to draw Japanese fighters into enormous dogfights.

On January 3, 1944, his sixty-plane fighter sweep was confronted by Japanese units that boasted over a dozen aces. Boyington scored three Zero fighters before he and his wingman were shot down. "Pappy" was captured by a Japanese submarine and spent the remainder of the war in a Japanese POW camp.

Major Boyington is credited with 22 victories with VMF-214 and two victories with the AVG Flying Tigers, plus four probable victories. He was awarded the following decorations: Medal of Honor and Navy Cross.

CDR GUY PIERRE BORDELON, JR, USN, was born on February 1, 1922, in Ruston, Louisiana, the son of Guy P. and Thurla Hearn Bordelon. Upon graduating from Bolton High School in Alexandria, Louisiana, he attended Louisiana Tech in Ruston. He later attended Louisiana State University in Baton Rouge, where he studied for a degree in law until he volunteered for Naval Aviation Training in 1942.

Guy Bordelon was commissioned ensign USNR in May 1943 upon completion of training in Corpus Christi, Texas. From May 1943 to May 1945 Ensign Bordelon served as Intermediate flight instructor in the SNJ "Texan" at Kingsville, Texas, and completed the flight syllabus at NAAS Sanford, Florida, where he was combat team leader.

From October 1945 to July 1948 he was in the original "Sundowner" Squadron VF-11. During this time he was commissioned Lieutenant on February 1, 1946, and transferred to Regular Navy on August 1, 1946. Lt. Bordelon joined the Naval Air Training Command for a second tour in August 1948 at the Advanced Training Command, Corpus Christi, Texas. It was here that he served first as an advanced fighter instructor in Corsairs and later as Administrative Officer on the staff of Naval Air Advanced Training.

When the Korean War began, Bordelon was ordered to the staff of Commander Cruiser Division Three, whose flagship was the heavy Cruiser *USS Helena*, and he served as staff Intelligence Officer, Assistant

After becoming the "Triple Threat Ace" of the Korean War by scoring night-intruding "Bed Check Charlies" in the eerie darkness of night with his F4U-5N corsair, Commander Guy Pierre Bordelon Jr, USN, held a series of important military positions. (U.S. Navy Photo, via National Archives)

Operations Officer, and Assistant Logistics Officer while *USS Helena* participated in gunnery actions against the North Korean land forces.

Lt. Bordelon was later ordered to Composite Squadron Three as an All-Weather night carrier aviator serving aboard the Attack carrier *USS Princeton* as Officer in Charge of the Night Fighter Detachment in combat operations against hostile forces.

As previously described, Lt. Bordelon scored five "Bed Check Charlies," making him the only Night-Fighter Ace, the only Navy Ace, and the only Ace who flew a propeller-powered plane.

All of Lt. Bordelon's victories were the five "Bed Check Charlie" night victories.

Lt. Bordelon was awarded the following decorations: Navy Cross, Two Silver Stars, and Four Air Medals. In addition, the Republic of Korea awarded the Ace the order of Military Merit Ulchi with Silver Star.

MAJOR GEORGE F. BRITT, USMC, was born in Portsmouth, VA, on September 24, 1914. He was commissioned 2nd Lieutenant in the Marine Corps after graduating from Georgia Tech University with a BS in Aeronautical Engineering and Naval ROTC. From July 1936 and May 1937 he was a student in the Marine Corps Basic School at the Navy Yard, Philadelphia, PA. From June 1939 to April 1940 he was designated a Naval Aviator after flight training at NAS Pensacola and promoted to 1st Lieut.

Capt Britt was XO of VMF-211, redesignated from VMF-2, and fighting in early Pacific battles such as Palmyra Island and Wake Island. He was given command of VMF-214 "Swashbucklers" which later became the "Blacksheep."

Chapter IX: Corsair Aviators and Decorations

Col George F. Britt, USMC, flew and fought in the early Pacific Islands at Wake and Palmyra. He became Operations Officer for Marine Aircraft Group 21 because of his sound planning ability. His Commendation Medal presentation for Meritorious Service reads: "For an acute awareness of the many complex inherent problems formulating the sound professional judgment for sound planning techniques." He flew an unarmed Corsair to conferences. (USMC Photo)

Capt William Earl Crowe, USMC, flew with VMF-124 off USS Essex. He remained in the Marine Corps after World War II and flew a combat tour in Korea. Promoted to Lt. Col on April 1, 1960, and, while attending a command and staff course, he was killed when his Douglas AD-6 Skyraider crashed. (USMC Photo Author's File)

Promotion to Major elevated Major Britt to Operation Officer for Marine Aircraft Group 21.

Col Britt flew over 50 combat missions, the majority in the high-speed Corsair "No-Bu-No" without an escort.

Major Britt was awarded the following decorations: Distinguished Flying Cross; Air Medal with six Gold Stars, commendation reads "For Leading escorts to Vila, Munda, Rekata Bay and Vanga Vanga during numerous missions and, on April 30, 1943, he led a highly successful strafing attack in which many enemy installations were left demolished and burning."; and the Commendation Medal for Meritorious Service reads: "for an acute awareness of the many complex inherent problems formulating the sound professional judgement for sound planning techniques."

CAPT WILLIAM EARL CROWE, USMC, was born in Austin, Texas, on February 11, 1918. William Earl Crowe joined the Marine Corps in 1941, graduating from flight training on February 9, 1942. Assigned to VMF-124, he arrived in Guadalcanal early in 1943, flying the F4U Corsair.

Lt. crowe scored his first victory on June 10, 1943, downing two Japanese bombers. After his promotion to captain he scored a Zeke on 15 August, followed by two Vals and a probable Zero three days later. Capt Crowe scored his last victory on 30 August.

After a tour in the U.S. Capt Crowe returned to combat in 1945 with his old squadron, VMF-124, flying off USS Essex; however, he scored no more victories.

Captain Crowe remained in the Marine Corps after the war, and flew a combat tour in Korea. He was promoted to Lt. Colonel on April 1, 1960. While attending a command and staff course for senior officers he was killed when his Douglas AD-6 Skyraider crashed in Texas.

Lt. Col Crowe scored seven confirmed victories, one probable, and one damaged.

He was awarded the following decorations: Navy Cross; Distinguished Flying Cross with four Gold Stars; and the Air Medal with 14 Gold Stars.

CAPT JAMES NORMAN CUPP, USMC, was born on March 21, 1921, in Corning, Iowa. James attended the University of Iowa for two years, and then he entered the Naval V-5 program in May 1941, graduating at Corpus Christi, Texas, on January 9, 1942, with a commission in the U.S. Marine Corps.

After assignment to aerial photography he transferred to fighter squadron VMF-213 "Hellhawks" at Ewa, Hawaii, in September 1942, flying Wildcats. By March 1943 he transitioned to Corsairs, covering the New Georgia landings on June 30, 1943.

James Cupp shot down a Betty bomber on 15 July for his first victory and scored an escorting Zero shortly after.

Corsair: The Saga of the Legendary Bent-Wing Fighter-Bomber

Capt James Norman Cupp, USMC, was shot down by an incendiary 20 mm cannon on Sept 20, 1943. The cannon was hidden in the bomb-bay of a Japanese Betty bomber, causing serious burns. He is shown here in his corsair prior to the serious accident. (USMC Photo via National Archives)

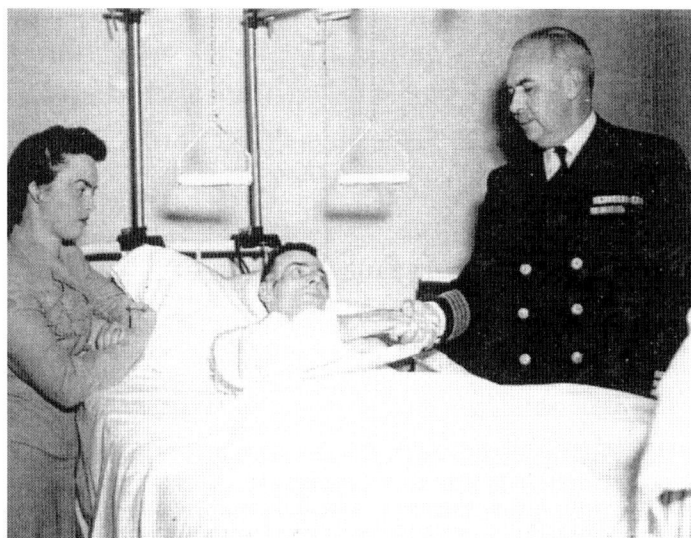

Capt Cupp recovered from his serious burns after fourteen operations and eighteen months in the hospital. He is shown here with the chief surgeon of Oak Knoll Hospital and the Ace's wife, Daphne. Cupp was released in February 1945 and served in the Korean War. (Oak Knoll Hospital Photo, Author's File)

On July 17, 1943, while on an escort mission, Cupp scored two more Zeros and shared another. While escorting on the following day over Kahili he shot down another Zero to become an Ace.

On 20 September Cupp was on a lone Dawn Patrol when he sighted a lone Betty on a reconnaissance mission coming from Guadalcanal and dropped a few bombs on the Allied airfield at Munda. By the time Capt. Cupp reached altitude the Betty was almost out of sight.

As the Japanese aviator went into a shallow dive to gain some speed Cupp gave chase for about twenty miles. Knowing that the Betty's tail gunner could not aim down at an angle greater than 45 degrees, Cupp's plan was to attack the Betty straight up under the belly.

As he swooped under the Betty, the bomb bay opened and a 20mm cannon began firing from that unorthodox location, hitting the Corsair repeatedly. Three shots hit the lower part of the cockpit, starting a fire, with the Corsair dropping at the rate of about 350 miles per hour. Jim Cupp could not bail out because he was standing on the rudder pedals and the holes in the fuselage fanned the small fire into a blowtorch onto Cupp's legs and face.

Capt Cupp finally raised his legs off the rudder pedals and throttled down his engine with both hands. Then he managed to bail out, badly burned. The hair was burned off his head, and pieces of skin hung around his lips. As he drifted with his parachute, James Cupp saw his corsair hit the water.

Cupp's wingmen Stewart and Avey spotted the Betty in the water with seven Japanese crewmen hanging on the wing trailing edge. Apparently Capt Cupp's last shots spelled the end of the Betty.

Jim Cupp was sent to Mobile Hospital No 8 on Guadalcanal until 6 December, when he was transferred to Oakland, CA, where a country club had been converted to Oak Knoll Hospital by the U.S. Navy.

Capt Cupp underwent fourteen operations and spent a year and a half in the hospital. He had gone through so much that his weight dropped to 68 pounds. His wife, Daphne, hardly recognized her husband. The brave warrior was released in February 1945 and served the rest of the war in Naval Flight Instructors School.

Remaining in the Marine Corps, he served with the First Marine Brigade during the Korean War and later with the First Marine Division,

After his release from Oak Knoll Hospital Major Cupp remained in the Marine Corps and served with the First Marine Brigade during the Korean War. He is shown here with his Corsair emblazoned with "Daphne C" in honor of his wife, who stood by him during his long hospital confinement. (USMC Photo Courtesy Vought Aircraft)

Chapter IX: Corsair Aviators and Decorations

Maj Marion Eugene Carl, USMC, was a licensed pilot by the time he graduated from college. He scored his first victory during the Battle of Midway flying the Buffalo and Wildcat. He was flying from Henderson Field by August 20, 1942, and became the first U.S. Marine Ace four days later. Captain Carl became CO of VMF-223 flying Corsairs, scoring a Zero and a Tony on that day. He scored a total of 18 ½ victories. (Defense Dept. Photo, via National Archives)

directing air support from the ground. Much of the air support performed by F4U-4 Corsairs during the division's fighting the retreat from the Chosin Reservoir in December 1950 was directed by Major Cupp.

Later, he performed staff duties in Quantico, Virginia, and Germany, as well as the Marine Corps Headquarters and in the 3rd Marine Air Wing. He retired with the rank of colonel in 1968.

Col Cupp scored twelve confirmed victories and two probables.

He was awarded the following decorations: Navy Cross; Distinguished Flying Cross with two Gold Stars and a third Gold Star for his activities at Chosin; Bronze Star and Bronze with "V"; and the Air Medal.

MAJ MARION EUGENE CARL, USMC, was born on November 1, 1915, in Hubbard, Oregon. He learned flying at an early age, and was already a licensed pilot when he graduated from Oregon State College with an aeronautical engineering degree in 1938. He applied for Naval Aviation Cadet training and received his wings and commission as a Marine Corps second lieutenant on December 1, 1939.

Lt. Carl flew the Brewster Buffalo and the Grumman Wildcat with VMF-221 on *Midway* for the first seven months of World War II, scoring his first victory on June 4, 1942.

He transferred to VMF-223 later that summer, and VMF-223 became the first fighter squadron to operate from Henderson Field on August 20, 1942.

Four days later Captain Carl became the first Marine Fighter Ace, scoring three Japanese bombers and a Zero fighter. By the time he left Guadalcanal in October he had shot down 11 ½ more Japanese planes for a total of 16 ½ victories by December 1943.

One year later he became the VMF-223 CO flying Corsairs, scoring a Zero and a Tony.

After the war Carl became a Navy test pilot, flying the jet-powered P-59, P-80, and German Me-262. In 1952 he established a world speed record in the Douglas Skystreak.

He returned to combat duty during the Vietnam War, commanding the 2nd Marine Air Wing.

Marion Carl retired with the rank of major general on March 31, 1973, having logged over 13,000 flying hours.

Marion Carl scored 18 ½ confirmed victories and 3 damaged.

He was awarded the following decorations: Navy Cross with two Gold Stars; Legion of Merit with three Gold Stars (one with Combat "V"); Distinguished Flying Cross with four Gold Stars; and the Air Medal with thirteen Gold Stars.

CAPT ARTHUR ROGER CONANT, USMCR, was born in Crystal Falls, Michigan, on October 21, 1918. He was raised in Marinette, Wisconsin, and graduated from the University of Wisconsin.

Captain Arthur Roger Conant, USMC, learned flying with the Civilian Pilot Training Program, joining the Navy in 1941. He received his wings on June 25, 1942, and scored his first victories flying with VMF-215 "Fighting Corsairs" on August 25, 1943. (USMC Photo, Author's File)

His first flights were with the Civilian Pilot Training program, and he joined the U.S. Navy in 1941, receiving his wings as a Marine aviator at Corpus Christi on June 25, 1942.

Assigned to VMF-215 "Fighting Corsairs" flying Corsairs from bases in the Solomon Islands, Conant scored his first victories on August 25, 1943, downing a Zero and a Tony, plus two Zero probables over Kahili. He destroyed another Zero three miles west of Vela Lavella on September 1, 1943.

After a short Rest and Recuperation (R&R) followed by ground support and strafing missions, Conant scored three Zeros on September 1, 18, and 22, 1943.

Capt Conant left the Marine Corps in 1945; however, he was called back to active duty in 1950 and spent one year in Korea flying Panther jets.

Conant went to work for Douglas aircraft as a test pilot in 1952 and remained at the position until he retired in 1985.

Arthur Conant scored 6 confirmed victories and 3 probable victories.

He was awarded the following decorations: Distinguished Flying Cross with 4 Gold Stars; Air Medal with 9 Gold Stars; and the Commendation Medal with Combat V.

LTJG DANIEL GERARD CUNNINGHAM, USNR, was born in Chicago, Illinois, on July 3, 1919. He graduated from Loyola University in Chicago in 1940 and joined the Navy on November 1, 1941, to enter flight training. He won his wings at NAS Corpus Christi, Texas, in October 1942.

Aviator Cunningham became a member of VF-17 "Jolly Rogers," the first Navy squadron to get the new Corsair. On 8 November VF-17 assumed morning CAP duty over Empress Augusta Bay. When the Japanese attacked, Cunningham climbed to guard against a high altitude attack and he found two Zeros and scored one for his first victory.

After a short R&R the squadron returned to action, attacking Rabaul. Cunningham scored two Zeros while he was part of a B-25 escort over Simpson Harbor.

Returning to the U.S. following his combat tour, Cunningham was reassigned to VF-10 and served aboard *USS Intrepid* before the war ended.

After the war he became an insurance man, and later became a member of the Chicago Mercantile Exchange, trading commodities.

Daniel Cunningham scored seven confirmed and 2 ½ damaged enemy aircraft.

He was awarded the following decorations: Navy Cross; Distinguished Flying Cross; Air Medal with two Gold Stars; and the Navy Unit Commendation Medal.

LIEUT PHILLIP CUNIFFE DELONG, USMCR, was born on July 9, 1919, in Jackson, Michigan. He graduated from the University of Omaha and entered the Naval Aviation Cadet program. De Long completed flight training, and was commissioned as a second lieutenant in the U.S. Marine Corps at Corpus Cristi, Texas, on December 16, 1942.

Assigned to VMF-212 "Hell Hounds" flying Corsairs in the Solomon Islands in June 1943, De Long scored his first victories in January 1944 when he scored two Zeros and damaged a third. He became a double Ace

LTJG Daniel Gerard Cunningham, USNR, won his wings in October 1942 and became a member of VF-17 "Jolly Rogers." During CAP duty over Empress Augusta Bay in November 1943 Cunningham scored his first of seven victories. He later served in VF-10 on USS Intrepid. (USN Photo via National Archives)

Lt Phillip Cuniffe De Long, USMCR, scored eleven victories in World War II and two victories in Korea. He flew with the "Hell Hounds" of VMF-212 flying Corsairs and retired with the rank of Colonel. (USMC Photo, Author's File)

Chapter IX: Corsair Aviators and Decorations

on 15 February by shooting down three Val dive bombers over Green Island.

De Long remained in the Marine Corps after World War II and flew Corsairs again in Korea with VMF-312, the Checkboard Squadron, aboard the USS Battan (CVL-29). Still flying Corsairs, De Long scored two Yak-9 in Korea.

During the remainder of his fighting career he was in command of five Marine squadrons and was commander of the Marine Corps Air Facility on Okinawa before retiring with the rank of Colonel.

Philip De Long is credited with 11 confirmed victories in WWII and 2 victories in Korea.

He was awarded the following decorations: Silver Star; Legion of Merit; Distinguished Flying Cross with six Gold Stars; Air Medal with 16 Gold Stars; and the Navy Commendation Medal.

MAJOR ARCHIE GLENN DONAHUE, USMCR, was born on October 24, 1917, in Casper, Wyoming, but moved to Texas as a young boy in 1934.

After studying three years of engineering at the University of Texas, he was accepted as an Aviation Cadet in the U.S. Navy. After training in Kansas City and Corpus Cristi Air Station, he transferred to the Marine Corps and was commissioned as a Second Lieutenant on December 16, 1941.

He was assigned to VMF-112, the "Wolfpack," in Guadalcanal on September 1942. His first victory was scored in a Wildcat, and eight subsequent victories were scored with a Corsair.

On May 13, 1943, while flying a Corsair, Achie destroyed five Zeros in a single battle. He returned to the United States in June and served as Flight Officer at El Toro Air Station in California. Donahue was then assigned to VMF-451 "Blue Devils" flying Corsairs, with the responsibility for making the squadron carrier qualified.

The "Blue Devils" began combat operations from USS Bunker Hill on February 16, 1945, and for the next three months the unit engaged in continuous strafing, bombing, and close support missions to cover the landings at Iwo Jima and Okinawa, plus raids against the Japanese mainland.

On 12 April Donahue scored five victories (two Zeros and three Vals) in a single combat over Okinawa.

The Bunker Hill was severely damaged by a Kamikaze attack and forced out of combat.

Donahue returned to CONUS to command a squadron at El Centro.

At War's end Donahue left active duty to enter the real estate business. However, he remained in the reserves until 1958, when he retired with the rank of colonel.

He joined the Confederate Air Force as director of flight operations and continued to fly World War II vintage fighters.

Archie Donahue is credited with 14 confirmed and one probable victories.

He was awarded the following decorations: Navy Cross; Distinguished Flying Cross with two Gold Stars; and the Air Medal with four Gold Stars.

MAJ JEFFERSON DAVID DORROH, USMCR, was born on March 14, 1921, in Corona, California. While attending the University of Oregon in September 1940 he enrolled in the U.S. Navy V-5 program, and in June

Major Archie Glen Donahue, USMCR, joined VMF-112 "Wolf Pack" in September 1942 and was assigned to VMF-45 "Blue Devils." His assignment was to make the Corsair squadron "Carrier qualified" on USS Bunker Hill. The "Blue Devils" engaged in continuous strafing, bombing, and close support missions. (U.S. Defense Dept Photo, Marine Corps, Author's file)

Maj Jefferson David Dorroh, USMCR, enrolled in the U.S. Navy V-5 program while he was attending college in September 1940. Enlisting in the Navy's pilot training program in Seattle, he was commissioned a second lieutenant. On April 22, 1945, Major Dorroh became an "Ace-in-a-Day" when he scored six victories in a row. (USMC Photo, Author's File)

1941 he entered the advanced Civilian Pilot Training program. He finished his course at Albany, Oregon, on July 8, 1941.

Dorroh then traveled to Seattle, Washington, to enlist in the Navy's pilot training program as a cadet.

He graduated at Naval Air Station Miami, Florida, on March 12, 1942, and was commissioned a second lieutenant in the U.S. Marine Corps Reserve.

After a position as flight instructor at several naval air stations, Dorrah was assigned to VMF-323 "Death Rattlers" at Cherry Point NAS in September 1943. By April 1945 he was the XO of the squadron and traveled to the Pacific Theatre as part of the unit.

On 22 April Major Dorroh became an Ace-in-a-day during a brief 20 minute encounter when he scored six victories in rapid succession.

Major Dorroh returned to private life on November 1, 1945, succeeded in attaining a law degree, and became a senior judge in Oregon.

Jefferson D. Dorroh is credited with six confirmed and two probable victories. He was awarded the following decorations: Navy Cross, Distinguished Flying Cross; and Air Medal with two Gold Stars.

MAJ GEORGE ELIJAH DOOLEY, USMC, was born on December 28, 1918, in Hopland, California. After graduating from San Francisco High School in 1935, he graduated with a BS degree from St Mary's College in 1939.

He joined the U.S. Marine Corps Reserve in July 1939 and completed basic Flight Training by the end of the year, and completed Flight School by 1941.

By October 1941, 2nd Lieut Dooley was a Squadron Officer in VMTB-131, MAG-11, the first Marine Torpedo Bomber Squadron. He became Assistant Squadron Operating Officer in October 1941, and by August 1943 Major Dooley became the CO of VMTB-131.

In view of the shortage of corsair squadrons Capt George Dooley transferred command of VMTB-131 to command of VMF-216 in the field. Many VMTB-131 aviators joined their leader in his move during January-March 1945.

From December 1945-July 1947 he was MCAS, El Toro, CA, Officer in Chief Instruments in several Squadrons, MAGs, Training Units, and CO Marine Training Squadron 2.

He retired with the rank of Lt. Colonel on October 16, 1947.

LIEUT OSCAR IVAN CHENOWETH, JR., USNR, was born in Salem, Oregon, on July 16, 1917, but moved to McMinnville, Oregon, as a young boy. He graduated from McMinnville High School in 1935. Enrolling in Oregon State University, he left college to join the Navy on August 7, 1939.

Receiving his wings and admission as an Ensign in 1941, Chenoweth was a flight instructor for a year. A combat tour with VC-21 in Attu, Alaska, was followed with a promotion to lieutenant on March 1, 1943.

He was then assigned to VF-38 flying Hellcats out of Segi Strip on Munda, from where he scored a Zero on September 15, 1943.

Returning from his first combat tour in January 1944, Lieutenant Chenoweth was assigned to VF-17 "Jolly Rogers" flying Corsairs. He scored a Zero near Rabaul on January 27, 1944, and downed two more three days later over Simpson Harbor. Chenoweth became an Ace when he downed another Zero on February 9, 1944. Ten days later the Ace downed two more Zeros and a Tojo over Rabaul to complete his scoring.

Major George Elijah Dooley, USMC, was assigned to a Torpedo Bomber squadron but transferred to VMF-216 in the field, while in action. Dooley soon led the squadron. He climbed the ladder of success until he retired with the rank of Lt Colonel in 1947. (Official USMC Photo, Author's File)

Lt Oscar Ivan Chenoweth Jr, USNR, received his wings as an Ensign in 1941 and was a flight instructor for a year when he joined the "Jolly Rogers" of VF-17 flying Corsairs. By the end of January 1949 he had scored three Zeros. He retired from the Navy with the rank of Commander having scored 8 ½ enemy aircraft. Chenoweth joined Chance Vought Aircraft as a technical representative for military sales. (U.S. Navy Photo, Author's File)

Chapter IX: Corsair Aviators and Decorations

Chenoweth returned to the U.S. in June 1944 to command a dive-bomber squadron. Later, he was in the second class of test pilot applicants to be accepted by the Naval Air Test Center at Patuxent River, Maryland.

He retired from the Navy with the rank of commander in 1954 and joined Chance Vought Aircraft as a technical representative for military sales.

Commander Chenoweth enjoyed life until he was 57 years old, when he had a heart attack on May 19, 1968, and expired.

Oscar Chenoweth is officially credited with having scored 8 ½ enemy aircraft.

Commander Chenoweth was awarded the following decorations: Silver Star; Distinguished Flying Cross; and the Air Medal with Two Gold Stars.

LIEUT PAUL CORDRAY, USNR, was born on September 4, 1919, in Grand Prairie, Texas. He joined the Navy on June 24, 1942, as an aviation cadet, and graduated from NAS Corpus Christi, Texas, in August 1942.

Cordray was assigned to *USS Bunker Hill* (CV-17) with VF-17 "Jolly Rogers"; however, the unit was land-based on the island of New Georgia instead during November 1943.

Flying Corsairs, Ensign Cordray scored his first victory on 17 November when he downed a Kate torpedo-bomber over Empress Augusta Bay. He completed his scoring for the day by destroying two Tony fighters.

Flying from Piva he scored a Zero fighter and damaged a second. On 28 January Cordray scored two more Zeros to become an Ace with five victories. He scored his sixth victory, a Zero, on February 18, 1944.

Promoted to lieutenant, Cordray returned to the U.S. in May 1944 to be assigned to VBF-10, flying Corsairs from *USS Intrepid* (CV-11).

Lt. Cordray scored another Zero on April 16, 1945, over an airfield in Japan.

He left the Navy at the end of World War II. He enjoyed life until October 20, 1963, when he passed away.

Paul Cordray scored seven confirmed victories, one probable, and three damaged.

He was awarded the following decorations: Distinguished Flying Cross with three Gold Stars, and the Air Medal with five Gold Stars.

CAPT HOWARD JAMES (MICK) FINN, was born on October 10, 1917, in Belmond, Iowa. He graduated from the University of Northern Iowa in 1941 with a Bachelor's Degree in the Industrial Arts.

Howard enlisted in the U.S. Marine Corps on July 9, 1941, and was accepted for flight training. Upon graduation at Pensacola on August 10, 1942, Finn was designated a Naval Aviator and assigned to VMF-124, flying the Corsair.

The squadron arrived at Guadalcanal in February 1943 and moved up the Solomons. "Mick" Finn's first victory was a Betty bomber on June 10, 1943.

During December 1944, VMF-124 went aboard the fast carrier *USS Essex* to reinforce Carrier Group Four raiding Japan.

Captain Finn was one of the few combat-experienced pilots in the squadron, scoring an Oscar and damaging another during a mission to shoot-up Japanese airfields in Japan.

"Mick" Finn flew Corsairs again with VMF-214 in the Korean War during 1950-1951.

Lt Paul Cordray, USNR, was assigned to *USS Bunker Hill* (CV-17 with VF-17 "Jolly Rogers"); however, the Corsair squadron was assigned to land-base duty during November 1943. Flying Corsairs, Ensign Cordray scored his first victory on November 17, 1943, when he shot down a Kate torpedo-bomber over Empress Augusta Bay. He destroyed his sixth victory, a Zero, on February 18, 1944. (U.S. Navy Photo)

When Capt Howard James "Mick" Finn graduated from college he enlisted in the U.S. Marine Corps and was accepted for flight training. He was assigned to VMF-124 flying Corsairs fighting up the Solomons. By December 1944 he was raiding Japan from *USS Essex*. "Mick" Finn flew Corsairs with VMF-214 in the Korean War. (USMC Photo, Author's File)

Major Joseph Jacob Foss, USMCR, took flying lessons while attending college. He entered Marine Corps Flight Training and received his wings in March 1941. Assigned as XO to VMF-121, he scored a Zero on October 13, 1942, and continued scoring until he became an Ace on 18 October. His score reached 23 by November 15, 1942, and continued until it reached 26 victories. (USMC Photo, Author's File)

Lt Clement Dexter Gile, USNR, enlisted in the Navy flight training program on November 14, 1940. After serving as a flight instructor he joined "Jolly Rogers" VF-17 on October 27, 1943. Ensign Gile became an Ace on January 26, 1944, when he shot down a Zero in addition to his previous four victories. (U.S. Navy Photo, via National Archives)

Further assignments included Allied Air Forces in Southern Europe 1952-1954; command of Marine Air Group 24 at Cherry Point, NC, Jan 1965-July 1966; and First Marine Division in Vietnam 1967-1968.

He retired with the rank of Colonel in 1969, and then taught electronics and retired in January 1983.

Major Finn scored six confirmed and one/half damaged victories.

He was awarded the following decorations: Distinguished Flying Cross with eight Gold Stars; Purple Heart; and the Air Medal with twenty Gold Stars.

MAJOR JOSEPH JACOB FOSS, USMCR, was born on a farm east of Sioux Falls, South Dakota, on April 17, 1915. He took flying lessons while attending college and, by the time he graduated from the University of South Dakota, he had over 100 hours of flying time in June 1940. Foss entered Marine Corps flight training and received his wings and commission at Miami, Florida, on March 29, 1941.

Assigned as a flight instructor at Pensacola, Florida, until November 1941, Foss was transferred to a reconnaissance squadron at San Diego. After requesting a transfer to a fighter squadron, he was assigned to VMF-121 as executive officer at Camp Kearney, California. Two weeks later the unit went to the Southwest Pacific, arriving on October 9, 1942.

Foss scored a Zero on 13 October and continued scoring until he became an Ace on October 18, 1942, downing two Zeros and a Nell bomber. His score reached 23 by November 15, 1942.

Returning to CONUS, Foss was promoted to major June 1, 1943, and assumed command of Corsair squadron VMF-115 upon his return to Bougainville in 1944.

Joe Foss left active duty in 1946 and returned to South Dakota. He organized the South Dakota Air National Guard, becoming its commander as brigadier general. He served two terms in the South Dakota house of representatives. This was followed by two terms as governor of South Dakota.

Major Joseph Foss scored 26 confirmed victories.

He was awarded the following decorations: Medal of Honor and Distinguished Flying Cross.

LIEUT CLEMENT DEXTER GILE, USNR, was born in New York City on January 30, 1918. He enlisted in the U.S. Navy on November 14, 1940, and completed the Navy flight training program. Following his tour of duty as a flight instructor, he joined VF-17 "Jolly Rogers" on October 27, 1943, flying Corsairs. The squadron was land-based in the Solomons at Ondonga and Piva Yoke.

Clement Gile's first combat experience came on November 1, 1943, when he shared credit for damaging a Zero during the Allied invasion of Bougainville. On 11 November he scored a Kate torpedo bomber over the Solomon Sea, and on the 17th he downed three Zeros over Empress Augusta Bay.

Chapter IX: Corsair Aviators and Decorations

Lt Robert Murray Hanson, USMC, was the leading corsair Ace of all time with 25 victories to his credit. This athlete bicycled all the way from India, where he was born, through Europe. (USMC Photo)

ENS Gile became an Ace on January 26, 1944, when he shot down a Zero over Rabaul. On 29 January Gile sent another Zero down in flames, raising his score to six confirmed victories. Two more Zeros went down to bring his score to eight on 18 and 19 February.

Gile was promoted to Lieutenant on October 1, 1943. The Lieutenant was assigned to VBF-10 aboard USS Intrepid (CVA-11).

This "Jolly Roger" was wounded in action by anti-aircraft fire on March 18, 1945, but never by enemy aircraft fire.

Lt. Gile scored eight confirmed victories.

He was awarded the following decorations: Distinguished Flying Cross with Three Gold Stars and the Air Medal with Two Gold Stars.

LIEUT ROBERT MURRAY HANSON was born on February 4, 1920, in Lucknow, India. Hanson was the son of Reverend and Mrs Harry A Hanson; Methodist missionaries in the Far East. Bob Hanson spent his early life in Lucknow, but returned to the family home in Newtonville, Massachusetts, to attend junior high school. He returned to India to finish high school. His interest in athletics prompted him to become the light heavyweight and heavyweight wrestling champion of the United Provinces.

In the spring of 1938, Bob Hanson bicycled his way through Europe on his way back to the United States, where he planned to attend Hamline University in St. Paul, Minnesota, where he was studying when the Japanese struck at Pearl Harbor.

Hanson enlisted for Naval flight training in May 1942 and won his wings and a Marine Corps commission as Second Lieutenant on February 19, 1943, at Corpus Christi, Texas. By June 1943 he was a First Lieutenant with VMF-215 in the Northern Solomons Campaign, and destined to become the leading Corsair Ace of all time.

Lt. Robert Hanson scored 25 victories (all with the Corsair).

He was awarded the following decorations: Medal of Honor; Navy Cross; and the Air Medal.

LCDR ROGER RICHARD (ROG) HEDRICK, USNR, was born in Pasadena, California, on Sept 2, 1914. "Rog" Hedrick attended Los Angeles City College before entering the Navy on October 26, 1936. He was accepted for flight training at Pensacola and graduated on September 10, 1937. The Naval Aviator was assigned to VF-4 on USS Ranger in May 1941; however, he was sent to Miami as a flight instructor. In January 1943 he was assigned to VF-17 "Jolly Rogers" flying the Corsair from USS Bunker Hill (CV-17).

Caught in the "We don't have Corsair spare parts" fiasco forced the squadron off the carrier and into combat as a land-based unit in the Solomons.

Hedrick was promoted to lieutenant commander late in 1943. On November 1, 1943, he shot down his first enemy aircraft (a Zero) in his first combat.

A week later he damaged three more Japanese aircraft, and then scored a Zero in each of his next five dogfights. "Rog" was now an Ace. Three more Zeros fell before his guns on February 18, 1944.

LCDR Roger Richard (ROG) Hedrick, USNR, was accepted for flight training on Sept 10, 1937, and assigned to VF-17 "Jolly Rogers" on USS Bunker Hill; however, the squadron was reassigned to land bases (because carriers had no Corsair spare parts!). He scored his first victory on November 1, 1943. Hedrick was placed in command of the 36 Corsairs of newly-formed VF-84. His final scoring was 12 confirmed victories with four damaged. (USMC Photo, Author's File)

Corsair: The Saga of the Legendary Bent-Wing Fighter-Bomber

Lt Alvin Julius Jensen paid for flying lessons by working in a printing office. He joined the Marine Corps Reserve and, following flight school, he joined VMF-214 "Swashbucklers" as a technical sergeant. After scoring two Zeros he was promoted to the rank of 2nd Lieutenant upon the recommendation of his commanding officer, Capt George Britt. On August 26, 1943, Jensen scored a dozen enemy aircraft on the Japanese Kahili runway! (Col Keith William Photo Courtesy Keith Williams)

Lieut Ira Cassius (Ike) Kepford, USMCR, smiles at his appointment as a Naval Aviation Cadet. Following flight training, Kepford was assigned to the soon to be famous VF-17 "Jolly Rogers," in which he became the top-scoring aviator. (Lt Ira Kepford Photo, Courtesy Ira Kepford)

Returning to CONUS, many "Jolly Rogers" aviators were transferred to the newly-organized VF-84, with LCDR Hedrick in command of the 36 Corsairs. The new squadron saw action over Japan, Iwo Jima, and Okinawa. Hedrick's final scoring was on February 25, 1945, when he shot down a Zero and two Franks.

After WWII Hedrick remained in the Navy, serving in a variety of staff and command positions. He retired from Military Service on November 1, 1958, with the rank of rear admiral.

Roger Hedrick scored 12 confirmed victories with four damaged.

He was awarded the following decorations: Silver Star; Distinguished Flying Cross with three Gold Stars; and the Air Medal with one Gold Star.

LIEUT ALVIN JULIUS JENSEN was born in Clemson, South Carolina, on June 23, 1920. After graduating from high school, he worked for the U.S. Printing Office and earned enough money to obtain a pilot's license.

On May 3, 1940, he joined the Marine Corps Reserve and experienced active service after the Pearl Harbor attack. Following flight school at Miami, Florida, he joined VMF-214 "Swashbucklers" as a technical sergeant, flying Wildcats.

During his first combat mission, on July 7, 1943, Jensen scored two Zeros. He was promoted to second lieutenant on recommendation of his commanding officer, Capt George Britt. 2nd Lt. Jenson continued his scoring on VMF-214's second combat tour, flying Corsairs.

He scored two Zeros and a Jake Reconnaissance float plane on August 6, 1943, and his fifth Zero on 26 August. Two days later he scored many parked aircraft on the Kahili Airfield runway, previously mentioned.

Lt. Jensen transferred to VMF-441 after VMF-214 became the "Black Sheep," and on June 22, 1945, he shot down his final Zero.

Promoted to Captain after the war, he was demonstrating a jet-powered Banshee F2H-1 fighter before a large crowd when the plane broke up in a dive over Chesapeake Bay. Captain Jensen was killed instantly on May 20, 1949.

Captain Jensen scored seven confirmed victories and one probable.

He was awarded the following decorations: Navy Cross; Distinguished Flying Cross with three Gold Stars; and the Air Medal with 16 Gold Stars.

LIEUT IRA CASSIUS (IKE) KEPFORD was born in Harvey, Illinois, on May 29, 1919, the son of George Raymond and Emma Mc Laughlin Kepford.

After completing high school, Kepford enrolled in Northwestern University in Evanuston, Illinois, where his athletic prowess enabled him to become the star halfback on the Northwestern football team. While still a student, "Ike" Kepford joined the U.S. Naval Reserve on August 18, 1941. He arranged to be honorably discharged on April 29, 1942, in order to accept an appointment as a Naval Aviation Cadet. Following flight training at Corpus Christi, Texas, and Miami, Florida, Ensign Kepford was assigned to the newly formed VF-17 "Jolly Rogers."

ENS Kepford's first taste of battle came on November 11, 1943, when he scored four victories protecting U.S. carriers that were attacking Rabaul. His four victories were a large portion of the eighteen Jolly Rogers victories of that day. Kepford was the first aviator to use the engine water injection system in combat.

The following month Kepford was returning to the United States and assigned to the Fleet Air Command at Alameda, California. That June saw the Ace transferred to Fighting Squadron 84 until December 1944,

Chapter IX: Corsair Aviators and Decorations

when Kepfrod was attached to the Staff of Commander Fleet Air, West Coast. He remained at this assignment throughout the remaining period of hostilities. On May 1, 1945, Kepford was promoted to the rank of Lieutenant. After the Japanese surrender, and a period of terminal leave, the ace was released from all active duty on November 7, 1945. He was transferred to the retired list of the U.S. Naval Reserve with the rank of Lieutenant Commander on the basis of combat citations on June 1, 1956.

Ike Kepford scored 16 confirmed victories, one probable, and one damaged.

He was awarded the following decorations: Navy Cross with one Gold Star; Silver Star; and the Distinguished Flying Cross.

LIEUT EARL MAY, JR, USNR, was born on June 1, 1920, in Milwaukee, Wisconsin. He joined the Navy on February 22, 1941, completing the Navy flight training program on October 1, 1942. Assigned to VF-17 "Jolly Rogers," he flew Corsairs from Piva Yoke, Bougainville, and Ondonga, New Georgia, from October 1943 to March 1944.

LTJG May shot down his first victory on January 27, 1944, with the Zero fighter falling near Rabaul. Two days later another Zero fell before his guns and, on 9 February, another Zeke fell in flames. On 19 February he scored three more Zeros that completed his scoring.

With his VF-17 tour complete, Lt. May transferred to VBF-10 aboard *USS Intrepid*, serving on board in March and April 1945.

Lt. May remained in the Navy following World War II, and trained to become a test pilot at NATC Patuxent River. The Ace was killed when he crashed while testing a Grumman F8F-1 Bearcat on October 22, 1951.

Lieutenant Earl May scored eight confirmed and one damaged enemy aircraft.

He was awarded the following decorations: Silver Star; Distinguished flying Cross with one Gold Star; and the Air Medal with one Gold Star.

CAPT ROBERT (BOB) WESLEY McCLURG, USMC, was born on February 9, 1919, in Coshocton, Ohio. The family moved to Pennsylvania, where Bob enrolled in Pennsylvania State College in 1939. He later transferred to Westminster College, from where he graduated in 1942.

He had joined the U.S. Marine Corps Platoon Leaders class at Pennsylvania State College, which made him eligible to apply for Naval flight training upon graduation from college. Bob received his wings and commission as a second lieutenant in the Marines on February 1, 1943.

Lieutenant McClurg was assigned to VMF-211 defending Wake Island. He was then moved to VMF-214 "Swashbucklers," whose squadron number was given to Major Gregory Boyington for his "Black Sheep" squadron.

McClurg often flew as Boyington's wingman, and they worked well as a team.

Captain McClurg remained in the Marines and earned a Master of Arts degree from the University of Pittsburg before he retired from the U.S. Marine Corps as a Lieutenant Colonel.

Robert McClurg scored seven confirmed and two probable victories.

He was awarded the following decorations: Distinguished Flying Cross with four Gold Stars, and the Air Medal with seven Gold Stars.

LT COL WILLIAM ARTHUR MILLINGTON, USMC, was born on August 28, 1914, at Ruth, Nevada, the son of Dr. William A Millington. After graduating from the University of Washington in 1936 with a Bachelor of Arts Degree, he enlisted in the Marine Corps and was assigned to pre-flight training at Naval Air Station, Seattle, Washington. Millington followed with flight training at Pensacola, Florida.

After completing flight training in December 1937, he was designated a Naval Aviator and assigned to VMF-2 at Naval Air Station, San Diego,

Lieut Earl May, Jr, USNR, joined the Navy on February 22, 1941, and, after flight training, he was assigned to VF-17 "Jolly Rogers." Flying Corsairs, he scored his first victory on January 27, 1944. Two days later he scored another Zero. He became a test pilot after the war. (Official U.S. Navy Photo via National Archives)

Capt Robert (Bob) Wesley McClurg, USMC, joined the U.S. Marine Corps Leaders class at college, which made him eligible to apply for Naval flight training upon graduation. Bob received his wings and commission as a second lieutenant in the Marines on February 1, 1943. Lt McClurg was assigned to VMF-214 "Swashbucklers" which became VMF-214 "Black Sheep." (Capt McClurg Photo, Author's File)

Lt Col William Arthur Millington, USMC, was the Commanding Officer of VMF-123 and VMF-124. He proved that Corsairs could be successfully operated in combat from aircraft carriers. (Defense Dept. Photo, Marine Corps, Author's File)

LTJG Robert Mims, USNR, joined the Navy and completed the Navy flight training program on October 1, 1943. Ensign Mims was assigned to the "Jolly Rogers" VF-17 in December 1943, flying from Ondonga, New Georgia, and Piva Yoke. (Official U.S. Navy Photograph, via National Archives)

where he was commissioned a Marine second lieutenant on July 5, 1939. He then went back to Pensacola, where he served as a flight instructor from November 1940 to May 1941, and then as flight instructor at Floyd Bennett Field in Brooklyn, New York, from May to July 1942.

Col Millington was CO of VMF-123 and VMF-124 in the western Pacific, flying Corsairs based on USS Essex (CV-9) in raids on Okinawa and the Tokyo area. During a raid on January 3, 1945, he scored 27 aerial victories, plus 207 aircraft destroyed by strafing, thereby proving that Corsairs could be successfully operated in combat from aircraft carriers. He then became Group Executive Officer for MAASG-44, Third MAW, until October, 1945.

Millington retired on September 30, 1956, after 20 years of service with the rank of Brigadier General.

Brig Gen Millington was awarded the following decorations: Distinguished Flying Cross with two Gold Stars; Bronze Star; Air Medal with two Gold Stars; and the Asiatic-Pacific Campaign Medal with one Silver Star.

LTJG ROBERT MIMS, USNR, was born in Dallas, Texas, on March 20, 1920. He joined the Navy on February 3, 1942, completing the Navy flight training program and receiving his commission as ensign on October 1, 1943. He was assigned to VF-17 "Jolly Rogers" in December 1943, in which squadron he flew Corsairs from Ondonga, New Georgia, and from Piva Yoke, Bougainville.

LTJG Mims was introduced to aerial combat on January 27, 1944, when he engaged Japanese aircraft over the large enemy base at Rabaul. He scored two Zeros and an unidentified enemy aircraft on that day.

On the following days he scored more enemy aircraft over Rabaul until his final score was six confirmed victories and three probable victories.

LTJG Mims was awarded the following decorations: Distinguished Flying Cross with one Gold Star and the Air Medal with one Gold Star.

LT JEREMIAH JOSEPH O'KEEFE, USMCR, was born on July 12, 1923, in Ocean Springs, Mississippi; however; the family soon moved to Biloxi, where he graduated from Sacred Heart Academy in 1941. Following graduation from Soulle Business College in New Orleans, O'Keefe entered Navy flight training. He received a reserve commission in the Marine Corps on June 16, 1943, at the age of nineteen.

Sent overseas with VMF-323 "Death Rattlers" in June 1943, he remained with the squadron until June 1945.

His first combat occurred over Okinawa on April 22, 1945, when he was one of three "Death Rattlers" that became an ace-in-a-day.

O'Keefe's score for the day was five Val dive-bombers, which was matched by his CO, Major George Axtell, and exceeded only by the XO, Major Jeff Dorroh.

Six days later O'Keefe scored two Nate fighter to bring his final score to seven.

Chapter IX: Corsair Aviators and Decorations

Lt Jeremiah Joseph O'Keefe entered Navy flight training after graduation from college and received a reserve commission in the Marine Corps on June 16, 1943, at the age of nineteen. This photo shows O'Keefe showing five fingers, the number of enemy planes that he shot down during his first aerial combat, plus two additional victories when the photo was taken. (U.S. Defense Dept Photo, Marine Corps)

He was awarded the following decorations: Navy Cross; Distinguished Flying Cross; and the Air Medal with one Gold Star.

MAJOR ROBERT GORDON (BIG "O") OWENS, Jr, USMC, was born in Greenville, South Carolina, on February 13, 1917. He enlisted in the Marine Corps Reserve after graduating from Furman University in August 1939. "Big O" was designated a Naval Aviator and commissioned a second lieutenant on June 12, 1940.

He had been assigned to a Marine dive-bomber squadron and assisted in the island's defense when the Japanese attacked Pearl Harbor.

Owens was a Major by 1943 and experienced combat as XO of VMF-215 "Fighting Corsairs" based at Munda. He finished the tour with three Zeros to his credit.

After R&R the squadron was relocated to Vella Lavella, and on December 6, 1943, "Big O" was named squadron commander. He shot down two Zeros on January 14, 1944, and another Zero on 22 January. Two days later he scored a Tojo and a probable Zero; however, he suffered shrapnel wounds and serious burns, forcing him to ditch his Corsair in the water. Picked up by a Catalina, he led VMF-215 until 28 February, when he returned to CONUS where he commanded VMF-481.

"Big O" remained in the Marine Corps following World War II, commanding VMF-215 and then VMA-323 "Death Rattlers." He then became commander of Marine Air Group 13 from August 1960 to September 1961.

Owens served two tours in Vietnam, following which he was promoted to major general on September 1, 1968. Then, he was commanding general of the 3rd Marine Air Wing in Japan until his retirement on August 1, 1972.

Robert Owens scored seven confirmed and four probable victories.

He was awarded the following decorations: Navy Cross; Legion of Merit with two Gold Stars; Distinguished Flying Cross with four Gold Stars; Purple Heart; and the Air Medal with eleven Gold Stars.

LIEUT THOMAS HAMIL REIDY, USNR, was born in Bethlehem, Pennsylvania, on April 20, 1913, and joined the U.S. Navy on February 17, 1942. He completed the Navy flight training program in October 1942 and was assigned to VB-83. When VBF-83 was organized on January 2, 1945, LT Reidy was transferred to the new unit and became its acting CO in April.

VBF-83 was equipped with Corsairs that were based on *USS Essex* (CV-9) until the end of the war.

Lieutenant Reidy was credited with his first victories on March 18, 1945, off the coast of Kyushu, when he scored two Zeros. On the following day he shot down a Myrt reconnaissance/bomber.

He continued with his success until August 15, 1945, when he scored the final victory by an Essex-based airplane, which was his tenth victory.

Major Robert Gordon (Big "O") Owens, Jr, USMC, was one of the most efficient and admired U.S. Marine squadron and group leaders. He enlisted in the U.S. Marine Corps Reserve upon graduating from university. Commissioned a second lieutenant on June 12, 1940, Owens was a Major by 1943 and became XO and then CO of VMF-215 "Fighting Corsairs," which spawned several high-scoring Corsair aces. Big "O" remained in the Marine Corps after WWII, commanding VMF-215 and VMA-323 "Death Rattlers." He then led Marine Air Group 13. Owens served two tours in Vietnam, followed by promotion to major general. He retired on August 1, 1972. Photo taken as CO of Fighting Corsairs. (U.S. Defense Dept Photo, Courtesy Gen Owens)

Lt Thomas Hamil Reidy, USNR, scored the last victory with a *USS Essex*-based Corsair on August 15, 1945. This victory is often claimed to be the last aerial victory of World War II. When Lt Reidy completed the U.S. Navy flight training program in October 1942 he was assigned to VB-83. He became the squadron's acting CO when the squadron was reorganized to VBF-83. (Official U.S. Navy Photo)

In fact, this is often claimed to be the last aerial victory of World War II.

Lt. Reidy was awarded the following decorations: Navy Cross; Distinguished Flying Cross with Four Gold Stars; and the Air Medal with Nine Gold Stars.

LIEUT JOE DRAPER ROBBINS, USNR, was born on March 24, 1921, in Chester, South Carolina. After attending Clemston College in South Carolina, he entered the Navy for flight training on February 10, 1942. After three months at Atlanta he was then transferred to NAS Jacksonville to complete his training.

Graduating in December 1942, Ensign Robbins completed carrier qualifications at Norfolk, Virginia.

By April 1945 Lieutenant Robbins was flying a Corsair with VF-85, aboard *USS Shangri La*, CV-38. On 11 May he encountered a flight of Zeros near Okinawa. He maneuvered into a favorable position and scored two of the enemy fighters and damaged another.

As the damaged Zero skimmed the South China Sea it bounced up and became airborne at a low altitude. Robbins, who had been following the damaged plane, fired a burst at the damaged Zero, and it struck the water again but bounced up again. Another burst from the American's guns forced the Zero down to the water, and it skimmed again but then sank out of sight.

Robbins remained in the Navy following the end of World War II and was promoted to lieutenant commander on February 1, 1952. LCDR Robbins retired from the Navy in June 1963 and entered the real estate business in Escondido, California.

Lieut Joe Draper Robbins, USNR, completed his U.S. Navy flight training at Atlanta and Jacksonville. During his term of service he was based on *USS Shangri La* CV-38 and scored five confirmed victories. (U.S. Navy Photo, Author's File)

Lieut John William Ruhsam, USMC, enlisted in the U.S. Naval flight training program and scored his initial victory during his first combat mission on April 12, 1945. Remaining in the Marines after WWII, he returned to combat in the Korean War and retired with the rank of colonel in 1969. He is shown adding Victory Flags to his Corsair. (USMC Photo, Author's File)

Chapter IX: Corsair Aviators and Decorations

Joe D Robbins scored five confirmed victories and one damaged adversary.

He was awarded the following decorations: Distinguished Flying Cross with one Gold Star and the Air Medal with seven Gold Stars.

LIEUT JOHN WILLIAM RUHSAM, USMC, was born on September 7, 1922, in Albert Lea, Minnesota. He enlisted in the Naval flight training program while he was still a student at Iowa State College. He received his wings and Second Lieutenant commission in the Marine Corps on October 1, 1943.

Lt. Ruhsam was assigned to VMF-323 the "Death Rattlers" of the Second Marine Aircraft Wing early in 1945.

Ruhsam scored his first aerial victory during his first combat mission on April 12, 1945, scoring a Zero. Three days later he scored a Tony.

Remaining in the Marines after World War II, he returned to combat during the Korean Conflict from April 17 to September 24, 1952. He retired from the Marine Corps with the rank of colonel in 1969.

John W. Ruhsam scored seven confirmed victories and three damaged enemy aircraft.

He was awarded the following decorations: Navy Cross; Distinguished Flying Cross; and the Air Medal with four Gold Stars.

HAROLD EDWARD SEGAL, USMCR, was born on Sept 1, 1920, in Chicago, Illinois; however, he grew up in New York City. He attended Pratt Institute in New York for two years. In September 1941 he enlisted in the U.S. Naval Reserve for aviation duty and, upon the completion of his training in October 1942, was commissioned a second lieutenant in the Marine Corps Reserve and designated a Naval Aviator.

Lt. "Manny" Segal was sent to the Solomon Islands in May 1943 to join VMF-221, flying Corsairs with the Fighting Falcons.

"Manny" scored a Zero and a Betty, and was credited with a probable Betty on 30 June.

Segal shot down three Zeros on 11 July with two more scored on 6 August.

VMF-221 was withdrawn from combat for a brief period and returned to action in October, when Segal destroyed three Judy dive bombers on November 17, 1943.

When VMF-221 was removed from combat, so "Murderous Manny" transferred to VMF-122 to complete his combat tour. He shot down his final pair of Hamp fighters on January 24, 1944.

He returned to the U.S. upon the completion of his combat tour, serving at MCAS El Toro until April 1945, when he returned to combat in the rank of captain with VMF-115 in the Philippines.

Detached from active duty in March 1946, "Manny" remained in the Marine Reserves. Promoted to major in September 1951, Segal retired on August 7, 1958.

Major Segal scored 12 confirmed victories and one probable victory.

He was awarded the following decorations: Distinguished Flying Cross with three Gold Stars; Purple Heart; and the Air Medal with three Gold Stars.

EDWARD OLIVER "BUD" SHAW, USMC, was born in Bloomer, Wisconsin, on January 20, 1920. "Bud" Shaw attended Gonzaga University in Spokane, Washington, before he joined the Naval Aviation Cadet program. He received his wings and was commissioned a lieutenant in the U.S. Marine Corps on September 4, 1942, at Corpus Christi, Texas.

"Bud" Shaw was assigned to VMF-213 Hellhawks, which he joined in Guadalcanal in 1943 under Major Gregory Weisenberger.

Flying Corsairs, Lt. Shaw scored his first three victories on June 30, 1943—three float biplanes. Another triple victory was attained on July 15, 1943, when Shaw scored two Bettys and a Zero. Two days later, on July 17, 1943, "Bud" scored a Zero, a float biplane, and a float monoplane. On the following day, Lt. Shaw was credited with two Zeros and a probable Zero.

The squadron was withdrawn from combat on July 18, 1943, for R&R and returned to Guadalcanal on September 5, 1943, at which time Shaw continued his scoring, along with a Zero on 11 September and a shared Zero on 23 September, plus a final Zero on 11 October.

This was his last victory and the last victory scored by VMF-213 in the Solomons. The squadron returned to the United States in December 1943, during which time he served as squadron commander.

On July 31, 1944, Squadron leader Shaw was testing a Corsair that had been reported erratic in flight, and the Squadron Leader put the plane through every conceivable maneuver without a problem until he put the plane into a dive from 20,000 feet. The expert aviator was unable to pull the Corsair out of the dive and perished in the crash.

Edward O Shaw scored 14 ½ victories and one probable victory.

He was awarded the following decorations: Distinguished Flying Cross with one Gold Star, and the Air Medal with two Gold Stars.

Harold Edward Segal, USMCR, was so short that his feet often slipped off the rudder pedals in the heat of battle; yet, this cool-headed "dogfighter" scored twelve confirmed victories and one "probable" (many of which were fighters). Lieut "Manny" Segal is shown with his Corsair. (USMC Photo)

Lieut Edward Oliver "Bud" Shaw, USMC, scored many of his 14.5 victories in doubles and triples. He received his wings and was commissioned a lieutenant in the U.S. Marine Corps on Sept 4, 1942. His first three victories were scored on June 30, 1943. His final victory, scored on October 11, 1943, was the final victory of his squadron (VMF-213) in the Solomons. (USMC Photo, Author's File)

Capt William Nugent "Luke" Snider, USMC, was assigned to fly with VMF-221 "Fighting Falcons," from which he scored most of his 11 ½ victories. When VMF-221 reorganized in January 1944 and embarked on USS Bunker Hill in December 1944, Nugent flew over Japan from USS Bunker Hill, scoring a Betty bomber and two fighters, which made him a double-ace. (USMC Photo, Author's File)

WILLIAM NUGENT "LUKE" SNIDER, USMC, was born in Cairo, Illinois, on December 12, 1918. Upon completing the U.S. Navy flight training program at Pensacola he was commissioned a second lieutenant in the U.S. Marine Corps on May 22, 1942, and assigned to VMF-221 "Fighting Falcons."

The Squadron departed for Guadalcanal on February 11, 1943, and was supplied with Corsairs.

"Luke" Snider scored his first victories during the Bougainville invasion when he downed three Zeros on April 1, 1943.

After his promotion to Captain, "Luke" scored two Zeros and a third as a "probable."

VMF-221 reorganized in January 1944 and embarked on *USS Bunker Hill* in December 1944.

The Squadron covered the Iwo Jima landings and the Okinawa Invasion. It also took part in the first naval mission against Tokyo.

Snider scored again when he shared the destruction of a Betty bomber over Japan on February 16, 1945.

"Luke" downed two Frank fighters and one Zero over Tomtaka airfield on 18 March and scored a Tony on 6 April near Kyushu. On 16 April Capt Snyder downed a Tojo and a Zero to make him a double Ace.

Capt Snider returned to civilian life following World War II and became employed by Stover Company until his passing in March 1969.

William N Snider scored 11 ½ victories and one probable victory.

He was awarded the following decorations: Silver Star; Distinguished Flying Cross with two Gold Stars; and the Air Medal with Five Gold Stars.

MAJOR EDWIN LAWRENCE "OLIE" OLANDER, USMCR, was born in Northhampton, Massachusetts, on March 27, 1917. He graduated from Amherst in 1938 and worked as a newspaper reporter before joining the Navy at NAS Glenview on September 26, 1941. After winning his wings at Opa Locka, Florida, on June 18, 1942, he served as a flight instructor from August 1942 to May 1943 at Jacksonville.

Lt. Olander was assigned to VMF-214 "Swashbucklers" on August 7, 1943. After training in the Corsair, the squadron moved to the Russell Islands on September 11, 1943, to begin its third combat tour; however, the squadron was disbanded and No. VMF-214 was given to the "Black Sheep."

Flying from Munda, New Georgia, as a "Black Sheep" Olander scored his first victory on October 10, 1943, when he scored a Zero. Another Zero fell to Olie's guns three days later.

Having completed his combat tour, Olander moved to Green Island and then back to El Toro to train in carrier landings for the planned invasion of Japan that was later deemed unnecessary.

Major Olander was released from active duty in November 1945.

He returned to Southampton, opened a building materials business and became mayor of Southampton.

Chapter IX: Corsair Aviators and Decorations

Maj Edwin Lawrence "Olie" Olander, USMCR, earned his wings at Apa Locka, FL, and was assigned to VMF-214 "Swashbucklers" in time to begin the squadron's third tour. Olander moved to the "Black Sheep" with the number VMF-214 as Swashbucklers disbanded. (U.S. Defense Dept Photo, Marine Corps)

Major Donald Hooten Stapp, USMCR, won his wings and commission as second lieutenant on June 3, 1941. He served with VMF-222 "Flying Deuces" in 1943 and scored his first victories on 14 September when he downed two Zeros. He became an Ace on Feb 3, 1944, when he scored a Zero and a probable. He was CO of VMF-122 at Peleliu from May 28, 1945, to the War's end. (USMC Photo, Author's File)

Edwin Olander scored five confirmed victories.

He was awarded the following decorations: Distinguished Flying Cross and the Air Medal.

Note: Don was born Donald Sapp; however, later in life he had his name legally changed to Stapp. Despite this, many official documents and records still revert to his original family name.

MAJOR DONALD HOOTEN SAPP (STAPP), USMC, was born in Center Hill, Florida, on December 29, 1915. After attending the University of Miami for four years he joined the Marine Corps Reserve in June 1935. Accepted as an aviation cadet in August 1940, he began flight training at Pensacola. He won his wings and commission as a second lieutenant on June 3, 1941.

As a major, Stapp was assigned to fly Corsairs in VMF-222 "Flight Deuces" in 1943. His first victories were scored on 14 September when he downed two Zeros. A third Zeke was scored over Kahili airfield on 11 October, and he destroyed a Helen near Bougainville on 20 November 20.

Major Sapp scored one Zero and a probable to become an Ace on February 3, 1944. During the next five weeks he scored five more Zeros.

On June 1, 1944, Sapp became commander of VMF-524 and then was CO of VMF-122 at Peleliu from May 28, 1945, to the war's end.

Promoted to lieutenant colonel in January 1951, Sapp was active in special projects and flew with the Navy's first atomic weapons squadron, VC-5, over the Atlantic and Pacific oceans.

Col Sapp also served as chief of staff, Ninth Marine Expeditionary Brigade, and deputy chief of staff, Third Marine Amphibious Force at Danang in Vietnam.

Donald Sapp retired from the Marine Corps with the rank of colonel on July 1, 1968.

Colonel Sapp expired due to heart failure on February 26, 1988, in Santa Ana, California.

Donald Sapp scored ten confirmed victories, four probable, and two damaged enemy aircraft.

He was awarded the following decorations: Navy Cross; Distinguished Flying Cross with one Gold Star; and the Air Medal with two Gold Stars.

CAPT HAROLD LEMAN "HAL" SPEARS was born on December 31, 1919, in Porsmouth, Ohio. Harold grew up in Ironton, Ohio, where the family moved when Hal was quite young.

While he was a senior football star at Ohio University, young Spears decided to enlist in the U.S. Naval Reserve as an aviation cadet and apply for Marine Corps flight training in 1940. He completed flight training at NAS Corpus Christi, Texas, on August 21, 1942, and became a Marine Reserve Second Lieutenant.

Capt Harold Leman "Hal" Spears, USMC, was one of the "Hot Aces" of VMF-215 "Fighting Corsairs." The former football star scored 15 victories before he died in an airplane accident. (U.S. Defense Dept Photo, Author's File)

Capt James Elms Swett, USMCR, won his wings and second lieutenant commission in the Marine Corps Reserve on April 16, 1942. Assigned to VMF-221 "Fighting Falcons," Swett scored seven enemy aircraft in one combat on April 7, 1943! Flying a Corsair, Capt Swett continued scoring multiple victories totaling eight, including one shot down while based on USS *Bunker Hill*. (U.S. Defense Dept, Marine Corps Photo, Author's File)

Hal was assigned to VMF-215 "Fighting Corsairs." The squadron arrived at Espiritu Santo in February 1943, and then went to Guadalcanal, in the Solomon Islands, on July 24 1943 supplied with the F4U-1 corsair fighter. At this time the Corsairs were used effectively by VMF-215 to strafe enemy positions and support Marine Troopers, as well as to destroy enemy aerial resistance.

Lt. Spears scored his first four Zeros over Bougainville on August 18 and 19, and on September 2, 1943.

Hal was promoted to captain in December 1943. As a division leader on February 3, 1944, he was responsible to escort bombers to their target. With the Corsairs heavily outnumbered, Spears went after the intercepting Japanese with relentless fury, breaking up the attack on the bombers. During the melee he shot down two more Japanese planes.

Spears destroyed his fifteenth and final Zero over Rabaul on February 7, 1944.

The Ace was ordered to the Marine Corps Air Station, El Toro, California, in February 1944. On November 1, 1944, Spears was integrated into the regular Marine Corps and planned to make a career in this outstanding service. He was assigned to training squadron VMF-462 as a flight officer, pending another tour of duty in the Pacific.

On December 6, 1944, Captain Spears had just completed a routine flight in an SBD-5 dive bomber and was landing when the plane crashed into the ground, killing the Ace and severely injuring his passenger, another VMF-215 Ace, Major Arthur T. Warner.

Capt Spears scored fifteen confirmed and three probable victories.

He was awarded the following decorations: Distinguished Flying Cross and the Air Medal with one Gold Star.

CAPT JAMES ELMS SWETT, USMCR, was born on June 15, 1920, in Seattle, Washington. He was attending San Mateo Junior College in California when he left, during his second year, to enter Navy flight training. He won his wings and was commissioned a second lieutenant, US Marine Corps Reserve, at Corpus Christi, Texas, on April 16, 1942.

Assigned to VMF-221 "Fighting Falcons," Swett arrived at Guadalcanal on March 16, 1943. It was less than three weeks later, on April 7, 1943, that he established a record-smashing day in the annals of aerial combat.

Leading a four-plane division of Wildcats, he spotted a large formation of Japanese aircraft flying below. Swett led his section down to attack Val bombers and scored three on the first run. As he regained altitude Jim Swett realized that his plane had been hit and began to return to base; however, he sighted five more Vals and dived behind the flight. He downed four, and as he planned to dispatch the fifth the Val's rear gunner damaged the Wildcat's windshield. This forced Swett to ditch his plane, and he was rescued by an American patrol boat.

Seven victories in one combat was deserving of the Medal of Honor.

Chapter IX: Corsair Aviators and Decorations

Ensign Frederick James Streig, USNR, joined the Navy on Jan 9, 1942, after completing the Navy's flight training program. He was assigned to VF-17 "Jolly Rogers" flying land-based Corsairs. LTJG Streig became an Ace when he shot down two Zeros over Rabaul. He remained in the Navy after WWII, serving on two aircraft carriers, and retired with the rank of Commander. (U.S. Navy Photograph, Author's File)

LIEUT Wilbur Jackson "GUS" Thomas, USMCR, enlisted in the U.S. Naval Reserve as a Seaman. He was accepted for U.S. Marine flight training in November 23, 1942. Lieut Thomas was assigned to VMF-213 "Hellhawks," which entered a major combat event on June 30, 1943, during which Lt Thomas scored four Zeros. His total of 18 ½ victories equaled the best Corsair aviators. (USMC Photo, Author's File)

When Capt Swett transitioned to the Corsair he continued scoring multiple victories that totaled eight, including a Jill that he scored when based on *USS Bunker Hill* in 1945.

James Swett scored 15 ½ confirmed victories, four probable, and ¼ damaged.

He was awarded the following decorations: Medal of Honor; Distinguished Flying Cross with five Gold Stars; Purple Heart with one Gold Star; Air Medal with 21 Gold Stars; Presidential Unit Citation; and a Navy Unit Citation.

LIEUT (JG) FREDERICK JAMES STREIG, USNR, was born in Sacramento, California, on April 24, 1921. After completing the Navy's flight training program at Corpus Christi, Texas, in October 1941, Ensign Streig joined the Navy on January 9, 1942. He was assigned to VF-17 "Jolly Rogers" flying land-based Corsairs in October 1943.

Ensign Streig's first combat experience was on November 1, 1943, when he shared a victory with LTJG Tom Killefer. He scored a Tony and a Zero, then damaged another Zero and a Hamp on 11 November.

On January 27, 1944, LTJG Streig became an Ace when he shot down two Zeros and shared credit for a third over Rabaul.

Streig remained in the Navy after World War II, serving on two aircraft carriers; served as aircraft maintenance officer at NAS Pensacola; and nuclear operations officer for CinCLant, Western Sea Frontier prior to retirement in July 1969 with the grade of commander.

Commander Streig died of tuberculosis in Livermore, California, on August 31, 1995.

LTJG Frederick Streig scored 5 ½ confirmed victories and two damaged.

He was awarded the following decorations: Distinguished Flying Cross with two Gold Stars and the Air Medal with five Gold Stars.

WILBUR JACKSON "GUS" THOMAS, USMCR, was born on October 29, 1920, in El Dorado, Kansas.

He enlisted in the U.S. Naval Reserve as a Seaman second class at Kansas City, Kansas, on September 18, 1941. "Gus" applied for U.S, Marine flight training in November 1941 and won his "Wings of Gold" and second lieutenant's commission on September 23, 1942, at NAS Corpus Christi, Texas.

Lieut. Thomas was assigned to VMF-213 "Hellhawks," Marine Aircraft Group Eleven, First Marine Wing. Little did "Gus" imagine that he was destined to become the Eighth ranking Marine Corps Ace of World War II.

Thomas was promoted to First Lieutenant in May 1943.

Capt Robert Wade, USMC, was no different from the readers and the author of this book. Bob spent weekends and summer vacation from high school working at the local airport to pay for flying lessons. Upon graduation from High School in June 1942 Bob Wade entered the Naval Aviation Cadet Program and emerged a Marine Corps second lieutenant. He won his wings on October 23, 1943. 2nd Lt Wade was assigned to Major Axtell's VMF-323 "Death Rattlers" on Okiwana. This "Corsair Jockey" scored his first victory on April 15, 1945, and when he shot down three Nate fighters on May 4, 1945, he was an Ace! (USMC Photo, Author's File)

Capt Kenneth Ambrose Walsh elevated himself from a Marine Corps aviation mechanic to a twenty-one victory flying Ace awarded the Medal of Honor. After the Pearl Harbor attack, Warrant Officer Walsh was sent to the Solomon Islands with VMF-124 as a second lieutenant. He became an Ace on May 13, 1943, and was promoted to first lieutenant. Multiple scoring and promotions led to the Medal of Honor. (Official USMC Photo, Author's File)

Led by Major Gregory Weisenberger, the "Hellhawks" entered their first major combat event on June 30, 1943, during which Lt. Thomas scored four Zero fighters of the 20 shot down by the squadron over Rendova.

On July 2, 1943, "Gus" contributed greatly to the destruction of a Japanese cargo ship by strafing it repeatedly.

Lt. Thomas scored two Zeros and a Betty on 15 July, plus three more Zeros over Bougainville on September 11, 1943. Twelve days later he downed three more Zeros.

By 1944 Wilbur Thomas was promoted to the rank of captain when VMF-213 deployed for its second tour, flying from USS Essex (CV-9).

Capt Thomas continued scoring until, at the end of the war, his 18 ½ victories equaled that of Major Marion Carl.

Thomas remained in the service following World War II. While based at El Toro, California, he was testing a Grumman Tigercat on January 28, 1947, when he was caught in a blinding rainstorm.

The Tigercat struck Old Saddleback Mountain at 4,200 feet, killing Capt Thomas and his passenger. So ended a life that had cheated death in mortal combat, only to succumb to it in an accident.

Capt Thomas scored 18 ½ confirmed victories, 3 ½ probables, and three damaged.

He was awarded the following decorations: Navy Cross; Distinguished Flying Cross with One Gold Star; and the Air Medal with one Gold Star.

CAPT ROBERT WADE, USMC, was born in Jenkintown, Pennsylvania, on October 31, 1923. As with many young air-minded youth, including the author, Bob Wade spent weekends and summer vacations from high school working at the airport to pay for flying lessons.

Upon graduation from Elkins Park High School, Pennsylvania, in June 1942, Bob Wade entered the Naval Aviation Cadet program. Upon completion of the program he was commissioned a Marine Corps second lieutenant and "won his wings" on October 23, 1943.

Originally assigned to fly Douglas SBD Dauntless dive-bombers, Wade was diverted to fly Corsairs with Major Axtell's VMF-323 "Death Rattlers" on Okinawa, arriving on the island in April 1945.

Wade scored his first victories on April 15, 1945, when he destroyed two Tony fighters. He followed this with two Val bombers and two Nate fighters, plus damaging three other Nate fighters on May 4, 1945. He was now an Ace.

Captain Wade was released to inactive duty in January 1946, but he returned to active duty that October for combat in Korea. He scored his final victory, a MiG-15, on January 20, 1953.

He worked for McDonnell Douglas after medical retirement and died on November 10, 1991.

Capt Wade scored eight confirmed victories: seven with the Corsair and one with the F-86 Sabre.

Chapter IX: Corsair Aviators and Decorations

He was awarded the following decorations: Navy Cross; Distinguished Flying Cross with one Gold Star; and the Air Medal with five Gold Stars.

CAPT KENNETH AMBROSE WALSH was born in Brooklyn, New York, on November 24, 1916. He enlisted in the Marine Corps as an aviation mechanic and radioman on December 15, 1933. Two years later he was accepted for aviator training, joining Class 89-E on March 1936 at Pensacola, Florida, and graduated in April 1937 as a Naval Aviation Aviator.

Promoted to corporal, he served in scout and observation squadrons for four years aboard USS *Yorktown*, *Wasp*, and *Ranger* before being promoted to Warrant Officer.

When the Japanese attacked Pearl Harbor, Walsh was serving with VMF-122 and transferred to VMF-124 in September 1942. He was shipped overseas in January 1943 for duty in the Solomon Islands as a second lieutenant.

Walsh was particularly active in aerial combat in the Vella La Vella area and, by 1 April, the Tyro scored two Zeros and a Val during a midday engagement and became an Ace on May 13, 1943, by destroying three more Zeros.

He was promoted to first lieutenant in June 1943.

Multiple conquests became the norm until Walsh was credited with twenty confirmed victories and was recommended for the Medal of Honor. Walsh was promoted to Captain in February 1944.

Major Gregory Weissenberger, USMC, was commissioned second lieutenant upon graduation from college. He became a major when he was CO of VMF-213 "Hellhawks" flying Corsairs in the Solomons. He retired as head of the personnel branch of the Division of Aviation with the rank of Brigadier General. (USMC Photo, Author's File)

After completing three combat tours Walsh returned to CONUS, where he served as an instructor at Jacksonville, Florida, until he was reassigned to VMF-222 "Flying Deuces" in April 1945, flying fighter-bomber missions from Samar, Philippines, and in the Okinawa campaign.

In March 1946 he was assigned to the Burean of Aeronautics, Navy Department. After more than three years with the Bureau of Aeronautics, Walsh joined the First Marine Aircraft Wing, Fleet Marine Force, in January 1949 as Assistant Group Engineering Officer at El Toro, Santa Ana, California. He also went overseas with this group on July 15, 1950, shortly after the Korean conflict as Assistant Engineering Officer. Capt Walsh returned to El Toro in late July 1951, remaining there until April 1, 1952, when he was transferred to Staff, Commander Air Force, U.S. Atlantic Fleet, Norfolk, Virginia, as Marine Liaison Officer for Aircraft Material and Maintenance.

He was promoted to Major during September 1955, when he was assigned as Aircraft Maintenance and Repair Officer and Transport Commander.

Major Walsh was the Wing Aircraft Maintenance Officer of the First Marine Aircraft Wing, Aircraft, Fleet Marine Force, Pacific, from January 1959 until April 1960.

The Ace retired on February 1, 1962, as a lieutenant colonel while serving in Japan with the first Marine Air Wing.

Kenneth A Walsh scored 21 confirmed victories and one damaged enemy aircraft.

He was awarded the following Decorations: Medal of Honor; Distinguished Flying Cross with 8 Gold Stars; and the Air Medal with 14 Gold Stars.

MAJOR GREGORY JOSEPH WEISSENBERGER, USMC, was born in Dallas, Texas, on August 16, 1914. He enlisted in the Marine Corps on June 7, 1934, after graduating from La Crosse high school and La Crosse State Teacher's College. He was commissioned as a second lieutenant on July 1, 1937.

Weissenberger began flight training at Pensacola, Florida, in August 1940 and was designated a Naval Aviator on February 25, 1941.

He had been promoted to a major by the time he became XO of VMF-213 "Hellhawks" in December 1942.

Weissenberger commanded VMF-213, flying Corsairs in the Solomons from April to August 1943. He scored three Zeros on 30 June before being shot down himself. Bailing out from below one thousand feet, he struck the tail of his Corsair but was rescued by an American destroyer. The Major shot down three Zeros on 11 and 18 July to become an Ace.

Upon completing his combat tour, the Major served as supply officer of MAG 11 and operations officer of MAG 12, followed by XO of Marine Corps Air Base on New Hebrides.

He returned to CONUS in 1944 as a lieutenant colonel.

After World War II he remained in the Marine Corps and was promoted to colonel in November 1951. In June 1953 he joined the personnel branch of the Division of Aviation, becoming its head in July 1953. He served in that capacity until his retirement on November 1, 1954, with the rank of brigadier general. He died on September 17, 1985, in California.

Gregory Weissenberger scored five confirmed victories.

He was awarded the following decorations: Distinguished Flying Cross with two Gold Stars; Purple Heart; Air Medal with eight Gold Stars; and the Chinese Service Medal.

A youthful Otto Keith (OK) Williams, USMCR, poses with his first Corsair. The smile on his face reflects the joy in flying this superlative fighter. He studied Maj Gen Geiger's order: "The reason Marines have airplanes is to assist the Marine Trooper." Williams was a "down to earth" Marine, facing withering antiaircraft fire at low altitudes. Keith's nickname at this time was "Pootwoodle"! (Col Keith Williams Photo, Courtesy Col Williams)

LT COL OTTO (OK) KEITH WILLIAMS, USMCR, was born in Tacoma, Washington, on December 10, 1918, and was raised in Ellensburg, Washington, where he attended local schools through Central Washington University, winning varsity letters in basketball and other sports.

Immediately after the Pearl Harbor attack he joined the U.S. Marine Corps during his second year at college. Williams conducted flight training at the Marine Corps Air Station in Santa Barbara, California.

He was assigned to VMF-214 "Swashbucklers" and discovered that the commander of the Marine Corps Air Force, Maj Gen Roy S Geiger, ordered that: "The reason Marines have airplanes is to assist the Marine Trooper."

Williams studied strafing techniques until he achieved perfection.

After serving two tours of duty in VMF-214 "Swashbucklers," Williams began his third tour in VMF-215 "Fighting Corsairs" because the VMF-214 squadron number had been given to Major Gregory Boyington's new squadron, "Black Sheep."

Lt. Williams continued his concentration on strafing military equipment and low-level troop support, obeying orders or volunteering. He was truly a "down to earth" aviator.

By 1944 Capt Williams transferred to VMF-351 "fighting Bulldogs," commanded by Lt. Col Donald Yost. The squadron was based on one of the first "Corsair Carriers," USS Cape Gloucester (CVE-109), which made a sortie from Okinawa to Shanghai, China.

After Williams was a veteran of over 100 combat missions he was honorably discharged in 1946, but remained in the reserves for seventeen additional years until he retired with the rank of lieutenant colonel.

Having concentrated in dangerous strafing, Col Williams scored no aerial victories; however, he was awarded the Air Medal.

LIEUT COL DONALD KEITH YOST, USMC, was born in Bethesda, Pennsylvania, on December 16, 1911. After graduating from Princeton University in 1934, he was accepted for flight training in July 1934; however, he was delayed until July 15, 1935, for lack of congressional funding. Donald Yost was commissioned as a second lieutenant in the Marine Corps on July 1, 1936. He made his first flight in October 1936.

Initially assigned to VF-9M, he was later transferred to VMF-2. Yost was on his way to Wake Island when the Japanese bombed Pearl Harbor and was assigned to VMF-111 when he arrived. Promoted to major on August 7, 1941, he became CO of VMF-111 on 5 October.

Transferred in Mid-December 1941, Don Yost led VMF-121 from Henderson field, Guadalcanal, into Japanese-held areas, scoring his first victories (two Zeros) on December 23, 1942. On the following day Yost shot down four more Zeros to become an Ace.

Promoted to lieutenant colonel on January 1, 1943, Yost commanded VMF-121 from 1 January to 12 March and MAG-51 from September 1 to October 17, 1944. After that, he commanded MCVG-4, flying Corsairs in the Okinawa area aboard USS Cape Gloucester (CVE-109).

Lieut Col Donald Keith Yost, USMC, was on his way to Wake Island when Pearl Harbor was attacked. He became an Ace when he led VMF-121 from Henderson field and commanded MCVG-4 flying from USS Cape Gloucester. He scored his two final victories over the East China Sea flying from USS Cape Gloucester. His final score was eight victories. (USMC Photo, Courtesy Col Keith Williams)

Chapter IX: Corsair Aviators and Decorations

He shot down his two final victories in the East China Sea when he scored a Judy on July 23, 1945, and a Francis on August 5, 1945.

Lt. Col Yost scored eight confirmed victories.

He was awarded the following decorations: Silver Star with one Gold Star; Legion of Merit with Combat "V"; Distinguished Flying Cross with two Gold Stars; and the Air Medal with 12 Gold Stars.

Corsair Mechanics and Technicians

It would have been impossible for the Corsair aviator to achieve their astounding victories and other successes without the maintenance and repair necessary to keep their complex fighter planes in the air.

The tireless efforts of the nameless, dedicated workers and craftsmen, working in blistering heat or freezing cold, are saluted here:

Seven VMF-213 aces pose before one of their Corsairs on July 30, 1943, at the end of the squadron's second tour. Standing (left to right) are: Capt James N Cupp (12.5 Vict); unidentified; Major Gregory Joseph Weissenberger (5.0 Vict); and 1st Lt Milton Norwood Vedder (16.0 Vict). Kneeling are: 1st Lt John Luther Morgan Jr (8.5 Vict); Lt Edward O Shaw (14.5 Vict); and Lt Wilbur J Thomas (18.5 Vict). (Dept of Defense, USMC, via National Archives)

This Corsair appears to be receiving a general inspection and overhaul, rather than repair of serious damage on Feb. 6, 1944. Note the aviator's seat on the ground and the inspector standing in the bladder fuel tank (arrows). Note that the Port (left) wing has been removed by the hoist. U.S. Defense Dept. (U.S. Marine Corps Photo by T Sgt Douglas White)

The Port (left) side of the Corsair receiving a general inspection on Feb. 6, 1944, reveals the portable hoist as an Ordnance specialist inspects the guns. Observe the two ammo boxes in the foreground. This Corsair was flown by members of VMF-211. (U.S. Defense Dept. U.S. Marine Corps Photo by T Sgt Douglas White)

Nose down in a drainage ditch, this Corsair appears undamaged; however, hidden damage could affect the propeller, engine mounts, engine cowl, and landing gear, plus other parts of the aircraft that only the mechanics can identify. (U.S. Defense Dept. U.S. Marine Corps)

Battle damage requires virtual reconstruction of the airframe by expert mechanics. Very often the mechanics must refer to factory drawings in order to reconstruct areas badly damaged by enemy fire or crashes.

In addition to repairing damage caused by accident or battle, periodical maintenance is most important to keep the Corsair in flying condition. Items such as as greasing, checking oil content, air in tires, wiping excess oil from guns, checking ammunition, and dozens of other important maintenance items are mandatory.

Probably the most important maintenance item is testing the boresight of the guns. The aviator often flew a different plane in each flight, and as

This FG-1A Corsair made a wheels-up landing on a crushed coral airstrip on Peleliu. The plane is being gently lifted by a portable hoist prior to an undersides inspection. Observe the men holding the horizontal stabilizer and the wing tips to steady the plane for the inspectors. (USMC Photo via Albert L. Lewis)

Chapter IX: Corsair Aviators and Decorations

Royal New Zealand Air Force mechanics work on Corsair engines in a temporary workshop shed. Observe the Marston Mat flooring on the earth. The shed is sturdy enough to steady the upright engine in the foreground. Note the chain attached to the propeller shaft. (RNZAF Photo, Courtesy RNZAF)

A USMC mechanic adds grease to Corsair landing gear fittings while another technician works on cockpit controls. The Ingersol-Rand air compressor (foreground-right) forces the grease into the lubricated joints. Grease is stored in the black, vertical tank near the mechanic. (Official U.S. Marine corps Photo by Tech Sgt Douglas White, Courtesy Ingersol-Rand Corp.)

Bore-sighting of the six Corsair machine-guns is a most important operation because the guns shift slightly when fired. The entire plane is trussed to a tail-high position in a cradle structure. Observe the block and tackle hoist and the supporting structure of finished lumber and coconut palm tree logs. (USMC Photo, Courtesy Col. O.K. Williams)

Many tasks are necessary to keep Corsairs in the air and fighting. This Marine Ordnance crew is unloading heavy crates of .50 Calibre armor piercing machine gun cartridges. Without the effort of these Marines the Corsairs would be impotent. (U.S. Defense Dept. Photo, Author's File)

soon as the aviator was assigned a plane he must check the boresight. Very often the new plane wasn't shooting dead-on—possibly two or three mils at 3 o'clock or 9 o'clock—and the aviator had to remember the guns' offset in the next fight. Not too good!

The guns also often shifted when fired. All six guns fired simultaneously; however, there might be one or more wild guns, in which case it didn't matter if the boresight was off! The ordance department had great responsibility.

Awards and Medals

Man's reward for acts of bravery, exceptional knowledge, athletic prowness, and outstanding military service are, and have been for centuries, certificates, colorful ribbons, and/or medals.

The following are the American awards presented to Corsair aviators for action beyond the call of duty or exceptional bravery:

MEDAL OF HONOR is the highest United States award for bravery to U.S. Army, U.S. Air Force, U.S. Navy, and U.S. Marine heroes. It is awarded for "gallantry and intrepidity at the risk of life above and beyond the call of duty."

NAVY CROSS is awarded only to U.S. Navy and U.S. Marine personnel, and is the second highest award in the United States. It is awarded for "extraordinary heroism in connection with military operations against an armed enemy."

DISTINGUISHED SERVICE MEDAL is the third highest United States Award for "exceptionally meritorious service to the Government in a duty of great responsibility."

SILVER STAR was first issued in 1932, and is the fourth highest United States medal; awarded to U.S. Army, Navy, and Marine personnel for "gallantry and intrepidity in action."

Chapter IX: Corsair Aviators and Decorations

LEGION of MERIT is the fifth highest United States medal. It is awarded for "exceptionally meritorious conduct in the performance of outstanding services."

DISTINGUISHED FLYING CROSS is the sixth highest among United States medals, and is awarded to Air Force, Army, Navy, and Marine aviators for "heroism or extraordinary achievement while participating in aerial flight."

AIR MEDAL is awarded for "meritorious achievements while participating in aerial flight." It is ninth highest among United States medals.

The ORDER of THE PURPLE HEART was established by George Washington in 1782 and was received in 1932. It is awarded to members of the armed forces who are honorably wounded in action against the enemy.

X

Surviving Corsair Aviators

We have met the brave and talented Corsair Aviators who tested the amazing corsair, and those who fought a determined enemy in the Bent-Wing Fighter in previous chapters. Now, we will meet the men who have escaped death in testing or in battle and survived the wars flying the Corsair.

The author omitted personal statistics, such as date and place of birth and so forth, during aviators' historical and personal coverage in order not to interfere with his heroic activities. Therefore, the personal information and other history is presented here for those readers who are interested in these statistics.

Special Note

The author believes that the aviator who flew the Corsair in its formative years and risked it all to convert this spectacular design into a one-of-its-kind fighter-bomber deserves to lead the list of great Corsair aviators:

BOONE T. GUYTON was the surviving Corsair aviator who was the Bent-Wing's Primary Test Pilot. He flew the Corsair on virtually all its early test flights and suffered the physical and mental anguish necessary to tame the racehorse into an obedient stallion.

Guyton entered the Navy's Aviation Cadet program in 1935 with Class 81C, graduating tenth in a class of 42 who completed the course out of 75 initial candidates.

During his three years of active service, Boone served in dive-bomber squadrons assigned to USS *Lexington* (CV-2) and *Saratoga* (CV-3). He was released to inactive duty in 1939 when he accepted the position of test pilot for Chance Vought Aircraft, where he tested the V-156 version of the SBU-1 Vindicator dive-bomber. He also trained French pilots on the Vindicator at the start of World War II.

After a brief job as an airline pilot, Boone returned to Vought to begin a long association with the Corsair.

He started with the XF4U-1 program and made the first flight of the F4U-1. Guyton continued test flying through World War II, testing the post-war Vought designs as the F6U-1 Pirate and F7U-1 Cutlass, as well as later models of the F4U and AU Corsair.

Upon leaving Vought, Guyton was briefly associated with Norden Laboratories before returning to Vought, where he assisted in forming United Aircraft's Missiles and Space Division.

After 46 years and more than 7,000 hours of flying he wrote several books and lived with his wife in Woodridge, CT, until he passed away on April 4, 1996.

COL JOHN F. "JACK" BOLT, USMC (Ret), is the only jet ace in Marine Aviation history and the only man in U.S. Naval Aviation history to become an ace in two wars: World War II and the Korean Conflict.

Following World War II "Jack" Bolt remained in the Marine Corps as an aviator, flying Corsairs based on the "Corsair Carrier" *USS Badoeng Strait* (CVE-116).

Boone T Guyton was the Corsair's Primary Test Pilot, and he flew the Corsair XF4U-1 and F4U-1 on most of the test flights. He also tested the Vought Pirate and Cutlass jet-powered fighters. (Vought Aircraft Photo, Courtesy Arthur L Schoeni)

Chapter X: Surviving Corsair Aviators

Lt Col John F Bolt flew Corsairs in the Marine Corps and F86 Sabre Jets in the Air Force, scoring six victories in each aircraft. He is shown with an F-86 named in honor of his wife, "Darling Dottie." (U.S. Air Force Photo, via National Archives)

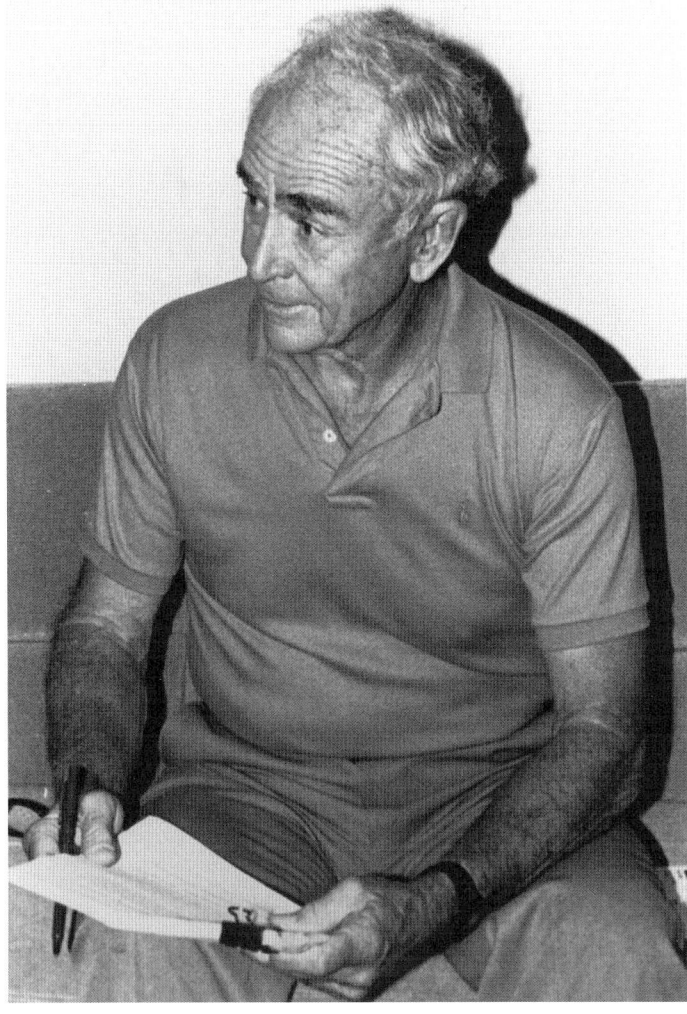

Retired "Jack" Bolt at the National Museum of Naval Aviation in 1992 during an interview regarding his wartime and post-war experiences. (National Museum of Naval Aviation Photo, Photo by Gibson)

When the Korean War started, Bolt was Flag Secretary for the Second Wing Group commander and was able to choose his next tour of duty.

He chose an Air Force exchange tour of duty flying F-86 Sabre jet fighters, scoring six MiG fighters to equal his World War II score.

After Korea, Bolt served three years at Fighter Design in the Bureau of Aeronautics, simultaneously attending evening classes for a BS degree from the University of Maryland.

He retired from the Marine Corps in April 1962 after twenty years of service and moved to Florida. He obtained a law degree and worked as a lawyer for twenty more years.

He retired in May 1991, enjoying hunting, ranching, scuba diving, and grandchildren.

CAPT JOHN THOMAS "TOMMY" BLACK BURN, USN, followed his command of VF-17 "Jolly Rogers" with an upgrade as commander of Air Group 14 on the Battle Carrier *USS Midway* (CVB-41). He soon became the captain of that large carrier.

Capt Blackburn retired with the rank of captain on August 1, 1962, to grow grapes in California Napa Valley. The Captain then moved to Florida and passed on in Jacksonville on March 21, 1994.

Capt John T Blackburn, former commander of the very successful VF-17 "Jolly Rogers" in the Solomons and commander of Air Group 14 flying Corsairs off *USS Midway*, has just landed in his personal Corsair as Air Group 14 Commander. (U.S. Navy Photo, Author's File)

Corsair: The Saga of the Legendary Bent-Wing Fighter-Bomber

Promoted to captain of USS Midway, Captain Blackburn retired to live in Napa Valley, California. (U.S. Navy Photo, via National Archives)

Two of Boyington's former Black Sheep aviators welcome "Pappy" upon his release from the Japanese POW camp. On the left is Robert W McClurg, and on the right is Alfred Johnson. Photo taken at the 1979 "Black Sheep" Convention in Atlanta, Georgia. (Syracuse Post Standard, Courtesy Peter Doyle)

LCDR GUY PIERRE BORDELON, USN, served with the Military Assistance Advisory Group in France at war's end, where he instructed French Naval Pilots in all-weather night fighting tactics with the Vought F4U-7 Corsair. He then became Air Traffic Control Officer at Moffett Field.

Bordelon completed the General Line Officers Postgraduate Course, followed by serving as Assistant Gunnery Officer on the carrier USS Yorktown.

On July 1, 1955, he was commissioned Lieutenant Commander, and in September 1959 Bordelon was attached to Airborne Early Warning Carrier Squadron Pacific as part of the DEW Line Defense system.

His last-known post was that of Public Affairs Officer on the Staff of Commander, Manned Spacecraft Recovery Force, Atlantic. At that time he became a full Commander.

COL GREGORY "PAPPY" BOYINGTON, USMC, found himself dogged by marital troubles, drinking, and unsuccessful jobs when he returned to "civilization" from the Japanese prison camp.

He finally conquered his drinking problem and wrote an autobiographical book *Baa Baa Black Sheep*, and his former squadron mates gathered around him to lift his spirits. Two of his closest buddies were Robert W McClurg and Alfred Johnson.

After a series of engagements, jilts, marriages, and divorces he found himself in a bed in Beverly Hospital at Montebello, California, for two years, destitute and recovering from abdominal surgery in 1967.

One of his marriages that appeared to hold was to a sincere, hard working woman, actress Dee Tatum, but he couldn't manage his monumental debts.

Boyington's plight reached America's hearts and pocketbooks with the result that contributions began pouring in to help the War Ace.

During 1980 Boyington was a guest of the Paul E. Garber Preservation, Restoration, and Storage Facility of the National Air and Space Museum, where the restoration of an F4U-1D Corsair was being completed. Col Boyington and some of his Black Sheep veterans were there to dedicate this Corsair to the National Air and Space Museum.

Many visitors to the NASM wonder how large aircraft are transported from the Paul E. Garber Preservation, Restoration, and Storage Facility to the Museum. The planes are transported in a relatively simple manner

After becoming the "Triple Threat Ace" of the Korean War by scoring five night-intruding "Bed Check Charlies" in the eerie darkness of night with his F4U-5N Corsair, Commander Bordelon held a series of important military positions. (Dept of Defense Photo, via National Archives)

Chapter X: Surviving Corsair Aviators

Col Gregory Boyington, USMC (Ret), in the cockpit of a restored Corsair at the National Air and Space Museum Paul E Garber Preservation, Restoration, and Storage Facility in Silver Hill, Maryland. Boyington and "Black Sheep" Squadron members dedicated this F4U-1D to the National Air and Space Museum in December 1981. (NASM Photo, Courtesy Col Walter J Boyne)

The beautiful Corsair reposes in the National Air and Space Museum for all to admire after a professional restoration. (NASM Photo, Courtesy Col Walter J Boyne)

Photo One: With the Corsair still in the Restoration Facility, the towing vehicle is outdoors but connected to the Corsair, ready to move. Photo Two: The caravan is halted to enable police-controlled traffic to pass using the opposite-direction lane. Photo Three: Arrival in Washington near the NASM, the caravan is stopped to change the towing vehicle into a pushing vehicle by turning it around. Photo Four: With the NASM doors wide open, the Corsair enters its new home. This photo affords a good view of the twin wheels that replaced the tailwheel. (NASM Photos, Courtesy Col Walter J Boyne)

The Commanding Officer
of Marine Attack Squadron 214
requests the pleasure of your company
at a
Ceremony
during which
Consolidated Freightways, Inc.
will present a bust of former commanding officer
Gregory 'Pappy' Boyington
on Thursday, the twenty-second of June
at ten o'clock in the morning
Building 97
MCAS Yuma, Arizona
Luncheon immediately following

R.S.V.P.
(602) 726-2701
A/V: 951-2701

Service
Appropriate Civilian Attire

The invitation to the Boyington commemorative included the "Black Sheep" patch because the "Black Sheep" Marine Attack Squadron 214 hosted the Commemorative on June 22, 1989. (Courtesy Col Keith Williams)

along conventional roads and streets, usually towed tail-first by a large open vehicle filled with sandbags for added traction.

Towing preparation on the Corsair consisted of replacing the small tailwheel with two large rubber-tire wheels arranged side-by-side on the towing tube. The outer wing panels were removed to clear overhead obstacles when folded and reduce the width of the plane if extended. The towing line is an eight-inch diameter tube, arranged to pull or push the Corsair in place. The rigid tube is preferred to a chain or rope because it prevents the Corsair from rolling into the truck in the event of a sudden stop. The rigid tube enables the plane to be pushed when necessary. Transportation is in the darkness of night when traffic is minimal.

"Pappy" Boyington died of cancer in a California hospice on January 11, 1988. Col Boyington was interred in Arlington National Cemetery on January 14, 1988, an American Hero.

From left to right at the Boyington Commemorative: the son of Dave Ekstrand; Gregory Boyington, Jr.; and Dave Ekstrand, VMF-214 Historian. (Dave Ekstrand Photo, Courtesy Col Keith Williams)

Left Photo: Col Tom Carstens, Commanding Officer of VMA-214 "Black Sheep" squadron and Jan Portugal, the artist who created the bronze Boyington bust, stand at each side of her work. Right Photo: The table of Boyington memorabilia at the commemorative was filled with two trophies flanking a large statue of a black ram (black sheep). Eight albums on the table record the history of the "Black Sheep" and Boyington. (Dave Ekstrand Photo, Courtesy Col Keith Williams)

Chapter X: Surviving Corsair Aviators

Invited guests at the Boyington Commemorative are, left to right: Dave Ekstrand, VMF-214 Historian; Marnie Williams; and Col Keith Williams, who was a Corsair aviator in the original VMF-214 (Swashbucklers) in the Solomons fighting. (Dave Ekstrand Photo, Courtesy Col Keith Williams)

Successor to the "Black Sheep" designation was squadron VMA-214 flying Harrier VTOL jets. As part of the "Gator Navy" the unit was based on USS Belleau Wood (LHA-3) amphibious assault ship. (Dept of defense Photo, R. Mazalan)

While Col Gregory "Pappy" Boyington had been languishing in a Japanese prisoner-of-war camp in Omori, Japan, he was presumed dead and was awarded the Medal of Honor posthumously.

His best friend in the POW camp was USAAF fighter pilot Capt Raymond "Hap" Halloran. While attending Boyington's funeral, Halloran resolved to do something special to commemorate his close friend. Halloran was senior vice president of Consolidated Freightways, Inc. and, working with the current "Black Sheep" Squadron VMA-214, it was decided that a life-size bronze bust of Boyington be commissioned and kept with other Boyington memorabilia.

The ceremony was held on June 22, 1989, at MCAS Yuma, Arizona, where Consolidated Freightways Inc. presented the bronze bust of the original "Black Sheep" commanding officer. A luncheon followed the ceremony for invited guests.

Among the invited guests were Col Boyington's widow, Josephine, and his son, Gregory Jr., who was a grown man by that time.

Oscar E (OE) Chenowith was a double-ace in "Tommy" Blackburn's "Jolly Rogers." In 1956 he joined Vought as a Sales Project Engineer. Photo was taken in 1958. (Vought Aircraft Photo, Courtesy Arthur L. Schoeni)

Jack Hospers will be remembered as the hard-working engineer who headed the task group which made the Corsair "Battle Ready" in the "field." By 1963 he was assistant to the Ling Temco Vought Chairman of the Board. He is shown here presenting a Corsair model to Marine Brig. Gen. Norman Anderson (L) and Marine Lt. Gen. John C. Munn in Washington, DC. (LTV Photo, Courtesy Paul Bower)

Corsair: The Saga of the Legendary Bent-Wing Fighter-Bomber

LCDR Ira C Kepford greets his mother, Mrs George Kepford, upon leaving the Naval Reserves on November 7, 1945. Having remained in the Naval Reserves, the sixteen victory ace retired from the Navy with the rank of Lieutenant Commander on June 1, 1945. Kepford joined the Rexall Drug Company, eventually becoming president of the eastern Division and of the Liggett Drug Company. He retired in 1967 and lived until January 19, 1987. (LCDR Ira C. Kepford Photo, Courtesy LCDR Kepford)

Several Corsair aviators and Vought employees joined the company or remained with the company after World War II ended. Many had "climbed the ladder of success."

At the end of World War II many veterans returned to their "loved ones" before "climbing the ladder of success."

The aviators of VMF-214 "Swashbucklers" and the aviators of VMF-214 "Black Sheep" shared a warm camradery, sharing each other's meetings and reunions.

CAPT. ALVIN J. JENSEN had been promoted by Maj George Britt from the rank of tech. sgt. to the rank of second lieutenant "in the field." 2nd Lt. Jensen was officially credited with seven victories.

By May 20, 1949, Jensen had become a captain. On that date Capt Alvin J Jensen was demonstrating a new F2-H Banshee jet fighter over NAS Patuxent, Maryland, and six-hundred spectators.

During one flight operation Captain Jensen climbed to 40,000 feet and dived to about two-thousand feet. As he started to pull out of the dive the wing gave a loud splitting sound as one half of the wing tore away. Captain Jensen died in the resulting crash.

Working his way up from a non-com to captain and scoring seven victories, then giving his life finding a flaw in the new jet fighter certainly proved Alvin Jensen a hero.

He was awarded the Navy Cross; Distinguished Flying Cross with three Gold Stars; and the Air Medal with 16 Gold Stars.

MAJOR DONALD H SAPP was promoted to lieutenant colonel in January 1951 after scoring ten official victories during World War II. He worked with special projects at Sandia Base, New Mexico, flying with the Navy's first atomic weapons squadron. Col Stapp retired from the Marine Corps on July 1, 1968, and passed away of heart failure on February 26, 1988, in Santa Ana, California.

MAJOR JOE FOSS led Corsair-equipped VMF-115 to Bougainville in 1944 and left active duty two years later, returning to his South Dakota home.

He organized the South Dakota Air National Guard, soon rising to command with the rank of brigadier general.

After serving two terms in the South Dakota House of Representatives he served two terms as Governor of South Dakota.

Left Photo: Left to right, standing before a Wildcat outside the Museum of Flight on Boeing Air Field, are: the Wildcat aviator; Keith Williams; Tom Tomlinson; and a mechanic in May 2002. Right Photo: Keith Williams (standing second from right) and Tommy Tomlinson (standing extreme left) were invited guests to join a "Black Sheep" reunion at the Museum of Flight on Boeing Air Field. (Col Keith Williams, USMC (Ret) Photo, Courtesy Col Keith Williams)

Chapter X: Surviving Corsair Aviators

Captain Alvin J Jensen was killed while he was demonstrating an F2-H Banshee jet fighter and the wing collapsed when the plane leveled off after a long dive. (Left Photo: Lt Jensen VMF-214 "Swashbucklers" Courtesy Col Keith Williams, USMC (Ret); Right Photo: U.S. Navy F2-H Banshee photo via U.S. National Archives)

Upon retiring from active duty Joe Foss organized the South Dakota Air National Guard and became the commander with the rank of brigadier general. This Aug. 1955 photo shows Gen Foss with a Lockheed F-80 "Shooting Star." Inset photo shows the General with an F-51 "Mustang." (Photos Courtesy of South Dakota Air National Guard)

Flying with the Navy's first atomic weapons squadron and special projects at Sandia Base, New Mexico, Lt Col Sapp is shown in his U.S. Air Force F-86 Sabre-Jet at that time. (USAF Photo via National Archives)

Corsair: The Saga of the Legendary Bent-Wing Fighter-Bomber

OK Williams' favorite sport is hunting. Shown here are two "down to earth" examples of his prey: a lion (right photo) and a Selous buffalo (left photo). (Keith Williams Photo, Courtesy Keith Williams)

Putting politics aside, Foss became commissioner of the American Football League and president of the National Rifle Association.

COL OK WILLIAMS (down to earth) remained in the U.S. Naval Reserves for seventeen years at the end of World War II as a veteran of over 100 combat missions.

Upon returning home, OK (short for Otto Keith) bought the recipe for cooking salmon eggs, for use as fishing bait, from his uncle Earnest Pautzke. Keith claims: "I boiled up a bunch and put them in jars but I had a hell of a time selling them."

Keith's wife, Marnie, suggested dying the eggs red, and they became an "instant success," in demand by American and European markets. The business expanded to include five more exotic marine baits.

Lt Col Kenneth Walsh retired from the U.S. Marine Corps in January 1962 after twenty-eight years of service. He was the first Corsair Ace. (Dept of Defense, USMC, Author's File)

Kenneth Walsh wrote this recollection on a beautiful notecard in remembrance of a fierce aerial battle in which he fought during the early Solomons campaign. This notecard illustrates the battle. (Courtesy Lt Col Kenneth Walsh)

Chapter X: Surviving Corsair Aviators

Left Photo: Congressional Medal of Honor recipient Col Ken Walsh and wife Beulah are photographed at the Congressional Medal of Honor Society Convention in Vancouver, WA, on November 9, 1991. The coveted medal hangs from the Ace's neck. Right Photo: Ken Walsh poses before paintings of Corsairs he flew in action: an original Machat at the left and an original Lapadura at the right. Photo taken at Dave Mocabee's "Air Museum" in Bend, Oregon. (Dave Mocabee Photos)

The success with the fish-egg bait gave Williams the time and ability to meet with other combat veterans; pay respects to the fallen heroes; and enjoy his sport of hunting and fishing.

Most retired Corsair aviators retained contact with retired comrades and attended many aviation, Marine, and Navy functions for many years.

DR. LOU ANTONACCI performed the amazing task of contacting VF-17 "Jolly Rogers" survivors for a reunion on the 40th anniversary of the squadron's founding.

The reunion was held in June 1983 at Oceans NAS, Virginia, and was the very first "Jolly Rogers" reunion.

Ken Walsh attended the 1994 Experimental Aircraft Association (EAA) 1994 Fly-In on 31 July. One of the attractions was this beautifully rebuilt F4U-4 Corsair finished in Ken Walsh's markings: White thirteen overlayed with twenty-one Japanese flags. The Ace, himself, autographed the plane and made notations on plane and photograph. (Dave Mocabee Photo)

Left Photo: Ken Walsh, extreme right, poses with four Aces in the Gallery of the Prop Shop in Bend, Oregon. The Aces are, L to R: Corsair Ace Roger Conant; Ace Rex Barber; Corsair Ace Jim Swett; and Corsair Ace Bruce Porter. Meeting was on October 11, 1997. With the Aces are two attendants of the Prop Shop aviation artifacts emporium in Bend, Oregon. Right Photo: Bobbie Mocabee joins Ken Walsh for refreshments in the Prop Shop Gallery. Ken seldom missed a meeting with Corsair aviators or Corsair enthusiasts. (Dave Mocabee Photos)

Corsair: The Saga of the Legendary Bent-Wing Fighter-Bomber

Upper Photo: Congressional Medal of Honor recipient Jim Swett is joined by Bobbie Mocabee at the Congressional Medal of Honor Convention in Irvine, California, on November 14, 1987. Right Photo: Jim Swett smiles at the photographer while he browses the Prop Shop in Bend, Oregon, on August 12, 1995. (Dave Mocabee Photos)

In honor of LTJG Jesse L Brown, who made an emergency landing in Korea and froze to death, it was decided to name destroyer escort DE-1039 in his name. Attending the launching on March 18, 1972, at Avondale Shipyards, Inc are, left to right: RADM John W Dolan Jr; Mrs Gilbert W Thorne, Sponsor; Henry Z Carter, Avondale President; and Capt Thomas J Hudner, Head, Aviation Technical Training, Office of the Chief of Naval Operations, who tried to rescue LTJG Brown. Capt Hudner made a valiant effort to save LTJG Brown for which he was awarded the Medal of Honor. (U.S. Navy Photo, Author's File)

Dr. Lou Antonacci performed the herculean task of contacting VF-17 "Jolly Rogers" survivors for a reunion on the 40th anniversary of the squadron's founding. Some survivors are posed here with Dr. Antonacci's Corsair that sports "Ike" Kepford's markings. The aviators are, left to right, standing: "Pete" Peterson; Harvey Mathews; Jack Chasnoff; Ward "Ace" Cole; Will "Country" Landreth; Dr. Lou Antonacci (Corsair owner and pilot); John T. "Tommy" Blackburn (VF-17 CO); Lyle "Doc" Herrmann, MD (Flight Surgeon); Dan Cunningham; Wilbur "Pete" Popp; Ira C "Ike" Kepford; and MW "Butch" Davenport. The remaining aviators are, left to right, kneeling: Harold "Bitz" Bitzegaio; Whit Wharton; Frank "Andy" Jagger; Robert "Hal" Jackson; Hap Bower; and Mel Kurlander. Photo taken at Oceana Naval Air station, Virginia Beach, Virginia. (Dr Lou Antonacci Photo)

Chapter X: Surviving Corsair Aviators

Major Marion Carl poses for the photographer in the Douglas D-558-1 Skystreak cockpit. Observe the smooth fuselage skin and vee shaped windshield to reduce air resistance. (Douglas Aircraft Co. Inc. Photo)

Major Carl is about to climb into the Skystreak. Note the pilot has no parachute to save weight; however, he is fitted with a face mask in the event that the windshield blows off at high speed. (Douglas Aircraft Co. Inc. Photo)

MARION CARL, who stated: "The Corsair was a great mount. It was head and shoulders above its contemporaries. An airplane like the Corsair only comes along occasionally," was rotated to the Naval Air Test Center at Patuxent River, Maryland, in January 1945. For the next 30 months he flew the early U.S. jets, such as the P-59 and P-80, as well as the *Luftwaffe's* Messerschmitt 262 and new helicopter designs.

While Carl was experimental testing, the Major was selected to fly the Douglas D-558-1 Skystreak to attempt a world speed record. He set a new world speed record of 650 miles per hour.

The Ace also set a world altitude record when he climbed to 83,235ft in a rocket powered version of the Skystreak, called the Skyrocket, after he was launched from a B-29 bomber.

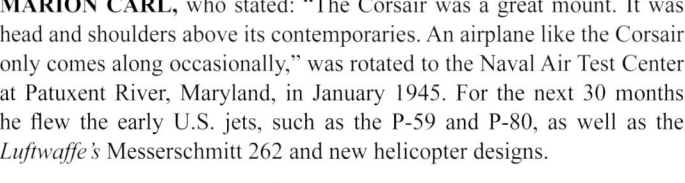

The Douglas D-558-1 Skystreak sets a world speed record of 650 miles per hour with Major Marion Carl at the controls. (Douglas Aircraft Co. Inc. Photo)

Lt Col Marion Carl suffered a serious accident when an F9F Cougar that he was testing had a flameout. Plane and aviator suffered broken backs in the crash. (Official U.S. Marine Corps Photo, Courtesy A.E. Ferko)

Gen. Wallace M Greene Jr, commandant U.S. Marine Corps (center), shakes hands with Col Marion E. Carl, Brigade Chief of Staff. Gen. Greene introduced to Brigade Special Staff Officers by Brig Gen. C.A Youngdale (Right). (Defense Dept Photo, Photo Sgt C.E Simmons)

Brig Gen Carl (center with cap) is being interviewed by John Wheeler of the Associated Press. Gen Carl's Fourth Brigade had just landed on Red Beach, Vietnam. (Defense dept Photo, USMC, Author's File)

Brig Gen. Marion E. Carl, USMC, led his brigade to Danang, Vietnam. (Official U.S. Marine Corps Photo, Author's File)

One of the last photographs of Marion Carl before he was shot and killed by a robber who burst into his home. The 83 year old Ace and American Hero was killed while protecting his wife from the shotgun-wielding robber. (Douglas County News-Review File)

Chapter X: Surviving Corsair Aviators

Left Photo: Brig Gen. Joe Foss, USMC (Ret), stands to the right with his arm around Lt Col Ken Walsh, USMC (Ret), before attending Brig Gen Marion Carl's funeral as Honorary Pallbearers. Both men are Medal of Honor recipients. (Dave Mocabee Photo) Right Photo: Maj Gen. Ken Houghton, USMC (Ret), left, poses with Lt Col Ken Walsh, USMC (Ret), prior to attending Brig Gen Marion Carl's funeral as Honorary Pallbearers. (Dave Mocabee Photo)

His closest brush with death was when, as a Lt. Colonel, he had a flameout in an F9F cougar jet fighter that he was testing. Attempting to deadstick back to Patuxent River, he landed short of the runway and broke the fighter's back as well as his own. Carl spent so much time in a cast that he missed the Korean war.

Promoted to Colonel, Marion Carl spent ten years in a variety of assignments which included Director of marine Aviation and the Air War College. By 1964 he was promoted to brigadier general. He became commander of the First Marine Brigade in Hawaii and took his Brigade to Viet Nam during the following year.

The Marine Hero retired in 1973, having flown 13,000 hours. Carl was awarded the following medals: Navy Cross with two Gold Stars; Legion of Merit with three Gold Stars; Distinguished Flying Cross with four Gold Stars; and the Air Medal with 13 Gold Stars.

The retired Ace and his wife, Edna, lived on a 37 acre tree-farm in Roseburg, Oregon. On the night of June 28, 1998, Edna Carl was reading in the living room shortly before eleven o'clock on that Sunday when an intruder with a sawed-off shotgun and wearing wraparound black sunglasses burst through the heavy Dutch doors.

The intruder screamed and shouted for money and car keys, and asked if she was alone. Edna Carl blurted "yes" as 83 year old Marion

Left Photo: Survivors of the original VMF-214 squadron known as the "Swashbucklers" celebrated a reunion in May 1993. The aviators who forced back the Japanese during the early Solomons fighting are, standing left to right: Keith "Down to Earth" Williams; Howard Cavanaugh; Doug McCall; Dave Rankin; and John Fidler. Sitting the "Swashbucklers" are, left to right: Lincoln Deetz; Col. George Britt, who flew "NoBuNo"; and Vince Carpenter. Right Photo: With their ladies, the survivors are standing left to right: Keith Williams; Howard Cavanaugh; Doug McCall; John Fidler; Vince Carpenter; and Dave Rankin. Center row is Lincoln Deetz and seated is Col George Britt, CO of the squadron. Observe the Corsair photo and "Swashbuckler" insignia. (Photos Courtesy Keith Williams)

Left Photo: 1943 photo of a lagoon in Espiritu Santo, New Hebrides, that VMF-214 Swashbuckler aviators enjoyed when not flying their Corsairs. (Photo Courtesy Keith Williams) Right Photo: Same lagoon in 1997, known as the "Blue Hole." When peace was declared, excess military equipment was unloaded into the lagoon, giving the water a bluish hue. It is said that the American actress, Dorothy Lamour, swam in the "Blue Hole" for one of her films. (Photo Courtesy John Regan, John Regan standing beside the lagoon)

burst in from the bedroom to protect his wife and jumped at the attacker. Angered at Edna's claiming she was alone, the gunman fired in panic, grazing the back of her head but striking the lunging Marion squarely in the head.

So died one of America's greatest combat aviators, test pilots, and record smashing fliers at the hands of a 19 year old worthless, morally corrupt individual.

Among the honorary pallbearers were Marion's son, Bruce Carl; Gen. J.K. Davis, USMC, Ret; Maj Gen Hal Vincent, USMC, Ret; Maj

VMF-215 "Fighting Corsairs" enjoyed their 2003 Reunion in Indianapolis, Indiana, and posed in front of an F4U-4 Corsair. The Squadron aviators are: (1)Roger Conant; (2) Dick Samuelson; (3) Ray Wolff; (4) Hap Langstaff; (5) Larry Smith; (6) Jim Warren; (7) O.K. Williams; (8) Bob Johnson; (9) George Brewer; (10) Walt Foust; (11) Bill Shaw; and (12) Reinhardt (Chief) Leu. The squadron ground crew members who kept the aviators and planes in the air are: (13)Ed Hershon; (14) Charles Fitzgerald; (15) Bill Yerks; (16) Jim Wudi; (17) Bill Mayer; (18) Clarence Thorn; (19) Ernie Mengler; and (20) Walt Bilimek. (Hap Langstaff photo and personnel identification, Photo contributed by O.K. Williams)

Chapter X: Surviving Corsair Aviators

Left Photo: Four American veterans place wreaths on the base of this granite stele. The stele is located on Guadalcanal and is inscribed as follows:
"THIS MEMORIAL WAS CONSTRUCTED BY
THE UNITED STATES OF AMERICA
IN HUMBLE TRIBUTE TO THE AMERICANS
AND THEIR ALLIES WHO LOST THEIR LIVES
DURING THE GUADALCANAL INVASION.
7 AUGUST 1942- 9 FEBRUARY 1943"
Right Photo: Marine Col Keith Williams (extreme right) of VMF-214 and VMF-215 has placed a wreath on the base of the stele. (OK Williams Photos)

Solomon Islanders were eager to meet Americans with whom they fought against the Japanese; however, they bore no animosity toward the Japanese visitors. Two Solomons Islanders greet Col Keith Williams on Guadalcanal in 2002. (Col OK Williams Photos)

Gen Ken Houghton, USMC, Ret; Brig Gen J. Hubbard, USMC, Ret; Brig Gen Joe Foss, USMC, Ret (MOH); and Lt. Col Ken Walsh, USMC, Ret (MOH).

Marine and Navy fighter pilots, most of whom had flown Corsairs, never missed the chance to meet and discuss past squadron life and future plans. Meetings could vary from necktie and jacket dress to informal picnic attire.

U.S. Navy, U.S. Army and, U.S. Marine veterans, as well as many civilizations, visited Guadalcanal in 2002 on the 60th anniversary of the battle to pay tribute to the Americans and their Allies who gave their lives during the Guadalcanal invasion, as well as during the fierce fighting when this island was the jumping-off point to invade other Japanese-held Solomon Islands.

Japanese Gen Akira Yabuki and his aide came to pay respects to the Japanese Fallen. (Col O.K. Williams Photo)

One of the American Veterans who listened to a local Solomon Islander war veteran, Billy Titiulu, was Col OK Williams. Titiulu exclaimed that:

"It is the first time that we have marked the events of the past with American and Japanese war veterans. This is good today when these nations are now allies allocating their time towards global peace and harmony."

During April 2005 more Solomon Veterans returned to Guadalcanal and continued to Vella La Vella, where many had flown from the fighter airstrip as the Japanese began their retreat.

 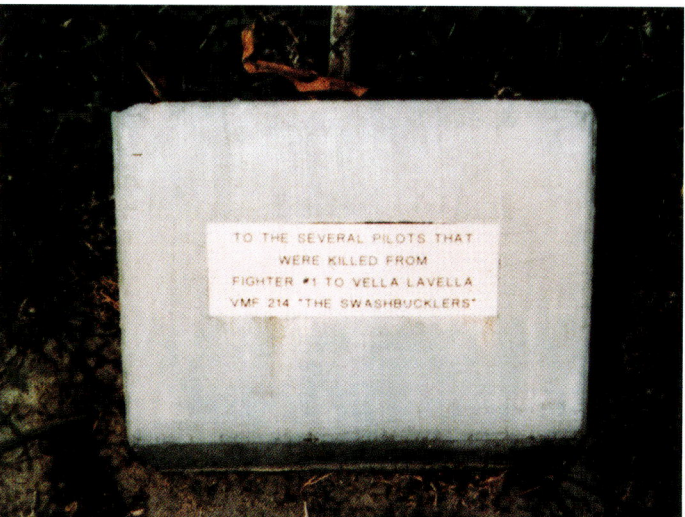

Left Photo: The Solomon Islands Memorial Gardens on Guadalcanal are approached by a broad pathway, bordered with plants, leading to an open rotunda. Right Photo: The open lawn contains memorial stones such as these. (Col OK Williams Photos)

Left Photo: The broad pathway leads to a guarded gate and the open rotunda. Observe the trained foliage encircling the property. Right Photo: The open rotunda to which the broad pathway leads consists of two inscribed obelisks, benches, and a broad shade-producing tree for visitors to meditate in comfort. (Col OK Williams Photos)

Chapter X: Surviving Corsair Aviators

Upper Photo: World War II Veterans are aboard an inter-island ferry traveling from Guadalcanal to Vella La Vella. Col Williams is wearing the dark jacket. Lower Photo: This is the remains of the fighter air strip on Vella La Vella, once one of the busiest fighter air strips in the Solomons. (Col Keith Williams Photos)

XI

Experimental Corsairs

Many experimental modifications were made to the Corsair: some in an attempt to improve the performance and potency of the design, while countless others were as a vehicle to test new ideas that would improve the efficiency and potency of other aircraft designs. The Corsair speed and lifting capability made it ideal as an experimental machine for other designs.

Upper Photo: This BAT-bomb; reposing in an aviation museum storeroom, presents a clear view of the missile. Observe the large triangular fin/ rudder. The body is dural while the wings, stabilizer, elevators, fins, and rudders are wood. (Photo Courtesy Cecil Weatherly III) Lower Photo: Installed under an F4U-1D; this BAT-bomb illustrates the transition from the large triangular fin/ rudders to small circular fin/ rudders. All installations and tests were conducted at Naval Aviation Ordnance Test Stations. Initial installations were accomplished in October 1946. (Defense Dept Photo, via Nat. Archives)

Chapter XI: Experimental Corsairs

Upper Photo: This view of an F4U-4B Corsair-mounted BAT-bomb illustrates the large size of the BAT-bomb. It is not known if the amount of white paint on the nose indicates the potency of the bomb. This BAT-bomb was installed at the Naval Aviation Ordnance Test Station in Chincoteague, Virginia. Lower Photo: It appears that this F4U-4 Corsair had two .50 cal guns removed to improve handling while carrying the BAT-bomb. Observe the circular fin/ rudders that became standard on subsequent BAT-bombs. (Defense Dept Photo, via Nat. Archives)

Japan and the United States experimented with heavy gliding bombs that were to be released and guided from large powered aircraft miles from the target beyond antiaircraft fire. The United States ended the experiments early in the tests, discovering that normal dive bombing and horizontal bombing were more efficient.

Military aircraft, especially fighters, must be capable of a rapid takeoff at all times, especially during an emergency.

During early 1944 Jet Assisted Take-Off was devised to shorten the take-off run using disposable rocket pods. Successful tests were performed in March and September of that year on F4U-1 and F4U-1A Corsairs.

Two rocket pods was attached to each fuselage side, near the bottom, just behind the wing. The pods were jettisoned when the rocket fuel was expended. This system is known as JATO (Jet Assisted Take-Off).

A single rocket pod generated thrust equal to approximately 230 horsepower.

Despite the superb performance of the Corsair, the U.S. Navy Bureau of Aeronautics (BuAer) could not satisfy its future need for increased top speed and high-altitude performance and, once again, looked to the Corsair on June 14, 1941. This quest led to the XF4U-3 Corsair, which began with Vought-Sikorsky proposal VS-331, followed by contract Number 198.

Large Photo: An F4U-1A Corsair streaks down the flight deck of USS *Altahama* during a solid fuel JATO test in March 1944. The wheels are ready for lift-off. (Official U.S. Navy Photo, Courtesy United Aircraft Corp.) Inset Photo: The wheels of this F4U-1 Corsair have just left the ground as the experimental liquid fuel JATO attains maximum thrust. Note the JATO fuel flask on the fuselage side. This test was conducted at Naval Air Station Anacostia in September 1944. (Official U.S. Navy Photo, via National Archives)

Inset Photo: This rebuilt F4U-1A is often described as the XF4U-3A; however, it is the XF4U-3B which was the second F4U-1A rebuilt into a high-altitude, high speed Corsair. White arrow points to the turbo-charger inlet. Main Photo: Except for the turbo-charger bulge (black arrow), the XF4U-3A and XF4U-3B could be mistaken for the F4U-4. (Defense Dept Photos, via National Archives)

The contract specified that two F4U-1A Corsairs were to be modified with larger, more powerful engines, turbochargers, four-bladed Hamilton Standard Hydromatic propellers, and torque-meters. The rebuilt F4U-1A Corsairs were to be redesignated XF4U-3.

The most visible external difference of the XF4U-3 was the four-bladed propeller and the turbocharger's large intake scoop located under the fuselage nose, with the inlet just ahead of the lower cowl flaps and terminating with a bulbous blister under the fuselage aft of the wing.

The powerplant consisted of the water-injected P&W XR-2800-16 engine Birmann-type two-stage turbochargers produced by the Turbo-Engineering Company of Trenton, New Jersey, and the previously-mentioned four-bladed propellers. This powerplant could develop 2,000 continuous horsepower from sea level all the way up to 25,000 ft.

Because of delivery delays for the P&W XR-2800-16 engine, Chance Vought suggested to the BuAer that the P&W R-2800-14W turbo-supercharged engine be substituted for the P&W XR-2800-16 and installed in the second XF4U-3, which was designated XF4U-3B, while the first conversion was designated XF4U-3A. Chance Vought also installed a water injection system that used water stored in an outer wing panel tank.

The Birmann turbosupercharger added over 300 pounds to the weight of the XF4U-3, and forced the elimination of the catapult hooks; however, at 25,000 ft altitude it gave the aircraft a top speed of 414 mph.

Vought test pilot Bill Horan, who had logged eighty-three flights between both planes, observed that, when the F4U-1A Corsairs were converted into XF4U-3 high altitude craft, the turbocharger and intercoolers were located on the bottom of the auxiliary section on the fuselage centerline, creating a large bulge in the airframe. He thought this might have upset the airflow, possibly adding to the compressibility factor. Horan is quoted as saying:

"Should compressibility have occurred, no matter what speed you traveled, you could always put the landing gear down. It wouldn't hurt the airplane a bit. Deploying the landing gear would double the drag; quickly slowing the aircraft". Horan also stated that he "had it up to 40,000 feet and it still had plenty of climb left in it. At rated power at 39,000 or 40,000 ft it came up to above 480 mph."

In December 1942 the BuAer decided to convert a "birdcage" F4U-1 Corsair into the third XF4U-3, and contracted Chance Vought to perform the conversion. Meanwhile, BuAer reconsidered its decision; however, before Vought could be instructed to remove the "birdcage" F4U-1 from the test program, Vought had completed the F4U-1 conversion into an XF4U-3, and had already flight-tested the craft, which crashed into the ground at the Stratford, CT, Chance Vought plant.

The remaining XF4U-3A flew for the last time at Chance Vought on March 29, 1945, before it was sent to the U.S. Navy for evaluation. The XF4U-3B followed three months later on June 29, 1945.

Goodyear Aircraft Corp. delivered twenty-six turbo-supercharged versions of the FG-1D, designated FG-3, to the Navy at Johnsville, PA,

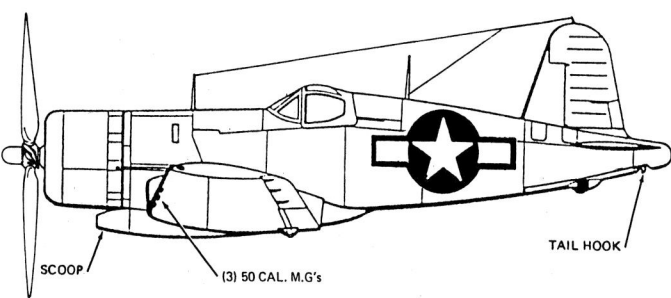

Vought XF4U-3 & Goodyear FG-3

The Vought XF4U-3A and XF4U-3B, as well as Goodyear FG-3, are virtually identical except for the powerplants. Observe the turbo-charger inlet (scoop) and bulge aft of the wing. (Vought Aircraft Artwork)

Chapter XI: Experimental Corsairs

During, December 1942 the U.S. Navy decided to rebuild a "Birdcage" F4U-1 corsair into the third XF4U-3 and ordered Vought to complete the conversion, shown here. Meanwhile, BuAer changed its mind; however, by the time it notified Vought to cancel work on the F4U-1, Vought had converted the plane into an XF4U-3 and test flew the prototype, crashing it onto the Chance Vought airfield. Observe the "Birdcage" canopy. (United Aircraft Corp. Photo, Courtesy Arthur L Schoeni)

between July 3 and 7, 1945. The planes were maintained and test flown in high-altitude work.

Two FG-3 aircraft were sent to Patuxent River for electronics testing in July 1947, and the last FG-3 was stricken from the U.S. Navy's list of active aircraft on July 31, 1949.

The high-altitude Corsairs were fine aircraft; however, they were developed at a time when very little Pacific aerial combat was fought above 20,000 ft. Further, it would cut into the badly needed production lines of the superlative F4U-4 that was less expensive and easier to produce.

What it did prove was that this excellent 1938 design could be modified to climb to 40,000 feet and attain 480 miles per hour!

The Corsair's ailerons were the pride of the design and gave the plane an amazing climbing roll. This was not achieved without meticulous designing and 110 laborious test flights. Famous test pilot and author Wolfgang Langwiesche stated that: "the roll rate was terrific; the ailerons were the factory's pride and joy."

In 1942, a Two-Place Corsair Trainer (V-354), converted from an F4U-1, was proposed in order to hasten the time required to train cadets to become Corsair aviators; however, it was discovered that they learned just as fast by flying the fighter itself. The Two-Place Corsair experiment was terminated at once.

Ever since the advent of propellers, efforts have continued to improve their efficiency as the driving force for aircraft and ships. The most recent efforts have been to eliminate the torque, or the twisting of air around the airplane's fuselage, or water twisting against a ship's hull, creating drag. This decreases the propulsion efficiency.

Torque can be best eliminated on airplanes by installing two contra-rotating propellers, with the forward propeller shaft running through a rear propeller tubular shaft. With the propellers turning in opposite directions torque is eliminated.

In 1943 two Hamilton-Standard contra-rotating propellers were tested on an XF4U-4. The propellers were also fitted with "cuffs," which are broad airfoils covering the propeller hubs to improve efficiency. No improvement was indicated with this installation.

Another experimental installation consisted of two Aero Products contra-rotating propellers on an XF4U-4 in the summer of 1945 for a vibration and performance test. As a result of the tests the original four-bladed propeller was retained because of its lower drag and weight.

After careful design and construction the Corsair's ailerons were flight tested to correct minor lateral instability. The test plane, shown here, had the elevator marked in a grid to aid in observation from the chase plane. The precise method of reading the grid is not known to the author. (Vought Aircraft Photo, Courtesy Paul Bower)

This Two-Place Corsair, converted from an F4U-1, was intended to train cadets to become Corsair aviators; however, it did not shorten training time as expected. (Vought Aircraft Photo, Courtesy Paul Bower)

Upper Photo: Hamilton-Standard three-bladed contra-rotating propellers were tested on an XF4U-4 in 1943. Observe the airfoiled "cuffs" on the blades that cover the hubs. No improvement was indicated with this propeller installation. Lower Photo: Aero Products' three-bladed contra-rotating propellers were tested on an XF4U-4 for vibration and performance tests in 1945. Results of the tests indicate that the original four-bladed propeller had lower drag and weight. (Ling Temco Vought Photos, Courtesy Arthur L Schoeni)

Chapter XI: Experimental Corsairs

This Goodyear FG-1 was used to experiment with the exhaust stack position and exit size and shape to provide thrust for an increase in speed. The effect was minimal so the experiment was ended. (Goodyear Aircraft Corp. Photo, Courtesy Nick Hauprich)

Speed at any cost is important in military fighters. Experiments using engine exhaust stacks to increase speed in rugged and heavy fighters is a rarity and usually ends in failure. However, aero engineers did not accept failure and continued to try to boost speed with properly designed and positioned exhaust stacks. This also ended in failure, despite the fact that record-smashing aircraft of the 1930s increased speed by using engine exhaust stacks and contra-rotating propellers.

As early as 1934, contra-rotating propellers and exhaust stacks angled aft on the Macchi-Gastoli speedster established a world's speed record of 475 mph. This event, no doubt, was remembered by the engineers of BuAer and Chance Vought.

The Macchi-Gastoli had a lightweight 6,410 lb wood and fabric structure, while the fighting Corsair weighed an all-metal 12,500 lbs (5.9 lbs/ hp). The Macchi-Gastoli was powered by two 1,500 hp vee-engines constructed in tandem in a single crankcase with each engine driving one contra-rotating propeller through a simple gearing system (2.14 lbs/ hp). This could not be duplicated with the 2,100 hp radial engine without a train of complicated, horsepower-consuming gears.

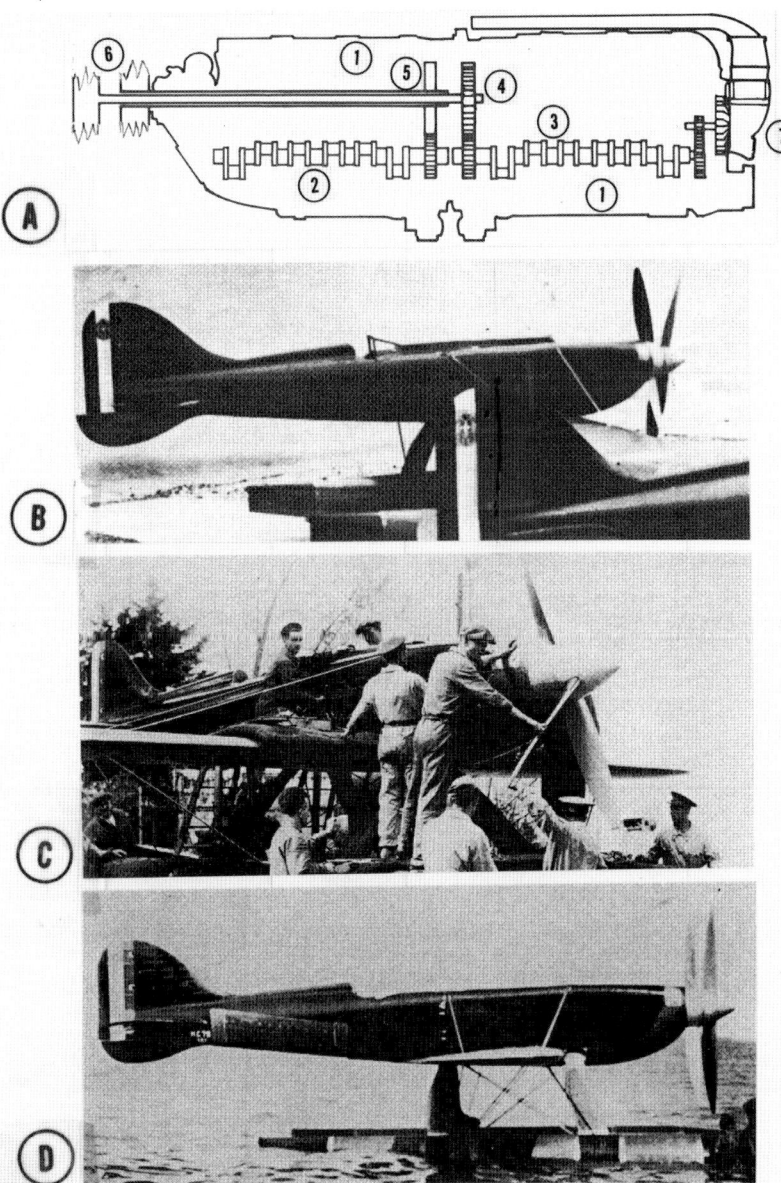

View A is a schematic of the Macchi-Gastoli contra-rotating propeller system: No 1. is the common crankcase for the two engines; No 2. is the forward engine crankshaft; No 3. is the aft engine crankshaft; No 4. is the aft engine propeller shaft; No 5. is the forward engine propeller shaft (tube); No 6. are the propellers; and No 7. is the turbo-supercharger driven by the aft engine. Engines rotated in opposite directions. View B shows the speedster with contra-rotating propellers at rest. The two engines in tandem, each driving one propeller. Simplicity! View C has a half-dozen mechanics servicing the amazing speedster. Observe the mechanic with his right hand on a forward propeller blade. View D shows the Macchi-Gastoli at anchor with the engines gently ticking over, clearly showing the first ever contra-rotating propellers in an airplane. (Courtesy Embassy of Italy, Washington, D.C)

This drop tank was developed by Firestone Rubber Co. Laminated like the bladder tank, the bullet is absorbed by the laminated construction and does not pierce the tank. The new tank was rejected because of excess weight and reduced capacity. (Ling Temco Vought, Courtesy Arthur L Schoeni)

The advanced wing tip fuel tank concept acted as an end plate by eliminating turbulence. The tanks also kept flaming fuel away from the aviator and sensitive parts of the aircraft. The new tanks were rejected because they were easy targets and because the folding wing would complicate the fuel line run from tank to engine. (Ling Temco Vought, Courtesy Arthur L Schoeni)

Fighter plane fuel tank location and material must be carefully considered during the design stage. Balance, protection, safety, and location are only a few problems the designer must solve.

In 1942 the Firestone Rubber Co. developed a Bullet-Proof Dropable Fuel Tank for the Corsair F4U-1A.

Construction was similar to the fuselage bladder fuel tank that had displaced the center of gravity cockpit location on the XF4U-1. The bullet is absorbed by the laminated construction and does not pierce the tank. This was not accepted by the BuAer. Excessive weight and reduced capacity appeared to be the reasons.

Ling Temco Vought developed wing-tip fuel tanks for an XF4U-4 (sometimes identified as F4U-4XB). The advantages were keeping a flaming fuel tank away from the aviator and sensitive parts of the plane. Also, aerodynamically tip tanks reduce or eliminate wing tip turbulence, acting as an end plate.

Conversely, the argument against the tip tanks was long fuel lines hinging at the fold in the wing, which were an easy target for the enemy to destroy the fuel tanks.

One of the most interesting Corsair experiments was the installation of a turbo-jet engine to test the engine.

By 1941 Germany and Britain had achieved jet powered flight and, although Britain had shared its technology with the United States, America began to develop its own jet engine.

In March 1941 the National Advisory Committee on Aeronautics (NACA) invited several steam turbine engine manufacturers, including General Electric and Westinghouse Electric and Manufacturing Company, to research new forms of military aircraft propulsion.

Westinghouse engineer Stewart Way submitted a proposal for a turbine engine that compressed air by an axial flow compressor which was externally started.

The Westinghouse "Yankee" 19-A jet engine was neatly faired into the F1-G Corsair belly by the Philadelphia Naval Air Material Center. This view of the installation shows the relative size of the engine to the Corsair. (U.S. Navy Photo 448762, Courtesy Arthur L Schoeni)

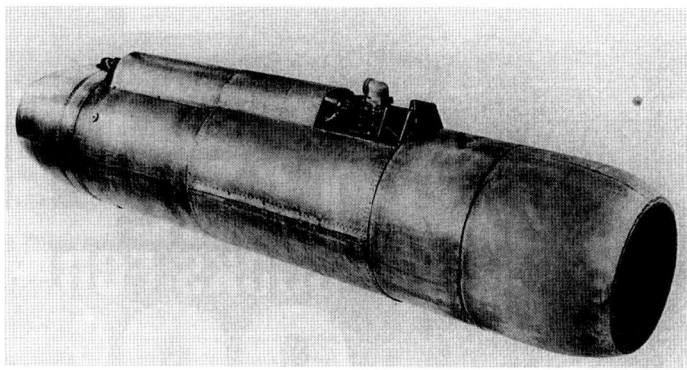

This is the Westinghouse "Yankee" 19-A jet engine. Dimensions were two feet in diameter and eight feet long. The right end is the air inlet, while the left end is the exhaust. When the unit is installed the exhaust end is insulated because the radiated heat could damage the Corsair. (Westinghouse Electric Photo, Courtesy Stewart Way, P.E.)

Chapter XI: Experimental Corsairs

FG-1 Corsair BU.NO.13041 at NAS Patuxant River, MD, starts engine prior to the initial flight. Observe the insulation on the rear of the jet engine. Flights were successful, leading to the early U.S. Navy jet-powered fighters. (U.S. Navy Photo 447430, Courtesy Arthur L Schoeni)

The compressed air then entered a combustion chamber where it mixed with vaporized fuel that ignited and expanded to produce a high-velocity exhaust, driving the turbine that drove the compressor which made a continuously operating engine. The high velocity exhaust became a high velocity thrust, and hence, a jet engine! This jet engine was called "Yankee" (Model 19A).

NACA was impressed, and the U.S. Navy contracted with Westinghouse to further research and develop the design. Rein Kroom, manager of Westinghouse engineering development and a steam turbine expert, continued refining the design with eleven selected engineers, naming the group "the twelve disciples."

After several failures, such as the tail cylinder collapsing on itself, a second Yankee was constructed and readied for flight. In January 1944 Westinghouse delivered the second Yankee engine to the U.S. Navy.

The eight feet long and two feet diameter jet engine could not produce enough power to take-off an aircraft by itself, but was expected to maintain flight once airborne by its carrier/ launcher "mother" plane.

The search was on to find a mother plane that could carry the second "Yankee" (Model 19A) jet engine and accelerate to a speed where the jet could start and propel the mother plane.

The Model 19A turbo jet was installed under a Corsair belly by the Philadelphia Naval Air Material Center in October 1943 and delivered to the U.S. Navy by January 1944.

The one-third size model of the submarine-fired ramjet cruise missile appears to be an aircraft-fired air-to-air or air-to-ground missile, as it is suspended from the F4U-4 Corsair. (Loral Vought Photo, Courtesy Rick Mac Donnell)

Corsair: The Saga of the Legendary Bent-Wing Fighter-Bomber

The combined FG-1 Corsair "Yankee" trials were very successful, leading to subsequent and more powerful versions of the "Yankee" that were selected to propel the McDonnell XFD-1 Phantom in the U.S. Navy's first carrier jet trials.

As we have seen, Corsair experiments were not always conducted for the improvement of the plane. This experiment is one in which the Corsair is used to conduct tests for a large submarine-fired weapon.

The weapon to be tested by Loral Vought Systems was a PA-6 one-third size ramjet powered model of a long-range cruise missile. The forward movement of the missile forces oxygen into the combustion chamber, hence the "ram"-jet.

Vought's Rick MacDonnell was in charge of designing and testing the one-third models. Three one-third size models were designed, constructed, and tested, and all were carried and test-launched by Corsairs.

The dependability of Corsairs made the design very adaptable to experimentation in attempts to improve its own performance or to improve the performance of other designs.

In a new experiment, a propeller-driven F4U-5 Corsair was fitted with large auxiliary fins in 1946 to establish whether they would assist the stability of the new Vought XF6U-1 "Pirate" jet fighter.

Eventually the final "pirate" design flew without the auxiliary fins, having made other modifications on the basis of the F4U-5 fin experiments.

Two views of the Loral Vought one-third size operating ram-jet of the submarine-launched long range missile that was launched from an F4U-4 Corsair. (Loral Vought Photo, Courtesy Rick Mac Donnell)

Left Photo: Rick MacDonnell, in white coveralls, eases a ramjet test model into place with a special cart before the test flights at Point Mugu test center, California. Right Photo: All smiles for the first missile test. A second missile design is in place for the next test. (Loral Vought Photos, Courtesy Rick Mac Donnell)

Chapter XI: Experimental Corsairs

Left Photo: Close-up of one of the two, newly installed experimental auxiliary fins on the F4U-5 test craft to assist in development of the XF4U-6 jet design. Upper Photo: Rear view of the fin installation on the F4U-5 Corsair showing the spacing of the test fins. (Ling-Temco Vought Photos, Courtesy Arthur L Schoeni)

Upper Photo: Test Corsair ready to test the new tail fins in 1946. Lower Photo: The Vought XF6U-1 "Pirate" on a test flight with the new tail fins; also note the wingtip blisters. Plane is flying from a Naval Air Test Center in 1946. (Ling-Temco Vought Photos, Courtesy Arthur L Schoeni)

XII

Surviving Corsairs and Racers

Despite the losses in combat, accidents, and intentional destruction, many Corsairs escaped obliteration to become the prized possessions of some, and powerful, prize-winning racing machines for many. Some Corsairs became monuments to the design in aviation museums where we can drink in this awesome and unique airplane almost within arm's reach.

In this chapter we will attempt to cover all aspects of existing Corsairs: non-flying, those flown for pleasure, and the sporting racing machines.

The fact that many "civilians" are able to fly this "dangerous" plane puts the "lie" to those who claimed it was impossible to fly when the Corsair made its appearance in the military.

One of the first non-flying Corsair exhibits was a monument erected on a tall pedestal at the Bridgeport, Connecticut, Airport in Stratford, Connecticut, across from the old Vought plant. Others found their way to existing air museums or new museums that mushroomed into existence during the post-war years.

Condemned! Among the World War II military aircraft crowded on Rukuhia Airfield, located seven miles south of the city of Hamilton, North Island, New Zealand, are almost two-hundred Corsair fighters scheduled for destruction! The Corsairs occupy the right hand portion of the airfield. (John Regan photo, Courtesy John Regan)

Chapter XII: Surviving Corsairs and Racers

This is Million Power Point, Esperitu Santo, in 1996. It is the site at which tons of excess United States military equipment, including many Corsairs, were dumped during the end of World War II. This photo was taken at low tide to reveal the corroded remains of military equipment, including Corsairs. (John Regan photo, Courtesy John Regan)

David Beisel Jr, Rex Beisel's grandson, holds his model Corsair aloft beneath the full size Corsair monument at Bridgeport, Connecticut. Photo taken in 1972. (David Beisel photo, Courtesy Tom Dickinson, MD)

This Vought Corporate Aircraft N63382 (FG-1D) was a private plane for the use of Vought executives and visiting aviators during the post-war years. (Olson photo, Courtesy Nick Hauprich)

Corsair: The Saga of the Legendary Bent-Wing Fighter-Bomber

This former New Zealand Air Force FG-1 Corsair was bought by Jim Landry and colored in the markings of "Big Hog," which was flown in action by CDR John T. "Tommy" Blackburn in 1943. (Jim Larsen photo, Courtesy Jim Larsen)

Corsairs were avidly collected, world wide, to rescue them from annihilation. New Zealand and Australia are closer to the War Zone where Corsairs fought than either the United States or Britain. This gave the Australian and New Zealand Corsair hunters an advantage over the more distant countries by saving Corsairs from the "postwar melting pot."

At least four Corsairs were saved in New Zealand, the most well known being an FG-1 registration number NZ5648. This Corsair was restored to taxiing status by members of the Waikato Aero club in 1962. The fighter was the stellar attraction when it was taxied at the opening of the Hamilton Airport by the owner, Jack Aspin.

The Corsair was sold to an American buyer, Jim Landry, in 1971. It was shipped to the United States, where it was restored to flying status as NX55JP in the colors of "Big Hog," which was flown by the commanding officer of VF-17, Commander John T. "Tommy" Blackburn, in 1943.

The only remaining airworthy RNZAF Corsair belongs to Ray Hanna as part of his warbird collection in Duxford, England.

Several Corsairs were sold by the U.S. government to South American and Central American countries and, after they served their purpose, were sold to U.S. civilians, such as movie companies and eager collectors, in the late 1970s. No.68 was one such Corsair that was sold to Howard Pardue, who apparently sold the F4U-4 to another enthusiast.

This magnificent formation of Corsairs was expertly photographed by Jim Larsen several years ago over Harlingen, Texas: No.167 is part of the Confederate Air Force flown by John Stokes.; No.5 is being flown by Merle Gustafson; No.68 is being flown by Howard Pardue; and No.115 of the Canadian Warplane Heritage is flown by Dennis Bradley. Note insignia is similar to Royal Navy and Royal New Zealand Air Force, with bar added and red center removed (for South Pacific sectors). (Jim Larsen photos, Courtesy Jim Larsen)

John Lane is caught in a steep bank over the sea in Gary Koh's F4U-4 Corsair by lensman Jim Larsen. There is nothing more beautiful than a Corsair in flight. The markings on this Corsair replicate those of an F4U-4 that flew with VMF-223 during the war. (Jim Larson photo, Courtesy Jim Larson)

Chapter XII: Surviving Corsairs and Racers

Dr. Antonacci keeps his FG-1D Corsair in excellent flying condition. Shown here are mechanics maintaining his Corsair in prime shape so he can fly whenever he chooses. (Dr. Louis Antonacci Photo, Courtesy Lou Antonacci)

Two views of Dr. Antonacci's Corsair, with the owner at the controls, reveal the markings of Lt Ira C. Kepford, the high-scoring "Jolly Rogers" Ace. Observe the sixteen Japanese flags arranged in a rectangle just forward of the plane number "29." (Dr. Louis Antonacci Photo, Courtesy Lou Antonacci)

This spectacular formation flight of Dr. Louis Antonacci flying his Corsair and CDR Joseph Daughtry, Jr, flying a Grumman F-14 Tomcat is a most difficult performance. Observe the positive angle of attack at which the Tomcat is flying in order to generate enough lift at its slow speed. (Dr. Louis Antonacci Photo, Courtesy Lou Antonacci)

Corsair: The Saga of the Legendary Bent-Wing Fighter-Bomber

```
AIRCRAFT: FG-1D CORSAIR, BUREAU NO. 88297
Contractor: Goodyear; Akron, Ohio
Contract No: NOa(s) - 1871, dated 10/16/44 and Amendment 10, dated 12/20/44
Contract Specs: FG-1D Type Aircraft with P & W R-2800-8W with an empty
                airframe wt. of 9600 pounds
Acceptance Date: April 9, 1945
Delivery Date:   April 11, 1945

Assignment/Unit:
May, 1945 - Enroute Guam
June thru Sept., 1945 - Aircraft Pool, Airwing 2, Guam
Oct., 1945 - Repair Depot, Samar
Nov. thru Dec., 1945 - Enroute return from Guam
Jan., 1946 - Aircraft Pool, San Diego, California
Feb. thru April, 1946 - Repair Depot, San Diego
May, 1946 - Aircraft Pool, San Diego
June, 1946 thru Nov. 30, 1947 - Naval Air Reserve, Minneapolis, Minn.
Dec., 1947 - Aircraft Pool, Jacksonville, Florida
Jan., 1948 thru Mar. 29, 1948 - Overhaul, Jacksonville
April, 1948 thru Nov., 1948 - Naval Air Reserve, Memphis, Tenn.
Nov., 1948 thru Aug., 1949 - Unknown (Possibly awaiting overhaul at JAX.)
Sept. 29, 1949 thru Oct., 1949 - Overhaul, Jacksonville
Oct., 1949 thru July 12, 1950 - Storage, Litchfield Park, Ariz.
July 16, 1950 thru Aug., 1950 - Overhaul, Jacksonville
Aug., 1950 thru Sept. 17, 1950 - Naval Air Reserve, Minneapolis
Sept. 18, 1950 thru May 30, 1952 - Naval Air Reserve, Miami, Florida
June 26, 1952 thru Jan. 9, 1953 - Overhaul, Jacksonville
Jan. 9, 1953 thru Jan. 16, 1953 - Minor Maintenance, Jacksonville
Jan. 15, 1953 thru Feb. 28, 1955 - Naval Air Reserve, Columbus, Ohio
March 14, 1955 thru Feb. 29, 1956 - Storage, Litchfield Park
March 1, 1956 - Placed for sale
                No record of combat assignments
                No record of direct carrier assignments
                Assigned USN: April, 1945 thru May, 1946
                Assigned USNR: June, 1946 thru March, 1955
                Total USN/USNR Flight Time: 1652 Hours Airframe
Jan. 7, 1957 Stricken from USN Records and sold surplus, Litchfield Park
        (Records from US Naval Air Station, North Island, San Diego.)
Jan. 23, 1959 - Litchfield Park, Sale Documents executed to:
                ALU-MET Smelters
                2056 Golden Ave.
                Long Beach, California
Jan. 9, 1960 - Sold to: Frank Tallman
                1821 Via Visalia
                Palos Verdes Estates, California
Feb. 18, 1966 - Sold to: Rosen - Novak Auto Co.
                2034 Farnum St.
                Omaha, Nebraska
March 13, 1967 - Sold To: Johan M. Larsen
                714 W. 77½ St.
                Minneapolis, Minnesota
Oct. 30, 1978 - Sold to: Dr. Louis E. Antonacci
                4PW279-1 Immelman Lane
                Hampshire, Illinois
```

The life of a Corsair in and after the military: This is the official record of Dr. Antonacci's FG-1D Corsair before he bought it. Observe it underwent four overhauls in less than one year and almost was destroyed in January 1959 (Saved by Frank Tallman). (Official Record of Bu Aer No. 88297, Courtesy Lou Antonacci)

Cook Cleland won sixth place in the 1946 Thompson Trophy Race flying this red and white Goodyear FG-1A. This was the first Corsair winner in a national Race. Name of the plane is "Lucky Gallon" in script on fuselage, forward of cockpit, partly hidden by wing. (Nick Hauprich Photo)

There are many Corsair lovers such as the author who, although they cannot afford a full size Corsair, content themselves with gazing at photographs of the "Bent Wing" or drinking the beauty of Corsairs at museums, or reading voraciously about them and their history. Many Corsair lovers, as the author, often content themselves by building models of the plane. It is a love affair.

Dr. Louis Antonacci satisfied his love of this beautiful bird by managing to buy a full-size Corsair that he flies whenever he chooses. His FG-1D is maintained regularly so it is ready to fly whenever he desires because his purchase of the Corsair was a matter of love and not an investment.

His Corsair is painted in the colors and markings of Lt. Ira C. Kepford, the high-scoring Ace of VF-17 "Jolly Rogers" U.S. Navy squadron.

One of the most amazing performances of Dr. Antonacci and his Corsair was the formation flight he arranged with CDR. Joseph Daughtry Jr, flying his supersonic Grumman "Tomcat" jet-powered fighter.

Both planes bore the "Skull and Crossbones" of the "Jolly Rogers" squadron.

The normal flying speed of the Tomcat is twice that of the Corsair. This forced the Tomcat to fly very slow and, in order to generate enough lift at the slow speed, CDR Daughtry was forced to fly at an excessive

Ths white and black Goodyear FG-1D placed 15th in the 1946 Bendix Trophy Race with Thomas Call at the controls, proving that the Corsair is capable of cross country racing. (Nick Hauprich Photo)

Chapter XII: Surviving Corsairs and Racers

This newly arrived F2G-2 "Super Corsair" awaits movement to shelter where it can be converted into a prize-winning racer. (Pete Doyle Photo)

This blue and white F2G-2 Super Corsair won the 1997 Thompson Trophy with Cook Cleland at the controls. Observe the clipped wing tips and large engine air scoop. (Nick Hauprich Photo)

287

Corsair: The Saga of the Legendary Bent-Wing Fighter-Bomber

Dick Becker's red and white XF2G-1 Super Corsair finished second in the 1947 Thompson Trophy Race. Note the bulging engine air inlet scoop atop the engine cowl. (Nick Hauprich Photo)

Flying his all-black F2G-1 Super Corsair with white number eighty-four in the 1947 Thompson Trophy Race, Tony Jannazo crashed to his death in the seventh lap. (Nick Hauprich Photo)

angle of attack. Conversely, Dr. Antonacci was forced to fly at maximum speed, yet he was forced to constantly adjust his throttle. The performance was a success.

CDR Daughtry was commanding officer of squadron VF-84 "Jolly Rogers," which adopted the "Skull and Crossbones" for the squadron insignia. Later, CDR Daughtry became a carrier captain and commanding officer of the Top Gun School, according to Dr. Antonacci.

When the U.S. National Air Races resumed in the post-war year 1946, the competing aircraft were modified surplus fighters, including Mustangs, Aircobras, and Corsairs, instead of the specially-designed and built racers that had become famous during the 'thirties.

Flying an FG-1A, Cook Cleland scored sixth place in the 1946 Thompson Trophy Race, while Thomas Call placed 15th in the 1946 cross country Bendix Race flying an FG-1D Corsair. These were the first Corsair winners in the post-war National Air Races that started a long string of Corsair racing victories and proved the Corsair could compete in cross-country as well as closed-course racing.

Corsair history was made when Cook Cleland won the Thompson Trophy Race in 1947 with an F2G-2 Super Corsair. The plane had clipped wingtips and was fitted with a special engine air scoop by Pratt & Whitney, the manufacturers of the engine.

Dick Becker placed second in the 1947 Thompson Race with his XF2G-1. The XF2G-1 is a Super Corsair that was converted from an FG-1A Corsair diverted from the Goodyear production line.

Tony Jannazo crashed to his death in the seventh lap of the 1947 Thompson Trophy Race while racing his F2G-1 Corsair. Many superstitious spectators blamed the all-black Corsair for the fatal accident.

Ron G. Puckett, flying a blue and yellow XF2G-1 Super Corsair "Miss Port Colombus" (also called "Betty"), was doing well in the 1947 Thompson Trophy race when, in the 19th lap, it suffered engine failure and dropped out of the race.

This blue and yellow XF2G-1 Super Corsair was flown by Ron G Pucket in the 1947 Thompson Trophy Race when it suffered engine failure in the 19th lap and was forced to drop out of the race. (Peter Doyle Collection)

Observe the dislodged engine air scoop on Cook Cleland's carefully engineered 1948 entry in the Thompson Trophy Race. This forced the Super Corsair out of the race. (Peter Doyle Collection)

Chapter XII: Surviving Corsairs and Racers

Cook Cleland's 1949 entry in the Thompson Trophy Race sports wing tip end plates and a fuselage tail cone that could have helped him win the race. (Peter Doyle Collection)

Bill Odom flew Jacqueline Cochran's highly modified Mustang in the 1949 Thompson Trophy Race against three Super Corsairs, but crashed into a house, killing two occupants and Odom. Three Corsairs forged ahead claiming first, second, and third places. (Nick Hauprich Photo)

This Cook Cleland Super Corsair won the 1949 Thompson Race, making Cleland the only man other than Roscoe Turner to repeat a Thompson Trophy first place victory. (Peter Doyle Collection)

Corsair: The Saga of the Legendary Bent-Wing Fighter-Bomber

Ron G. Puckett scored second place in the 1949 Thompson Trophy Race with his blue and gray XF2G-1 Super Corsair at an average speed of 393.5 mph. (Peter Doyle Collection)

The stellar attraction at the 1948 Thompson Trophy Race was Cook Cleland's XF2G-1 Corsair.

Cleland had removed all military equipment; covered all steps; faired over all fuselage main fuel tank panel Dzus fasteners with filler; faired all cowl latches with stainless steel; removed the auxiliary rudder and replaced it with a fixed section; and he installed FG1-D outer wing panels from "Lucky Gallon" and replaced the fabric covering with .025 Alclad Skin. (This became the only racing Corsair with metal-skinned wings). He also installed a 28 gallon fuel tank in each gun bay and a 54 gallon fuel tank in each outer wing panel, and removed eighteen inches from each wing tip and closed each tip with a fairing cap. Flaps were faired in and a solid tire tailwheel was installed. A custom designed and built engine air intake air scoop and special propeller spinner were also installed.

As the super-engineered racer entered the fifth lap the air scoop loosened and shifted, forcing Cleland to drop out of the race, and allowing Anson Johnson to win with his P-51D Mustang.

The principal challenger to the Corsairs was the P-51 Mustang, and one of the best-modified Mustangs was owned by the world-famous airwoman, Jacqueline Cochran. The deep belly radiator was traded for two barrel-shaped wingtip radiators. This not only streamlined the fuselage and acted as end plates on the wing, but also made the ailerons more effective, which should be an asset when rounding the pylons. Cochran engaged experienced Bill Odom to fly the plane because he had previously won the Sohio Race in that Mustang. Now, it challenged three Corsairs in the 1949 Thompson Race.

Ben McKillen, Jr, chief pilot at Cook Cleland's Willoughby, Ohio, airport, raced this red and white F2G-1 Super Corsair to third place in the 1949 Thompson Trophy Race. Ben McKillen, Jr, also won the 1949 Tinnerman (close course) Race with this plane. (Peter Doyle Collection)

Chapter XII: Surviving Corsairs and Racers

After the termination of the Thompson Trophy Races in 1949 some of the former racers were scrapped. That was the fate of the red and white F2G-1 Corsair flown by Ben McKillen, Jr. With wings folded the beautiful plane was left to deteriorate by the forces of nature. Photos taken July 1963 in Chardon, Ohio. (Nick Hauprich Photos, Courtesy Nick Hauprich)

As Odom rounded the No. 2 pylon on the second lap, his oversensitive ailerons banked the sleek plane too sharply to the left. In an effort to correct to a right bank, the plane rolled over onto its back and, at this low altitude, dived into a house, killing two occupants and the famous aviator.

The Three Super Corsairs surged ahead: Cook Cleland won the 1949 Thompson Race at an average 397.071 miles per hour in his XF2G-1; Ron G. Puckett scored second place with his XF2G-1 at an average 393.5 mph; and Ben Mc Killen Jr, chief pilot at Cook Cleland's Willoughby, Ohio, airport, took third place in one of Cleland's F2G-1 Corsairs with an average speed of 387.6 mph. This beautiful red and white No.57 also won first prize in the 1949 Tinnerman Race.

Cook Cleland's 1949 Thompson victory made him the only man other than the legendary Roscoe Turner to repeat a First Place Thompson victory.

The high qualifying time at the meet was made by Dick Becker at a speed of 414.592 mph in a third Cleland Corsair; however, he was eliminated from the race because an oil fire destroyed his engine after the qualifying run.

Taken during a Thompson Trophy Race, this is how the red and white F2G-1 Super Corsair No.57 appeared before and after deterioration and restoration. Upper Photo is original No.57. Lower Photo is Restored No.57. (Upper Photo- Jim Larsen, Lower Photo- Nick Hauprich)

Corsair: The Saga of the Legendary Bent-Wing Fighter-Bomber

Pilot Lynn Winney crashed to his death before the time trials of the 1965 Los Angeles National Air Races (29-30 May 6 June) when flying Lou Kaufman's FG-1D Corsair, (N4719C). (Jim Larsen Photo)

Bob Guilford's beautiful F4U-7 is outfitted with long range drop tanks, wing rocket rails, and spiral painted propeller hub that suggests scale authenticity, but with the cowl number he might have had racing in mind. (Jim Larsen Photo)

It is interesting that all of the Corsair aviators wore oxygen masks as a precaution, since the crash of a similar plane in 1947 was blamed on engine fumes.

The 1949 Thompson Trophy race and Bendix Trophy Race were the last race for both famous races. The terrible accident of Bill Odom and the resident's death led to the end of the races.

Championship Races were resurrected at Reno in 1964 and were dominated by Mustangs and Bearcats. Super Corsairs were not entered. They had made their mark in racing and retired gracefully.

After the races ended in 1949, hearts were broken when many of the former racers were scrapped because most of the owners could not afford the upkeep of a 2,000 plus horsepower racing plane, while some of those who could afford the maintenance lost interest or looked for other exciting "toys." Those that were not scrapped for the price of the metal in their airframes were left to slowly deteriorate. A few found their way into museums; however, such was not the kind care that befell No.57, that beautiful red and white F2G-1 Corsair.

With wings carefully folded No.57 was abandoned in a lot near Chardon, Ohio, with other "trash," and in a few years all the fabric covering was in shreds—but all was not lost.

Bob Mitchum (owner/ pilot) in his FG-1D (left photo) and flying his converted F2G-1 Super Corsair in September 1970 (right photo). (Tom Piedmont Left Photo, Jim Larsen Right Photo)

Chapter XII: Surviving Corsairs and Racers

Bob Guilford's beautiful F4U-7 is devoid of long range drop tanks and rocket rails, but has false machine gun barrels, suggesting scale effect. (Nick Hauprich Photo)

John Trainor, who owned other military aircraft and raced at Reno, bought No.57; however; before he could put his plans into action he was killed in a flying accident.

Harry Doan, a Florida businessman and warbird collector, bought No. 57 and owned the plane from 1984 through 1990, when he was also killed in a flying accident. During the time Harry Doan owned No.57 most of the components had been disassembled and parts from other Corsairs had been collected to help in the rebuilding.

The Corsair next moved to the Lone Star Museum in Texas, where more work was done on the airframe.

Eventually, by 1996 No.57 was in the possession of Robert Odegard, an experienced warbird restorer who owned an Avenger bomber that he had restored.

Missing parts consisted of the engine, engine mounts, propeller, most of the fairings, and the canopy. Every system had to be created using manuals. Parts that couldn't be found had to be made by hand. The Crawford Auto-Aviation Museum of Cleveland, Ohio, loaned Odegard the engine from Cleland's No.94 Racer that was part of its collection.

Finally, engine tests were complete and taxiing passed. The first flight was completed on August 18, 1999, and Odegard was elated at the performance.

After more test flights it was agreed to make the long flight to the Reno National Championship Air Races. A half century before, Ben McKillen Jr. flew No.57 at the Cleveland National Air Races and Odegard felt that it would be proper to have No.57 at America's only active air races to celebrate that anniversary.

In addition to commorate the Ben McKillen, Jr. victory at the Cleveland National Air Races fifty years ago flying No.57, Bob Odegard planned to compete for the prestigious Rolls-Royce Aviation Heritage Trophy. Presented by Rolls-Royce, the National Aviation Hall of Fame, the

From 1982 to 1984 this SuperCorsair was sponsored by "Budweiser Light Beer." During this time the SuperCorsair campaigned respectfully as the crew gradually improved the racer. Then All-Coast Forest Products, Chino, CA, took up the sponsorship. (Courtesy The Air Museum Planes of Fame)

Corsair: The Saga of the Legendary Bent-Wing Fighter-Bomber

Two views of the SuperCorsair as sponsored by "All-Coast Forest Products." Plane is colored silver with blue trim and red striping. Observe the massive four bladed propeller and the long strake on the wing fillet. (Courtesy The Air Museum Planes of Fame)

Smithsonian National Air and Space Museum, and the Reno Air Racing Association, the trophy was conceived as an incentive to encourage the preservation of aviation history through the restoration of historically significant aircraft.

A panel of five expert judges examined the fifteen entries with authenticity as the criterion. Bob Odegard's No.57 won over a field of well-restored entries.

The hand-made, four-foot tall trophy was initially displayed at the National Aviation Hall of Fame, Learning, and Research Center in Dayton, Ohio, and now resides at the National Air and Space Museum in Washington, D.C.

The rebuilt No.57 also won the National Aviation Hall of Fame's "People's Choice Award" co-sponsored by Rolls-Royce. This award guarantees that No.57 is one of the most beautiful airplanes ever.

It required about 12,000 hours of skilled labor and restoration experts to do what seven previous owners did not do. The restoration is mute testimony to what can be done with skill and determination to restore a beautiful airplane to its former glory.

Opposite: This detailed rendering shows the color scheme, layout, and markings of the Super Corsair. Note the long strake extension on the wing/ fuselage fillet.
"Thanks" notes are amplified thus: Upper note on Drawing
John Sandberg - Pete Lain
Bruce Boland - Tilidyne Corp
Joan Mc Guire - Consolidated Aero
Bruce Baims - Karen Hinton
Bay Por - Aircraft Cyl.
Lt Christophire - Lawrence Fagey
R.A. Saus Co. - Frank Lie
Rick Brickert - Merrill Wien
"Thanks" notes are amplified thus: Lower Note on Drawing
Charles Dame - KKW Trucano
Otto's Instruments - Lawly Boats
Randy Scomis - Sudlis Aircraft
Vanesa Air Corps - Frank Taylor
John Paul -Walley Mc Bonnill
John Bealamaint - Bob Reed
Joe Maley - Dave Lyon
Marci Di Marino
Brandon Kenicky - Brian Mortin
(Courtesy The Air Museum Planes of Fame)

Chapter XII: Surviving Corsairs and Racers

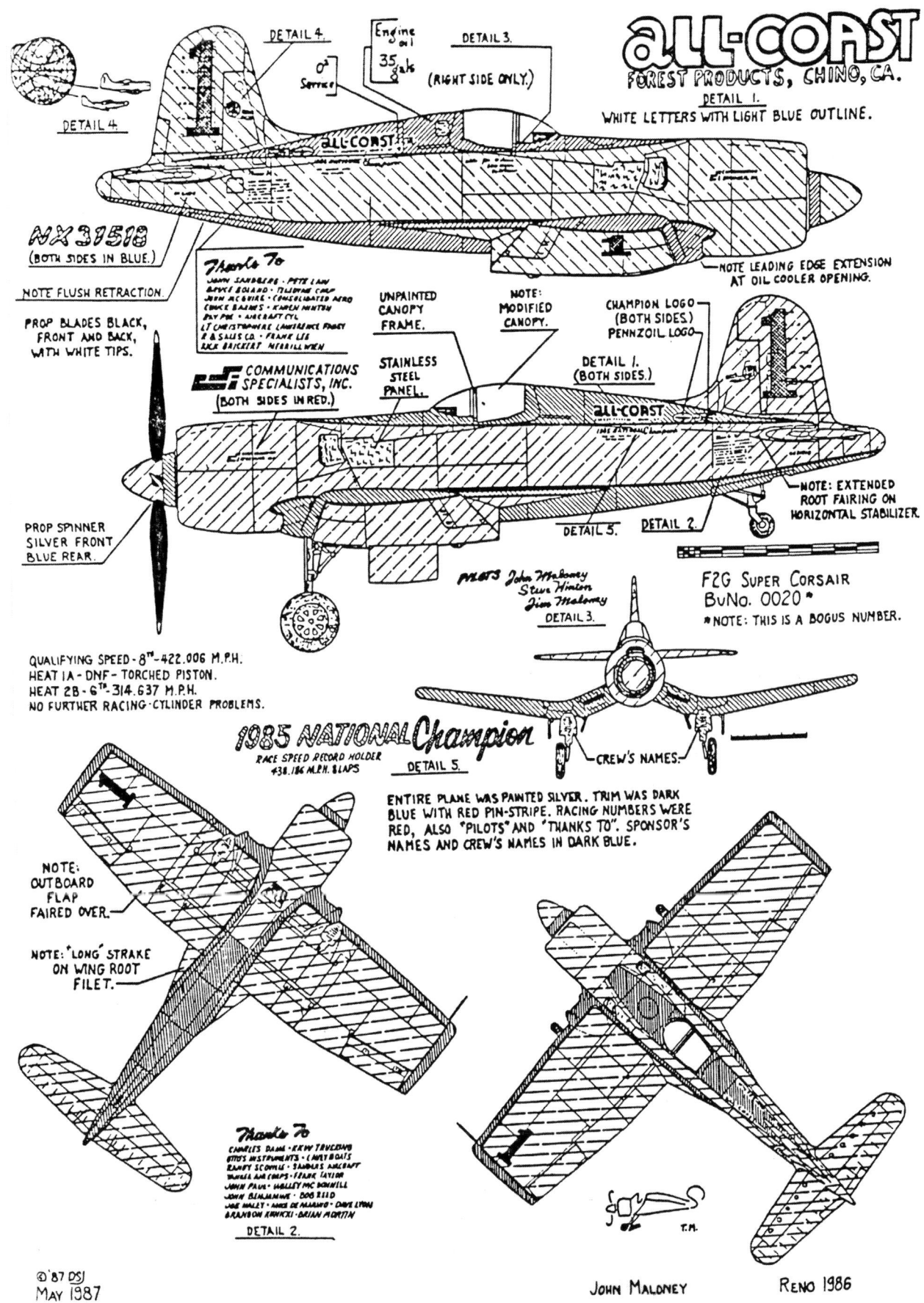

This view of the "Super Corsair" reveals that it is virtually an enhanced corsair. Observe the absence of a flap on the wing outer panels, lengthened fuselage tail, and the dorsal on the fin. The scene is probably the Phoenix 500 Air races for Unlimited Propeller-Driven Aircraft. The lettering beneath the cockpit reads as follows:
Pilots: John Maloney
Steve Hinton
Jim Maloney

Lettering under stripe under ALL-COAST:
1985 National Champion
(Courtesy Phoenix 500 Racing Committee)

Several air races followed the end of the Thompson and Bendix Races. Some of the races included the Phoenix 500; Los Angeles National Air Races; Reno Air Races; and Mojave 1,000 mile Race.

In the spring of 1982, two young crack pilots and experienced mechanics decided to build a really competitive unlimited class racing plane. One of the young men was Jim Maloney, son of the founder and director of the Air Museum Planes of Fame, Ed Maloney. The other young pilot was Steve Hinton, a race pilot of great ability.

The Air Museum Planes of Fame is located on the Chino airport at 7000 Merrill Avenue No.17, Chino, California, 91710. The Planes of Fame Museum was the first permanent air museum in the Western United States. Ed Maloney has also been a pioneer in the concept of restoring display historic aircraft to flying condition.

The museum is manned by a core of dedicated volunteers. Ed Maloney has supported its operations for the past fifty years with admission fees, donations, and proceeds for the use of its aircraft in various productions, such as motion pictures.

The museum also has a special membership program available to the public, with one of the benefits of membership being the opportunity to experience the thrill of orientation flights in genuine historic warbirds. Information regarding the museum can be had by calling (909) 597-3222.

Years before, Ed Maloney had acquired an old F4U-1 Corsair that had been used as a movie prop over the years and had become a derelict. Since the Air Museum already had a flying Corsair, the derelict was pushed into the back lot and ignored. Jim and Steve looked the derelict over once more and decided it could be the foundation for a new racer.

Over the next few months, with help from their friends, Jim and Steve put together what was to be the ultimate "Airplane Kit."

While Jim and Steve concentrated on the structure, Dennis Sanders built up a new wing and, in the process, cut almost four feet off each side and reduced the flap area!

John Sandberg donated a massive Pratt and Whitney R-4350 engine, converting the plane from an F4U-1 to an F2G and nearly doubling the power! Due to the engine size it was necessary to adopt the engine cowl from an A-26 medium bomber. In order to absorb the power of the larger engine a Skyraider propeller was installed. The propeller hub was covered with a Mustang P-51K spinner. A new streamline canopy was made to fit the new lower fuselage profile to complete the new airplane.

(Left Photo) When the "SuperCorsair" caught fire Kevin Eldridge was ordered to "bail out"; however, the slipstream sucked him out of the cockpit and slammed him against the stabilizer. The wounded Kevin is floating to earth. (Courtesy The Air Museum Planes of Fame) (Right Photo) After bail-out, the "SuperCorsair" continues its plunge to earth, crashing into an unpopulated area. (Courtesy The Air Museum Planes of Fame)

Chapter XII: Surviving Corsairs and Racers

The improvements made the derelict F4U-1 virtually a new airplane. Many aircraft designers and craftsmen had insisted it could not be done, but in only five months the Super Corsair was ready to race!

The magnificent machine raced from 1986 to 1994 (John Maloney 1986-1991 and Kevin Eldridge 1992-1994). The crew gradually improved the Super Corsair until it was ready for the 1985 Unlimited Class Air Racers at Reno, where the Super Corsair became the world's fastest Corsair by becoming the World Champion Unlimited Class Air race winner at a speed of 438 mph with Steve Hinton at the controls.

In the spring of 1994, the inaugural Phoenix 500 Air Races for Unlimited Propeller-driven Aircraft was announced, and the fastest corsair in the world was expected to enter with Kevin Eldridge at the controls.

Kevin Eldridge was the youngest active pilot competing in the Unlimited Category of air racing at the age of thirty-two years. He had already flown most of the World-War II racing fighters, and this was Kevin's seventh air race.

The race was separated in three heats of six laps each, and the second heat was scheduled for March 19, 1994.

Six World War II fighters were scheduled to race on that day: three Mustangs; two British-built Sea Furies; and one Super Corsair.

With three of the six laps completed, Howard Pardue's Sea Fury was in the lead with the Super Corsair close behind. Flying an oval pattern with speeds up to 430 mph and an altitude as low as fifty feet above the ground made flying this race a harrowing experience.

Entering the third of six laps, Kevin Eldridge felt a shudder, but assumed it was a burble from the high "G" forces or the slipstream from the Sea Fury he was closely chasing.

Following vibrations were more severe, and they felt like a car riding over a rocky road.

The violent shaking was followed by a sudden loss of engine power! Kevin pulled the stick into his belly and closed the throttlem trading engine power for altitudem and reached 5,000 feet, simultaneously calling "Mayday! Mayday! From Race One. Looks like I've got an engine failure."

The response from both the ground crew and the airborne race coordinator was "Roger your Mayday. Race One."

The violent vibrations had diminished but, at idle, the powerful engine could not deliver enough power to sustain flight. His ground crew reported trailing smoke, and at the same time the cockpit started to fill with smoke. Before Kevin could plan his next move he received his next message from the ground crew, "Race One, you're on fire! Bail out! Bail Out!

Kevin felt heat coming from the engine and more smoke entering the cockpit. He quickly removed his oxygen mask and radio cables, released his safety belt and shoulder straps, and banked the Super corsair away from the grandstand. As he stood up in the cockpit to dive over the side or bail out, the 250 mph slipstream literally blew him out of the cockpit and slammed his body into the stabilizer, knocking off his helmet and opening his parachute.

As he drifted downward, he observed that two panels of his parachute were torn. He also discovered that his right arm was broken, as was his left leg! He landed well on his right leg and was relieved to see that his falling Super Corsair fell in an open field, causing no injury or damage.

Kevin Eldridge is shown out of the hospital with a broken right arm fitted with a steel plate, compound fracture of the left leg, and a broken neck which required wearing a "halo" head and neck stabilizer for three months. The "halo" prevents head and neck movement with four steel needles screwed into the skull. (Courtesy The Air Museum Planes of Fame)

Kevin's injuries healed well, except that his broken neck required that he wear a head and neck stabilizing "Halo" for three months to prevent neck and head movements.

This chapter started with the destruction of hundreds of lovely Corsairs and ended with a triumphant Corsair, rebuilt from trash. The Corsair knows no death; it will live on forever.

Despite his injuries, Kevin Eldridge continued to race for at least a dozen years in very advanced racing planes.

Epilogue

Rex B Beisel, the designer of the Bent-Wing Corsair, was a quiet man and not a "Bragadocio." In fact, his son Rex Jr. claims that his father never talked about the clever designs he developed at work when he came home from the office at the end of each day, regardless of inquiries from his son.

This quiet attitude could have been the reason why the National Museum of Aviation was not aware of Rex Beisel's outstanding aircraft designs that would make him worthy of enshrinement in the Hall of Honor.

Many writers credit Mr. Chance Vought with the design of the Vought F4U Corsair when, in reality, Mr Chance Vought died in 1930, ten years before the Vought F4U Corsair was designed by Rex Beisel. This illustrates how otherwise informative writers assume that Chance Vought designed the Corsair.

The list goes on and on, because Rex Beisel never owned his own company and, therefore, never made the "headlines."

Leaders in the Aviation Industry, naval aviation officers, aviation authors, and many others pressed for Rex Buren Beisel's enshrinement in the National Naval Aviation Museum Hall of Honor.

Finally, Mr Rex B Beisel's achievements were recognized and his enshrinement ceremony was held on Thursday, May 4, 2000, in the National Museum of Naval Aviation Hall of Honor.

Close family members were the honored guests at Rex B Beisel's enshrinement in the Hall of Honor, and a large bronze plaque of Rex

"Once an engineer, always an engineer." Despite Rex Beisel's position as Vice President of United Aircraft and Vought General Manager he took an enthusiastic interest in the design and production of all contracts. He is shown here stressing a point with Bert Taliaferro, Vought Factory Manager (right), and John Hemmert, Assistant Factory Manager (arrow). Observe the Vought F6U Pirate jet fighter under construction in the background. (Vought Aircraft Company, Author's File)

The 1951 Vought F7U-3 "Cutlass" U.S. Navy tailless fighter featured a pressurized cockpit and engine afterburners. It was the last design that kept Beisel fully involved. (Vought Aircraft Company, Author's File)

Epilogue

WALTER A. MUSCIANO 110 UNION STREET   LODI, NJ 07644 ● (201) 472-7545

● AVIATION, NAVAL & MILITARY HISTORY ●

Captain Robert L. Rasmussen
Department of the Navy
Naval Aviation Museum
Naval Air Station
Pensacola, Florida 32508

February 4, 1993

Dear Captain Rasmussen:

It has come to my attention that Rex Buren Beisel is, once again, to be considered for election to the National Naval Aviation Museum Hall of Fame. I was disappointed and saddened to learn that the committee had failed to elect Rex Beisel to the Hall of Fame in the past.

I wish to add my endorsement to his election because I earnestly believe that Rex Beisel is eminently deserving of admission into the museum's Hall of Fame and, therefore, I implore the committee to carefully research the man and his many contributions to the advancement of U.S. Naval Aircraft. This is most important because, once aware of the man and what he had to overcome to create his wondrous aircraft, it is impossible not to realize that Rex Buren Beisel deserves to be elected into the museum's Hall of Fame this year.

For over a half-century I was engaged in the design of naval combat aircraft as well as aircraft carriers for the U.S. Navy. I am now a full-time author of articles and books on aviation subjects and am presently completing my twenty-first book which is about aircraft carriers and their brood of Warbirds. The story also includes Rex Beisel's contributions to naval aviation. My twenty-second book is to be the comprehensive story of the Vought F4U Corsair and Rex Buren Beisel. Both books are under contract with Schiffer Publications Ltd. In the late sixties I had published one of the first if not the first book about the Vought F4U Corsair, "Saga of the Bent-Wing Bird", and it was during that time that I discussed Rex Beisel with George Page who had worked closely with Beisel at Curtiss. Page had nothing but praise for Rex Beisel's technical ability and determination. My "Corsair Aces" was published in 1979 by Arco Publishing and a second edition in 1989 by TAB/McGraw-Hill.

From the very first U.S. Navy airplane designed specifically for carrier operation to a successful advanced tailless jet-powered carrier-based interceptor/fighter/strike aircraft Rex Beisel's designing genius produced some of the finest naval aircraft in the world and he deserves a prominent place in the National Naval Aviation Museum Hall of Fame.

It is unfortunate that many otherwise knowledgeable persons believe that Beisel's only claim to fame is the Vought F4U Corsair and, admittedly, the Bent-Wing Bird is, indeed, enough for Rex Beisel to qualify for the museum's Hall of Fame. However, there is more! In order to correct this unfortunate assumption I have taken the liberty of enclosing a brief outline about Rex Beisel and some of his outstanding designs that have contributed immeasurably to the advancement of Naval Aviation.

As can be deduced from this information, Rex Beisel deserves admittance into the Museum's Hall of Fame.

Sincerely,
Walter A. Musciano

WAM/ MM
Enclos.

This is the author's letter to Captain Rasmussen, USN, endorsing Rex Beisel's enshrinement in the Hall of Honor of the National Museum of Naval Aviation. (Author's File)

DEPARTMENT OF THE NAVY
NATIONAL MUSEUM OF NAVAL AVIATION
1750 RADFORD BLVD
SUITE C
PENSACOLA FLORIDA 32508-5402

28 JUN 1999

Rex Beisel Jr.
617 Longfellow Drive
Branford, CT 06405-5811

Dear Mr. Beisel,

It is my distinct pleasure to advise you of the selection of your father, Mr. Rex B. Beisel, for enshrinement in the Hall of Honor of the National Museum of Naval Aviation. The Hall of Honor selection was made in the early spring of this year by a committee appointed by the Chief of Naval Operations. As one of the four selectees for enshrinement in 2000, Mr. Beisel will be joining a distinguished group of Americans who have made major contributions to Naval Aviation. A list of honorees, named in ten previous selections along with those chosen this year, is enclosed.

The enshrinement ceremony will be part of the Museum Foundation's Fourteenth Annual Naval Aviation Symposium, which will be held at the Museum from Thursday, 4 May through Friday, 5 May 2000. The enshrinement ceremony will be held on Thursday, 4 May, at 0900. A copy of the Symposium schedule is enclosed. We hope you will be able to attend.

For the Hall of Honor Enshrinement and Symposium, you and one guest of your choice will be hosted by the Naval Aviation Museum Foundation. All expenses for air and ground transportation, meals and lodging will be covered for you and your chosen guest for the entire period of the Symposium. We will also provide assistance in making all of the related reservations for you both.

Please advise us at your earliest convenience whether or not you will be able to join us for this very special event. After we hear from you in this regard, we will send you further detailed information, and our Public Affair Officer, Ms. Jean Tarnok, will contact you to assist in making all appropriate arrangements. If you have any questions at this point, please feel free to contact her at (850) 452-3604, ext. 130 and I can be reached at ext. 119.

Congratulations and I am looking forward to hearing from you soon.

Sincerely,

R. L. RASMUSSEN
Captain, USN (Ret)
Director

Encl:
(1) List of Honorees
(2) 2000 Symposium Schedule

This is Capt. Rasmussen's letter to Rex B Beisel, Jr, announcing the approval of Rex B Beisel's enshrinement in the National Museum of Naval Aviation Hall of Honor. (Courtesy Rex B Beisel Jr)

Mr. Walter A. Musciano
110 Union Street
Lodi, NJ 07644

Dear Walt,

Herewith a copy of the True Word from Pensacola.

The entire family expresses its gratitude for your generous contribution of your writing skills to this project.

And, finally success!

Best regards,

Rex B. Beisel, Jr.

July 08, 1999

Rex B Beisel's son, Rex B Beisel, Jr, sent this note of thanks to the author with Capt Rasmussen's announcement of Rex B Beisel's selection to enshrinement in the Hall of Honor. (Author's File)

Corsair: The Saga of the Legendary Bent-Wing Fighter-Bomber

This large bronze plaque was placed on display during the Rex Beisel enshrinement in the Hall of Honor of the National Museum of Naval Aviation. It will be displayed permanently. (Photo Courtesy National Museum of Naval Aviation)

B Beisel's portrait was on display and will probably be displayed permanently.

The National Museum of Naval Aviation Band played appropriate music for the occasion.

The splendid naval aircraft collection of the National Museum of Naval Aviation includes select aircraft designed by Rex Buren Beisel that span three decades:

Beginning with the TS-1 of 1921 that set the pace for early U.S. naval aircraft, the Naval Aircraft Factory constructed five, while Curtiss made thirty-four known as FC-1. It was the first U.S. plane designed to operate from an aircraft carrier. Beisel also experimented with a metal framework versus the conventional wooden framework and discovered that the TS-1 was lighter and stronger with the metal framework!

One of the longest-lasting and recognizable of Beisel designs was the Curtiss "Hawks" that started with the Curtiss F6C (Navy) and P-1 (Army). This design progressed into the Navy "Goshawk" and Army "Hawk P-6E" of the 'Thirties. This 1926 design was also produced with radial engines in the "Goshawk."

(Left Photo) The enshrinement ceremony of Rex B Beisel was conducted by RADM Mark M Gemmill (standing). Seated (visible L to R) are: RADM Michael T. Bucchi; VADM Mike Bowman; VADM J.W. Crain, Jr.; and Chaplain Wiggins. (Right Photo) The National Museum of Naval Aviation Band played appropriate music at the ceremony. (Photo Courtesy National Museum of Naval Aviation)

The honored guests at the late Rex B Beisel's enshrinement in the Hall of Honor of the National Museum of Naval Aviation were Beisel's close relatives (Left Photo), from left to right: Rex B Beisel, Jr-son; and James H. Mac Naughton, Jr-son-in-law. (Right Photo) From left to right: Kimberly Day Proctor-granddaughter; Mark Smedley-Fiance to A.R. Oliver; Amy R. Oliver-Granddaughter; Jonathan K. Day-Grandson; James H. MacNaughton, Jr.-son-in-law; and Stephan D. Day-Grandson. (Photos Courtesy Rex B Beisel, Jr)

Epilogue

(Left Photo) Working with the Naval Aircraft Factory, Rex Beisel created this diminutive single-seater biplane to operate from America's only Aircraft Carrier, USS Langley. With a 25ft wingspan it was the smallest U.S. Navy plane and the first U.S. Navy single-seater. It was also one of the first air-cooled radial engine-powered planes in the U.S. Navy, designated Curtiss FC-1. (Right Photo) This Curtiss F6C Hawk, designed by Beisel in 1925, evolved to the radial engine powered Goshawk of the 1930s. The same design for the U.S. Army (P-1 Hawk) evolved to the beautiful Hawk P-6E. Good designs do not die! (Photos Courtesy National Museum of Naval Aviation)

(Left Photo) This jaunty, swept-wing, radial engined biplane fighter won the 1929 Curtiss Marine Trophy. The F7C-1 "Sea Hawks" were flown by the U.S. Marine Corps. One "Sea Hawk" was used for experiments on cowlings, propellers, and spinners. Another Beisel design. (Right Photo) This 1928 Curtiss N2C-1 "Fledgling" trainer won a competition over fourteen other companies' designs. Observe how Beisel strengthened the wings with two sets of struts and two sets of flying and landing wires in the event that the student makes an error in maneuvering. Note the air-cooled radial engine. (Photos Courtesy National Museum of Naval Aviation)

(Left Photo) As Vought Chief Engineer, Beisel designed the first U.S. Navy monoplane scout-bomber, the SB2-U (with a cockpit-operated upward folding-wing), known as the "Vindicator." The Museum display features the upward folding wing. Other companies' folding wings required a three to six-man crew to operate the folding wing at that time. (Right Photo) The Museum display of the OS2U-1 "Kingfisher" is suspended on cables in order to appreciate the design of the single float. Rex Beisel pioneered aircraft spot welding in this design. (Photos Courtesy National Museum of Naval Aviation)

The museum exhibits a wonderfully preserved F6C "Hawk."

In 1928, Beisel's Curtiss N2C-1 "Fledgling" trainer design was selected over fourteen competitive designs from other aircraft companies to become the Naval Reserves' standard primary trainer. A beautifully preserved Curtiss Fledgling Trainer is an exhibit in the National Museum of Naval Aviation collection.

Rex Beisel became Assistant Chief Engineer of the Chance Vought division of United Aircraft Corporation in 1931, and by 1932 he had designed the U.S. Navy's first scout-bomber, the SBU-1 biplane.

In 1935 Beisel was promoted to Chance Vought Chief Engineer while he was working on the design of a monoplane scout-bomber, the SB2-U. This plane is exhibited on the floor of the museum with upward-folding wings. This plane became known as the early World War II "Vindicator." It also featured one of the first trapeze bomb racks.

Two years later his knowledge of seaplane hull design helped Beisel create the first monoplane to regularly catapult from shipboard, the OS2U-1 "Kingfisher." Known for its extraordinary strength when rescuing up to a dozen downed airmen in rough seas is often credited to the "Kingfisher's" spot-welded fuselage and float pioneered by Beisel and applied to the future "Corsair."

The "Gull-Winged Marvel" is featured in two positions in the National Museum of Naval Aviation: one high in the air, with retracted landing gear, and the other on the floor with wings folded, showing all aspects of the Corsair in the display.

A visit to the National Museum of Naval Aviation in Pensacola, Florida, is most rewarding, not only for those who want to feel close to Rex Beisel's creations, but for those who enjoy airplanes in general and Naval Aircraft in particular. Treat yourself and those you love with a visit.

(Upper Photo) Suspended high above other displays, this checkerboard "Corsair" appears to be the "King of the Hill" in the National Museum of Naval Aviation. With retractable landing gear, we can almost hear the engine roar. (Lower Photo) Another Marine "Corsair" on display with cockpit-operated wing folded could be imagined in the carrier's hangar ready to be serviced. Spot welding was used in the fuselage construction. (Photos Courtesy National Museum of Naval Aviation)

Appendix A:
Corsair Fighter Organization

The principal U.S. Marine Aviation tactical, administrative, and commanding organization in World War II was the Marine Air Wing (MAW), which comprised from two to five Marine Air Groups (MAG).

The MAG, in turn, consisted of two to six squadrons.

Col or Lt. Col ranks were in command of MAW or MAG combat units. Air wing commanders were in control of all aircraft on an aircraft carrier because all aircraft on a carrier form a wing. A wing also governs the general air operation in a given battle area.

The basic administrative and tactical unit of any air arm is the squadron: VMF= fighter; VMSB= scout bomber; V= heavier than air aircraft; M= Marine; F= fighter; and SB= scout bomber (scout and dive bomber).

United States Navy and Marine fighter squadrons consisted of 18 aircraft prior to the Japanese attack on Pearl Harbor. The 18 aircraft were divided into six flights or sections of three planes each. The flight operated as the smallest unit, each with its individual leader. The flight flew in a vee formation, with the leader at the apex (front/center). Very often, one or both of the wingmen obstructed the leader's view from the center/apex of the Vee.

As new fighter tactics evolved during the Spanish Civil War and the Battle of Britain, the universally employed three-plane flight was discarded and replaced with a four-plane formation called a Division that was divided into two two-plane flights. Each two-plane flight is called a Section. One plane in each Section was the Section Leader, while one of the Section Leaders is also the Division Leader.

This typical Division is engaged in a turn to port (left turn); however, each Section is using a different technique in making the turn. The wingman normally flies slightly above, outboard, and to the rear of the Section Leader. When making a turn, the wingman must assume a position in which he can make the turn at the same speed as his Section Leader without increasing or decreasing his speed, and resume the normal combat relationship with his leader at the end of the turn. The Upper Division illustrates the Wingman dropping behind his Leader to assume the same speed. Lower Division illustrates the Wingman sideslipping over the Section Leader, which is the more acceptable maneuver. (U.S. Navy Photo via National Archives)

Three-plane flights are unusual unless one of the four aviators is taking the photo, which is the case in this high-flying Corsair division. After completing a high-flying flight beyond the sight of the ground for landmarks a special map is necessary to guide the aviators to their base. (Goodyear Aircraft Photo Approved by U.S. Navy, Courtesy Nick Hauprich)

The second plane in each section is the Wingman, who flies outboard and slightly above and behind his Section Leader. With this formation, all pilots have an unrestricted view in all directions, thereby thwarting a surprise attack. When viewed from above, the Division is arranged as the fingernails of the four fingers of the right hand when widely spread and viewed from above. In fact, the Royal Air Force calls this formation "Finger-Four." This is the formation in which Corsairs flew in World War II and the Korean conflict. Very often the Sections separate from each other in the heat of battle; however, they soon join with each other to re-form the Division.

In the event that the flight or a lone aviator is flying so high that the ground is beyond sight, or in the event that combat with the enemy led the aviator over unfamiliar territory, every aviator is equipped with a homing map that will guide him back to his home base.

Both U.S. Navy and U.S. Marine squadron leaders were removed from duty as squadron leaders after one tour or, at times, two tours of duty, regardless how well they led their squadrons. Commander, Air Solomons (Comairsols), made this decision because of the unacceptable rate in which squadron leaders were being killed in action. They were later assigned as CO of other squadrons, or into other high-ranking operational positions.

The entire organizational pattern was quite flexible, especially with land-based units. This proved to be an asset, especially in the Solomons campaign, where extra squadrons and double-strength units were formed as needed depending upon the enemy resistance.

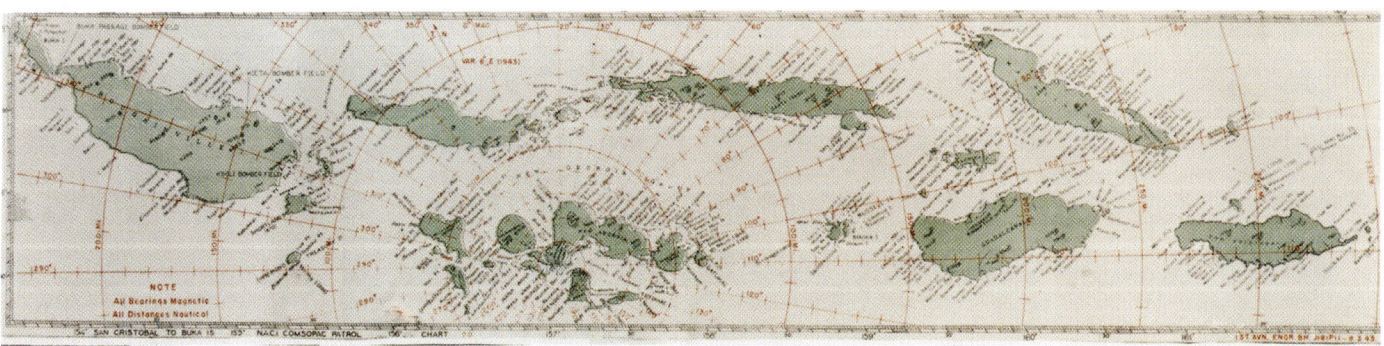

Every U.S. Marine aviator was equipped with a map similar to the one shown here that would guide him back to his base. The concentric circles gave the aviator nautical mileage to his base while the radiating lines indicated the magnetic compass bearings to his base from wherever he might be in that war zone. (U.S. Marine Corps Chart Courtesy Col. OK Williams)

Appendix B:
Corsair Squadron Histories

The following digest of U.S. Marine Squadrons that were active with Corsairs on several fronts in the Pacific will reveal that names of Squadron Leaders emerge leading several different units from time to time:

Marine Fighting Squadron One-One-One (VMF-111) "Devil Dogs"
Organized at Quantico on July 1, 1937, as VMF-1, this was changed to VMF-111 on July 1, 1941. Arrived at Samoa on March 11, 1942, and went to Makin March 9, 1944, then moved to Roi and Kwajalein, in the Marshal Islands, during November 1944.

First commanding officer was Maj. Thomas J Walker Jr. (July 1, 1941, to Feb 28, 1942), followed by: Capt Daniel W Torrey Jr. (Mar 1, 1942, to Sept 30, 1942); Maj Harold J Mitchener (Oct 1-4 1942); Maj Donald K Yost (5 Oct to Dec 17, 1942); Maj Leonard K Davis (Dec 18 to Sept 19, 1943); Maj Frank cole (Sept 20, 1943, to April 6, 1944); Maj William T Herring (Oct 28, 1944, to Mar 1, 1945); Maj Robert D Kelley (March 2, 1945, to July 18, 1945); and Maj Thomas A Todd (July 19, 1945, to Japanese surrender).

Marine Fighting Squadron One-One-Two (VMF-112) "Wolf Pack"
VMF-112 was formed on March 1, 1942, in San Diego under the command of Major W J Huffman. Major P J Fontana succeeded Huffman on 11 May and left camp Kearney, California, with his squadron for New Caledonia on 13 October. The unit arrived in Noumea 15 days later, and by 2 November the first echelon landed on Henderson Field, Guadalcanal, and actively engaged in the drive toward Rabaul. On March 27, 1943, Captain R B Frazer took command and was replaced by Major H Hansen, Jr., on 9 July. Major G Boyington led the Squadron from 26 July to 11 August, when Major H Hansen Jr. took the unit to Miramar, California. VMF-112 was retrained for operation from aircraft carriers and was then based on the *USS Bennington*. Remaining under the command of Major H Hansen Jr., the unit participated in the Iwo Jima and Okinawa campaigns and made air strikes against Tokyo until July 1945, when it returned to the U.S. Lt. G Leonard took command on 26 August until the Japanese surrender. VMF-112 downed a total of 140 enemy aircraft, which makes it the third most successful Marine Fighter Squadron of the Second World War in number of enemy aircraft shot down.

Marine fighting Squadron One-One-Three (VMF-113)
"Whistling Devils"
Organized January 1, 1943, at El Toro and commissioned on September 15, 1943, at El Toro. In January 1944 the squadron was ordered to Tarawa and Kwajalein, and it was in action at Engebi by February 1944. Covered Central Pacific landings of Wotje, Mille Atoll, Maloelap, and Jaluit. Covered landings at Okinawa from July 16, 1945, until Japan surrendered.

The first Corsair squadron (VMF-113) commanding officer was Capt John H King Jr. (Jan 1 to Feb 4, 1943), followed by: Lt. Frank C Drury (Feb 5-6, 1943); Capt Loren D Everton (Feb 7, 1943, to Sept 7, 1944); Maj Charles Kimak (Sept 8 to Dec 18, 1944); Maj Philip R White (Dec 19, 1944, to Feb 20, 1945); and Maj Hensley Williams (Feb 21, 1945, to Japanese surrender).

Marine Fighting Squadron One-One-Four (VMF-114) "Death Dealers"
Squadron organized at El Toro on July 1, 1943, and arrived at Ewa, Hawaii, on October 23, 1943. From Dec 18, 1943, to Feb 27, 1944, flew CAP and escort missions from Midway. Went to Green Is. March 28, 1944, striking at the Bismarcks until May 8, 1944.

In October 1944 the squadron began strikes against Yap and Babelthaup, where it earned the name "Death Dealers" under the leadership of Capt Robert F Stout during Sept 18, 1943, to March 3, 1945.

Maj Herbert H Long led the squadron from Aug 2, 1945, to the date of Japanese surrender.

Marine Fighting Squadron One-One-Five (VMF-115)
Squadron organized at Santa Barbara on July 1, 1943, and arrived at Emirau in April 1944 after three tours of combat in the Solomons. Moved to Leyte in December 1944 and covered Ormoc Landings and Mindoro Landings in the Philippines.

Commanding Officers were Maj John S Mac Laughlin Jr (July 1 to 16, 1943); Maj Joseph J Foss (July 17 to Sept 20, 1944); Maj John H King Jr (Sept 21, 1944, to May 29, 1945); Maj John S Payne (May 30 to Aug 17, 1945); and Maj Thomas M Coles (Aug 18, 1945, to the Japanese surrender.)

Marine Fighting Squadron One-Two-Two (VMF122) "Kayo Tojo"
Organized at Camp Kearney on March 1, 1942, and arrived at Henderson Filed on Jan 17, 1943; fought in the New Georgia campaign during June and July 1943.

Landed in the Palaus in August 1944 for strikes against Babelthaup, Koror, and Yap. Also covered U.S. Army landings at Pulo Anna in November 1944. The Squadron remained at Peleliu until the end of the war.

The first commanding Officer was Maj Gregory Boyington (April 20 to June 7, 1943), followed by: Maj Herman Hansen Jr (June 8 to July 7, 1943); Maj Robert B Frazier (July 8 to Aug 21, 1943); Maj Joseph H Reinburg (Aug 22, 1943, to Jan 31, 1945); Maj Frances E Pierce Jr. (Feb 1 to March 14, 1945); Maj Quintus B Nelson (March 15 to April 15, 1945); Maj Israel E Boniske (April 16 to 18, 1945); Maj John R Bohnet (April 19 to May 27, 1945); and Maj Donald H Sapp (May 28, 1945, to date of Japanese surrender).

Marine Fighting Squadron One-Two-Three (VMF-123) "Eight Balls"
The squadron was organized on Sept 7, 1942, at San Diego and began operations from Guadalcanal on Feb 4, 1943, where it served two tours. It was operating from Munda during Sept 1943 and left for the West Coast on November 28, 1943, arriving on December 14, 1943, for reorganizing and training.

The squadron was aboard the aircraft carrier *USS Bennington* from Jan 1 to June 1945 flying strikes against Tokyo and supported the Iwo Jima landings, as well as the entire Okinawa Campaign.

Commanding Officers started with Capt Richard M Baker (Sept 7 to 21, 1942); Maj Edward W Johnston (Sept 22, 1942, to April 20, 1943); Maj Richard M Baker (April 21 to Sept 11, 1944); Maj Everett V Alward (Sept 12, 1944, to Feb 25, 1945); and Maj Thomas E Mobley Jr (Feb 26, 1945, to date of Japanese surrender).

Marine Fighting Squadron One-Two-Four (VMF-124) "Death Heads"
Squadron organized at Camp Kearney on Sept 7, 1942. Departed San Diego on *SS Lurline* on Jan 8, 1943, and arrived at Guadalcanal on Feb 11, 1943.

VMF-124 was the first Marine squadron supplied with Corsairs.

The squadron participated in the Russells, New Georgia, and Vella Lavella operations. Returned to the U.S. on Oct 13, 1943, to reorganize and train at Mojave until Sept 18, 1944.

Trained on carrier *USS Ticonderoga* at Pearl Harbor.

On board *USS Essex* (Dec 28, 1944, to March 24, 1945) supporting Lingayen landings, striking Tokyo, covering Iwo Jima, and pre-invasion strikes on Okinawa.

Except for one officer and 47 enlisted personnel who remained on *USS Essex*, the Squadron reorganized and trained before embarking in *USS Tripoli* on Sept 1, 1945.

Commanding Officers were: Lt. Cecil B Brewer (Sept 7 to 23, 1942); Maj William E Gise (Sept 24, 1942, to May 12, 1943); Capt Cecil B Brewer (May 13 to June 25, 1943); Maj William H Pace (June 26 to July 13, 1943); Maj William A Millington (July 14 to March 23, 1945); and Maj James M Johnson (March 24, 1945, to date of Japanese surrender).

Marine Fighting Squadron Two-One-Three (VMF-213) "Hellhawks"
Organized at Ewa, Hawaii, on July 1, 1942. Arrived at Espiritu Santo March 1, 1943, and the first Corsairs followed ten days later.

The "Hellhawk" aviators went to New Caledonia, where they catapulted 39 Corsairs from CVE *Copahee* for the first time without an accident.

On June 17, 1943, the Squadron relieved VMF-124 in the Russell Islands and covered the New Georgia landings. Squadron was transferred to Guadalcanal on Sept 5, 1943, from where it started strikes against Kahili on Sept 11, 1943.

Embarked on *USS Kittyhawk* on Dec 9, 1943, for CONUS to be reformed and re-equipped at Majave. Squadron boarded *USS Franklin* on February 4, 1945, and began operations off Japan on March 18, 1945. On the following day *USS Franklin* was bombed with great loss of life, after which VMF-213 retired to El Centro, California, where it remained until the war ended.

Commanding Officers were Capt Herbert T Merrill (July 1 to Aug 31, 1942); Maj Charles N Endweiss (Sept 1 to 30, 1942); Maj Wade H Britt Jr (Oct 1, 1942, to April 13, 1943); Maj Gregory J Weissenberger (April 14 to Aug 21, 1943); Maj James R Anderson (Aug 22 to Oct 21, 1943); Capt Leonard W McCleary (Oct 22 to Nov 4, 1943); Maj Stanley R Bailey (Nov 5 to Nov 16, 1943); Capt James R Wallace (Nov 17 to Dec 10, 1943); Lt. Edward O Shaw (Dec 11, 1943, to Jan 12, 1944); Maj Sherman A Smith (Jan 13 to 31, 1944); Maj Donald P Frame (Feb 1, 1944, to Jan 28, 1945); Maj Louis R Smunk (Jan 29 to Feb 4, 1945); Maj David E Marshall (Feb 5 to July 9, 1945); and Maj Conrad G Winter (July 10, 1945, to date of Japanese surrender).

Marine Fighting Squadron Two-One-Four (VMF-214) "Swashbucklers"
Squadron was organized July 1, 1942, at Ewa, Hawaii, with a nucleus of Midway Veterans. "Swashbucklers" arrived at Espiritu Santo in February 1943 and was based on Guadalcanal from March 10 to May 17, 1943, under Capt George F Britt. After training in their new Corsairs on Efate during June and July 1943 the squadron moved to Munda in Sept. 1943. The "Swashbucklers" flew from Munda in Sept and Oct 1943 and flew to Vella Lavella on Nov 28, 1943.

Major William H Pace led the "Swashbucklers" in action on August 6, 1943. Maj Pace was succeeded by Capt J R Burnett, who took the squadron to Munda.

At that time Major Gregory R Boyington was demanding his own squadron. VMF-214 "Swashbucklers" had suffered losses, and several members were on leave after serving two consecutive tours of combat duty.

When the "Swashbucklers," who were on leave, returned, they were shocked to learn that they were no longer "Swashbucklers!" Their Squadron number VMF-214 became "Black Sheep" under the leadership of Maj Gregory R Boyington.

Many of the former "Swashbucklers" joined other Marine Squadrons; for example, Lt. Robert M Hanson and Lt. OK Williams joined VMF-215 "Fighting Corsairs."

Marine Fighting Squadron Two-One-Four (VMF-214) "Black Sheep"
On September 3, 1943, Major Gregory R Boyington assumed command of VMF-214 "Black Sheep," staffed with many of his long-time flying friends.

In November, VMF-214 "Black Sheep" was based on Vella Lavella when it made the first fighter sweep against Rabaul in an attempt to draw Japanese into the air to engage the "Black Sheep" in "dogfights." This tactic continued until January 3, 1944, when Major Boyington was shot down and captured.

The Squadron returned to CONUS for carrier training. Major S R Bailey led VMF-214 on raids over Japan and Okinawa from the aircraft carrier *USS Franklin* during February and March 1945 until the Japanese severely bombed the carrier with great loss of life. This forced the remnant of the unit to return to the United States, where it remained until the Japanese surrender.

Marine Fighting Squadron Two-One-Five (VMF-215)
"Fighting Corsairs"
With 137 official victories, this unit is the fourth ranking Marine squadron of the Second World War. It was organized on June 3, 1942, and originally designated V-MSB-244 (scout and dive bombing unit), but by mid-September VMF-215 had been created.

Appendix B: Corsair Squadron Histories

The unit had arrived at Midway in April 1943 under the command of Capt J L Neefus. During July the squadron was based on Espiritu Santo and began attacking Japanese bases in the Northern Solomons. It moved to Munda on August 12, 1942. The second tour of active duty began in early October on Vella Lavella. Lt. Col H H Williamson led the Squadron on strikes against Rabaul and Kavieng until 5 December, when Major Robert C Owens took command.

Owens remained in command as the Squadron spawned several great aces until February 1944. Maj J K Dill was CO when the Unit was reformed at Turtle Bay and then moved to Emerau during the summer. The Squadron continued to hammer at the Japanese under the command of Major B S Hargrave Jr. from early June to late August 1944. On 14 September the Squadron moved to Guadalcanal, and then departed for CONUS (having earned a rest) on the West Coast on October 20, 1944.

VMF-215 acted as a replacement training squadron until the war's end.

Marine Fighting Squadron Two-One-Six (VMF-216) "Bulldogs"
The Squadron organized on January 1, 1943, at El Centro and Commissioned on Sept 16, 1943, when it departed for Pearl Harbor. Relieved VMF-211 in Russells on Nov 23, 1943, and after Bougainville the squadron arrived at Guam on Aug 4, 1944, to attack Rota and Pagan.

Arrived on Oahu in December 1944 for carrier training and boarded *USS Wasp* at Ulithi on Feb 5, 1945. Supported Iwo Jima landings and made strikes on Japan and Okinawa.

VMF-216 left for U.S. on March 26, 1945, and remained at Santa Barbara until Japanese surrender.

Commanding Officers were Capt William P Addington (Jan 1 to 26, 1943); Capt Max R Read Jr. (Jan 27 to June 23, 1943); Maj Rivers J Morrell Jr. (June 24, 1943, to Jan 22, 1944); Maj Benjamin S Hargrave Jr (Jan 23 to May 4, 1944); Maj John Fitting Jr (May 5 to Oct 30, 1944); Maj Richard L Blune Jr (Oct 31 to Dec 7, 1944); Maj George E Dooley (Dec 8, 1944, to April 18, 1945); Lt. George F Kelley (April 19 to May 20, 1945); and Maj Robert L Anderson 21 May to date of surrender.

Marine Fighting Squadron Two-One-Eight (VMF-218) "Hellions"
Organized at Mojave on July 1, 1943, and commissioned on Sept 15, 1943, the Squadron arrived at Espiritu Santo on February 1, 1944.

Covered Green Island landings on Feb 15, 1944. Departed for Leyte, Philippines, in late Nov 1944, making attacks on southern Luzon during December 1944. In the following month the Squadron engaged in convoy cover at Tacloban and troop support missions on Cebu

On March 10, 1945, VMF-218 flew close-support missions at Capisan and made pre-invasion strikes on Bongao and Jolo, continuing attacks on Mindinao until the Japanese surrendered.

Commanding Officers of VMF-218 included: Capt Robert R Read (July 1 to 15, 1943); Maj Horace A Pehl (July 16, 1943, to Sept 28, 1944); Maj Robert T Kingsbury III (Sept 29, 1944, to Jan 30, 1945); and Maj John M Massey (Jan 31, 1945, to date of surrender).

Marine Fighting Squadron Two-Two-One (VMF-221)
"Fighting Falcons"
"Fighting Falcons" was organized on July 11, 1941, in san Diego and sailed for Hawaii on Dec 8, 1941. Upon arrival at Pearl Harbor the squadron was ordered to the relief of Wake Island and sailed on *USS Saratoga* the next day. When Wake Island was lost to the Japanese the squadron was diverted to Midway, where it fought in the attack of June 4, 1942.

Following the Battle of Midway, the squadron moved to Ewa, Hawaii, where it remained until February 11, 1943, when the forward echelon went to Guadalcanal. VMF-221 operated at Guadalcanal for two combat tours. A third tour was spent at Vella Lavella. The squadron covered the Treasury Island landings on Oct 27, 1943, and supported the later Bougainville invasion on 31 October.

The squadron relocated to Munda on November 4, 1943, and supported carrier strikes on Rabaul seven days later.

The "Fighting Falcons" sailed for San Francisco on Dec 14, 1943, and was reorganized at Miramar. The squadron went to Santa Barbara for carrier training and boarded *USS Bunker Hill* in Dec 1944.

The squadron conducted the first naval air missions over Tokyo and covered the Iwo Jima landings. During April and May 1945 the "Fighting Falcons" supported the Okinawa invasion.

On June 9, 1945, the carrier echelon joined rear echelon at El Centro, where the squadron remained at war's end.

Commanding Officers included: Maj William G Manley (July 11 to Oct 5, 1941); Maj Verne J Mc Caul (Oct 6, 1941, to April 18, 1942); Capt James L Neefus (April 19 to May 7, 1942); Maj Floyd B Parks (May 8 to June 3, 1942); Capt Kirk Armistead (June 4 to July 31, 1942); Capt Robert R Burns (Aug 1 to 7, 1942); Lt. Col Luther S Moore (Aug 8 to Oct 5, 1942); Maj Harold J Mitchener (Oct 6 to Feb 18, 1943); Capt Robert R Burns (Feb 19 to May 31, 1943); Maj Monfurd K Peyton (June 1 to Aug 16, 1943); Capt John S Payne (August 17-24, 1943); Maj Nathan T Post Jr (Aug 25, 1943, to Oct 11, 1944); Maj Edwin S Roberts Jr (Oct 12, 1944, to July 31, 1945); Capt Frank B Baldwin (Aug 1-17, 1945); Lt. Harry Pierkowski (Aug 18-28, 1945); and Lt. Franklin T Hovore (Aug 29, 1945, to date of Japanese surrender).

Marine Fighting Squadron Two-Two-Two (VMF-222) "Flying Deuces"
Commissioned at Midway on March 1, 1942, and sailed for Espiritu Santo in July. The "Flying Deuces" participated in the first fighter sweep over Rabaul. Based at Efate, Emirau, and Green Island, the Squadron transferred to Samar in January 1945 and participated in the liberation of the Philippines. Relocated to Okinawa on May 22, 1945.

Commanding Officers were Capt Robert M Hayes (March 1 to Sept 5, 1942); Lt. Ralph Martin (Sept 6-27, 1942); Capt Max J Volcansek Jr (Sept 28, 1942, to Nov 4, 1943); Maj Alfred N Gordon (Nov 5, 1943, to April 5, 1944); Maj Roy T Spurlock (April 6, 1944, to April 27, 1945); and Maj Harold A Harwood (April 28, 1945, to date of Japanese surrender).

Marine Fighting Squadron Two-Two-Three (VMF-223) "Rainbow Squadron"
Organized on May 1, 1942, at Ewa, and sailed from Pearl harbor on August 3, 1942; became the first fighter squadron in the Solomons.

Departed Guadalcanal on Oct 16, 1942, arriving in San Francisco on Nov 1, 1942, then to El Toro. Arrived in Midway in July 1943 and in Vella Lavella. Transferred to Piva Yoke in Feb 1944. Based on Bougainville June 24, 1944, to neutralize Rabaul.

Located in Samar, Philippines, Jan 14 to May 15, 1945, then to Okinawa.

Commanding Officers began with Capt John L Smith (May 16 to Dec 31, 1942); Lt. Conrad G Winter (Jan 1 to 13, 1943); Capt Howard K Marvin (Jan 14 to 25, 1943); Maj Marion E Carl (Jan 26, 1943, to Feb 3, 1944); Maj Robert P Keller (Feb 4 to July 2, 1944); Maj David Drucker (July 3 to Oct 13, 1944); Maj Robert F Flaherty (Oct 14, 1944, to March 24, 1945); Maj Robert W Teller (March 25 to April 16, 1945); Maj Howard E King (April 17 to July 23, 1945); and Maj Julius W Ireland (July 24, 1945, to date of Japanese surrender).

Marine Fighting Squadron Two-Two-Four (VMF-224)
"Fighting Wildcats"
Commissioned at Ewa. Trained at Barbers Point until Aug 14, 1942. Arrived at Henderson Field, Guadalcanal, on August 30, 1942.

Squadron traveled to San Diego in December 1942 and arrived in Pearl Harbor on Aug 5, 1943, via San Diego. Arrived on Roi in Feb 1944 for strikes against Marshall Islands via PagoPago and Funafuti.

Arrived at Yontan airfield on April 7, 1945, and began operations from Chimu airfield in early 1945.

Commanding Officers were Maj Robert E Galer (May 1 to Dec 4, 1942); Maj James W Poindexter (Dec 5, 1944, to May 30, 1945); Maj Robert C Hammond Jr (May 31 to June 14, 1945); and Maj Allen T Barnum (June 15, 1945, to date of Japanese surrender).

Marine Fighting Squadron Three-One-One (VMF-311) "Hell's Belles"
Squadron organized at Cherry Point on Dec 1, 1942. Moved to Parris Island on April 18, 1943, and left for Miramar on Aug 31, 1943. Arrived at Roi, Marshall Islands, on Feb 6, 1944, via San Diego and Pago Pago.

Flew missions against the Marshall Islands from Roi from May 1944 to Jan 1945 and continued operations from Yontan Airfield, Okinawa.

Commanding Officers were Maj Ralph K Rottet (Dec 1, 1942, to Jan 31, 1943); Lt. Harry B Woodman (Feb 1 to 5, 1943); Lt. Roy A Neundorf (Feb 6 to 15, 1943); Lt. Michael J Curran Jr. (Feb 16 to 26, 1943); Capt Jack D Kane (Feb 27 to May 31, 1943); Maj Harry B Hooper Jr (June 1 to July 5, 1943); Maj Jack D Kane (July 6 to Aug 31, 1943); Maj Robert L Anderson (Sept 1 to 13, 1943); Maj Harry B Hooper Jr (Sept 14, 1943, to Oct 23, 1944); Maj Charles M Kunz (Oct 24, 1944, to Feb 10, 1945); Maj Perry L Shuman (Feb 11 to June 15, 1945); and Maj Michael R Yunk (June 16, 1945, to date of Japanese surrender).

Marine Fighting Squadron Three-One-Two (VMF-312)
"Checkerboard Squadron"
Organized at Parris Island on June 1, 1943. Arrived Miramar in Jan 1944, and on Feb 28, 1944, embarked for Ewa. Following three months training, the unit departed for Espiritu Santo. Arrived in the Admiralty Islands on Oct 12, 1944, and flew to Guadalcanal on Nov. 15, 1944.

Landed on Okinawa April 6-9, 1945. Supported Iheya Shima landing and flew strikes against Japan.

Commanding Officers: Maj Richard M Day (June 1, 1943 to May 13, 1945); Maj Hugh I Russell (May 14-24, 1945); and Maj J Frank Cole (May 25, 1945, to date of Japanese surrender).

Marine Fighting Squadron Three-One-Three (VMF-313)
"Lily Packin' Hellbirds"
Commissioned on Oct 1, 1943m at El Centro. The Squadron arrived at Ewa on March 22, 1944, and arrived at Midway Island on April 13, 1944, remaining there until June 1944, then returned to Ewa.

Transferred to Emirau for operations against Kavieng, on New Ireland, in Sept 1944.

Relocated to Leyte, Philippines, in Dec 1944 and covered Mindoro operation and Zamboanga landings. "Lily Packin' Hellbirds" remained in Philippines until decommissioned on June 1, 1945.

The first Commanding Officer was Maj Hugh I Russell (Oct 1 to Nov 9, 1943), followed by Maj Philip R White (Nov 10, 1943 to Feb 23, 1944); Maj Joe H Mc Glothin Jr (Feb 24, 1944, to April 26, 1945); Capt Jay E Mc Donald (April 27-29, 1945); and Lt. John M Lomac (April 30 to June 1, 1945).

Marine Fighting Squadron Three-One-Four (VMF-314) "Bob's Cats"
Commissioned on Oct 1, 1943, at Cherry Point, "Bob's Cats" sailed for Ewa on June 18, 1944, and then to Midway. Returned to Ewa until April 1945. Moved to Chimu Airfield, Okinawa, where it remained until the war's end.

Commanding Officers were Capt Theodore E Olsen (Oct 1 to Nov 1, 1943); Capt Raymond A Rogers Jr (Nov 2 to 10, 1943); Capt Frederick G Steckelberg (Nov 11-19, 1943); Capt Robert E Schneider (Nov 20-28, 1943); Maj Robert E Cameron (Nov 29, 1943, to Aug 1, 1945); and Maj Christian C Lee (Aug 2, 1945, to date of Japanese surrender).

Marine Fighting Squadron Three-Two-One (VMF-321) "Hell's Angels"
Commissioned on Feb 1, 1943, at Cherry Point. Trained at Oak Grove and headed for the South Pacific via Samoa.

By Jan 1, 1944, the "Hell's Angels" were operating from Bougainville, and by April they were based on Green Island, striking New Ireland.

In August 1944 the "Hell's Angels" were on Guam for strikes against Rota and Pagan.

By December "Hell's Angels" were in Mojave and Santa Barbara for carrier training, and were operating aboard USS *Puget Sound* by July and August 1945.

Commanding Officers were as follows: Maj Gordon H Knott (Feb 1 to Sept 30, 1943); Maj Edmund F Overend (Oct 1, 1943, to Oct 28, 1944); Maj Justin M Miller Jr (Oct 29, 1944, to Mar 22, 1945); and Maj William P Boland Jr (March 23, 1945, to date of Japanese surrender).

Marine Fighting Squadron Three-Two-Three (VMF-323)
"Death Rattlers"
Commissioned on Aug 1, 1943, at Cherry Point and trained at Oak Grove until Jan 19, 1944, then moved to El Centro. Departed San Diego July 21, 1944, and arrived at Ford Island in the following week. In Espiritu Santo by November 29, 1944, and arrived in Okinawa by April 9, 1945, with entire Squadron operating from Kadena airfield, striking against Japan in June 1945.

Commanding Officers were Maj George C Axtell Jr (Aug 1, 1943, to June 14, 1945) and Maj Martin E W Oelrich (June 15, 1945, to date of Japanese surrender).

Appendix C:
Corsair Targets and Destruction

U.S. Marine Maj Gen Roy S Geiger expressed, many times, that "The reason Marines have airplanes is to assist the Marine Troopers."

As seen in Chapter Five, the Corsair replaced the dive bomber and torpedo bomber, giving birth to the present day fighter-bomber.

Having usurped the role of the dive bomber and torpedo bomber, many scenes of destruction are attributed to this bent-wing bird: ship sinkings, parked aircraft destruction, gutted runways, concrete bunker demolition, and blown ammunition stowage are only a few of the results from Corsair attackers, plus, of course, shot down enemy aircraft.

Probably the most dramatic assistance to the Marine Troopers is low-level Corsairs flying over the charging Americans' heads and firing at the enemy troops from altitudes as low as fifty feet! Trooper friends have told the author that Corsairs flew so low that it "rained" .50 Cal. cartridges ejected by the firing Corsair machine guns.

U.S. Marine Corsairs could help Marine troopers in addition to engaging in the strafing support described in the previous paragraph. In fact, Corsair fighter-bombers often destroyed airfields, sunk ships, and exploded ammunition depots hours and days before the American attack in order to reduce the enemy's ability to combat the troopers as the Marines pressed on against the weakened defenders.

Preparation for a U.S. Marine offensive consisted mainly of arranging thousands of large bombs on bomb carriages so they were ready to load on the Corsairs' hard points when the Marine offensive began.

Armed with six .50 Caliber machine guns and ten five-inch diameter HVAR (High Velocity Air Rocket) missiles, the Corsair was a potent weapon against man and machine, in the air or on the ground.

Hundreds of 500lb bombs on a Bougainville field await final adjustment before Corsairs deliver them to Rabaul. Note the technicians working on a bomb. (Official U.S. Navy Photograph via U.S. National Archives)

A Corsair is firing all ten of its five inch diameter HVAR missiles into an enemy hillside emplacement. The missiles can destroy men and machines. (Official U.S. Navy Photograph, Naval Photographic Center Naval Station, Wash. D.C.)

This pockmarked Roi-Namur airfield in the Marshall Islands is strewn with destroyed aircraft after Corsair fighter-bombers completed their attack with bombs, rocket missiles, and machine guns. (U.S. Navy Photo via National Archives)

Wotje, in the Marshalls, was Corsair-bombed on aircraft runways, antiaircraft gun emplacements, and significant buildings. Bombing such as this required overlapping raids by several squadrons dropping 500lb. bombs. (U.S. Navy Photo, Author's File)

Corsair bomb craters in the Marshall Islands Mille Atoll runway prevented Japanese aircraft from taking off against landing U.S. Marine Troopers. (U.S. Navy Photo)

Appendix C: Corsair Targets and Desctruction

Strafing, if done carefully with adequate planning and talent, can score outstanding results, as can be seen by this row of severely damaged Zero fighters. Damage was wrought with Corsairs' 50 cal guns. (U.S. Navy Photo Courtesy Air Progress via Al Lewis)

Upper Photo: The salt air around small Pacific islands quickly turned slightly damaged Japanese aircraft into skeletal remains. U.S. servicemen are examining the structure of this damaged Japanese plane that had been strafed. (International News Photo via Al Lewis) Lower Photo: This Zero appears intact and could have force landed after the pilot was wounded by Corsairs. Note bent propeller blades, suggesting a belly landing. (Acme Photo via Al Lewis)

Corsair bombing of Japanese-held airfields and airstrips prevented them from being used by enemy planes against the landing Marines.

Efficient coordination by Corsair squadrons produced an uninterrupted carpet of destruction.

The dangerous and skillful art of strafing has been perfected by few fighter aviators; however, the importance of the maneuver cannot be overestimated.

The strafer is usually met by heavy defensive fire from rifles to machine guns and heavier AA guns as he flies lower into their range.

Dive-bombing Corsairs can sink merchant ships with bombs and seriously damage them with .50 cal. machine-gun fire and/or missiles. Three burning Japanese merchant ships have beached themselves to save the precious cargo of arms and/or food. (U.S. Navy Photo via National Archives)

Relatively thin steel hull plating on ships, such as freighters and destroyer escorts, can be seriously damaged by .50 cal. gunfire and sunk by five-inch diameter HVAR missiles. It was very important to destroy the enemy's freighters because they delivered food, medicine, small arms, and ammunition, without which the enemy troops could not exist as a fighting force.

Scoring bomb hits on ammunition depots not only destroyed surrounding structures, but also deprived the Japanese of ammunition that would eventually be used against the Americans.

Flying low to assure direct hits adds peril to the operation because the explosion is sudden and enormous, spewing hot streamers generated by the ignition.

Strong, fast, and agile Corsairs proved themselves well-suited for this task.

After an objective has been bombed or rocketed it is photographed, analyzed, and marked regarding the target's condition, and whether it requires additional attacks.

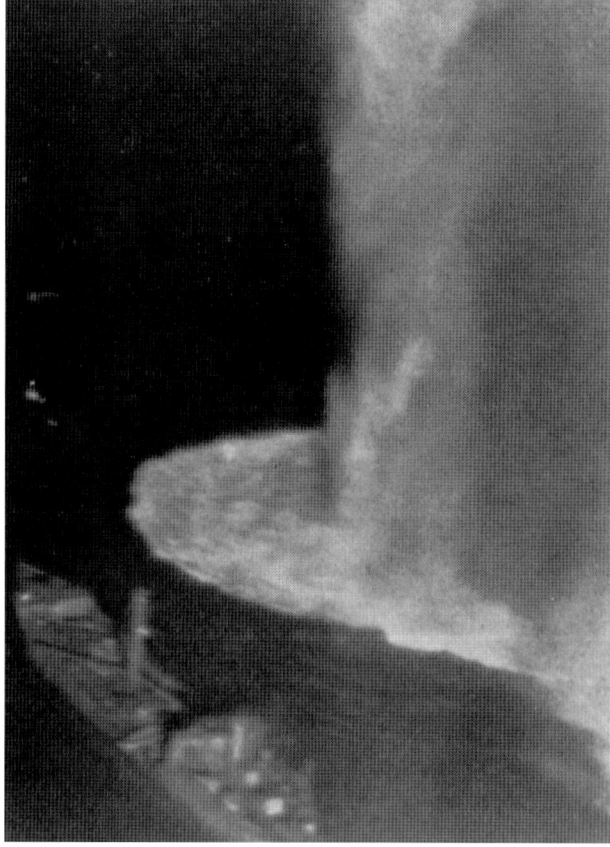

Upper Photo-Left Side: A Japanese cargo ship is afire after strikes by Corsair rocket missiles. Upper Photo-Right Side: A Japanese cargo ship is grounded after receiving Corsair strikes. Meanwhile, Corsairs destroy harbor facilities to prevent the Japanese from unloading the stricken cargo ship to save the cargo. Lower Photo-Left Side: "Lyon Maru," sunk in Simpson Harbor after Corsair bombing, rests on harbor bottom of shallow water. Lower Photo-Right Side: A one-mile range "Tiny Tim" missile, fired by a Corsair, explodes near a Japanese cargo ship, causing untold underwater damage. (U.S. Navy Photos)

Appendix C: Corsair Targets and Desctruction

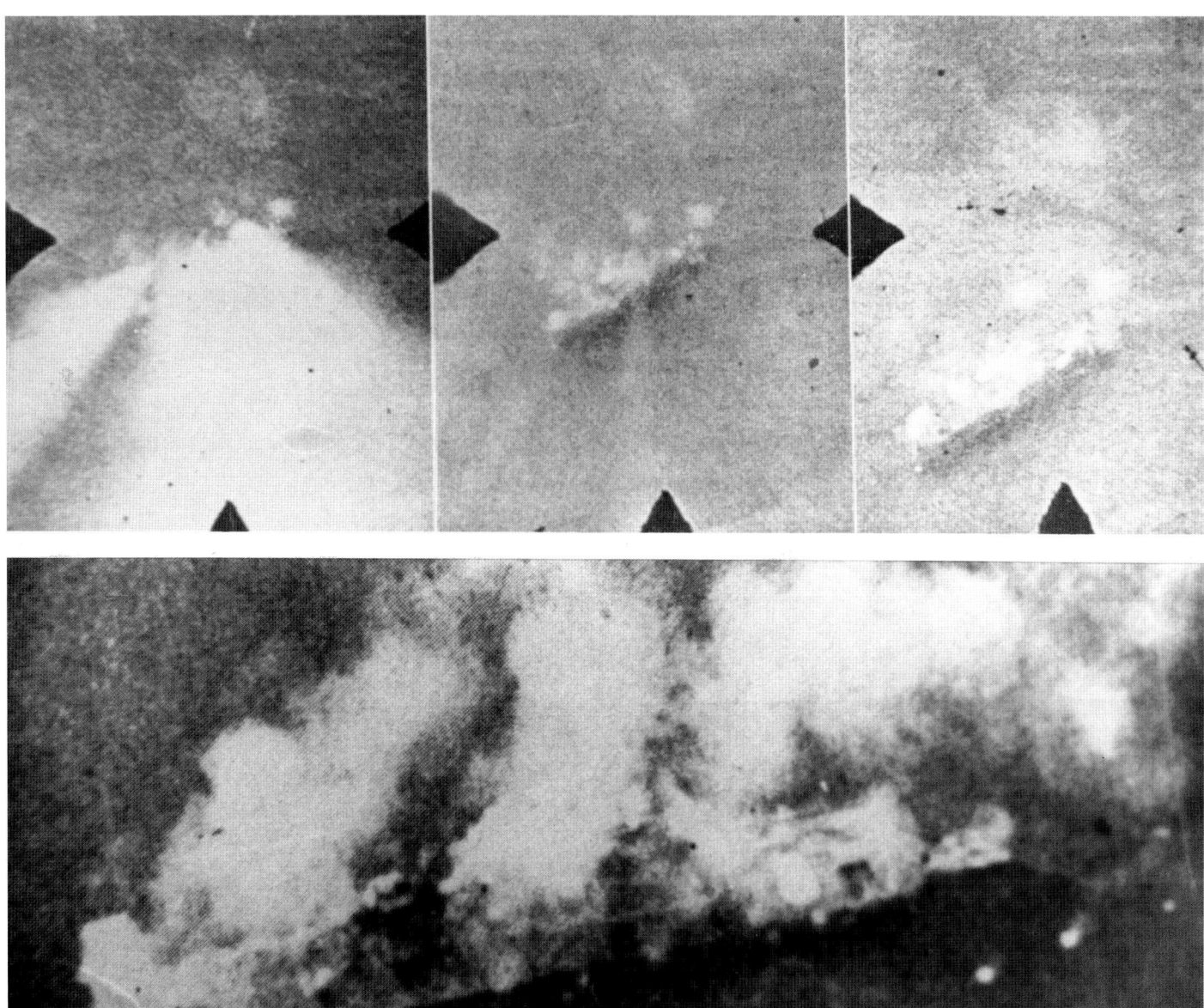

VMF-451 "Blue Devils" flew to the Japanese Naval Base at Kure, Japan, on March 19, 1945, to attack the Japanese aircraft carriers *Ryuho*, *Amagi*, and *Katsuragi*. The Corsairs were armed with five-inch diameter rocket-powered missiles, eight to each plane, plus bombs; other Corsairs were armed with two "Tiny Tim" missiles. Flying with the 24 Marine Corsairs were four Navy Corsairs, 12 Scout Bombers, and 14 Torpedo Bombers. *Ryuho* suffered the most damage of the three carriers and never sailed in combat again. Upper photo (left) caught missiles headed for *Ryuho*. Upper photo (center) shows several hits on *Ryuho*. Upper photo (right) has *Ryuho* almost hidden in smoke. Lower Photo shows three fierce fires on *Ryuhu*. (U.S. Navy Photos Courtesy Al Lewis)

Corsairs of VMF-211 "Wake Avengers" bombed two large Japanese ammunition depots on Rabaul that exploded with unbridled fury. (Photo by Lt. Loren Stricklin VMF-211, Courtesy Lt. Loren Stricklin)

This close-up of the ammunition explosion indicates the loss of ammunition that would normally be used against the Marine troopers. ("Wake Avengers" Photo Courtesy Lt. Loren Stricklin)

Corsair Targets and Losses During World War II

Sortie Targets	Sorties (A)
Enemy Airfields	10,210
Strafing Military Targets	34,887(A)
Land Transportation	2,818
Harbor Areas	2,095
Armored Warships	- 263
Unarmored Warships	245
Merchantmen (more than 500 tons)	799
Merchantmen (less than 500 tons)	3,172
Misc. Ships	<u>23</u>
	54,512

Activity	Corsair Losses
Air Combat	189
Enemy Anti-Aircraft Fire	349
Operation During Action Sorties	230
On Misc. Flights	692
Aboard Ships or on Ground	<u>164</u>
	1,624

(A) Sorties are the number of individual aviators, each in one plane, and not the number of targets: 34,887 Corsairs and Corsair pilots strafed an unknown number of Military Targets, and not only 34,887 Military targets.

Closer still is the expanding firestorm, destroying everything in its wake. Note the Japanese bomber and fighter plane, suggesting that the explosion was near an airfield. ("Wake Avengers" Photo Courtesy Lt. Loren Stricklin)

Appendix C: Corsair Targets and Desctruction

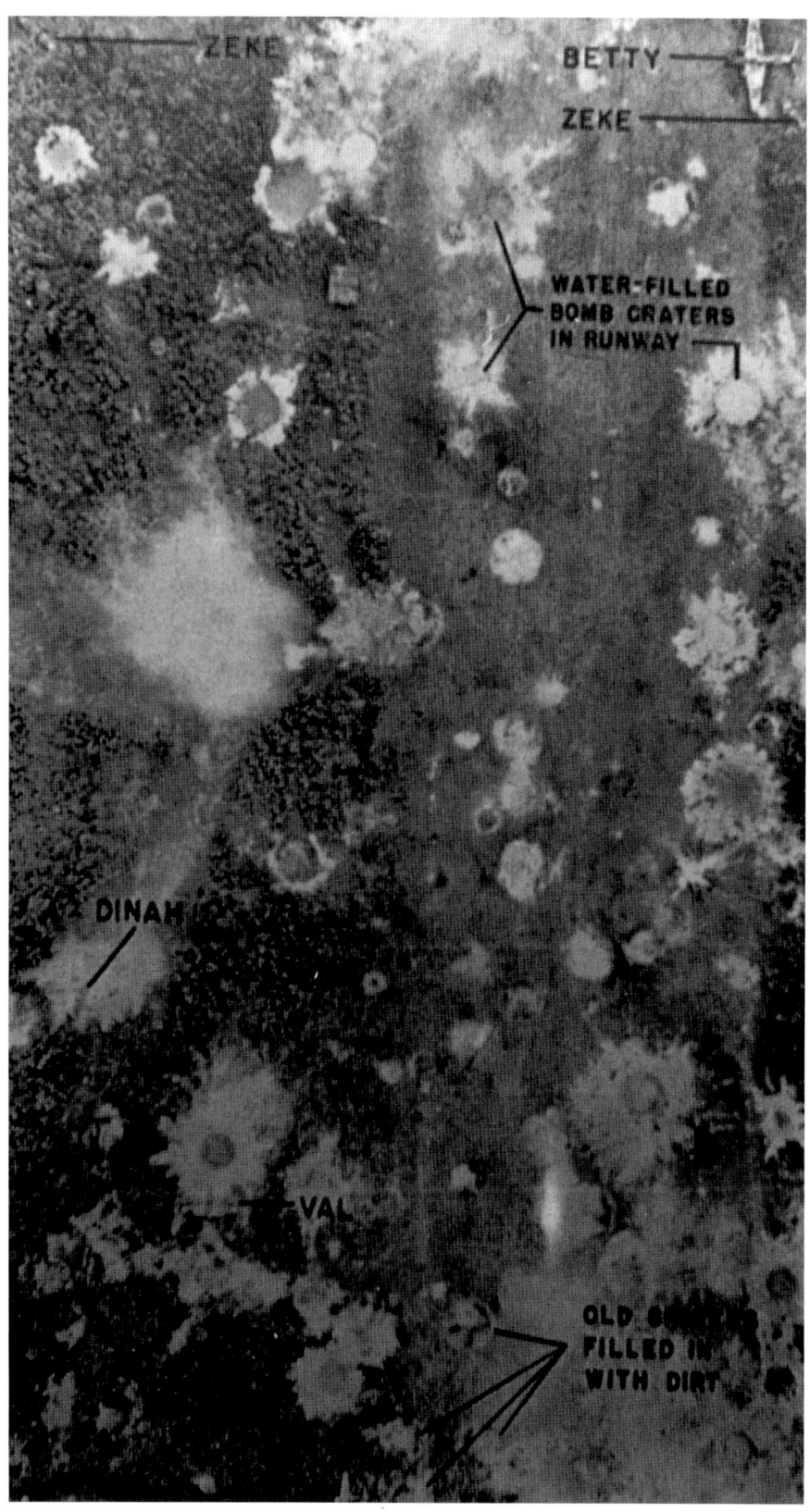

After an objective is bombed, strafed, or rocketed, it is aerial photographed and the photos are analyzed by military experts regarding the results of the attack; whether it is necessary to repeat the attack, or whether the objective has been destroyed. The photographs are marked by the experts to reflect the condition of the target after the raid. This is an example of a post-attack marked-up photograph. The photograph shown here is the Gasmata Airfield runway on New Britain, Bismarck Archipelago. (U.S. Navy Photograph Courtesy Lt. Loren Stricklin)

Appendix D: Corsair Crash Sites

Most of the earth over which the Corsairs were flown during World War II was either uncharted rainforest or unattended overgrown coconut plantations. It was also impossible to fly any distance without flying over tropical waters, which was also a hazard. A forced landing for any reason could result in a fatal crash, or death by abandonment, if rescuers failed to locate the downed aviator.

From the air, the rainforests and coconut plantations appear to be the ideal "cushioned blanket" for a forced landing; however, a 12,000lb fighter crashes through the foliage as though the foliage does not exist.

After crashing through the upper leaves and fronds, the plane's forward speed reduces slightly as it crashes through trees and the heavy vines below. As the Corsair crashes to the ground it loses its engine, outer wing panels, and machine guns that have torn loose. It is truly a miracle if the aviator survives this crash landing.

In the event the aviator survives the fall through the higher fronds and lower trees on the plane's fall to the ground, it is most difficult to find the wreckage from the air because many of the fronds and smaller trees have either fallen on the wreckage or sprung back to cover the hole made by the falling plane as vines drape themselves over the wreckage.

It appears that the best way to locate the wreckage is on foot cutting through the underbrush, which is an arduous task.

If the crash site is not discovered at once, nature begins to cover the airplane and aviator. The longer the site remains undiscovered the more difficult it is to find, adding to the Corsair's decomposition.

Thanks to men of vision, craftsmen, and artists, many Corsairs have been rescued from crash sites and scrap yards, rebuilding them into flying condition for Corsair addicts to suck in their breath and sigh in admiration.

Very often a Corsair "Classic" is bought and sold, crossing from nation to nation and continent to continent to finally arrive where it can be admired by enthusiasts.

According to records, of 32 Corsair crashes in the Southwest Pacific area between Oct. 22, 1943, and July 30, 1945, ten were shot down by antiaircraft guns; seven were shot down in combat; two were destroyed in collision with other planes; eight crashed because of aircraft malfunctions or aviator errors; and five were listed as missing.

This photo was taken two days after RNZAF F4U-1A Corsair NZ 5211 crashed through the umbrella of tall trees on July 12, 1944, near Cape Torokina, Bougainville. Observe that the outer wing panel and engine have torn from the fuselage and the displaced machinegun ammunition boxes have ejected the .50 cal ammunition. Interesting is the heavy amount of foliage, growing close to the ground, that the Corsair has displaced in the crash. If this crash site had not been located so soon, the small trees and vines would have hidden the plane from view. The aviator survived the crash and is identified as RNZAF Sgt P.M. Malvieney or an American technical advisor. The three investigators are checking the Corsair's damage and speed at the moment of impact. (RNZAF Photo Courtesy John Regan)

Appendix D: Corsair Crash Sites

Left Photo: U.S. Marine 2nd Lt Wayland Bennett crashed at Turtle Bay, Espirito Santo, on October 22, 1943, while flying F4U-1 Corsair Bu No.02608 on a training flight. Overhead coconut palms have darkened the area. The crash site was discovered in 1996 and was hardly recognizable. Observe the machine guns in the lower right-hand corner of the photograph and the native standing at the extreme left-hand side to the left of the arrow. The arrow points to Lt. Bennett's remains. Right Photo: This photo is an enlargement of the lower right quarter of the upper photograph. It reveals some of the Corsair's structure amidst growing plants after a half-century. Researcher John Regan examines parts of the Corsair's wreckage. (Photos Courtesy John Regan)

Left Photo: Partially assembled, this Corsair is undergoing restoration in the RNZAF Museum workshops at Wigram, New Zealand, in February, 1988. Donated to a town in Utah, USA, by the American Government, the plane was displayed outdoors for years until it was moved to the local junkyard. The plane was rescued in 1966 by aircraft collector Harry Doan, restored to flying condition in Florida by 1979, and shipped to New Zealand. The plane was grounded with hydraulic problems and was sent to the RNZAF Museum at Wigram in 1992, where it was prepared for display. Lower Photo: Completely assembled, the Corsair is fully painted in the colors and number NZ 5201, which was the same as the RNZAF's very first Corsair in 1944. John Regan holds the U.S. Marine Squadron VMF-215 identification patch of the famous "Fighting Corsairs." (Photos Courtesy John Regan)

Southwest Pacific Area Corsair Wrecks

Serial Number	Wreckage Location	Crash Date	Discovery Date	Cause of Crash
US 02608	Turtle Bay	Oct. 22, 1943	1996	Training
US 17804	Kangu Beach (Buin)	Nov. 21, 1943	April 9, 1968	Crash
US 40652	New Ireland	?	(NOT	Crash
US 37114	Rabaul	?	Discovered)	Shot Down
NZ 5221	Buka	Oct. 17, 1944	"	AA
NZ 5255	Kara	Aug, 29, 1944	"	Missing
NZ 5236	Henry Reid Bay	Sept. 14, 1944	"	AA
NZ 5207	Seem Sum	June 30, 1944	"	Shot Down
NZ 5271	S.E. Mokerang	Dec. 15, 1944	"	Collision
NZ 5241	Talili	June 28, 1944	"	AA
NZ 5271	S.E. Mokerang	Feb. 24, 1945	"	Missing
NZ 5274	Kurakakui Pl.	June 20, 1944	"	AA
NZ 5276	Cape St. George	July 11, 1944	"	Missing
NZ 5283	Green Island	Jan. 15, 1945	"	Missing
NZ 5287	Sea	Jan. 15, 1945	"	Missing
NZ 5292	Guadalcanal	Aug. 8, 1944	"	Shot Down
NZ 5306	Torokina (Sea)	Sept. 18, 1944	"	Crash
NZ 5317	New Ireland	April 12, 1945	"	Crash
NZ 5319	Sea	Sept. 30, 1944	"	Crash
NZ 5336	?	Oct. 17, 1944	"	Shot Down
NZ 5376	Torokina	July 4, 1945	"	Crash
NZ 5379	Torokina	July 30, 1945	"	AA
NZ 5400	E. Shortland	March 2, 1945	"	Crash
NZ 5402	Ulu Island	June 21, 1945	"	Shot Down
NZ 5412	Green Island	Jan. 15, 1945	"	AA
NZ 5413	Beehives	Jan. 15, 1945	"	AA
NZ 5414	Sohano	Mar. 26, 1945	"	AA
NZ 5415	Rabaul	Mar. 26, 1945	"	AA
NZ 5429	Vanapope	Dec. 30, 1944	"	Collision
NZ 5464	Mt. Balbi	Dec. 30, 1944	"	Shot Down
NZ 5480	In Sea	June, 20, 1945	"	Shot Down
NZ 5211	Torokina	July 12, 1944	July 14, 1944	AA

Appendix E:
Foreign Flag Corsairs

In addition to the U.S. Navy, U.S. Marines, Royal New Zealand Air Force, and the Royal Navy previously mentioned, the Corsair was flown in combat by the French *Aeronavale* (Naval Air Force), Argentine *Aeronavalde Combate* (Naval Air Fighter Force), *Fuerza Aerea Hondurena* (Honduran Air Force), and *Fuerza Aerea Salvadorena* (El Salvador Air Force).

The F4U-7 was the last of the bent-wing Corsair line. This post-World War II hybrid was prepared at France's request to combat ground forces, yet it had to maintain a superb performance at high altitudes.

In August 1945 the retreating Japanese forces gave the rule of Indochina to the Communist leader Ho Chi Minh, director of the Vietminh revolutionaries, who began deadly reprisals against the French inhabitants. The French had governed Indochina since 1887 as "French Indochina," but lost control to the Japanese during the beginning of World War II.

In view of the fact that the Vietminh had no air force, the French needed a low-level attack plane for antiguerrilla work using bombs, cannon fire, and Napalm. The Corsair AU-1 was ideally suited for this task; therefore, the U.S. aircraft carrier *USS Saipan* unloaded twenty-five AU-1 Corsairs that were left over from the Korean War at Tourane (Da-Nang) to help France, a U.S. ally.

The F4U-7 Corsair is Born

The French also used the AU-1 to cover the evacuation of troops and civilians, but France needed more. They also required a high altitude fighter in addition to the AU-1; however; instead of designing a new high altitude Corsair, Rex Beisel's design team combined the solid AU-1 structure and firepower with the high altitude ability of the F4U-4 engine into one machine! This was the F4U-7, and only the *Aeronavale* flew this plane.

In 1954 the AU-1s were returned to America who, in turn, replaced them with 94 F4U-7 Corsairs in the context of the MDAP (Military Defense and Assistance Program) to equip 12F, 14F, 15F, and 17F *Flotille* (Squadrons). These aircraft were needed to combat the general state of insurrection in France's former colonies. The only change in the combined design of the F4U-7 was the bubble canopy, similar to the F4U-5, which again facilitated raising the seat, considerably improving the visibility.

Armed with four 20mm rapid-fire cannon and eight HVAR missile launchers, the hybrid Vought Corsair F4U-7 could also carry large bombs on underwing hardpoints. Note how high the aviator sits in the cockpit for maximum visibility. (United Aircraft Corp. Photo, Author's File)

This profile photograph of the Corsair F4U-7 can be mistaken for the F4U-4 because of the chin air inlet and the four-bladed propeller. Ninety-four F4U-7 Corsairs were delivered to the French *Aeronavale* and were flown in action over Indochina, Egypt, and French North Africa. (United Aircraft Corp. Photo, Author's File)

Corsair: The Saga of the Legendary Bent-Wing Fighter-Bomber

The *Flotille* 14F F4U-7 Corsairs were successful fighting the Indo-China Viet-minh troops who fought from countless trenches, underground bases, and camps hidden near native villages. Thus, the French troops were able to come to a favorable agreement with the Viet-minh Communists. (ECP Armies, *Aeronavale*)

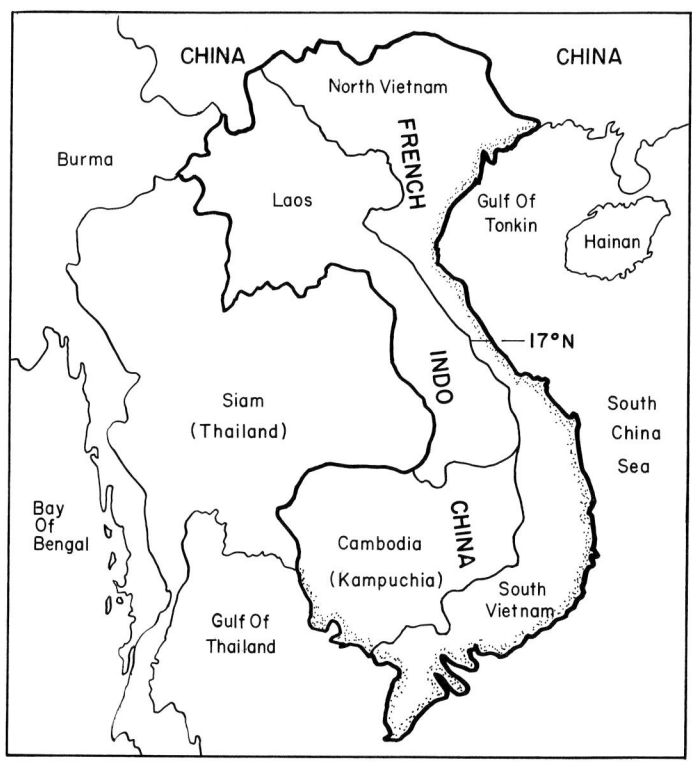

Indo-China as it appeared at the end of the post WWII Vietnam War. The division of North and South Vietnam was to be the source of fighting for several years to come. This map illustrates the first division, at the Seventeenth Parallel.

Corsairs in Indochina

The French *Aeronavale* flew the F4U-7 in action over Indochina, Egypt, and French North Africa. The F4U-7 was the last Corsair to be designed and built.

Despite the efforts of the F4U-7 Corsairs, the overwhelming numbers of Communist troops of the Vietminh pounded the advancing French troops from the countless trenches, underground bases, and camps hidden near native villages.

The bloody and tragic conflict in Indochina officially ended on July 21, 1957, with the result that Vietnam was divided into North Vietnam and South Vietnam along the 17th Parallel.

Corsairs in Egypt

Meanwhile, on October 29, 1956, fighting flared in Egypt involving Royal Navy aircraft, the U.S. Sixth Fleet, the Soviet Navy, and the French *Aeronavale* known as the Suez Canal Crisis.

It all began when Britain and the U.S. had withdrawn their promised aid to Egypt for the Aswan Dam Project on July 18, 1956. This prompted President Gamel Abdel Nassar of Egypt to nationalize the Suez Canal eight days later, planning to use the canal revenue for the Aswan Dam construction.

On 24 October Britain and France (both were investors in the canal as well as frequent users) reached a secret agreement with Israel for a covert attack on Egypt. Israeli troops attacked through the Sinai Peninsula on October 29, 1956, while the Anglo-French invasion flotilla left for Egypt.

Upper Photo: Having just landed on the carrier *Arromanches*, this *Aeronavale* F4U-7 Corsair is just starting to fold its wings. Observe the air inlet at the bottom of the cowl. (ECP Armies, *Aeronavale*) Right Photo: Racing down the flight deck of *Arromanches* with tail high, this F4U-7 is ready to leave the deck at any moment for the "Suez Crisis." (Service Cinema Des Armies)

Appendix E: Foreign Flag Corsairs

The U.S. Sixth Fleet was in the port of Valencia, Spain, when it learned of the above attack, and steamed eastward across the Mediterranean Sea at once.

The suthor was sailing with the Sixth Fleet in an advisory capacity regarding modifications to ships of the fleet as a civilian ship designer at that time and had a "grandstand" view of the activity.

The Royal Navy carriers HMS *Eagle*, *Bulwark*, and *Albion*, plus the French Navy carriers *Lafayette* and *Arromanches* launched dive-bombing jets and Corsairs to bomb Egyptian airfields, while Egypt intercepted the attackers with jets and Corsairs.

The U.S. disapproval of the attack revealed itself when the U.S. ships of the Sixth Fleet left Valencia and sailed so close to the Royal Navy and French carriers that it appeared the U.S. intended to disrupt the attack.

When the British Task Force Commander, Admiral Durnford-Slater, requested the U.S. Sixth Fleet Commander, Vice Admiral Charles R Brown, to distance his ships from the British and French ships, Adm. Brown held fast and even illuminated his ships at night!

Egypt accepted a U.S. call for a cease fire with Israel on 2 November; however, the Anglo-French bombardment of Egyptian airfields continued unabated. Four days later an Anglo-French amphibious force landed at Port Said. More and more Soviet ships also began appearing in the Mediterranean and, using the Sixth Fleet for subtle intimidation, President Eisenhower joined with the Soviets in pressuring an Anglo-French cease fire and withdrawal.

The Royal Navy jet-powered Hawker Sea Hawk and de Havilland Sea Venom fighters were supported by Royal Navy Corsairs and *Aeronavale* Corsairs. Several Sea Venoms and Sea Hawks were shot down by Egyptian anti-aircraft fire as well as by Egyptian Corsairs.

On November 2, 1956, the 15F *Flotille* Corsairs bombed the airfield at Alexandria Dikheila. Heavily loaded with 500lb bombs, the fifteen F4U-7 Corsairs were catapulted from the carrier *Lafayette*. After destroying the hangars, the Corsairs completed the mission by destroying the runways. All returned to the carrier safely.

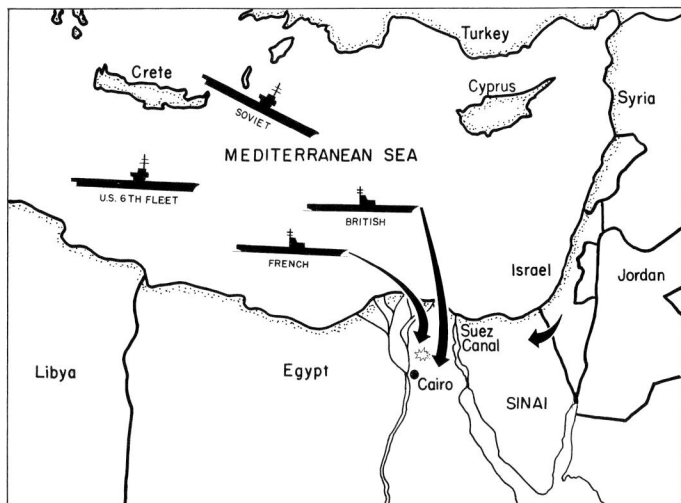

British and French shipboard aircraft attacked Egypt while Israeli troops invaded the Sinai peninsula because Egypt nationized the Suez canal. The U.S. Sixth Fleet and a Soviet flotilla approached the British and French flotillas to indicate their displeasure at the attack. The four nations' ships are each shown as one aircraft carrier in this symbolic illustration.

Shortly thereafter, because of diplomatic pressure from the USA and the USSR, and because of the disapproval of the international community, who feared the situation would flare into enormous proportions, the Franco-British expeditionary force was ordered to halt operations.

Although in a short "War" the "obsolete" Corsairs were still viable weapons in the beginning of the "Jet Age" flown by experienced aviators, the Corsair proved it could score against the emerging jet fighters.

The Franco-British forces were humiliated because, at the moment of victory, they were forced to stop fighting and be replaced by UN peacekeeping forces.

Left Photo: A jet-powered Hawker Sea Hawk fighter of No. 802 Naval Air Squadron makes a forced landing aboard HMS *Albion* after an underwing auxiliary fuel tank was smashed by Egyptian anti-aircraft or a Corsair interceptor. Right Photo: A de Havilland Sea Venom jet-powered strike-fighter of No. 893 Naval Air Squadron is making a belly landing on HMS *Eagle* because its landing gear was damaged by Egyptian anti-aircraft fire or a Corsair interceptor. (Imperial War Museum)

Corsair: The Saga of the Legendary Bent-Wing Fighter-Bomber

Two F4U-7 Corsairs of *Flotille* 12F that were engaged in the North African fighting at Algeria and Tunisia await rearming prior to engaging the enemy again. Note the fuel drop tanks used not for long range but for endurance. (ECP Armies, *Aeronavale*, Courtesy United Aircraft Corp)

Corsairs in North Africa

The Anglo-French reversal in Egypt gave Nassar a victory "by default." The effects of the Suez offensive's failure gave renewed energy to the Algerian-Tunisian revolts which saw the promise of a future victory against the Franco-British "Imperialists."

Seventy acts of murder by "revolutionists" on October 30 and November 1, 1954, marked the real beginning of the fighting in Algeria. During these events four Flotilles comprising 12F, 14F, 15F, and 17F F4U-7 Corsairs from the *Aeronavale* took part in keeping order on Algerian soil. The Corsairs were based at BA (*Base Aerienne*= Air Base) at Telergma. and were also based at Algeria-Maison Blanche, Karouba, or Biskra.

A mixed bag of AU-1 and F4U-7 was applied in devastating ground support, with bombing and strafing missions in Algeria and Tunisia. These were carried out under harrowing conditions, with the Tunisians pounding French airport runways with mortars and cannon, and actually building a high wall to prevent the *Flotilles* from using the Bizerte Airport!

The *Aeronavale* lost fourteen aviators in Algeria caused by in-flight collisions, human error, and unexplained crashes.

The *Aeronavale* suffered no losses in Tunisia and, thanks to the splendid design of the F4U-7 and AU-1 Corsairs, the conflicts ended amicably.

Corsairs in Central America

Two neighboring Central American countries purchased surplus Corsairs from the United States: El Salvador bought FG1-D Corsairs and Honduras bought the newer F4U-4 and F4U-5.

The two adjoining countries were always hostile to each other, both disposition-wise and politically; therefore, the very small argument between the countries caused by the disputed result of a soccer match between the two countries erupted into war! For one hundred hours both countries pitted their Corsairs against each other. The conflict was often humorously called the "Soccer War."

The outstanding aviator of the war was Honduran Captain De Soto Henriquez, who shot down a Salvadoran Mustang and two Salvadoran FG-1 Corsairs with his F4U-5 Corsair in this shortest of all wars.

El Salvador flew its Corsairs until 1969, while Honduras flew its Corsairs until 1977.

Left Photo: A Honduran F4U-4 Corsair "on the prowl" for Salvadoran aircraft or ground targets to "beat up." Observe the drop tanks to extend the range of his "prowl." (United Aircraft Corp. Photo, Author's File) Right Photo: A two-plane flight of Honduran F4U-5 Corsairs are patrolling the skies near the Salvadoran border with a third Corsair in the distance. A Honduran Corsair aviator scored two Salvadoran Corsairs and one Salvadoran Mustang during this 100-day war. (United Aircraft Corp. Photos, Author's File)

Appendix E: Foreign Flag Corsairs

Corsairs in South America

Argentina bought twenty-two F4U-5 and F4U-5N corsairs from the USA for the Argentine Navy in 1962. The planes were based on the aircraft carrier *Independencia* (former *HMS Warrior*) from 1956 to 1966.

During an "incident" with Chile in 1965 an Argentine Corsair was shot down.

The last Argentine Corsair F4U-5N, identification code 3-A-211, is an exhibit in the Navy Museum in Bahia Blanca, Argentina.

Flown world-wide for both offensive and defensive tactics, in dogfights, or strafing and dive bombing, the Corsair was in demand, world-wide, for many years by numerous air forces.

Upper Photo: An Argentine F4U-5 Corsair of the *Armada Nacional* is taking off from the carrier *Independencia*. Note the black anti-exhaust coating on the fuselage side to protect the dural from the heat and soot of the engine exhaust. (Vought Aircraft Company Courtesy H.J. "Jerry" Dalton, Jr.) Lower Photo: An Argentine F4U-5 Corsair caught at the moment its hook has snared the carrier's arresting cable. (Vought Aircraft Company Courtesy H.J. "Jerry" Dalton, Jr.)

Appendix F: Corsair Colors and Insignia

Color photographs and carefully researched artwork reveal aircraft colors and markings that the reader will find interesting.

The following gallery of Corsair color plates is intended to inform as well as entertain the reader regarding Corsair color schemes.

Upper Photo: This shot of the original Corsair XF4U-1 (Bu No. 1443) reveals that the wing is colored yellow on the upper and lower surface. When the Corsair was created, the U.S. Navy had specified that all naval aircraft have the upper surface of the wing (upper wing for biplane) be colored chrome yellow. This gave rise to the assumption that only the upper surface of this Corsair wing was yellow. This photo, taken on April 19, 1941, proved otherwise. (Vought Aircraft Photo) Lower Photo: Boone Guyton stands beside the first production corsair (Bu No. 02153) preparing for the first test flight on June 25, 1942, as workmen make last minute adjustments. (Vought Aircraft Photo)

Appendix F: Corsair Colors and Insignia

Left Photo: This F4U-1A shows off its profile and the three color camouflage: sea-blue top, non-specular blue mid-point, and white fuselage bottom. Note that bottom of the wing is dark blue like the fuselage top so it blends with the fuselage when folded. (U.S. Navy Photo Courtesy Vought Aircraft) Right Photo: The F4U-1D was the first Corsair variant to sport a glossy sea-blue overall color. (U.S. Navy Photo Courtesy Vought Aircraft)

This F4U-1A carries a 500lb. bomb on a Brewster bomb rack. A bomb rack is not merely a hook. It must release the bomb quickly and completely without any twist or fore and aft delay. (U.S. Navy Photo Courtesy Vought Aircraft)

This is how an F4U-4 Corsair appears to an enemy aviator in wartime when there is no escape! Ace aviation photographer Jim Larsen risked it all to take this amazing photograph. Closing speed is about 400 miles per hour! (Jim Larsen Photo Courtesy Jim Larsen)

It is hard to believe that this beautiful AU-1 Corsair is an "angel of death" to enemy troops, tanks, parked aircraft, gun emplacements, and tanks. The bottom of the aircraft is well armored. (U.S. Marines Photo Courtesy Vought Aircraft)

Vought-Sikorsky technicians put the final work on a Pratt & Whitney R-2800 engine that has been mounted on a Corsair fuselage. Photo taken in March 1943. Note the engine cooling air outlet deflector ring. (Vought-Sikorsky Photo via National Archives)

Below right: SSgt. L. Toner, USMC, is checking the .50 cal. machine gun mechanisms on a U.S. Marine Corsair. Note that the wing is in the folded position for the convenience of SSgt Toner's important work. (U.S. Navy Photo via National Archives)

Aviation Ordnanceman NF Nitishin, USMC, carries two belts of .50 cal. machinegun ammunition to arm the guns of a Corsair fighter. Observe the bullet mix of one tracer (Red Nose) and four armor piercing bullets (Black Nose). Apparently the target was to be a ship or a motor convoy. (U.S. Navy Photo via National Archives)

Appendix F: Corsair Colors and Insignia

The olive and gray fuselage and wings, plus white undersides, contrast greatly with the U.S. colors. Planes are Corsair II (F4U-1A/D) at Naval Air Station Squantum, Mass. in 1943. Observe the plane numbers quickly added. (Royal Navy Photo, via National Archives)

Two Royal Navy armorers service the .50 cal. machine guns prior to installation in the Corsair in the background, during Sept. 1943. Corsair insignia still has the red center prior to removal of red center and added wings. Photo taken at Naval Air Station Quonset Point, Rhode Island. (Royal Navy Photo, via National Archives)

Upper Photo: The basic structure of the F4U-1A/D became an entirely new airplane when fitted with the new P & W water-injected 2,100 hp R-2800-18W engine. The photo is one of the two F4U-4X prototypes. U.S. Navy test aircraft usually had yellow noses and quite often yellow tails as well, as shown on this F4U-4X Corsair. (U.S. Navy Photograph Courtesy Vought Aircraft) Lower Photo: This photograph shows the 3,650 hp powered Goodyear FG-1 Super Corsair in a speed test at 426 mph. Observe the bubble canopy, reduced turtle deck, and enlarged vertical tail surfaces. (Goodyear Photographs Courtesy Nick Hauprich)

Corsair: The Saga of the Legendary Bent-Wing Fighter-Bomber

The following color plates cover Corsair colors, bomb racks, action, engine installation, armament, Royal Air Force colors, and test Corsairs modified from previous Corsair models and more.

The U.S. Marine squadron insignia shown here depicts a sample of the transfer of Marine aviators from squadron to squadron during World War II. As previously mentioned, VMF-214 "Swashbucklers," who fought in the early battles of the Solomons, was dissolved in order to give the number 214 to Maj. Gregory Boyington's new squadron, "Black Sheep." Some "Swashbucklers" became "Black Sheep," while others joined Maj. Robert Owens' VMF-215 "Fighting Corsairs." When the Corsair Carrier USS cape Gloucester (CVE-109) was commissioned, squadron VMF-351 "Fighting Bulldogs," commanded by Lt Col Donald K Yost, was aboard. Several "Fighting Corsairs," including former "Swashbucklers," also joined the 'Fighting Bulldogs" aboard USS Cape Gloucester.

Aircraft national insignia of the United States and Britain underwent considerable revision from 1915/1921 to 1947. The more recent changes stem from 1942/1943 and progressed throughout World War II. Most changes were made to avoid confusing the U.S., British, and New Zealand insignia with the Japanese red disc. The Americans eliminated the red color in their insignia, while the British and New Zealand not only eliminated the red, but added the American bars to their roundel on aircraft that were to engage Japanese planes.

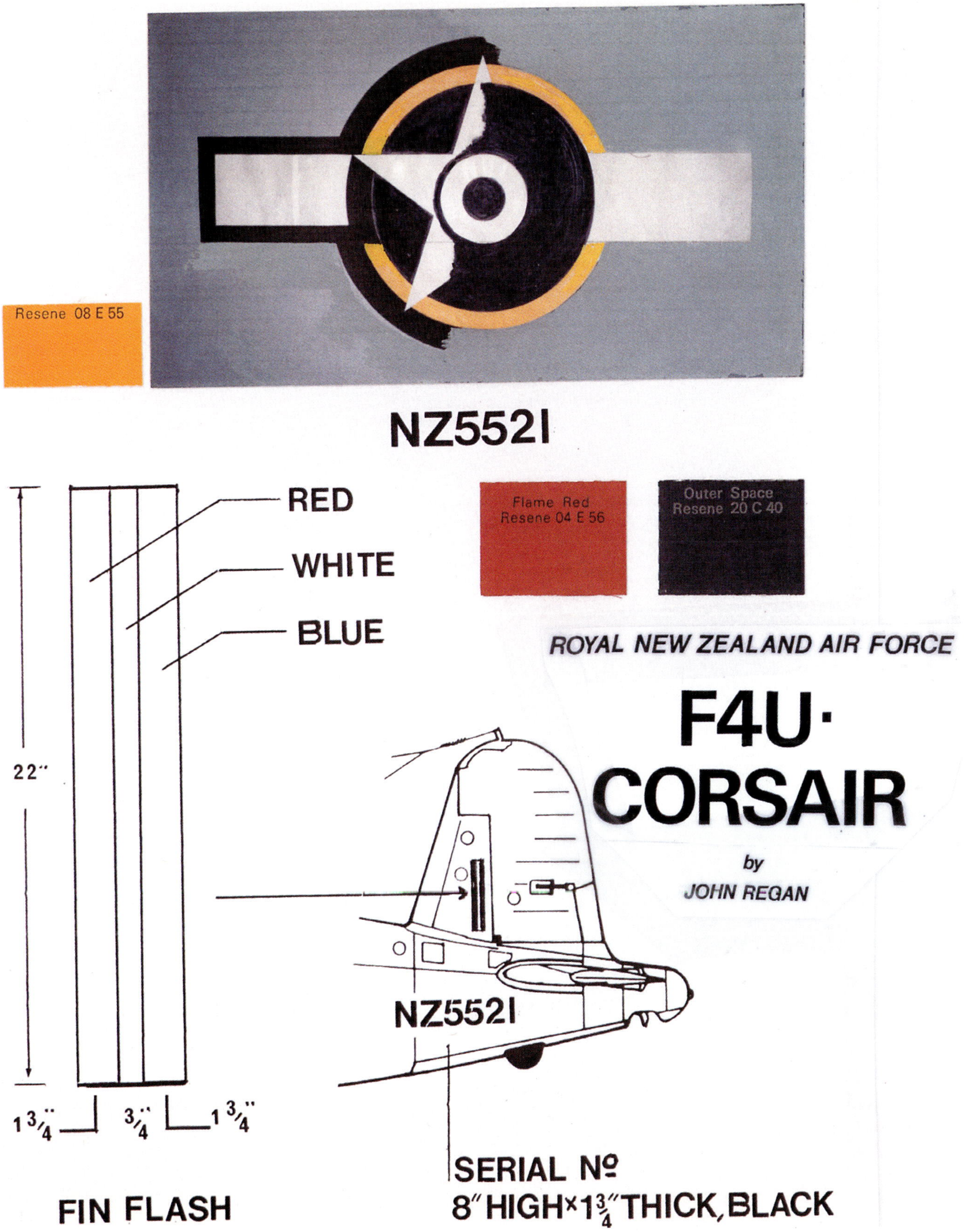

Appendix F: Corsair Colors and Insignia

This artwork gives an overview of the Royal New Zealand insignia during World War II. Color plates for the yellow, red, and blue colors used on the insignia are shown for those who have an interest in World War II colors. The size and colors of the fin flash are shown here. (John Regan artwork, Courtesy John Regan)

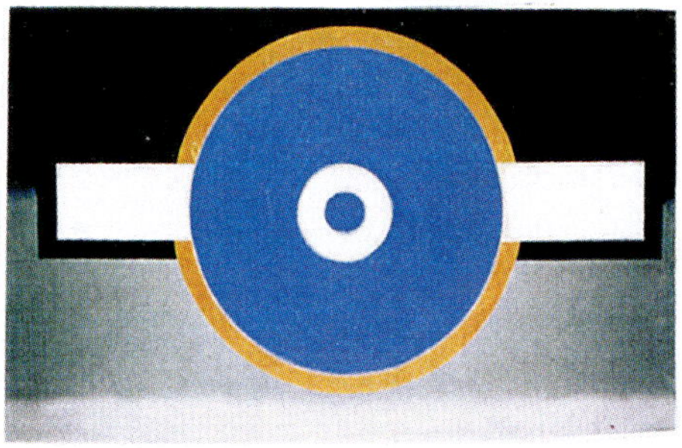

ROYAL NEW ZEALAND AIR FORCE
F4U-CORSAIR

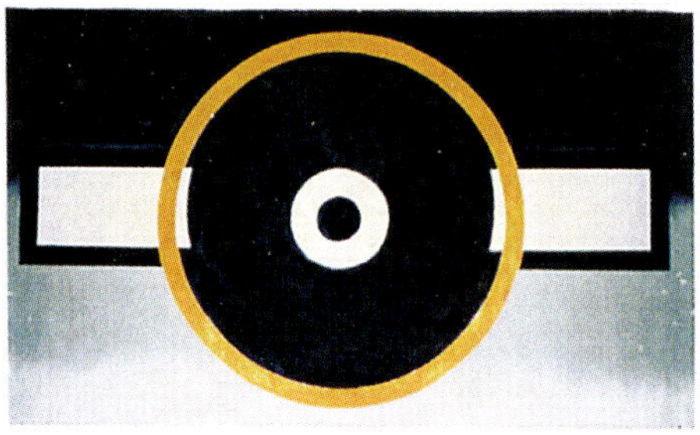

Roundel Details Etc 1944-45

by **JOHN REGAN**

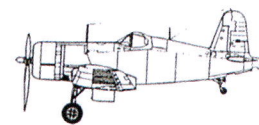

The difficult conversion of the U.S. star insignia into the Royal New Zealand roundel and bar is illustrated here: The Royal New Zealand Air Force Roundel is smaller than the U.S. Star and Bar. Roundels No.1 and No.2 are early conversions done in haste, whereby the roundel was inlarged to cover the star, completely. The U.S. Bars were left untouched. Roundel No.5 illustrates that the U.S. Star is larger than the RNZAF Roundel. The left side bar is the U.S. Bar, while the right side bar is the RNZAF bar. Drawings No.3 and No.5 illustrate the steps in converting the U.S. star and bar into the New Zealand Roundel. No.3 has the left side of the Roundel against left edge of the star background. The yellow circle is made first, then the small white circle is made from the white star. White bars are added last. No.4 illustrates how the white star is painted over to form the blue disc of the insignia. The remainder of the U.S. insignia is painted over in the color of the plane. (John Regan Artwork Courtesy John Regan)

Appendix F: Corsair Colors and Insignia

Upper Photo: The French *Aeronavale* modified their insignia twice in order to clarify their roundel insignia. The original insignia superimposed a black anchor over the red, white, and blue *cocarde* (roundel) that obstructed too much of the insignia. This was remedied by using a slender anchor stretched across the *cocarde*. A third modification used a larger and more slender anchor. Lower Photo: This post World War II French Vought F4U-7 sports the intermediate anchor insignia design. Observe the anchor on the white rudder stripe. The F4U-7 fought in the Suez Crisis, Algeria, and Tunisia conflicts. (*Aeronavale* Francais Foto)

The color plates that follow illustrate progress in British, American, and French national insignia, plus the interesting conversion from the U.S. star to the Royal New Zealand Air Force roundel. Also shown are four U.S. Marine squadron insignia that depict the transfer of aviators between them.

This newspaper clipping reports that the Governor of Connecticut, Gov M Jodi Rell, signed a bill naming the Corsair the state's official airplane. (Courtesy Thomas G. Dickinson, MD)

Connecticut's Cadillac In The Sky

By JEFF HOLTZ

GOV. M. JODI RELL on Monday signed a bill making the Connecticut-made, World War II-era Corsair F-4U the state's official airplane.

"This measure is a terrific way to honor the war effort and the achievements of the men and women of Connecticut's aircraft industry at United Aircraft, Pratt and Whitney, Hamilton Standard and Vought-Sikorsky," she said. "Some 12,500 Corsairs were built between 1938 and 1945 — the longest production of any World War II-era aircraft. I was proud to sign this bill."

State Senator George (Doc) Gunther, a Republican from Stratford who introduced the bill in January, said the plane had long deserved the honor.

"When the country was experiencing a crisis in the South Pacific, it needed a plane that could take on the fast Japanese airplanes," he said. "The Corsair was that plane. It was designed and built here. Ninety percent of the components were built here."

Mr. Gunther said the Corsair was also special because women played a major role making it. With so many men being drafted, it was hard to build them at first, he said. "So they brought women in and found that they were better on the production line than the men," he said. "This designation is a salute to everyone involved with this aircraft, not just the heroes who flew it."

The plane will also be celebrated at an event called Corsairs Over Connecticut at Sikorsky Memorial Airport in Stratford June 3 through 5. It will feature flights by six Corsairs, a recreated production line, a display of World War II uniforms, a remembrance tent with photos of veterans and appearances by former Corsair pilots and people who built the aircraft. It will culminate with a fly-by over the Barnum Festival Parade in Bridgeport.

Nick Mainero, 82, of Bridgeport is a former pilot who will be at the event. He was hit by enemy fire numerous times during his 51 Corsair missions in World War II and said that he flew the plane over 200 miles of water in the South Pacific with the tail blown off. "They took pictures when I got back and put a caption on them that said: 'Our plane flies without a tail,'" he said.

Obviously, Mr. Mainero had great praise for the Corsair.

"At 21,000 feet, it could fly 425 miles per hour and it was stable," he said. "You could trim it up and fly it with no hands. And it could carry a thousand-pound bomb and would still fly like a Cadillac."

Last Monday, the Corsair became the state's official plane. Thousands were made by men and women in Connecticut during World War II.

Corsair: The Saga of the Legendary Bent-Wing Fighter-Bomber

The United States Postal Service issued a First Class stamp showing a U.S. Marine corsair in flight in full frame. This included the word "Corsair" on the stamp. (Courtesy David A Mocabee)

Very few World War II aircraft have been so celebrated as has the Bent Wing Corsair in moving pictures, magazines, advertisements, and newspapers. Even the name "Corsair" has become synonymous with "Navy Fighter Plane." In addition; the United States Postal Service has printed a first class stamp of the Corsair to celebrate this magnificent naval fighter.

The Corsair attraction was used in advertisements by the companies that designed and assembled the entire plane, as well as the firms that built the smallest but most important parts of this complex machine.

The U.S. Navy also used the Corsair to recruit aviators, as well as mechanics and other technicians to maintain these important aircraft.

Following are examples of the firms that were involved in the construction of Corsairs, as well as those who conferred accolades upon the Corsair.

Corsair color schemes varied considerably, depending upon the terrain and the colors dictated by experience in combat.

One dozen Corsair profiles in full color ranging from the F4U-1 to the F4U-7 and spanning the years 1943 to 1969 from the Pacific shores and Indo China to North Africa, plus South and Central America, are presented in this segment of the color Appendix.

The U.S. Navy used the Corsair in their recruiting advertisements because of the attractive qualities of the plane: beautiful and brute strength in one machine. (U.S. Navy Photo Courtesy U.S. Navy Recruiting Bureau)

United Aircraft Corporation used this early low-key advertisement for its Corsair, Pratt & Whitney engines, and Hamilton Standard propellers. Observe the "birdcage" canopy that "dates" this advertisement. (Courtesy United Aircraft Corporation)

Appendix F: Corsair Colors and Insignia

Goodyear Aircraft and Brewster Aeronautical were coproducers of the Corsair with Vought. This is the striking action advertisement featuring the Goodyear "Birdcage" Corsair. Observe the sketch of the Corsair and Blimp, both made by Goodyear for the war effort. (Goodyear Photo Courtesy Nick Hauprich)

The Nash-Kelvinator corporation was renowned for its Nash automobiles and Kelvinator refrigerators; however, they retooled to construct Pratt & Whitney engines and Hamilton Standard propellers for Corsairs. Observe the dramatic last paragraph which tells it like it was. (Nash-Kelvinator Photo Courtesy Nick Hauprich)

333

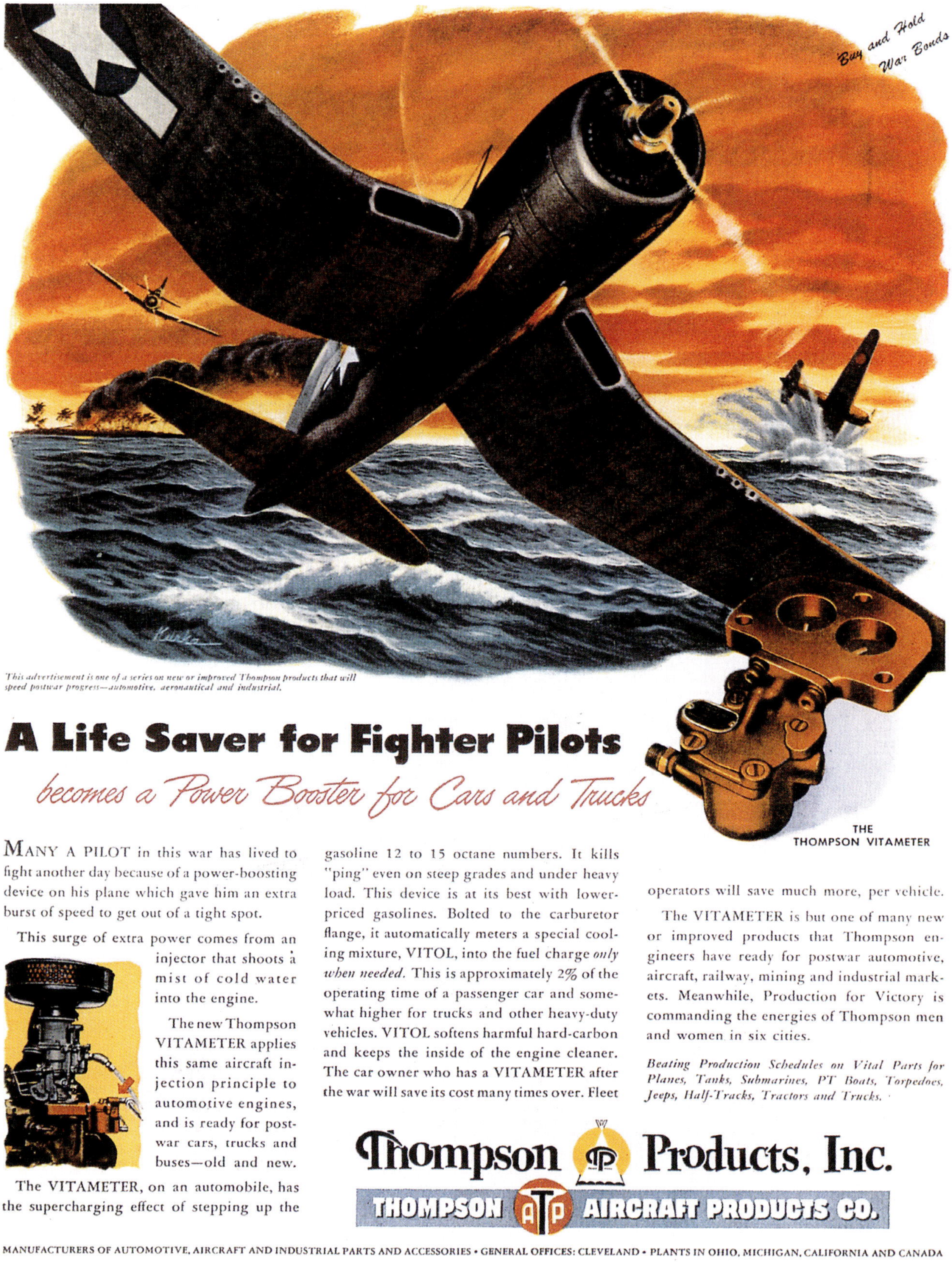

A Life Saver for Fighter Pilots
becomes a Power Booster for Cars and Trucks

MANY A PILOT in this war has lived to fight another day because of a power-boosting device on his plane which gave him an extra burst of speed to get out of a tight spot.

This surge of extra power comes from an injector that shoots a mist of cold water into the engine.

The new Thompson VITAMETER applies this same aircraft injection principle to automotive engines, and is ready for postwar cars, trucks and buses—old and new.

The VITAMETER, on an automobile, has the supercharging effect of stepping up the gasoline 12 to 15 octane numbers. It kills "ping" even on steep grades and under heavy load. This device is at its best with lower-priced gasolines. Bolted to the carburetor flange, it automatically meters a special cooling mixture, VITOL, into the fuel charge *only when needed*. This is approximately 2% of the operating time of a passenger car and somewhat higher for trucks and other heavy-duty vehicles. VITOL softens harmful hard-carbon and keeps the inside of the engine cleaner. The car owner who has a VITAMETER after the war will save its cost many times over. Fleet operators will save much more, per vehicle.

The VITAMETER is but one of many new or improved products that Thompson engineers have ready for postwar automotive, aircraft, railway, mining and industrial markets. Meanwhile, Production for Victory is commanding the energies of Thompson men and women in six cities.

Beating Production Schedules on Vital Parts for Planes, Tanks, Submarines, PT Boats, Torpedoes, Jeeps, Half-Tracks, Tractors and Trucks.

MANUFACTURERS OF AUTOMOTIVE, AIRCRAFT AND INDUSTRIAL PARTS AND ACCESSORIES • GENERAL OFFICES: CLEVELAND • PLANTS IN OHIO, MICHIGAN, CALIFORNIA AND CANADA

Possibly, the smallest, but one of the most important mechanical parts of the corsair powerplant was the Thompson Products, Inc. water/alcohol power booster injection system. It will be remembered that "Ike" Kepford of "Jolly Rogers" actuated the engine injection booster system to score Japanese Zero and Tojo fighters in Chapter Four. (Thompson Aircraft Products Co. Photo Courtesy Nick Hauprich)

Appendix F: Corsair Colors and Insignia

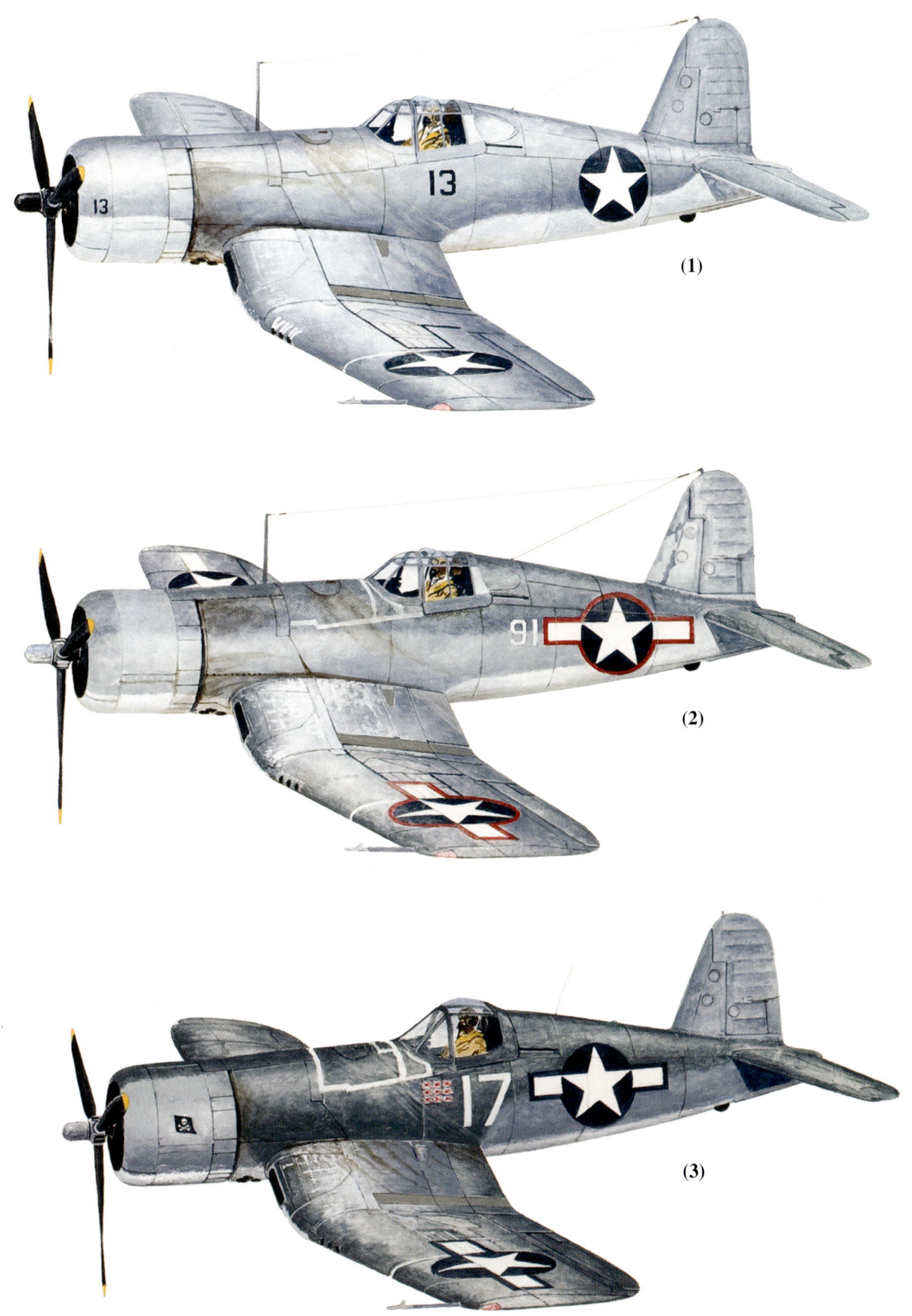

(1)

(2)

(3)

335

(4)

(5)

(6)

Appendix F: Corsair Colors and Insignia

Corsair: The Saga of the Legendary Bent-Wing Fighter-Bomber

(10)

(11)

(12)

Appendix F: Corsair Colors and Insignia

(1) F4U-1 BuNo 02350 - A/C black 13 of VMF-124, the first U.S. Marine squadron to take the Corsair into combat on Guadalcanal, Solomon Islands. Black 13 is displayed in markings of February-March '43 era. The "birdcage" canopied A/C was originally flown by Lt. Ken Walsh, the first Corsair ace and subsequent recipient of the Congressional Medal of Honor for 20 victories confirmed at the close of his extended seven month tour.

(2) F4U-1 BuNo 02591 - A/C white 91 of VMF-214 *"Swashbucklers"* based at Munda airfield, New Georgia Island, at the close of their first tour in August '43, which produced 30 aerial victories. In their second tour as the legendary Boyington's *"Blacksheep"* from October '43 to March '44, they would triple the first tour's score, which resulted in the only Presidential Distinguished Unit Citation to be issued to a Navy/Marines squadron in the war. Veteran white 91 is typical of the weathered, recycled Corsairs flown by any number of pilots, including units simultaneously operating from the same rustic packed coral air strip. Refreshed camouflage and tactical markings were wholly inconsistent. Unit insignia and personal markings were typically subdued. Victory flags were most commonly applied for publicity events and the tallies were rarely current.

(3) F4U-1 (A) BuNo 18005 - A/C white 17 of VF-17 *"Jolly Rogers"* based at Ondonga air strip on New Georgia Island in their October '43 to April '44 combat tour. In contrast to random A/C assignments in the Marines' squadrons, each "Jolly Roger" was assigned a "Hog number" emulating A/C "Hog 1" of CO Lt.Cdr. Tom Blackburn. Hence, "Hog 17" seen here is suspected of being the last of three "17s" flown to attrition by the *"Jolly Rogers"* XO Lt.Cdr. Roger Hedrick with nine confirmed kills. Later, as CO of VF-84's Corsairs aboard the USS *Bunker Hill*, Hedrick would score three more aerial kills and damage four others. Although VF-17 is purportedly the first unit to receive "1A" Corsairs with modified cockpits and "bubble" canopies, the "A" designator is not a U.S. Navy Bureau reference. Many "Dash 1" Corsairs were upgraded to "1 (A)" status at any number of Naval air stations throughout the South Pacific. There are no sequential Bureau Numbers that designate a specific block of "1A" types. Hence, both the "birdcage Dash 1" and "bubble 1(A)" types sortied side by side in the Solomons campaign.

(4) F4U-2(N) BuNo unknown - A/C Black 12 of VF(N)-101 led by Lt.Cdr. "Chick" Harmer attached to VF-10 aboard CV-6 *USS Enterprise* for the January to October '44 extended tour in the Southwest Pacific. Ironically, of the three night fighter squadrons simultaneously sent into action, Lt.Cdr. Harmer's diminutive four-plane squadron would be the very first U.S. Corsair outfit to operate from a carrier. With less than a dozen junior grade pilots flying in rotation, only the commander and Lt.(jg) Bob Holden were rated for night flights. In the ensuing seven months, from New Guinea's north coast to the Philippine Seas, their night sorties over *Enterprise* resulted in two enemy bombers being shot down by Harmer and three by Holden, plus several other airborne targets being heavily damaged. Corsair "black 12" seen here is unique in its "non-specular sea blue" upper camouflage and its retention of the early "birdcage" canopy. The "2Ns" of VF-101(N) likewise were modified in the deletion of the starboard outer .50 caliber gun to compensate for the weight of the radar blister, plus the extended exhaust flanges to suppress the exhaust flames.

(5) F4U-1D BuNo unknown - A/C white 153 of VMF-217 based on Peleliu Island in support of the Philippine operations of late '44. The "1D" introduced in the Central Pacific island hopping campaign proved to be what was arguably the most capable fighter bomber of WWII. With reinforced shackles installed beneath the inner ramp of the gull wings plus the center line hard point, the glycol-injected 2800 Hp Pratt & Whitney could heft three 1000 lb. bombs to a fortified target, albeit within minimal range. And as the ultimate interceptor of the dreaded kamikazes, the Corsair "1D" truly became the Marines' "bent-wing angel."

(6) CORSAIR II [F4U-1(A)] s.n. JT-410 - A/C T8-H of 1836 Squadron aboard *HMS Victorious* in 1945. Despite the U.S. Navy's reticence, the Royal Navy's Fleet Air Arm (FAA) readily took Vought's big fighter aboard its carriers in the mid-'44 operations against the *Kriegsmarine* trapped in the Baltic Sea. Once the German naval threat was eradicated, the Royal fleet returned to the Orient in late '44 to fully re-engage the Japanese. The FAA's only "ace" to score five confirmed kills in a Corsair was Canadian Sub-Lt. Don Sheppard, who often flew T8-H shown here. Being a typical British Corsair II with clipped wingtips, "H" also had its radio masts removed, and it was equipped with a small cine-camera set in the lower rear fuselage to record air strikes in the Indian Ocean operations of January '45. Sheppard flew another Corsair for his last aerial victory in May as part of Task Force 57 strikes against the Japanese home islands.

(7) F4U-1C BuNo unknown - A/C white 74 aboard CV-9 USS Essex in the January to March '45 tour of VMF-124/231 led by Lt. Col. W.A. Millington, presiding CO of VMF-124 from the Solomons campaign of late '43. The colonel's combined units now formed the first Marines wing of Corsair fighter-bombers supporting their TBD bomber brethren, all to operate from a single aircraft carrier. The Essex group, TF 38, swept into the China Sea raiding airdromes and port facilities, first against Okinawa and Formosa, and then for a major strike on Luzon. They next raided the far shores of French Indo-China and quickly turned eastward to retrace their route for yet another strike back on Japan's home islands. Renamed as TF 58, for two months they would rage over Iwo Jima, Okinawa, and even Tokyo. VMF-124/231 crews struggled with a high rate of operational accidents far more costly than combat losses to their opponents. Within the fierce influx of replacement A/C, the "1C" armed with four long-barreled, Hispano M-2 20mm cannons made its debut, as with white 74 shown here. The A/C likewise bears a white nose cowling tactical marking for TF 58 carrier fighters sent against central Japan, particularly over the heavily defended shorelines of the Inland Sea. The "1Cs" joined the "1D veterans" in gunnery strafing missions, markedly sans ordnance. Strafing runs were often executed by an entire squadron in line abreast formation intent to overwhelm anti-aircraft defenses.

(8) F4U-4B BuNo 07157 - A/C white 306 of VF-53 aboard CVA-45 *USS Valley Forge* as the first U.S. Navy Corsair unit to be deployed against North Korean targets in June 1950. So like its ancestors just five years before, the prop driven "U-4s" proved to be the most resilient tactical fighter available in significant numbers to aid the tactically challenged United Nations. The Navy had accepted the "U-4" with the last of its series dedicated to the upgraded quartet of short-barreled M-3 Hispano 20 mm cannon, lighter in weight with a higher rate of fire, and better suited to "high-G" maneuvers. Regardless, in the ensuing three years, whether land based or carrier borne, whether engaging MiGs or enduring arctic combat conditions, Navy and Marines Corsairs flew in every campaign of the United Nations' first "police action."

(9) F4U-5NL possibly BuNo 12435 - A/C red 5 of VMF(N)-513 *"Flying Nightmares"* from the *USS Bataan* and detached to Wonson Air Base, South Korea, as of April 1951. The "Dash 5" with its late generation "E" series P&W R-2800-32W could handle a myriad of tasks, and specifically excelled in the night intruder role. A/C red 5 is finished in matte black to make it virtually invisible to the search lights of anti-aircraft defenses. Over 3000 night sorties alone out of 34,000 sorties overall were executed by the *"Nightmares"* in the first year of the conflict, flying a mix of "Dash 5s" and twin-engine F7F-3N Tigercats. Their resident 11-victory "Solomons" ace, Capt. Phil Long, dispatched a pair of No. Korean Yak 9s with his "Dash 5" on 21 April to underscore that a U.S. Marine in his Corsair was still a deadly aerial adversary.

(10) F4U-7 BuNo 133599 - A/C white 20 of France's *Aeronavale 1 Flotiile 14F* aboard the CVA *Arromanche* in the Suez Crisis of 1956. France adopted a number of surplus U.S. Marines AU-1 Corsairs at the outbreak of the Korean War in 1950, and eventually deployed them to the ill-fated Indo-China uprising. To meet the attrition of the popular AU-1, France contracted for ninety-four new F4U-7s, which were roughly equivalent to the F4U-4. Four *Flotilles* received the "Dash 7," as with the 14th *FiotUle* A/C shown here in its bold tactical markings employed during the Suez Incident of 1956. *Aeronavale* Corsairs made their last hostile sorties briefly in the Algerian rebellion in 1961.

(11) FG-1 BuNo unknown / serial # FAS-219 of the *Fuerza Area del Salvador* (FAS) in the "One-hundred Hours War" in July 1969. In the boundary dispute between El Salvador and Honduras, the former's military junta resorted to the desperate acquisition of surplus U.S. aircraft from several private sources in order to circumvent a prevailing North American embargo. Over a period of many weeks, at least two dozen vintage fighters reached El Salvador, more than half their number being Vought and Goodyear Corsairs. Of only six Corsairs that were serviceable, FAS-219 was one of the few to be heavily camouflaged to aid in its close support of Salvadoran troops. It was lost to Honduran anti-aircraft fire on 17 July at the height of the "*La Guerre del Ciento Horas.*"

(12) F4U-5 BuNo unknown / serial # FAH-609 of the Fuerza *Area de Honduras* (FAH) in the "One-hundred Hours War" in July 1969. Though the Honduran forces were numerically fewer, its FAH command wisely persisted that air power be its predominant weapon. The most potent element of the FAH was the nine F4U-5Ns and the eight F4U-4 Corsairs that were flown by a comparatively well disciplined group of flyers. Ironically, a World Cup qualification soccer match played in El Salvador in June between the quarrelsome neighbors degenerated into a riot. The furor deepened as the Honduran government launched an aggressive expulsion of Salvadoran immigrants in the borderlands. When El Salvadoran troops mobilized, the Honduran response proved to be more effective strategically. On 17 July, the third day of the war, three FAH F4U-5N Corsairs encountered a pair of FAS F-51 Mustangs and one was dispatched by Major Fernando Soto-Henriquez flying FAH-609. On the major's second sortie of the day his Corsairs met a trio of Salvadoran FG-1D types. Major Henriquez prevailed over two of the opposing Corsairs, and as of the ceasefire the next day, he was the aerial champion of the war the local gente would call "*Lo Guerra de Futbol.*"

Abbreviations

AAM –	Air-to-Air Missile
Air-Wing –	Total aircraft complement on an aircraft carrier
ASM –	Anti-Ship Missile
ASR –	Air-Sea Rescue
AVG –	Aircraft Escort Vessel (U.S. Navy)
BPF –	British Pacific Fleet
Bu Aer –	Bureau of Aeronautics
Bolter –	An aborted landing in which aircraft tail hook fails to engage the arresting cable and the plane climbs away to try again.
CAP –	Combat Air Patrol
CCA –	Carrier Controlled Approach
CASD –	Carrier Aircraft Service Detachment (Marine)
Cin C Pac –	Commander in chief Pacific
CIWS –	Close In Weapons System
CSA –	Commander Support Aircraft
CONUS –	Continental United States
CVE –	Escort Aircraft Carrier
CBCB –	Communist Border Constabulary Brigade
CCF –	Chinese Communist Forces
CV –	Aircraft Carrier
CVL –	Light Aircraft Carrier (U.S. Navy)
ETO –	European Theatre of Operation
FAA –	Fleet Air Arm (Royal Navy)
FOD –	Foreign Object Damage
Fouled Deck –	When flight deck is not ready to receive oncoming aircraft.
Gen –	General
HOTAS –	Hands On Throttle And Stick
HVAR –	High Velocity Air Rocket (missile)
JCS –	Joint Chiefs of Staff (US)
KNOT –	Nautical term for ship's and airplane's speed at sea (Knot equals 1.15 statute miles per hour).
MAG –	Marine Air Group
MCVG –	Marine Carrier Air Group
MPH –	Miles per Hour
MAW –	Marine Air Wing
MTO –	Mediterranean Theatre of Operations
NAPALM –	Aluminum Soaps Thickener For Gasoline (Napthene and Palmitate)
NAS –	Naval Air Station
NATC –	Naval Air Test Center
NASM –	National Air and Space Museum
NKPA –	North Korean People's Army
PORT –	Port Side (Left Side) of ship or aircraft
ROK –	Republic of Korea (South Korea)
R&R –	Rest and Recuperation
STBD –	Starboard (Right Side) of ship or aircraft
USMC –	United States Marine Corps
USMCR –	United States Marine Corps Reserve
USAAC –	United States Army Air Corps
USAF –	United States Air Force
VMA –	Attack Squadron (U.S. Marines)
VMF –	Fighter Squadron (U.S. Marines)
VF –	Fighter Squadron (U.S. Navy)
VMSB –	Scout Bomber Squadron (U.S. Marines)
VSB –	Scout Bomber Squadron (U.S. Navy)
VMTB –	Torpedo Bomber Squadron (U.S. Marines)
VTB –	Torpedo Bomber Squadron (U.S. Navy)

Abbreviations

Ranks

ADM –	Admiral
ATCO –	Air Tactical Control Officer (U.S. Navy)
AGC –	Air Group Commander
Air Boss –	Officer in charge of all operations on hangar deck and flight deck including take off and landings on an aircraft carrier.
Airdale –	A flight deck crewman such as plane handlers.
Capt –	Captain
CO –	Commanding Officer
Col –	Colonel
Cpl –	Corporal
CWO –	Chief Warrant Officer
CDR or COMDR –	Commander
CAG –	Commander Air Group
CINC –	Commander-In-Chief
ENS –	Ensign
ETO –	European Theatre of Operation
FADM –	Fleet Admiral
VADM –	Vice Admiral
Gy Sgt –	Gunnery Sergeant
LCDR or (Lt. Comdr) –	Lieutenant Commander (U.S. Navy)
LT or (Lieut) –	Lieutenant
LTJG –	Lieutenant (Junior Grade); (U.S. Navy)
2nd Lieut –	Second Lieutenant; US Army & Marine
Maj –	Major
LTC or Lt. Col –	Lieutenant Colonel
Brig Gen –	Brigadier General
Lt. Gen –	Lieutenant General
Maj Gen –	Major General
MSG –	Master Sergeant
Gen –	General
LSO –	Landing Signal Officer
VADM –	Vice Admiral
RADM –	Rear Admiral
Sgt –	Sergeant
CMS gt –	Chief Master Sergeant
SMS gt –	Senior Master Sergeant
SSG or SSgt –	Staff Sergeant
T Sgt –	Technical Sergeant
XO –	Executive Officer

Awards

AM –	Air Medal
DSC –	Distinguished Service Cross
DSM –	Distinguished Service Medal
DSO –	Distinguished Service Order
DFC –	Distinguished Flying Cross
DSM –	Distinguished Service Medal
DSO –	Distinguished Service Order
DSC –	Distinguished Service Cross
MOH –	Medal of Honor

Bibliography

Publications

"Air War Over Korea", Robert Jackson, Scribners, New York, 1973.

"Aircraft Museums and Collections of North America", R. Ogden. The Aviation Hobby Shop, West Drayton; Middlesex, England.

"American Fighter Aces Album", Col. J Ward Boyce USAF (Ret), American Fighter Aces Association, 4636 Falcon Circle Drive, Mesa, Arizona 85205.

"Air War Over Korea", Robert Jackson, Scribners, New York.

"British Navy's Air Arm", Owen Rutter, Penguin, New York, 1944.

"Baa Baa Black Sheep", Gregory Boyington, Bantam Books, New York.

"Battle for Leyte Gulf", C. Vann Woodward Mac Millan Co. N.Y.

"The Corsair and other Aeroplanes Vought", Gerard P. Moran, Sunshine House, 1978, Terre Haute, Indiana.

"Carrier Operations in World War II, Vol. I: The Royal Navy", David Brown, Naval Institute Press, Annapolis, MD.

"Corsairs and Flattops", Gen John Pomerory Condon, USMC (Ret) Naval Institute Press, Annapolis, MD.

"Chance Vought Aircraft. Corsair IV". Stratford, Conn; 1944.

"Corsair, 30 years of Filibustering, 1940-1970", Bruno Pautigny, Histoire & Collections, Paris, France, 2003.

"Directory of Unlimited Class Pylon Air Racers", Jim Larsen, Kirkland, Wash. : American Air Museum, 1971.

"Fleet Air Arm", Lt. Cdr. P.K. Kemp, Herbert Jenkins, Ltd.

"Fleet Air Arm at War", Ian Allen, Shepperton Surry, England, 1982.

"Forgotten Fleet: The British Navy in the Pacific", John Winton, Coward-Mc Cann, New York, 1969.

"Goodyear Aircraft", Hugh Allen, Corday & Gross, Cleveland, Ohio, 1947.

"History of Marine Corps Aviation in World War Two", Robert Sherrod; Combat Forces Press, Washington, D.C. 1952. Also; The Nautical and Aviation Publishing Company of America, Baltimore, M.D. 1987.

"History of United States Naval Operation in World War II. Vols. VI, VII, X, & XII", Samuel Eliot Morrison; Atlantic, Little, Brown, Boston, Mass.

"The Naval Air War in Korea", Richard Hallion, The Nautical and Aviation Publishing Company of America, Boston, M.D. 1986.

"Pilot's Handbook for Navy Model F4U-5 Aircraft, AN 01-45 HD-1 including F4U-5P and F4U-5NL 1947." Contact: U.S. Govt. Printing Office Washington, D.C. for availability.

Bibliography

"Queen of The Flat Tops, USS Lexington at Coral Sea Battle". Stanley Johnston, Jarrolds.

"Top Guns: America's Fighter Aces Tell Their Stories", Joe Foss and Mathew Brennan. Pocket Books, New York, 1991.

"United States Naval Aviation 1910 to 1980" NAVAIR 00-80P-1 Washington, D.C.: U.S. Government Printing Office, 1981.

"US Navy and Marine Corps Fighters", William Green, Arco, N.Y. 1977.

"Unlimited Air Racers", Don Berliner, Motorbooks International, Osceola, Wisconsin.

"US Navy Aircraft 1921-1941 and US Marine Corps Aircraft 1914-1959", William T Larkins, Orion Books, New York, 1988.

"USN/USMC Over Korea", Thomas E Doll, Squadron/ Signal Publications 1988.

"Vought: Six Decades of Aviation History" Arthur L Schoeni, Plano, Texas: Aviation Quarterly.

"Whistling Death" Boone T Guyton, Orion Books, New York.

"Wings over the Pacific" Alex Horn The RNZAF in the Pacific Air War.

"Wings for the Navy: A History of the Naval Aircraft Factory, 1917-1956" Annapolis: Naval Institute, 1990.

"Wartime Journals of Charles A Lindbergh". Harcourt, Brace, Jovanovich, New York, 1970.

"Zero", Okuniya Masatake, Balantine, New York, 1971.

Articles

"Old Hog Nose", Boone T Guyton, Airpower, January, 1971.

"Fleet Air Arm Fighter Operations in World War II", C.F. Shores and J.D. Brown, Air Pictorial April, 1971.

"RNZAF Corsairs", John Regan, Wings (New Zealand) Sept. 1972.

"What It's Like to Strap Me On an F4U", Wolfgang Langewiesche; Flying, June 1977.

"Sweathogs of the Solomons", Hap Langstaff, Airpower, January 1978.